The Sniper's Log

Architectural Chronicles of Generation X

Alejandro Zaera-Polo

ACTAR

Introduction

It was around 1985 when I started to indulge in occasional writing engagements for various publications. Since then, writing has been a parallel activity present throughout my professional life. This book is a non-exhaustive compilation of the publications, lectures, academic briefs, project descriptions, and theorizations of my own practice which I produced since 1990. During the collection and editing of these materials I became aware of the link between the various documents and the situations for which they had been constructed. The connection between contingent biographical events and theoretical constructs slowly became central to the edition of this collection of textual *artifacts*, aimed to perform in specific occasions and under certain circumstances, addressed to multiple and contingent targets. As my own position drifted constantly through this journey, this book has taken the shape of a *sniper's log* rather than a strategic battle plan. It became a register of actions and their attachments to the world outside a register of events for tactical analysis rather than the construction of a consistent worldview.

I have never viewed writing as an instrument for producing a comprehensive doctrine or a definitive truth; rather, I see it as a model for engaging with subjects that have attracted my attention in the course of other practices. I believe we theorize because we need to bring order to the realms we operate within, to hypothesize how reality works, and to create a re-interpretation of facts that may alter reality. Rather than in an internal truth or virtue, theory is ultimately grounded in the contingencies of a certain situation, which often lie outside the practice in question. It may optimize operative protocols, or establish a polemic; what is important is that it does something to the world out there.

And if theory is a practice aimed to enable agency rather than to find truth, we must be capable of dropping theories once they cease being useful. Thus, theory is both ineluctably contingent and, therefore, disposable, while philosophy is purportedly not. What is universal in such a situational ethics is that all definitions of the *universal* or *utopian* have proven sadly contingent, time after time. I follow here a well-known epistemological lineage where a theory is abandoned when a better one—one with more instrumental content over its predecessors—develops. Competing hypotheses will try to increase content and predict novel facts. But no advantage for one side can ever be regarded as conclusive: this method has an intrinsic evolutionary character. And as such, it also invokes the *involutionary*, the secret exit from nihilism, and the advance of the radical project of architecture as a self-evident, fully naturalized endeavor toward and for the always deferred *real*. What passes here, then, is a series of essays approaching the *now* of material agency. A new *now-time*, perhaps, but also a strange intimation of a type of post-utopian directionality.

This is where the sniper returns as a model. Unlike the philosopher or the scientist, the sniper's maverick profile appears as a better protagonist for a contemporary epistemology of the now. Shooting from changing locations at constantly moving targets, following a ruthless path of tactical movements without a necessary alignment with other agents, directly engaged with a permanently changing ground... The sniper hides and hits by stealth, avoiding direct confrontation with the enemy, bypassing the battlefield's rules of engagement. When correctness—be it political or moral—becomes the quickest path to conformism, the sniper's moral ambiguity constitutes a promising model for a new form of theory that never falls into complacency.

The ideological—or, more properly, *ideational*—ambiguity across these texts stands as one of their distinctive qualities. They move from political engagement to disengagement and back, from a rejection of meaning and representation to their redemption... Therefore, consistency can only come from  an external convergence upon their theoretical content, the alignment of forces that exceed the purpose of every action. Instead of threaded by an ideology, these texts are linked by a *milieu* determined by temporal and geographical factors: this is very much a discourse of the *Zeitgeist*, although perhaps one that is primarily determined  by geopolitics, the new form of the ultra-historically indeterminate *genius loci* (not the Norberg-Schulz version, but rather Dilthey's historical unconscious).

As I was trying to construct an argument to circumscribe this set of incongruous texts under some sort of biographical umbrella, I discovered that I am an early member of a generation with an ambiguous identity, born between 1961 and 1981, labeled *Generation X*.[1] The so-called Xers are the generation that follows the

---

1   "*Nomads* are ratty, tough, unwanted, diverse, adventurous, and cynical about institutions. They grow up as the underprotected children of an Awakening, come of age as the alienated young adults of an Unraveling, become the pragmatic, midlife leaders of a Crisis and age into tough, post-crisis elders during a High. Generation X and the Lost Generation are examples of Nomad generations." Strauss and Howe state that generations last the length of time of one phase of life—the same length of time as a turning. Like turnings, generations come in four different archetypes, defined in "The Fourth Turning" as prophet, nomad, hero, and artist. William Strauss and Neil Howe, *Generations: The History of America's Future, 1584 to 2069* (New York: Harper Perennial, 1992).

baby boomers and are supposed to be "*a Reactive* or *Nomad* generation, composed of those who were children during a spiritual awakening, whose members tend to be pragmatic and perceptive, savvy but amoral, more focused on money than on art..." That's hardly a complementary description, particularly when our small dark-horse demography is sandwiched between two larger generations characterized by visionary and collective drives and a desire to be identified: the so-called *baby boomers* and *millennials*. Allegedly, Gen Xers are reluctant to define their identity and form a lost generation, hardly recognizable as a consistent social force. Julian Assange is a paradigmatic example: a nomadic agent with an unsettling aura in pursuit of transparency, who uses morally questionable weapons to attack the status quo. Yet to be seen is what will happen with Gen Xers' mistrust of authority after the more domestic types begin accessing power: Barack Obama, Dmitri Medvedev, and David Cameron are all early Gen Xers, equally caught in the crosshairs of history, or the crosscurrents of modernity and anti-modernity. Indeed, Gen X relativism is an anti-modernist bias, or—as Latour and Eisenman say—"we have never been modern..."

I am not sure yet if there are architectural tendencies within Gen X, but I could recognize myself in the social picture: I also despise bureaucracies and armies and dislike moralists, prophets, and heroes, let alone artists . . . I'd much rather remain a sniper, a nomad, and a cynic. I have a fondness for mischief and I am content to belong to a certain population that does not move in unison. Gen X architecture may actu-

ally be in need of a *theory of misbehavior* capable of defining an elective amorality as a higher moral stance. Despite Gen X reluctance to comply to an alignment, a generational analysis seemed to be a good alternative to the prevailing model of the *star-system* and its theory of exception and uniqueness; that is, of *privilege* a priori. Even if we live in an age when our life path is no longer bound to national, cultural, or political imperatives, I am suspicious of the idea of late-capitalism freeing us from both the dictates of tradition and the totalitarianisms of modernity. I am skeptical of the discourse of individualization as the primary trait of a contemporary subjectivity. Precisely because of the emancipation of subjectivity, we are more carefully classified than ever before. We appear to be targeted by selective marketing that seems to inevitably identify us as likely consumers of certain products, for example. Even within our bubble, we are *co-isolated* and *co-dependent*.

Despite some crucial exceptions, generations are a useful reference by which to frame individual tendencies within a populational consistency. For example, my youth had little to do with "being an underprotected child of an Awakening."[2] There was little awakening going on in Spain during the Franco dictatorship, where I grew up. Unlike the majority of my colleagues from the first world I was not born in a democracy, but, despite my peripheral upbringing, my early memories are also the Apollo 11 landing on the moon, the Vietnam demonstrations, May '68, Nixon resigning, the Concorde... We Gen Xers are probably the first generation that grew up sharing global events on TV. And those media were, whether we like it or not, American. We are an American generation as much as the next one may be Chinese. Gen Xers' proneness to drift is perhaps catalyzed by an unprecedented connectivity across different cultures enabled by mass media. But it was also shaped by the disillusionment with the collapse of communism, the dissipation of the family as a nuclear structure, the decay of the welfare state, the failure of the experimentation with individual freedoms in the '60s... By the time we were grownups, the late baby boomers had successfully reconfigured social freedoms into market freedoms. If the boomers gave up and sold utopia down the road, perhaps the ultimate goal of Gen Xers must be to retrieve a purpose from the ruins of utopianism. These documents also expose the characteristic themes of my generation: nomadism

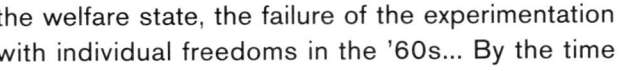

and rootlessness, the debate between the critical and the pragmatic, the relationship between architecture and the market, the computational as a new craft, the relation between speculative practice and the profession, theory and practice ... The generational reading of the work collected here aims to set up consistency with a whole population, enabling a form of authorship that transcends the individual agent and turns it into a collective, mediated one. Rather than forming an ideological manifesto, I hope this document will become an index of tendencies—and, in so doing, stimulate others. It is an early entry into an architectural chronicle of Generation X.

I have classified the documents into four basic parts that address the type of performance they were seeking. In some of them I aimed to locate myself in the field by

2   Ibid.

analyzing the practices of the previous generation of architects (the boomers). Some others are reflections on my own practices, both the academic and the professional. Some are an attempt to locate the practice of architecture within a political context. These four parts are: Global Positioning Systems; Nomad Practices; Breeding Sciences and Material Politics. They are framed by what I call a biographic calendar, which aims to describe the cultural, political, social, and economic milieu within which the texts were produced. The biographic calendar is assembled with a series of events of a global nature that for some reason have affected my biography or drawn my attention. They draw from multiple sources: politics, economics, technology, arts... A graphic texture of images that captures the temporal framework of these texts is provided as a background to trigger associations, which are often of a private nature. This radiation invokes the absolutely relative nature of the time—the passage through both the end of a century and the end of a millennium.

In essence, the drive of this series of essays is to capture the idea of performance through its multiple registers—from affordances to affects to political aesthetics—as the key to all pre-personal, anti-humanist, or non-ideational forces in architecture... It is performance that determines the last wave of innovation in architecture, and, most importantly, is the precursor to *material agency*—the ghost in the machine of all pre- and post-utopian architectures. The shadow in these essays is a function of having to overcome a generation of idealists with the attendant reversal of what precedes their own time. What emerges, by degree and by an irreducible historical agency, is a *new vitalism* insofar

as an interior is invoked while the division between inside and outside—representation and its other—is elided. This is the somewhat momentous path of two generations at war with ideology, without invoking absolute non-ideological bias (or not abandoning "ideas" altogether). What is momentous by 2011 is the apparent return of the Real as fully synthetic resolution of old antinomies and outmoded dialectical operations given to nihilism. Thus, these essays invoke a moment, not an answer for all times. They are *performative* and *pro forma*. Definitive answers await another day. The story is not ours to finish...

The images in this text are dedicated to the raise of Generation X and its unlikely heroes, as the context of these writings. Since the early press identified the emergence of a new generation after the seemingly incombustible Baby-Boomers, it came the identification of a few characters and their dubious achievements: The public figures displayed here epitomise the tampering with some powerful contemporary instruments and its likely pitfalls: drugs, cars, the music and film industry, the stock market and the internet.

Acknowledgements

For Milagros, Maider and Mina

I would like to thank the people who either gave me the chance of exploring text as a vehicle to research and to contribute to a public discussion, or those who inspired or directly contributed to discuss these texts and perfect them. Without them, this book would not have happened.

I would like to first thank Milagros Polo for triggering my interest in reading and theorising as a strategic withdrawal from the real. To Josep Quetglas and Charles Jencks, whose texts revealed to me that architecture could be connected, through writing, to a much wider world than originally thought. (before I ever met them in person) To Alberto Campo Baeza, who gave me the first chance to actually publish something. To Josep Lluís Mateo who showed me the opportunity to theorise the contemporary as a strategic tool for practice. To Fernando Márquez and Richard Levene who gave me that chance to experience directly the workings of the precedent generation of architects and to test my ideas with their work. And for giving me the exposure that made me well know as a global theorist. To Cynthia Davidson for her continuous encouragement to remain a writing architect. To Albert Ferré and Ramon Prat for over 20 years of generational editorship. And to the team who worked hard to make this project possible: Andrés Flajszer, Rosa Lleó, David Lorente, Tomoko Sakamoto, Manuel Távora and Anna Tetas. To Lluís Ortega and Bill Saunders who took the risk to publish my written work. To Alan Balfour, Ole Bouman, Ricky Burdett, Helen Castle, Marc Garcia, Manuel Gausa, Nikolaus Kuhnert, Ben Pell, Moisés Puente, Robert Stern, Richard Sennett, Ken Tadashi Oshima, Harm Tilman, Bernard Tschumi, Philip Ursprung and Albena Yaneva who thought I had something to say. To Peter Eisenman and Rem Koolhaas, whose example convinced me that writing was somehow important for practicing architects. To Arata Isozaki for his enormous generosity and support in diffusing many of these ideas. To Hchioh Seung Sang who became a friend after being criticised. To Sanford Kwinter who in a seminar in 1990 gave me sufficient theoretical ammunition to survive for twenty years. To Jeff Kipnis for being a most inspiring coach on many of my theoretical endeavours, this book amongst them. To Manuel de Landa for making things evident. To Sylvia Lavin for her support and engagement in a few of these controversies. To Vedran Mimica, Roemer Van Toorn and Pier Vittorio Aureli who took me out of postcapitalist political apathy. To Lucy Bullivant, Cristina Díaz-Moreno, Efrén García-Grinda, Jeff Inaba, Peter Macapia, John McMorrough, Ciro Najle, Nina Rappaport, Fernando Samaniego, Roemer Van Toorn and Anatxu Zabalbeascoa, who asked me the right questions. To Sarah Whiting for her supreme editing which developed ideas way beyond what they originally were. To Penelope Dean, Tina di Carlo, Jeannie Kim and Jennifer Siegler for their patience and help to streamlining ideas. To Maider Llaguno who set my radar a generation forward. Very special thanks to Gavin Keeney, who took on the biblical task to edit these texts to make them more resilient to time, and to Stan Allen for making this and a few other projects possible.

Table of contents

Global Positioning Systems — **16** USA 1990: Survey of an Artificial Territory, *Quaderns d'Arquitectura i Urbanisme*, Barcelona, 1990 — **26** The Material Organisation of Advanced Capitalism, *AD Monographs*, London, 1994 — **37** Frank O. Gehry. Still Life, *El Croquis*, Madrid, 1990 — **52** OMA: Notes for a Topographical Survey, *El Croquis*, Madrid, 1992 — **69** Herzog & de Meuron: Between the Face and the Landscape, *El Croquis*, Madrid, 1993 — **81** Jean Nouvel: Intensifying the Real, *El Croquis*. Madrid, 1994 — **93** Eisenman's Machine of Infinite Resistance, *El Croquis*, Madrid, 1997 — **103** A World Full of Holes, *El Croquis*, Madrid, 1998 — **127** The Alchemical Brothers: A Compact Material History of Herzog & de Meuron, *Natural History*, CCA, Montreal/Lars Müller Publishers, Zürich, 2001 — **132** RGBGlobal™, Installation at the Spanish Pavilion at the Architecture Venice Biennale, Venice, 2002 — **139** In Memoriam: Cedric Price, *AA Files*, London, 2003 — **141** A Scientific Autobiography + Post-¥€$ Postscript, *A+U*, Tokyo, 2002 and *Harvard Design Magazine*, Cambridge, 2004

Breeding Sciences — **164** Generative Processes and New Material Agencies, Sampling of *The Virtual in Architecture*, Tokyo University Virtual Architecture Exhibition Catalogue, Tokyo, 1996; *Generative Processes* in The Journal of Architecture and *Building Science*, Tokyo, June 1997; *The Computer as a Tool*, AIJ magazine, Tokyo 1997; and *Mind After Matter*, Jyvaskyla Symposium, 1997 — **178** Abstract Matters, Unpublished, 1999 — **183** Message to the Engine Drivers. *Quaderns d'Arquitectura i Urbanisme*, Barcelona, 1999 — **188** Back to the Hard Core, Studio Brief Columbia GSAPP, New York, 2001 — **192** The Material Grain of Geometry: A Conversation with Alejandro Zaera-Polo, *Log*, New York, 2004 — **205** Methodological Proposal for the Staedelschule Frankfurt, Unpublished, 2001— **214** The Berlage Menu: A new "productive" rather than "critical" paradigm, *Arch+*, Berlin, 2002 — **230** Five Points for Now, British Pavilion at the Architecture Venice Biennale, Venice, 2002 — **232** Processes, Materials, *Prototypes*... Symposium at UCLA, Los Angeles, 2002 — **237** AZP Crib Sheets Glossary, Symposium at UCLA, Los Angeles, 2002 — **242** Mediating Between Ideas and Matters: Icons,

Indexes, Diagrams, Drawings, and Graphs, *AD Monographs*, London, 2009 — **248** Architectural Education in a Global World, International Architectural Education Summit, Tokyo, 2009 — **255** Ecotectonics, Yale School of Architecture Studio, New Haven, 2010 — **260** Localizing Networks: Physical Terminals for Web 2.0 Engines, Princeton School of Architecture Studio, New Jersey, 2011 — **268** Theory of the Excuse, *Harvard Design Magazine*, Cambridge, 2012

Nomad Practices — **276** Forget Heisenberg. A Discussion on the Formless, Anybody Conference, Buenos Aires, 1996 — **284** The Virtual House, *Any Magazine*, New York, 1997 — **288** New Platforms, Anyhow Conference, Rotterdam, 1999 — **301** Remix 2000, *2G*, Barcelona, 2000 — **333** Roller-coaster Construction, *Verb Processing*, Barcelona, 2001 — **346** Species/Phylogenesis, *Phylogenesis*, Actar, Barcelona, 2003 — **356** United We Stand (The Bundle Tower™), Installation in the Graz Latent Utopias. Graz, 2001 — **361** Grunge Olympics, Unpublished, London, 2004 — **365** 30 St. Mary's Axe: Form isn't Facile, *Log*, New York, 2004 — **369** The Hokusai Wave, *Quaderns d'Arquitectura i Urbanisme*, Barcelona/*Volume*, New York, 2005 — **383** High-Rise Phylum 2007, *Harvard Design Magazine*, Cambridge 2007/*The Endless City*, London, 2008 — **408** Patterns, Fabrics, Prototypes, Tessellations, *AD Monographs*, London, 2009 — **421** Opportunity Conversation with Jeff Inaba, *Volume*, New York, 2008

Material Politics — **436** For an Ecology of High Metabolic Rate, *A+U*, Tokyo, 1997 — **440** Disciplines, *Hunch*, Rotterdam, 2003 — **440** Rethinking Representation, *Hunch*, Rotterdam, 2005 — **450** Mediators, *Hunch*, Rotterdam, 2006 — **459** Local Smart, Lecture series at the Berlage Institute, Rotterdam, 2006 — **463** Architecture and Power, *Hunch*, Rotterdam, 2007 — **466** Re-empowering Architecture, Berlage Institute's installation at the Architecture Venice Biennale, Venice, 2006 — **471** The Urban Age, *El País*, Madrid, 2007 — **477** The Politics of the Envelope, *Log*, New York, 2009 and *Volume*, New York, 2008 — **541** Bare Life, No Frills: Cheapness and Democracy, *Log*, New York, 2010

Book Structure

This book has been structured in four main areas of performance, into which the texts have been distributed:

–Global Positioning Systems (GPS): address primarily questions of location in time and space **–Breeding Sciences (BS)**: address the production and transmission of knowledge and the theorisation of skill **–Nomad Practices (NP)**: contains some reflections and proposals for architectural practices **–Material Politics (MP)**: aims to the empowerment of material agency.

These four chapters have been treated graphically with a different color ink. The sum of the four colors adds to black, as if the black ink had faded into four different hues which denote a primary area of performance.

Within these four sections, the texts also distinguish themselves in 8 formats according to their genre. Each category has a different page layout, so the outlook of the texts responds to the chapter they fall in and the category they belong to:

–Journalistic (J): double columned, justified, serif **–Theoretical (T)**: single columned, justified, serif, centered, occupying maximum of page space **–Epistolar (E)**: single columned, non justified, serif, positioned towards the bottom of the page, and towards the outer part of the page **–Manifestoes (M)**: single columned, justified, sans serif, bigger font size, occupying maximum of page space **–Instructive (I)**: single columned, justified, sans serif, positioned towards the outer part of the page **–Notarial (N)**: single columned, justified, serif, centered, white margins on both sides **–Propositive (P)**: single columned, non justified, serif, positioned towards the inner part of the page **–Conversational (C)**: double columned, non justified, sans serif.

The texts are set in a background of images which is aimed to pin them down to a wider context, a sort of timeline of events, objects and characters which emerged during my lifetime. The selection of the images is basically driven by personal interests and memories. They are not aimed to illustrate the texts, but to produce assemblages with them. The attachment between a text and the images that "staple" it to its wider context are based on associations of private nature. A brief explanation at the end of each text tries to give account of those associations that can be rationalised or simply publicly disclosed.

A biographic calendar of events which are personally relevant and a weighted glossary complete the structure that I hope will allow the readers to navigate through the complex web of relations and attachments that constitute this book.

Global Positioning Systems

The texts included under this section were aimed to explore the positioning—technical, cultural or geographical—of a contemporary practice of architecture. I wrote these texts primarily during my time as a student at Harvard GSD, my engagement at OMA, the period in which I taught at the AA and the early years of FOA. In these texts I was interested in exploring the new brave world of globalization and its associated technologies and locations. The analysis of the work of the architects of previous generations, triggered by my early involvement with *El Croquis* was a crucial positioning tool. The early exposure to multiple building cultures—Spain, USA, The Netherlands, the UK and Japan—was also an important trigger of some of these reflections. In either case, the objective was to set up a system of reference for a practice within the emerging economic and technological context of late-capitalism and globalisation.

USA 1990: Survey of an Artificial Territory

Was Darwin an American?
Darwin, not *Descartes,* was the American. America has nothing to do with hyper-rationalist speculation, the achievement of a secular or religious utopia, or the mad dream of reason. It has toyed with and discarded all three. It is concerned, instead, with the construction of an *artificial paradise*—a workable, okay version of the world, albeit totally transformed in the process into a type of hallucination of ends chasing means (and vice versa). In America, virtue lies neither in rationality nor in the possibility of absolute knowledge, but in pure *effectiveness.* It is no coincidence that the local philosophical lineage tends towards *pragmatism* and is not keen on epistemology per se. If truth is an axiom, efficiency is a quotient, an operation that depends on ends (will) and on means (power).

In the USA, the characteristic approach to a culture of colonization (arguably the outcome of the mad dream of reason and the Enlightenment proper) becomes radicalized due to the power its civilization has unleashed: given the power of instruments, it is no longer essential to know, only to decide. *Decisions* shape the world to the image of its desires. In America is necessary to construct the landscape before settling. The artificiality of North American landscape can be appreciated upon flying over the geometrical designs created by the harvesting machines and irrigation systems of the Midwest. Perhaps the break with tradition that lies at the core of the American ethos is just a manifestation of a civilization whose origin does not work organically and never will.

In America, science itself has ceased to be an instrument of knowledge and has instead become a mechanism or unitary apparatus to verify efficiency of means. The "nature" that technicity once processed has become enclosed in a cycle that swings between science, knowledge, and technology—that is, power. It is the perfect embodiment of the end foreseen in Heidegger's *Question Concerning Technology*; the world as a flatscape with containers.

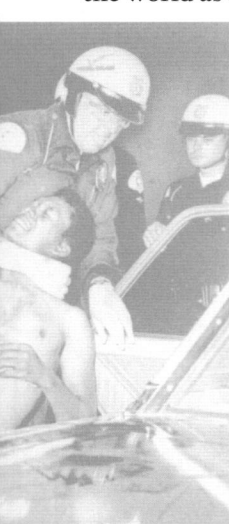

In the large software campuses of Silicon Valley, California, computers are becoming randomizing machines a thousand times more potent than the archaic roulette wheels of Las Vegas; the same gamble occurs, East and West, in the gigantic academic research centers at MIT or Stanford. In America singular progress is not produced by precise reasoning but by *natural selection*, each technological or cultural breakthrough emerging from a greater number of *mutations*. For this reason, scientists, artists, and architects are becoming engaged and, in some cases, enraptured with *chance*. Anyone who achieves a successful mutation is catapulted to the *cathodic heaven, reproduced* to the extreme. *Fashion* and *advertising* thus become perfect regulators of this *artificial evolutionary process*, liberated from the circularity of nature and the axioms of abstract truth, from the physical and the metaphysical. It is a culture driven by the linear chain of *decision making*.

The Productive Strategy: X-ray of a Vivisection

The production strategy of North American architecture divides the parties involved into those who play and those who choose. While the *architect-artist* has evolved to become an efficient machine that generates randomness, at the other extreme of the spectrum—and practically without steps in between—the *developer-architect* devotes his time to choosing, absorbing, and reproducing the successful mutations. The symbiotic relationships between both groups are a characteristic aspect of this biological reproduction.

While Peter Eisenman, Frank Gehry, and Daniel Libeskind strive to produce indetermination, individuals such as James Rouse, Gerald Hines, John Portman, and Donald Trump seem to have perfected the characteristically demiurgic attitude once attributed to architects; both their power to transform the world and their megalomania are well known. But these new *artificial gods* play no dice; that is what they pay architects for. In such a rapidly changing economy, the capacity to provide immediate answers is the quality most appreciated by those who award "princely" commissions. It is precisely the time restrictions involved in preparing and executing the project that impose the linear structure characterizing the typical American corporate structure. Although larger entities are admittedly going through a bit of a crisis, this productive structure continues to function in mid-sized offices that have recently permeated the North American market with the potential to become the most efficient way to meet new demands in simply building amidst the challenges of new media.

The process consists of a chain in which each step is taken on the basis of decisions made previously on a higher echelon, and according to increasing levels of abstraction. Thus the *principals* practically limit themselves to providing the spirit; beneath them, the *project manager* 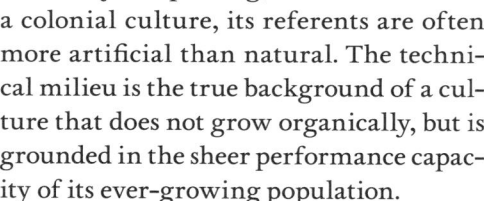 decides on the organization of work and the use of the firm's resources in terms of the project—here is where the economic variable comes in as a determinant in the project process. The first person to be concerned with the concrete materialization of the building is the *project leader,* who decides upon the general layout of the projects and supervises the production of the different work teams. Below these, the *designer-in-charge* is entrusted with leading the project teams, the true design task. This tree can become simpler or more complicated with intermediate figures, depending on the dimensions of the structure. The interesting thing here is that the basic decisions made concerning the project are severed from its concrete formalization as part of a strategy, thereby limiting any feedback between design decisions and global decisions, and dismantling the traditional circularity that made the project an organism that grew through a series of adjustments. The organic paradigm—the world as city, as house, as body (all anthropomorphic projections given to the humanist project of architecture)—has been abandoned in this linear process and replaced by a *heterotopical* model in which the parts and the whole are essentially disconnected, and the only link between them is an act of will, technical or otherwise. The building is no longer an organism: it is a Frankenstein, the product of a vivisection, the sign of the threshold of the *posthuman* world to come.

From Bricolage to NASA

The following poststructuralist theory developed in contemporary American architectural culture is hardly surprising; as a colonial culture, its referents are often more artificial than natural. The technical milieu is the true background of a culture that does not grow organically, but is grounded in the sheer performance capacity of its ever-growing population.

The roots that American culture has

in the artificiality and the complexity of its processes, even in the sphere of everyday life, imply certain specificities in the approach to technology, which becomes, by way of its omnipresence, a *second nature*—a new form of the *pensée sauvage*.

Given the mutability of the technological milieu in contemporary American culture, the architectural project can no longer be addressed as a whole; there is no room for an activity that simultaneously builds the object and the language; within this artificial nature, we can only work like *bricoleurs*, without a previously defined project or set language.

In the USA, technology does not have the heroic, socially marginal, even subversive character that it has in Europe: technology is there to make your life easy. The process of technical refinement with engineering ambitions that animates a wide spectrum of contemporary European architecture could be interpreted as a traditional approach where there is confidence in the language and the project, and a system of inherited values. Such finesse is only possible in a well-settled culture, both geographically and politically. It may be precisely the mistrust of language and tradition—characteristic of former colonial cultures, due to the disparity of backgrounds amongst members of the community, and the territorial instability—that has pushed the architectural project toward a pure *making* in contemporary American architecture. Verification occurs after the fact, rather than referring to previous traditions, and a project's efficiencies determine its ultimate value. Against rationalist thought, American architecture embraces statistical reason: it is the difference between the *Concorde* and the *jumbo jet*; between the high-tech and the low-tech; the sharp and the blunt.

American blunt technology is based on an artificial evolutionary process that ranges from domestic *bricolage* to NASA, at levels that do not exist in the old world, where evolution is produced as a result of Cartesian reason within well-controlled and delimited environments.

The fact that certain radical proposals, such as the tensegrity models of Robert le Ricolais and Buckminster Fuller, have been absorbed and rendered operative by more orthodox engineers (for example, Fazlur Khan and W. J. LeMessurier), is a testament to the capacity of the American system to integrate technological mutations, albeit often with imported talent.

Transparency versus Resistance
The radical detachment between practice and academia in the USA indexes a higher level of schizophrenia between *culture* and *civilization* than in the Old

World. The classic Adorno/Benjamin debate regarding the autonomy of "intellectual work," or Umberto Eco's polemic contrasting *apocalyptic* and *integrated* intellectuals, has a very direct translation into the American building industry.

What is interesting about the American situation is the clarity with which the extremes appear: those who want to retrieve organicity and the circularity of value and reestablish the bond between action and thought are opposed by those who do not want to be critical but prefer to engage with economic and social reality; that is, in the latter case, to be *transparent* and indulge the vortex of consumerism, the instability of values, and capitalist *spectacle*. Against the heroic stance of the resistant, they seem to claim: "If you can't avoid it, then relax and enjoy."

Regionalism versus Difference

We may be witnessing the American Empire's decadence. If the capacity of a culture to expand depends on its operativity beyond its geopolitical limits, or its autonomy with respect to its original substrate, this is precisely what American culture is questioning now. And it is far from clear what the outcome may be.

The fact that Rockefeller Center has been sold to Mitsubishi Estate (a real estate company of the Mitsubishi Group) may have something to do with the drop in the stock value of corporate architecture generally. American corporate architecture was essentially a colonizing device, a solidly average product typical of American industry, not unlike Wonder Bread, which fed the country during the 1950s. What is now being called New Regionalism is a return to the prewar age of Bernard Maybeck, H. H. Richardson, McKim, Mead & White, Greene & Greene, and others—or the era when local flavors were rediscovered after the *first colonization* of the territory by exceedingly pragmatic architectures, the railroad, and early industrialization. The difference now is that there has been another postwar colonization, implemented through the construction of the interstate freeways, and the rapid development of air transport and *mass media*.

This second wave of banal colonization has introduced a new layer of consistency and homogeneity based on techno-economical factors (the first was primarily political and legal, wresting control by displacing natives and taming the anarchic elements of the first colonists). This new techno-economical wave enforces a general state of mobility or rootlessness that neutralizes geographical space, replacing traditional regional tectonics with the abstraction of numbers and the fictive *frisson* of spectacle (mediatic capitalism). This is the ideal exemplification of Guy Debord's statement that the collapse of real space performed by technological society has created the need to reproduce the distance internally, as a *spectacular distance*. Cultural precedents, traditions, and experience are now replaced by sheer will in the construction of *difference*. No longer grounded in need but in pure *desire*, the American dream now materializes technically and "phantasmatically," rather than tectonically. Or, as a type of "cinematographic" fiction (illusion), America now inhabits what Umberto Eco has called a form of "hyper reality" (simulacra upon simulacra).

The Picturesque South

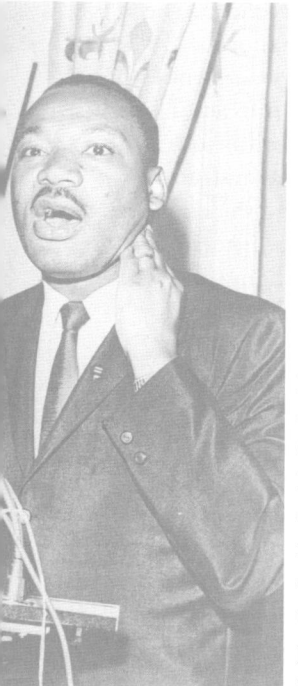

Houston, Atlanta, and Miami are cities crossed by money, suspended in the landscape by the green sap of the greenback. Houston is a corporeal diagram of economic forces, the most radical manifestation of the American will to power. Ground does not exist as such; it is an invention of its inhabitants. The only regulations are those that successive owners have written in their property contracts; the materialization of desire. Perhaps it is for this reason that Houston possesses the most impressive skyline of any modern North American metropolis—that is, it grew without restraints (without zoning or any other means of rational planning).

In Houston, CRS (Caudill Rowlett Scott, a.k.a. CRS-Sirrine), one of the most potent architecture-producing machines in the US, turns black gold (oil) into (artificial) stone, while its reach as an A&E firm extends all over the country and into the reinsurance business (through CRS Capital). Its rootedness is in its anodyne ubiquity. On the other hand, with a population of around three million, Atlanta is the city with the greatest volume of air traffic in the world—rootlessness personified. This velocity of means allows only a superficial appreciation of actually existing things, producing a reality that is no longer terrestrial ("archaeological" or of the earth) but simply aerial ("picturesque" or fabricated out of thin air). As metaphors, Houston and Atlanta epitomize the explosive growth that occurred across the American South in the latter half of the twentieth century, giving it, in turn, excessive *political* clout. The architecture of Atlanta is as dense and humid as William Faulkner's novels.

A good example of this southern way of thinking is the architecture of Scogin Elam and Bray (founded in 1984), another refined mutation of the random system of great corporations, in this case grown within

Heery & Heery International (established in 1952), a local corporate behemoth. With obscene southern gentility, the buildings by Scogin Elam and Bray are essentially energetic, sharp-pointed, and shining, like the nose of a Corvette.

Nature and artifice merge in the kingdom of the *mortal gods*. Atlanta is the city of the great developers: Portman and Hines are characters of a nearly divine nature where the desire for riches has been replaced by sheer megalomania. The most interesting aspect of these tycoons is precisely that *their power takes a physical form*. Their domain is not limited exclusively to what is erected from ground level: the fantastic natural forms that grow at the feet of the skyscrapers of Atlanta are, to a large extent, artificial and powerful amplifications of the *picturesque* method par excellence.

In Miami, the great "colonial" style—that is, the International Style—bursts at the seams with pure richness in the work of Arquitectonica. The buildings by Bernardo Fort-Brescia and Laurinda Spear embrace a picturesque elaboration of the images of modernist architecture: the most cosmopolitan manifestation of *sunny-funny*, without the regionalist tectonicity of Antoine Predock or the moral scruples of Gehry.

The Resisting East

In New York City, a monument should be erected to the Unknown Artist, fallen victim to ambition and misfortune. New York is the city with the greatest density of ideas per square foot in the world: each apartment that is modified sustains a highly sophisticated interpretation of the world; each minimal gesture commits the whole person. Contrary to what occurs in Texas, where the vastness of open space results in an essential indetermination of actions, the lack of space in Manhattan forces their over-determination. The whole movement of the city is produced in the hidden, interstitial area of the stock exchange, the credit card, and the fax. Between the proximity of the body or the gesture and the infinite velocity of transactions, the city's daily life evolves. This duality between the presence of the body and the abstraction of money characterizes the schizophrenia of its architecture.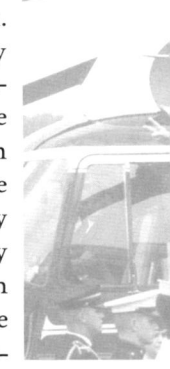

SOM, is changing not only the postmodern skin but also the bones: chain production is no longer adequate in the age of computers and telecommunications, and the tendency now is to divide the office up into small workgroups.

Steven Holl is a perfect example of faith in hermeneutics. A declared heir of the *resistant* school, he has become the paladin of right-minded society, having spent several years living a bohemian life in order to prepare for combat. Taking firm anchor in disciplinary questions of geometry and construction—with a certain degree of New York regionalism, and even a dose of social conscience while brandishing the sword of phenomenology—he is determined to resist the advance of international capital. May the force be with him.

For his part, Harry Wolf has achieved a perfect blend of *resistant aesthetics* and commitment to the world of finance. His office carries out the fundamentally pragmatic task of high-quality design but without the theoretical ambition that characterizes New York output at it grandest.

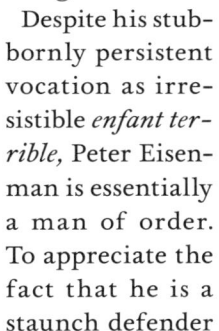

Despite his stubbornly persistent vocation as irresistible *enfant terrible,* Peter Eisenman is essentially a man of order. To appreciate the fact that he is a staunch defender of the episteme, one need only contemplate his efforts to understand and explain the contemporary world through pursuits such as deconstruction, fractal geometry, the structure of DNA, or the semi-mythic architectural world of Andrea Palladio. The great fallacy of so-called deconstructivist architecture was the attempt to include in its ranks a pragmatist such as Gehry or someone so far removed from zero-degree architecture as Rem Koolhaas. In the meantime, John Hejduk and other brilliantly nostalgic minds construct highly sophisticated mythologies from the safe reserve of the ivory tower, resisting the consumer avalanche and sidestepping spectacle.

For its part, Chicago seems to have lost the ability to produce good architecture without great intellectual pretensions. The aftermath of the *Miesian school,* an extraordinary precedent in the exercise of apparent *heroic resistance* in harmony with economic opportunism, appears finally to have burnt itself out. Its heirs, such as Krueck & Olsen, produce a kind of watered-down version. The work of Helmut Jahn, who seems to have connected with the commercial vein of the city that gave rise to its characteristic architecture, lacks the qualitative sophistication that such quantities of architecture should produce.

The Destiny of the West
If New York is reputably the kingdom of self-righteous self-consciousness, and California is the territory of anti-intellectual currents, or easy ecstasy, then the Midwest

is easily explained as the pragmatic heart of America, caught between the two extremes and trying nonetheless to define that middle ground as *the* ground. At the edge of America (the so-called right coast), California embraces not the easy romantic ecstasy of nature, but rather the *uneasy* voluptuous ecstasy of technical media, speed, traffic, and images. Nature and artifice are intimately mixed, as Reyner Banham explains in *The Architecture of Four Ecologies* (1971).

Technology becomes the new *mastery of revelation,* it acquires *biological* qualities. Silicon Valley's children stitch together complicated computer programs; they are employed because in certain areas they are more effective than more expert programmers; they are better able to play, advantageously lacking in preconceptions, causal considerations, and experience—that is, self-consciousness itself. Work has become play in a technical environment so complex that it invalidates old European reason. Technicity seems (for the moment) to be the antidote to age-old existential and metaphysical questions. Why worry when you can compute?

Buildings, like computers, are born, become sick, are vaccinated, become old, and die... Corrugated sheet metal, cardboard, plywood, asphalt, chain link: all proliferate now as only plants once did. They form the "garden" in which the city grows.

Gehry is a typical product of the system: a successful mutation, a quirk of fate. No brilliant academic curriculum, no meticulously constructed career; he might simply have been an anonymous quality professional. His great talent is for taking advantage of opportunities, for letting currents pass through him, for being transparent. The extraordinary force of his work, and the difference that separates him from his ingeniously artful epigones lies precisely in his authenticity, in his *naturalness.*

As has occurred throughout the history of Western culture, its center of gravity is moving farther west, even crossing the Atlantic, except that in California Western thought seems to be touching the edges of the East, as it also does geographically (the breadth of the Pacific notwithstanding). If the gradients that indicate the evolution of Western culture can be measured as the passage from *pagan mystery* to *Christian revelation,* from *collective communion* to *individual self-consciousness,* or, more generally, from *faith* to *reason,* in California these parameters seem to be becoming inverted, perhaps in preparation for sliding into and crossing the Pacific.

The images in this text illustrate the strangeness of the world that grew from the success of the American post-war period and the development of corporate global modernism, which grounds the early experience of a generation: the theme parks and the riots, Vietnam and the civil rights struggle set the scene for a form of modernity that, far from the principles of rationality that inspired early modernism, gave rise to the phenomenology of globalisation.

The Material Organization of Advanced Capitalism

Unveiling the *Phylum*
This document aims to describe the forms of the production of capitalist space at the end of the twentieth century, recognizing the importance of an urban phenomenon that, merely because of its quantitative extent, has an enormous impact in the contemporary world. The collection of practices described below aim to unveil a phenomenon of almost *geological* magnitude, avoiding ideological or social critique, suspending judgment temporarily in order to engage with this new urban phenomenology. The aim here is to initiate a redescription of the processes of urban production and to propose models of distribution, capturing the orders of the emerging urban *phylum*,[1] identifying organizations, and geometries that rule contemporary urbanity in the search for material and formal determinations suitable for the transformation of the urban.

---

1   *Phylum* is the term used by Deleuze and Guattari to describe the evolution of a material culture, the series of singularities and traces of expression and the processes of transformation associated to a given state of evolution of nonorganic matter. The term inaugurates a purely materialist, nonhumanistic history of technology. See Gilles Deleuze and Félix Guattari, "1227: Treatise on Nomadology:—The War Machine" in *A Thousand Plateaus. Capitalism and Schizophrenia*, trans. Brian Massumi (Minneapolis: University of Minnesota Press, 1987).

We examine the casuistic of the cities where we live, where we can no longer identify the indexes of an urban behavior as we used to know it. Paraphrasing Lefebvre,[2] this is the sign of a schism between *spatial practices* and *representational spaces*, between the way we envision urban space and the way we produce it.

There are several ways in which the schism between urban production and urban representation has been addressed in the past. For example, in 1990s Berlin, every new development was effectively submitted to strict rules of aesthetic control in the name of urban correctness and cultural consistency. In contrast, several Asian cities have been celebrating the chaotic nature of uncontrolled urbanization as the liberating essence of the contemporary metropolis. Certain forms of radical pragmatism have suspended the need for intelligibility and, therefore, of appraisal of the resulting environment. And yet, despite the mysterious nature of these landscapes of pure production and the multiple possibilities they open (as opposed to the over-coding that characterizes ideological urbanism), it is impossible to renounce altogether the desire to project some sensibility, to speculatively imagine potential orders, or to envision forms of control. The eulogies for conventional urbanism predicting chaos and impotence suggest the post-ideological city will only lead to the demise of planning, the preferred agent for the possible transformation of urban reality. In order to avoid leaving the city solely in the hands of the so-called free market, it is necessary, then, to initiate the reconstruction of potential orders, looking at the contemporary city as a process whose order has still to be identified somewhere between that of Berlin and Tokyo.

In parallel to the changes affecting the nature of the contemporary urban environment, a new scientific paradigm arises to replace the long-lasting validity of *conservative systems*—those based in models where systems are considered isolated and matter and energy are assumed to be constant—by

---

2   Henri Lefebvre, *La production de l'espace* (Paris: Anthropos, 1974).

systems of vaguely delimited locations crossed by flows.³ By extension, the demise of the Enlightenment-Modernist project of universal rationality may be a matter of spatial organization, a matter of geometry:⁴ *the emergence of a global space that enhances local differences.*

Flexible Accumulation: Spatial Organization as Economic Strategy

The urban phenomenology we are addressing here emerges with the crisis that affected the economies of developed countries at the end of the 1960s parallel with the implementation of the forms of economic integration devised to overcome the problems of over-accumulation inherent to capitalist development, which have now consolidated into new forms of urbanity.

If urbanization has historically developed as a process of *accumulation* and *location of surpluses* within the late-capitalist regime, the urban milieu is now determined by its capacity to *incorporate* a *circulation of surpluses.* David Harvey has described as a "regime of flexible accumulation" that  form of economic integration characteristic of advanced capitalism where over-accumulation is solved through *mechanisms of spatial and temporal displacement.*⁵ Within the regimes of flexible accumulation, periodical redistributions of capital through time and space are set to absorb the over-accumulation inherent to capitalist development. The areas required for the system's growth are produced not through direct territorial expansion, but through an increasing mobility of resources and capital, and the massive development of transport and communications.

---

3   As René Thom writes, any form of knowledge is an operative tool, where the data we register and manipulate (*pregnances*) do not correspond to any essence of reality but with our ability to capture entities into an *intelligible* and therefore *operable* domain. René Thom, *Structural Stability and Morphogenesis* (Reading, MA: The Benjamin/Cummings Publishing Company, 1975).

4   Michel Serres proposes geometry as the origin of thought and knowledge, precisely because it is the most direct, operational, and pragmatic form of knowledge. Michel Serres, *Les origines de la géométrie* (Paris: Flammarion, 1993).

5   Mechanisms of temporal displacement are those that permit the instant conversion of fixed capital to moving capital, using loans, bonds, mortgages, etc. These mechanisms require the existence of financial institutions capable of guaranteeing the validity of these conversions. Mechanisms of spatial displacement are those that continually allow for the opening of new areas of growth to absorb surpluses in production, capital, and labor. Technological and educational research, and construction of transport and communication infrastructures are exemplary processes. These are the processes that are most interesting in relation to the rethinking of urbanism and territorial organization. See David Harvey, *The Urbanization of Capital* (Baltimore: John Hopkins University Press, 1985).

The growth of the *organic composition of capital*,[6] which once characterized capitalist development in its Fordist regime, reverses direction within late capitalism: the quotient of *variable-to-fixed* capital increases to enhance the flexibility of production. The evolution from economies of *scale* to economies of *scope* implies that production is no longer competitive through a good cost/price relationship, but through its diversification and capacity to adjust to a constantly evolving demand. As a result of this growing *disorganization* of the composition of capital, and, therefore, of the *location of surpluses*, new urban structures tend toward less organic structures.

Despite the systematic weakening or erasure of spatial boundaries, the production of urban space seems to acquire a central position within late capitalism: a periodical restructuring of capitalist space requires urban structures to maintain *flexibility* in order to absorb constant spatial reformulation without losing specificity and centrality. In this situation, the success of contemporary urban topographies will probably rely upon the ability to articulate this all-pervading *space of flows*,[7] requiring the consolidation of centralities with sufficient *critical mass* to ensure structural stability.

Globalization as Trigger of Difference

In the urban models generated by industrial and Fordist capitalism, the stability of the economic and productive structure, the homogeneity of technologies, and the uniformity of the social composition were projected onto *stable*, *homogeneous*, and *continuous* spatial and material organizations where exchange and flow processes had only a relative importance in the construction of urban topographies. In contrast, the late-capitalist city is characterized by the coexistence of heterogeneous economies, technologies, and cultures, and the growing importance of flows and exchange. The globalization of financial markets is a crucial factor in the formation of contemporary urban topographies: capital and resources operating on a global scale have resulted

---

6   Namely, the ratio between fixed capital and variable capital within a productive structure. In Marxist theory, that quotient is supposed to increase over time, following the development of a productive structure in order to improve its productivity. It implies a tendency toward monopolistic forms of capitalism and an economy of scale.

7   See Manuel Castells, *The Informational City* (Oxford: Blackwell, 1989).

in the devaluation of spatial boundaries. Simultaneously, but inversely, urban centers evolve into poles of attraction whose success depends on their offer of specialized services. In the late-capitalist city, centrality is established through connectivity rather than through accumulation.

Contrary to the homogenization of urban topographies that could be expected from these processes of globalization, the mobility of capital and resources develops into a sharp consciousness for the specificity of each enclave. The locations that offer more developed mechanisms of spatio-temporal displacement (improved transport and communications, developed research and educational facilities, more trustworthy credit systems, and fiscal advantages) will become poles of attraction of labor and surplus, and consequently locations of urban centrality. By increasing the awareness of *difference* we witness an *artificial regionalization, where the local flavor has become synthetic*. This process of territorial competition within advanced capitalism has given supremacy to the material over the social: the political battlefield has become spatial rather than classbased.

Intensive Coherence: Constellations, Networks, Lacunary Distributions

Traditional urban structures were developed through an organic growth scheme; modern urban structures were based on techniques aimed to produce *extensive coherence* of the urban territories. Both models implied techniques operating through the linear application of a formal order—centrality, axiality, repetition, homogeneity—over the full extension of the field of operation.

As late-capitalist modes of production and economic integration began to consolidate, urban topographies exposed to the instability of the system could no longer maintain the rigidities of an organic structure articulating urban events within a global structure, whether in a programmatic or geometric sense. As a result of this, a whole new urban phenomenology arose in the hope of producing more operative spatial paradigms. Abandoning the premise of coherence that formed the core of modernism, these attempts tried to construct new urban structures through difference and incoherence: Collage City, critical regionalism, deconstructivism, postmodern historicism, and other proposals posited alternative modes of constructing difference. However, these strategies left us with an epistemological oxymoron: an operation purely based on difference. As an alternative to these early late-capitalist spatial models, the positions described here are based on a model of *intensive coherence*, where the urban field remains coherent and yet allows for differentiation through variance in intensity.

The territorial organization derived from a *liquid economy* disintegrates the urban body and spreads it over the territory in a multiplication of centrality, structured on the transport infrastructure as a vector of mobility. It is no longer the isotropic extension of the modern city; the city is being built around *lines of displacement and connection*, operating as a *connective topology* that turns urban structures into *conductive milieus*. A model like this that manipulates intensities is more suitable to register and manipulate the progressive erasure of the classic *city/territory opposition*.

The polycentrality of the Parisian Ville Nouvelles, the cities of the American Sunbelt, and the Central European conurbations such as the Ruhrgebiet and the Randstaat are all examples of the type of continuous, heterogeneous, and polycentric structure of emerging urban fabrics. Cities constituted as constellations of *attractors*,[8] which defy both the *gravitational* criteria of traditional urban models and isotropic, decentralized *modernist* expansions. Within emerging urban models, the *center/periphery*, *full/void*, and *exterior/interior* oppositions tend to disappear, evolving toward polycentric, often sprawling non-hierarchical systems—*networks or rhizomes*[9]—that are arguably more productive and operative within the chaotic and unstable conditions of flexible accumulation.

The projection of the Parisian Ville Nouvelles is a paradigmatic case of manipulation of the forces at play in the late-capitalist city through the determination of its spatial structure as an *intensively coherent, inorganic*

---

8   We use the term *attractors*, taken from contemporary physics, to determine certain areas of structural stability within an evolving system. This allows us to understand the system's behavior without having to resort to "centralized" or "constant" models. See René Thom, *Structural Stability and Morphogenesis*, op. cit.

9   This term, proposed by Deleuze and Guattari, characterizes material or conceptual structures that articulate multipliers. See Deleuze and Guattari, "Rhizome" in *A Thousand Plateaus*, op. cit.

structure. The plan originates in a political decision that sought to solve the sclerosis of the overcrowded metropolitan area of Paris without decreasing its weight within the network of European cities. Paul Delouvrier, Prefect of the Parisian Region, set in motion an ambitious program for the Île de France that would connect, through a densified transport infrastructure, five Ville Nouvelles and an airport zone.[10] Unlike the English New Towns, the political nature of the Île de France operation did not just try to solve the growth of the urban structure, but also to keep Paris as the capital of Europe. Delouvrier designed a system where the distance between the primitive nucleus and the new centers would maintain their interdependence and, therefore, the unity of the structure: the "flexibilization" of the urban structure without the loss of its critical mass.

Another interesting example of this type of urban structure can be found in the cities of the American Sunbelt—those placed in the band that crosses the continent between the forty-second parallel and the Mexican border (Los Angeles, Phoenix, Dallas, Fort Worth, Houston, Atlanta, Washington, and Miami). These cities witnessed explosive growth and development during the 1960s and 1970s while the great cities of the American East were stalling. Contrary to what was happening simultaneously in Paris, the development of the Sunbelt cities occurred with a remarkable lack of state control, driven mostly by economic demands. The Sunbelt cities were created on the territory generated in the second colonization of America sponsored in part by the construction of the interstate freeways in the 1950s, but indicative of the postwar boom visited upon the USA. If the first colonization established the cities of the East and West coasts, and on the Great Lakes, the network of coast-to-coast interstate freeways opened up the interior of the country. New accessibility, a good climate, and cheap land were the reasons for the flow of investment that produced one of the quantitatively most important urban developments in recent history. The

---

10 See the analysis of the construction of Île de France in H. V. Savitch, *Post-Industrial Cities: Politics and Planning in New York, Paris and London* (Princeton, NJ: Princeton University Press, 1988).

Sunbelt cities have generally developed a characteristic polycentric structure of dense cores, approximately ten miles away from each other, where the urban structure is determined by the topological continuity of the infrastructure (the connective tissue) versus the integrity of the geometric urban fabric (the body itself). Cities begin to resemble cyborgs—half-human, half-machinic entities. The characteristic flatness of the topography and the benign climate of the Sunbelt were determinant factors for the development of these newly wrought or newly expanded cities. Among these urban attractors, motorways and open spaces serve as a *buffer*, allowing the system to evolve and providing the flexibility required by the emerging financial climate.

But connectivity is not the only driving force of the late-capitalist urban milieu. The very creation of a connective structure of transport and communication becomes the reason for the increase of *differentiation* within a milieu where spatial boundaries and metrics are becoming increasingly ineffective. The conurbations of the Ruhrgebiet and the Randstaat are a paradigmatic case of such an effect. Neither of them originates directly from a political decision (as in Paris); instead they are triggered as mutations of preexisting urban structures via a new accessibility. What in both cases was a Medieval network of small cities evolves, by way of the development of transport infrastructure during the 1950s, into a series of urban enclaves that operate as a unitary urban structure. Each one of the existing centers undergoes simultaneously an important growth and a functional specialization: for example, within the Ruhrgebiet, Dusseldorf becomes the service center, Bochum the industrial one, Essen the commercial area; in the Dutch Randstaat, Rotterdam assumes the industrial role, Amsterdam specializes in services and culture, and The Hague hosts administrative functions.

If in the Northern European conurbations differentiation occurs on a programmatic level, the polycentrality of cities like Tokyo or Kuala Lumpur demonstrate an associated phenomenon. The urban acupuncture of the so-called Fashion Buildings in Tokyo belongs to the same strategy of intensification. This is an intervention within the existing fabric that simultaneously blurs the structure of uses, through the introduction of *hybrid* complexes, and singularizes points through physical *differentiation* and *densification*. The proliferation of hybrid structures is certainly one of the consequences of the demand for a greater flexibility within late-capitalist urban structure. Urban events can no longer be captured as typological definitions once the integrating ability of

The Material Organization of Advanced Capitalism

urban structure has disappeared. *Hybrids* are programmatic structures able to *capture* erratic flows of *surpluses* (franchises are, for example, the preferred clients of the fashion buildings) and fix them in specific topographies, bypassing the mediation of an organic urban structure. The Tokyo hybrids become paradigmatic of the complex nature of the contemporary city, which no longer responds to simple linear models (that is, metric distance, center-periphery gradients, public-private structure, inside-outside boundaries). Each point on the territory is determined by superimposition of laws whose effects cannot be analyzed as linear functions. Hybrids are to complex processes what types are to linear processes.

Complex Dynamics:
Qualities of Urban Morphogenesis

So far, we have tried to depict through some examples how the dynamics of late-capitalist urban phenomenology register the emergence of complex orders that cannot be resolved by traditional urban models. These regimes of flexible accumulation bring the variable conditions of the urban structure to the forefront, opening a field that was largely ignored by both the structural and the organicist proposals. The emerging urban topographies exhibit an extraordinary increase in the external links of these urban structures that calls into question the validity of urban planning strategies based on traditional models. The models of material organization that emerge from these conditions of change and exteriority resonate with the contemporary sciences of complexity, where the consideration of *non-conservative* systems prevails. The most interesting quality of these models is that in these systems there is no equilibrium and yet, there is structural stability.

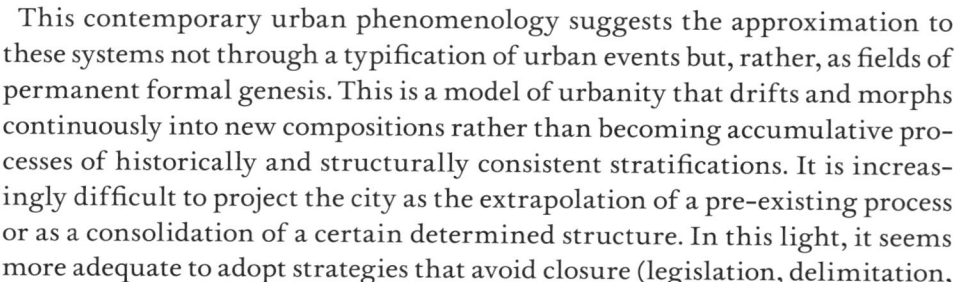

This contemporary urban phenomenology suggests the approximation to these systems not through a typification of urban events but, rather, as fields of permanent formal genesis. This is a model of urbanity that drifts and morphs continuously into new compositions rather than becoming accumulative processes of historically and structurally consistent stratifications. It is increasingly difficult to project the city as the extrapolation of a pre-existing process or as a consolidation of a certain determined structure. In this light, it seems more adequate to adopt strategies that avoid closure (legislation, delimitation, and the assignment of competencies through rigorous taxonomies of space or the imposition of geometrical structures). To prioritize change and transformation and address contemporary urban structures as systems liberated from origins and ends seems a more appropriate approach.

The consideration of the temporal variable within a process of urban morphogenesis approximates the preexisting urban structure as a base for evolution subject to potential modifications. It does not imply the completion of an *originary* situation nor a final goal. Originating crimes and redemptive utopias are forgotten. The temporal extension becomes the space where the *asymmetries* of the process are registered. Urban processes are irreversible and never in equilibrium, and *types* and *structures* become obsolete planning instruments under such a new regime because of their insistence on the *constancy* of form and function. *Density*, *size*, and *topological structure* are much more important in contemporary urbanism than the traditional relationships of *scale*, *measurement*, and *proportion*. (For example, scale relates to a fixed reference—man, state, place—and is consequently a non-reliable approach within the unstable geographies of late capitalism.)

The loss of an organic and hierarchical structure for both city and territory (as complex) produces the fragmentation of the urban system into singularities. Instead of *homogeneous*, *equilibrated*, and *segmented*, the new urban forms spread over the territory as a *heterogeneous*, *unbalanced*, and *uneven* yet *connective* essence.

These urban changes are taking place simultaneously with the evolution away from static, central, or linear models toward more complex ones in contemporary science and mathematics. Contemporary urban structures are now operating as multiple-attractor fields with *automorphic* properties across different scales[11] —or at least this is the theory. From the competition between metropolises on an international scale to the polycentric structure of metropolitan areas, including the polymorphic and polycentric spatiality of hybrid buildings, we always find analogous polycentric compositions organizing connective space, where differential intensities share a common space.

11 Referring to the concept used in fractal mathematics, in which automorphic structures are defined in each of their scales. Benoit B. Mandelbrot, *The Fractal Geometry of Nature* (New York: Freeman & Co., 1977).

Multiple agencies now perform where once there was one or (at best) two at play. Not unlike particle physics, urban phenomenon now takes many forms under different conditions. It is not long before human agency follows course.

New faces of geometry arise from the necessity of operating within this late-capitalist material culture. If we look at maps that register the nature of contemporary urban structures we will find that the correspondence between the formal structure of the city and the urban systems (the communication systems and public space) are not regulated, as they are in traditional urban systems, by a common *metric* and *geometric* structure. Irregular geometries versus ideal forms, compositions of traces rather than *closed forms* and boundaries, these seem to be the manifestation of the complex formal logics of emerging urban systems. The predominance of flows, deformations, and dimensional and dynamic heterogeneity within late-capitalist production calls into question the static spatiality, homogeneity of magnitudes, and consistency of form over time that once characterized traditional urban structures and planning methods. What remains to be seen is whether human agency can maintain and control these new structures or whether they spin out of control—as is implicit in the hubris of the over-wrought city.

The images along this text set a counterpoint to the heroic tone of the writing, which marks the realization that we had exited modernism and that the new brave world of late capitalism was opening multiple opportunities for a reformulation of spatial and material organizations. Instead, the images refer to a series of man-made disasters of global reach that punctuated the last three decades: Seveso, Exxon Valdez, Chernobyl, Bhopal, Deepwater... demonstrate the devastating effects of the new paradigm when it got out of control.

Published in *El Croquis* n. 45,
Madrid, 1990

Frank O. Gehry, Still Life

An Anthropological Analysis
Frank Gehry's extraordinary success in the 1990s may actually be due to his capacity to attend to the object and the detail without falling into the disciplinary discussions that have otherwise monopolized "cultivated" architectural debate since the mid-1970s.[1] Gehry is one of the few architects of his generation in the USA who has been able to escape the narrow confines of the academic debate while remaining experimental and culturally relevant. The energy driving his practice comes primarily from a direct connection to the socio-economic and productive structures in which he operates, rather than from an "artistic" approach to the practice. Gehry's talent has been to understand and take advantage of the hidden potential of this work, creating an architecture that is both popular and *authorial*.

The links between Gehry's work and the more populist currents of North American architecture are well documented: it is no accident that he labored for people like Victor Gruen, John Portman, and Bruce Goff during his early career. The con-

---

1   This essay intends to approach Gehry's work through an "anthropological" analysis. To this end, I have structured the text as a fragmentary collection of ideas focusing on the polemical charge of each argument, rather than on resolving the contradictions between them. I must recognize here a debt to Luciano Rubino's monograph on Gehry [Luciano Rubino, *Frank O. Gehry Special* (Rome: Edizione Kappa, 1984)], which was crucial in setting up my critical perspective, a form of critique that sees architecture as a coherent process with a social structure, and not as an autonomous discipline that produces objects with a signature.

nection to popular culture as a source of inspirational fire-power was advanced by Robert Venturi and Denise Scott Brown in *Learning from Las Vegas* (albeit under the guise of a more democratic "architecture without architects"). However, in practice, they have not been able to match the popular success achieved by a less intellectual sensibility such as that of Gehry, who has succeeded to project the approach into an entirely new dimension.[2] The interest of Gehry's work is to have gone beyond commenting on Palladian or Corbusian aesthetics, or to becoming the architectural translator of the poetics of Richard Serra, or the incarnation of a deconstructivist cosmology. Rather, it lies in a very specific strategy that exploits the generative potential of certain local social and cultural demands.

Attending mass in Johnson's Crystal Cathedral or riding the elevators in Portman's Hotel Bonaventure are very different architectural experiences from those proposed by politically correct "critical" architects to raise the spirit of the consuming masses. Gehry has recognized that exquisite compositions and subtle, theoretical mannerist gestures are systematically destroyed by the *Doppler effect* of accelerated consumption, with a consequent loss of intelligibility. The return to a more literal architecture, closer to the techniques of advertising than to academic rhetoric, has been integrated by Gehry into work that remains experimental while connecting with the desires and possibilities of a certain socio-economic sector; that is, the California of the Reagan era, "in which what used to be stigmatized as mass or commercial culture is now received into the precincts of a new and enlarged cultural realm."[3]

Architecture as Second Nature

"The only problem is to know if the natural systems which we call living beings should be assimilated into the artificial systems that science develops from prime material, or if they should not more correctly be compared to that natural system which is the totality of the universe. That life could be a kind of mechanism I can clearly see. But is the mechanism of artificially isolated parts within the totality of the universe, or is it within the totality of the real?" —HENRI BERGSON

2   See Fredric Jameson, "The Politics of Theory," *New German Critique* 33 (Fall 1984).
3   Fredric Jameson, Ibid.

When Frank Gehry began, in the mid-1960s, to work with low-cost and industrial materials—chain link, corrugated metal, and corrugated cardboard, for example—he contacted various producers, seeking precise information and proposing a *new* use of these materials. Whether it was chain link, cardboard, or plywood, the response was always the same: "Listen, we sell more of this stuff than we can make, so we're not looking for new ideas." Far from abandoning his experiments, this reply only got him more interested in the potential of materials so perfectly integrated into the consumerist maelstrom. The anecdote summarizes Gehry's attitude: the laws of the system are taken as a basis for operation. The architect's task is to develop potentials rather than subverting the system. This attitude no longer relies on meaning or ideology. Gehry's very choice of materials indicates a willingness to work within an *artificial nature* where matter itself is totally artificial, industrially produced and consumed on the scale of a geological event. Gehry's attention to these forms of materiality denotes a strategy of engagement with a local structure of production and consumption, but it also expresses the metabolic cycle of production, consumption, and recycling that constitutes the late-capitalist ecology of Los Angeles. Chain link, corrugated cardboard, plywood, and metal siding share certain characteristics that make them a consistent choice as a material palette. First, they are cheap; in Marxist terms, their *intrinsic value* has been shamelessly replaced by *exchange value*, rendering them a statement for artificiality, but also a clever subversion of traditional architectural value. Second, they are all produced in sheet format, lacking in principle the malleability of wood or plaster. Third, they manifest a constitutive discontinuity; the voids in their mass are visible at a macroscopic scale; they no longer claim the noble integrity of iron, stone, clay, or glass. Their discontinuous sheet structure gives them a visual quality similar to surfaces of biological epithelia, cellularly built. These constitutive characteristics are precisely deployed with experimental intent, as is patently clear in Gehry's proposal at the

Frank O. Gehry, Still Life

invitation of the Formica Corporation to use their homogeneous plastic laminate in an experimental design. Gehry first destroyed the homogeneity and continuity of the material, creating an object from its splintered fragments. This act is indicative of a sensibility toward construction that generates intensity from the juxtaposition of nonidentical elements, more than in the imposition of an overall order that defines each element, as if the contingencies of natural textures were being sought in certain artificial aggregates, intentionally avoiding artificial materials with a regular finish.

The use of industrial materials also draws upon an established tradition in California, whose best-known manifestation may be the Case Study Houses. But, contrary to the aesthetics of Richard Neutra or Pierre Koenig, architects who were more interested in expressing the artificiality of industrial production, Gehry strives for a certain degree of naturalism. His interest in a *povera* technology is obviously connected to California's 1960s counterculture and the ironic critique of consumerist society and the establishment by moving intentionally down market. *Povera* technology implies a liberation of collective creativity through embracing the detritus of culture and eschewing the refinements of high culture, but it also alludes to the metabolism of materials as perishable consumer goods: the production and the recycling of a second nature, a reestablishment of the organic cycles of construction and destruction that the linearity of production–consumption had previously discarded as an aesthetic possibility, but which has always been embedded nonetheless within California's radical-chic counterculture since the "Revolution." This includes, but is not limited to, the absorption and decontextualization of technology, the removal of its *exchange value*, and its ultimate integration with natural ecologies. Plastic and wire were mixed with plaster and wood in the domes modeled on Fuller's polyhedrons, whose non-Cartesian geometry and heterogeneous use of industrial materials reappear in Gehry's work, giving ad-hoc expression to the artificial ecology of Los Angeles noted by Reyner Banham in his *Los Angeles: The Architecture of Four Ecologies*.[4]

---

4   Reyner Banham, *Los Angeles: The Architecture of Four Ecologies* (New York: Harper & Row, 1971).

A New Vitalism

"I am for an art that grows not knowing that it is art, an art that has the chance to have zero as a starting point. I am for an art that imitates man, that is, cosmic and if necessary violent or any other being that is indispensable. I am for an art that takes form from the lines of life itself, that contorts, extends and accumulates and sticks out and drips, that is heavy and rough and sweet and stupid as life itself." [5] —CLAES OLDENBURG

Gehry's work deploys an ironic register that ranges from furniture design to the recycling of vulgar materials. This anti-heroic attitude is parallel to the investigations of Claes Oldenburg or John Cage, where art ceases to function as a social model, as it had in the avant-garde period, becoming instead the engine of personal creation. If modern architecture made itself a stronghold of the hope for social change, Gehry, like Cage and Oldenburg in their respective fields, appears to resort to the banal in order to regenerate a moribund architecture. This attitude relates to a series of socio-political movements that proliferated in California in the 1960s, an era when the most globe-trotting multinational executives crossed their first frontiers as *drop outs*, and expert computer programmers made their first connections with the infinite thanks to LSD.

The formation of these radical ideologies was consolidated in the postwar period with the landing of the Frankfurt school on the West Coast. Horkheimer, Adorno, Marcuse, and Reich imported a Marxist-Freudian social criticism that successfully took root in the United States, particularly in California, in the 1960s. Despite belonging to the same seed of modernism, the ultimate derivation of these theories in their Californian embodiment was finally aimed at the *elimination of culture*; that is, understanding culture as all the moral, aesthetic, or religious values that limit the freedom of judgment and action of the individual: a *new naturalism* takes the place of cultural determinations as the regulator of contemporary civiliza-

---

5   Claes Oldenburg, from "I am for an Art", 1961, in Harrison, C. and Wood, P. *Art in Theory, 1900-2000: an Anthology of Changing Ideas*. 2 ed. (Malden, USA: Blackwell Publishing, 2006).

tion. Anti-establishment battles in the 1960s turned to aesthetic posturing in the 1970s. By the early 1990s, capitalism had fully appropriated the entire apparatus of countercultural "ad hocism."

In the arts, the rejection of a merely positivistic or utilitarian description of reality was assembled through the decontextualization of objects of everyday use, their estrangement through alterations in scale, and the rejection of closed languages in favor of mechanisms that generate meaning through semantic distortion: these are some of the operative methods shared by Oldenburg, Cage, and Gehry. Gehry's characteristically *vitalist* approach to architecture, and his capacity to transgress linguistic conventions—except perhaps lately his own—can be tracked to his antecedents within 1960s radical culture. The temporality of architecture as consumer good, a commodity whose "representativity" is closer to advertising than to monumentality, is one of the consequences of this heritage. Gehry's taste for the unfinished is determined by a conception of architecture as a *life process*: the stages of development and decrepitude come to substitute for that idea of *plenitude*, of mineral eternity that has characterized Western architecture since the Renaissance. Gehry's association of the building *as* a living being—so evident in his iconography—is symptomatic of an architecture with a shelf life and expiration date, a result of its inclusion in the cycle of production-consumption-recycling that comes to substitute, as an artificial ecology, the linear mechanism of an earlier, more primitive conception of industrial production.

In Gehry's own words, his intention is to implicate the inhabitant or spectator in the actual construction of the architectural object, which thereby acquires organic qualities. The subject of architecture is always present in his work, from the first moments of design: it is sufficient to recall his insistence on his relation with the client as the decisive factor in the design process. A physical empathy between the body and the object is thus clearly perceived as one of the aims of this animal architecture on the edge of movement, of metamorphosis. The difference between his work and that of other contemporaries interested in the possibility of an organic architecture resides in the fact that Gehry's work is not biomorphic: a simple formal mimesis of natural forms makes no sense when naturalism is understood from the beginning as artificial.[6]

Despite the later evolution of his work, Gehry used to state that an ambition for an invisible architecture is implicated in the ambiguous corporeality of his buildings, conceived as the fluid materialization of variable forces.[7] Gehry's work explores the association between the processes of industrial production, capitalist consumption, and the phenomenology and psychology of the contemporary subject in a bid to coordinate *desire* and *production, Eros and Civilization*.[8]

Poetics of Extraterritoriality

"It's too pretty, it's not dealing with reality. I see reality as harsher, people bite each other. My take of things comes from that point of view."[9] —FRANK O. GEHRY

It is difficult to discern whether Gehry's work refers to its surroundings (the California of the Reagan era), to his foreignness (as transplanted Canadian), or to a happy juxtaposition of both. Gehry's organicism is not rooted in an idealized nature (like the pantheistic spirit of the architectures of Greene & Greene, Rudolf Schindler, or Charles and Ray Eames), even if there is a lineage to these architects. For example, with very few exceptions, Gehry's buildings have a tenuous relationship with the literal ground.

The fact remains that Gehry's buildings do not relate organically to their surroundings, despite sharing the organicity that has characterized California's architecture in the past. This is especially clear in his domestic work as the expression of an *extra-territoriality* of habita-

6   "What I like doing best is breaking down the project into as many separate parts as possible... So, instead of a house being one thing, it's ten things. It allows the client more involvement, because you can say: 'Well, I've got ten images now, that are going to compose your house. Those images can relate to all kinds of symbolic things, ideas you've liked, bits and pieces of your life that you would like to recall...' I think in terms of involving the client." Frank O. Gehry, Interview with Barbaralee Diamondstein, *American Architecture Now* (New York: Rizzoli, 1980), 34.

7   This, in turn, would give him an automatic way out of being charged with empty formalistic or ritualistic architecture insofar as it signals an interest in what is always buried in architecture anyway; that is, formal rigor of one kind or another, even when it is a disheveled or impoverished formal rigor.

8   Herbert Marcuse, *Eros and Civilization: A Philosophical Inquiry into Freud* (London: Routledge, 1987)

9   Frank O. Gehry, Interview with Barbaralee Diamondstein, *American Architecture Now*, op. cit., 34.

tion—perhaps the *linguistic disharmony* between habitation and the surroundings that impregnates Jewish thought—which is more inclined to anthropological than geographic references, except that, in Gehry's case, not much remains of the original community. One could say that the perilous journey—his personal *héjira*—before achieving the recognition he now enjoys is reflected, not without a certain tardiness, in the discomfort with which his disheveled creatures settle in the artificial territory of California. For Gehry, as for Emmanuel Lévinas (and contra Heidegger), habitation implies the *discovery of a world* (an *outside* or an *otherwise than being*) more than the process of taking root organically *within* it and *commanding* it.[10]

Gehry's drawing notation is also indicative of a specific attitude. As opposed to most of his contemporaries, Gehry started publishing conventional working drawings rather than architectural (pure representational) drawings. In that choice he was making a statement that drawings are more the description of building technologies than graphic or compositional devices to sell an image or idea. The function of drawings as mechanisms for compositional verification has been violated in order to become a register of constructive instructions. The very density of merely technical information makes a visualization of the compositional structure nonviable. Measure and proportion have been replaced by quantitative data, where the function of spaces is superimposed over topographic description.[11] For Gehry, the habitation is not organic and composed, as the carefully tended modern compositions of his California predecessors intended. Rather, it is an act of colonization: Gehry's own house features metal bumpers and asphalt paving; the Ron Davis house, a metal box containing a series of disconnected, floating rooms connected via gangways appears like a container to be completed in the process of habitation. In these residences there is

---

10 See Emmanuel Lévinas, *Totality and Infinity: An Essay on Exteriority*, trans. Alphonso Lingis (The Hague: Nijhoff Publishers, 1979). See also *Otherwise than Being, or Beyond Essence*, trans. Alphonso Lingis (Pittsburgh: Duquesne University Press, 1998), the sequel to *Totality and Infinity*.

11 Deleuze and Guattari propose *enregistrement* (registry) as characteristic of contemporary systems of production. See *The Anti-Oedipus: Capitalism and Schizophrenia*, trans. Brian Massumi (Minneapolis: University of Minnesota Press, 1983).

no nostalgia for the organic habitation that animates the utopia of modern living inherited from the Central European modern tradition.[12]

Semantic and Syntactic Inversions

"Consequently, the relation between diachronic and the synchronic is in a certain sense inverted... mythic thought, a bricoleur, builds structures on the basis of phenomena, or better said the residues of phenomena, while science, functioning simply in virtue of its own being, creates its own form of phenomena, its own means and results thanks to structures that it elaborates constantly, and which are its theories and hypotheses." —CLAUDE LÉVI-STRAUSS

One of the most popular sides of Gehry's work has been his use of figurative elements. This is very much a surrealist technique, aimed to expand the frontiers of immediate reality towards the realm of the unconscious. Although the objectives of this practice are coherent with other strategies, they constitute an important index for the interpretation of the work as a whole rather than as an effective technique in itself. Gehry's work is perhaps a last attempt to maintain the possibility of a representation of reality, just before it disappears into simulation; an essential slackening of the anchoring of the signifier with the hope that a widening of representational systems will permit the possibility of an architecture that is not entirely simulated. Gehry's strategies have been fundamentally directed toward the implication of the subject in the experience of architecture, an implication that is not limited to a purely formal, spatial, or material experience, but one that attempts to include realities external to its pure objecthood. Gehry's work invades the

---

12   In this respect, see the theories on habitation developed during the avant-garde proposed by Francesco Dal Co, as a manifestation of the nostalgia for the loss of harmonious relation with the surroundings created by industrial production. Francesco Dal Co, *Abitare nel moderno* (Bari: Laterza, 1983).

domain of the *signifier*, as much as it explores the sensual and the phenomenal. The architecture of an artificial nature cannot rely merely on the construction of the object; it must at the same time contemplate its anthropological attachments and machinations.

In order to address those engagements, Gehry resorts to analogic, magic, or mythic thought: the famous fish, snake, and Lockheed 101 belong to a mythology that is partly personal, partly tribal or totemic, and with which Gehry can confront the re-semanticization of everyday reality. The use of these strategies has as its end the dissolution of the barriers between reality and desire—to quote André Breton, "The reintroduction of desire in the very center of our existence." The destruction of any single system of reference and representation, of any ingenious rationalism, with the object of transcending the mere material or formal quality of architecture and approaching the internal realms of a liberated subjectivity is the modus operandi invoked.

The distorted geometry that characterizes his work is designed to subvert the conventional spatial and constructive syntax, and thus enlarge the range of representation. The exploration of multiple orientations in space impedes the apprehension of the object within a single system of representation. It is not likely for the objective of this strategy to be the mannerist distortion of perspectival systems—as has been proposed in some interpretations of the work. Rather, they aim to replace the perceptual distance such systems introduce to produce a more expressionist experience, a more direct relation between space and the body, an eroticization of architecture. Gehry himself speaks of Romanesque churches as being among his favorite buildings, evidence of his return to a pre-Renaissance, pre-perspectival understanding of space.

Only in the *assembly* of a series of heterogeneous natural materials—in the discontinuites between their fragments—can new quantities of information, or of meaning, appear, as Gehry explains: "I guess I approach architecture somewhat scientifically; there are going to be breakthroughs and they are going to create new information. It's adding information to the pot, not necessarily regurgitating other older ideas."[13]

The reconstruction of reality in fragments takes us back to Levi-Strauss' bricoleur, who, in contrast to the engineer (who constructs the object and its meaning simultaneously), acts in a finite and heterogeneous universe, in which each element does not contain the project in its entirety because it is simply impossible to design when time becomes part of the work: a diachronic reality is constructed in the pure act of making, on the boundaries between nonhomogeneous parts. The organic nature of the building's components, the relationship between the whole and its parts, is altered when the work has to become part of a production system subject to systematic planning. The indexical references to supplementary specification that populates construction documents (which Gehry chooses to

underline) prompt the segregation between the parts and the whole, where the composition of the architectural object dissolves into the cycle of the artificial. It was in the making of the metropolis that we first witnessed the crisis of the organic paradigm. Yet the romanticism of the European avant-gardes struggled to keep the organic paradigm alive. Gehry mobilizes an American tradition of independence between urban planning and building (through the grid) and between the building and its details (as in balloon-frame technology) and develops their expressive potential.

13 Frank O. Gehry, Interview with Barbaralee Diamondstein, op. cit.

Epistemology of the Instrumental

*"The fundamental event of the modern age is the conquest of the world as a picture (*Weltbild*). The word 'picture' (*Bild*) now means the structured image (*Gebild*) that is the creature of man's producing, which represents and sets before. In such producing, man contends for the position in which he can be that particular being who gives measure and draws up the guidelines for everything that is."*[14]
—MARTIN HEIDEGGER

Gehry's work unfolds on the border between materiality and *affect*, construction and signification. He operates very much as a traditional architect, committed to the object's representative value, a rare commitment at a time when architecture seems irreversibly split between absolute technological determinations and the production of simulated environments. Gehry's work still moves within the traditional categories of architecture, understood as an activity that mediates between the resolution of structural, environmental, and functional problems, and the production of *meaning*. The extraordinary expressiveness of the work is achieved through the poverty of expressive means. His understanding of the object as a subjective experience relates to neo-expressionist attitudes, where the physical, spatial, or material traits are empowered as modes of communication. Nevertheless, his projects are not designed with the sole intention of exercising a specific effect on the subject; they communicate effectively with the surrounding community and are not reducible to mere icons. His permanent consideration of architecture as a consumerist product gives primary place to those aspects of the building that refer to its expressive capacity or *character*, as opposed to those aspects intrinsic to its constitutitive structure or *composition*.

Gehry combines a refined material sensibility with a powerful capacity to com-

---

14   Martin Heidegger, "The Age of the World Picture," in *The Question Concerning Technology and other Essays* (New York: Harper Torchbooks, 1982), 134.

municate through architecture. His work for the Temporary Contemporary in Los Angeles—where an industrial building was converted into a museum of contemporary art without even removing the original signage—reveals a conceptual rigor and flexibility that reaffirms the crisis of objectivity that lies behind more conventional readings of his work.

The interest of Gehry's representational techniques lies in his particular combination of media strategies with the affects of the architectural object. If one of the bases of representational architecture is monumentality, Gehry's seems to be the exploration of instrumentality. While monumentality mobilizes material and geometric qualities associated with a continuation of geography, instrumentality is not associated so much with the permanence of structure as with mobility—it resides closer to the organic world than to the mineral, geological quality of the monumental. The monument implies taking charge of a territory, taking measure, hence the importance of composition and measure in its constitution. In the paradigm of instrumentality the knowledge of *essence* or *meaning* is no longer important; what counts is *service* and *performance.*

Rather than seeking to reveal the world (*being*) through representation, as occurs with the monument, *performance* addresses the benefit to be obtained from a *thing*. In an era given over to the nostalgic venture to establish composition via the monumental—from deconstructivism to the neo-Miesian, even neo-Rossian tendencies now flourishing in Central Europe—the retrieval of *character* that we find in Gehry's best work opens the possibility of an architecture genuinely integrated with a contemporary culture.

Productive Chance

"When the artists and sculptors I know work, there's sort of a free play idea. You try things; you experiment. It's kind of naive and childish, it's like kids in a playpen. Scientists work that way too—for example, genetic scientists that I have been involved with (through a genetic foundation that I work with) seem to work similarly. It's kind of like throwing things out and then following the ideas, rather than predicting where you're going to go."[15] —FRANK O. GEHRY

---

15   Frank O. Gehry, Interview with Barbaralee Diamondstein, op. cit, 34.

Frank Gehry's career has not followed the academic path that most of the American experimental architects have, but has instead developed within a conventional professional practice; and yet, despite his customary claims to contingency, his biography reads as an almost paradigmatic reflection of the world that surrounds him, a rigorously constructed curriculum vitae.

Gehry's work is perfectly expressive of the economic model in which it is inscribed, where chance has finally been integrated into the productive process as a mechanism able to continuously modify the internal structure of the system, integrating chance as a factor of controlled, dynamic disequilibrium that permits its continuous modification. The post-Keynesian economic theory behind California's evolution under Ronald Reagan appears close to the models of thermodynamic processes or to the process of biological evolution based on unstable, asymmetrical systems. California has become the paradigm of those processes that are characteristic of certain forms of the contemporary; it has the most exuberant and uncertain territory combined with the most prosperous and accelerated economy: a perfect embodiment of Deleuze and Guattari's proposition that the world of nature and that of capitalist production follow parallel paths. Gehry's position demonstrates the dissolution of the opposition between order and chaos, one of the principal motors of avant-garde experimentation.

In the disappearance of the architect as ideologue (a consequence of late capitalism), there are two extreme alternatives. One is a pathetic *resistance*, a desperate attempt to maintain an ideological position, openly confronting capitalist development. The other, represented by the work of Gruen and Portman in the 1950s and 1960s, involves playing with the system via the control of economic structures without ideological pretensions. In this situation Gehry's choice of a design method allegedly based on chance is surprisingly coherent: needing to integrate with the system, but in the simultaneous impossibility of producing an efficient *plan*, Gehry appears to turn himself into a producer of chaos, something that, in turn, has become highly marketable within the range of *culturally astute* clients he cultivates.

The organization of the productive process—a crucial task within the modern project—has been replaced by the function of creating the disequilibrium necessary to maintain the constant evolution of the system; it bespeaks the very hyper-capitalist system it resides within. By embracing chaos as a productive mode, Gehry integrates himself in the neo-organicist melting pot of late- and post-capitalist production—something that Cage had also tested in his introduction of chance to musical composition.

We could perhaps object to the relative immediacy of Gehry's work, its occasional limitation to superficial appearances more than an authentic integration of chance in his design method. But what is truly revolutionary in his position is the fact that his work may be seen as a derivation of the most conventional of commercial architectures. His integration in the reality of systems of production is precisely what distinguishes him from deconstructivist or neo-constructivist postures whose academic affiliation result in a concentration on academic linguistic experimentation than in an engagement within productive processes.[16]

The definitive proof that the role of the architect as a producer of chaos functions much more organically within the contemporary North American system of production than the ideological positions of resistance lies in the proliferation of intermediate-sized firms that have begun to occupy positions similar to Gehry's position nearly fifteen years ago. Whether Gehry's form of integrating chance in the design process is the most adequate, or whether this model could be directly translated outside the North American system, are questions that could be raised at this point, but there can be no doubt that Gehry's proposal is one of the most important and theoretically consistent of contemporary architecture.

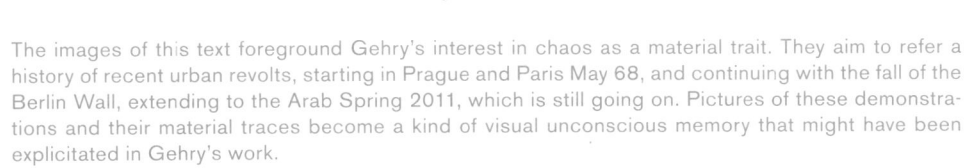

The images of this text foreground Gehry's interest in chaos as a material trait. They aim to refer a history of recent urban revolts, starting in Prague and Paris May 68, and continuing with the fall of the Berlin Wall, extending to the Arab Spring 2011, which is still going on. Pictures of these demonstrations and their material traces become a kind of visual unconscious memory that might have been explicitated in Gehry's work.

16 I refer to the keen analysis of the problem of contemporary architectural production in Manfredo Tafuri's "Problems in the Form of a Conclusion," the final chapter of *Architecture and Utopia. Design and Capitalist Development*, trans. Barbara Luigi La Penta (Cambridge, MA: The MIT Press, 1979).

Published in *El Croquis* n. 53, Madrid, 1992

OMA: Notes for a Topographical Survey

"The rites of passage are no longer intermittent; they have become permanent." —PAUL VIRILIO

Metropolis: The Topography of Flexible Accumulation

In spite of Rem Koolhaas' explicit rejection of the adjective *metropolitan* in the name Office for Metropolitan Architecture,[1] it is hard to find a better description for OMA's activity, insofar as it directly affects the conditions of production that have collectively turned metropolitanism into a qualitative or universalizing category rather than a restricted, geographically based territoriality. In the hyper-geography of advanced forms of capitalism, East and West, *metropolis* equals *world*. The metropolitan paradigm has surpassed the city/territory duality, restructuring the dichotomy into a developed/underdeveloped modality.[2] One no longer speaks of cities as unitary things but as states of mind and, by inference, states of capital translatable to *culture*.

1 Rem Koolhaas, lecture at Columbia University, November 1989. Reprinted in the exhibition catalogue *Rem Koolhaas: Proyectos Urbanos 1985–1990* (Barcelona: Gustavo Gili, 1990) for the exhibition held at the Col·legi d'Arquitectes de Catalunya, Barcelona, January 1991.
2 See David Harvey, "Cities, Surpluses and the Urban Origins of Capitalism," in *The Urbanization of Capital* (Baltimore: The John Hopkins University Press, 1985).

While the *city* has been historically built as a geographic accumulation of surplus value, the *metropolis* is the product of a mode of economic integration based on the circulation of surpluses. One of the important aspects of recent work by OMA lies precisely in the exploitation of the spatial and material implications of metropolitan culture. Within this paradigm, neither time nor space—the basic categories of experience—can be considered either *abstract* or *natural*, as they have become closely related to the late-capitalist processes of material organization.[3] The recent work from OMA focuses upon a redefinition of material practices, initiating a new approach to the discipline of architecture and urban planning within late capitalism.[4]

Such a redefinition may be seen as a consequence of the processes of *temporal and spatial displacement*, developed to overcome capitalism's inherent problems of over-accumulation, and whose epistemological implications have been summarized by David Harvey as a tendency toward *time-space compression*.[5] In surpassing Fordist models that are structured on supply and demand correspondences, and a precise geographic and social location of resources, goods, and profits, the regime of flexible accumulation questions the models built on well-established territorial boundaries, prevalent within Keynesian economics, and alters their space-time parameters: the more flexible and inarticulate the local structures (spatially, temporally, or socially), the greater the overall stability of the system.[6] The close links between economic planning and the spatial and territorial structure within late-capitalist produc-

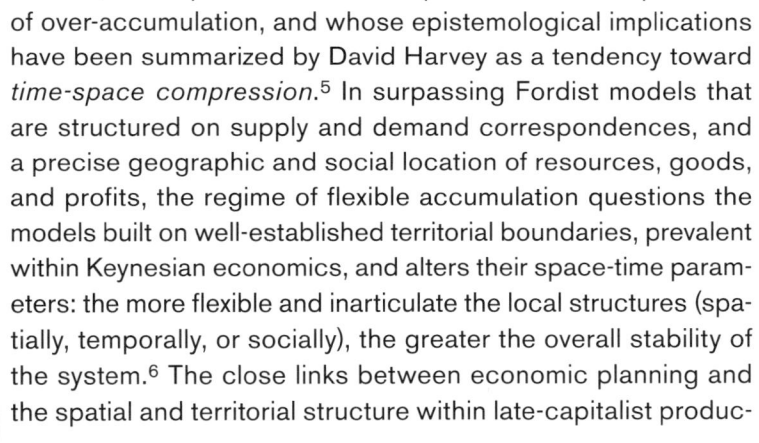

3   See David Harvey, *Explanation in Geography* (London: Edward Arnold, 1969).

4   "Flexible accumulation, as I shall tentatively call it, is marked by a direct confrontation with the rigidities of Fordism. It rests on flexibility with respect to labour processes, labour markets, products, and patterns of consumption. It is characterized by the emergence of entirely new sectors of production, new ways of providing financial services, new markets, and, above all, greatly intensified rates of commercial, technological, and organizational innovation… It has also entailed a new round of what I shall call 'time-space compression' in the capitalist world—the time horizons on both private and public decision-making have shrunk, while satellite communication and declining transport costs have made it increasingly possible to spread those decisions immediately over an ever wider and variegated space." David Harvey, *The Condition of Postmodernity: An Enquiry into the Origins of Cultural Change* (Oxford: Blackwell, 1989).

5   See David Harvey, "Theorizing the Transition," in ibid.

6   "An analysis of (contemporary) production shows that we have passed from the production of things in space to the production of the space itself." "The past left its marks, its inscriptions, but space is always present space, a current totality with its links and connections to action. In fact, the production and the product are inseparable sides of a process." Henri Lefebvre, "Space, Social

tion enforces spatial organizations over temporal sequences. As Lefebvre puts it, space has become the key product of contemporary civilization.[7]

OMA's work approaches the processes of mutation, flow, and disorder, all characteristics of regimes of flexible accumulation, to develop the instruments required for an adequate and consistent material practice. An analysis of OMA's work from a *topographic* perspective, shying away from genealogies of form or linguistic analogues, reveals a focus on material organizations as products of an epistemological break.

Anti-formalism: The Rhizome

Only after the recent work by OMA does Koolhaas's schizophrenic dedication to both Leonidov and Coney Island become understandable as part of a precise agenda. His first experiments with the languages of modernity reveal a self-deprecating strategy aimed at the clearance of language as an architectural problem: a carefully designed program to finish architectural representation by exhausting its two possible fronts at once: signifier and signified. One might imagine Koolhaas's wry grin upon witnessing the suicide of the architectural language as posited by his ex-partners Zaha Hadid and Elia Zenghelis. His narrative excesses in *Delirious New York*[8] could be seen as the last stroke in the assassination. By turning architecture into pure *tracing* or pure *text*,[9] early OMA work dislocated architecture *and* language. The end of

Product and Use Value," in *Critical Sociology*, ed. J. W. Freiberg (New York: Irvington Publishers, 1979). On space as a consumer product, see Harvey, *The Condition of Postmodernity*, op. cit.

7   See David Harvey, "Time-Space Compression and the Postmodern Condition," in *The Condition of Postmodernity*, op. cit.

8   Rem Koolhaas, *Delirious New York: A Retroactive Manifesto for Manhattan* (Rotterdam: 010 Publishers, 1994).

9   See Deleuze and Guattari, "Rhizome," in Deleuze and Guattari, *A Thousand Plateaus. Capitalism and Schizophrenia* (Minneapolis: University of Minnesotta Press, 1987), 12-15. The term tracing is used by Deleuze and Guattari to classify any representation of the real operating as an abstract coding that fixes structures, rules, measurements, or compositions. The tracing is the opposite of the map, which is rather an instrument of engagement with reality, always in constant evolution, made for experimenting with reality. The tracing is a tool used to determine competences while the map is an instrument of "performance." The graphic approach to the project that

representational architecture is served by simultaneous reduction to the purest formalism or the most conceptual narrative.[10]

OMA's truly metropolitan work emerges from the calculated ruins of the representational city. Within the representative paradigm, *forms* were instruments of reproduction, mechanisms for the establishment of hierarchies and genealogies, machines of codification or capture.[11] Such techniques of control and supremacy over a static, tamed reality are ineffective when applied to a domain structured on the continuous process of mutation, such as late capitalism.

OMA's latest work could be defined as rhizomatic;[12] that is, determined by its operativity.[13] The clearest example of this condition is the project for Melun-characterizes the work of Hadid and Zenghelis is probably closer to the tracing, as a formal abstraction of reality.

10   "Once art (architecture) was materially inserted into the mechanisms of the universe of production, its own experimental character, its own character of co-reality, was necessarily compromised. It is at this point that there occurred a break between linguistics and architecture, proven by the personal and dramatic experience of the most coherent of the Russian architects who tried to translate into an architectural method the thesis of Sklovsky or Eichenbaum. In fact, the communicative system refers only to the laws of its internal structure, if architecture can be interpreted—in its specific aspects—only as linguistic experimentation, and if this experimentation is realized only through an obliqueness, through a radical ambiguity in the organization of its components, and finally, if the linguistic 'material' is indifferent and matters only in the way the various materials react with each other, then the only road to be followed is that of the most radical and politically agnostic formalism." Manfredo Tafuri, *Architecture and Utopia: Design and Capitalist Development*, trans. Barbara Luigi La Penta (Cambridge, MA: MIT Press, 1976).

11   "Forms relate to codes and processes of coding and decoding in the parastrata; substances, being formed matters, relates to territorialities and movements of deterritorialization and reterritorialization of the epistrata." Deleuze and Guattari, *A Thousand Plateaus. Capitalism and Schizophrenia* (Minneapolis: University of Minnesotta Press, 1987).

12   Heidegger's concept of *Gestell* (enframing) as the essence of modern technology comes to replace the "Idea" as epistemological basis. While the "Idea" relates to a representational or formal knowledge, enframing is associated with a relational, utilitarian, and operative concept of reality. See Martin Heidegger, *The Question Concerning Technology and other Essays*, trans. William Lovitt (New York: Harper & Row, 1977).

13   "The rhizome is an anti-genealogy, a short-term memory or anti-memory. The rhizome operates by variation, expansion, conquest, capture, offshoots. Unlike the graphic arts, drawing or photography, unlike tracings, the rhizome pertains to a map that must be produced, constructed, a map that is always detachable, connectable, reversible, modifiable, and has multiple entryways and exits, and its own *lines of flight*. It is tracings that must be put on the map, not the opposite. In contrast to centered (even polycentric) systems with hierarchical modes of communication and preestablished paths, the rhizome is an acentered, nonhierarchical, nonsignifying system without a general and without an organizing memory or central automaton, defined solely by a circulation of states." Deleuze and Guattari, "Rhizome," in *A Thousand Plateaus. Capitalism and Schizophrenia*, op. cit., 8.

Sénart, a strategy to generate a system apt for development, rather than the determination of a formal result. An initial distinction between areas of control and indetermination,[14] and the explicit rejection of any urban ideology for the plan, implies the acceptance of the impossibility of absolute control over the materialization of the city,[15] or perhaps abdication of control in favor of hybridity and mutation. There are no compositional preconceptions (no formal master plan): the core of Melun-Sénart is purely operational. Melun-Sénart's system is made out of bands—or lines[16]—that intersect at contingent points and create a "nonsignificant" urban structure; the points of articulation do not determine the nature of the lines. It is a type of structure that could illustrate the *principle of connection and heterogeneity* used by Deleuze and Guattari to characterize rhizomatic systems: "Any point in the rhizome might and should be connected to any other."[17]

The urban topography of Melun-Sénart is organized in lines or vectors instead of points, centers, or positions; each line has a particular determination in terms of speed, direction, or activity: a multitude of measurements and directions. There is no spatial reference, orientation, or measurement. It is a disorganized topography that does not impose regulations on the correspondences between elements and positions, a rigorous fulfillment of the *rhizomatic principle of multiplicity*: "In a rhizome there are no points or positions like on a tree, simply lines. There are no units of measure, only multiplicities or varieties of measurement."[18]

14 "Un projet d'urbanisme ne peut être confondu avec un projet de développement bien qu'il intègre les différent éléments de ce dernier: ils ont chacun leur logique." "An urban project should not be confused with a real estate operation, even if it includes the different elements of the last: each one has its own logic." Rem Koolhaas, text for Melun-Sénart in *OMA, 6 Projets*, ed. Patrice Goulet (Paris: Institut Français d'Architecture, Editions Carte Segrete, 1991). My translation.

15 "Nous refusons de produire une nouvelle idéologie urbaine et prenons comme base de réflexion la réalité architecturale et urbanistique de Melun-Sénart. Notre proposition s'interroge sur l'hétérogeneité construite de la ville moderne et en profite pour affirmer le rôle déterminant du paysage dans une société où pratiquement tout le territoire est potentiellement urbain." "We refuse to produce a new urban ideology while taking as a point of reflection the architectural and urban reality of Melun-Sénart. Our proposal questions the heterogeneity of the contemporary city and uses it to affirm the crucial role of landscape in a society where practically all territory is urban." Rem Koolhaas, "Text for Melun-Sénart," in *OMA, 6 Projets*. My translation.

16 See the definition of smooth space proposed in "The Smooth and the Striated" in Deleuze and Guattari, *A Thousand Plateaus. Capitalism and Schizophrenia*, op. cit., 474; that is, a vectorial space, formed by lines rather than points.

17 Deleuze and Guattari, "Rhizome" in *A Thousand Plateaus. Capitalism and Schizophrenia*, op. cit., 7.

18 Ibid., 8.

The lines that structure Melun-Sénart would be extendable, able to grow, since their definition is neither syntactic nor figurative. There are no formal codifications of links or limits. Here we find the third principle of the rhizome, or the *principle of asignifying rupture*: "A rhizome may be broken, shattered at a given spot, but it will start up again from one of its old lines or on new lines. It will not have the over-significant breaks separating structures or cutting across a single structure."[19]

The graphic representation of the design is simply delightful in its linguistic variety. As in cartography, we may find different codes corresponding to different inputs: lines of movement; fragments of different fabrics; figures indicating densities; figures that represent activities; logotypes of companies; etc. The plan becomes a modifiable document, operative rather than legislative or determinant of positions and hierarchies. The strictest application of the *rhizomatic principle of cartography and decalcomania*: "A rhizome is not amenable to any structural or generative model. It is a stranger to any idea of genetic axes or deep structure. A rhizome is a map, not a tracing. It does not follow the tree logic, aimed at reproduction and the establishment of powers, but rather the rhizomatic logic, aimed at experimentation and action. It has multiple entrances rather than a single viewpoint."[20]

In its radical rejection of urban ideologies and in its abandonment of any genealogical, historical, structural, organic, or formal relationship, the OMA plan for Melun-Sénart is a paradigm of the rhizomatic principles in urban practice, and probably the most important urban planning proposal of the last twenty years.

Melun-Sénart is the most explicit, but not the only recent OMA plan to respond to these principles. Most of the OMA projects of the last five years relate to them in one way or another. In the plan for the City Hall of The Hague we could also recognize the rhizomatic *principle of asignifying rupture*: the search for formal stability within programmatic instability. The spatial inarticulation in projects such as the Zeebrugge Sea Terminal, the Très Grande Bibliothèque in Paris, and the ZKM in Karlsruhe complements the disruption of linear sequences in favor of experiences of simultaneity or indetermination. The proliferation of non-articulated connections and the proposal of heterogeneity are ultimately tactics of formal deregulation: the logical consequence of a coherent material practice within the regimes of flexible accumulation.

19   Ibid., 9.
20   Ibid., 12.

Epistemology of Desire: Multiplicities, Projections, Deformations

Koolhaas refers often to surrealist methodologies in *Delirious New York*. Salvador Dalí's paranoid-critical method is an alternative epistemology, a method of analysis/synthesis that escapes objective logic: reality is a construction of desire, there is no clear boundary between subject and object. As in Heisenberg's Principle of Indetermination, it is not possible to separate the knowledge of reality from the instruments of analysis: science collapses into ideology.

Delirious New York builds an epistemology of desire for the metropolis. The Vitruvian natural orders (*utilitas, firmitas, venustas*) are ruthlessly eliminated through the application of modern tools: gravity warped by anti-gravitational structures and devices; beauty replaced by cosmetics; need replaced by desire.

As a crystallization of this argument, recent OMA production comprehends the development of a series of tools for the analysis and construction of reality. A systematic reformulation of space-time categories becomes unavoidable when the *short circuit of metropolitanism* spreads throughout late-capitalist territory to occupy the different facets of our everyday experience.

Whether by establishing a multitude of speeds within a single space, or through a diversification of connections between two spaces, the space-time experience undergoes violent deformations in the latest OMA projects. Examples of such effects may be found in the circulatory structure of the design for La Villette,[21] or the spatial juxtaposition of systems of movement (access ramps for motor traffic, escalators and elevators) in the Zeebrugge Sea Terminal, the Très Grande Bibliothèque, and the ZKM in Karlsruhe. OMA experiments with the simultaneity of different speeds of movement and the juxtaposition of spaces, questioning the validity of the homogeneous and linear concept of spatial and temporal categories within an artificially enhanced environment. The Piranesian space of

---

[21] "L'opposition entre les diverses perceptions est aussi exploitée sur les axes majeurs de circulation qui forment la 'Promenade' et le 'Mall.' Opposition entre le montré et le caché, le but de la 'Promenade' est sans cesse détourné; parcontre, le percours du 'Mall' s'effectue sans surprise, les diverses étapes sont délibérément explicites. La Promenade est surprise, le Mall, certitude."
"The opposition between the different perceptions is also exploited along the main circulatory axis formed by the *Promenade* and the *Mall*. Opposition between the visible and the hidden, the end of the *Promenade* is constantly displaced; on the contrary the experience of the *Mall* is completed without surprise, the different stages are deliberately explicit. The *Promenade* is surprise, the *Mall* certainty." Rem Koolhaas, text for Parc de La Villette, in *OMA, 6 Projets*, op. cit. My translation.

Lille or the robot in the ZKM Karlsruhe, where various movements at different speeds coincide within the same space, are examples of a conceptual use of mechanical implementation.[22]

In the same way that profits are increasingly independent from work within the late-capitalist techno-corporate model, the human scale ceases to be applicable to a mechanically enhanced topography: the phenomenological relationship between human body and built space becomes irrelevant. The distortions in scale we find in these projects are an intentional and expressive use of technology and its incorporation within an artificially constructed body. In the recent OMA work, space-time categories have ceased to be homogeneous extensions, to become molded into multiplicities of intensity. Space is structured into distances rather than magnitudes. Time is quantified by *duration* rather than *interval*. Far from the Cartesian, Kantian, or "modern" space, recent OMA work treats space as a nonmodular, diverse, directional, and smoothly fluid.[23] Projects such as the Agadir Conference Centre, the Très Grande Bibliothèque, or the Karlsruhe ZKM do not belong to the striated, uniform, linear space characteristic of modernism, nor do they belong to the fragmented space of postmodernity. They break ground toward a differential, variable, and vectorial space-time.

Topological or projective geometries replace the Euclidian orders in these projects, in what appears as an epistemological rupture. In the Très Grande Bibliothèque and the Agadir Conference Centre, measure and proportion, the basic instruments of classical architecture, are replaced by fundamentally topological relationships: connections, adjacencies, or distances instead of measurements, magnitudes, or properties.[24] OMA operates with a geometry of the inexact, a *proto-*

---

22 "At the complementary and dominant level of integrated (or rather integrating) world capitalism, a new 'smooth space' is produced, in which capital reaches its 'absolute' speed, based on machinic components rather than human labor." Deleuze and Guattari, "The Smooth and the Striated" in *A Thousand Plateaus. Capitalism and Schizophrenia*, op. cit., 436.

23 "In 'striated space,' lines of trajectories tend to be subordinated to points: one goes from one point to another. In the 'smooth space,' it is the opposite: the points are subordinated to the trajectory." "The line is therefore a vector, a direction, and not a dimension or metric determination. It is a space constructed by local operations involving changes in direction... 'Smooth space' is directional rather than dimensional or metric." Ibid., 478.

24 It is important to distinguish between distance and magnitude, as explained by Bertrand Russell; for Russell, a distance is not visible without altering the nature of its subdivisions, while a magnitude is composed by homogeneous units. Bertrand Russell, *The Principles of Mathematics* (New York: Norton, 1964).

geometry,25 a geometry of deformation and distortions rather than conservation. This belongs to a science of the eventual rather than of the essential, of the problematic rather than theoretical.

There are no precise proportions in the Très Grande Bibliothèque or the Karlsruhe ZKM but, rather, a desire for "cubicness" which belongs to an operative logic rather than a formal or linguistic codification: the desire for minimum contact between inside and outside. The Zeebrugge Sea Terminal and the Agadir Conference Centre are also examples of this geometry of flows and changes of form in time and space. As early as the City Hall of The Hague there is an intention to avoid forms that may be reduced to the translation of a floor or section to occupy space.

The metrical indetermination with which these projects are produced is an alternative to the imposition of form over homogenized matter: as an exploitation of the singularities of matter and space, the recent OMA projects are defined through a gradient of precision in which certain areas of the design are intensively determined and others extensively abandoned. It is a selective strategy of control over detail.

Unarticulated Topography: The Disorganized Body

Koolhaas's progress since *Delirious New York* tracks an evolution from textual to material discourse, through an intermediate stage of linguistic experimentation aimed at dismantling architectural language. In *Delirious New York*, the natural laws were systematically transgressed. The gradients of gravity, ventilation, and illumination were warped in parallel with the rhythms and rituals of everyday life in the metropolis. Technology and artificiality become the origin of indetermination or freedom, rather than the instrument of optimization and mechanical determination. In this book, technical implementation leads to topographical, social, or psychological disorders: deformity, instability, and schizophrenia respectively—prescriptive or analytical, it hardly matters.

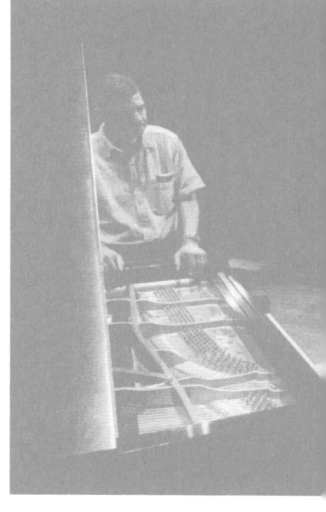

The techniques used in the recent OMA projects—such as sudden fluctuations of scale and measurement, rupture of linear sequences, simultaneity and juxtaposition, spatial heterogeneity and functional displacement—are *deterritorializing* or

---

25 Edmund Husserl, *Ideas: General Introduction to Pure Phenomenology*, trans. W. R. Boyce Gibson (New York: Humanities Press, 1976).

destratifying tools[26] that dismantle the articulations between different sections of material or social reality, allowing their recombination, densification, or dissolution. These techniques are aimed at the production of a *disorganized body* rather than a structured composition of parts.

Analyzing the Karlsruhe ZKM, the Très Grande Bibliothèque, the Agadir and Lille conference centers, the Zeebrugge Sea Terminal or the Rotterdam Kunsthal, one notices a common initial deterritorializing tactic: the compactness and seclusion of most of the built volume. Plans and sections tend to a nondirectional shape, distilling the coincidence between facade surface and built volume to a minimum. This internalization of the building exploits the possibility of generating large areas of artificially controlled space, thereby liberating the destructuring potential of technological implementation. It is not by chance that the use of this procedure is consistent with the contemporary development of speculative typologies: *fat buildings*, with a low ratio between perimeter and useable area, have emerged over the last ten years as a prevailing type of tertiary space where large structural spans have become a default choice in commercial buildings to increase flexibility and permit a maximum of technical implementation.

The density acquired by the Karlsruhe ZKM, the Agadir Conference Centre, and the Zeebrugge Sea Terminal through their extraordinary compactness leads to a mutation of their structures, as if after attaining a certain *critical mass*, a *liquefaction* of the internal spatial articulations ensued. The latest generation of OMA buildings is probably explained better as a collection of gel containers or hydro-pneumatic mechanisms rather than a series of geological formations or piles. This liquefaction of space also occurs in domestic projects: Fukoka is configured as two shapeless bodies that float without geological or urban links. The roofs of the dwellings produce unoriented daylight to enter by reflection, drilled through the dark mass. In Villa Dall'Ava and Villa Linthorst, similar dissolutions of space occur with water and light.

One of the main areas of research in OMA's recent work addresses the load-bearing structure. The structural concepts of many of these recent projects

---

26 This is again grounded on Deleuze and Guattari, "Rhizome" in *A Thousand Plateaus. Capitalism and Schizophrenia*, op. cit.

reinforce the initial strategy of compactness and liquefaction: the achievement of an unarticulated corporeality; an efficient strategy for the disorganized late-capitalist structure.

The Vierendeel concept in the Karlsruhe ZKM is a strategy of *destratification*. The beauty of the concept consists of enlisting the structure as space, inverting the traditional full/empty categories, and architecturally embodying the discontinuity of matter. The Vierendeel beam is at the same time a real instrument of destratification in the most literal sense of the term: it is the mechanism capable of completely changing the geological, gravitational, and natural order, shifting the material presence of the structure from the base of the building to its coronation, dissolving the continuity of the lines of gravitational force. The material quality of the building structure, which evolves from steel at the lower levels to concrete above, insists on the transgression of natural orders; again a radical affirmation of artificiality.

The structural strategies in both the Agadir Conference Centre and the Rotterdam Kunsthal are also weapons of spatial disarticulation. In Agadir, one also finds a Vierendeel-type structure that adapts to the proposed space. The spatial anisotropy composes a structure with elements that adapt to the forces crossing them; the material/form duality evolves towards the strength/material unity.

In the Rotterdam Kunsthal, the strategy followed is similar, through the use of functionally specialized structures included in a single volume. The inclined columns challenge the gravitational lines of attraction to align with the topography generated in the design, in a radical declaration of freedom and independence from natural orders: a materialization of *clinamen* which would have delighted Lucretius.

Smooth Space: Cash Flows, Data Channels, Drive-throughs, and Other Flows
OMA's Dutchness is not irrelevant: The Netherlands is the *terrain vague* par excellence,[27] the artificial territory, the domain of flows: hydrodynamics and commerce. Koolhaas's metaphor of the surfer is a global version of the Dutch heritage;[28]

---

27 See Paul Virilio, *L'insécurité du territoire* (Paris: Stock, 1976).

28 "We are a bit like a surfer on the waves; he does not control them, but he knows them; he knows how to make use of them and also how to go against the current." Rem Koolhaas, in "We are like a surfer on the waves," *Rem Koolhaas: Proyectos Urbanos 1985–1990*, op. cit.

OMA's Dutch heritage lies not in the *nieuwe zakelijkheid* (new objectivity) and modern Dutch rationalism, but rather in the merchant's or sailor's tradition of nomadic knowledge and strategic operativity, an important advantage when operating in the smooth space of flexible accumulation.

OMA works from a nomadic science, more appropriate to the constant confrontation with new terrains than to the consolidation of stable knowledge, power, and regulations; a science of irreversible processes rather than constant laws of an atemporal nature. The need to operate in late-capitalist reality (shaped by flows and change) requires the development of design techniques that can tackle deformations, distortions, and variations of form in time and space. The stochastic and differential geometries used to model turbulence, are closer to the epistemological evolution that OMA is opening within material practices.

In this paradigm, architectural form is a changing entity through time and space: it envisions reality as a constitution of flows or deformations, embodiments of post-capitalist smooth space, the space of individualized production and diversified networks, moving away from the treelike, reproducible hierarchies of the Euclidian geometry of the striated space of the assembly line and the mass media.[29]

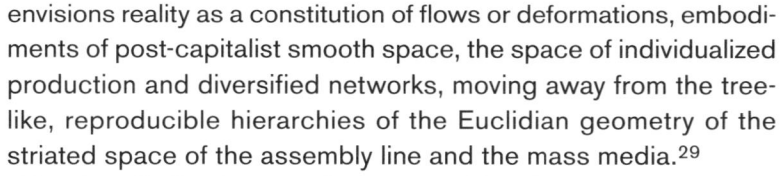

The Agadir Conference Centre and Lille Congrexpo are good examples of this spatial *smoothness*. Both are paradigmatic of a reality sculpted by flows of money and information, and the consequent reformulation of material and spatial determinations. Both designs are examples of a challenge to traditional objectivity and its tectonic embodiments in which the buildings become *disorganized bodies*, superconductors capable of being restructured to engage different types and directions of flows. These experiments explore alternative forms of material and spatial organization to challenge the formal codification of established typologies, without retreating to a material substrate.

---

29 "At the complementary and dominant level of integrated (or rather integrating) world capitalism, a new *smooth space* is produced, in which capital reaches its 'absolute' speed, based on machinic components rather than human labor. Multinationals fabricate a kind of deterritorialized smooth space in which point of occupation as well as poles of exchange becomes quite independent from the classical paths to striation. What is really new are always the new forms of turnover. The present-day accelerated forms of circulation of capital are making the distinction between constant and variable capital, and even fixed and circulating capital, and the way in which the former gives rise to the latter through complexes that cut across territories and states and even the different types of spaces." "Surplus labor, capitalist organization operates less and less by the striation of space-time corresponding to the psychosocial concept of work." Deleuze and Guattari, "Rhizome" in *A Thousand Plateaus. Capitalism and Schizophrenia*, op. cit. 439; italics mine.

The Agadir Conference Centre is probably the best example of this new corporeality of flows and the connectivity of smooth space. No more segmentation between spaces or homogeneity: a continuous variation of form through space, the generation of a vectorial, directional, and anisotropic space. Agadir forms a differential space rather than the articulation of homogeneities that we find in postmodern collage. By eliminating the structural grid, spatial and metrical references are neutralized: in Agadir, space and matter are treated like dynamic flows rather than stable forms.

One of OMA's favorite themes is the exploitation of flows: the figure of the *drive-through*, a road infrastructure cutting through the building in a contingent manner as if slicing a destructured, informal mass, is a regular theme in the recent projects. The Lille Congrexpo is a good example of this form of slippery syntax aimed at capturing a flowing reality. So is the Zeebrugge Sea Terminal, where a varied number of infrastructures and flows cross the soft body of the building, whose informal rotundity insists, as in Lille, on an inarticulate, superconductive corporeality, capable of being oriented correctly to permit the passage of flows. The form of a head insists also on a lack of orientation, predominant direction in space, or "faciality" structure. In the Rotterdam Kunsthal we can see another example of the same approach where vehicular and pedestrian traffic cross inside the mass of the building without any resistance.

In the Très Grande Bibliothèque there is a related strategy of liquefaction: here it is not a flow of traffic infrastructure that crosses the building, but the change of phase between diverse states of information: from the solid phase of storage to the liquid state in its active phase. An allegory of the laws of entropy and the irreversibility of physical processes, the amount of information is inversely proportional to the structure of the system.

The Très Grande Bibliothèque and Agadir use geometries of phase change, expressing epistemology, a phenomenology of turbulence, and general instability. The elevations of both buildings refer almost directly to dynamic, natural organizations: waves, dunes, or clouds. The recent OMA work is a return to the Heraclitean, chaotic world view, irreducible to form and meaning; a retreat from modernist arrogance into an acceptance of the lack of absolute power and sovereignty over reality.

Topographies of Indetermination

Already in *Delirious New York*, Koolhaas had identified uncertainty as one of the constituent characteristics of metropolitan culture, initiating research into determination and indetermination. In Koolhaas's words, "architecture is a mixture of power and impotence."[30] Such enthusiasm for uncertainty is an index of alignment with the cultural tendencies of the early 1970s, triggered by the first great crisis of over-accumulation. Simultaneously, there is a parallel development in the natural sciences: theories of chaos, catastrophe theory, etc. are contemporary with these politico-economic developments and similarly propose a radical revision of traditional sciences. Such sciences experimented with nonlinear complex models, determined by a multiplicity of interrelated processes.

If the function of science vis-à-vis the means of production is the creation of models or languages for the production of the real, OMA's new sciences are aimed at the generation of new spaces, new territories of expansion, rather than the consolidation of the status quo. Architectural technique thus becomes an instrument for the production of indetermination rather than uncertainty.

Recent OMA production registers the application of these models to the practice of architecture. The topographies proposed by OMA since 1985 refer to material organizations similar to those that the theories of chaos address: a new approach to the dualities of texture/figure, symmetry/asymmetry, structure/information, and dimension/measure through which the irreversibility of morphogenetic processes is approximated.

The inversion of the traditional terms between texture and figure, figure and background, full and empty is one of the techniques explored in the recent work. As attractors establish certain conditions of stability—regardless of a central, causal, or gravitational materiality—OMA's urban projects are shaped into galaxies of plankton that gravitate around random configurations. Melun-Sénart, the '89

---

30 "Architecture is a very bizarre profession in the sense that it is a poisonous mixture of omnipotence and impotence. It is obviously true that our dreams and fantasies are megalomaniacal, and we are doomed to wait passively for occasions where we can realize fragments of that megalomania." Rem Koolhaas, lecture at Columbia University, November 1989. *Rem Koolhaas: Proyectos Urbanos 1985–1990*, op. cit.

Paris Expo, La Villette, etc., are all examples of these topographies that combine architectural specificity with formal indetermination.[31]

OMA's urban proposals are not structured around the center/periphery duality, nor as a uniform extension. They rather respond to the proposition of fields configured in accordance with fluctuating orders produced by a series of attractors. The inversion of full and empty proposed in Melun-Sénart or the oscillations between texture and figure proposed in the City Hall of The Hague and the '89 Paris Expo reveal the same type of order via fluctuations as those discovered in natural forms by nonlinear scientific models of analysis. In recent OMA work, form is not the result of a mechanical or linear process, or of a static law.[32] The topographies proposed by OMA are neither determinist nor Gaussian, but Brownian configurations whose overall stability depends on their ability to integrate local fluctuations on a global level.[33]

Melun-Sénart is obviously one of the best examples of these models. The acceptance of the uncertainty in which the urban phenomenon is produced, and the renouncement of formal control over such developments is leveled with the establishment of operative limits.[34] Melun-Sénart is an attempt to avoid the over-codification of the urban fabric that has characterized urban design since its emergence as a discipline in the 1950s. The impact of the phasing of design in the final outcome indexes a fluid perception of the urban. Formal synthesis depends on (and constantly summarizes) the development of the design and expresses the implementation of the generating idea. In La Villette, and even in Melun-Sénart, form is produced as a dependent result of an irreversible temporality.[35]

31   Rem Koolhaas, text on La Villette. *OMA, 6 Projets*, op. cit.

32   "Statistic" and "mechanical" in Claude Lévi-Strauss's sense: in the mechanical model, elements have the same scale of phenomena, while in the statistical model the scalar symmetry breaks up, allowing for the independence between elements and phenomena. That means that certain parts of the system behave randomly while at a certain scale there is structural stability. See Claude Lévi-Strauss, "Methodes et Enseignement," in *Anthropologie structurale* (Paris: Plon, 1969).

33   See Benoit B. Mandelbrot, *The Fractal Geometry of Nature* (New York: Freeman & Co., 1977).

34   "Le bâti, le plein, est désormais incontrôlable, livré tous azimuts à des forces politiques, financières, culturelles, qui le plongent dans une transformation perpétuelle." "The built, the filled is incontrollable, exposed from all angles to the political, financial, cultural forces that subject it to a constant transformation." Rem Koolhaas, explanatory text for Melun-Sénart, in *OMA, 6 Projets*, op. cit. My translation.

35   "In consideration with the continuous re-elaboration, rather than thinking in terms of *design*, we would rather propose a *method* capable to combine architectural specificity with programmatic indetermination. In other words, we conceive the concept as a strategy rather than as a *design*: it

In projects such as the '89 Paris Expo, Melun-Sénart, Scientopia, etc. the very presentation of the design implies the proposal of topographies where information prevails over structure; topographies in which color and material diversity overcome the need for a stable formal codification.

In these works, the process of formal synthesis is closer to morphogenetic processes than to the classical precepts of hylomorphism.[36] Morphogenesis is an approach to form in its fluid state rather than in its eternal or ideal state—or, form as a temporal configuration within a process of entropy, rather than in an invariant or solid entity.

Postideological, Postlinguistic: Performative

Koolhaas's proposal has been driven since *Delirious New York* by the intentional exploitation of ideological ambiguity and a contempt for linguistic coherence. The retroactive manifesto proposes modernity as a sensibility, rather than a plan of action, an ideological program, or a stylistic affiliation.

The relevance of recent OMA work lies precisely in the evolution from those attitudes that have developed since the economic-ideological crisis at the end of the 1960s, when avant-garde architecture was confined to a superstructural position and restricted almost exclusively to linguistic manipulations or utopian formulations. This autonomy is increasingly unsustainable when the engagement with infrastructure, in whatever meaning one may give to this term, seems unavoidable. One of the frequent strategies used by Koolhaas is the resort to contradictory or simply unfit ideological formulations, probably with the purpose of undermining their legitimacy as architectural tools and the inadequacy of autonomy as a premise for architecture.

If ideology has traditionally been a form of legitimization and validation of action, constituting a type of social cement able to provide the social processes of production and reproduction with standards and values, the idea that late capitalism requires ideological consensus to survive is questionable.[37]

---

is a matter of optimising the benefits of the location of a number of facilities while simultaneously offering a relatively stable aesthetic experience. At the base of the formal concept, the principle of programmatic indetermination allows any sort of mutation, modification or replacement, without altering the departure hypothesis." Rem Koolhaas, text on La Villette, in *OMA, 6 Projets*, op. cit. My translation.

36   René Thom, *Structural Stability and Morphogenesis* (Reading, MA: The Benjamin/Cummings Publishing Company, 1975).

37   "There is little evidence to suggest that certain values or beliefs are shared by all (or even

The aperture of OMA's ideological diaphragm permits exposure to a whole series of specifically contemporary phenomena that can only be addressed from outside traditional political ideologies, and, consequently, the renunciation of linguistic coherence.[38] The eclecticism of the prospective manifesto becomes the operative basis that drives the recent production of the firm from the simultaneous rejection of ideological and linguistic coherence to the articulation of multiplicities with performative aims.[39] OMA's architecture is crucially focused on the performative, as its validation is not grounded in functional, representational, or reproductive effects, but in operative exactness, adequacy, or efficiency. Rather than posing ideological or semantic questions, OMA's effort is concentrated on material, topographic, and spatial organizations. OMA's work must be seen as a strategic retreat, the cessation of ideological resistance to the developments of contemporary culture.

The images on this text have a more biographical nuance. They refer to the personal experience of working at OMA, which happened in parallel with the writing of this text. The feeling of working in an insultingly young office experimenting with important projects without the usually required experience illustrated an increasingly common phenomenon across different practices in the last few decades. The defiance of experience, initiated in the mid 20th century by the film and music industries had become a global phenomenon across more mainstream industries. Even architecture, a famously gerontocratic practice was beeing affected. After the model of Bill Gates and Steve Jobs—both Boomers—arrived Sergei Brin and Larry Page's Google, Mark Zuckerberg's facebook, all of which are examples of this tendency. Other disciplines such as arts, music or even sports have also been traditionally prone to this trend.

most) members of modern industrial societies. On the contrary, it seems more likely that our societies, in so far as they are 'stable' social orders, are stabilized by virtue of the diversity of values and beliefs and the proliferation of divisions between individuals and groups. The stability of our societies may depend, not so much upon a consensus, but at the very point where oppositional attitudes could be translated into political action." John B. Thompson, *Studies in the Theory of Ideology* (Cambridge: Polity Press, 1984).

38 "To explore the interrelations between language and ideology is to turn away from the analysis of well-formed sentences or systems of signs, focusing instead on the ways in which expressions serve as means of action and interaction, a medium through which history is produced and society reproduced." Ibid. The close relationship that links ideology and language has been extensively analyzed by Jürgen Habermas, Fredric Jameson, and Pierre Bourdieu.

39 On the subject of "performativity," see Jean-François Lyotard, *The Postmodern Condition: A Report on Knowledge* (Minneapolis: University of Minnesota Press, 1984).

Herzog & de Meuron: Between the Face and the Landscape

This text is neither a description nor an interpretation, judgment, or manifesto. I think that the most productive function that an architectural critique may have is to act as a deterritorializing machine, using architecture as *pretext* to speak of something else, to create assemblages establishing networks with other territories, extending architecture's zones of influence, systematically transgressing the boundaries of other sciences in search of new metaphors—to operate like a television camera on a battlefield, altering the course of events by simply being present.

Materialization of the Face

Hermann Rorschach was a Swiss psychiatrist who, at the start of the twentieth century, gathered a collection of inkblot sheets as an instrument for the analysis of personality.[1] These plates, initially produced at random, were ultimately reduced to ten inkblots through the analysis of the associations produced by such figures in the imagination of more than 40,000 subjects, both sick and sound.

---

1   Hermann Rorschach, *Psychodiagnostics: A Diagnostic Test Based on Perception* (Berna: Huber, 1942). See also Rudolf Arnheim's analysis in *Towards a Psychology of Art: Collected Essays* (Berkeley, CA: University of California Press, 1966).

The Rorschach test is classified as a projective test where the inkblots become screens upon which the structures of personality are projected. The method is a scientific rationalization of a long history of perceptual explorations: primitive paintings as completion of the figures formed by the rocky shapes of caves; the contemplation of the capricious forms of clouds which delighted the romantics; the interpretation of flaking and damp stains used by Leonardo da Vinci to train his disciples, etc.

The interest of the Rorschach method resides in the foregrounding of material organizations as the locus of meaning that precedes the constitution of a representative language. Somewhat similarly, René Thom's *sémiophysique* explains that significant effects—*pregnances*—have nothing to do with the essence of things but, rather, their ability to enter an intelligible and thus operable world.[2] Nature is continuous and inchoate; it is human conscience that is capable of individualizing discrete entities, *figures*, in order to operate on reality.

Both theories have particular repercussions in the work at hand. In Herzog & de Meuron's work, the emergence of material organization becomes a pregnant entity, without requiring conventional semiotic vehicles. Rather than describing phenomena, humans provide them with *pregnance*, or intelligibility. The strategy occasionally includes dissolving the forms of experience; weakening structuring capacity in order to retrieve the freedom of exploring matter. Herzog & de Meuron's ambiguous interest in figuration—the use of figures with established pregnance—is, in itself, proof of this interest in mediating between emergences and pregnances.

Herzog & de Meuron oscillate between being portrait architects and landscape architects; between the Italian and the Flemish school. Their work possesses

---

2   "Instead of establishing Geometry on Logic, it is a question of establishing Logic within Geometry. Thus, we produce an overall scheme of a world made of emergences and pregnances: emergences are respectively impenetrable objects; pregnances are hidden qualities, efficient virtues that, emanating from source forms, impregnate themselves with other emerging forms and produce visible (figurative) effects." René Thom, *Esquisse d'une sémiophysique* (Paris: InterEditions, 1988).

the precision and structure of those who find light years of difference between slight deformations of outline and gesture. But their work also shows the richness in texture and sensuality of those who are able to abandon themselves to the disorder of matter. It is a matter of genre.

Herzog & de Meuron's projects evidence an effort—also noticeable in their writings—in the construction of surfaces as preeminent elements of architecture. The *envelope* becomes their primary research field, beyond structural or spatial organizations. The envelope is the area of articulation between interior and exterior, where the public values of the architectural object are registered: the face of the building. As opposed to the determination of modern architects to make this boundary disappear, Herzog & de Meuron concentrate on defining it, without nostalgia for the form-function identity.[3] Their work displays a determination to operate within a paradigm—that of *faciality*—that has the potential for the release of the body from its natural determinations even to its cancellation.

The sensuality of surfaces in the work of Herzog & de Meuron does not originate in the primitive sincerity of those who aimed at the disappearance of veils—the pure manifestation of the naked body and the *primitive head* as the source of significance.[4] Nor is it identified with the *faciality* that has traditionally constituted the academic architectural discipline, based on the virtuous application of certain codes and conventions established to subject the body of the building to adequate public morals. It thus escapes a system of significance with a long tradition dating back to the Renaissance: Leon Battista Alberti divided

---

3   On the distinction between the body-head system and the faciality system as machines of significance for material organizations, see Deleuze and Guattari, "Year Zero: Faciality," in *A Thousand Plateaus. Capitalism and Schizophrenia* (Minneapolis: University of Minnesotta Press, 1987).

4   See Leon Battista Alberti, *On the Art of Building in Ten Books*, trans. Joseph Rykwert, Neil Leach, and Robert Tavernor (Cambridge, MA: MIT Press, 1988), book IV. See also Victor Burgin's "Perverse Space" and Mark Wigley's "Untitled: The Housing of Gender," in *Sexuality & Space*, ed. Beatriz Colomina (New York: Princeton Architectural Press, 1992).

architecture into alignments, deriving from the mind, matter, and nature. The body of a building should be covered by a skin made of several layers of stucco that must "shine like marble" and subject the material body of the building to the dominance of an appropriate visual order that is manifested in the organization of the surface, which ultimately serves as a canvas or a screen for the deployment of the signifier.[5]

This historical form of faciality is structured around defining the edges of the plane—base, body, and coronation—toward the goal of appropriately organizing the duality between holes and screens: determining unequivocally the function of each hole (signifying doors, windows, etc.); framing the screens (molding panels, adding ornaments); establishing centers and symmetries; and graciously overcoming the discontinuities produced by the corners in the application of a type of faciality over the body of the building. In short, historical faciality enacted a range of policies aimed at the strict control of the expressiveness of the building's body, an expressiveness that reappears and generates new percepts when we immerse ourselves in noncoded, raw matter. Herzog & de Meuron's determination to operate from the surface is readily apparent in their design process, which originates in characteristic lead pencil drawings on paper, where two-dimensional organization is asserted as the seed of the project. The notable absence of perspectival or three-dimensional representations in the elaboration and presentation of projects is an evident manifestation of a specific style that is clearly exemplified in projects like the Stone House in Tavole, where the figure of a cross is projected and rotated successively to constitute the central feature of the project. And yet the figure of the structural cross is immediately transferred to the faces of the building. The facial traits in Herzog and de Meuron's buildings are very much affected by the presence of material textures, as if the face of the buildings was permanently oscillating between the figure and the matter. The

5   Deleuze and Guattari, "Year Zero: Faciality", in *A Thousand Plateaus*, op. cit.

faces of Herzog & de Meuron's buildings are, therefore, unstable. The architects try to diffuse edges, borders, or frameworks into the materiality of the surface; they blur the limits between holes and screens; the component parts of the surface are not functionally specialized.[6] Herzog & de Meuron's work is on the cusp between the face (what is ordered, pregnant) and the landscape (the chaotic, emergent).[7]

In the Schwitter Building in Basel, the Ricola Europe Factory and Storage Building in Mulhouse, and the Signal Box Auf dem Wolf in Basel we find a strategy of liberation from the classical forms of faciality: an instability of the visual order—like the deliberate effect found in an op art composition—undermines the configuration of the facade plane, releasing control over the identity of the face. In the case of the Sandoz Laboratories in Basel, a visually destabilizing moiré effect is produced through the serigraphy of the insulation texture on the enveloping glass.

In the residential building on the Hebelstrasse and the Schwitter Building, both in Basel, we find yet another form of dissolving traditional structures of facade organization: the serial order that constructs the main elevation is suddenly interrupted, revealing the discontinuity of the corner. To obviate the need for a specific treatment of the edge of the surface and the definition and articulation of its boundaries is a strategy that was foreseen in the Stone House (1991) through the concealment of the corner structure. Through this operation, the structure becomes a form that does not delimit an interior domain. The lack of an edge definition targets a reduction of the hierarchic structure of the surface in the absence of a framework.[8] The best example of this operation

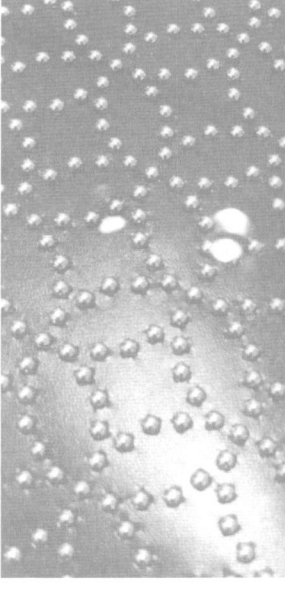

---

6   I refer here to the distinction that René Thom makes between form as the figure that defines an interior and an exterior, distinguishing itself over a background, and trace as the figure that does not outline an interior, and therefore has an ambiguous relationship with the background, even when it is expressed as pregnance. According to Thom, topological connectivity of form is one of the characteristics that enables its individuation by definition of an interior domain. René Thom, *Esquisse d'une sémiophysique*, op. cit.

7   "A landscape is something essentially chaotic, but is found in the scale of sizes amongst the ordered forms of, let's say, a flower and the globe." Arnheim, *Towards to Psychology of Art*, op. cit.

is probably in the configuration of the corner of the Ricola Europe Factory and Storage Building (1991), where both planes meet directly, without any component that resolves their edge, turning the facade elements into traces instead of individualized forms. As in Jean-Luc Godard's films, the joint is made through direct (*jump*) cut, without fade-outs.

Herzog & de Meuron express their deep disgust with "white models" and "conventional architectural perspectives" that reduce architecture to volume and geometry.[9] Instead of considering matter as essentially inexpressive and unintelligible, Herzog & de Meuron propose the inclusion of material singularities in the construction of the face. Material specificity is pitched at the dissolution of figures of hylomorphic faciality: binary configurations of holes and screens[10] are replaced by textures that overcome the duality of figure-ground. Already in the Blue House (1980), the simple application of the intense International Klein Blue on the plane of the facade negates the stability of the wall as a screen. Similar pictorial mechanisms can be found in the Schwarz Park Apartments (1988) project and the Student Housing for the Université de Bourgogne, Dijon (1991). In both projects, the alternation of light and dark horizontal bands—a mechanism often found in pre-Renaissance Italian architecture and perhaps the origin of modern faciality—disintegrates the plane of the facade as a surface for the deployment of the signifier.

Other strategies to dissolve the figurative occupation of the surface can be found in the attempts to undermine the functional determination of certain elements of the facade. Doors, windows and panes are often disfigured. How does one distinguish between the doors and windows

---

8   "However, all hierarchic distribution presupposes two steps: framing and filling. One outlines the field or fields, and the other organizes the resulting space." E. H. Gombrich, *The Sense of Order: A Study in the Psychology of Decorative Art* (Oxford: Phaidon, 1979).

9   See "The Hidden Geometry of Nature," in *Siedlung Pilotengasse Wien: Herzog & de Meuron, Steidle + Partner*, ed. Adolf Krischanitz (Zurich: Artemis, 1992).

10 See Deleuze and Guattari, "Year Zero: Faciality," in *A Thousand Plateaus*, op. cit.

of the residential building on the Hebelstrasse (1988)? Where is the entry to the Ricola Europe Factory and Storage Building in Mulhouse (1993), the Blois Cultural Center (1996), or the Goetz Gallery (1992)? They have been subsumed as texture—their faces transmuted into landscapes. Centralities, symmetries, and recognizable hierarchies have disappeared to release the power of repetition,[11] turning the face into a territory, into a landscape of rhythms.

As in Rorschach's inkblots, a material organization that is not determined by significant structures becomes a surface for the projection of meanings. The disfiguration of the face enables Herzog & de Meuron to return to the landscape of matter in the search of new *percepts* without having to abandon intelligibility.

The Sensorial Difference: Repetition and Self-Similarity

Herzog & de Meuron's work is distinguished, especially in comparison with the vast majority of contemporary architecture, by the use of repetition as a compositional technique. At the other extreme of the spectrum, the historicist, regionalist, and deconstructivist architectures have been presenting themselves as incorporations of difference, a crucial category of contemporary politics.[12] It is precisely repetition that enables them to approach the specificity of the work in a more consistent mode, instead of operating via the systematic proliferation of different forms. Here, repetition is what produces difference, proposing textures and rhythms as material, temporal, and spatial organizations with signifying performances beyond mere linguistic coding.[13] The use of repetition in the work of Herzog & de Meuron

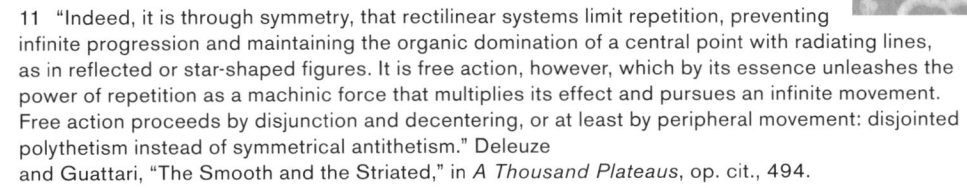

---

[11] "Indeed, it is through symmetry, that rectilinear systems limit repetition, preventing infinite progression and maintaining the organic domination of a central point with radiating lines, as in reflected or star-shaped figures. It is free action, however, which by its essence unleashes the power of repetition as a machinic force that multiplies its effect and pursues an infinite movement. Free action proceeds by disjunction and decentering, or at least by peripheral movement: disjointed polythetism instead of symmetrical antithetism." Deleuze
and Guattari, "The Smooth and the Striated," in *A Thousand Plateaus*, op. cit., 494.

[12] Instead of difference as a temporal identity (Popper/Rowe), difference as regional identity (Heidegger/Frampton), and difference as linguistic identity (Derrida/Eisenman), the work of Herzog & de Meuron approaches repetition as a sensorial form of difference, or as Deleuzian "non-representative difference." See Gilles Deleuze, *Différence et répétition* (Paris: Presses Universitaires de France, 1968).

serves as an illustration of an operation that affirms particularity rather than generality, while rejecting the preexisting concepts and figures of linguistic space. For Herzog & de Meuron, repetition is the supreme manifestation of freedom and particularity, the dynamic order that creates a space, a time, a rhythm, and a temporal synthesis that includes past and future and avoids both narrative arguments and chaotic succession.

Rather than evoking the reification of objects in the process of industrial production, repetition has an intention that goes back to the most basic operations of the construction of space and territory: the rhythm of the tam-tam, territorial signs, and ornamental motifs of tattoos. Repetition in Herzog & de Meuron is only related incidentally—vaguely in the effects and never in the intentions—to reproduction, to the model-copy system. This is where their work is also distanced from architecture that insists upon serial production or repetition as identity. In Herzog & de Meuron's work, repetition is the instrument that permits the generation of a space in which differential intensities become expressed. Like variations in the intensity of ritual chants through body movements, it is the repetition of the detail of the facade in the Ricola Europe Factory and Storage Building that enables one to appreciate the gradient of intensity that produces the specificity of the object. The curve of the Schwitter Building is made visible precisely because of an obsessive repetition of the facade element rather than the faithful representation of programmatic differences. In the residential building on the Hebelstrasse, the repetition of the tie structure and the corresponding pillars makes expressive the change in the alignment of the enclosure. Repetition here works by contraction; this is where we find the specificity of a rhythm, where difference is manifested sensorially. This is quite unlike the occupation of space through differentiated configurations—that is, historicist, regionalist, or deconstructivist architecture—and also distinct from the hierarchic

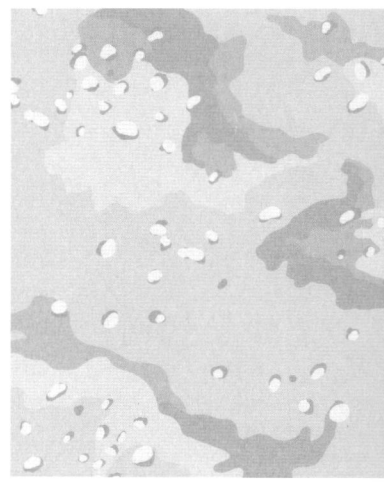

13 "Repetition not only does not exclude differences, but begets them, produces them. Sooner or later, repetition finds the phenomenon that arises, or rather happens, through its relationship to the whole or repetitively produced series. In other words, the difference." Henri Lefebvre, *Rhythmanalysis: Space, Time, and Everyday Life*, trans. Stuart Elden and Gerald Moore (London: Continuum, 2004).

organization and occupation of a framed milieu (as in high-tech architecture).[14]

Herzog & de Meuron's architecture works effectively through the reduction of material organization to a core that constructs the specificity of the architectural object through repetition. It is not a question of imposing forms on matter, but of elaborating an increasingly rich and consistent material logic, designed to engage with an ever-complex set of attachments. Herzog & de Meuron's architecture is rich in polyrhythmic (and polyphonic) effects, which produce the specificity of a territory without predefined boundaries: the vertical bar railing or the repetition of structural elements on the facade of the Schwitter Building that serve to highlight the curved volume; the series of railings, fusi-form columns, and metal rods on the panel-shutters that explain the change in alignment of the balconies of the residential bulding on the Hebelstrasse; the overlapping rhythms of the structure and the divisions on the enclosure in the Ricola Europe Factory and Storage Building. As in the Nonius (Nóniusz), difference is synthesized and materialized in the overlapping of different series, in *polyrhythmia*—through "line-breeding." The metaphors are telling: we have, in a sense, *in architecture*, the polyphonic waves of indistinct and discordant musical structures washing over one another and the fusion of distinct genotypes as found in the Hungarian art of horse-breeding to account for what, *in effect*, is an intense combinatory practice. The result is invariably spellbinding (not unlike the symphonic excesses of Mahler or Bartók, or the stellar breeds emerging from the stables at Mezöhegyes).

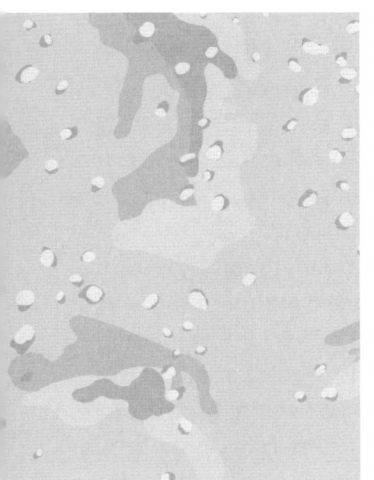

---

14   Rhythm is opposed to meter because its significance is registered on a different plane [from] that of actions. Its meaning must be found beyond the plane where the action takes place, that is, not in the nature of the component that is repeated, but rather in the mode in which the repetition is produced. I do not think so. "The territory is not primary to the qualitative mark; it is the mark that makes the territory. Functions in a territory are not primary; they presuppose a territory—producing expressiveness. In this sense, the territory and the functions performed within it, are products of territorialization. Territorialization is an act of rhythm that has become expressive, or of milieu components that have become qualitative. The marking of a territory is dimensional, but it is not a meter, it is a rhythm. It retains the most general characteristic of rhythm, which is to be inscribed on a different plane than that of actions." Deleuze and Guattari, "Of the Refrain," in Deleuze and Guattari, *A Thousand Plateaus*, op. cit. 313-314.

Herzog & de Meuron's work often uses self-similarity as an organizational structure that is manifested in both the syntactic structure of the object, and in its relationship with context. The correspondence between spatial organization and envelope in the Stone House, Redevelopment of the Gaba Block, Basel (1988), and the Sandoz Technology Development Centre, Basel (1993); the formal similarity between the structure, facade, and detail of the railings in the Schwitter Building; and the resonance between the form of the main body and the beams that sustain the hangar roofs of the Railway Engine Depot Auf dem Wolf, Basel (1995) are all examples of this self-similar organization. It is as though the specificity of each project is materialized in each of its parts or organizational levels, eliminating the need for an overall hierarchy. The part is freed syntactically from the whole to become its synthesis.

A self-similar architecture is particularly efficient when working in an unstable environment; it provides the object with extraordinary resilience against change (for example, a potential amputation or enlargement) and independence from context by eliminating scale as a constituent essence of a project. Scale depends on a reference system and is thus ineffective as a compositional mechanism in an unstable milieu. Projects such as the Ricola Europe Factory and Storage Building, and the Signal Box Auf dem Wolf (1994) are examples of the scalar indetermination which is often a feature of Herzog & de Meuron's work. In these projects, scale is not a constant, linear function as in classical architecture, but a differential function that depends on its border conditions. It is not that there is no scalar relationship with context in these projects, but rather that this relationship is ambiguous and not endemic to their material organization.

Decodification of *Milieus*: Disfigured Figuration
There is a third operative strategy in the work of Herzog & de Meuron that is closely related to the procedures analyzed previously. In light of the arguments that we have maintained, how can one explain the serigraphy of religious icons on the alabaster envelopment of the project for a Greek Orthodox Church in Zurich (1989)? How can one explain the facades of the projects for the Flowtec Office and Laboratory Building in Reinach (1990), the Suva Building in Basel (1993), and Sandoz Technology Development Centre in Basel (1993), where the envel-

oping surface is printed with images or text? How can one explain the electronic letter bands of the Arts Centre in Blois (1991), the Berlin Zentrum contribution to the exhibition Berlin: Morgen (1991), and the gallery for a private collection of modern art in Munich (1992). Is the apparent abandonment of abstraction a slide toward representational strategies? The categories advanced in the previous sections are precisely those that permit us to establish continuity between both operational modes, beyond the traditional artistic categories of the abstract and the figurative and the classifications or codifications of the milieus where they may be deployed. Herzog & de Meuron's work can be understood better as occupying the ambiguity between emergence and pregnance, existing between what is revealed and what is projected, mediating the distance between chaos and the appearance of specific territories.

The categories of figurative and abstract are produced in the domain of representation; figuration is already a form of abstraction of reality, a form of art. It is the crisis of representation that ultimately erases the figurative-abstract duality.[15] The introduction of figurative motifs in Herzog & de Meuron's projects occurs as an inverse procedure to the abstraction needed to produce order or intelligibility in a chaotic material organization (the process in the Rorschach inkblots, for example). Figuration is disfigured to become texture, to abandon its representational nature, just as pregnances become emergences through repetition and juxtaposition.

This is a process that has an interesting precedent in some of Andy Warhol's works, such as the Car Crash, Campbell's Soup Cans, and Marilyn Monroe diptych series, where an image of socially high pregnance disintegrates into a texture from which color stains and dispersed parts emerge. (It is not coincidental that Warhol was also attracted by the Rorschach as an artistic process.) This ambivalence between abstract

---

15 "The abstract is not directly opposed to figurative. The figurative as such is not inherent to a 'will to art'; In fact, we may oppose a figurative line in art to one that is not. The figurative, or imitation and representation, is a consequence, a result of certain characteristics of the line when it assumes a given form." Deleuze and Guattari, "The Smooth and the Striated" in A Thousand Plateaus, op. cit. 497.

and figurative languages is what distinguishes Warhol and Herzog & de Meuron from, for example, Oldenburg and Venturi, Rauch & Scott Brown. In the former, the figurative component tends to disappear in a texture, while in the latter, it is used as a recognizable and pregnant—albeit recontextualized—element. The work of the latter is still produced within the linguistic-representative paradigm, while in both Warhol and Herzog & de Meuron's work the figure becomes a rhythmic incident, precisely what produces the transfer between milieus, connecting a cultural iconography to a material structure.

The inclusion of text in the surface of buildings occurs within this same operative mode. With text, the maneuver is even more obvious in the sense that words are the paradigmatic representative code. In Herzog & de Meuron's work, text functions as a significant texture, rather than as another sign among the different linguistic operations that construct the significance of the building (as is the case in many projects by Venturi, Rauch & Scott Brown, where text or iconography refers specifically to the content of the building). In the Arts Centre, Blois (1991) or the two libraries for the Université de Jussieu, Paris (1992), text becomes a social texture, not necessarily determined by the signification or character of the building. The work of Herzog & de Meuron is therefore independent of milieus, traveling in both directions along the vector that links order with chaos, nature with artifice, emergence with pregnance, or matter with signs; connecting the abstract and the figurative—in short, *making the face as the landscape*.[16]

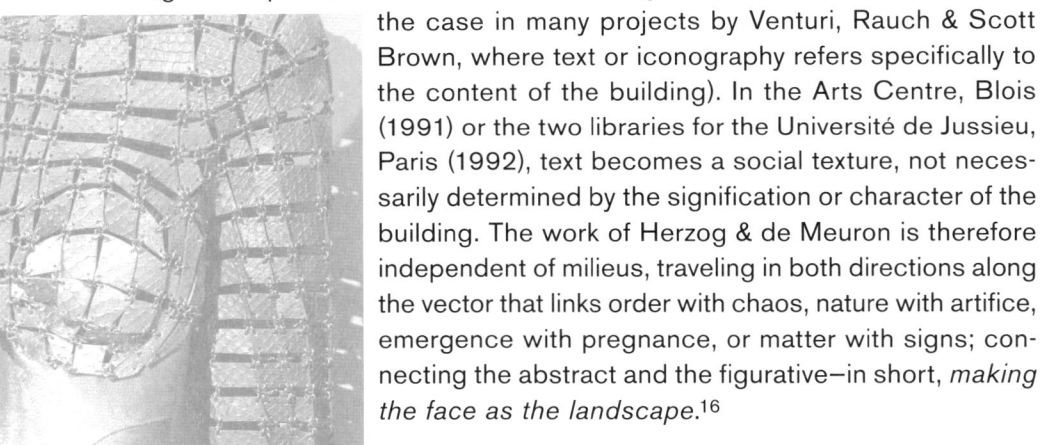

The images along this text address the intense focus on the surface that the practice of H&dM developed since the 80's, in advance to the avalanche of surface-related experiments that were to take place in the late 90's and in the new century. I have used the space of this text to illustrate a short history of the fashion patterns, since the 1960's. From the Chanel fabrics, through the Paco Rabanne metallic fabrics and the Barbour padded clothes to the Miyake pleats, the images enclosed aim to refer the recent history of pattern.

16 To "make the face as the landscape" is a direct translation of the Spanish *poner cara de paisaje*, which is a colloquial expression for "keeping a straight face," "to dissimulate," "not wanting to show our attitude," etc.

Jean Nouvel: Intensifying the Real

"To the tenth degree of virtuosity, mind is free!
Risen from the prison of humanism."[1]
—*DOWNTOWN SCIENCE*

The first time I saw Jean Nouvel's design for the Tokyo Opera House, it reminded me of Saint-Exupéry's *The Little Prince* and the story of the snake that had swallowed an elephant.[2] This reference, in turn, triggered a reverie on the work of Jean Nouvel, an architect who belongs to a certain intellectual lineage and sensibility with deep roots in French culture, of which Saint-Exupéry doubtlessly belongs, but which also includes Deleuze and Guattari, Michel Serres, René Thom, Paul Virilio, and others given to an equally fantastic sense of expressive force. This reverie is, in fact, an *assemblage* between texts and theoretical agency,[3] structured at the level of logistics, strategies, and tactics in an effort to describe Nouvel's work as a continuum with the material culture of which it is part and parcel.

1   From the song "Radioactive," Def Jam Music Inc./Sam I Am Songs Inc./Money Makin' Music Inc., 1991.
2   Antoine de Saint-Exupéry, *Le petit prince* (Paris: Gallimard, 1946).
3   Here, assemblage is a translation of *agencement*, used by Deleuze and Guattari to explain operations that link signs and contents (declaration and production), territories and movements (interiors and exteriors). It describes an operation of assembly, joining, and mixture, or one able to produce a new entity through the association of diverse elements. See Deleuze and Guattari, "Rhizome," in *A Thousand Plateaus. Capitalism and Schizophrenia* (Minneapolis: University of Minnesotta Press, 1987).

The legend goes that, after reading a picture book on life in the jungle describing how boa constrictors swallow their prey without chewing as part of a digestive process that can last for six months, young Saint-Exupéry produced his first childhood drawing: a shape that represented a boa that had swallowed an elephant and was sleeping through its digestion. He showed it to his parents, who interpreted it as a hat. Disappointed, Saint-Exupéry drew a second picture of a snake with transparent skin, showing the elephant inside to make the concept more explicit. The response was advice to forget his artistic pursuits and concentrate on the study of geography, history, calculus, and grammar. Faced with the prospect of having to follow a strict discipline without deformations, mixtures, or evolutions of forms, Saint-Exupéry learned to fly and became an air force pilot, writer, and artist. He also came to love the desert, where he met the *petit prince*, the only person able to understand the drawing of the boa constrictor that had eaten the elephant; a primitive case of what a few decades later was to be called *morphing*.[4] The "snake who swallowed an elephant" and "the whale that swallowed the Kaaba"[5] are examples of geometries that have escaped from the discipline of type to delve into the formal implications of a reality determined by intensities rather than extensions—into the geometry of navigation, flight paths, deformation, accidents, and affects that characterizes Nouvel's work.

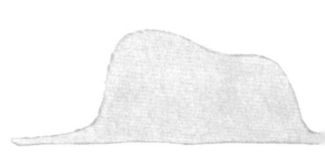

Logistics: Abstract Machines

Jean Nouvel practices a form of guerilla logistics; in his own words, his method of operation is one of *migration* or *movement*,[6] through multiple deterritorializing and reterritorializing operations. His fondness for exteriority is a device to reengage his discipline with reality. Disciplines belong to a culture structured on hard segmentations that produce schools, factories, and garrisons,[7] but the emerging global space of late capitalism can

---

4   *Morphing* is the informational technique that enables hybrid forms to be produced, for example, 60% Great Dane and 40% Volkswagen, or halfway between the faces of Michael Jackson and a wolf. Morphing has been used most effectively in cinema and typesetting.

5   This is how Philippe Starck describes the Tokyo Opera House project. See Patrice Goulet et al., *Jean Nouvel* (Paris: Electa Moniteur, 1987).

6   Ibid.

7   The construction of an appropriate space-time for the development of industrial society has been analyzed rigorously by Foucault. See Michel Foucault, *Discipline and Punish: The Birth of the Prison*, trans. Alan Sheridan (New York: Vintage Books, 1979).

no longer be interrupted by the modern notions of space and time based on the assembly line. In the emerging global order, entities are fundamentally defined by their *exteriority*.⁸

Nouvel operates with *abstract machines* that afford him a conceptual mobility and the transversal engagement with different segments of reality.⁹ His architecture is grounded on a level that operates beyond the disciplinary; many of his projects can be enunciated through a verbal statement:

—An opaque monolith floating adrift in the asphalt of a parking lot sunken into a lake (Onyx Cultural Centre).
—A facade like the diaphragm of a camera (Institute of the Arab World).
—A whale that has swallowed the Kaaba (Tokyo Opera House).
—A tower without start or finish (Tour Sans Fin).
—A case for three musical instruments (Tours Convention Centre).

The specificity of Nouvel's method spanning across milieus becomes evident when we try to describe other architects' work in the same terms. For example, if we compare his method with Le Corbusier's, we can see the specificities: the *plan libre*, the *fenêtre en longueur*, the *terrasse jardin*. These labels all refer systematically to specific descriptions of architectural components, lying within the nineteenth-century disciplinary paradigm. Moreover, Le Corbusier's words define generic prototypes, never specific concepts. In Nouvel's work, specificity becomes the other face of exteriority: on the one hand he practices deterritorializations; on the other, those abstract enunciations are applied in a very specific manner to a concrete assemblage or situation—they are immediately territorialized. These dual logistics are aimed to escape both from the Medieval space, where global equals empty, and from the enlightened, modern space, where local equals disconnected. By simultaneously addressing the concrete and the abstract, the work is able to operate in the emerging space of late-capitalism, where the emergence of a global financial order tends to intensify differences instead of increasing uniformity.

8   See Jean-François Lyotard, *The Inhuman: Reflections on Time*, trans. Geoffrey Bennington and Rachel Bowlby (Cambridge: Polity Press, 1991).

9   "Abstract machines work in specific assemblages: they are defined by the fourth aspect of assemblages, i.e., by the maximums of decodification and deterritorialization. They outline these maximums; they also open territorial assemblages on to an exterior, to other assemblages—molecular, cosmic, and constitute becomings." Deleuze and Guattari, "Conclusion: Concrete Rules and Abstract Machines" in *A Thousand Plateaus*, op. cit., 510.

Strategies of Desire: The Production of *Affects*

Musical genres often evolve through the devaluation of form and technique in order to increase the integrative capacity of expression.[10] Contemporary music is a good example of this: consider rap's replacement of melody with speech, or techno's mixing board techniques—sampling and scratching—where multiple segments of reality are literally included in the musical construction, suspending previous forms of disciplinary virtuosity. Jean Nouvel works in a similar way through a preliminary suspension of aesthetic judgment, moving away from modern ideals, rejecting their precepts of rationalization, secularization, and equality. Nouvel's pragmatic aesthetics eliminates the boundaries between science and art, collapsing the estrangement that permitted the humanistic construction of an active subjectivity and a passive objectivity. There is a lineage of artists that goes from Marcel Duchamp to Jeff Koons, or from Nicolas Le Camus de Mézières to Jean Nouvel, and which exploits desire as a mediation between subject and object through strategies of sensationalism, seduction, and fascination.[11] In Deleuzian terms, this mediation lies in the capacity to *affect*. An *affect* is an empowerment, and not a simple change or modification. Affects, according to Deleuze, are not simple affections, as they are independent from their subject. Artists create *affects* and *percepts*—blocks of space-time—rather than functions or concepts.[12]

10   See the analysis of rap techniques and ideologies as a prototype form of creation of a pragmatic aesthetics in Richard Schusterman, "The Fine Art of Rap," in *Pragmatist Aesthetics: Living Beauty, Rethinking Art* (Oxford: Blackwell Publishers, 1992).

11   "What happens when what you see, even from a distance, seems to touch you with a grasping contact, when seeing becomes contact at a distance? What happens when what you see is imposed on your gaze, as if the gaze were touched, captured, put in touch with appearance?" Maurice Blanchot, *The Gaze of Orpheus: And Other Literary Essays*, trans. Lydia Davis (Barrytown, NY: Station Hill Press, 1981).

12   Following Deleuze, *affects* are "pre-personal intensities" that are transmitted by empathy between material organizations rather than through codes, signs, or conventional forms of representation. Gilles Deleuze, "Percepts, concepts, affects," in Gilles Deleuze and Félix Guattari, in *What is Philosophy?* trans. Hugh Tomlinson and Graham Burchell (New York: Columbia University Press, 1996).

Nouvel's method is scenographic: with the scenographer Jacques Le Marquet, he works by constructing situations instead of topographic or geometric models. The Situationists described these techniques as the *elimination of artificially generated distances*.¹³ Nouvel explores the dense materiality of desire through the intensification of dubious aesthetic pleasures, often verging on the *kitsch*, finding delight in reproducing the most banal scenographies of consumer society—coating a cultural center with the skin of a supermarket, designing the highest tower in Europe, dressing a rock venue in heavy-metal icons—and using the cheapest tricks, including catwalks, paints and screens, vertigo and bedazzlement, violent compressions and expansions. These are strategies with neither depth nor rhetoric, offering no social redemption. It is not an aesthetic of disappearance but rather of intensification, grounded on the production of affects. Nouvel works through an intensification of the real rather than a simulated aesthetics or nostalgia for reality.

Local Strategies: The Accident as Essence

Michel Serres writes that modern sports such as surfing, hang gliding, and rafting all describe lines with neither start nor end, where virtuosity applies to using currents, *haecceities* of matter,

13   This way of operating refers us to the urban techniques of working that were born from the surrealists and developed at the hands of the Situationist International, one of the most influential ideological associations of the 1968. The situationists believed that the only way to react against the modern bureaucratic state and the society of spectacle was to generate situations or events that could force us to reestablish emotional contact (desire) with our surroundings. They experimented with psycho-geography, a mediating epistemology between subject and object (a science of feelings). Psycho-geography is the study of precise laws and specific effects in the geographic environment, organized consciously or unconsciously on the basis of emotions and the behavior of individuals. See Guy Debord, "Introduction to a Critique of Urban Geography," in *Situationist International Anthology*, ed. and trans. Ken Knabb (Berkeley, CA: Bureau of Public Secrets, 1981). It is nonetheless important to distinguish between the surrealist insurrection and the situationist insurrection. Debord famously wrote in "Report on the Construction of Situations" (1957), published in *Situationist International Anthology*, op. cit., the document that led to the merger of various avant-garde protest movements and the foundation of the Situationist International, "We must advance the keywords of unitary urbanism, of experimental behavior, of hyper political propaganda, and of the construction of environments. The passions have been interpreted enough [surrealism]: the point now is to discover others."

rather than covering a precise distance in less time, like in the 100-meter dash.¹⁴ In Nouvel's aim to collapse the subject-object duality he is also attacking another fixture of Western thought: the distinction between essence and accident. His work follows the accidents in the project, with the purpose of turning them eventually into the essence of his work.¹⁵ His architecture develops neither thickness nor depth: it rides on the crest of the wave, operating on the materialization of the contingent rather than the crystallization of essence. Nouvel declares himself to be radically contemporary: his forms aim to develop the potentials of the accident rather than to legislate a process.

Nouvel is fundamentally opportunistic. He defines his tactics in relation to a specific situation—an accident—rather than to universal norms; hence his rejection of style and his aspiration to the hyper-specific. His methodology cannot be described as either essentialist or phenomenological, as he identifies accident with essence. In the Anne Frank School, the need to build with a prefabricated component becomes the essence of the project. In La Coupole, there is an acritical appropriation of the forms of the surrounding buildings—the swimming pool and the supermarket—into the core of the project. The Institute of the Arab World uses the formal coincidence between the repetition of a photographic diaphragm and an Arabic lattice. However, as the projects get bigger, the accident loses importance as a premise. Instead, the buildings tend to produce scenographies. In the Tokyo Opera House, the Tours Conference Centre, and Tour Sans Fin, the project acts as the producer of an accidental nature rather than as a prototype.

Differentiating Tactics: Topologies and Tensors

Tactics are the most basic operations of a war machine and they crucially inform the shape and the organization of the armed body; they determine its consistency and flexibility, as well as the hierarchy, geometry, and speed of movements. Tactics are concerned with solving problems of friction or resistance, ways of controlling

14   Michel Serres, *Les origines de la géometrie* (Paris: Flammarion, 1993).
15   "Are we prepared to accept an inversion of every philosophical sense in order to consider the accident as absolute and necessary, and substance, whatever substance, as relative and contingent, thus understanding the catastrophe not as a substantial deformation but rather as an unexpected accidental formation [à] la René Thom" Paul Virilio, *L'espace critique* (Paris: Christian Bourgeois, 1984).

and transmitting commands and information. Tactics always mediate between the ideal and the real; they are what distinguish a *phalanx* from a *platoon*.¹⁶ Most architectural practices work solely on a tactical level, at the most purely pragmatic level. But even more sophisticated approaches such as Nouvel's need a tactical level of operation.

In this sense, Nouvel operates through diagrammatic rather than geometric functions. His method favors topological over geometric relationships, the relative position and the connections between programmatic areas over systems of regulating proportions and measurements, or spatial modeling. In contrast to geometric space, topological space has the advantage of being able to solve one of the fundamental problems of contemporary experience: incommensurability.¹⁷ Topology is geometry without scale or measure and, therefore, it is a useful tool for designing structures requiring a high degree of flexibility.

Nouvel's proclivity toward topological operations is patent in a project such as the INIST-CNRS, where the essence of the project relies upon the direct volumetric expression of the diagram of the different functional packages of the program. The manipulation of space through expansions and contractions in the Institute of the Arab World is realized as a topological continuum determining relationships of proximity, segmentation, or orientation instead of compartmentalizing the spaces in the building. The Galleries Lafayette in Berlin is an example of pierced space, another topological model. Expansions and compressions of space, and spatial sequences with violent contrasts are common in Nouvel's projects. They have a topological rather than a geometric determination, unfolding an *inexact* geometry and an unstable corporeality.¹⁸

16 For a more precise description of the tactics, see Carl von Clausewitz, *On War*, ed. Anatol Rapoport, trans. J. J. Graham (New York: Penguin Books, 1982).

17 Incommensurability is one of the basic problems of the postmodern theory of knowledge. See Jean-François Lyotard, *The Postmodern Condition: A Report on Knowledge* (Minneapolis: University of Minnesota Press, 1984).

18 See Edmund Husserl, *Ideas Pertaining to a Pure Phenomenology and to a Phenomenological Philosophy*, trans. F. Kersten (The Hague: Martinus Nijhoff, 1982)

A diagram does not set a geometric shape, but rather proposes a field of intensities. Unlike a space occupied by geometric or linear functions, a diagrammatic function only determines a precise shape when it has been applied to specific conditions.[19] A diagrammatic function discerns a field of intensities that finds mathematical description in *tensors*. Tensors are instruments that enable the differentiation of the field and, unlike linear equations, they are not imposed on an isotropic space, but produced by the space itself. Nouvel's interest in the context and its specification in addition to his proposal of an architecture of tension explains his fondness for certain types of intensive geometry;[20] both the Tokyo Opera House and the Tours Conference Centre develop from a logic of deformation. *Deformations* and *tensors* are differentiating operations. They articulate a global form with local conditions: the local ceases to be an isolated space and becomes defined by a differential and its surroundings.

Integrating Tactics: A-Dimensionality and Hybridization

If topological performance and inexact geometry were tactics of differentiation that enabled intensive local spaces to be built within coherent global orders, Nouvel simultaneously developed an inverse set of tactics aimed at the globalization of accidents.

For example, he refers often to *a-dimensionality* as one of his preferred architectural effects; his projects tend to oscillate between two-dimensionality and three-dimensionality. This tactic operates primarily on the perception of the object and the discernment of measure and proportion. Like Benoit Mandelbrot's famous example of the thread ball,[21] dimen-

---

19   "Each abstract machine is a consolidated set of matter-functions (Filum and diagram). This is seen clearly in a technological *plan*: this type of plan is not simply made up of formed substances and organizing forms, programs, prototypes, etc., but rather a set of non-formed materials that only present certain degrees of intensity (resistance, conductivity, heating, extension, speed or delay, induction, transduction, etc.) and diagrammatical functions that only present differential equations or more generally, *tensors*." Deleuze and Guattari, "Conclusion: Concrete Rules and Abstract Machines" in *A Thousand Plateaus*, op. cit., 511.

20   In Patrice Goulet et al., *Jean Nouvel*, op. cit.

21   "A ball of thread has different dimensions depending on our position with respect to it: at a great distance, it has a null dimension–it is a dot. As we draw closer, it starts to have two or three dimensions, and then two again." Benoit Mandelbrot, *The Fractal Geometry of Nature*, (New York: Freeman & Co., 1977).

sion is a variable that depends upon the position of the observer. It is a pragmatic, rather than essential or objective, quality of spaces or objects. Dimensionality concerns the degree of resolution, the distance, and the intentions with which we perceive the object. In a-dimensionality we face once again the elimination of the distance between subject and object, this time via a perceptual tactic: the manipulation of perceived dimensions. An architecture that pays such close attention to topological relationships, routes, and spatial sequences is destined to operate through dimensional ambiguity and "surfacial" qualities of architecture. In the project for Tête Défense, we move from a frontal vision as a flat background to the Arc de Triomphe, a three-dimensional vision as one enters the building. This technique recalls Sol LeWitt's installations, similarly playing constantly with dimensional ambiguity.

There is a whole range of tactics in Nouvel's work that address the building envelope as a communication interface in a clear reference to his Virilian lineage, as if architecture had evolved into a pure interface.[22] This is apparent in the competition entry for the Nîmes Cultural Centre, the IMA, the offices for the publishing house DuMont-Schauberg, and, finally, in the Fondation Cartier project, where the play of transparency between the three-dimensional body of the building and the screen that shields it constitutes its primary compositional device. Alternatively, in the Cologne Media Park and the Lille buildings, the surface becomes a plane of coincidence between divergent realities: a mechanism for collapsing distances rather than establishing limits. Nouvel was a pioneer of inscribing text and images on building enclosures, pursuing a consistent line of research that starts with his early collaborations with François Seigneur on the expressive use of signs and their problematization as architectural devices.

By treating the building envelopes as surfaces of registration, external realities are grafted onto the object. If the projects mentioned above demonstrate the

---

22 Paul Virilio, with the term *the overexposed city* (from *L'espace critique*), presents a vision of the modern city as a vectorial space, where the materiality of the limits gradually fades away into intermediate or *interface* surfaces, which demonstrates a close sensibility to Nouvel's own approach.

Jean Nouvel: Intensifying the Real

use of a-dimensionality and inter-faciality, there is a third tactic that operates at the scale of objects. This is particularly visible in the projects for Tête Défense, the Tokyo Opera House, Hotel Saint-James, Onyx Cultural Centre, and Jussieu Library. In the Tokyo Opera, Onyx, and Saint-James, the object explores an ambiguity of scale by eliminating any volumetric or textural articulation of the envelope. In Tête Défense and Jussieu, the references to self-similar structures and fractal dimensions appear quite explicitly.

The tactics of a-dimensionality, inter-faciality, and non-scalarity tend to produce instability in the formal determination of the architectural object, thus connecting it to external realities. Similar formal logics have been used by contemporary artists such as LeWitt with parallel aims: the construction of a global space with differential intensities and the articulation of local and global traits—tackling as it were the Gordian knot of contemporary space.

Phylum of the *Unexpressive*

Manuel de Landa hypothesizes the history of technology as a process of organization of matter into increasingly complex systems going through three steps: the clockwork, the motor, and the network.[23] All three have decisive influence upon the spatiality of cultures and forms of thought and action. Each state of the material culture—or phylum[24]—implies specific traits of expression, spatiality, and temporality. Clockwork implies a power based on the deformation of matter, a centered spatiality and rigorous space-time measurement. The motor derives its force from flow and changes of state, implying a decentralized but still rhythmic space-time with linear sequences. The network is the most recent phase in the process of material organization. It feeds upon information exchange; it has simultaneous, disjoined, and unstable space-time sequences, and a topological, nonlinear spatiality. Following his argument, we

23 See Manuel de Landa, *War in the Age of Intelligent Machines* (New York: Zone Books, 1991).

24 *Filum* is a term de Landa borrows from Deleuze and Guattari to describe the evolution of a material culture, the series of traits of material expression and the operations of transformation and usage associated with a given state of evolution of nonorganic matter. What is interesting about this term is that it begins a story of technologies and purely materialistic, not humanistic, culture. See Deleuze and Guattari, "1227: Treatise on Nomadology:–The War Machine" in *A Thousand Plateaus*, op. cit., 497.

could analyze architecture as the medium of the different expressive forms of material culture formed as a historical sequence of a differential nature,[25] prioritizing the organizations of matter (liquefaction, crystallization, folding, disfiguring, and facialization) appropriate for a given technological state.

Nouvel's work tackles the aesthetic dimension of a technological state we could label the *unexpressive*, following Germano Celant's definition of *unexpressionism* as the tendency toward a lack of articulation between material organizations and performances.[26] The unexpressive could well become an appropriate description of the technological and sensorial phylum that nurtures Nouvel's work: the assemblage of enunciation for the disorganized spatial and temporal sequences characteristic of the network paradigm. It produces architectural expressions where the organicity of the architectural object is abandoned, turning instead toward an inorganic, a-teleological, a-genealogical, body, a matter for *development*.[27]

The exploration of a phylum of the unexpressive entails the production of affects rather than expressing the performance of the architectural body. Nouvel's work ranges from the most obscene transparency to the most seductive concealment.[28] The violent polarization between these extremes becomes evident in the comparison between projects such as the Tokyo Opera House and Onyx, or the Fondation Cartier and the building for DuMont-Schauberg. Sequences of radical change in the lighting conditions of the environment are often found within a single project: the contrast between the glass envelope and the black volume of the conference hall in La Coupole;

25 Or the *assemblages* of enunciation of the *filum*, using Deleuze and Guattari's terms.

26 Celant uses the term to explain the work of a group of contemporary artists, some of whom are mentioned in this text. See Germano Celant's introduction to *Unexpressionism: Art Beyond the Contemporary* (New York: Rizzoli, 1988).

27 Performative is the form of legitimization of knowledge and operativity that Lyotard associates to the late-capitalist order. It relates to fundamentally pragmatic reasons of adequateness and efficiency, which govern a process of development—that is, a process unlimited by an original state or a teleological aim. See Jean-François Lyotard, *The Postmodern Condition*, op. cit.

28 For a clarification of the metaphysics of development, see Jean-François Lyotard, *The Inhuman*, op. cit.

the step from the mysterious black exterior to the shining interior in the Tokyo Opera House through a curtain of dazzling light; the illuminated and transparent facades surround the reflecting bubbles of the rooms in Tour Sans Fin. Both extremes of overexposure and concealment, or the range from total transparency to complete opaqueness, perform Nouvel's sensual intensification of the building body. His frequent resort to lighting as an expressive material indexes his interest in mobilizing sensual, atmospheric effects that do not involve a physical presence, but the production of affects (light exposure being a powerful inducer of erotic activity).

Weight and balance also become part of this general strategy of sensorial intensification that characterizes Nouvel's work: the Foundation Cartier, the Saint-Imier offices and the Nemausus, or the Institute of the Arab World, the Onyx Cultural Centre, and the Lyon Opera House explore these "gravitatory" affects, and the violent compressions and expansions of space.

The critical distance that was the trademark of modernism and the possibility of *re-presentation* have been replaced by shock techniques aimed at the intensification of sensorial effects, pure physical excitement—in short, an intensification of affects as architectural content.

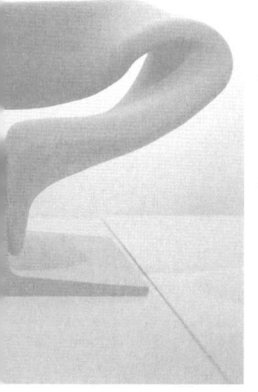

The images illustrating this text seek to relate Nouvel's work with the tradition of French super-modernity, as the alternative reference to America when searching for the origins of contemporary culture in Europe. The aesthetic sophistication of this tradition is very much a background for Nouvel's interest in the phenomenology of the super-modern: the glare, the speed, the transparency, the formal elegance, the experiential paradoxes of new technologies were already explored in the Citroen DS, the TGV, the Concorde, in the furniture of Pierre Paulin, but also in the fashion of French *coutouriers*, Brigitte Bardot's cool or in the ramps at Charles de Gaulle Airport.

Eisenman's Machine of Infinite Resistance

"The sciences do not try to explain, they hardly even try to interpret, they mainly make models. By a model is meant a mathematical construct which, with the addition of certain verbal interpretations, describes observed phenomena. The justification of such a mathematical construct is solely and precisely that it is expected to work."[1]
—*JOHN VON NEUMANN*

The practice and career of Peter Eisenman have reached paradigmatic status within contemporary architecture. From the very beginning, Eisenman's progress has been one of consistent research directed at the potential of a contemporary critical practice; that is, a practice whose product is fundamentally *architectural knowledge* rather than literal architectural production. His work on Giuseppe Terragni's Casa del Fascio and his House series are clear confirmations of this approach, and also early indications of the focus of his research on

---

1   John von Neumann & Oskar Morgenstern, *Theory of Games and Economic Behavior* (Princeton, NJ: University of Princeton Press, 1980).

processes of formal manipulation. Eisenman's work inherits—via Rowe, his direct master—a lineage that originates in Heinrich Wölfflin and the discussion of form as the primary category of architectural practice. But, contra Rowe's approach, Eisenman's research focuses on the autonomy of form.

These are pursuits that Eisenman has followed in his architectural and discursive (written) practices but also in his extended academic engagement. He was director of the legendary Institute of Architecture and Urban Studies, an institution that is credited with rescuing American architectural culture from the hands of corporate practice, and a widely admired and replicated model. The direction indicated by the work at the Institute is resonant with Eisenman's own position as a speculative practitioner, more interested in critical practice than in the straightforward production of architecture.

Is architectural knowledge possible in the age of triumphant late capitalism, in the ascendance of new media and the wholesale unleashing of market forces? Is architectural knowledge possible in the absence of ideologies, Eisenman claims that a critical practice has to necessarily occupy a position of resistance, and yet remain within the *Zeitgeist*. At a time where the critical practice of architecture is clearly divided between those embracing and those resisting the forces of the market and the media (hyper-consumerist, global culture), his position is a paradigmatic alternative, as those occupying a position of resistance typically tend to reject the *Zeitgeist* with the same enthusiasm as those who try to construct a critical practice from *within* the capitalist regime essentially end up embracing it, and *facilitating* it. The niche that Eisenman has defined for himself within the space of this debate is, therefore, unique, in that it attempts to construct a position of resistance—we could even say of *absolute* resistance—without rejecting the *Zeitgeist* as an operative space. If most of the contemporary architects who claim to occupy a position of resistance operate by finding a point of leverage from which to oppose the dominant forms of spatial organization given to architecture complicit with capital—whether this means the embrace of specialized techniques or idiosyncrasies, local history, or simply through authorial self-affirmation as the origin of a counter-movement—Eisenman has constructed an even more radical form of resistance by discarding the points of leverage under the suspicion of potential alliance or derivation from power structures, regrounding his practice in the autonomy of architecture *as a discipline*. It is his allegiance to formalist measures that both embrace and distance the prevailing episteme that makes his work, at once, a critique and an answer. *Zeitgeist*, in this instance, indicates an inordinate sense that within the prevailing episteme another order is possible or at least *latent*.

His absolute resistance to dominant forces is produced not by exerting subjective opposition to them, but rather through the replacement of the subject—always assumed to be the medium of some form of power—by a *machinic* (semi-deterministic) process. By replacing origin, presence, and author with arbitrariness, absence, and machinic behavior, he has found the recipe for a non-conservative resistance; that is, *criticality* performed from within the *Zeitgeist*. Eisenman is the first truly machinic architect, not in the productivist sense, but in the purely ideological.

"I have been always interested in control, not in power,"[2] he states. Eisenman's machine aims to disengage the traditional coupling between power and control, to remain in control of the project without becoming an instrument of the dominant forces of the *Zeitgeist* while remaining a critical force within it. It is the difference that obtains between the *Zeitgeist* and the episteme that determines the location of this engagement with power. And it was, after all, Michel Foucault who demoted the somewhat mystical *Zeitgeist* to the episteme, in order to make it conform to *disciplinary* logic.

Eisenman's project tries to operate neither as the tautological application of forms based on accumulated disciplinary knowledge, nor as the embodiment of the paradigms of the *Zeitgeist*: it is neither an act of opposition nor a *revolution* in the Kuhnian sense (that is, as a form of paradigmatic knowledge operative within *emerging* forms of production or economic integration). His is a process engineered to generate accidental emergences and affiliations, to reveal

---

2   From Eisenman's presentation to the Complexity Seminar held at the Architectural Association, London, 1994. Author's notes.

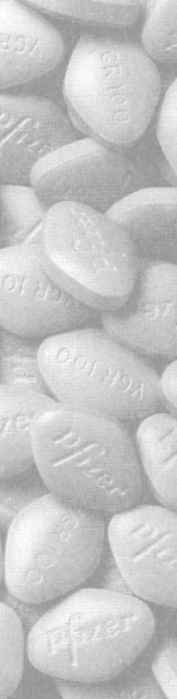

latent potentials rather than to meet the requirements of an emerging demand. Rather than trying to discover specific achievements, or naming unique qualities of space and/or material distributions within the project (post-Cartesian space, supple geometries, and folds), what instead emerges as the signature moment of his work is the mere fact that architecture, traditionally subjected to dominant, "natural" orders (structural, functional, symbolic, or linguistic) is now liberated from them, without necessarily abandoning the idea of disciplinary rigor and control. Along his extended career, Eisenman has obstinately explored the possibilities of an "artifactual" intelligence, rather than complying with the dominant orders that establish the limits of architectural practice. "Architecture" can only emerge once we are able to disengage the discipline from its historical and local context, when we can start thinking of the sequence of architectural practice as a purely artificial construct. This implies speaking with a metalanguage, obviating the need for language altogether; in Eisenman's words, the "architecture of architecture."[3]

Eisenman's buildings are, in their obstinate compliance with an alienating program, in their deliberate contradictions and negotiations with the site, and in their structural, technical, and functional requirements, a critical manifesto about the limits of the building industry, typological determination, context and, ultimately, architectural language. His buildings cannot be assessed in conventional terms, vis-à-vis accumulated disciplinary knowledge; nor can they be judged by the specificity of their response or their adequateness to the *Zeitgeist*. Ultimately, Eisenman's projects can only be viewed as fragmentary comments about the "interiority" of architecture—arguably where performative agency resides and all forms of absolute resistance to purely diachronic concerns are possible (by election).

The DAAP (a.k.a the Aronoff Center for Design and Art Building, University of Cincinnati) occupies a distinctive place among the projects that constitute Eisenman's career-long search. The project explores techniques that have been present since the early work—the juxtaposition of multiple grids as traces of different parameters and the generation of an architectural object as a structure with multiple affiliations. However, compared with his Checkpoint Charlie project,

3   Ibid.

Romeo and Juliet project, and the Wexner Center, the DAAP does not explore the contradiction between multiple rigid, abstract, orthogonal grids as the geometrical argument of the project. The grid is generated here through the transformation of specific traces of the site and the program. If in the other projects Eisenman proposed that the building is determined by its affiliations to a contradictory multiplicity of grids extending far beyond the specific domain of the project, in the DAAP project the object is embedded in the web generated through the transformation of local traces: the curves of the site's natural topography, the borders of the existing buildings, the geometries of the "chevrons," and the spatial "quantums" of the given program. What is interesting here is the exploration of parameters that are specific to the most traditional definition of the discipline. The DAAP is the first of a series of projects—the Greater Columbus Convention Center and Emory University Performance Center will arrive later—where Eisenman's work approaches concrete architectural parameters and, therefore, his research comes closer to defining an architectural knowledge beyond a mere compliance with the prevailing forms of the *Zeitgeist*.

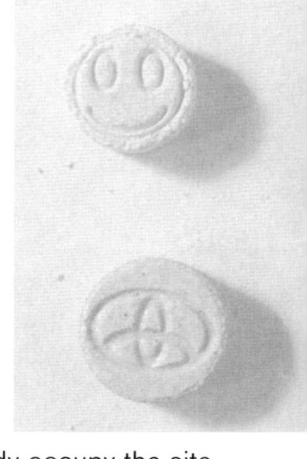

In the DAAP there is a new formulation of Eisenman's anti-modern tendency to enforce coherence between the field and the object, the figure and the background. More significantly, here we witness one of his first attempts to redefine the background as a figure, initiating a *figure-figure* dialogue. The most important evolution vis-à-vis his previous projects—and, remarkably, to its closest ancestor, the Wexner Center—is the use of fields that are no longer abstract, but determined by objects that already occupy the site in a literal sense. What is interesting about the DAAP within Eisenman's overall project is that it becomes the inflection point between research developed before the Wexner Center, based on the contradiction between *different* external fields, and the latter phase, where the import of accidental, singularized, coherent, and internal but differentiated fields constitute the basis of the projects. In Rebstock Park, the Max Reinhardt House, and the Haus Immendorf, models extracted from other disciplines—the so-called soliton wave and Fredericks transition, for example—are grafted onto the project *top-down*, to generate a coherently differentiated spatial effect. In the DAAP there is an attempt to construct a singularized field of artificial specificity out of inherently contextual affiliations, a *bottom-up* construction process performed through the encoding of the accidental qualities of the site/program as indexical traces, and their subsequent transformation, through a set of geometrical operations, into the web that will ultimately constitute the structure of the project.

The DAAP is therefore a moment of emergence in the work of Eisenman. The techniques used in its construction achieve a double effect by operating with specifically architectural parameters in a non-conventional manner, and by avoiding the application of external models that, even if singular and contingent to the specific problem, ultimately involve some form of negotiation with the *Zeitgeist*. Eisenman develops a series of techniques in the DAAP that prefigure the later developments of his work, coinciding with his initiation with the computer as a design tool that makes available geometries that are more complex than the orthogonal grid that was a constant metric of his early work.

The DAAP's generative process begins with a seemingly arbitrary selection of specific data from the site: the curves that define the northern border of the plot are adopted as a contingent geometrical origin that is not committed to a precise geometric law or function; the borders of the existing buildings and the basic formal structure of the DAAP building—a chevron—are taken as indexes, devoid of their functional or significant content; a quantum of classrooms (A × B × C) is taken as a concrete, latent quality of the site. This is the concrete material of the project, replacing the more abstract, substantial references that originated previous projects.

Two parallel sets of serial transformations are applied to the data in order to produce the erasure of a potential conflict between the new and existing building. This affords the generation of a seamless structure between the site and the existing buildings, and the production of a non-homogeneous, non-linear, latent spatial structure. The transformations involve two types of operations that Eisenman had already employed in previous projects—displacements and reorientations—aiming to erase the oppositions between the three incoherent buildings that constitute the structure to be extended (the DAAP building itself, the Alms Building, and the Wolfson Building). These techniques do not alter the internal structure of the organizations they affect, but their location in space and orientation. By processing the borders of the building complex and the "idealized chevrons" as parallel processes, the resulting transformation eliminates any potential hierarchy between the generated structures. The "idealization of the chevrons" and the alignment on the site—first to the Alms and then to the Wolfson Building—serve to produce a more global structure out of latent existing traces on the site. The manipulation of the data from the natural topography is serial rather than parallel, as if Eisenman's interest in the natural topography were as a landscape where an evolutionary process will generate the primary traces of the project. The first operation is to couple the curved lines with the programmatic quantum to erase the opposition between the program and the site. These quantums of programmatic space are inserted along the curved line with an "exponential overlap" regulated by a factor of 1.6 that introduces in the project a differential, oriented system of intervals, suggesting a very different space from the repetitive metrics of the abstract grid that characterize Eisenman's previous projects. The subsequent operation, an "asymptotic tilt" of the programmatic quantums regulated by an arbitrary factor of 1.2, is an operation that introduces a local disjunction in the relative orientations of the volumes. The third operation, a vertical stepping of the boxes with respect to the original line, pursues a similar effect, aimed this time at subverting the horizontal datum as the global order of the project, and reintroducing the sloped topography of the site. The next operation, the "exponential torquing" of the volumes, serves to differentially distort the programmatic quantums themselves. The final transformation of the topographic line involves a shift into three layers of program, introducing a similar localized differentiating effect in the sectional relations of the resulting complex grid. The use of exponential overlaps, asymptotic tilts, and phase displacements is also geared to turn metrics of closed intervals—a striated space—into a vectorial smooth space with locally differentiated metrics, although regulated by a coherent law.

The "architecture of the architecture" of the DAAP is formed by two parallel processes of "accidental," rather than "substantial" topographic data from the site. The data resulting from the registration of the existing buildings is manipulated through an "integrative" parallel process, in which the new structure is derived from the proliferation of traces into multiple locations. The data resulting from the natural topography and the site is processed serially, generating a spatially differentiated grid.

If we drew a flow chart of the operations, the architecture of the architecture of the DAAP would look like this:

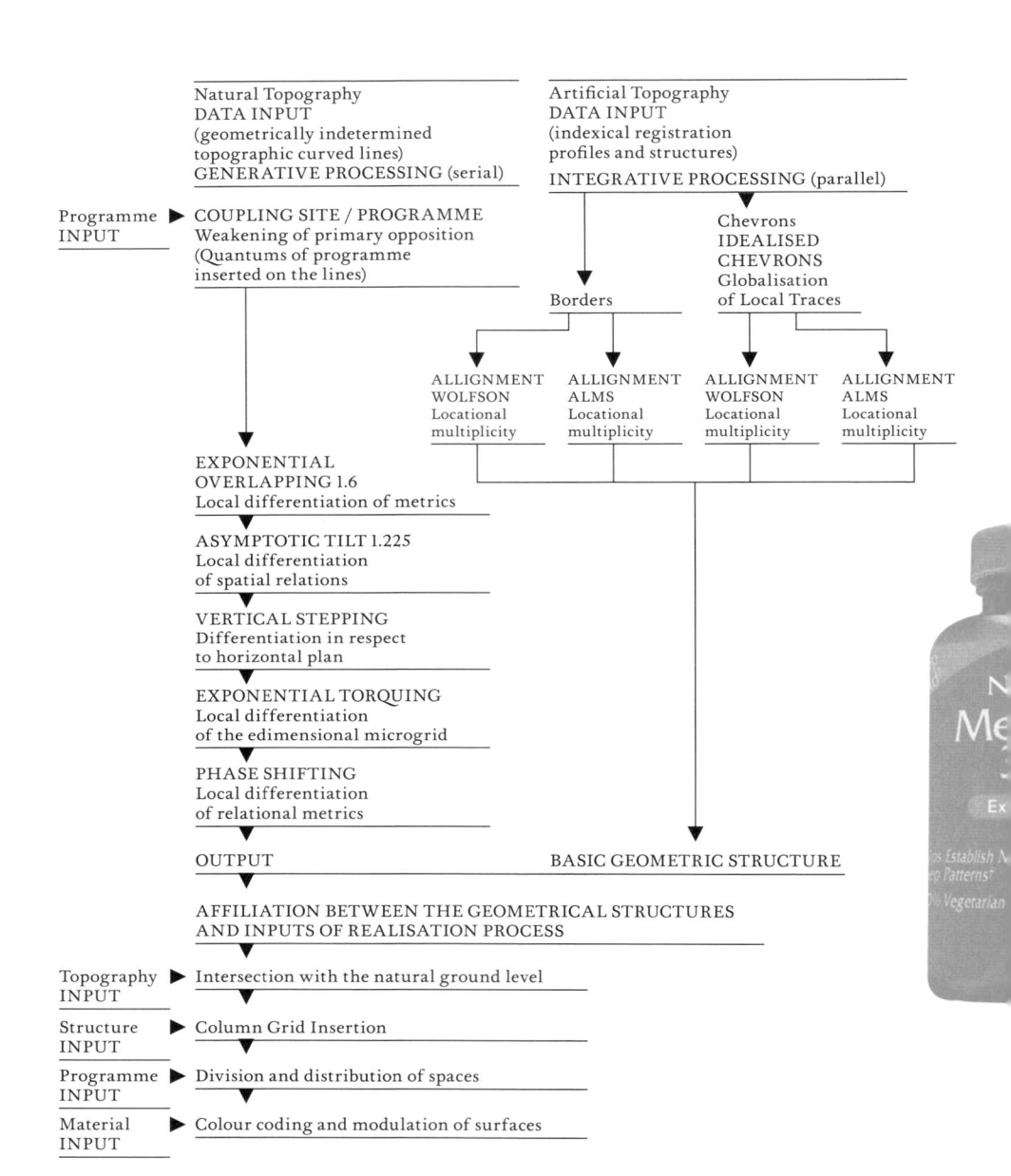

```
                            Natural Topography                  Artificial Topography
                            DATA INPUT                          DATA INPUT
                            (geometrically indetermined         (indexical registration
                            topographic curved lines)           profiles and structures)
                            GENERATIVE PROCESSING (serial)      INTEGRATIVE PROCESSING (parallel)
                                        │                                   │
                                        ▼                                   ▼
Programme  ▶  COUPLING SITE / PROGRAMME                         Chevrons
INPUT         Weakening of primary opposition                   IDEALISED
              (Quantums of programme                            CHEVRONS
              inserted on the lines)                            Globalisation
                                        │                       of Local Traces
                                        ▼                                   │
                                        Borders                             │
                              ┌──────────┴──────────┐         ┌─────────────┴─────────┐
                              ▼                     ▼         ▼                       ▼
                         ALLIGNMENT          ALLIGNMENT   ALLIGNMENT            ALLIGNMENT
                         WOLFSON             ALMS         WOLFSON               ALMS
                         Locational          Locational   Locational            Locational
                         multiplicity        multiplicity multiplicity          multiplicity
              ▼
              EXPONENTIAL
              OVERLAPPING 1.6
              Local differentiation of metrics
              ▼
              ASYMPTOTIC TILT 1.225
              Local differentiation
              of spatial relations
              ▼
              VERTICAL STEPPING
              Differentiation in respect
              to horizontal plan
              ▼
              EXPONENTIAL TORQUING
              Local differentiation
              of the edimensional microgrid
              ▼
              PHASE SHIFTING
              Local differentiation
              of relational metrics
              ▼
              OUTPUT                                            BASIC GEOMETRIC STRUCTURE
              ▼
              AFFILIATION BETWEEN THE GEOMETRICAL STRUCTURES
              AND INPUTS OF REALISATION PROCESS

Topography  ▶ Intersection with the natural ground level
INPUT
              ▼
Structure   ▶ Column Grid Insertion
INPUT
              ▼
Programme   ▶ Division and distribution of spaces
INPUT
              ▼
Material    ▶ Colour coding and modulation of surfaces
INPUT
```

The results of both parallel processes are then juxtaposed on a graph where unexpected local affiliations start to emerge between the different geometries. Functional, structural, and constructive data of a conventional nature will be now deployed on the geometrical frame. This becomes the most dubious—and perhaps most revealing—stage of the process as the geometrical frame of the building, elaborated with such sophistication, is colonized by conventional "elements of architecture": columns, doors, toilets, stairs, and elevators. All previous resistance to the dominant forms of space is abandoned at the moment in which Eisenman's program states that the building should be built with the most conventional technologies; the embodiment of the project is regulated not through negotiation but in contradiction with the geometrical diagram. From the charmed spaces within the *Zeitgeist* he moves back outside to the prevailing episteme of present-day building.

However, the way these elements colonize the spatial web unveils the rigidity of the system where these elements are typically engaged: the position of the windows relative to the ground; the proportions of *poché* space and usable space; the use of color in respect to the architectural elements, etc. These are the moments that automatically lead us to abandon possibilities when faced with a design problem; this is, therefore, where the most direct critique of conventional architectural traits appears. Another interesting effect of Eisenman's machinic construction of the DAAP is the fact that the complexity of the result—depicted by some critics as smoothness—had to be implemented through an extreme example of striation, as all the trades of the building (the various subcontractors and material logics of the actual construction) were controlled through a three-dimensional coordinate system implemented by electronic meters on site. If, typically, the coordination of the trades is relational and projective, determined by local relationships between elements on the site, in the DAAP this relationship is generated by a global metric organization with an arbitrary system of reference. In this sense—and in the absence of any other consistent criteria of legitimization—the building succeeds in opening new alternatives to normative practice and launching a critique of the conventional systems of architectural thought. But the most interesting aspect of Eisenman's *machinic* critique is that it is not produced as another consistent alternative, but rather from *all over the place*—from the random encounter between arbitrary decisions and the banal social conventions of the construction industry.

However, viewed from the perspective that the most important purpose of architecture is to produce space, and not necessarily the possibility of an architectural knowledge (or that there is a possibility of producing architectural knowledge from within pure production), one could imagine an alternative development of the construction process of the DAAP, where building techniques and functional requirements are not deployed without mediation on the spatial diagram, but are something more pliant, and modified in the process. Looking at some of the encounters between the concrete structure and the spatial envelopes of the north elevation and the internal common space, one wonders if the choice of a steel cage-like structure internal to the enveloping surfaces—in a straightforward "balloon-frame" style—would not have been less obtrusive spatially and more able to negotiate their verticality; one wonders whether stairs could have been designed by negotiating functional metrics with an arbitrary logarithmic order; or if the gridded metric of the curtain wall could not have been reduced by eliminating the mullions or restraining them to one direction.

The air-conditioning facilities display a more appealing result of Eisenman's machine: a *supple* rather than contradictory negotiation between the geometrical determination of the grid and the incorporation of technical requirements. As the ceiling space occasionally becomes too narrow for the air-conditioning ducts, the air-flow regimes have to suffer violent changes in speed and geometry; sometimes the ducts become technically non-viable, and an alteration of the geometry of the graph has to be performed.

The most difficult question when addressing this project is finding the criteria to assess the results of a process that does not recognize any origin and embraces arbitrariness as an operative mode; our references to judge remain necessarily suspended. However, in spite of the arbitrariness of the origin and the development of the project purely by reaction "like in a chess game,"[4] where the decisions are dependent on the affiliations discovered during the process, the building is successful in achieving its original goals: "to blur the opposition between the extension and the existing buildings, to accommodate to the existing topography, to eliminate the homogeneous layering and the homogeneity of the space."[5] One does not know ultimately whether the assessment of this building from an experiential perspective would be legitimate, as the specific objectives of this particular project, unlike Eisenman's overall project do seem to intentionally target specific criteria about *building* (rather than Architecture). And this may reveal a potential fracture between Eisenman's long-term critical project and his short-term practice: a global and local Eisenman at odds within the same project.

The images along this text relate to Eisenman's position as a voluntary withdrawal from power in order to attain maximum control over the work, even at the expense of an artificial exile into autonomy. After the image of Carl Lewis on stilettos under the motto "power is nothing without control" there is a small history of artificial life in the last 30 years, from the Pill to LSD and Extasis, from Prozac and Valium to Viagra.

4   Author conversation with Peter Eisenman, Donna Barry, and Michael McInturf, Interview in *Eleven Authors in Search of a Building*, ed. Cynthia Davidson (New York: The Monacelli Press, 1995).

5   Ibid.

A World Full of Holes

About five years ago, when I still had time to think, I proposed a special issue of *El Croquis* entitled *Worlds* to its editorial team. The idea was to compile a record of the most important works from recent years in a single volume, in order to present a synchronic cross-section of the spectrum of positions that characterize current architecture from a global perspective. My interest in this task was to present a map of the different practices that define the spectrum of possible approaches to contemporary architecture, to investigate the emergence of a landscape of architectural practice, which seemed to be increasingly fragmented. It was also an attempt to *short circuit* the editorial principles of *El Croquis*, which had been documenting this panorama sequentially in a series of monographs that described each of the so-called worlds that had managed to accumulate a certain critical mass. The editors received my proposal with skepticism, and said they would think about it. Four years later, almost a year ago now, when I had forgotten about the project, they returned it corrected and expanded, for me to draft a text.

Now, the hardest thing has not been determining what to write, or how to write it, but rather the purpose for doing so. It has taken me nearly a year, without writing a single line, to find the reason. The main reason for my inability to write this text has been that my interest in the spectacle of this fragmented landscape had disappeared. The task was not worth the effort if this description did not produce an impetus, a direction capable of making the exercise useful; something that went beyond the pure pleasure of the spectacle. Furthermore, I became aware that the task bore a considerable resemblance to Charles Jencks' description twenty years ago in his famous map of the coming millennium.[1] What was the basic difference between Jencks' analysis and the one that should be done now? What was the difference between his viewpoint and mine, twenty years later? What is the reason for drawing a map? Despite having been harshly criticized, the architectural taxonomy proposed by Jencks is nonetheless one of the bravest and most successful attempts at describing 1960s and 1970s architecture and the multiplication of architectural discourses that characterized the end of the modernist scene. Of course, as with any other taxonomy or classification, it was doomed to be superseded, but naming the phenomena is the first step into producing knowledge.

A map is always an object of controversy rather than the description of an absolute truth. Perhaps the key difference between his classification and the one I am trying to construct here is a question of attitude: *Architecture 2000* was a manifesto in favor of diversity, of the fragmentation of culture following the collapse of the modern paradigms; a great fresco of postmodern architecture dictated by the pleasure of the spectacle more than by the aim of indicating a direction, prescribing an attitude, or proposing a model. It is, in spite of its rigor, a manifesto in defense of pluralism rather than the production of an instrument. It is an invitation for architects to follow their instincts since there are no defined paths. This was the purpose behind

1   Charles Jencks, *Architecture 2000: Predictions and Methods* (New York: Praeger, 1971).

Jencks' manifesto. His merit lies in having been able to capture the spirit of his times before and better than anybody else.

The map I wish to propose here is more directional than his. It is for a specific purpose rather than just a description, however performative that may eventually become. The idea is the following: It is true, we do live in a world that appears fragmentary to us—a world made of worlds. It is no longer enough to look at the projects of Mies and Le Corbusier, or Bramante and Palladio, to guide our practices. Now that there is no longer a single world or a single truth, architecture magazines have become a much more powerful instrument for contemporary practice than the old manuals. This condition has emerged since the decline of corporate practices as they were understood in the 1940s and 1950s, that is, as an optimization and concentration of a series of techniques and processes fundamentally defined by the practices of the modern masters. That model of corporate practice ultimately became a stratification of the modern masters' architecture, in which expression was sacrificed to technical efficiency.

In the mid-1970s, a new generation of architects that included Peter Eisenman, Arata Isozaki, José Rafael Moneo, Aldo Rossi, Robert Venturi, and others, began to develop an alternative form of practice, essentially characterized by a small-scale, speculative approach and the simultaneous pursuit of intellectual and academic activity. Although perhaps much more closely interconnected than the architects of the previous generation through the use of publications and academia as a communication system outside the production structure itself, this generation was much more reluctant to identify itself with a common definition of "contemporary practice" than CIAM or Team X. On the contrary, the birth of what is known as the *star system* is characterized by the intensification of differences between practices, even when the influence of fads such as historicism or deconstructivism had such an obvious effect on the evolution of the respective speculative agendas of these practices. A series of slightly younger architects (Jacques Herzog and Pierre de Meuron, Toyo Ito, Rem Koolhaas, Jean Nouvel, et al.) has perpetuated this new species of architect striving to investigate different potentialities rather than defining the program of contemporary architecture as a whole.

The perspective of the map I wish to propose is based on the model of the market, as opposed to the bureaucratic tendencies that characterized classical criticism. Instead of stratifying practices into minimalists and formalists, for example, we shall try to define a series of variable parameters that overcome apparently stable alignments. The map has the virtue of making operative the fragmented landscape that *Worlds* tries to describe under the hypothesis that the sum of the niche markets is quantitatively larger than those with the biggest market share. In other words, it is potentially more productive to invest in hitherto unexploited domains than in the areas that already generate high profits. *Worlds* is not an instrument for discovering *what's cool* but, rather, what is yet to be exploited.

The niche-seeker map I propose attempts to originate a new way of reading magazines in which one does not try to identify models to follow but, rather, holes in the fabric of contemporary architecture. The exploitation of the holes is possibly the only alternative in the implosive post-capitalist space to the expansive capitalist "fashion system": although avant-gardes are necessary, they work in the interstices of the space instead of being applied to the expansion of the field.

In order to see the holes, however, we must first produce the criteria that enable us to weave this fabric. The map we shall draw tries to establish forms of congruence between the different scopes that define the landscape to construct figures on which we may operate. The instrument we shall use is a system of opposites—a distinctly structuralist technique, in which opposites do not operate in a binary manner as a system of switches, but, rather, as fields with gradients formed by the extremes of each opposition. The spectrum of these fields is thus not defined as an ideal, but as a specific case, practice, or projection on which our way of using the system depends. It establishes the end point of each gradient and can be updated successively with information that is fed into the system. It is like reading the stock market report and looking at the different categories: shares, bonds, securities, futures, raw materials, etc. Or like looking for a partner in a contacts magazine, where the classification of personal traits and desires has reached such a degree of sophistication that one can find ads like this:

"36yo, SLPF NS ND C 36-24-36, 5'4", ISO 35-45yo, SW\LPCM 5'5"+, MB, D\D free for LLR." (Meaning: 36-year-old, single, Latin, professional, female, non-smoker, no drugs, Catholic, 36" bust, 24" waist, 36" hips, 5'4" tall, in search of 35- to 45-year-old, single, white\Latin professional, Catholic male over 5'5" tall, medium build, drug\disease free, for long-lasting relationship).

In both cases, the practice is defined by the reference to a series of parameters in which we have captured the information necessary to carry out certain actions, such as investing or coupling. These forms of information classification are one of the most powerful instruments for even more committed practices than architecture, despite the logical limitations of their resolution and duration. What follows is a selection of a series of categories relevant to contemporary architectural practice, one that will serve to establish the different gradients on which each of the practices or projects of these fragmentary *worlds* can be located.

Power/Potential
The differentiation between *potential* as the pure capacity to act, reveal strength, and produce affects, and *power* as its stratified, institutionalized form, regulated through codes, is one of the main problems of modern practices from Nietzsche to Foucault and Deleuze. A creative practice is characterized precisely by its ability to destabilize established forms, its ability to produce *virtuality*. Between power and potential lies control, as claimed by the famous Pirelli ad featuring Carl Lewis in stiletto heels under the slogan "Power is nothing without control." The way of exercising control is one of the modes of a discipline, and one of the possible forms of differentiation

between contemporary architectural practices that are capable of producing virtuality. If modernist architecture was an attempt to discipline, architecturally speaking, the formidable forces of industrial capitalism—silos, factories, and freeways turned into the new production models for the city—the architecture of the 1960s was a critique of the sclerosis that the modernist models had started to develop. An entirely new type of architect developed during this period. Team X, the Japanese post-metabolists and the American postmodernists subverted the modernist identity between power and control in order to induce new potentialities. For example, Alison and Peter Smithson identified social, cultural, and natural functions that were not included in the modernist program not as a disjunction between power and control, but rather as a critique of the forms of power as they had been defined in modernism. Isozaki introduced new possibilities into the metabolist dogma through the intensification of the functions toward an excessive regime that produces indetermination.

Perhaps the most radical case was Philip Johnson, who always worked via the contingent deployment of power as a source of pure potentials. An anecdote told by Koolhaas is an interesting sample of the techniques used by Johnson. While studying at Cornell, Koolhaas visited Philip Johnson in his office for an interview. The interview began, and Johnson answered the questions while moving spasmodically and making facial gestures, gazing downward under his desk. After a few minutes Koolhaas, unsettled by Johnson's attitude, spat out "Mr. Johnson, you seem nervous. Are my questions or my presence upsetting you? Would you rather I left for a while and came back later?" Johnson raised his head with a saintly smile and invited the interviewer to come round and look under the table, saying, "No, no, don't worry, it's just that while I'm doing the interview I'm trying to sort out this project. Look, look, what do you think of this distribution?" while he used his feet to move some wooden blocks around a model under his desk, which appeared to be the place for a skyscraper complex. Johnson, always prepared to sprint one hundred meters in high heels, eliminates control in order to turn power into pure potential.

If the disengagement between power and potential is a mode of producing the virtual, *critical* practices constitute an alternative to Johnson's regime of contingent excess by generating forms of *resistance*. Feminist, regionalist, environmentalist, and militant architectures—or simply so-called politically correct practices—are examples of this approach. Critical architecture is defined as a negative feedback mechanism, tending to correct deviations or excesses of the prevailing forms of power. When Moneo, Kenneth Frampton, or Steven Holl complain about the erosion of local or historical specificity of commercial practice, or when feminist theorists criticize the phallocentric and fetishist architecture of the high-rise, they are trying to release potential from the consolidated forms of power through the construction of an alternative critical model, by encouraging the forms of difference.

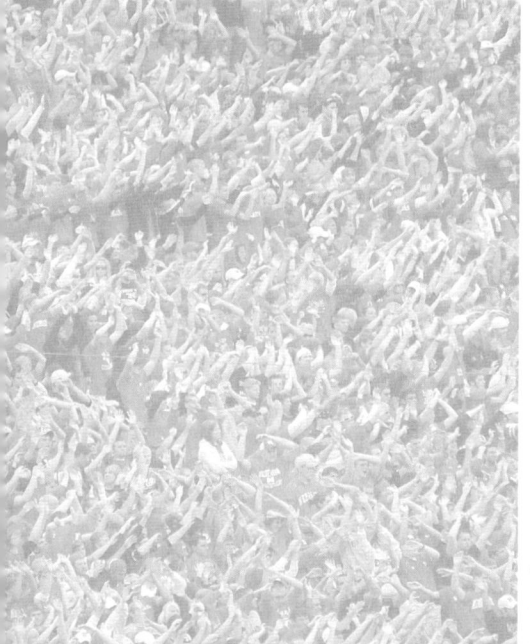

In an initial reading, Eisenman would fit in this same group of critics of the status quo. Eisenman's resistance, however, works from within the discipline instead of becoming a vehicle for an external discourse. His proposal is a radical schism between power and control, effective through the exercise of arbitrary control. Following his approach, the more difficult the assimilation of a work of architecture, the greater its value. This position of resistance through the application of a series of arbitrarily produced control mechanisms negates the local, historical, political, or psychologically specific nature that characterizes other resisting discourses.

The architects who have adopted what we might define as positive feedback might also include those who, instead of opposing dominant tendencies (globalization, media control, complexity of production processes, etc.), have received them as the origin of unprecedented potentials. Koolhaas would probably be the most paradigmatic of this tendency, proposing positive feedback as a trigger of virtuality. In a text published in the *Harvard Architectural Review* in 1996, Koolhaas makes the following statement: "If we are in this job, it is because one way or another we are interested in *power*." His defense of the *generic city*, of banality, of linearity, etc., proposes that an extreme, intensified practice of the forms of power may end up opening potentials, at least within the "educated" architectural practice, often shrouded in well-stratified forms of resistance to that very genericity.

Although Nouvel and Ito have less precisely articulated positions, they are probably close to Koolhaas in their approach to power, understood as the strategic intensification of the predominant trends that are capable of projecting new architectural potentials.

Herzog & de Meuron, who are often mentioned by *critical* architects as one of the best examples of resistance to the disappearance of the material qualities of contemporary architecture, are nevertheless in other aspects perfectly capable of avoiding friction between power and potential. In the discussion following a 1997 speech at the AA, a politically correct member of the audience accused them of having become architects of refined, closed envelopes for the powerful and wealthy. Herzog's disdainful answer was: "We *star architects* often get amazing projects that enable us to explore fields that are unknown to the majority of architects." Herzog & de Meuron's ability to maintain a constantly experimental and yet accommodating practice has made them one of the most interesting practices on the contemporary scene.

In contrast to the production of virtuality through the fracture between control and power, it is worth also accounting an entirely different casuistic: the assimilation or *capture* of certain architectural discourses by forms of political or economic power which, rather than exploiting the disintegration between power and control, turn this correspondence into a generator of architectural culture. The examples we shall now analyze lie at the opposite extreme from the group of virtual practices that have been described above.

The first notable case is that of assimilation by the international corporate culture of the British *high-tech* architects, the natural heirs to the modernist, functional, efficient tradition. It is only the dose of Anglo-Saxon pragmatism and Victorian stricture that distances architects like Norman Foster, Nicholas Grimshaw, and Richard Rogers from modern idealism. The replacement of modern ideological principles with a pragmatic attitude toward the specific conditions of each problem, without relinquishing technical efficiency as a fundamental stratum of architectural practice, generated the proposal for flexible, multifunctional structures. The consideration of environmental and regional factors as part of the functional requirements of the buildings were the perfect recipe for their total assimilation by the Thatcherite culture of economic and social deregulation, making them perfect architects for the implementation of a new international corporate culture.

Another peculiar example of contemporary relations between architectural discipline and political power is the so-called Berliner Clique, an active group of O. M. Ungers's disciples in Berlin, composed of architects such as Max Dudler, Hans Kolhoff, and Jürgen Josef Sawade. In the early 1990s they came to be recognized as the architects of the new Berlin thanks to an aesthetic and ideological alliance with City Councilor Hans Stimmann. At a time when Germany had to forge a new *post-reunification* image to be implemented in the new capital, this group of architects became a perfect product for the new urban image of united Germany. The synthesis of references to Schinkelian and Miesian architecture (abstract, material, and static), along with Berlin metropolitanism and early twentieth-century American capitalist architecture was a highly powerful mix. The scale and efficiencies of capitalist architecture were perfectly blended with *gemütlich* tree-lined avenues and repetitive orders of spans on facades, to produce one of most consistent and powerful manifestos of contemporary architecture. Attempts by Günter Behnisch (whose new building for the Bundestag was the first victim of the political process) and Libeskind to establish alternatives to this crystallization of the urban forms of repetition and stability have hitherto been incapable of producing a consistent alternative.

In an almost opposite architectural direction from Berlin, where the political requirement of architecture was the need to reconstruct an image of the power purportedly diluted ever since the end of WWII, Olympic-era Barcelona experienced another moment of convergence between an emerging political and economic structure and a new architectural proposal. In contrast to Berlin, where the thrust was to unify, solidify, and centralize, the political situation of Barcelona in the 1980s demanded an almost opposite structure, which could provide a new independent identity to post-dictatorship Catalonia. The new identity of Catalan architecture was constructed on the basis of difference and periphery, through an outward-looking view toward the rest of Europe instead of inward to the Iberian Peninsula. The Barcelona of Mayor Pasqual Maragall provided the opportunity for a generation of architects to construct one of the most consistent urban manifestoes of the second half of this century, through the production of an identity that was ambiguous and elusive, landscapist, and geometrically complex.

Determination/Indetermination
The relationship of a project to cause and effect has traditionally been one of the crucial questions of the discipline. The *modern project* attempted to rationalize these relationships in order to free architectural production from historically constructed determinations. The *postmodern* revision tried to construct practices outside of dominant cause-effect relations, using linguistic deconstruction, psychoanalysis, etc., to reveal *latent*, *repressed*, or *unconscious* content. These techniques appeared to be an alternative to the sclerosis that the structures, categories, and methods of modernism had reached during the first half of the twentieth century, as they became dominant forms of language or culture. With the appropriation of the more aggressive aspects postmodern (anti-modernist) insurrection by late capitalism, subsequent iterations of its various means to ends became increasingly mired in the hot-house of its own production. In the case of Berlin, it is obvious that otherwise good rationalist architects

were co-opted by a conservative regime hell bent on building a picturesque "unified" Berlin tailored for the complete conquest by the corporate hegemon that rules Germany.

A considerable part of architectural speculations after the 1960s has been committed to the exploration of this type of technique and argument. In Europe, the attempts at liberation from cause-effect relations can be found in the work by groups such as Archigram and Archizoom, where the modernist dogma was challenged by intentionally introducing a degree of indetermination within the design process, allowing architects to operate by integration rather than exclusion. The contemporary ideals of political freedom were translated by these anarchic and comic-book practices into models of absolute flexibility; that is, proposals for the open conception of the architectural and urban project as *heedlessly* mutable and *endlessly* extendable. Not dissimilarly, in America, movements emerged in the post-'60s climate—for example, The New York Five (Peter Eisenman, John Hejduk, Charles Gwathmey, Richard Meier, Michael Graves), or individual architects such as Venturi and Charles Moore—wherein, while all nominally "serious postmodernists," the idea of play or ambiguity was set free, and an irreverent manipulation of modern language ensued, both innocently and ironically, yet always already emptied of its supposed functionalist bias. In Japan, Isozaki, Kisho Kurokawa, and Kazuo Shinohara, educated in and following on the postwar metabolist tradition of the late 1950s and early 1960s, also began to explore alternatives to structuralist models through the recourse to random processes and the subversion of modernist architectural language, in many cases directly influenced by contemporary Western thought (including Gilles Deleuze and Félix Guattari).

The challenge to causality took a turn in the 1980s with the work of architects such as Coop Himmelb(l)au, Eisenman, Frank Gehry, Zaha Hadid, Koolhaas, Libeskind, and Bernard Tschumi. These so-called deconstructivist architects constitute a group that, while continuing along the anti-deterministic line of the previous generation, used abstraction rather than the manipulation of language, to escape from recycling architectural languages in a deliberate shift away from architectural history as a referent.

Some of these architects, such as Coop Himmelb(l)au, Gehry, and Hadid, operated from a less intellectual position, subverting the causal relationships by using authorial or artistic sensibility as a destabilizing factor. On the contrary, Tschumi was closely linked to the architectural and intellectual precedents of the 1960s: his attack on sameness of form and function constantly cross-references processes of transgression, excess, and violence as part of the anti-structuralist discourse of Roland Barthes and Georges Bataille. His ideological connection with the Situationist International is another of the abstract references that served to structure his architectural proposal: his use of the *dérive*, *direct action*, and *happening* as indeterminate programmatic structures formed the backbone of a proposal that aimed to escape determination. The proposal of a series of programmatic figures (*trans-programming*, *cross-programming*, *dis-programming*) that elude the simple determination of *modernist* functions and their formal correspondences is probably one of this group's most interesting contributions to the disciplinary body. The aperture inherent to Tschumi's pronouncement does not necessarily imply a position of indetermination, but precisely the possibility of exerting determination at a higher level while retaining an indeterminate expressionist defamiliarization of the known. Indeed, many of these practices eventually confirmed their determinist bona fides, especially when they were established as working models and easily assimilated by the architectural apparatus (the market, architectural media, and academia).

In the case of Libeskind, the attack to causality is mounted from an alternative reading of time. Tschumi's *event*—an ephemeral, unpredictable program—is replaced in this case by the *palimpsest*, a register of spatial and material structures applied to space over an extended period of time, in order to display the contingent and accidental nature of the archaeological overlap. Other forms of subversion of architectural determination in Libeskind's work include the use of random or "occult" devices such as the Kabala.

A higher level of abstraction that shies away from narratives and programs arises in the work of Eisenman, who utilizes arbitrary but rigorous processes to produce indetermination. For Eisenman, the purpose of these protocols is to reveal *latent* or *repressed* content that cannot be unraveled by intentional action (the Jamesonian reading of texts applied to architecture personified), as any conscious perception is tainted with cultural, political, and/or psychological determinations that are in themselves manifestations of power. Compared with Tschumi and Libeskind, Eisenman's process is precise and enables a more direct translation into architectural form.

Koolhaas occupies a particularly caustic area within the postmodernist regime. Despite the fact that he has made some of the most lucid declarations about indetermination as an architectural mechanism, he has consistently sustained a more ambiguous position towards indetermination. While he claims the impotence of the architect to determine the built environment, his work and discourse could possibly support the opposite proposal. His claim towards *programmatic indetermination and formal stability* in the City Hall project for The Hague suggests that, beyond his attempts to engage with the instability of the modern world, there is a drive to find forms of determination capable of operating even within the unstable organizations of postmodern or late-capitalism. His discourse contains a notable ambiguity that seems to suggest that the architects' lack of power is caused by poor or sloppy adaptation to the often vague determinations of building. His therapy for architectural practice, following the collapse of modern causal models, does not seem to point to the implementation of techniques aimed at the *liberation* of repressed content in dominant forms but, rather, to an anti-psychoanalytical technique of engagement and surrender in its radical sense. The exploration of quintessentially modernist techniques such as statistics and diagrams indexes a search for alternative forms of determination.

Although Ito was not part of the deconstructivist camp, he is probably worthy of inclusion in this category as somebody who has consistently researched contingency as an architectural effect, not so much as a subversion of structural determinations (transgression, violence), but as phenomenological possibility. The use of the ephemeral or temporal as an argument for producing architectural indetermination is one of the subjects most thoroughly explored by Ito, especially in projects like the Tower of Winds, the Dwelling for the Nomad Girl, the Nomad Restaurant or the "Visions of Japan" exhibition. Time as a factor of indetermination arises again and again in these projects on a different scale from the palimpsest or the event, and probably has a more literal, plastic translation.

Curiously, both Ito and Tschumi see the need to program events or phenomena through the design of fireworks or lighting sequences, while Koolhaas develops techniques to use time as a factor in the determination of space: the infamous graph of activity on the basis of which he constructed his Yokohama Masterplan competition entry (1992) aims to integrate time into processes of architectural formalization. Finally, an intriguing option in the range between determination and indetermination is occupied by the British high-tech architects. While the most innovative architectural proposals in recent years have primarily concentrated on questioning the causal laws that had formed the program of modern architecture, architects like Foster, Grimshaw, Renzo Piano, and Rogers have maintained research that is essentially a continuation of the modern project in terms of formal determination as a causal process between function or construction and form. However, they have dropped *both* the exploration of the expressive possibilities of the modernist language (given to some of late-modernist or postmodernist experiments) and, to some extent, the ideological agenda that existed within the modernist dogma. After growing in an atmosphere of antagonism toward the modern project (developed in the UK during the 1960s by fundamentally ideological groups like the cadre of new brutalists and Archigram), the British High-tech architects chose to maintain a causal relationship between function and form, using a radical reduction of the control parameters. In British high-tech architecture, the construction of open organizations is not aimed at producing indetermination or revealing latent subversive possibilities to the status quo, but at reducing determinations to a minimum. The pragmatic attitude that characterizes this group of architects arises through a renunciation of ideological programs to concentrate on developing technical solutions capable of hosting the widest range of functions. The explorations of the concepts of flexibility or multi-functionality in Foster's Sainsbury Centre or Piano & Rogers's Centre

Pompidou serve as manifestos of this possibility. The orders of production, site delivery, and construction sequences in stages are the new determinants of an architectural proposition where research is focused on establishing the basis for local relationships between the parts and the whole, rather than in the figuration of the indeterminate, which we have seen in other practices. The orders of figuration are replaced in these practices by a composite algebra in which the interface between parts often constructs the whole by repetition. In the most advanced examples of these practices, such as Grimshaw's Waterloo Station, Piano's Kansai Airport or Bercy Shopping Centre, this repetition is differentiated to incorporate orders that are not merely constructive.

This might be a table of the possible combinations within the parameters that we have defined in the two preceding sections:

		David Chipperfield	Daniel Libeskind
F	NEGATIVE	Peter Zumthor	Peter Eisenman
E			
E		Steven Holl	
D			
B			
A		Norman Foster	Frank Gehry
C			
K	POSITIVE	Jean Nouvel	Zaha Hadid
		Rem Koolhaas	Coop Himmelb(l)au
		POSITIVE	**NEGATIVE**
		DETERMINATION	

Process/Effect

Another possible categorization of contemporary architectural practices can be established in terms of the nature of the instruments used. These may be external or internal to the products themselves. We can either use procedures aimed primarily at the internal construction of the project, or construct the project to produce effects that are extrinsic to its own extension. A classical example of this distinction is the friction between the marketing and the engineering department of an industry. While marketing techniques are driven to assess the product's impact on a system extrinsic to its own material constitution (that is, the market), engineering techniques address the control of manufacturing processes and the relationship between diverse components. Often, the determinations of the project are of an entirely different nature. The epistemological distinction between pure and applied research is parallel to this differentiation: pure research is generally internal to the discipline, while applied research trespasses the disciplinary borders, driven to achieve performances external to the disciplinary frame. Mies van der Rohe writes about this dichotomy as the opposition between *what* and *how*, stating his personal preference for the second type of question as the origins of the architectural project.

Another possible classification related to the issue of exteriority has a long tradition in aesthetic theory: *Baukunst* versus *Kunstwollen*, or the argument between Gottfried Semper and Alois Riegl. Riegl described this opposition as the *internal coherence* of a work when its productive requirements are sufficient to determine the product, and as *external coherence* when a product can only be understood and completed in a complex of factors that exceeds its pure materiality, whether it be authorial expression or an engagement with cultural codes.

The distinction suggested by Rowe between *character* and *composition* may also be a form of this opposition: if an architecture driven by composition concentrates on the relationships between its parts, character architecture is primarily concerned with the complex of social uses, idiosyncrasies, symbols, types, etc. external to the actual material construction of the architecture.

There is a link between an instrumentality intrinsic to the discipline and the internal coherence of the project, and between the use of extra-disciplinary techniques and the production of objects with external coherence. However, this is not necessarily the rule, and it might be interesting to consider the spectrum of possibilities resulting from the cross-breeding of these determinations. Four basic models of practice thus arise. The first model works in both spheres within the forms of the discipline, both in the effects sought and in the instruments used. Here we can include all those speculative practices aimed primarily at producing alterations to the structure of the discipline itself, such as formalism, or metalinguistic experiments that explore autonomy as a position. A second mode goes beyond the limits of the discipline at both levels: commercial practice, participative design, and "direct action" are some of the types of practice that have tried to dissolve the edges of the discipline, both in terms of the effects produced and the instruments used. In a third option, the practices include extra-disciplinary instruments with the aim of affecting the disciplinary field, as we see in certain "pop," "regionalist," and metaphoric practices, which incorporate images, rituals, idiosyncrasies, etc., in order to produce extensions within a fundamentally disciplinary object. A fourth mode might use specifically disciplinary mechanisms, seeking effects and determinations outside the disciplinary domain. This mode is populated with what we might call pragmatic or functionalist practices.

A map of these possible locations might be:

INSTRUMENTS			
	EXTERIOR	Commercial Practice	Regionalist
		Direct Action	Pop
	INTERIOR	Pragmatic	Formalist
		Functionalist	Linguistic
		EXTERIOR	**INTERIOR**
		EFFECTS	

Authorial/Machinic

Another possible polarization between contemporary architectural practices exists between those based on the expression of an authorial subjectivity and those practicing a demise of authorship. This dichotomy is particularly relevant at the moment where architectural practice has shifted toward the so-called *star system*. In the absence of utopia or a solid reference frame for the project, contemporary avant-garde practices need to rely on the author's sensibility, or on a series of protocols designed to ground the work in itself.

Within the first tendency we may identify a series of practices in which authorial sensibility becomes the primary argument of validation; for example, practices like Hadid or Coop Himmelb(l)au, for whom the project is a projection of the author's psycho-physiological make-up. Coop Himmelb(l)au has often resorted to techniques aimed at eliminating consciousness in order to make the projection more literal, becoming a radical exploration of the author's psycho-physiological drives. There is a curious automatic component in these techniques: by doing sketches blindfolded, or under the influence of other disinhibiting mechanisms, the authors try to capture their psycho-physiological condition in its purest state, which is then proposed as the ultimate reason for the project. The case of Hadid's early work or Gehry's recent projects belong to a more traditional expressionist lineage, where more consciously controlled transmission devices—paintings in Hadid's case, models in Gehry's—are used as vehicles of authorial projection. It is what Gehry himself calls *the eye-hand relationship*.[2]

One case of a less *wild*, more controlled expressionism that is culturally mediated through images or types can be found in David Chipperfield's and Álvaro Siza's work: The project's argument is often ciphered in direct response to a series of personal decisions regarding the use of materials or geometry. These decisions never come solely from the author but, rather, from a broader context which the author interprets. In the case of Siza, the presence of a specific local cultural tradition in his work is quite obvious, and might be interpreted as an expanded concept of authorship. Chipperfield's case is not grounded in local culture but rather in the choice of a certain minimalist aesthetic developed through a sophisticated, pragmatic materialization that distances him from the reductive rigor of other minimalist architects like John Pawson.

Herzog & de Meuron also work toward the expansion of the minimalist aesthetic. Their approach, however, is radically different. Whereas in Chipperfield's work the project is often determined by decisions related to an authorial sensibility via a series of concrete decisions, Herzog & de Meuron's projects are often driven by orders that place them beyond authorial expression. Buildings such as the Warehouse for Ricola, the Signal Box, and the Dominus Cellars can be explained by a diagram, an order that automatically structures the decisions of the project, almost without any need for involvement by the author. In this sense, despite the powerful aesthetic thrust of the work, Herzog & de Meuron's production is primarily mediated and determined by a material and constructive concept despite its often powerful phenomenal effects. If Herzog & de

---

2   Author interview with Frank O. Gehry published in *El Croquis*, n. 74/75, Madrid, 1995.

Meuron's work is conceptual and generated from a diagram that controls the totality of the work, the work of Enric Miralles has an obvious expressionist lineage that leads to the deployment of geometric and constructive control mechanisms that somehow manage to overcome their initial tendencies. In Miralles' work, rigorous geometric and material construction act as machinic devices that create objective distance between the author and the work. Despite undeniable authorial and expressive tendencies, Miralles' work operates by proliferation, addition, and complexification of rigorous processes which operate fragmentarily, and haptically, on the parts rather than the whole.

Libeskind represents the next degree of mediation; despite his enthusiasm for a process-driven architecture, there is always an initial negotiation with history, language, and cultural specificity at the origin of his policies.

Eisenman, set at the extreme of this spectrum, is probably the architect who has most radically applied machinic processes to produce the fracture between authorial consciousness, the project's constraints, and its determination. In this radical search, the architect becomes a contingent agent, responsible for preserving the autonomy of architecture as a discipline. In this gradient, Koolhaas occupies a position where the author becomes a *medium* to deconstruct his authorial identity. Through the uninhibited—some would say uncritical—immersion in production processes, the author becomes an agent for the intensification of certain logics that exceed the established forms of disciplinary control. In his radical intensification of borrowed logics, Koolhaas's work belongs to the *un-expressionists*. (Perhaps Nouvel and Ito sustain a similar approach, trying to capture and intensify contemporary processes as a source of architectural expression.) In his case, the agents of determination are neither internal to the discipline—such as the relationship between figure and form in Eisenman's work or the question of axiality in Libeskind—and they are not produced as a form of criticism or negation but, rather, as the intensification of an external logic. As in the modernist dogma, in Koolhaas's case the *machine* is a function that relates external processes to internal operations, rather than a critical machine that questions its own operations from within.

Integration/Differentiation
If the traditional models of the discipline tend to be based on extensive models of space with a constant, hierarchical distribution of the parts in the whole, the contemporary modes of economic integration seem to operate via intensive models of organization in which it is not easy to identify parts, scales, or levels of hierarchy. This has led to the obsolescence of certain disciplinary arguments such as symmetry, axiality, and sequence in favor of alternative techniques.

In the construction of intensive organizations, there are two directions of processing information with which we shall try to classify contemporary practices. One works from a single entity that is differentiated to integrate new solicitations. The other tries to integrate a multiplicity of conditions. These directions correspond to the alternatives in systems theory: top-down and bottom-up.

The processes of integration and differentiation are common to several forms of contemporary organizations that operate intensively: in finance we have mergers and acquisitions and delocalization. On a geopolitical scale, the simultaneous operation of globalizing processes and cultural differentiation has had an immediate effect on architectural positions: the debate between specific and generic (or local and global) is common to architecture and other disciplines. Frampton's proposal for *critical regionalism* and Koolhaas's defense of globalization are a good illustration of this dichotomy, one that addresses the emergence of spatial organizations that no longer consider local space as an isolated fragment with an identity of its own, nor the global space as an undifferentiated, homogeneous space.

The opposition between integration and differentiation as an organizational structure includes a series of oppositions that illustrate the range of possibilities for contemporary architecture: for example, specific versus generic, local versus global, and difference versus repetition.³

In the work of Miralles, the topography of the site, the views, the presence of shadows, vegetation, paths, pavements or construction materials, and other mutually incongruous material structures often take on a critical role in the construction of the project. The groups of trees and the topography at the Igualada Cemetery, the stand of pine trees opposite the sports complex in Alicante, the excavated material in Reus Boulevard. In all of these projects, the initial information is not a programmatic one but, rather, a multiplicity of material or topography, which the project attempts to integrate.

The alternative case occurs when a simple programmatic organization differentiated by the project relates to the classical typological operation; that is, where a type deforms to adjust to the specific requirements of the site or the brief. Operations of this sort can often be found in the work of Siza, who almost systematically works with simple, well-defined programs; that is, social housing, libraries, swimming pools, etc. As Siza has often stated, architecture works through the *transformation* of existing models. This can be seen in several of his projects, such as the Carlos Ramos Pavilion or the Porto School of Architecture, where a traditional type is distorted through the manipulation of the ground plane and the position of the entrances, opening the type to

---

3   In his article "Toward a New Architecture," Jeffrey Kipnis proposes to differentiate between *deformation* and *information* architectures, two architectural modalities that do not rely on an archive of architectural forms. In the globalized world of intensive space, the whole is no longer a hierarchical organization of parts, but rather an intensive congruence, a logic of affiliations through diagrammatic operations, and it is the nature of these relationships that determines the quality of architecture. In an analysis that relates to the categories we are proposing in this text, Kipnis appears to associate differentiation to matter and integration to program, claiming that deformation architects such as Eisenman and Gehry tend to differentiate a basic figure to incorporate multiple orders. On the contrary, information architects like Ito, Koolhaas and Tschumi begin their projects from a diagram of events or programmatic relations that become a consistent organization through the emergence of repetitions (the mesh or the container). Kipnis's taxonomy is at the core of a series of possible categories. See Jeffrey Kipnis, "Toward a New Architecture," in *AD: Folding in Architecture*, ed. Greg Lynn (London: Academy Editions, 1993).

new programmatic possibilities. It is not unlike an anamorphic operation where scalar or projective deformations of an existing typological structure are used to produce new possibilities of occupation. The manipulation of the Dutch residential types in his social housing in Schilderswijk, the patio-houses in Evora, and the deformation of the facade plane of the Schlesisches Tor project in Berlin, are similar sorts of operations where a well-defined programmatic structure is geometrically or topologically deformed to incorporate new effects or extend the potential of the original program.

In this light, we might conclude that from a constructive or material strategy, a project such as Herzog & de Meuron's Signal Box is organized top-down in a process of differentiation, while the Igualada Cemetery by Miralles is constructed bottom-up in a process of integration. From a programmatic perspective, OMA's ZKM in Karlsruhe was built as a heterogeneous aggregation of programs, integrated through an idea of structure, while Siza's Carlos Ramos Pavilion is built top-down, from a programmatic type (the classroom) in which certain surfaces are specialized as enclosure walls or illumination walls, the scale is reduced, and certain typological components such as the differentiation between corridor and classroom are eliminated.

Building by differentiation or repetition are some of the architectural possibilities that emerge in relation to the tendencies towards programmatic or topographic integration or differentiation, and can help to distinguish between practices which otherwise would be pigeonholed in the same category. Returning to the "minimalists" category, it is interesting to compare the tendency in Herzog & de Meuron to work with serial elements as a means of canceling-out supposed figures in the composition even through the repetition of images, as opposed to Chipperfield's tendency to construct figures using the differentiation of constructive elements, or differentiated surface treatments. Basically, depending on the way that the repetitions are produced—the type and number of symmetries, for example—they can be used to construct a texture or a field, or to generate a figure. Neither pure repetition nor pure differentiation is capable of constructing.

Returning to Miralles, to use an example taken from a radically different "aesthetics," an analysis of his Archery Range project immediately reveals an enormous number of repetitions of geometric and physical construction mechanisms that interact with the existing topography to construct the project. This form of construction is radically different from what we find in architects who at a first glance might be considered part of an aesthetic of formal proliferation—say, Eric Owen Moss or Thom Mayne, for example—and where the idea of difference has been radicalized to an extreme in order to hide the organizational plot of the project. A comparison between the work of Ito and Kazuyo Sejima, especially in the last two years, can also be articulated on the basis of this differentiation: even when both have the same language in common and probably a series of interests as well, Ito always tends toward the proliferation or differentiation of forms, whereas Sejima tends more and more towards repetition.

One possible classification of projects that work within this sense of opposition is the following:

MATTER		PROGRAMME	
INTEGRATION	DIFFERENTIATION	INTEGRATION	DIFFERENTIATION
Igualada Cemetery (Miralles/Pinós)	Tokyo Opera (Nouvel)	La Villette (Tschumi)	Thermal Bath at Vals (Zumthor)
Guggenheim Museum (Gehry)	Signal Box (H&dM)	Kunsthal (Koolhaas)	Carlos Ramos Pavilion (Siza)

Instructions for Use

The niche-seeker map can be used to classify practices or projects. This can have a range of uses such as deciding the long-term direction of a practice, or simply presenting oneself in a competition. Depending on the user, it can help to synthesize a practice or to adjust a preestablished practice to market trends. Depending on the objectives, the map must take on different form; augmenting in resolution certain areas of particular interest, or utilizing certain projects or practices as classificatory material. The following steps are necessary to construct the map:

1. Read the definition of the suggested categories and choose those that are relevant to particular objectives.
2. Establish a grading between the extremes of each category, and draw each one as a line on a single sheet of paper. DIN-A0 landscape is a good format for the map, although a spreadsheet program is a better choice to update

the map continuously with new information or focus on certain areas at a closer resolution.
3. Place files with the names of architects or projects you wish to use as references along the lines at the points where you believe each case fits into each of the categories. This is the most difficult and laborious stage of the map-making process, as it requires a degree of sensitivity to evaluate the material available.
4. Identify the areas with the lowest density of names. These are probably where you are likely to find gaps in each distribution. If you are interested in a certain ethos, you will have to increase the map resolution around the areas of practice that interest you (for example, around local practices). The secret of this step is to know how to mediate between the areas that interest you and the opportunities that can be detected in the map.
5. Take note of the "niche" coefficients you have identified (for example, gradient 3 between determination and indetermination + gradient 7 between information and form + gradient 2 between apocalyptic and integrated). The sum of all of these categories defines the coordinates of the niche that you have found.
6. Try to apply these instructions in the design of a project, or to the ideology or structure of your practice. This is a very complicated process, and is often faced with insurmountable psychological, ideological, or instrumental resistance, although it is nevertheless an extremely interesting exercise in understanding one's own position in this world full of holes. Good luck…

The images in the background of this text are aimed to illustrate the text's description of the contemporary world as a swarming field full of eddies and vortexes, or "holes", where niches can be found. The images are a recollection of famous crowds of the last few decades, from Woodstock, Glastonbury, Monterrey and the Love Parade to the Barcelona and Beijing Olympics ceremonies. The patterns of these crowds provide a graphic image of the world in the border between the 20th and 21st Centuries.

The Alchemical Brothers: A Compact Material History of Herzog & de Meuron

A few years ago, when I was still a student, there were no ambitious architects who did not sprinkle their work with quotes from the latest conceptual artists as some form of crucial reference. To this day one bumps into architects in their fifties who seem to be more interested in art than in architecture, and take great pride in collaborating with artists in their work. As a diligent student at the time, I had a go at it myself, only to conclude that architecture was actually much more interesting, because it operated with the wildest (and widest) palette: structure, symbol, space, function, and money. It can also be sold in many markets; including the *art market*. In fact, the art market is one of the *best of all possible markets* because it generally has good budgets and enlightened clients. Yet there is nothing more boring than architecture made like art; that is, works conceived within a purely subjective frame, freed from external constraints and given over to art for art's sake (architecture for architecture's sake, architecture for art's sake, or what have you).

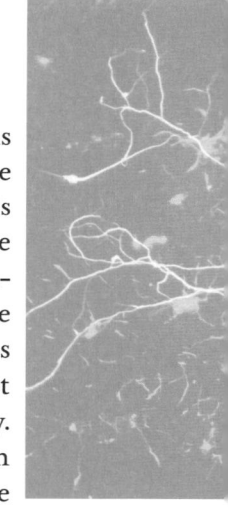

I could not care less whether Herzog & de Meuron hang out with artists or not; in fact, I think they are rather focused on architecture. Their fundamental strength is their capacity to achieve higher levels of consistency within the material organizations they produce; that is, to make matter alive. And that

1. Herzog & de Meuron. *Natural History*, ed. Philip Ursprung (Montreal: CCA/Zurich: Lars Müller Publishers, 2001)

makes them sound more like alchemists than artists, which suits them fine, since they come from Basel. Herzog & de Meuron are hometown kids gone global, like Ciba-Geigy.

What was good about the alchemists of the near past is that they were just excellent apothecaries gone mad. They did not only know how to turn base metal (lead) into gold (like artists), but also how to undertake the most prosaic of tasks, such as preparing aspirin, perfume, and other artificial devices to produce physical affects at the service of *someone else's* will. Unlike patronized and patronizing artists, their gains came out of their relation to an open world, rather than to their own subjective obsessions. Herzog & de Meuron also range from the mystic to the kinky: they are the architectural equivalent of the swerve negotiating between Gerhard Richter and The Spice Girls; Federle and Manchester United; Prada and Versace. Anything goes as long as it yields excitement. To truly understand matter's erotica, you need to taste it in its most disciplined arrangements or in its utmost state of chaotic dissolution. To be a good general, you also have to be lucky; they got lucky. Very early on, they came across an artist who wanted to be an alchemist. Joseph Beuys certainly triggered some latent capacities. As an alchemist deeply involved with matter in the broadest sense of the term, he manipulated symbols, energies, ideologies, processes of materialization, crystallization, and dissolution—negotiating the "hallucinatory" assemblage of matter and flows set in a permanent field of transformation, exchange, and *entropy*.

For a while Herzog & de Meuron toyed with Rossian archetypes, even figurative analogues. They also rediscovered their own urban background in the boredom and greyness of 1950s, Northern European rationalism, and experimented with Swiss concreteness: wood construction and precast concrete; material research that would prove much more productive than the more cultural or figurative references of their earliest works. Very early on they had some stuff to build, so they could not linger forever in Beuys' slightly demented, wild and abject *cosmology*. They were lucky again to have commissions before they had a clear manifesto. As they were pouring concrete and piling wood, their alchemical perspective on architecture was being formed. The making of Herzog & de Meuron had begun...

To get lucky you have to hunt opportunities with the strongest determination. The commission for the Ricola Buildings would provide the opportunity to push the work definitively onto the right path. The problem of stacking, storing, distributing matter would finally give Herzog & de Meuron the opportunity to move away from the more figurative vein and sink *deeper and deeper* into material agglomerations. When the building becomes the outcome of a process of accumulation or construction it disappears into a process or a pattern. It becomes primarily a form of organizing matter that turns the object into a field, or into a *material texture*. The Ricola project exploits the repetitive nature of material accumulation to produce an elemental rhythm. As in the songs of the Swiss mountain shepherds, the rhythmic repetition of a motif and its echoed resonance in the valley produces figures and landscapes, constructing an "ulterior" or "anterior" territory. After Ricola, the figural doubts of the early work would slowly disappear and make the rationalist and concrete background productive on an *affective* level. Even the figural details of the plywood house or the wooden flats would not reappear in the work. the residence in Dijon, the Auf dem Wolf Depot, Eberswalde, and the storage of bodies, trains, and books, would proliferate this research through the subsequent work. The alchemical project gains strength in engaging new, disparate forms of lead. Buildings become a direct output of the construction process of a complex assemblage. Is not the true role of *art*, after all, the construction of territories through the reorganization of the components of a milieu? Is not *art* the making of increasingly complex and consistent material aggregations possessed with a *primary* force that has the ability to develop different functions, even within the finite parameters of *a single project*? What is interesting about Ricola is the conversion of mere functions—the distribution and accumulation of matter—into primary rhythms of expression and emergent affect. True artistic production has nothing to do with human subjectivity per se; it is an intrinsic quality of matter, of complex material organizations. And, as Deleuze and Guattari have taught us, much to our collective chagrin, human agency is not *everything*.

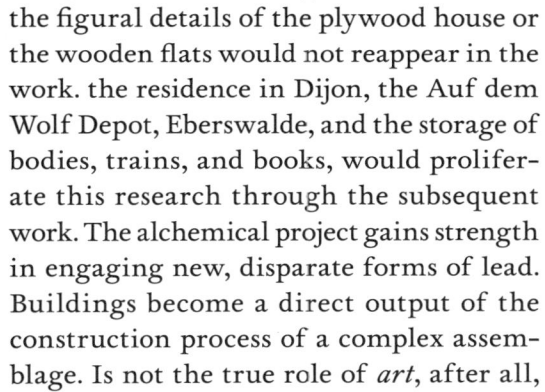

But every consistent material composite also requires a destratification of components; for example, stains, radiographs, tracings or marks. In the work of Herzog & de Meuron one can immediately *feel* that intense alchemical pleasure of following the path of a liquid dissolving into another or filtering through a sponge, of rain dripping down a wall. Seen or *unseen*, it still *drips*... What if that casual imprint started to produce a figure, becoming deterritorialized, consistent with an external process? What if we project figures on a complex imprint, as in a Rorschach (another Swiss invention)? What if we cast a figure on a construction element so that it becomes a stain, making the figure consistent with a building component? What if we do it not once, but serially, so that it produces a rhythm, a territory that disappears into a texture, into a field of matter? The Ricola Production and Storage Building would spearhead research into images becoming part of matter, becoming consistent with building elements—it would release the hidden affects *in* building that would, in turn, trigger the *expansiveness* of a building-that-is-*no-longer-a-building*. This is distinct from ornament, from a signpost, from a mark, because the ornament is subordinated to the building material rather than enveloping the body. The ornament is *not* rhythmic—instead, the *whole building* is a metric suffused with the rhythmic. This is, therefore, no longer the problem of an either/or proposition: decorated shed *or* duck, an always-false dichotomy anyway, given that the "cheaper" forms of postmodernist rhetoric were premised upon a usurpation of populist sensibilities. Thus, we are faced with complexity through consistency, rather than contradiction. The point of alchemy is, after all, synthesis and renewal. The ornament becomes a stain in the material composition; it becomes submissive to a construction system; chopped, repeated, and alienated, pushed toward abjectivity with a secret exit as *specular affect*. The alchemy of corroding frames and strata through serial composition is deployed here, turning the molecular accumulation of candies into a molar flow. *Serious cavities* do not seem that far off...

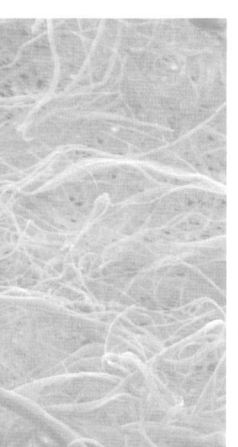

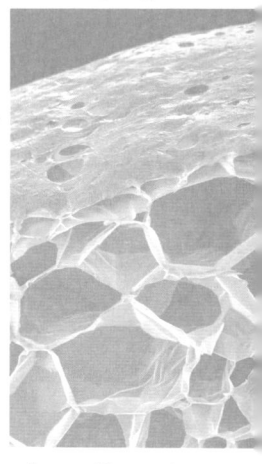

A territory is constructed through a regrouping of forces... Similarly, maps are constructed through a tissue of lies that become truths. Often indefinable forces are what make the material aggregations consistent beyond the stratified state of the different components in a medium. It is in channelling these forces or allowing them to play out within a defined set of conditions (the alchemist's "furnace") that makes matter stand up and pay notice to creative will. Matter is a medium for the play of indeterminate and diverse energies. In the Signal Box Auf dem Wolf, the facade is a material of *superior*

consistency; it not only limits the outside, but regulates the ingress of light, water, temperature.

The facade of the Signal Box Auf dem Wolf not only signifies the appearance of the building, it serves as a literal Faraday cage, a copper-wire envelope that deflects electric charge should one hit the building. The compound of stones and steel rods (modular gabions), light and shadow, weight, and *air* in the Dominus Winery becomes the complement to an even more sophisticated composite "reality," that is to say, *French* grapes growing in a *Californian* valley, fermenting in *American* oak barrels, and marketed *around the world*. All that is solid does, indeed, melt into air... Making wine is a sophisticated form of alchemy, a complex form of arranging matter into a consistent organization that excites our taste buds and slows down neural connections: more complex than making aspirin. It involves the earth, the landscape, the sun, the weather, the containers, the order of actions, the rhythms... Dominus is not about making a building but about making wine. I remember Herzog & de Meuron saying, during the design of the building, that the wine was so good that it was likely that it would become a good project. And how could one make a heavy lattice, with earthy thermal inertia, that lets the air and light through to produce the fresh and shady environment needed for the wine to mature? The sorting of caged stones in different sizes increases the material complexity of the aggregate and introduces a further degree of complexity that extends the suppleness of the constructive orders. A gradation of the qualities of the surface is made possible, differentiating the air penetration, quantity of light, and thermal inertia of the wall. This gradated surface may well become the next step in Herzog & de Meuron's path toward a more sophisticated territory, an even more consistent hyper-materialist practice.

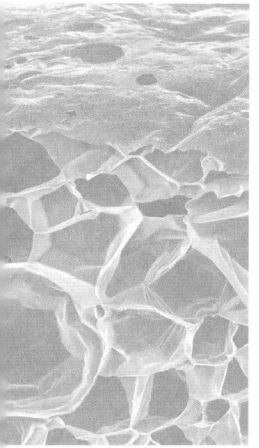

They are cooking something right now. I have seen glimpses of drawings that do not look like the standard Herzog & de Meuron... Further shape-shifting is to come. Just get ready for the next generation of architectural *pheromones*!

The images in this text aim to illustrate H&dM's interest for the material as an area of architectural experimentation. The idea of alchemy which the title addresses, refers both this interest of H&dM for the material, micro-texture of architecture, and their location in Basel, one of the global centers of the chemical industry. A series of microscopic photographs, made with technologies developed primarily after the 1960's have made available to us an experience of the world that did not exist before, and that I consider a crucial and important experience. This chapter displays some of these images that constitute a critical part of my generation's visual memory.

Text for the installation in the Spanish Pavilion at the 2002 Architecture Venice Biennale, developed with Lluís Ortega, Toni Montes and programmed by Enrique Romero Merino

RGBGlobal™ (version 2.00)

RGBGlobal™ is a prototype tool that will allow architects to position themselves strategically in an increasingly global, complex and fast-changing market. A must-have in the architect's office of the 21st Century.

In the same way that politicians are no longer operative without opinion polls, and investment bankers don't make decisions without expert data-mining systems, the time has come for architects to understand that they are no longer the great designers of the world and to accept that taste is neither personal nor eternal, but rather an unstable substance that depends on markets. If architecture has been traditionally a local business, it is increasingly important to be able to take positions in the global market, even if the operation of architecture always happens within a local domain.

RGBGlobal™ is a tool that allows architects to position themselves aesthetically in the global market. The tool is geared to process global data, while providing the possibility of developing local specificity by training the tool itself. Like any other value, architectural quality is a vector that negotiates an increasingly complex system of forces operating on a local but globally determined scale. A contemporary project needs to build its possibilities and potentials within environments with high levels of variation and indeterminacy; and, as in any other professional field, operativity is increasingly dependent upon processes of automatization.

The processes of automatization allow individuals to make real choices in a globalized environment by allowing them to navigate effectively through the increasingly complex layers of information that characterize decision-making processes in such milieu, albeit without getting captured by the systems of local belief. **RGB-Global**™ is a tool that enables architects to engage in this most contemporary mode of machinic sensibility. **RGB**Global™ has been designed as a tool that will enable users to process global information efficiently and develop machinic sensibilities by linking a global data processing system to an interface where the user can train the machine toward certain behavior in tune with individual inclinations.

In order to design **RGB**Global™ we have made two hypotheses about a system to dynamically model architectural value:

1. That architectural value is not just dictated internally by professional media, but always bears a relation to external factors (economy, politics, social structure, etc). Practices need to situate themselves in this field and to construct the condition of possibility for actualizing their potential organization.

2. That architecture is the engineering of material life and therefore architectural value relies fundamentally in qualities derived from material organizations, distributions, and formations. For this version of the tool, we have temporarily excluded any linguistic and representational considerations in favor of intrinsic material properties. One could imagine that the tool could acquire increasingly sophisticated levels of output (selecting materials from catalogues, distributing programs, deciding upon massing options, etc.). For this exercise, we propose to use a plasma screen or a projection as an output device. We will structure the architectural qualities of **RGB**Global™ around a few factors that exploit the possibilities of the tool. The advantage of this simple output is that the tool could be made universally available to run on any PC.

Technical Description

RGBGlobal™ organizes information as a variable material and identifies differential qualities of density and organization where the opportunities and potentials for a project may be identified. It is a tool that encodes global information into material organizations that reveal architectural qualities. The selection of categories and parameters that determine output has been limited to a few parameters, but it would be possible to inform **RGBGlobal™** with a more complex set of parameters to cater to specific architectural effects. The selection of the output levels of this version is the following:

A. **Geometry**: The qualities of architectural definition depend largely on the amount of information used in the definition of architectural form. The level of information used in an architectural organization determines its qualities, which are regulated by the following parameters:

1. The level of repetition and variation in the geometrical pattern. Within this parameter we determine whether the form is constructed with repetitive units, what level of differentiation in position exists, and what degree of similarity is evident. This parameter will distinguish, for example between a more industrialized and a more artisanal architecture, or between a more collage-like and a more homogeneous one.
2. The level of resolution of the form across scales. This parameter will identify the relevance of geometrical definition of detail in the whole.
3. The level of deviation from the orthogonal reference system that has come to constitute the default architectural construction mode and the consistency of any deviation.
4. The amount of information consumed in the definition of architectural form (i.e. defined by two points, a straight line, center and radius, a simple curve, by a simple function, sine, cosine..., by a complex function, using NURBS, or by a raster of a certain level of resolution).

B. **Texture and color**: The other series of parameters that define architecture regulate the levels of information that describe the superficial material effects on different qualities. More continuous distributions tend to imply a higher level of information, while more repetitive or discrete distributions require a lower level of information.

1. The range of the color hue, level of saturation of the material palette, and its level of deviation (i.e. whether the output architectural quality is monochromatic or polychromatic, and to what degree it varies).
2. The average scale and standard deviation of the standard texture (i.e. what is the scalar relationship between the overall profiles and the micro scale of material definition, and what is the range of variation).

These architectural qualities will be coupled in **RGBGlobal**™ with other matter, generated through information about global markets, and supplied to the device via real-time connection to specialized information systems on the world wide web.

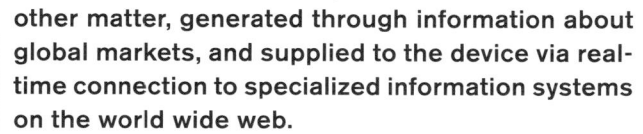

The selection of these fields of information and their encoding and weighting into material aggregates has been driven by hypotheses that rely upon our observation of the last twenty years of architectural practice and its related sectors of production, as well as our knowledge of architectural history. We will sample across several fields of global data that we identify as relevant in the construction of global taste. They constitute the input into the machine, and their relationship with the behavior of **RGBGlobal**™ as an index of global adequacy of architectural organizations are the following:

1. Index of global level of communication, which indexes the amount of information that is exchanged globally per unit of time. In our hypothesis, its rate of increase will generally induce a global aesthetic behavior that tends toward a high level of geometrical complexity due to the accessibility of data and the generation of a desire of a more information intensive environment. However, beyond certain levels in its absolute value, we have applied a sudden correction behavior in which the need for information-poor environments will suddenly reverse the tendency. This index rate of increase will also have a positive effect in the level of chromatic information of the organization, mitigated suddenly above a certain threshold by a sudden return to poor chromatic information (as an example of this behavior, see black dress code and preference for minimal design in extreme information-rich environments, such as London, New York and Tokyo, while moderate and fast-growing information

supply in Kuala-Lumpur generates a preference for formal and chromatic information excess).
2. Index of global energy consumption, whose high absolute value will tend to diminish the richness in material texture, but increase chromatic complexity, thanks to the availability of artificially produced materials, which usually present a more homogeneous surface but a more differentiated chromatic range. Again, corrections beyond a certain threshold of consumption will induce a revaluation of rough natural textures and crude tones.
3. Index of global agricultural growth, which indicates the availability of food supplies and general well-being on a global scale at the most basic level of the economy, having a diminutive effect in the manpower cost in a sector of the economy traditionally sustained through low-cost, low-skill manpower.
4. Raw materials price index, which indicates a composite index of the cost of raw materials. Our hypothesis is that a fast rate of increase in the value of material costs will induce a tendency toward a low level of geometrical information and textural richness, as the cost of production of construction material will force the careful elaboration of raw materials, aimed at a minimization of material costs. The resort to orthogonal geometry and linear repetition of building parts will be a likely outcome of this global tendency. The parallel increase in the level of artificial manipulation of construction materials will increase the chromatic ranges of available products.
5. Chemical industry and metals composite index, which will have a proportional effect on geometrical and chromatic complexity as the availability of refined materials will induce the use of a more sophisticated level of profiling and a wider color palette, while diminishing the ruggedness of material patterns.
6. Construction index, which will indicate an increase of the availability of funds for construction, and again will imply a positive change in the level of geometrical complexity of the output.
7. Composite global interest rate index, which will induce a revaluation of urban and built infrastructure capitals, increasing real estate prices and construction budgets and resulting in an increase in geometrical complexity, as well as a preference for "true" materials that will decrease the chromatic range and increase the textural complexity.

8. Real estate index, which will affect the output by decreasing the level of geometrical and chromatic and textural complexity. Large investment in real estate is an index of mass demand that results in a neutralized, default product.
9. Global consumption index, which will affect the output by increasing the level of geometric and chromatic complexity proportionally to its rate of increase. As global consumption grows, production prices decrease, allowing for a higher level of elaboration and a demand for sophistication of the products.
10. Technology index, which will mirror its gains in the raise of the levels of geometrical and chromatic complexity, and reduce the textural complexity of the output. As the model of taste is very complex and not easily explained, we will design **RGBG**lobal™ using a neural network, in order to incorporate the real-time complexity that defines architectural value, and to be able to customize the tool and to accumulate the knowledge produced over time. A neural network is formed by a series of cells, called neurons, usually organized in layers interconnected through adjustable parametric correspondences, defined by the weighting of those connections. The input layer is activated by the incoming sampled data, while the output layer reflects the results of the network calculation. This output result is mediated through the weights as well as the connections between cells and their activating functions, which will also be subjected to a parametric transformation. All of this will constitute the knowledge embedded in the network.

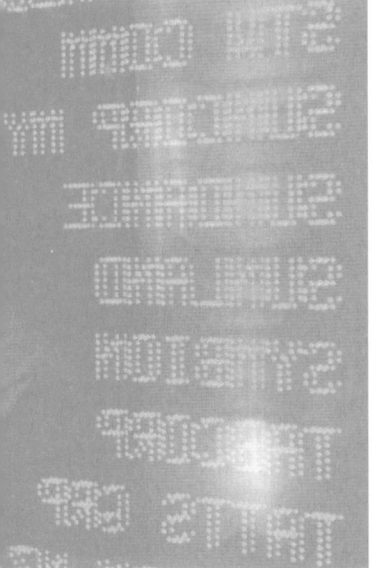

The process of training of the neural network consists of the adjustment of all its parameters in order to optimize its control function. The most commonly used control function is the quadratic error. The training is usually performed through a series of input samples obtained from a representative sample of the problem in question. In classification problems, the neural network output is closely linked to the probability *a posteriori* of pertinence to each one of the classes in the output layer. In problems of regression, neural networks perform as universal approximators. This makes the neural modeling a very adequate theoretical framework to deal with problems of Artificial Intelligence, where the complexity of the function to model is usually unknown.

In order to capture the temporal, variable dimension of architectural value, we will design **RGB**Global™ as a dynamic system. A dynamic system is a mathematical entity defined as a succession of states of continuous or discrete nature. In the best case scenario, there is a physical law that characterizes them. In other cases, like the problem at hand, we do not know the laws that regulate the system, but we can define their evolution by using the evolution of a series of parameters. The most relevant aspect of a dynamic system is its asymptotic behavior, which means that it tends towards a final state, favoring the *attractors* of the system.

The first criteria that we have used to train **RGB**Global™ assumes an asymptotic behavior that selects the most common screen types produced during the duration of this show, therefore identifying an attractor for the output layer, which will indicate what is cool now, generally speaking. The second criteria has been to provide to the system a level of sensitivity toward data variation which will turn the screens into an intriguing display for the type of user it will have in this location. (These targets or control functions could obviously be challenged by the user in future applications of the system.)

The neural network allows us to frame the behavior of our codification software; beyond certain limits the format of the information becomes illegible and requires an adjustment to new limits that will return the code back to the communication field (i.e., a record played on a CD player is illegible and needs to be adjusted back to its native communication mode).

RGBGlobal™ will be trained with specific consumer tastes. Its neural network performance will allow it to optimize its behavior to get closer and closer to its initial criteria but, of course, just by changing the trainer profile, **RGB**Global™ can also readjust itself. This learning capability increases its software information management efficiency and life potential.

At this point, we do hope that the spectators will find the screen an interesting aesthetic experience...

The images of this text are extracted from the device that I designed for the Spanish Pavillion of the Venice Biennale 2002 with Lluis Ortega, Toni Montes and programmed by Enrique Romero Merino, under the title RGBGlobal ™.

Published in *AA Files*,
London, 2003

In Memoriam:
Cedric Price

I had the chance to meet Cedric Price several times during the years we were both teaching at the Architectural Association, and I was always surprised by his perfect gentlemanly manner. In a place where, more often than not, one encountered people who would go out of their way to demonstrate their superiority, passion, and originality, Cedric's relaxed manner and real intelligence was very refreshing. He used to look at projects as a patient scientist, waiting calmly for something to happen, rather than trying to demonstrate how much he knew or making virtuous interventions or demeaning remarks. When something did actually happen, he would become visibly excited and make truly lyrical readings of the work. He was, most of all, a very generous critic, not interested in judging or evaluating, but in contributing to the work from the distance of his position. He was able to sustain the weirdest arguments without blinking. He had perfected the role of the eccentric, to the point where eccentricity becomes truly productive.

But the image of Cedric that appears most vividly in my mind occurred one sunny, spring morning when I was walking up Tottenham Court Road in the middle of the day, a time when it characteristically buzzes with students and people shopping, getting a sandwich, or going about their business. For some strange reason, everybody was young and everybody was running in the same direction, northward. I was almost being carried forward by the crowd, enjoying being part of the swarm, when suddenly I could see a few yards ahead that the swarm had encountered an obstacle and people were moving aside and lowering their speed. I moved forward cautiously, as one does in a swarm, watching the speed of the guy in front, and suddenly a gap in the crowd appeared and, in the middle of it, Cedric, walking in the opposite direction with characteristic parsimony, bouncing from one side to the other in slow motion. Same stripy shirt with white neck, blue blazer, and grey trousers; same aerodynamically gelled hair, smoking a cigar and looking bleakly to the horizon, as if he could not see anything in front of him. There he was, the prophet of flows and change, the tracker of trends and movement, suddenly turned into a blind obstacle to the swarming crowd. I remembered Paul Virilio's *aperçu* that the most intense travel is motionless... Perhaps we needed Cedric's consistency for everything to change.

Only two images in this text: one from Cedric Price himself, and another from the first human stepping on the Moon, which is a reminiscence of Cedric's outlandish character.

A Scientific Autobiography + Post-¥€$ Postscript

In recent years, the old struggle between theoretical and practical knowledge has become (again) a critical subject in architectural discourse. Within a field traditionally focused on practice, theoretical discourse (especially during the 1990s) expanded exponentially, while the borders of the discipline dissolved into neighboring fields. The convergence of architecture, planning, and landscape architecture is just one example of this mutation of the discipline.

To describe the possibility of a relationship between theory and practice in which they are no longer understood either in opposition or in a complementary, dialectical relationship, but, rather, as a complex *continuum* in which both forms of knowledge operate as devices capable of effectively transforming reality, is in many respects begging trouble. The antagonistic positions noted are also discursive and non-discursive *fiefdoms*, one figuring the other, and in which the erasure of boundaries or the co-optation of one by the other typically enrages one or the other party, if not elements of *both*. Such *secret* corollaries—apparent camps opposing one another—belong, nonetheless, to a complex *engine*

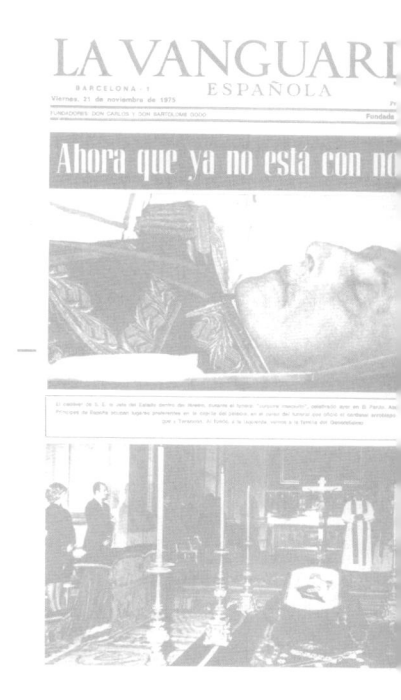

where sheer (versus *adequate*) performance is dependent upon the harmony of conjoined circumstances.

To say that practical knowledge is devoid of significant theoretical content is as false as stating that theoretical knowledge lacks pragmatic purpose. I would rather describe their assemblage as two alternatives within a particular discipline and a particular domain of reality, one trending toward virtualization (theory), the other toward actualization (practice). In this capacity, theory is never generic or universal; it relates very directly to real, even prosaic things; things such as currency (and its exchange), cultural traditions (and their mutations), and geopolitics (and its cycles of transformation), all of which one could argue are not quite things, but complexes, but—ultimately—an argument that just returns to the old battles between ideal and pragmatic worlds held in tension plus the attendant clash of ideologies given a *historical* stalemate. Theory has, just like practice, a site and an age. Virtualization often operates within the site of theory as reality's vector of change, as an index of tendencies. Similarly, however, practice is never a pure form of local knowledge. On the contrary, pragmatics often relies upon the repetition and generalization of preexisting ideas (it inherits *previously expounded* and *assimilated* theory).

Having traversed some of the more stimulating milieus for architecture (at the border between centuries)—Spain in the '80s, American academia in the late '80s/early '90s, Holland in the mid-'90s, London in the late '90s, and Japan at the dawn of the twenty-first century—it is in these very different milieus that I would like to ground these reflections.

Spain in the '80s: *El Croquis* and the Non-critical Virtual

I grew up as an architect in Madrid in the early '80s. The Spanish economy was thriving through a period of simultaneous political and social development, and architecture found in this climate one of those historical and geographical singularities in which opportunities and expectations grew to unprecedented levels.

The formula was: a powerful, guild-driven, professional structure (inherited from the dictatorship) + a booming economy (generated by the new democracy) + a process of cultural and political revolution (produced by the new regime and by the repressed ambitions created during the old one) = interesting architecture.

Architects had become confident and optimistic to a degree that I have elsewhere experienced since only in South Korea—another ex-dictatorship—before the economic slump of the mid-'90s. Most of the knowledge needed to operate in such a newly burgeoning milieu is practical: architects just need to keep pace with external processes and actualize their potentials to produce innovation: there is no need to establish strategies of "virtualization," to unduly question this new-found freedom, since influencing reality seems always already beyond anyone's wildest dreams anyway. Born into a new freedom, why belabor its splendid appearance with a critical dissection of its premises? Yet questioning things does occur, and it is usually done with kid gloves; that is, the *inquisition* proceeds by standards that remain "involutionary," given to the discipline and not aimed at the world per se.

Within the Technical School of Architecture in Madrid, those who were committed to virtualize or theorize the discipline could be put in two camps:

—An older group of great designers, well-oiled by years of intense "holistic" practice (the average size of practices was about three, which meant that everybody did everything: structures, detailing, site supervision, environmental systems, etc.)—designers who drew their inspiration from sports cars, sail boats, poetry, sculpture, holidays in Majorca, and beautiful women (they were obviously all male); a type of indulgent critique, typical of operating within a fixed range of aesthetic manipulation of desire.

—The younger generation, more intellectual and influenced by historical and linguistic studies; a group that focused their experiments on evolving the disciplinary language. For them, a sublime form of practice engaged in the evolution of block typologies, design of innovative corners, perversion of conventional fenestration orders, and so on: a more discursive and metacritical critique indulging the perennial exercise of performing architecture's autopsy, pretending it has died and that a proper dissection will prove therapeutic for all that *might* come.

In typical Oedipal manner, I became critical of both groups and resorted to extra-disciplinary fields—that is, philosophy and literature—as a strategy for virtualization. Since nobody was very interested at that time in virtual activities, at an early age I was given the opportunity to participate in an emerging industry of professional publications, grown in the shadow of the building industry and the ambitious cultural policies of Architects' Associations across the country. Writing at that time was considered a bit too intellectual (something for wimps), and some of my tutors, informed of my literary activities, would tell me with a skeptical grin, "What really matters is the site supervision."

One of my early engagements was with *El Croquis*, a magazine that started up as a pamphlet publishing the thesis work of students in Madrid so that other students could learn how to organize a graduation thesis (a complicated technical enterprise at the time). *El Croquis* was then shifting toward the professional market, with the same zest and focus in the description of details that they had used for the student market. Then lacking a particular theoretical agenda—as far as I could tell—they had a vague notion that they needed some *text* to go with the illustrations. In this situation, writing allowed me enormous freedom, as long as I remained within the word limit. Most importantly, I could not be overtly critical (I was never told this explicitly, but got it pretty quickly anyway). Some of my friends who were also interested in a more theoretical approach criticized me for working in that most "pornographic" of architectural magazines. Yet, now all of them want to be published in it... Others accused me of not being critical enough, which was entirely true (but also the very point of the exercise, and certainly the operative basis for what I have been doing ever since as a critic). Once the possibility of judgment of somebody's work has been removed, you can use the work only as a raw material to construct your own affirmative statements. Relating it to other dimensions or domains suddenly appeared as a broad field of potential. Once writing abandons the role of the critical—that is, establishing benchmarks, comparisons, judgments, and value systems—it becomes a projective tool in itself, an instrument that processes others' work into one's own.

To some degree this was the secret of the phenomenal success of *El Croquis*: the lack of a critical agenda and an extreme commitment to the detailed portrayal of architectural artifacts, encompassing their innermost secrets. The magazine made an art of describing work, independent of age, trend, or situation. In the same way, *El Croquis* had complete independence from institutions, professional or academic power groups, and individuals. (To the editor's credit, I witnessed some rather important architects begging for a monograph and being consistently ignored far beyond political tactfulness.) One may question whether its choices have been right, but that is beside the point: once they chose something, they turned it to gold. The case of *El Croquis* is a lesson about the power of production versus that of critique.

Not only did these activities provide me with the opportunity to construct a theoretical approach, they also allowed me to mount one of the largest operations of industrial espionage ever carried out in this profession: there is nothing more revealing than meeting architects and visiting their offices to learn about their techniques. It was only after a few years of these activities that I decided to stop writing about the work of others, since doing so was hampering my own career as an architect—people tended to associate my name automatically with writing, and practice never forgives that mistake.

American Academia in the Early '90s: Economic Recession and the Empowerment of Theory

In a radical change of milieu, in August 1989 I landed at the Harvard Graduate School of Design to do a post-professional degree. The favorable exchange rate between peseta and dollar after a few years of economic crisis in the US presented me with a good opportunity to maximize a scholarship and find a more benevolent climate in which to theorize.

In the American academic environment, the smartest guys from the then "around forty" generation had already figured that, given the economic conditions of that period, the practice of architecture had become impossible. After the great corporate architecture of the first half of the twentieth century, Americans had invented more profitable forms of creating public "space" than architecture—that is to say, they had diverted their investment to movies, art, information technology, advertising, marketing, and the like. As a result of this, the emerging generation of architects shifted to film theory, art criticism, cybernetics, cultural studies, graphic design, and economics, producing an era in which theory became substantially empowered.

A shrinking demand for quality architecture in the USA had neatly split American practice between the "stars" (also known among the politically correct newcomers as the Boy's Club) and the usual corporate suspects (big- and medium-sized A&E firms, for the most part). With an economic milieu rapidly deteriorating after the excesses of the '80s (after the crash of 1989), this new generation was left with little opportunity to grow through familiar modes of architectural practice. Exchanging production-driven practice for critical practice, they discarded both forms of practice (the celebrity circuit and the corporate suite) as corrupt and politically incorrect, and devoted themselves, instead, to more noble enterprises than making buildings.

Theory, critique, and cultural production appeared as the most promising field of potential for this secretly *power-hungry* generation. Its members grouped very much in the old boys' style; promoting the least threatening, least manipulative institutions, publications, and *worlds*, all from behind the veneer of the politically correct. Bred in the yuppie generation, they had perhaps learned a couple of lessons from their luckier high-school classmates who became brokers during the '80s: the more remote your practice is from the making of real goods, the less overhead and the more flexibility, money, and power you *might* have. As the stock market became the Mother of All Things, the new generation of American architectural thinkers moved to high-theoretical speculation, becoming, in turn, progressively estranged from anything merely physical. "Critical practice" was the *only* thing to do if one wanted to do anything relevant in architecture, and that meant to nag about everything and try to architecturally embody all sorts of psychological and political perversions and subversions.

After an initial shock at the brightness of the ongoing discourse (all the greater due to my then poor command of English), I became suspicious of this brave new world, and particularly of the fact that projects that in Spain would provoke immediate disdain were able to trigger hour-long debates about Lacanian psychology, poststructuralist semiotics, and the like at juries. For the first time I was facing the symptoms that I would face repeatedly across several educational institutions worldwide, where the "empowerment of theory" had been translated into an artificial detachment from architectural production, resulting in legions of bad novels, bad sociology, bad psychology, bad philosophy, and bad movies, all presented at juries as advanced architectural *research*. The fundamental problem was the systematic exile of architectural effects outside the discipline, leaving the architectural capacity of the students in a precarious state. (Some years later, as an antidote and act of defiance, I removed from my Architectural Association studio bibliography everything but Ernst Neufert's *Architects' Data* and *Architectural Graphic Standards*.)

Skeptical about the proliferation of cultural studies and *arty-farty* seminars on the menu at the GSD, and unable to understand them due to my language handicaps, I defaulted (to much contempt from my classmates and some of the faculty) to the very uncool options of real estate, construction management, and especially computer-aided design, all of which, at the time, was a subject reserved for nerds with no real interest in architecture.

However, I could not completely escape theory: within my focused assault on the American production technologies, I did come across with some potentially useful neo-Marxist urban theory, most notably that of David Harvey and Henri Lefebvre, and most importantly, I bumped into Sanford Kwinter, a lunatic who curiously did not speak about scopophilia, gender, and other issues related to the construction of the subject, but about all sorts of multiplicities—that is, swarms, forests, glaciers, and other unorthodox matters. He gave a seminar on complexity with a reader full of Henri Bergson, Ilya Prigogine, Gilles Deleuze, Manuel de Landa, and the like. I was so excited to discover external fields that could at last become excuses for new architectural effects that I toyed with the idea of enrolling in a PhD program, profiting from the possibility of extending my scholarship. But another encounter at the GSD with another outsider, Rem Koolhaas, aborted a promising career as a theorist: he offered me a job.

Rotterdam '91–'93: OMA and the Super-Dutch—The Engineering of Cultural Production

I landed in Rotterdam in August 1991 loaded with my recently acquired American arsenal: on one hand, CAD proficiency; on the other, a cocktail of Deleuze's materialism and Harvey's neo-Marxist globalization theory.

The first missile, CAD production technology, failed miserably: My computer skills were at odds with OMA's company policy at the time of a radical split between designers and computer operators; since I wanted to be a designer, I had to go back to the parallel bar and the foam cutter for two years.

The second missile, the theory cocktail, was far more successful: Koolhaas was amused at my attempt to wrap the stuff going on in the office in pretentious new words. Previous theoretical encapsulation dated from Foucault and Barthes, extending towards Derrida, so it was time for an update. Paradoxically, production at OMA was remarkably non-theoretical by American standards. The pressure of deadlines did not leave much time for constructing critical arguments before diving into the blue foam. Discussions were only about matter-of-fact stuff. It was like undergoing detox treatment against the critical thought that by the end of my American residency was threatening to paralyze my architectural nerves.

Holland was an artificial paradise. Everything was new and worked—trains, doctors, highways, telecommunications, architects... Certainly the happiest population in Europe and maybe the world, the Dutch looked like the Americans in the '50s. Beefed-up Europeans, sporting permanent Caribbean suntans and perfectly gelled hair, were drinking in fashionable cafés and shopping their hearts out at *reasonable* prices. These people were the very best example of Dutch engineering: everybody was friendly but fast, smart but cool, daring but responsible, liberal but effective. The *Super-Dutch* were already there before Bart Lootsma coined the term.

Among the architects, a new generation of busy bees was emerging, excited by the international success of their local star, Rem, as everybody seemed to call him in a bout of spontaneous collective familiarity later to be exported worldwide. No wonder, because Koolhaas had put together the recipe for international stardom as an ingenious assemblage of theory and practice, speculative vision and ruthless realism. After Rem, the typical path of a Dutch architect was to do a few of those projects growing everywhere in Holland, put together some theory, write a book with a cool name—branding is one of the best skills of the Dutch—and sell it all *worldwide*. As opposed to what happens in the USA, Dutch architects, given the level of opportunity in Holland, get physical very quickly, and write after—or at best during—the fact. And some of them even evolve their own customized publishing programs to construct, through language, a discourse of the actual. Maybe they do so also to undercut the critical, but even that seems to be consistent with a form of virtualization focused on production.

Unlike in Spain, where the potential for virtualization in architecture was primarily developed from the mighty Associations of Architects and was, therefore, enslaved to practice, and unlike in America, where virtualization resides within the walls of academia and never gets out lest it contaminate everything, in Holland architecture was being taken care of by much higher authorities: the Ministries of Culture and Spatial and Economic Planning. As I arrived in Rotterdam, the Netherlands Architecture Institute was under construction and the Berlage Institute was just starting, both generously funded by the government as brand new infrastructures for architectural speculation and, most importantly, networking and dissemination. All deserving Dutch architects made books subsidized by the Ministry, and all architectural startups progressed with governmental funding. This high-level management has devised a system in which cultural production and speculation have become perfectly integrated in the making of the environment, and this arrangement is paying handsome dividends. Dutch architecture is considered—with good reason—one of the most innovative today. A highly industrialized and effective construction sector mobilizes important resources, while producing large benefits that are severely taxed by the government (I was paying 40% of my income on a less than ideal salary!). In return, the administration provides generous support for those who decide to speculate further (I was eligible to collect start-up funds, even as a foreign citizen, and was generously compensated by the Berlage Institute as a visiting critic). Advanced speculation is then disseminated worldwide through subsidized magazines, schools, and museums, and absorbed back by the construction industry and the public. Architects' cultural production becomes essential as a way to place architecture in the wider cultural context and the politics of space so that, in return, culture and politics are aware of architecture's potentials. In response, Dutch theory is deeply committed to the actual. Koolhaas formulated, if not invented this approach, theorizing after the fact on case studies (New York, Atlanta, Singapore, Lagos) or on method (critical paranoia, bigness).

Out of modernist Dutch planning, a new architectural culture of progress and difference has emerged and is being colorfully interpreted by the super-Dutch generation, which is obtaining worldwide success and is acclaimed by local developers. It is so varied and progressive that one sometimes wonders whether the variations are mere scenography, like the choices at McDonald's. But it is an incredible achievement that such a smooth marriage of theory and practice has been engineered not by historical coincidence—as in the Spain in the '80s—but by the artificial arrangement and ruthless determination of the *competent* authorities.

London in the Late '90s: The AA— Eccentrics and Pragmatics

Out of the Dutch artificial paradise and into the British gloom, I landed in London in August 1993 to teach at the Architectural Association, at the rock bottom of the recession. The city was literally falling apart, especially in comparison with the shining Dutch environment. The AA—and the other academic institutions in London—were filled with '60s-era debris of the ideological, methodological, and even personnel sorts. Archigram heroes were doing odd jobs in the dark corners of academia—for a Spanish architect educated in the '80s, it was like watching Mick Jagger sweep floors. Generally well-preserved in alcohol, these heroes were no longer able to understand what was going on and kept a distant air, like bankrupt aristocrats. What happened to all those wonderful ideas? How could they have vanished like that, into thin air?

After a year at the AA, I started to understand (and worse still, *feel* like one of them). The AA, which originated as a club, had become an ivory tower for the English eccentrics. This typically local figure had developed a unique model of education of enormous success, exported everywhere during the 1980s. Its uniqueness, especially in comparison with the stale, continental polytechnic model, was assembled as a hybrid between a liberal arts school and a gentleman's club. It gave support to the most outrageous experiments and the most unique personalities, and produced work of an intensity difficult to match within any other academic infrastructure. The very British system of local allegiances and networks of defensive legitimization had produced in the AA a powerful vehicle for architectural experimentation and a precinct where the eccentrics and other outsiders (many of them foreign) were given a socially productive role.

The price to pay was the certainty that none of it would ever effectively transform reality. In this most peculiar pact with the Devil, the English eccentrics knew that their job was to form an alibi for the system to remain as unaltered as possible. In this scenario, the more outrageous and removed from reality, the more effective work becomes as a legitimization of the otherwise conservative reality of British architecture. The reason why those wonderful ideas never touched down on Earth is because their makers, totally committed to their social role as true eccentrics, never actually believed in them as a potential reality. Or rather, these ideas were actually being developed by the other side of the British mind: the pragmatic. Through the Thatcher era, the high-tech lords were actually having a ball exploring the most pragmatic aspects of the 1960s and exporting them worldwide.

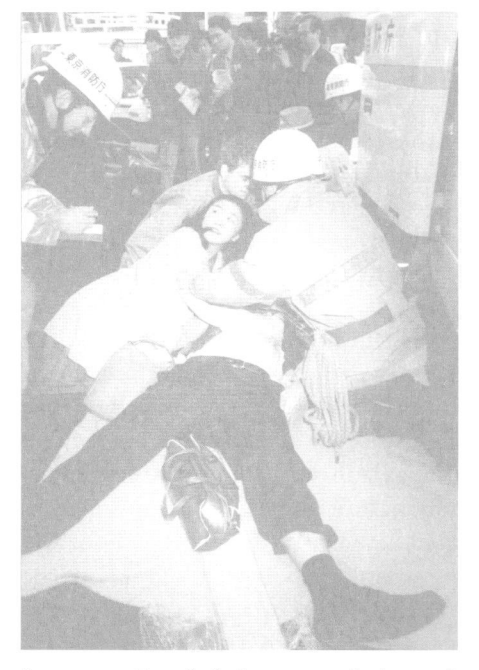

Partly out of survival instinct and partly out of the fear of becoming an eccentric—a capital sin for a Castilian—the more I heard the continuous dismissal of their work inside the ivory tower, the more interested I became in the pragmatic lords. All they actually needed was to grow a virtualizing branch, just as the eccentrics needed to grow an actualizing one; all they required was *somebody* to read their work as an actualization of potentials of building technology rather than as optimal solutions of technical problems. But this would have probably endangered their public profile; meaning the fiction they were selling worldwide of *carefree* technical proficiency. Being truly pragmatic, they were never truly interested in spreading confusing virtualized messages.

After escaping from the Spanish polytechnic education and attempting to find solace in the Anglo-American liberal arts tradition, I had found the limits of liberalism and the advantages of a less individualistic, more technically oriented education. Diploma 5, the unit that I co-headed at the AA for seven years, was precisely an attempt to virtualize pragmatics. Built upon a mix of Jacobin radical faith in the transformation of reality with a Calvinistic commitment to production and rigor, the ethos of Diploma 5 was aimed at exploring and proliferating the potentials of a technical repertoire for contemporary practice. Curiously, Lord Foster was to become the single largest employer of ex-Dip 5 students after our own office, which became an extension of the people and ideas in the unit.

This continental departure from local liberalism did not go down very well with the 1960s derivatives, who immediately understood our radicalization of pragmatics and technique as a threatening force to individual self-statement and free thinking. To make matters worse, I met and immediately aligned myself with Jeffrey Kipnis, one of the most volatile explosives concocted by American academia through the *empowerment of theory* phase, who encouraged me to abandon my pseudo-multi-disciplinary approach to concentrate on the irreducible secrets of the discipline. Echoes of Spanish brutality resonated in his words, as he also blasted the 1960s debris. (I would later introduce Kipnis to *El Croquis,* and he would become a local legend: the first intelligible American theorist after transplant-to-America Kenneth Frampton.)

Diploma 5 was to become a kind of sect for techno-freaks who wandered around the school with blood-shot eyes speaking in a strange jargon. After all, and despite the initial mistrust, at least a few students understood that exercising dexterity in sophisticated techniques and temporary submission to rigorous and alienating regimes might become as powerful a weapon of virtualization as the cult of personality and extravagance had been during the 1980s. The quality and amount of work they were able to produce was legendary and *dizzying*. It was, *arguably*, the first realization I ever had of the power of a *specific* (that is, narrowly defined) culture *within* architecture to operate as an engine for unparalleled experimental production *for* architecture. All false modesty aside (and, after all, some credit goes to the AA for being the best school for the synthesis of architectural cultures), not since the Bauhaus had such selfless *frisson* produced such a leap in architectural *science*.

Yokohama 1999–2002: A Matter of Culture

After more than four years of doubts, the Yokohama Municipality decided in January 1999 to proceed with the construction of the Yokohama International Port Terminal Building, a project we had won in 1995 in an international competition. After a period of incredulity on the client's part, we finally realized that this time the project was being taken seriously and that the only way to do it well was to move our entire project team to Japan. In London we formed a team styled like British military intelligence, with a core constituted mainly of Japanese "Sherpas" (operators with local knowledge), who had either worked in the London office for some time or been our students at the AA or the Berlage Institute. Their job would be to guide us through the difficult Japanese terrain. We also took with us some Spanish "Gurkhas"—a fierce deterritorialized contingent, ignorant of the basic rules of local behavior and capable of the worst atrocities—to crack the local boundaries. And in August 1999, FOA was at last at large in Japan.

Japan is an interesting place in which to speculate about the relations between theory and practice since it is by Western standards a particularly theory-proof environment. The architect as an agent almost completely detached from the literal process of construction is a Western import dating from the age of metabolism. In Japan, the contractor (responsible for material actualization) is officially the architect, even linguistically; there is no split between a theorizing agency and an actualizing practice, for better or worse. Material organization can reach unbelievable levels of excellence in Japan, since the cultural and industrial commitment to material perfection is unmatched, but it can also produce the most incongruent assemblages, since there are no means in place to provide consistency fast enough in response to an exponentially growing capacity to build. This produces a particular form of architecture that can be seen in local architectural magazines where one can witness hundreds of truly inspired moments of material assemblage (sometimes several in the same project) without any consistency across them. Western architectural culture could live for a month with the ideas in a single Japanese magazine, using them one by one, rather than all at once.

The production of the detail design of the Yokohama Project was an exhausting process in which we had to concentrate all our energy for seven months, followed immediately by an equally demanding supervision phase. No time for theorizing, and yet the key for success was the theoretical consistency of the team. The Yokohama team's core was built up with very talented, mostly Japanese architects, who had gone through further training in the West. We kept a small team with whom we had close communication, since its members had been part of the cultures of either our academic or our professional practices in London. Practically trained in Japan and theoretically trained in the West, these people made up the only workforce capable of producing the cultural synthesis that the project needed. Together we could discuss topological grids, intensive tessellation, the differentiation of systems, diagrammatic performance, and many other techniques that we had been developing jointly for the practices of material organization. The design process became in itself a process of creating knowledge. The Yokohama project not only gave us the possibility of actualizing a theory we had been developing for some time across academic and practical endeavours, but also started growing its own lines of virtualization, surprising us at every moment with how the technical requirements were organizing themselves into arrangements that we could not predict at the onset of the project.

Our most important role as project directors was to assemble the team members and defend them from unavoidable attacks from the different professionals involved in the project, who would naturally dismiss them because of their age. Most difficult and yet most crucial in allowing the growth of the project was to resist forming a corporate bureaucracy in which team structure is aimed at maximum efficiency in decision making. The Yokohama team shared an extreme work ethic, and anybody who did not share that had to be dismissed to avoid contaminating others, to keep the energy focused. To have given the power to "experienced" architects, as most of the conservative forces around us were demanding, would have been catastrophic, since it would have destroyed the team's cultural consistency. Our main task was to synthesize and maintain a team culture through an exhausting process. As an architect, one can either operate within a linear structure where decisions are made in a hierarchy of command, or within a culture in which a more complex system of relationships between the team members allows much greater flexibility, innovation, and feedback. It was as important to introduce Jeff Mills, Autechre, Miles Davis, and Boulez to the other members of the team as it was to design the structural grid or the wood deck pattern on time. As such a building had not previously been experienced, the Yokohama project had to be "grown" and could not be "designed." The team had to grow with it: nothing grows without a culture.

The experience of Diploma 5 at the AA was critical for our constructing a culture aimed at the exploration of material organizations that simultaneously develop a project, a series of techniques, and a group of individuals. What constitutes a building culture? Is not this what we create whether we work as experimental architects, as critics, or as teachers? The Yokohama project has not only been both a great architectural experiment and a producer of virtuality; we hope it has also been a producer of some very fine architects. Japan is, like Britain, a country of pragmatics and eccentrics: you succeed either through maximum compliance or through the most outrageous behavior. Having gone to Europe to maximize their potential individual eccentricity, our Japanese colleagues had come across some Europeans fascinated by the Japanese population's intensive, machine-like behavior. Yokohama was an experiment in how to evolve a systematic, rigorous, alienated, and technical approach to produce the most outrageous architecture.

Recently, I heard from Arata Isozaki—who has been, together with Toyo Ito, our Japanese godfather through the project—that young Japanese architects have lost the appetite for design and beauty. As an improbable link in the chain of architectural lineage in Japan, I would like to think that this generation has perhaps favored realizing the potentials of growing designs, rather than making decisions or manifestos. And that the Yokohama project has not only been an experiment in growing buildings, but also an unlikely multicultural graft that will open an alternative for Isozaki's sceptical grandchildren. We just hope that the economy will allow them to actualize it. A culture always needs a material substrate, too.

2004: Post-¥€$ Postscript

The preceding text was published in a somewhat different form in the February and March 2002 issues of *A+U*, but was actually written in the last half of 2001 and finalized in the aftermath of September 11th. In retrospect, this temporal coincidence seems to acquire unexpected relevance. The text was a personal account of the milieu where my generation grew up and had to practice and theorize, an attempt to index a paradigm of carefree optimistic globalism and opportunism that was being challenged—if not severely questioned—by the events taking place as the text was being written.

Many things have changed in the two years since the text was published, both on a global and on a personal level—and in a curiously intertwined manner—that lend themselves to reflection, as they become an interesting verification of the ephemerality and temporal and local specificity of any theoretical or practical proposition. This, in turn, introduces a historical dimension to my argument, beyond its initial focus on the geographical diversity of certain modes of practice and theory.

Koolhaas, who was the first to theorize the processes of global capital and the effects and potentials *for* architecture, branded these emergent trends the "¥€$ regime." He subsequently started to criticize it as soon as its phenomenology became apparent. The outcome was: architecture henceforth is deprived of any utopian potential and is to be subject, *whether it likes it or not*, to the whimsical and capricious reign of global capital and its accelerated processes of estrangement, alienation, and discipline. With characteristic speed, he created AMO and the *Content* project to escape such enslavement and the onslaught of *junkspace*. The Harvard Project on the City, like Content and AMO, shifted from shopping and the Pearl River Delta to Rome, Lagos, and communism as new domains of knowledge and operation where there might still be chances for architecture to be utopian and work for collective well-being. That very few could see that this shift was anything more than rote opportunism is the result of Koolhaas's permanent state of mutating within definable boundaries: that is, his penchant for never standing still. Yet what better protagonist to take on big capital than one who has mastered its inversions and slides toward totalitarianism?

Koolhaas may very well be right about contemporary conditions, although the current delays in the CCTV project suggests that the pace of evolution in those domains is even faster than he calculated and the new political establishment has already learned about overheated economies, soft landings, and democratic demagogy, without completing the phase of mad development: Hu Jintao has allegedly stated more interest in "people" than in "big projects."

In the light of this, what I would like to do as a follow-up to my slightly cynical argument about the ephemerality and local diversity of theoretical and practical operations is to revisit some of those well-trodden architectural scenarios in which I am directly involved before venturing into those brave new worlds of the wild Far East, post-communist Eurasia, and darkest Africa.

In Spain, for example, after two decades of architectural prowess and orthodox commitment to the ¥€$ regime, the country achieved full acceptance as a distinguished member of Mr. Rumsfeld's New Europe and the Azores Summit. Spain has now fallen under the spell of the architects' star system and become easy prey for the international design elite. (As a Spanish architect, I am fortunate to be able to stalk from the outside.) *Newsweek* has saluted Mr. Aznar's model of public-private partnership as a new model for a European sustainable economic and urban development, and pointed to Barcelona's Forum 2004, where I have been directly involved, as the maximum expression of this regime, despite the very public conflicts between Barcelona Local Government and Mr. Aznar's Central Government.

But after the dramatic March 11, 2004 bombings in Madrid, Mr. Aznar was democratically dismissed and replaced by what the critics have already described as "the first democratic European government of al-Qaeda." Mr. Rodríguez Zapatero, new president-elect, has set the two first important policies for the new government: pull all Spanish troops out of Iraq immediately and create a new Housing Ministry—an institution revived from General Franco's technocratic era—aimed at rescuing a housing-handicapped population.

After two decades of dogged commitment to the ¥€$ regime, 17% of the country's GNP is produced in the real estate and construction sectors, and Spain has become Europe's main investment zone for real estate, setting the prices of housing out of control. The municipalities of both Barcelona and Madrid, from different political positions, and under the pressure of potential total collapse if the prices of residence are not brought back under control, are developing massive programs of publicly funded urban housing at a scale not seen for decades in Europe, and involving some unusual architects—like ourselves—in the process. Will this revival of socially controlled urbanism bring back also the need for utopian thinking and replace the ¥€$ regime by a kind of new urban fundamentalism?

In the meantime, in New York, the Ground Zero saga has been proceeding wonderfully. At the epicentre of the struggle of the ¥€$ regime and where the potential for architectural fundamentalism should have been maximum, things are looking a bit bland. After popular clamor trashed the proposals of Beyer Blinder Belle, the Lower Manhattan Development Corporation was forced into an international competition to search for proposals for what should become the future embodiment of Western culture. Koolhaas and Frank Gehry were sidelined, allegedly for not being willing to participate without being *properly* paid. Political fundamentalists hammered them for their shameless commitment to the ¥€$ regime and lack of a moral stance. SOM, who had been working for Larry Silverstein practically since *the day after* the tragedy, resigned officially in order to enter the competition. The list was reduced to two corporate behemoths camouflaged in mixed teams, a British Lord of impeccable reputation and size, a highbrow-intellectual Old Boy, a group of pre-critical Old Boys, and an international group of post-critical Young Turks (including myself). Each team was paid a miserable $40,000. Allegedly the communications company in charge of the process was paid a cool $3,000,000. Architects lost again to the ¥€$ regime. In such cases, and given the *historical* assimilation of all difference by the machine of big capital, we should have known it was all coming (or that the *apparent* pluralism of the middle years—the 1980s and 1990s—would be hijacked by conformity *and* reaction). Neo-liberal capitalism, originating in the 1970s, is now heading toward its natural station as global hegemon.

A few remarks on the shortlist, then, are in order. The Old Boys and Young Turks had to join forces in order to be accepted. Critical architects from the intermediate generation were remarkably excluded. The corporate establishment, determined to regain the intellectual legitimacy that they lost in the 1970s to the Old Boys, resorted directly to the very keen Young Turks as camouflage. But the strategy did not work properly the first time around, and Daniel Libeskind, an Old Boy with an inappropriate CV for the job but an *apparently* impeccable moral trajectory, won the contest (with some inside help from the governor's office, if the rumor mill has any validity whatsoever). David Childs, the retired corporate captain contemporary of the Old Boys, returned from his grave to publicly dismiss the SOM entry—which had been entrusted to a younger generation within the company—and resigned from the competition to work again for Larry Silverstein. A public fight ensued between Libeskind and Childs for control over the project. Libeskind's *apparent* moral stance was by now very worn out by years of confrontation with the ¥€$ regime and was surprisingly ready for conciliation: he abandoned his trademark slurry wall and, with Childs looking over his shoulder, produced the Freedom Tower, the new phoenix of Western architecture for an alleged "genius fee" of one million dollars (effectively invoking his own "kill clause"). Childs' very real management genius, on the other hand, succeeded in returning cultural legitimacy to the corporate establishment in America after thirty years *slaving* in the margins. Both Old Boys and Young Turks were erased from the scene. Meanwhile, other birds are landing on Ground Zero in what promises to become an interesting architectural spectacle. Whether it will remain an expensive cosmetic operation *à la* Times Square dictated by the ¥€$ regime or it will actually become an urban manifesto for the emerging late-capital, post-9/11 fundamentalisms is yet to be seen.

The Netherlands has become a victim of its own success: the highway system is permanently clogged, trains are systematically delayed after the privatization of the rail network, Schiphol airport is coming apart at the seams... Even the Royal family is plagued by infighting. The Social Democrats, who reigned for decades over the economy, the welfare state, and the culture, have collapsed. Wim Kok resigned over the failure of Dutch troops to prevent the massacres of Sarajevo. My own official nomination as the new dean of the Berlage Institute was severely delayed by the period of political turmoil that followed the election. In the middle of the process, Pim Fortuyn, the maverick right-wing/gay politician poised to become the prime minister, was shot dead by an animal rights activist in front of MVRDV's VPRO campus in Hilversum. The newly elected Christian Democrat government of Jan Peter Balkenende has very serious doubts about whether it belongs to the Old or to the New Europe and is posting the worst GNP growth expectations in the Eurozone...

In 2003 a widespread scandal involving many developers and contractors exploded, revealing dubious morals and systematic price rigging in an industry regarded for years as very profitable, well organized, and efficient—one of the pillars of the Dutch economy. The enormous office-space pool developed during the last ten years remains 60% empty. The current state of the economy and the new liberal government are threatening to cut down severely the expenditure in cultural subsidies that made the Netherlands a mecca for emerging artists in Europe. The NAI and the Berlage Institute, the two institutions set up in the 1980s to reflect on the city and architecture, are on the firing line, despite being a potential source of regeneration for the whole of the real estate sector after the price-rigging scandals. As the miraculous balance between the welfare state and the ¥€$ regime that became the trademark of the Dutch for a few decades collapses, Dutch architects are selling their expertise in welfare management, becoming especially appreciated in master planning, social housing, and open public grounds and landscaping. This expertise is particularly appreciated in those countries moving *forward* toward a welfare state, like those in Eastern and Central Europe, and those moving *backward* toward a welfare state after deregulation, like the UK. Many Dutch architects can also be found in China bidding for work.

In the UK, the so-called urban renaissance is on a roll. Birmingham, Brighton, Bristol, Leeds, Leicester, Liverpool, Manchester, and Newcastle are all discreetly turning their city centers into massive shopping malls. ¥€$ urbanism has finally come to rescue the dormant British cities... But is it too late? The real power behind the urban renaissance movement is not ideological but purely pragmatic: inner-city land values in mid-sized cities have dropped so far that land costs for building there has become negligible. Why keep building suburban shopping malls when whole city centers are for sale and come with great transport infrastructure, central locations, and captive populations? The merit of Richard Rogers and his Urban Task Force is to have identified these commercial potentials and set up a synergy between them and a politically sellable agenda. Creating new high-density city centers, plus redeveloping urban brownfields and the like, are all *probably* less polluting, more sustainable and community-friendly than simple laissez-faire urbanism, yet they are also, *obviously*, able to produce larger commercial revenues for inner city landowners. ¥€$ urbanism in Britain has given rise to a new breed of more pragmatic and efficient architecture that does not comply with the categorization of conservatives and eccentrics that has become the legacy of years of welfare-state and conservative-planning policies. ¥€$ density is moving wealth from the Tory-voting, fox-hunting, Barbour-clad, Euro-sceptic farmland to the Labor-voting, jet-setting, metro-sexual, Europhile urbanites. The prince's and English Heritage's rhetoric has been replaced by the Task Force and the Commission for Architecture and the Built Environment, a body formed by developers, architects, planners, journalists, and academics with a rather pragmatic approach, veiling the new ¥€$ urbanism in Britain, and actually enticing developers to look for more experimental architects as a source of *added value*.

Under the advice of Lord Rogers, Ken Livingstone, a colorful politician expelled from Labor for opposing party discipline and then warmly readmitted once he had become mayor of London as an independent candidate, is implementing some advanced—if not awkward and risky—urban governance policies: he has managed to implement the first congestion charge scheme in Europe, has been fighting in court with the government for a new policy to fund metropolitan transport, has imposed a quota of 40% social housing on all housing developments in London, and has initiated the most ambitious extension of London (since Queen Victoria's time) through the Thames Gateway scheme.

Rogers' and Livingstone's achievements of dressing ¥€$ urbanism with light-hearted ideology are mirrored by Blair's commitment to take the ¥€$ regime to new post-ideological heights. His confrontation with the traditional forces of the Old Europe led him to the even more traditional fundamentalism of Bush's evangelical crusade, internalizing the potential contradictions of the regime within his government to catastrophic effects.

Blair and Livingstone's twin versions of the ¥€$ regime have, however, found a common *grand project*: the London Olympic bid for 2012 and a master plan for the Lea Valley, in which we have become involved. After having discovered our potentials as camouflage material through our involvement in the Ground Zero project, we decided to accept the invitation from a team formed between the local chapters of two American corporations (EDAW and HOK Sport) and a British one (Allies & Morrison) to bid for the project. Our camouflage is spread very thinly, since every other partner is on average ten times our size, but this mix of 75% corporate *savoir faire* and 25% *experimental naïf* was able to beat not only the naiveté of some important international bidders, but also both pragmatic lords! In other words, it is a triumph of meritocracy over pedigree whose effectiveness has still to be proven; but so far so good. The lords are cool about it, and we have found that the corporate monsters are made of reasonable people of more or less our generation with a slightly different career path with whom it is easy to work. The question now is whether this ¥€$ team will be able to deliver the architectural ideology needed to represent Britain in front of the International Olympic Committee and to provide some soul to the 50,000 housing units that Mr. Livingstone wants to place in the Lea Valley. Is there an architectural future for a post-¥€$ Britain?

No news from Japan except from the *Financial Times*: after amassing a fortune in dollars trying to keep the Yen at bay, Heizo Takenaka, Koizumi's finance superminister, is well on his way to clearing up the bad loan mess. There is a record number of IPOs as people move their money out of the banks to become minority shareholders in those emerging companies. Keiji Tachikawa, the CEO of mobile communications company NTT DoCoMo, is close to getting W-CDMA transmission technology adopted as the third generation global standard after years of heavy unilateral investment. Carlos Ghosn has turned around Nissan from a liability to the economic engine of the Renault-Nissan group. Koizumi is sending troops to Iraq, rebuilding the Japanese army, and paying honors to war criminals. The arrival of Shintaro Ishihara (in 1999), as charismatic neo-nationalist governor of Tokyo City, signals an emergent new national pride to be materialized in the creation of a super-airport in Tokyo Bay. The economy is rebounding and so is national self-esteem not as a result of ¥€$ alignment but, on the contrary, as the result of charismatic, disciplined ideological and financial commitment to ideas.

Lucid architectural output is not emerging yet. Roppongi Hills' fanfare eclecticism failed catastrophically as a mirror for post-¥€$ Japan as six-year-old Ryo Mizokawa was crushed to death as he tried to slip through one of the automatic revolving doors, bringing public confidence in architecture to its nadir after the government declared the end of big public projects. All well-known Japanese architects are working mostly abroad, and our only commission there after Yokohama was the Spanish Pavillion in Aichi. But in the same way that savings are moving toward minority stakes in emerging companies, a new generation is starting to produce work of carefully measured effects and small private commissions. I sense that they are on the verge of a secret fundamentalist revolution... I am itching to go back.

The images that populate this text are global milestones of my personal history: from Franco's death, through the Barcelona Olympics, the fall of the Berlin Wall, Greenspan's tenure, Diana's Death, the rise of Labour in the UK, the Sarin attacks in Tokyo, the 09/11, the Azores summit, 11-M, the assassinations of Pim Fortuyn and Theo van Gogh, and the tenure of Junichiro Koizumi.

Breeding Sciences

The texts included under this section were written primarily as reflections on my academic practice and research, developed across my successive engagements at the AA, Columbia, Princeton, UCLA, Yale, my tenure as Dean of the Berlage Institute in Rotterdam, or my participation in international conferences such as the Any Conference, Urban Age, the Venice Biennale, the International Architectural Education Summit and others. These texts were mostly written for presentations in conferences, academic programs, and other stages where architecture and urbanism were discussed as disciplines. They constitute a collection of proposals, and reflections on the production and transmission of knowledge on material practices.

This essay incorporates sections from my texts "The Virtual in Architecture", Tokyo University Virtual Architecture Exhibition Catalogue, Tokyo, 1996; "Generative Processes" in *The Journal of Architecture and Building Science*, Tokyo, 1997; "The Computer as a Tool", *AIJ magazine*, Tokyo 1997; and "Mind After Matter," Jyvaskyla Symposium, 1997

Generative Processes and New Material Agencies

While the game of architectural tag is often played with different media and within different registers of the discipline, passing from one hot spot to another, and while IT seemed to be "it" in the 1990s, as linguistic games were certainly the "thing" in the 1980s, it would seem that many of the issues first raised then (both with the linguistics model and the IT model) have since passed closer to a more grave and serious body of knowledge: the intense gravitational pull of *material agency*. This latter concern represents the full magnitude of the revolution occurring within architectural agency since the collapse of *modernism* in the 1960s and the subsequent echoes of that collapse in the 1970s and 1980s in *postmodern* instances of questioning architectural complicity with regimes above, beyond, or *outside* its own inherent concerns. It is pure material agency that almost always calls from within architecture as a means of escaping its instrumental regimes (its appropriations by other regimes of power and demagogy). Let me explain by both revisiting some of those first movements within architecture to assimilate the IT revolution and the subsequent outcome of this "turn" in a type of new formalism or determinism that drew on both the innovations given to the IT juggernaut plus its production of a new language of autopoietic measures; measures that seem wholly given to the production of new material agency and new formal agency for architecture—that is, the possible and impossible measure of all architectures that approach the real with an urgency to engage worlds in order to transform them in entirely *positive* terms.

In the Beginning...
In the beginning was information, 0s and 1s conferring a new Year Zero... Theorists from different fields have already baptized the period of the late 1970s through the late 1990s as the Information Age, an era when the production, manipulation, and exchange of information became more important than the production of goods. The cities where we live have also been radically affected by the introduction of technologies—such as telecommunications and computers—aimed at the manipulation of information, much like industrialization altered the world at the end of the nineteenth century. The arrival of the Internet (in the 1990s) further expanded this new digital horizon toward a wholly wired and interlocking world constructed of worlds.

The computer has become the paradigmatic tool of this era, as the production line became the paradigm of production in the past century. In spite of all this, it seems that architecture was relatively impermeable to assimilate computer technologies. This in part had to do with the necessity of writing software of any use to the profession and the re-education of the architect to integrate computational theory to a discipline notoriously slow to change with the times. When in the 1990s, while studying at the Harvard Graduate School of Design, I decided to take courses in Computer-Aided Design (CAD), there was yet great resistance to admitting that computers would become the go-to tool in architectural practice, especially among the largely computer-illiterate lecturers. Computer knowledge was understood as a distraction from the practice of design proper. Yet, at the Architectural Association, in London, by the mid-1990s, most students were fluent in CAD, and in my office we did not bother to look at applications from people who could not use IT fluently, as they had become completely ill-equipped to enter into the process of design.

Those of us entering practice in the early to mid-1990s were the first generation able to enjoy information technology developed to such a degree that it could be efficiently incorporated into design practices. Just a decade previous, designers who ventured into the computer world had to spend so much time learning the interface that they had to specialize rather than simply use the tool as part of the day-to-day process of design development.

But this was only the beginning: by the end of the 1990s I had already become incredibly clumsy, at this critical juncture, compared to students in school or just emerging who had been born into the digital maelstrom. In this matter—as with many other aspects of contemporary culture—the younger you are, the better.

What was making computers increasingly important for architects, both in professional practice and research processes? First of all, the computer is obviously an incredibly powerful *productive* tool. And that is not a minor detail, but it also is not the core of the question. The real potential of the computer, then as now, is that it can open new possibilities in the very way we *think* about architecture. If we contemplate the relationship between how we think in architecture and how we work, we will realize that the computer allows us to *act*, quite literally, *as we think*, cutting out costly backtracking. When we are designing an elevation, we think, "These windows are too small and have the wrong proportion." If we are using drafting tools, we will have to go one by one and redraw every window with a new size and a new proportion. If we are using a CAD program, we will simply draw one unit of the new type and apply it to all the windows that were drawn previously.

Even the most primitive of the three-dimensional computer applications from the early years was a potentially explosive device that conventional two-dimensional design tools could not quite match: the construction of architectural objects occurs in three-dimensions, and traditional drawing systems imply a process of abstraction in respect to the object. The first 3-D CAD systems allowed us to produce precise architectural instructions directly in three dimensions and to test spatial organization without having to reduce the information to two-dimensional drawings. Yet somewhere lurking within the resistance of the academy to the introduction of computers was not simply a resistance to the new, but also a slight fearfulness that the destruction of drawing might also be the destruction of a "humanist" component in design.

In short, computers allowed us to act more expansively in real time to the very way we think and process design decisions. At that moment, as with most such moments of techno-revolution, any downside was outweighed by the upside.

But even this close integration of design thinking and technical execution is not where the real strength of informational technology as a design tool lies; it is not the tool's ability to operate following the way we think per se, but rather its ability to help us to explore dimensions that we have not yet even thought of; computers are the quintessential new modeling tool. CAD short circuits more conventional architectural representation, introducing whole new vectors to architectural design. Within ten years of the introduction of IT came an entirely new genre within architecture—the *computational*—and wholly new syntheses of formerly disparate disciplines; for example, the entire operative success of topographic and topological architectures (and the assimilation of landscape by architecture).[1]

We live in a culture in which the rate of change has accelerated to such a degree that production is actually being driven more by innovation than by servicing existing paradigms: In marketing terms, the "niches" are becoming a larger market than the "mass." "Types" are losing currency as a production tool, as we can no longer rely on what is already proven (received truths), but rather imagine alternatives to trigger emerging sectors of the market and perhaps, in the process, throw out some of those measures we have toyed with and found wanting. Change implies the devaluation of certain levels of experience; that is, historical, typological, or what have you. Precedents fall into decay, and new *models* emerge as crucial decision-making tools across different disciplines, as cultures shift as much within singular disciplines as all at once or across multiple disciplines, the spectrum of *all* cultural activities. A model is an analogue capable of predicting the behavior of a system in

---

1   In retrospect, and in the context of the present remix of past essays, this story is already too well known to reiterate here, but what is less well known is the insistent and persistent objections that something else was and is always possible, versus a simple new determinism however theoretically substantiated or propped up by borrowings from parallel disciplines. This *otherwise than determinism* seems, today, too in many ways salvage both the promise of the IT revolution and the critical or intelligible forms of architectural thought that were jettisoned in the early and heady days of "the revolution."

the absence of verifiable data. Models (topological and wholly experimental) are what appear at times of dramatic change. Is this not the very origin of hedge funds? It is always risky. Technology is given to forcing changes in the prevailing episteme. Yet, as we already can see, all change is not necessarily positive change and some changes require constant recalibration to remain productive.[2]

Architectural design and education have been traditionally based on the study of historical precedents and typological studies, but as those became less operative within so-called late-contemporary modes of production (and it is this shifting sense of contemporary that is truly problematic), they were replaced by modeling and simulation as design tools. Informational Technology was *the* ideal modeling tool, as it allowed us to construct unprecedented organizations and images.[3] The computer is, ultimately, a device that allows us to *see* things that we could not see before, and therefore, to *imagine*. In Greek, "idea" and "image" are the same word; if we can only think of what we have already seen, we are doomed to operate through rote mimesis, to repeat what we already know. Creativity becomes a matter of interpretation, or redescription.

The possibility of escaping from simple and reductive mimetic or eidetic modes through the use of IT implies to use these tools to construct, rather than to represent. For example, computer-graphics applications allowed us to see the airflow distribution within a large space, or to model the pattern that a large crowd will follow when escaping from a fire alarm. The irregular geometries that populate contemporary architectural magazines are the indexical figures for a changing, plastic sensibility triggered by computer graphics. Cities may eventually resemble the patterns of a cloud or waves than to a series of platonic solids. This perhaps unavoidable new *terrain vague*, should it ever arrive, will be a direct outcome of computational architecture combined with computational finance.

2   Again, in retrospect, critiques of parametric architecture have subsequently begun to circle the simple problem that there is no apparent subject given to these hyper-topological compositions and that the entire idiom (if not quite a genre) is sorely lacking in *political* (or *ethical*) agency. While epistemes come and go, and with increasing frequencies these days, it is the return of all that was bracketed in the early days of the IT revolution that is most interesting today. What we see, now, is parametric architecture developing a theoretical edge that transcends merely formalistic *edginess*. The return of the political in the late 2000s has begun to produce yet another shift in the paradigmatic excesses of IT-inflected architecture.

3   Twenty years later, more or less, we have decided to address what was always missing—or, to turn that model now toward what was always forthcoming. In dropping historical or typological concerns we inaugurated a passage through and toward material agency

One of the most important capacities of the computer is that it allows us to visualize and operate on multi-dimensional systems. The same capability that allowed early CAD operators to directly control three-dimensional data will potentially allow us to introduce other parameters into architectural drawings. *Already such ineffable qualities such as time, light, and temperature are beginning to be modelled and played with as affective, material measures.* This possibility has not yet been thoroughly explored for architectural practice, but it will potentially open formal and material consequences from systems comprising complex sets of parameters. For example, if a standard "ray-tracing" program can allow us to produce visualizations that model the multiple reflections of light over surfaces of different qualities (such as transparency, reflectivity, ruggedness, and color), taking into account the relative position of the lights and the surfaces, we can easily imagine that a program of a similar complexity will be able to evaluate the patterns of growth of an urban structure depending on a series of parameters, such as land value, solar radiation, topography, location of infrastructure, etc. What has always existed as *speculative expertise* might become a physical science. Early on it was evident that a simple rendering program could be used to test the effect of different values and different parameters, and get immediate answers to questions such as: "What will be the result of reducing the reflectivity of all the materials by 45%?" or "What will happen if the intensity of the light doubled?" Moreover, we could also increase values to an "unreal" limit; in other words, models allowed us to test the behaviour of the system under conditions that were not experientially verifiable, to explore situations beyond the accumulated knowledge that we had at hand from urban or architectural systems.

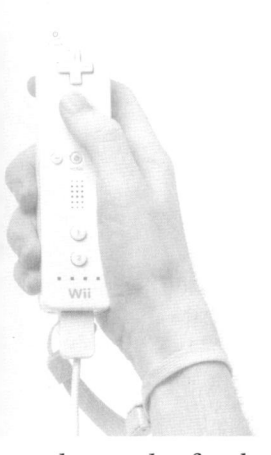

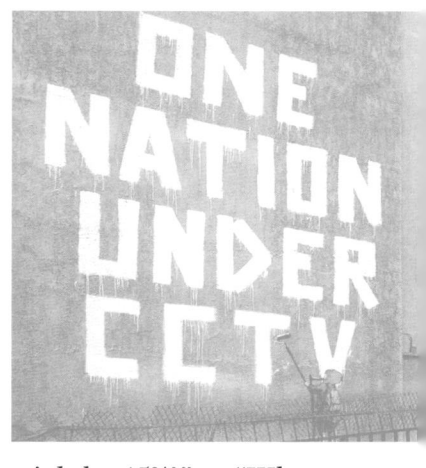

If design practices have been traditionally based on accumulated knowledge and experience, IT tools have introduced the potential for turning the process into a multiple-choice system. This does not mean that IT will make decisions for us, but that it will present us with possible alternatives, giving us the choice to make informed decisions.

Another very promising capacity of Information Technology applied to architecture in the first wave of innovation was the use of computer-graphic applications to transfer numerical data to graphic data. This capacity made possible crucial advances in the field of the sciences, as it enabled one to transform abstract orders or n-dimensional functions into forms, or, conversely, to scan forms or objects into abstract orders or mathematical functions. This eliminated the representational mediation through which knowledge of complex systems had traditionally passed. There was no longer a need for linguistic mediation between an idea and a spatial or material organization: computer language has a level of abstraction that removes mediation by cultural, historical, or local factors in the construction of a form. This capacity of computer-graphic applications had a double potential for architectural practice. On the one hand, data originating from domains external to architecture could be introduced into the design process for the generation of forms and structures. Statistics or data coming from other fields, such as economics, social sciences, or engineering could be introduced into the design process as determining factors. On the other hand, the development of numerically controlled manufacturing was beginning to make it possible to communicate directly between computer archives and manufacturing processes with a considerable reduction of manpower.

What was even more promising about IT in the design practices was that numerically controlled manufacturing allowed us to alter the repetitive nature of industrial production to make it more flexible and more specific to the particularities of a given situation.

Information and Architecture: Idea and Image

As already noted, *idea* in Greek equals *image*. To have an idea, one must *see* an idea. Images in this sense prefigure ideas (or language proper). Yet this manner of seeing or thinking is not the same as simple mimesis; that is, it is not reducible to eidetic images, mnemonic images, or any faithful replication of simple sensory stimuli. We are not speaking of perception. It instead implies a process that is interpretive and given to the productive agency of images *as* ideas. Although computers have mimetic capabilities, their innovative aspect relies precisely in their capacity to construct new images in n-dimension that do not exist in nature as images, as *preexisting* ideas. Constructing images in other dimensions has opened the possibility for us to understand the structural properties of images that, if seen only in one phase or dimension, would remain as pictures that mimic certain *predictable* behaviors. It is the *unpre-*

dictable that calls... Weather maps and air-flow charts in a room mapped in phase space are only two of hundreds of images that have led to the construction of new knowledge. This is now typical of how computers have quickly revolutionized our world of ideas by expanding our world of images. We are, as a result, moving toward the atypical—and it is the atypical that is both promising and threatening.

The overlapping of multiple cultures, languages, and codes within a singular space in the late-capitalist environment necessitates new techniques aimed at the construction of spatial and material organizations that are continuous but *differentiated* spatialities. As a result of the changes unfolded by late capitalism, it is necessary for us, as architects and urbanists, to recover the coherent aspect of urban structures. Within this realm many previous methods of design become less effective as operative tools.

The *romantic* conception of the designer as the creative individual expected to battle through opposition, preserving his or her creativity, the reference to previous fixed types, or interpretative techniques aiming to unveil new possibilities through an individual's interpretation appear *conservative* insofar as they depend on *received knowledge*. While all that is new is not necessarily better, it is also axiomatic that all that is outmoded is, more or less, *in the way*. The use of symbols, signs, theories, and rhetoric—classical or otherwise—as ways of grounding the ideal or the rational conception of architecture are, arguably, critical modalities that have become inadequate by depending on consensus for their success. Productive of the status quo, though often perceived as *opposed* to the status quo, such measures have within them certain functions that might be extracted. For example, typology has, ever since it was reintroduced in the 1970s, been incapable of explaining or accounting for the production of meaning, which seems to float over architecture anyway and never quite reside within it in any predictable way. The excesses of such methodologies come over to computational architecture in the form of an affective excess that has of late been used to great effect—an excess that indicates that even the most mathematical or "scientific" processes cannot escape some manner of figuration or accumulation of desired or undesired cultural agency. What this indicates is that within material agency is a secret reserve or blank space that allows projections of all types, whether intentionally or accidentally imposed. This sets up the next issue for material agency in that it describes a project of bringing to bear that very cultural agency but without its ideological baggage. Techniques using language and text are also obsolete *as radical operations* since they identify an oppositional priority and seek to introduce the contradictions within such an opposition into the production of built space. Technology has, strangely, unharnessed certain repressions within architecture, and it is only natural that they come floating to the surface as autonomous or sinister affect. To drive the unwanted affect or residue away, in turn, will mean to find and introduce affects that are wholly real versus spectral but without a return to "psychoanalyzing" architecture. Successfully repelling renascent forms of spent and spectral ideology depends on harnessing new forms of knowledge. If engendering outmoded or useless affects within the design of the environment *before the fact* (in an a priori fashion) is problematic, *and it is*, then the central issue for design today becomes the elucidation of methods that generate coherent, non-representational forms that lend themselves to affiliative relationships *after the fact* (in a posteriori manner); that is, techniques that generate projective, progressive arguments rather than interpret, mimic, or represent existing, repressive, or outmoded ones. In such an argument, forms are neutral, or forms that are developed in a neutral manner are then given positive value by their instantiation of progressive environmental and political agency. This is not in itself an anti-historical argument, but it is an argument based on a definitive bias for technical agency and its very own historical path of productive and often radical innovation. Political agency returns without the ideological deformations typical of a priori "arrangements" insofar as the material agency engages a datum that is not anti-ideological but *neutral* and given to the increasingly "rarefied" world of the real. An architectural sensibility, as much as an architectural technology, that embraces the real is effectively also an ethical architecture.

Space-Time and Time-Space
Perhaps the second most important contribution the computer has made to the sciences is the ability to model space and time—to permit it to be compressed into smaller and smaller units creating multiple worlds within multiple worlds, and to paradoxically flip it, creating out of space-time its mirror image in time-space (and vice versa). Not a simple rhetorical device, this distinction indicates that in flipping space-time, virtual worlds also flip conventional

wisdom regarding which came first. Time has always been considered a result of space (even within the continuum defined by Einstein), yet now in the virtual worlds of computational architecture we see the nature of time as First Cause, and we sense literary or artistic antecedents (where time is the metric that defines any space of writing or painting) returning to architecture by the back door. So much for expunging linguistic models? No... The return we sense is the return of artistic agency, not linguistic science, not grammars and certainly not syntactical operations. Beyond structuralism there was always a more austere territory: actually existing things and our exceptional relationship to them (and our exceptionally alienated turn against them in all forms of rote domination), a double bind we have yet to resolve.

Technologies do not merely meet needs but are implicated in the defining and redefining of practice. The role of an architect in this process becomes one of establishing criteria and identifying concepts. The architect is further liberated by being enabled to bring in concepts that are external to the discipline to inform architecture. It is *which* concepts are imported that matters.

Mind after Matter

Every time the relation between ideas and their materialization becomes the subject of discussion, the traditional humanistic positions emerge to claim again the primacy of mind over matter, of the supremacy of the subject to the object. Why? Such a position is increasingly difficult to maintain, as the concept of the *human* has been stretched so far and so thin that it is increasingly difficult to make this definition eventful of anything other than the domination of nature. This increasingly problematic position can be made only from a somewhat nostalgic claim that there is something exceptional called human nature, defining mankind precisely by its artificiality (and divorce from the world as such). Given a religious or theological origin, this problem set is increasingly useless. Giorgio Agamben has referred to it as the "anthropological machine,"[4] and it is mostly, today, an apology for being "human, all too human."

Specifically, within the discipline of architecture, the constant reference to a supposedly eternal "human scale" can be made only from the most con-

4 Giorgio Agamben, *The Open: Man and Animal*, trans. Kevin Attell (Stanford: Stanford University, 2004).

servative of antediluvian positions. It is quite remarkable that such claims are usually made as an ethical crusade that warns us against the dangers of the out-of-control proliferation of materialism, that which leads us into the abyss of the loss of scale, order, ethics, etc. Such a position does not realize the dangers of anthropocentrism, logocentrism, Eurocentrism, or any other version of the claim of an insuperable "human nature" (always backloaded with ideology and ready for war), usually molded upon dominant forms of artificiality. Let us change the subject, then, talk about human agency instead.

The necessary, antithetical approach to this anthropological machine is to define mankind and nature (or mind and matter) as essentially interrelated and *mobile* categories. This is not new. We can point to all manner of philosophers, sages, and mystics, if you like, who have attempted the same destruction of the classical humanist agenda. Rather than understand humanism and materialism (or naturalism) as fundamentally opposed attitudes, the idea is to find a definition that allows a constant feedback between the processes of material transformation that we are undergoing and the structures of thought that inform our *worldly* practices. Basically, the idea is to accept that airplanes, automobiles, computers, statistics, markets, etc. are essentially human, and should therefore be included in the process of defining of the human. This subsumes everything we have touched as part of *our* problem, and therefore part of *our* responsibility. It does not absolve us of caring for the natural world in/for itself, insofar as that natural world is our origin (at least biologically) and our life-support system.

But how does this apply effectively to the practice of architecture—architecture being an activity that is strongly determined by the forces of gravity, the laws of construction, and ergonomic determinations? In all these processes of material organization that characterize our age, is it really possible to find the energy to modify a discipline that has been constructed on the basis of permanence and natural determination?

It is very difficult to make a definitive argument regarding the integration of external factors in the reformulation of the discipline of architecture or, more critically, the reconfiguration of the very ground beneath our feet. This subject becomes even more significant when we are talking about the relationship between the way we think and the domain in which we operate: One could only refer to an eternal or ideal human realm if the field of operation was also of a permanent nature, a Garden of Eden, perhaps. But what happens when the ground—in the broadest sense of the word—shifts, becomes artificial, and ends up utterly fabricated out of the wilful mists of human agency? It would seem to signal the end of paradise, of expulsion from the garden, and of the arrival of endless grief, except it is our condition. As the processes of material organization characteristic of our age are increasingly determined by what economists or sociologists, such as David Harvey, define as regimes of "flexible accumulation," the so-called ground—the extension where our practice unfolds in time and space—becomes deformed, manipulated by a series of mechanisms of temporal and spatial displacement, aimed at controlling the processes of material accumulation in a more flexible manner than previous economic models. How, then, do we develop an architectural practice able to address the potential changes behind these fast-moving processes? If we have been expelled from the garden, and we are all somehow guilty and must be punished, how might we redeem ourselves?

Virtual and Virtuous Architectures

Recently we have witnessed renewed interest in the idea of the *virtual*, triggered perhaps by the increasing availability of Information Technology. Yet this is not enough to explain the massive shift underway as of the last two decades of the twentieth century. The capacity of this technology to model and simulate the behaviour of complex systems and the dynamic representation of built environments raised expectations to the stratosphere that are only now returning to earth with samples of what's out there. What's out there seems to be "unseen" new worlds, worlds that will have to be constructed out of thin air and pixels, before they can then be planted firmly in the earth and be used to any positive effect. This is the now much-vaunted possibility of producing synthetic, virtual environments that will eventually replace reality in the form we know it.

But if this virtual fever is a recent phenomenon associated with the development of Information Technology, the idea of the virtual is not new: virtual stems from the Latin *virtus*, "potential" or "force." The virtual becomes actual once it is made effective, perceptible, or operative. Gilles Deleuze, one of the philosophers most abused by architectural misappropriation in the 1980s and 1990s, explains that the actualization of the virtual is not the same as the realization of the possible. As Brian Massumi has pointed out elsewhere (and Massumi was the translator of Deleuze and Guattari's two-volume *Capitalism and Schizophrenia*), the virtual is just a new name for the "imaginary." Where the realization of the possible is a process of achievement, a development of an existing model, the actualization of the virtual can never reach a state of closure. The virtual always has a multiplicity of possible actualizations and is always the *origin* or the limit of a new lineage rather than the implementation of the possible. This opens up a whole new field of possibilities for the virtual, beyond its more conventional misconception as mere simulacrum or the replacement of the real. The virtual is an artifice that produces a whole new construction or constellation of material agencies, *of the real*; it coexists and intersects with the real, rather than become an alternative reality. It also notably (as the reconstituted imaginary) *reconstructs* worlds. It is not simply a fantastical sideshow to the real or a futuristic "cyclotron" of affects parading before the imagination of possible other worlds. In Deleuze's world, virtualities always already exist. The virtual unfolds potentials beyond the given identities of form, function, and place. As such, it is the very locus of the answer to the problem posed above: what are we to do about being tossed out of the garden?

The poetics of the "aesthetic of disappearance" and the "precession of simulacra," so well described by Paul Virilio and Jean Baudrillard, describe a certain conception of the virtual as the dissolution of the body and space in an emerging virtual world of screens, images, and simulacra. This sort of sinister super-modern aesthetic, which is usually qualified as virtual hell, is actually not at all related to Deleuze's positive conception of the term: rather than constructing a sophisticated surrogate of the real, the virtual would imply opening unprecedented forms of reality, proliferating the real in unexpected directions. It is important to note that, in so turning away from the negative form of virtuality, Deleuze and Guattari also turned against psychoanalytical theory (from Freud to Lacan), as it is the foremost means of negating the real and sublating everything in a system of repressions and superimpositions—the very definition of the *Names-of-the-Father*, Lacan's preferred name for the place of the faceless, demiurgic superego and Lacan's means of dislocating the real and replacing it with the erotic and distended reflections of his version of the everyman, the incurable, neurotic subject.

Information Technology has become a crucial tool for contemporary architecture, if not a new Name-of-the-Father. Yet not so much as a tool for the simulation of reality, but rather as a tool for "modeling" reality, it in the broadest sense of the term allows the architect to model worlds in the absence of verifiable data, simulating new behavior for new and old, or new-old, systems. Information Technology becomes in this way an ideal tool for the production of the virtual, not for the reproduction of the real. Computers allow us not only to mimic a pre-existing reality but also to construct organizations and images that we had never seen before, and that we never could have seen—and, therefore, could never have imagined—without the model. If the realization of the possible is a matter of interpretation, or re-description of a given set of identities, the actualization of the virtual has to escape resemblance and requires tools that will allow us to see—and, therefore, to imagine, to conceptualize—what we have never seen before. Virtuality is the liberation of repressed agency in such a scenario, and fully comports in Deleuzian terms with materiality (purely immanent orders freed of humanist agendas or interpretive apparatuses that render them—in classical terms—mere representations of reality). Virtualities present a back door to Eden in the form of a reconstituted freedom from both benign and malignant historical agency. The virtual potential of IT is a Lacanian Name-of-the-Father only in the sense that it has the potential to swerve toward the production of its own set of repressive machinations, enslaving where it once might have performed the opposite function. It is all about mechanism or apparatus versus anything purely virtual. Virtuality is innocent; apparatuses enslave.

The images along this text are related to the progressive automation of human activities that we have witnessed in the last decades. From the robotization of the factories and the radical advances in prosthetics to the CCTV surveillance systems that have become a part of contemporary public space; from the digitalization of sound and motion image and the explosion of sensing technologies to the mechanization of war, we have witnessed since the 1970's the progressive replacement of human agency with machines, of which these images are a testimony. If Generation X emerges with the Vietnam war, we are now in a world where wars are fought remotely by machines.

Abstract Matters

The debate that followed the development of serial composition in the postwar era constitutes one of the most interesting discussions about composition and organization within artistic practices, and lays down important foundations for the clarification of these subjects, not only within the musical discipline, but across most artistic practices. Having been asked to discuss about the role of abstraction and informational technologies in architecture, I believe that the musical model presents a very clear picture of the range of possibilities that abstraction can produce in an architectural practice.

The figure of Boulez is crucial within this debate, not only because of his frenetic theoretical activities but also because of the multiplicity of perspectives from which his practice unfolds. Boulez, who had already become the *enfant terrible* of postwar French music at the tender age of twenty-five, developed his career through several simultaneous practices: composer, orchestra director, critic, teacher of analysis and composition, organizer of concerts, and director of IRCAM. It is possibly this position across different activities that forced him to develop a unique capacity to operate on an abstract level: That was probably the only way of producing a certain level of coherence across the spectrum of his diverse activities.

Moreover, his capacity to operate at a high level of abstraction is the instrument that produces the necessary degree of alienation to radically question the established sensibilities, without having to abandon the specificity of his discipline. Boulez is by no means an unconscious creator, but rather somebody who is able to project a high degree of awareness and technical skill beyond the limits of established discipline, to turn them into productive, rather than reproductive processes. He remains constantly aware of his evolution and the historical, theoretical and technical framing of his work.

Speculative activity is a constant requirement of his creative practice, as the instrument able to project techniques beyond their merely reproductive role. Consequently, his activities as interpreter and teacher will take a similar projective—rather than retrospective—direction. When Boulez directs Wagner, he is not trying to be faithful to a particular historical moment or to incarnate the composer, but rather to project Wagner's work onto his own work, to problematize rather than recreate. Rather than a reconstruction of historical truth, his interpretative practices are a research into the virtualities within older forms, and their possible resonance with his contemporary practice as a composer. Time and history become a web of possible links with no single direction containing simultaneously various forms of development. It is the capacity of abstraction that allows Boulez to advance the techniques of serial composition, not by growing them organically but by proliferating them to the extreme in order to extract new effects. The neutralization of a tonal center extends towards the subversion of rhythm, pitch, volume, and pulse. Yet what is even more interesting is the comparison between Boulez, Stockhausen, and Cage, as describing a whole range of possibilities for abstraction as a musical matter.

Both Boulez and Stockhausen were disciples of Messiaen, and both inherited his interest in rhythm and his ambition for unity in the work. Both chose as a departure point in their research the late work of Webern, characterized by a radical athematicity, a high degree of abstraction, and extremely rigorous serial techniques. From this precedent, they both developed the intellectual rigor necessary to use formal analysis not as a technique of reproduction but as a projective tool.

However, while Stockhausen focused on research with electro-acoustic media, Boulez remained within the most conventional musical textures, wary of the effectiveness of electronic media to produce musical affects. It is through the reflection on the question of coherence and compositional unity, and the different kinds of technical apparatus, that they explored what increasingly defined the domain of research for each one of them.

The question that appears in front of both composers relates to the ambition of challenging the traditional forms of musical matter, their centers and striations. The codification of musical matter is based on the establishment of a grid of a certain resolution—the scale, the compass—able to capture time, vibration, and accent in recognizable forms. The great discovery of Stockhausen was to realize that the real potential of electro-acoustic instruments was the possibility of increasing the resolution of the striation grid of pitch or rhythm beyond the human capacity of perception, so that form becomes pure matter, and matter the plane of consistency of every form. All of this without having to abdicate absolute control over these matters.

For Boulez, who was deeply involved in the questions of interpretation, fidelity, etc. as a director, the real challenge was the possibility of constructing new musical forms of such complexity that they would reach consistency at a level beyond consciousness. His reflection on the subject of consistency is the origin of his categorization of time in smooth and striated terms, the core of his system of rhythmic forms. If the scale or the compass allows the codification, and therefore the reproducibility of a composition, they also imply radical limitations in the possibilities of local differentiation of musical space, as these differentiations are limited to those established by an overall, generic, striated structure. In the case of Stockhausen, the unity of the composition is achieved through the transformation of every acoustic phenomenon—pitch, rhythm, attack—to vibration. In the case of Boulez, the consistency of the work is achieved through the form of organization of musical matter. His preference for pitched percussion, probably the most striated form of music, is remarkable in this attempt to produce smoothness with striated musical matter. In his *Structures*, the idea of total serialism—not only of the tonal intervals but also of the rhythmic structure—raises the complexity of the structure to a point where the most striated kind of matter acquires a smooth consistency, in which it becomes difficult to recognize parts or striations of musical space.

Smoothness or consistency is reached here at a different level from the one where the musical phenomenon is perceived through the generation of a vectorial space within the striated orders.

No less revealing is the correspondence between Boulez and Cage. Both were interested in experimental practice, in the logic of production as the very basis of composition. Both also shared a fascination for the impersonal, for the alienation of authorship. In both of them there is a consequent rejection of causal technique, and neither of them will set as an objective the a priori achievement of certain musical effects or the expression of the authors' subjectivity, but rather the resort to some form of automatic process or device, capable of producing the unexpected, to trigger the virtual. Both start the composition as a diagram, as an open form that will define itself only in the process of construction, keeping the work open and mutable, even after the composition has taken shape. Both operate through matrices, diagrams, numbers, and other techniques of abstraction, as a vehicle of alienation and exploration of new musical effects. However, their paths diverge to occupy radically opposed positions. For Cage, the diagram was determined purely by the matter of the composition, basically organized as a series of patterns or groups to take definitive shape only in the moment of performance, in order to incorporate the contingencies of every situation. On the contrary, for Boulez the diagram was in itself the vehicle of determination of the composition, providing internal consistency to every element within the overall structure. It is also the mechanism that maintains the work in a permanent state of openness and development, as in an infinite process of construction. In fact, most of his work remained unfinished, typically being performed before reaching a state of completion, and remaining in constant evolution throughout his career.

Cage developed his method through the introduction of arbitrary and random processes as a mechanism of openness and search for the unknown, but also as a technique that is able to integrate the specific situation of every performance, making contingency a crucial productive force. Flipping coins, employing the I Ching, or simply giving enormous freedom to the interpreter to reorganize the composition becomes part of his usual technique. There is in these techniques an implicit recognition of the factors that prefigure the composer's work, and the explicit attempt to liberate every moment or element of the composition from the overarching structure of the composition.

Boulez followed the opposite path by proliferating compositional techniques in an extreme degree of abstraction and complexity, by using mathematical algorithms, diagrams, and other devices able to trigger the virtual, the latent underneath established forms and sensibilities. The search for absolute coherence between matter and form, and between the various elements and the overall structure, is the fundamental aim of his compositional method. The unknown emerges through the systematization of the compositional process, as a form of retaining control and determination, while falling neither into the reproduction of forms, nor into expressionism. Unlike Cage's dissolution of the author in arbitrary processes, Boulez constantly states the determining role of the composer in the construction of the work, and the crucial role of the compositional technique in any possibility of innovation.

Despite his broad cultural affiliations, Boulez's project was an attempt to escape from any form of translation or interpretation of parallel disciplines or processes. There is no desire to translate poetic, scientific, or philosophic language into musical structure, as in Stockhausen, or to incorporate life into art, as in Cage. Composition is for Boulez fundamentally a process of construction and internal consistency, and despite his multi-disciplinary texts, his work is always concerned with problems of strictly disciplinary nature. In opposition to Cage's mysticism and pantheistic acceptance of the event and the contingent, and to Stockhausen's conceptualism and romanticism, Boulez chooses to be a craftsman, a sophisticated builder.

The images illustrating this text refer to the composers that held some of the most interesting debates about electronic music: Boulez, Cage, Stockhausen and Xenakis. The discussions are particularly relevant to the discipline of architecture, and are one of my most cherished references.

Published in *Quaderns d'Arquitectura i Urbanisme* n. 205-206, Barcelona, 1994

Message to the Engine Drivers

I cannot say much about the whole fifty years of *Quaderns* because my biography is far shorter than that, but I can certainly reflect on the last ten.

My interest in the journal was instrumental at first: when I was a student in Madrid. *Quaderns* was the only Spanish journal which determinedly opted for a more abstract form of discussion, beyond mere factual description of works or figures within strictly disciplinary categories. Thus *periphery, void,* dirty realism... suddenly became problems of architecture, and architecture became a form of cultural debate.

This made *Quaderns* a major source of information for those of us who were interested in expanding the cultural and political potential of the practice of architecture. Later, a casual encounter with Josep Lluís Mateo in Berlin gave me the opportunity to collaborate occasionally with the journal and to get to know the engine from a different viewpoint.

One of the journal's distinctive strategies was the adoption of an abstract thematic structure which made it possible to approach the discussion from a multitude of different positions, neither strictly disciplinary nor strictly local. The problem of the periphery as an operative space—a logical object of attention by a Catalan cultural institution at a time of redefinition of the national space—was made extensive to techniques of analysis and modeling on the territorial, urban, cultural and disciplinary levels.

The success of this strategy of deterritorialisation was its outward orientation—outside of the discipline and of the local scene—, instead of trying to re-establish a centre based on the construction of a local identity. This redefinition of the *periphery* through an *externalisation* of references is probably the key to the success of *Quaderns* as the only journal of a Spanish professional association to achieve international recognition: a veritable machine of productive articulation between global processes and the local sphere.

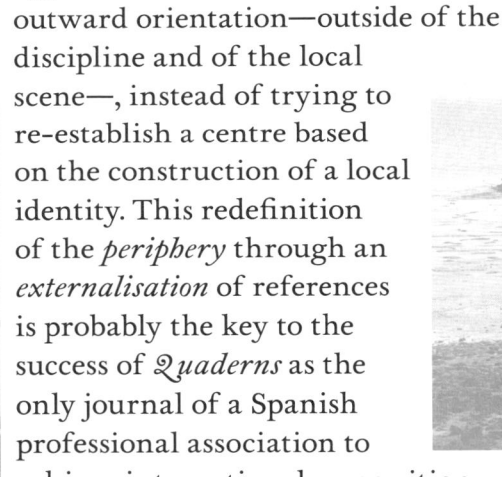

This for me is the most important characteristic of the engine which Josep Lluís Mateo managed to assemble and which the current editorial staff has inherited. Not only them, but probably many other architects of my generation, in the sense that *Quaderns* is a paradigmatic structure of a contemporary space where global does not necessarily mean void and *local* is not synonymous with disconnected.

I am not proposing here a tradition to follow, but rather trying to identify which are the most effective traits of the engine, those with most future for the magazine. It is like deciding which line of microprocessors is worth developing: a strategic error here would mean the firm's bankruptcy.

The most lucid architects from the generation that preceeds mine pointed instinctively towards the possibility of a new practice, but in no way have they resolved the question; indeed the structures that embraced these practices exist only in very precarious forms. A first reason for congratulating *Quaderns* in this 50th Anniversary is on the fact that it has managed to survive intact from a period which saw the demise of many periodical journals that originated within the milieu of the Spanish professional associations as a result of the euphoria of the eighties.

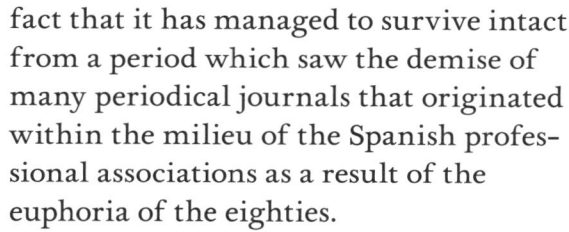

If Josep Lluís Mateo managed to use that energy to create a new *assemblage,* we have Manuel Gausa to thank for having steered a straight course through the backlash of the waves. There are two editorial strategies which I consider critical for this success. The first is the slowing down of the engine through a certain *re-territorialisation* in the discipline as revealed in the previous period (the territory, the landscape, the void, technology...). Keeping to the same strategies as in the eighties would have been inappropriate in times of crisis—and possibly catastrophic, as other experiences have shown—if it was to deal successfully with a profession mostly entrenched in positions of resistance.

The second intelligent strategy is the maintenance of a segmented and more rigidly regulated thematic structure than in the previous period, with possibly less brilliant though undoubtedly more solid results, more adapted to the rigors of the nineties.

I believe that the maintenance of *Quaderns* as an institution of international articulation through an adaptation of strategies is one of the great achievements of the present editorial team. I know from experience the type of resistance which one encounters in any attempt to question the limits: to my surprise, I have recently verified how even those "international" institutions least suspected of being provincial systematically develop areas of bureaucratic resistance to the globalization process. Not to mention the degree of nervousness reached in institutions supposedly devoted to culture when one is not a local resident...

Those who still use bureaucracies as the means to construct a local or disciplinary identity should be reminded that such forms of identity tend to be ineffectual in an inevitably globalised space. In this sense, the contribution of *Quaderns* to the construction of an identity for Catalan architecture has been crucial and paradigmatic for what some theorists already call the *post-colonial* space: the construction of local identity through its estrangement, the production of landscapes instead of *places,* as Lyotard says. Landscape as a domain without meaning, origin or destination, the result of estrangement (*depaysement*): "There is a landscape when the mind is transported from one form of sensitive matter to another, but the mind still retains the sensorial organization characteristic of the former, or at least memory of it: the Earth seen from the moon for a terrestrial.[1]

As a machine for estrangement and *deterritorialisation*, as an instrument with which to build landscapes, *Quaderns* has proven to be most effective when it comes to establishing a local identity. It would be hard to derive the identity of the much acclaimed Barcelona School from a series of vernacular traditions or as an attempt to construct a *place* through the identification of pre-existing types, figures or idiosyncracies. It might be carrying things too far, but there are odd analogies of style between the emblematic characteristics of the Barcelona School—a preference for complex geometry, for traces as opposed to figures, for a delicate, nearly ephemeral construction...— and the techniques of estrangement and abstraction, of construction of *landscapes*—instead of places— which characterises *Quaderns*.

This text, written on the occasion of the 50th anniversary of Quaderns, the magazine of Barcelona's Architects' Association, aims to depict Catalonian architecture in the last 40-50 years as deeply interested in landscape, in the broader sense of the term, and Quaderns being an integral part of that perspective. The illustrations have been selected from contemporary artists involved with land-art and environmental art: Olafur Eliasson, James Turrell, Richard Long and Robert Smithson represent those parallel tendencies which have been developing in art since the 1970's.

1   Jean-François Lyotard, "Scapeland" in *L'Inhumain: Causeries sur le Temps* (Éditions Galilée, Paris, 1988).

Brief of a studio at Columbia University's
GSAPP, New York, Fall 2001

Back to the Hard Core

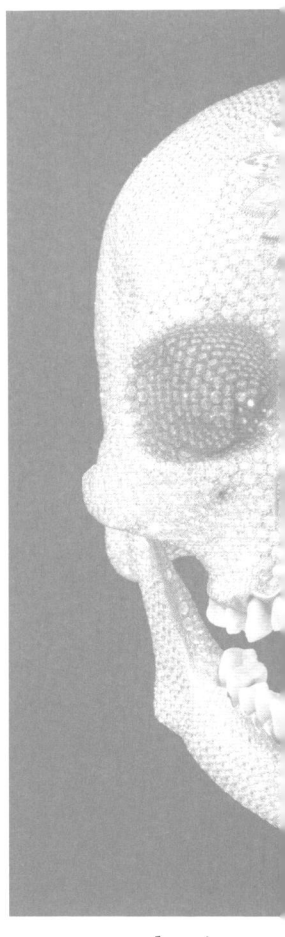

During the past fifteen years, the most interesting architectural experimentation has coalesced around the possibility of broadening an excessively hardened discipline to include a variety of concerns of an external nature, many of which might further its operative capacities in the face of ever-changing demands. This has been implemented by resorting to abstraction as a mechanism, deliberately operating outside of the manipulation of architectural language. Two types of abstract devices, theoretical discourse and data processing, have constituted the two fundamental mechanisms aimed at the inclusion of economic, social, political, or psychological factors into the discipline. However productive this process may have been in terms of generating architectural knowledge, it has failed to define a system of assessment that is internal to the discipline, or to explain how the inclusion of those concerns has caused the architectural qualities of the products to evolve. A progressive architecture is supposed to erase the gender divide, increase the sales of a mall, or decrease the level of CO_2 in the atmosphere, but, even if successful in identifying new fields of operation, however prosaic, this approach does not guarantee the quality of the architectural product, and, in fact, does not even question it. Social equality, net profits, or environmental sustainability can certainly be achieved without the involvement of architecture. One wonders, as a result, about the very nature of cyclical fashions within architecture; and theory and technology are but the two most obvious examples.

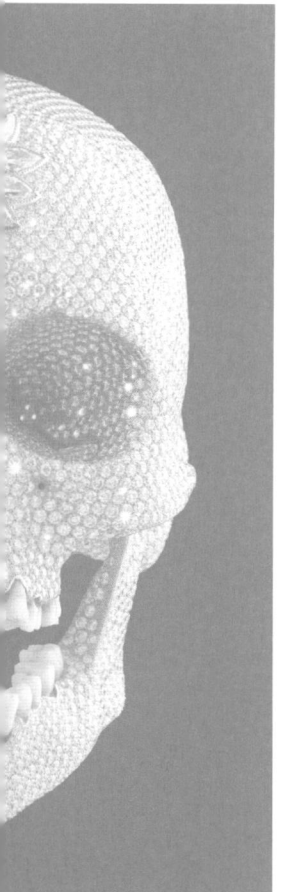

Architecture is primarily a discipline of material organization, and the purpose of architectural research is fundamentally the synthesis of new materials, in the broadest sense of the term *material*. What escapes mere fashionable turns *in and out* of material research is what is always operating in the background anyway: material agency. As Lenin said, one cannot have a revolution without a revolution. Yet most revolutions in architecture are not really revolutions at all, but, instead, *fashion statements*. The true revolution always occurs through the *substrate* (material agency) not the *superstructure* (theory).

Without renouncing the achievements of abstraction, an admittedly powerful tool to broaden the field of operation, the discipline needs to reset its frame of reference, using as raw material the accumulated knowledge of the field. To pursue our analogy further, theory is Lenin in Zurich, and practice or material agency is Lenin in St. Petersburg.

Typological precedents are both the essence of those materials that architectural knowledge has managed to synthesize in the past (as archive), examples of complex material organizations, and they need to become the subject and object of architectural research: A church is a material assemblage of ritual choreographies and structural systems; a skyscraper is a hybrid composite of real-estate processes, structural technology, and mechanized circulation and environmental control; an airport is a mix of circulation systems and security systems... A typology is a particular blend of selected materials with a certain performance; the history of typologies already constitutes an invaluable resource for understanding how the material organization of a particular scale performs and is constructed. The adoption of a typological form is, in essence, a *neutral* gesture, though most often it is also a *conservative* gesture. To submit typology to a materialist critique is a *radical* gesture. The appropriated form might undergo manifold changes to its recognizability, but it remains part of the equation nonetheless. Such changes are materially and historically determined.

Within a type, the proportions and hierarchies between the different components can be abstracted and rendered diagrammatic in order to be purposefully modified, distorted, or diversified in the process of being adapted to a particular environment. Hierarchies, scales, proportions, critical ratios, or thresholds regulate the performance and consistency of the synthesized materials: beyond a certain scale, an airport grows satellites because the walking distance between the check-in and the gates becomes excessive to maintain in a single envelope; Gothic cathedrals evolve from single to multiple vaults to increase their capacity; auditoriums grow balconies to increase their capacity without losing acoustic qualities; an I-beam evolves into a Boyd beam and then into a truss as its depth increases to span larger distances, and its flange becomes structurally ineffective; a skyscraper shifts from post-and-beam structure, to cross-braced, to stability cores, to multiple tubes as it reaches higher... Material qualities become the vehicle that establishes continuity across the different typologies of material organizations.

There are already quite precise thresholds that explain these kinds of *becoming*, and perhaps this is where we could measure architectural performance; learn to operate from within the discipline, at the hard core.

In order to do this, rather than trying to synthesize new materials from scratch, we need to depart from existing typologies as our raw material—those will be our "primitives"—and try to develop them in a certain environment. Underlining the phenotypical side of typology—not as a mechanism for reproduction, but as material for proliferation—allows us to establish a basis for assessment within the discipline. It is the equivalent of arriving at Finland Station.

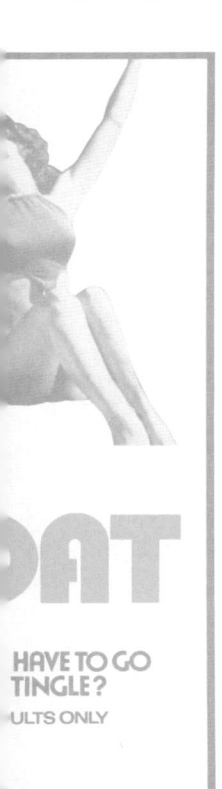

Abstracting a typology into material parameters, understanding its scale of operation, and its critical thresholds, may enable us to extract its prototypical qualities. Prototypes are technical and material mediators, able to transfer information into form and constituting responsive devices of internal transference of information. Prototypes contain in themselves the potential to absorb interference, the capacity to adjust to local contexts, and the potential to incarnate as much as to virtualize and export information into other material components. In this context, projects become as generic as they are specific, as models for internal differentiation and responsiveness constitute the core, relevance, and interest of the project. Only a beginning, the rediscovery and redeployment of material agency against the conservative and hybrid practices of the past and the present is the beginning of "the revolution." Where it might lead is the question that remains, ineluctably, *unanswerable*. Yet material agency leads straight back into historical agency, and, therefore, it is the *march of time* and the *laws of motion* that will provide the answers.

There are two image illustrating this text that refer to the idea of Hard Core: one is a photograph of Damien Hirst's *For the Love of God*—a diamond-encrusted skull—which refers to the return to the basics that is preached in the brief of this studio in Columbia University in 2000. The proposition of returning to a typological approach, as the skeleton of the discipline, and the necrophilic tendencies denoted by this return to the type, resonate deeply with Hirst's skull. The other is the poster of Gerard Damiano's *Deep Throat*, a film that inaugurates an era of massive development of the hard core porn industry which shadows the growth of a generation, and that bred some deep typological lineages of its own.

Peter Macapia, Interview with Alejandro Zaera-Polo
in *Log* #3, New York, Fall 2004

The Material Grain of Geometry: A Conversation with Alejandro Zaera-Polo

Introduction
One of the crucial problems in late 20th century architecture is consistency, from, say, the diagram to construction. But it is also an ancient problem of methodology. One finds an interesting version of this and its relation to design logics both general and specific in Vitruvius's account of the Greek temple. An ontologically consistent and therefore beautiful design, he suggests, depends on pure Platonic geometric forms. This general law has its basis in another general law, the proportional relations of the human form and harmony. But once the temple is constructed, geometry has a tendency to drift, and now certain interventions become necessary, such as *entasis*, in order to provide consistency between concept and performance, law and event, truth and sense. In other words this second introduction of geometry covers not general laws but rather that which is too specific, the remainder that disturbs the equilibrium of the general. And while it is true that this remainder is folded back into the building's general performance through the economy of a geometrical "technique," the word "geometry," indeed the concept of geometry, and all that it implies by technique, no longer means the same thing. It operates between a general law on the symbolic level of

form (*eidos*) and ideality, and as specific instrument of intervention which leaves us with the question of consistency.

—**Peter Macapia:** You are interested in the methodological problem of "consistency in performance," but how does the consistency of geometry, for example, function in your practice with regard to the general and the specific?
—**Alejandro Zaera-Polo:** I think I am interested in consistency in its most general sense. Probably this is a reaction to the architectural culture where we were educated, which was more interested in questions of fragmentation, disjunction, juxtaposition, etc. I believe that to devise arguments of consistency has become a critical contemporary question, on a political, social, and cultural level. This is a paradigmatic problem of our time, between cultures, geographies, populations… A similar problem appears in space between a whole and a singularity, not only in terms of performance but also in terms of physical organization. And geometry plays a primary role in establishing consistency across spatial domains at every scale. I would claim that geometry is related to the specific and to the solution of specific questions, but always as an argument of consistency with larger domains. I am not interested in Vitruvius's introduction of what one might call the reparative; Vitruvius thinks that what is important for an architect to do is operate or perform on a more, I wouldn't even say generic, but rather paradigmatic basis.

In fact you could also talk about general geometry in different terms, in terms more operative than the ones Vitruvius uses. You can talk about Modernist or Gothic types of generic geometry that are not necessarily grounded in some kind of theoretical relationship to, say, a system of universal proportion, but rather that function in terms of a generic mode or geometric operation that relates to a non-specific domain.
—**PM:** What is interesting about the Gothic period is the reason why… Geometrically, it is an exception to classical theories of geometry. I mean that although certain types of symbolic geometry were retained in plan, the structural logic was not. That type of geometry emerged from the logic of material organization in such a way as to locate structure and, let's say, drainage as expressions of the same system (and here the connection between Aquinas's *Summa Theologica* and Aristotle's logic and *Metaphysics*—the comprehensive connection between the general and the specific—is important). In the 19th century one begins to see a different order of geometry.
—**AZP:** Within the history of the discipline, geometry has been a means of description. But as a theoretical problem the issue is quite different. People who theorize architecture only theorize geometry when it is related to some kind of paradigm that is somehow ideal. Or rather, geometry only acquires a specific set of meanings when it is identified as a paradigm.

I would argue that in the 19th Century, for example in Durand, there is another form of geometry that is neither the specific geometry to solve purely local problems, nor is it an ideal geometric paradigm. It is a generic type of geometry that operates across a multitude of cases. And in some ways I wonder if the more formalized geometrical paradigms or more formalized theories about geometry are nothing but a sort of dressing of some kind of generic or typological modes of geometrical practices. Durand represents an operative geometry that didn't emerge out of an aesthetic theory of architecture, but rather functioned as a means of extracting certain modes of operation that had to do with real practice, and which were to some degree generic. They develop consistency across multiple cases rather than proposing an ideal, formal geometry to be deployed onto specific cases. The Enlightenment produced certain modes of geometrical performances that are generic and not simply theoretical. Or let's say that they are only theoretical as far as some of these generic modes of geometric operation have been somehow captured into a theoretical machine.

—**PM:** Yes, but that means Durand is simply emblematic for advanced 19th century architectural thought. Hübsch, Bötticher, Viollet-le-Duc, Semper, Choisy, and even Ruskin are part of the legacy of Durand; they effectively overturned previous classical theories that based the logic of design on mimesis, on the ideality of nature's general laws.

—**AZP:** Do you mean that after the 19th Century the notion of method or technique somehow becomes emancipated from a certain logic of representation?

—**PM:** Yes; the concept of architectural "style," they would claim, emerges not from some idealized paradigm, as in Blondel, but rather from specific material relations operating within a given sociocultural context that emerged historically, over time. They were relations not of any representative content, but rather functions. Typology and style are, they would say, the material expression of these relations. For example, when Viollet-le-Duc attempted to reinvent the typology of the market hall, he did it around features of pure performance, i.e., managing emerging urban density—he raised it off the street. This of course brought with it new structural concepts, but also new material ones. The new typology derived from a specificity always latent in the urban condition, but previously unavailable. Or rather, this strategy, this type of analysis, allows for moments of specificity to accumulate.

Similarly, the geometry that emerged in the construction phase of Yokohama, as opposed to the competition design phase, acquired, I would say, a new kind of specificity. Its ontology has changed. Or rather, you invented a new ontology within it.

—**AZP**: So, you think that the competition part of the project is somehow a more generic form of geometry, and in the second part of the development the different design that the geometrical notions of the project become transformed because of a set of more concrete problems? Maybe it is an idealistic perception, but I would like to think there is no substantial difference in the approach to geometry between the two phases. The fundamental difference lies in the *type* of geometry that we used. Geometry is a device that enables us to construct the project, construct the form, to generate the form. And I think this is in some ways similar between the two phases, and the idea, for example, of using a single geometry to generate consistency across the project also continues between the competition stage and the construction stage.

—**PM**: That's true. But as a tool it no longer means the same thing. The instrumental features by which it captures continuity—topological, programmatic, and structural, not only laterally and axially, but also vertically and horizontally—that has changed.

—**AZP**: Perhaps. The geometry during the construction phase is in my opinion more sophisticated at producing continuity than the geometry we had at the competition time. At the competition time we used a geometry that is fundamentally Cartesian in the sense that it is referenced to a center, to an origin, and to a kind of orthogonal axial reference system. When we swap to what we call the "topological grid," the geometry is more referred to the moment in which we are joining pieces so it becomes locally referred. So there's no longer an overall reference system, although there is continuity, consistency across the different sections of the building. The nature of the geometrical problem is just different. But maybe you should insist on this difference; I'm actually very interested in that kind of reading, if you think there is a fundamental change in our approach to using geometry as a device for generating the form of the project.

—**PM**: But there is no consistency when you move from a series of folding surfaces, from which you extract sectional cuts—which defined the original design logic—into a curve that is based on a template of seven radii. That is an inventive move, not reparative. The project emerged under a new type of geometrical specificity and, at the same time, consistency. It is quite common for designers to generate a form, then take cuts, and then derive a constructional geometry. But this is reverse engineering, and in the end you did not do that.

—AZP: And I think that is also a certain geometrical system that relates to the achievement of particular architectural effects; you chop up the building in planes, and those planes then provide the structure as a series of free sections... We simply shifted the geometrical system because the types of problems that we encountered on the scale of assembling the building were of a different nature than when we had to assemble the program and the circulation. And so it is true that there is a change of intention but a very fundamental change of geometrical system. But it is not a change in how we use geometry: We always use geometry as a way of generating form. The question is, what are the problems in the generation of form that you encounter in the process of implementation of a project?

—PM: But this points to an interesting question: Is the cut a geometrical operation or rather a diagrammatic one?

—AZP: First of all, it is not the cut, but rather a series of cuts. And with those cuts you blend, or you eliminate a kind of lamination of the section. This is a technique to produce certain architectural effects that we probably picked up from Rem. Look at the project of the Grand Bibliothèque, where the technique allows him to move freely in section... This is very much the point of departure for Yokohama: If we do many parallel sections, we will be able to blend the levels, and then we are going to be able to erase the striations of the section.

—PM: But one doesn't usually design 300 sections and *then* acquire a folded surface. One starts with the surface as an organization of specific qualities. The cut is a generic notation, and then it becomes geometricized. It is operational, it is descriptive, before it is geometrical. I think that within the construction phase, you reinvented geometry's specificity. This is what you said:

"The primary challenge was how to reconcile three-dimensional geometry with a geometry that, through folding, was essentially axial. Thus far, we have discovered unique geometric and formal emergences that have evolved form within the project itself, and have pre-empted external formal or geometric ideologies imposed from without."

This is about geometry's specificity as much as it is about the relation between the general to the specific, but with one important difference. One begins to define that relation from the side of the specific. The paradigm comes to be written from within the empirical rather than the conceptual domain. That is what you did with geometry.

—AZP: For me, geometry is a device to

achieve certain effects of the assemblage of materials. It is purely instrumental, and its theorization emerged a posteriori. This is a different approach to what, let's say, Peter Eisenman will do. He will say Cartesian geometry is wrong, is obsolete, and we should change it. It may even differ from Greg Lynn's insistence in the technical milieu as the primary source of disciplinary evolution… you have to use splines to produce contemporary buildings… Despite the fact that I share with them many common interests, we probably operate in a slightly different mode. And it's a very interesting idea to talk about the difference between a generic and a concrete or local form of geometry.

—**PM**: What is interesting is when the ideality of geometry loses its consistency, but consistency itself is not lost; it has migrated to a different geometry, a different material organization. I think that is what you did, but I think it can also be located in other types of architectural performance, such as Tati's *Playtime,* where he finds moments where the orthogonality of grid begins to oppose itself. He locates specific material organizations that point to a very different diagram than modernist rational planning. The tilt window or the door become spatial hinges for comic dialogue—between programs, spaces, economic classes, professions, as well as sites… Without that consistency, continuity and, I would argue, geometry is lost, at least its instrumentality. Without that consistency you have a mélange. Lynn's Presbyterian church certainly aimed at that consistency, but you notice the problem when the envelope behaves more as an attached surface, and you get an awkward lamination of I-beams.

—**AZP**: The fact that you are adjusting a complex surface geometry to series of striated conventional elements, as in Greg's church, is not inferior as a kind of technique to the one that we used in Yokohama. It's just an assemblage of a different type of materials that produce a different effect. The Yokohama is different simply because we had the luxury of using a less conventional construction system. It opened for us the freedom to operate with a certain type of geometry. But if we couldn't get the budget or if we had a different project manager that didn't allow us to go to into the exploration of these techniques, I am not sure what the effect would have been.

This has been in the past the object of several discussions with Peter

Eisenman. When you talk about operative geometry, forget the paradigms, forget about genericness, or theoretical approaches. One has to think more specifically about the concrete problems of assembling the building. Peter will say "Well, finally the building has to define somehow the conventions of doing architecture. And if you are telling me if anything goes because it doesn't matter for this kind of problem of putting together things in a consistent manner, then it doesn't matter whether you are using the conventional profiles to build the surface or not."

And in a way I would sustain that. I would say well, if the problem is that you cannot do anything but use profiles, then you have to define the system so that it becomes a generative process. But it is not necessarily less interesting as a problem or less consistent as a result.

—PM: But I think Greg is also interested in that consistency (he calls it rigor). The Predator house generates that correlation at the very beginning of the design process, rather than reverse-engineer it. If you look at the geometry of the Predator, it utilizes a kind of geometrical specificity identified by Bernard Cache. Cache applied Euclid's fifth axiom not to straight lines, but rather to lines with embedded curvature. As a result, the lines ran parallel *and* self-intersected—a point at which the geometrical begins to acquire the potential of a diagram—and thus pointed to something inconsistent within the general law, something too specific. I think Greg looks for an inconsistency in geometry in order to produce a new specificity, and then, I would say, he uses that specificity to redefine, for example, "envelope" and its relation to "site." It's no longer about the experimental technique, it's no longer about simply generating technique, it is about transforming certain general categories of architecture according to its internal criteria.

—AZP: Yes, that is what Eisenman would say: "Operation, operation, but so what? Finally, how are you addressing the problems of architecture as a discipline? In order to approach discipline you will have to make some kind judgement."

—PM: So the question is, how do you define that interiority of geometry in your practice?

—AZP: There is a certain predisposition—even in the work we developed before Yokohama—for using geometrical diagrams as devices for generating the form of the building. For me the idea of geometry has always been the same, the vigorous constraints that geometry gives you: I like the feeling that you cannot move a lot. Composition, for example, doesn't allow for similar forms of research. I think one of the inventive things about Tati and his description of the modern world is this kind of strange effect of certain generic organizations being applied to everyday life, the kind of new psychological situation that they produce. This is also something I'm very interested in. I am interested in it because I think that otherwise your activity becomes almost tautological. It is as if you say, "I'm a creator," "I'm an author," "I want to do this, and I'll do it." Full stop. There's no generative moment in the process. Whereas if you are able to set up the problem so that the geometrical production of the object mediates your intentions, the results have at least the potential to become more interesting than what you could have imagined. I believe that just by using interferences between systems, you will not be able to release latent potentials without necessarily rejecting intentionality and authorship. It's always a kind of mediated authorship. For example, Libeskind has often tried to set up a system that is not readily claiming effects in the architectural realm but on an external realm to produce unexpected effects in the architecture realm. (Even if the final reason is obviously to produce architectural effects…) In the case of Eisenman, he will tell you that the purpose is to produce architectural effects, but the techniques he uses are more a kind of detour from architectural problems in order to come back to them with a fresher mind. Probably the difference with them is that we are setting up our targets within the architectural realm —hence we do not deny authorship or intentionality—and we are using the mediation of specifically architectural techniques between the statement of our intentions and the product.

—**PM**: Do you think this rigor is generalizable, or is it becoming inherent to some particular category of your work?

—**AZP**: I think it's more the emergence of "fields of operation" that we were not aware of or thought irrelevant; we had not embedded them into our system to the point where we would think about them as generative. They were simply something to resolve. The exposure that we had the last few years in the sense of being involved in the processes of construction has been mainly productive to opening other domains of generation of form and organization that we were not aware of. You now understand how these forces too can become generative.

The Material Grain of Geometry

One of the things I would like to discuss is the issue of developing from the bottom up with regard to particular local emergences. Currently we are using some of the ideas that started to emerge out of the Columbia studio about typologies. The studio concerned itself with rediscovering an interest in typology and then trying to formulate a way in which typology is not just a device or an instrument or a tool to replicate organizations, but a tool that allows you as an architect to generate a basic material for the production of architecture. And one of the things I am more and more interested in now is the idea of the species as a potential reformulation of problem of type.
—**PM**: Can you say more about what you mean by species? I mean the term is of course related to both Aristotle and Euclid. For Aristotle, species is linked to that which is "specific," something that exists, in the mundane sense of that word. In fact the Latin term *specere* means to perceive, and it is ontologically distinct from that which is general, *genesthai*—to be born, origin. It also appears in Euclid's theory of forms. What is interesting is that Aristotle distinguished between that which was specific, and that which was too specific, which he called the accidental, and of which he said there can be no science. This is why I was interested in Vitruvius's statement in the first place.
—**AZP**: I think this is related to the general and the particular and the problem of process as something that organizes from the top down or the bottom up. When we started working at the AA we were very interested in the idea of generation from the bottom up, and the use of materials that were extra-disciplinary. You look at certain material organizations, you abstract them, you manipulate them with certain intentions, and you evolve the product into something that you don't know exactly what it's going to become but that almost generates itself out of certain materials that you have discovered in the brief. But the assessment of the work is always very difficult. Difficult to say why a product becomes relevant, in what way you can test it. And I think what came out of working like this for a few years was that we needed to establish some form of reference that was external to the bottom, to the kind of material that starts assembling through a number of procedures into a product. And that's when we also started thinking that the only device with which we were able to assess the work was actually our own disciplinary education.

I went through a typical Spanish education that was actually very type-based. You study how to do a house, and then how to do a school, etc., and you learn architecture by experimenting with types that are already more or less consistent as formal organizations. And that way you can assess the work in respect to an evolution of the type; you have a system of reference. The trouble with the non-typological education that I was myself practicing at the AA is that it removes possible disciplinary references and therefore makes it difficult for the students to assess their work beyond the consistency of the operations, in a wider perspective. This was one of the main reasons to try in Columbia a kind of typological research, simply to provide that kind of background. Not as a recipe, but rather as raw material to produce… And after that, we became interested in developing some of the ideas of speciation into a methodology, or at least a reflection, on our own practice.

So, I developed a genealogy of projects that we can trace almost as if our practice was a genetic pool of possibilities that are reacting and expanding as they are deployed on certain environments. So then, the process, and this has to do a little bit with what you have said about the general and the specific, you realize that the potential of a practice, in this case of our practice, is formed by a process that works in two directions. I work from the bottom up. I work with the materials that we find in a project, the economics, the technology, etc. You synthesize certain organizations, and then these organizations mutate into another project. And once they mutate in another project, they become almost material mediators of the materials that you find in a new situation, in a new site, a new program, and a new location. And through that process the lineage of species becomes broader, but you can almost trace how ideas have been generated. They're specific architectural ideas, but they are not ideas specific to one project.

There is a kind of branding of a practice by setting its potentiality in a number of techniques or in a number of gestures or the use of a certain language, etc. Meyer or Graves based the consistency of their practice in some form of top-down, almost stylistic core that is deployed in different conditions, and maybe reacts to some local material, but doesn't really integrate, doesn't become mediated by the local problems. Then there is the reaction against this, which is probably something that people like Rem or Nouvel have explored, which is to say there is no style and no consistency in the technical or linguistic repertoire. The project is grown out of a specific situation. That means every project is a new project, where you have to reinvent everything, you have to reinvent techniques, language, approach, etc. I think it is almost an impossible situation. First of all, it's not valuable to sustain a practice that doesn't have a certain degree of repetition.

It is actually a model of constructing the practice that constantly moves between a generic approach on the one hand—the DNA of the practice, its genetic pool—and the specific problems that you encounter through practice. And this is actually quite interesting, because it allows you to develop a certain perspective in which you can see your work and the projects that you are engaged in as some form of accumulated knowledge. I am recently much more interested in the possibility to develop a certain consistency in the work, a kind of style that you can construct, that others can reproduce, so that it ceases to rely in some sort of mysterious, black-box process.

There was a moment in which we thought the most important core in the office was the technical arsenal, the methodologies, the different techniques or approaches that I had developed. I wanted to rely more on some methodological body rather than on the use of a language. It was almost as if the consistency of the work was in the techniques I was using. And we are progressively moving away from it into the acceptance of a sort of consistency in the work that enables us to be more effective and more efficient and more precise. The interesting potential behind the concept of speciation is that the projects become part of a family. Looking back at the projects, you can see there is a number of organizational structures and forms that transcend the approach and the techniques, making the work consistent across projects. It is almost as though we are not designing but rather growing or breeding projects out of a genetic pool that we are increasing through our experiences.

—**PM**: But that is also one of the important differences with Eisenman, because his work on geometry is tied to the problem of the Gestalt to such an extent that it almost can't make sense without that critical relation. In your work, the grammar of geometry is quite different, and I think that it is a grammar implied in Tati's film, but explicit in Foucault, which sees geometry first and foremost as a diagram of material relations, as in the Panopticon. Your recent Columbia studio takes a similar approach to geometry, technique, and typology, but how do these operate empirically and architecturally or instrumentally *before* they operate theoretically? I mean, isn't this one of the distinctions with Eisenman?

—**AZP**: The answer to that will be that the geometrical structures are kind of the core of architectural operation. For example, a whole array of architects practicing very successfully now in

Holland and in Spain do not generally formulate their discourse on a geometrical code. Or at least they tend to default to the orthogonal, geometry, because the core of the projects lies outside its physical entity; they make obviously important statements on a cultural, political, or environmental level. But finally, you have to be able to bring those observations into what we could call a material construct. A material construct is something with material properties: scale, grain, geometry, distance... If we want to construct a certain way of assessing architecture beyond whether it fits the programmatic requirements, budget constraints, sustainability requirements, then we need to necessarily go through a transformation of all those cultural, political, social, economic processes into material operations.

—**PM**: But what is the relation in your work between a material logic on the one hand and a geometrical code on the other?

—**AZP**: Of course! Materials have very strong geometrical properties...

—**PM**: Even as you've said, I think, in one of your lectures, the dinner conversion is material organization...

—**AZP**: Exactly, like the distance between us in this interview. I think this is really the core of the work of an architect. I think that if we are trying to do something, it is to set things in a certain order, at a certain distance, with certain organization, with a certain hierarchy. And unless we are able to formulate cultural arguments into that kind of plane, we remain outside of architecture. It doesn't happen to Rem as an architect because he has the resources to do it, although he never talks about them. But I think many of his followers, who haven't been able to develop that other side in their practices, are failing to produce moving buildings. There are legions of architects doing Photoshop collages and multicolored charts, saying that architecture is program... That's why for us, geometry is crucial. It's not interesting to see architecture either as an icon, as a form, nor as ambient. Yes, architecture is about program, but unless you're able to geometricize program, unless you're able to extract the physical qualities of program, understand its grain, and learn to operate within that material, you're not making architecture.

What is interesting in geometricizing programs is providing them with particular material performances, without defining a priori the envelope in which they have to perform. I have grown weary of hybrids in architecture. This pretence that great architecture is about hybridizing or mixing programs... The question is not whether programs are mixed, but *how* they are mixed. And in order to know how you mix them, you need to provide them with material qualities, diagrammatize them, study their geometrical qualities, and set them up in such a way that they start forming something *else*.

—PM: Which is one of the interesting aspects of Gehry's practice. He starts out with colored cubes of program that are compositionally organized and dispersed. That is one kind of geometry. The other is the envelope he wraps around it. One way of mediating this ontological conflict in the process of design is to work with geometrical information that is neither too specific nor too general and representative, and that is to work with pattern. Is this what you mean by genetic development of material?

—AZP: Probably what differentiates my work from Gehry's is a tendency to operate with patterns. Our work is very much based on patterns. I am much more interested in material organizations that have a certain degree of repetition, a certain pattern, a certain systematicity. And, somehow, the friction between that systematicity and the conditions or specificities that generates the project. This is probably because one of the qualities of material is repetition; every material has a certain structure that repeats in space. And also differentiates. It's kind of a play between that repetitive pattern and the way it differentiates through space and maybe through time.

Just like a piece of wood, every matter has a certain structure or certain grain that, for example, alternates layers of cellulose that has been solidified. This happens with certain regularity through space. If you are working with wood, you know that sanding in a certain direction is more efficient. What architects ultimately do is to assemble materials with a higher level of consistency, putting together new materials. To generate a material, you need to understand patterns. And this is something that happens systematically in every one of our projects. This is again a tendency towards consistency rather than contradiction.

The images illustrating this text are a collection of images of the globe: modeling or satellite imaging have made available to the general public an imagery of the world that did not exist before: from wind movements to temperatures, to tectonic plates, to networks, we have now several images of the world that insist on continuity and gradation, rather than as a collection of locales.

Unpublished, 2001

Methodological Proposal for the Staedelschule Frankfurt

An Alternative to the Polytechnic and the Liberal-Arts Models
The approach to architectural education that I will try to implement for the Staedelschule Frankfurt, is an intermediate to the polytechnic model that predominates in Continental Europe and Asia and the liberal-arts model that characterizes the Anglo-American schools. This new model would attempt to articulate the relationships between education and research and theory and practice into a more operative assemblage.

The polytechnic model is efficient in maintaining a close relationship between the educational and the practice modes of the discipline of architecture, as it provides students with a solid technical background to operate in a particular domain of practice. However, it fails to produce an adequate environment for a research-based educational model able to render the disciplinary techniques truly productive. This model fails also to provide the theoretical background that allows the students to question the boundaries of disciplinary knowledge and to develop it further, becoming able to operate in increasingly unstable conditions, or broaden the field of technical possibilities beyond the conventional modes. As a model of education based in the uncritical training of skills and techniques, devoid of specific project or objective, it tends to sclerosis and is often unable to offer alternatives to the practice of architecture. Its devastating effects can be seen in Germany, France, and in several Asian countries.

The liberal-arts model has been the fastest-growing model in architectural education during the past twenty years, as a result of the increasing instability of disciplinary models that demand a more research-oriented, educational system. The liberal-arts model is more efficient in providing students with the necessary critical background to question, search, and select the appropriate skills to approach a specific architectural problem. It also produces students that are more capable of independent thinking and research. However, this model has evolved into a path of internalization where the success of the projects relies purely upon their critical capacity and eccentricity, rendering it unable to operate effectively in the practice of the discipline, and generally outside academia. As the disciplinary content to this model diminishes in favor of the critical and ideological content of the education, the academic work focuses on the ideological or stylistic contents instead of developing operative techniques for architectural production. The no-less-devastating effects of this process can also be witnessed in America and the United Kingdom, where the schizophrenia between theory and practice is such that academic experimentation has been devoid of any real transformative effect on the practice. Moreover, it has become an alibi for the conservativism of the real practices, those that effectively transform the built environment. While an old problem, it nonetheless deserves tackling anew.

Frankfurt, as the home of both the Frankfurt kitchen and the Frankfurt school, domain of radical technical rigor and radical liberal thinking, seems to be an ideal place to grow this new model of architectural education. That is the opportunity that this proposal attempts to exploit.

A Focus on the Discipline

As an alternative to other graduate schools in Europe, the opportunity at the Staedelschule relies precisely on the possibility to reestablish a strong relationship with the world outside the school, to construct an academic environment capable of generating again real transformative possibilities for architecture. Rather than focusing the postgraduate studies on theorizing other disciplines and trying to make a translation into architecture, a research program primarily applied to the production of architecture and the problematization of its techniques will offer an alternative to the current proliferation of fuzzy, multidisciplinary approaches. Rather than looking for architecture in other disciplines, a retreat into architectural materials and techniques would explore how to look at everything from an architectural perspective and how to search for architectural instruments in other disciplines. This is, I believe, an approach that was already initiated by the work of Enric Miralles at the Staedelschule, and that should be continued. By researching and theorizing specifically the discipline and its operative role within the urban, cultural, and economic processes in which it needs to perform, the Staedelschule will hopefully be able to regain an operativity that has been progressively closed to academia and establish effective relationships with the architectural practice. Architecture, more than other arts, cannot exist outside the processes of economic, cultural, and urban transformation, and any serious proposition of an architectural school should take this relationship very seriously.

Moreover, the most interesting debate on architectural theory today is about operativity and technique, about how a new pragmatic approach may become the most productive in generating alternative forms of practice. After a period when the debate about language, style, or ideology has dominated the architectural debate, the return to the discipline as an alternative and more operative domain of research seems to appear as an innovative approach. A "school" used to be given coherence by the use of a certain language or certain ideological position. Today it seems perhaps more adequate to find consistency in the production of architectural effects and the instruments used in their production, or to research the instrumental; that is, to make the discipline grow toward integration with emergent economic, cultural, and social structures versus retreat to the suspect ground of autonomous production.

A Laboratory of Architecture

The focus on the development and problematization of architectural operativity will not be sufficient without the constitution of a true laboratory, where every member will have to develop independent research within a common framework. The difference between this model and a master class is that the consistency that establishes the framework is based on an area of research and an objective, not on the reproduction of a master's style or procedure. In opposition to a traditional polytechnic school, where technique is explored without a specific purpose other than developing skills, and in opposition to a traditional liberal-arts school, where critique and individual positions are explored devoid of operational content beyond the academic domain, a laboratory has primarily a specific, operative purpose. A laboratory is not constituted by a closed series of techniques or an infinitely open series of possible individual positions, but by an infinitely open field of technical and theoretical positions with a specific purpose. The objective of a laboratory is to produce a solution for a problem; any technique or position is legitimate as long as it serves to achieve the purpose that is targeted. The discovery of a vaccine for a certain illness, a new theory of physics to explain a particular phenomenon, or the manipulation of certain types of rhythms to produce musical effects are purposes similar to the development of an architectural prototype for an emergent urban condition. In a laboratory, anything is adequate to reach the purpose; there are no borders to the approaches and techniques used to solve the problem, and the creativity of the participants is located precisely in their originality in defining their approach to the problem. My proposition to construct an architectural laboratory at the Staedelschule is based on two foundations:

1. Identify a concrete architectural problem or possibility that can be researched in order to exploit a certain condition or improve a certain product, method, or operation. The way to enlarge the discipline and to integrate multidisciplinary techniques into an architectural project is not to attempt the translation of them into architecture (making installations and trying to turn them into architecture, or discussing science or cultural theory and then using architecture as a milieu to embody statements that have been made in a different field). It is exactly the opposite: having defined an architectural performance, select the fields of knowledge that will help to develop the project, no matter how far removed they become from conventional architectural practice. That is also the way of learning to look at other disciplines as an architect, not to look at architecture as a philosopher, a sculptor, or a biologist.

2. Select specialists that have the knowledge required at every particular moment in the projects to support specific research. An architecture laboratory cannot be constituted by subscribing to a particular brand of architecture, engineering, or theory. That will be far too limiting and inefficient to reach a certain purpose. It is necessary to select the experts that will contribute to the experiments that are being carried with a specific purpose, whether they are geometers or economists, filmmakers or biologists, musicians or sociologists. Contributors and collaborators to the work of the laboratory will be chosen on the grounds of coming from a field of knowledge that collectively emerges as critical, as the projects in the studio evolve.

A Domain of Operation
Every successful school of architecture is characterized not only by a consistent series of procedures, languages, and approaches, but also by a strong relationship to a domain of real practice. This field or place of external reference becomes the framework of operation, the object of research, and the testing ground of this experimentation: for example, London in the '70s; Barcelona and Los Angeles in the '80s; or Rotterdam and Zurich in the '90s. If the work of the school does not have an effect in real practice, the school remains an academic institution with no real capacity to transform reality. A real school needs a project that is operative beyond the academic domain. Otherwise it produces only further schizophrenic dysfunction between theory and practice, limiting the possibility to test the work of the school as an effective device to transform reality. If the Staedelschule is to become an important school in the coming years, it will have to choose a domain of practice and draw up strong links with it in order to focus the research and be able to test the results. My proposal is to choose, in cycles of two or three years, different domains of operation that will focus the research of the school and provide the frame for speculation. For the first two or three years, our project will be Europe, the continent surrounding Frankfurt—potentially Frankfurt's hinterland—and undergoing an intense process of transformation and reinvention, culturally, socially, and economically. Processes of negotiation and hybridization between traditionally strong cultures, articulation between entrepreneurial economies and interventionist policies, integration of the former communist countries, massive immigration of North African and Asian workers, the emergence of unprecedented relationships between work and leisure, all of these processes put forward a rich field of possibilities that can be exploited architecturally, or considered from an architectural perspective.

Double Agenda

The academic program that I am proposing establishes a clear structure with different programs for the first and second years, aimed at both the development of a consistent but constantly evolving body of architectural knowledge and skill and the construction of independent individuals with the capacity of becoming operative agents beyond the academic realm. This structure is aimed at dismantling the polarization between the collective and engaged polytechnic education, and the individual and detached approach of the liberal-arts model. There is no reason to think that both the engagement with the reality of the architectural practice and the development of individual and independent thinking are mutually exclusive. In fact, they complement each other. The model I am proposing is aimed at producing a vital continuum between an elastic, yet consistent school framework (architectural laboratory), a constantly evolving realm of practice, and the development of individual and operative research.

Year One: Making a School

The first year at the Staedelschule will aim to provide incoming students, with diverse origins, with a common body of techniques and approaches, constructed ad hoc to face the challenges of a common project to be individually developed. The particular approaches of the members of the group will inspire different technical procedures to be discussed collectively to build by accumulation the arsenal of instruments that will constitute the school. This common project will be a real one, and developed in close communication with an external interlocutor, a community, enterprise, or institution (a city council, a development corporation, an interest group), facing a project paradigmatic of those European processes that will be the objective of the discussion inside the Staedelschule. This relationship with the outside world could even take the form of a commission to the school, helping to fund the resources to develop the projects or the publication of the work.

Within this model, the work of the students will have to be accountable both to the internal discussion about the adequacy, effectiveness, and precision of the instruments and approaches, and to the external demands for specific performance. Accountability does not mean compliance but consciousness about the effects of a practice. Accountability can also be subversive. To understand the degree of compliance implicit in a certain procedure beyond the academic realm is one of the benefits of this double accountability in an educational institution.

The wealth and consistency of the school will grow as the range of techniques explored by the students and the consciousness of their effects are accumulated through the different generations, rather than as a pre-existing series of technical or formal recipes to be provided by the teaching staff. The school will also grow as the research becomes instrumental in discussing or producing knowledge that can be operative outside the school, and the work reaches a public dimension.

Year Two: Proliferating the School

In the second year, graduating students will be required to develop entirely independent research, and to individually customize and extend the range of skills and approaches that should have been developed collectively in the first year. They will be requested to select a project of their choice to be developed, also in contact with an external interlocutor of their choice, with whom they will test particular developments of the experiments they developed during the first year. This individual research will not necessarily be based in Europe or be part of the internal core of the school. Europe, or whatever other field is being targeted by the school, will become too limiting for the kind of individual work that will be expected from graduating students. The objective is for students to develop a critical stance to the framework developed in the first year that will hopefully serve to diversify and proliferate the research in different directions. Those could in return be incorporated or used as a critique by the next group of incoming students, making the school's constitution evolve constantly. This strategy is also aimed at preparing graduating candidates for their future professional life outside the school by developing research into an area or a location where they aim to practice in the future, making a particular practice, a particular scale, a particular type or approach, or even a particular academic realm or public institution the target of the research. There is nothing sadder than witnessing brilliant overeducated postgraduates drifting for years after graduation, captives of their academic work, searching for a place to deploy their skills and knowledge without success, or entering the professional market as raw generic manpower.

The request from candidates to target in their second year an area of individual interest and develop a consistent research that they can exploit after graduation will give them an advantage in their professional careers by producing sophisticated research that cannot be sustained outside the academic realm, and asking them to become independent agents. A school is also measured by the capacity of its scholars to succeed outside, and by its capacity to update its techniques and discourse to react effectively to the external world. Again, a double agenda that will simultaneously benefit the school's internal debate and its capacity to produce operative individuals beyond the academic realm.

To master and understand the disciplinary procedures is the only way to take architecture to a superior level. Like pilots, football players, and musicians, to be a virtuoso, to produce the magic, you need to know the technique so well that you do not need to think about it anymore.

The images illustrating this text attempt to link a proposal for the generation of a design culture—which is the object of every school of architecture—with the processes of mass migration that have characterised geopolitics since the late 1960's. If the school has a direct association with the swarm, the migratory movements create also instant consistency across large populations which develop entirely new skills and behaviours in the process. The images refer the extraordinary rate of contemporary population shift, be it through tourism, political or economical reasons.

Alejandro Zaera-Polo in conversation with Roemer van Toorn.
Published in *Arch+*, Berlin, 2002

The Berlage Menu: A new "productive" rather than "critical" paradigm

—**Roemer van Toorn:** Universities and schools of architecture help people to become architects, in the same way they learn to be lawyers or doctors. With Wiel Arets as dean the Berlage Institute was after another kind of teaching. The students who apply at the Berlage Institute are already practicing architects and come here—after years of frustration being in an office working for other architects—to develop their own agenda. While he stressed the making, Wiel also brought in more theoretical reflections. The Institute was furthermore not only providing a service for each individual to develop his or her thesis; we confronted the students with assignments from within the Netherlands. What will be the next step for the Berlage Institute, according to you, Alejandro, as the new dean?
—**Alejandro Zaera-Polo:** I was invited to the Berlage Institute by Wiel Arets in the very beginning of his term. During those first contacts I met some of the students who were at the Institute during the deanship of Herman Hertzberger, who were still in the system. My impression is that the Hertzberger period was a very exciting time, almost the hippie period of the Berlage, orgy-like... Probably it did not yet have a very clear structure, nor a clear didactic program, but great excitement and very motivated people. Typical heroic period... I think Wiel's term has been a period of consolidation, both of academic and financial consolidation. He has provided a more structured organization and probably a more focused direction to the research in the Institute.

I think that what we should aim for now is to develop a more special profile that will make the Institute a unique international institution.

As a postgraduate laboratory, the Berlage should find a specificity that distinguishes it from a school that makes it specific in respect to American schools but also in respect to other European postgraduate programs. Obviously the Berlage has already built up an important and globally-known reputation and network. There are no such institutions in America or Asia.

The fact that the Berlage Institute is in Holland—and obviously Holland has been for the past 15 years one of the most interesting places generating new architecture—makes it a very strategic location in the international debate. Maybe this is a kind of optimistic perspective, but I believe as the European consolidation advances, industries tend to concentrate in certain regions: automotive industry in Germany, luxury manufacturing in Northern Italy, telecommunications in Scandinavia… Why not imagine that Rotterdam may become the center of architectural and urban planning services in Europe, taking advantage of a very well-built local, cultural, and productive infrastructure? If so, the Berlage may become a crucial part of this infrastructure. The target would be to make the Berlage a European research institution based in the Netherlands, rather than just a local architectural school.

—**RvT:** During Wiel's period, the Berlage Institute became famous for its urban research, for its architecture critique, bringing cultural studies into the field of architecture, and for its critical brief-writing from the perspective of the program of architecture and urbanism. What kind of directions have you in mind with the Berlage Institute, Alejandro?

—**AZP:** I am also fundamentally interested in the Berlage as a laboratory rather than as a school. I am interested in doing more applied research, rather than defining general themes of research. Searching for opportunities of research in specific cases of reality. I am interested in a kind of opportunistic research that is able to engage very directly in the processes of transformation of the built environment. I am interested in reality as a field of research that is able to offer a certain level of friction to the research and that can provide certain accountability to the work in the Institute. I am interested in developing an institution that will have a transformative impact, both on the built environment and in the contemporary culture, in a very concrete and direct manner. In order to produce the convergence of speculative practice with realistic performance, the identification of concrete domains of operation, either geographical zones, media, formats, or subjects is crucial. Both the knowledge and the debate within the Institute should have an effective capacity of transformation, rather than remain as a purely speculative practice.

I am not at all interested in visionary projects, or in individual authors.

Contemporary postgraduate architectural education is basically formed in the '80s author-centred practices rather than focusing on subjects or problems. Students seem to go to postgraduate schools looking to become the next great prophet of architecture without realizing that not only are the statistic probabilities for that to happen very small, but also that even the greatest figures need to develop a great capacity to understand the situation where they operate and its relationships with their field of interest. We are in an expanding disciplinary field, and obviously, what you can better teach to people—aiming at a higher level of education—is how to be resourceful in getting information and how to put things together, rather than telling them what architecture is, as a recipe, that is obviously something of the past. All the good schools, like the AA and Columbia, are based on this model. However, the model they have developed is largely based on the '80s model of architect with strong character and "vision." The architect-artist or the architect-performer. That type of architect is unable to engage effectively in the swarm-like, complex reality in which most architects have to operate today. Is not about constructing individualities but about understanding multiplicities. Is not about visions but about opportunities. I am convinced that the liberal arts model in which all these schools are based is exhausted and has reached its limits by delving into the systematic production of eccentricity and authorship rather than developing models to handle the generic, the multiple, the impersonal... Understand the effect on the swarm that small changes of direction may have, rather than embracing vision and originality as our operative mode. In this sense the '80s "à la carte" postgraduate education is unable to generate solid knowledge able to be used outside the institutions, and at worst produces overeducated professionals who are usually unable to engage productively in anything for several years, doomed under the weight of their own personal visions.

Also, I am interested in exploring a new breed of architectural knowledge that in a way has been left aside by the educational institutions in the past 10 years. Individuals are formed as a by-product of knowledge rather than the other way around. Contemporary research is typically directed towards fields of knowledge that are basically supra-disciplinary (economics, sociology, philosophy...) or sub-disciplinary (engineering, construction management...). In this landscape, the possibility of producing knowledge able to effectively analyze and articulate both levels of knowledge is a niche to exploit, for which the structure of the Institute is particularly adequate.

Furthermore, I believe that postgraduate education as we know it and as it is defined at most important institutions, is starting to become a little bit obsolete. In recent years there has been an ever-expanding domain in the architecture discipline that has lead the research or experimental practices to direct themselves very closely to discuss theoretically what architecture is, what the discipline is formally. What is lacking now in the current landscape is an institution that focuses more on structuring the thinking on how to make a project. Now it seems that when you talk about "research" in an architectural school it means reading, theorizing, doing cultural studies, or gathering statistics. Issues of technology, geometry, structural design, and typological analysis have been overlooked by current research. Research is very much equal to the production of text and graphics. Text is not necessarily the only form of research that you can do. Architectural research has to deal specifically with the tools and matters of architecture, and has to be fundamentally aimed at architecture as a product.

—**RvT:** Perhaps the trick of the strategic

devices Wiel put forward each year—challenging everybody at the institute to define, to interpret, to give meaning to a word like "conflict," "forces," "field," or "double Dutch" is that this culture of different expert interpretations promoted a stimulating culture of debate and research. The climate of confrontation and support by different voices—positions in and outside architecture—helps the student to orient him/herself beyond mainstream platitudes, to develop his/her own cultural agenda and mentality. You can learn the technique of making rather easily, while it is much more difficult to develop an independent and critical position towards society. How would you see the focus of the Institute? Would you allow the same kind of wide range of interpretations as Wiel put forward to orient and challenge the student? Or would you prefer more specificity because the educational method of the past didn't bring deep enough research results?

—**AZP:** If you are able to channel the research more then the output would be more sophisticated. I am not at all interested in students who think they know what they are about but in those who are prepared to find out by engaging in research they did not even know before. I am 15 years older than them and I am happy not to know what I am about yet. And what I am involved in now I hope will change in the future. If you are truly interested in learning things, you have to keep your mind open and let things happen, learn to fly in a swarm… This idea of the "à la carte" school is a product of the consumer education and produces products like McDonald's. When you go to McDonald's, especially in the U.S., they make you believe you have enormous choice, when at the end everything tastes the same. I would rather go to a Kaiseki restaurant where there is only one menu and you cannot choose, but everything is extremely sophisticated and new. I am more interested in that approach to the design of the future Berlage menu, and I am more interested in a clientele open to experiencing new flavors rather than rejoicing in the ones they know.

—**RvT:** How do you see the relationship between the development of the thesis of the student and the institutional research the Berlage is interested in? Is there a conflict between what the institute wants and what the student is looking for or, earlier, a synergy (and how do you see that synergy)? How do you guarantee good education and high-profile research at the same time?

—**AZP:** I think a thesis is a format that belongs to other disciplines, like philosophy, literature, physics... An architect's thesis is a kind of imposition on the dynamics of the architectural practice that I am not yet sure it works... I would rather structure architectural research around a concrete project, the development of a prototype, a new technique for synthesizing hybrid programs or to design with viscoelastic joints... When you talk about a thesis you are already limiting the output to a written one. You are giving priority to nonarchitectural technology. Firstly, I am much more interested in developing research that is specific to the discipline and its instruments. Secondly, I do not think that more than 5% of the students engaged in postgraduate education are capable in two years of producing a truly interesting piece of research by themselves. To think that as a single individual you can compete in terms of producing architectural research with offices, companies, and institutions with large and experienced teams and abundant resources is kind of naive. When you have been in the academic circuit for 10 years, like myself, you get really bored with traveling 7,000 miles to be in a jury where you see the same kind of smart guys trying to impress you with original and unique research that you have already seen 10 times in other schools. It is much more informative, for example, to talk to people from the research department of a construction company on how to reduce manufacturing costs by using a certain arrangement... A certain awareness that the relevant subjects in a certain age are few and that the real sophistication and originality is to find a new personal perspective on them, is a very necessary reflection to offer to the students. If a student comes to you with research on, let's say, the Ionic order, you should try to dissuade him or her from proceeding. You may be foreclosing groundbreaking research and suppressing the desires of an individual, but the likelihood that it will not lead to anything worthwhile is too large to risk valuable time and resources on it. To identify those frames of relevant research is the job of the dean of the Institute. And of course, to be able to identify when someone is proposing something that is worth considering despite not being included in the main frame of research. But to take for granted that every individual in the school will make a significant individual research is not only unbelievably optimistic but also irresponsible as a management strategy. I believe that individualism to that degree has been a dead end culturally already for a few decades. Real education consists today in constructing individuals who are able to understand their multiplicity and the mediation and construction of all desires through a very complex network of relations, and to be able to operate within these constraints.

—**RvT:** Herman Hertzberger's philosophy was that students should do 15 designs in one year and should learn to do a lot of things at the same time. The Berlage Institute should prepare the student for an architecture practice where you have to act fast, be creative, present well, do research, work in teams. In simple words, the education program was mimicking a high-quality innovative architecture practice. The students were always very busy even when they did not know precisely what they were doing themselves.

—**AZP:** Postgraduate education, as it is defined now in the most sophisticated institutions, is very much based on a star architecture model, in which students go to Columbia, the AA, or the Berlage Institute to study with a certain guy or personality, because that's what you see in the magazines. Students want to become another star architect. Things don't work like that. There are a lot of very bright architects from my generation who didn't hit the big time, while other, less capable ones have managed to get their own practices. I am much more interested in developing a type of research, and therefore education, that is based on issues and subjects that are out there, and by doing that being engaged with the production of the institute in the process. You don't come to work here to work with a certain person. You come to the Berlage because you are interested in certain issues you would like to work on with highly qualified experts. Maybe that will be a certain drawback—without branding the Institute through stars it could be a problem to get students in—hopefully we will be able to come up with challenging research proposals engaged in reality that counteracts the '80s education; turning education around. Looking for research not so much with someone but aiming directly at affecting the world outside.

Another important point for me in my program is that we will work with third parties outside the institute. Like municipalities, institutions, the government, developers, etc., who say, "We have a problem here, can you help us solving it?" Whereby the Institute will research a problem that is directly involved with reality. I am very interested in the model of direct action as opposed to the ivory tower that speculative research tends to become. That is the opposite of going to ask a well-known personality, because he or she is famous and cool, "What do you want to do?" I am much more interested in looking outside and getting clients involved who will tell us what is needed, where the opportunities are for action.

—**RvT:** The Institute teaches students to be independent researchers in the field of architecture and urbanism, to present, and foremost to intervene with projects in society in an innovative, independent, critical, and relevant manner. How can we, as an institute, move beyond an agenda set by the much-needed independent, innovative, and critical individual practice?

—**AZP:** I must say that the paradigm of the "critical" is in my opinion part of the intellectual models that became operative in the early 20th century and presumed that in order to succeed we should take a kind of "negative" view towards reality, in order to be creative, in order to produce new possibilities. In my opinion, today the critical individual practice that has characterized intellectual correctness for most of the 20th century is no longer particularly adequate to deal with a culture determined by processes of transformation on a scale and complexity difficult to understand. Talking about the critical individual may be even demagogic, especially when selling it to the students. I would rather be more sincere, avoid making false illusions, and talk about a new, "productive" rather than "critical" paradigm in which the critical decisions cannot be made on the whole system—let's say capitalism versus Marxism or democracy versus fundamentalism—but on a much more concrete and haptic level. That means that you have to be fundamentally engaged in the processes and learn to manipulate them from the inside. You never get that far into the process as a critical individual. If we talk in terms of the construction of subjectivity, the critical belongs to Freud and Lacan, and what I called "productive," to Deleuze.

—**RvT:** On the occasion of the farewell of Wiel Arets and your welcome as new dean of the Institute, I asked many architects, theoreticians, curators and alumni of the Berlage to reflect upon the question, "What will/should the architect enact tomorrow?"

Elia Zenghelis talked about the need to "start again" in architecture and urbanism. "The retro-active manifesto has come to an end," he said. The systematic idealization of data (often subversive in its contradiction) generated by the latest phase of capitalism —which made Dutch architecture (in developing new concepts) for our Second Modernity so famous—is no longer able to propose innovative and progressive prototypes. The culture of sprawl, in which everything is submerging in consumerism and atomization (even in its most subversive or ironic pragmatism), but also the inherent political climate of corporate globalism, are both developments that people more and more start to question as being inappropriate to project alternatives for live-in space. Elia Zenghelis, like Peter Eisenman, believes that the structure, the language of architecture, the formal instead of the programmatic is capable today of countering the culture of sprawl. What they propose is to investigate the syntax of matter instead of the sociology of space.

—**AZP:** I think that this is a polemical statement that is interesting in some ways, as a whole generation of architects, to whom I belong, has grown up thinking that to be idealistic, to be visionary, to try to impose formal visions onto the world is nonsense. If you were to ask 15 years ago, architects of the generation that today is around 55 what they thought about developers, shopping malls, etc., they would have probably said it was bad. They looked at themselves and at architecture as an activity of "resistance." If you ask today any of the around-40 generation, we would all tell you that we think those are very interesting worlds to engage with and that contemporary architecture is about surfing in those worlds. Rem was probably the first architect of that generation who changed the chip and started to propose that complicity was a far more productive attitude than resistance, and he used the "retroactive manifesto" to explain that precisely the most insane and mundane conditions have produced the most interesting architecture, by looking at New York, Singapore, Lagos. The engagement of my generation with complicity, quantitative analysis, factual data, consumerism, and so on is a development of that shift initiated in the retroactive manifesto, and I still believe in it; I still believe that visionary architecture and political resistance are very unproductive attitudes to sustain for architects who lead a whole generation of architects to lose the chance to effectively engage in the transformation of the environment. So I believe that the path open by the retroactive manifesto is a good one, and complicity is a good antidote for idealism and barren visionary attitudes. I think that going back to language and formalism would be to forget the valuable lessons of the retroactive manifesto. What I would say after 10 years of data and shopping malls, is that the

retroactive manifesto is not enough, and that we need to set up new references so that people do not think that the fact that they use data, build shopping malls and deal with developers conclude that they are making substantial contributions
to the world of architecture. Those worlds do not need architects to exist. What is important to define is what an architect does within those worlds, and how can we assess its performance from the perspective of the discipline of architecture.

The fundamental question here is how to operate beyond a fixed system of values and conventions, in order to survive the constant changes of conditions in which we have to operate. The practice of architecture as a reference to discourses, a system of values or conventions, as a language, etc., has been greatly destabilized by the processes of change that characterize our productive context. In this context, operations on productive processes appear to be more appropriate as creative postures and generators of new possibilities than criticism. Architecture today is more than ever an experimental activity given the growing difficulty of operating with a priori discernment, either of a critical or a visionary nature. To practice like a judge, or as a theoretician who reflects on reality and questions what has up until now been considered as good practice. But to judge we need references, systems of value, comparisons and these are more than ever before difficult to find in solid form.

The problem is that we can't absolutely give up judgement a posteriori either. The question is how to overcome the operative paradigm that has come to dominate all disciplines and the intellectual or productive practices: the critical process. The solution perhaps lies within the interior of the construction process; to be able to construct sequences of micro-judgements that operate on very specific and concrete aspects of the project. To take down the great paradigms of references into chains of small local decisions in time and space, that we can realize without resorting to grand visions, or absolute references.

—**RvT:** Isn't there a risk that architecture, by concentrating on its technique, forgets the engagement with the social? Lars Lerup answers one of the questions

I asked him to write about in *Hunch 6* with a statement: "Our task is to build and rebuild the democratic city. Operate beyond the borders of your project. Make a gift to the street! Ethics!" Are you not afraid that with the much needed "start again" manifesto the Berlage ends up celebrating the autonomy of architecture? That the designed (sublime) object can either solve it all or can just be self-referential or provide a service? (I fear the Swiss and Singaporean democracies.)

—**AZP:** I do not know if there is a risk, but in any case it would be a risk worth taking if the outcome were good architecture. You do not need to keep reminding yourself that you are engaged with the social: The social is one of the materials of architecture, and you need to work with it. What I do not believe is that the purpose of architecture should be set in social or political objectives.

All of the cultural analysis that architecture went through in the '80s does not seem particularly adequate to deal with the production of an architecture that has to operate in an increasingly mixed and unstable cultural background. Perhaps as a reaction to that sort of architectural discourse, focused almost exclusively on social, political, and cultural developments, we have tried to put the emphasis of our practice on the architectural construct, on the materiality of the project, and on its organizational qualities. Geometry, construction, organization, materiality, technique, and pragmatics have become an alternative for a temporary suspension of the exclusivity of cultural analysis. This is not to neglect the value of a theoretical perspective for the practice of architecture. Those architects who are not able to construct a theoretical perspective on their work die very young, and run out of possibilities to develop. To think theoretically generates a certain capacity to look at the work not purely from inside but to see it in an economic or social context. What is less evident is the kind of thought that can actually contribute to the practice of architecture. There are certain theoretical approaches that are completely inoperative as a focus for an architectural practice. At most, what these approaches can do is to turn an architectural practice—fundamentally a form of production—into a practice of cultural critique. This can also be interesting, but as a practitioner I am more interested in a perspective that allows us to problematize architectural techniques specifically, to develop an architectural discourse out of the productive rather than out of the critical.

As an architect, involvement in those external processes finally becomes significant if they are used as an excuse to open new architectural potentials. It is irrelevant whether we are doing malls and transportation buildings or churches and schools. Malls or theme parks do not need an architect to come into being: They happen spontaneously. We need to make these developments internal to the logic of the discipline, and you don't do that by writing more and more about minorities, migrations, gender, globalization, or new cultural patterns but by finding a correlation between the emergent political, economic, and social processes and certain architectural techniques, geometries, and organizations.

We have been through a decade of political correctness in architecture that has not produced a single good architect. If I look at the architects that interest me, Le Corbusier dealt with Vichy, Mies sold himself to American corporations, Rem is an accomplice of commercial interests, and Jacques Herzog is making beautiful enclosures for the international high culture… And so what? They are all inevitably engaged with the social, it is part of the materials they handle, but the driving force of their practice is not to produce social effects but architectural ones. Lars' statement seems to me totally irrelevant in terms of defining what architecture should be, and Swiss democracy has produced a generation of the best architects in the world.

—**RvT:** How do you relate the fact that we need to know more about the life and times surrounding buildings and the much-needed revitalization of the profession with its own specific language?

—**AZP:** I am not sure if I understand the question properly. If you refer to the relevance that program has acquired as an architectural material in the past 15 years, it is obvious that we can no longer ignore that programmatic factors are of great relevance in the assemblage of materials of different sorts that construct architectural organizations. I think they always have been, the difference between now and let's say, the Enlightenment, when the array of building typologies started to have entity as an urban science, society's rhythm of change has accelerated enormously, and the life cycle of buildings decreased substantially. This means that we have to rethink the nature of the assemblage between material program and other materials to increase the capacity of buildings to deal with the different consistencies that those components acquire in contemporary conditions.

However, the idea that an architecture is interesting simply because it has an innovative program is somehow overvalued. Legions of architects are now trying to justify their projects by the programmatic composition. Certain forms of architectural programs are very interesting as cultural or social phenomena, but that does not guarantee their architectural value. For example, in Tokyo there are thousands of buildings with really weird program and very little architectural value. Even worse is the way in which architects usually talk about programmatic composition. Even in the highest academic circles, it is embarrassingly imprecise. There are several disciplines that can talk about this matter with far more precision. To be serious about our capacity to operate with program, we should be able to look at the techniques that other disciplines use to deal with activities, to learn how to quantify, to use statistics, and to model the effects of a programmatic distribution. And not only to develop forms of engineering program, but to discern the capacity to produce architectural effects. That is what the prophets of program have not answered yet.

The hybrid as program has become one of the key themes of contemporary architecture culture. Nevertheless it is treated with a laughable degree of imprecision. It seems that the mere joining together of an office with a tennis court or a discotheque with a church is sufficient to have made architecture with "hybrids." One of the aspects of real interest, which we have concentrated our academic investigation on since 1993, is the possibility of understanding that activities have physical, material and geometric properties: weight, friction, hardness, cohesion, durability, and texture... For this reason they can be used to construct in a way similar to how we use traditional physical materials. The objective would be to transcend the social and linguistic consistency of the program, to learn its material properties and the form of building with them. At the current time, there is an absurd proliferation of colored plans with scattered activity keys or pictograms that attempt to become the new instruments for the making of an architecture of "the program." This is a mistaken instrument that will probably never produce any architecture of value. From designing restaurants, we have learned a lot about the physical properties of this type of program. Now we know that the proportion and scale of the dining hall is crucial in producing determined ambient affects; the distances between fellow diners or the geometry of the tables and the service circulation. We know the material and we can manipulate it to produce certain effects, although these effects are effectively determined by the culture where the program is situated. So you want to join a gymnasium with an office? Very good, but as of yet, we are not talking about architecture. If you ask me why, I'll tell you if you are making architecture or a social commentary or writing a movie script.

—RvT: After September 11, architecture will be confronted more and more with social and political issues. Does architecture have to choose a certain side? Or is surfing the contemporaneity of late capitalism enough, the only possibility?

—AZP: This is a very complicated question and difficult to answer in a short time. I am not so sure if the world after September 11 is going to change so drastically. However, I think that we will go through some time in which we will be increasingly held accountable for the forms we produce beyond the architectural domain. I don't think that it will help very much when an architect justifies his or her practice by the fact that it has a particular political orientation, or that it aims to yield a particular "political effect." Good architecture produces fundamentally interesting or new architectural effects, and those have an effect in politics and the economy, but as a secondary stage. That doesn't mean that politics are not a huge force from all these various forces that we have to deal with when we are doing a commission or a project. So you need to be conscious that what you are doing has a political color and has a political effect and to some degree also the result of a political context, but it is difficult to justify your architectural performance by your political alignment.

—RvT: Perhaps the problem is not so much to make political architecture as to make architecture politically? Or in the words of Benjamin: "Instead of asking, 'What is the attitude of a work to the relations of production of its time? Does it accept them, is it reactionary? Or does it aim at overthrowing them, is it revolutionary?'—Instead of this question, or at any rate before it, I would like to propose another. Rather than asking, What is the attitude of a work *to* the relations of production of its time? I would like to ask, What is its true position *in* them? This question directly concerns the function the work has within the literary relations of production of its time. It is concerned, in other words, directly with the literary *technique* of works. In bringing up technique, I have named the concept that makes the literary product accessible to an immediately social, and therefore materialist, analysis. At the same time, the concept of technique provides the dialectical starting point from which the unfruitful antithesis of form and content can be surpassed."

—AZP: I always rejected giving my students any kind of political direction. I was educated in a very politically charged environment. I consider myself someone with a very strong political awareness simply for a biographical reason: I grew up in Franco's Spain, I was 12 years old when Franco died, and I remember very clearly that we had to learn "how to vote" at school. Learning democracy was a very important part of my upbringing, and that is an experience that most of the people I meet from my generation in this profession have not gone through. I have a very clear consciousness that political freedom and democracy are not a given; you have to construct them. At the architecture school, your work had to be loaded with political content, but this did not necessarily lead to very interesting production. My friends who became more actively involved in political action are no longer architects today. They became politicians or developers. I think that no matter how politically motivated we are as architects, the pleasure we get and give out of building is not political. Our work is finally relevant because we managed to do something that relates to a certain architectural tradition and architectural discipline. I think that today, after a decade of cultural theory and political correctness, there is a very important task in finding the intrinsic values of architectural organization.

—**RvT:** Zaha Hadid, Patrick Schumacher, but also Hans Ulrich Obrist, are organizing exhibitions around the issue of utopia. They believe, and I agree with them, that every time needs its utopia(s). Zaha and Patrick write in their introduction of the exhibition "Latent Utopias" that "There is no sense anymore in projecting and articulating the Zeitgeist. Every architectural concept or trope is relative with respect to divergent perspectives and interests. Every architectural form multiplies in the kaleidoscope of multiple, temporary audiences. The total social process has become far too complex to be anticipated within a single vision and utopian image. Other strategies are called for." Although the utopian speculation is rather dubious today, how do you see the much-needed principle of hope (as Ernst Bloch put it)?

—**AZP:** I would rather operate with the principle of "no hope, no fear" as Michael Speaks puts it. I agree with the idea that utopias can only be multiple and ephemeral today. They relate to specific environments or situations, and can be used only temporarily, as a guideline. However, I still believe that there is a certain Zeitgeist, a certain consistency across all those multiple environments that we need to be able to effectively understand. Call it capitalism, democracy, or worldwide web, those locales that are not connected through

them are outside the domains that everybody who will read this interview operates within. Yes, there are aboriginal tribes out there that may be very interesting from an anthropological perspective, but are beyond our field of operation; there are also fundamentalisms that decide not to enter into these global processes and remain local in time and space. But they are not interesting to me; they are not multicultural by ignorance or will. The idea that everything is local and that there is no Zeitgeist, no consistency across locales is finally very dangerous to sustain because ultimately it will lead us to a position of no discussion and no debate.
There is a Zeitgeist that cannot be any longer represented in a singular utopian vision, but in a multiplicity of, let's say, local utopian tendencies. In the show, in which we are represented too, there will be a great deal of consistency. Leon Krier, and the Prince of Wales, nor the Taliban, are in the list of exhibits.

The images illustrating this text focus on the idea of menu, in the title of the conversation, to address the subject of food; simultaneously to the development of globalization, there has been an increasing global availability of local foods: sushi, dim-sum, falafel, tapas or kebab have now become global foods. A series of images of these local foods becoming global seek a resonance with the programming of an international design institution.

A version of this text accompanied the opening of the British Pavilion at the 2002 Architecture Biennale in Venice

Five Points for Now

1. Frameless. Architecture has traditionally been loaded with functions, conventions, and meanings. But now that identity, value, and purpose are in constant fluctuation, buildings have been freed of such heavy, *immaterial* loads; and, as such, they are increasingly difficult to define physically. Because they now bleed into the field, figuratively they blend with the background. Buildings are becoming "landscapes," devoid of functional or representative content, until we add that content—such as when we look for figures in clouds or go for a picnic in a park. It is in this milieu of building and landscape that the potential for new architecture resides.

2. Intensive. Architecture used to be about clearly defining extensions: making walls, gates, roofs, etc. But now that time and space are subject to constant processes of compression and expansion, architecture may have to embrace intensity rather than extension: building links, connections, bifurcations, or continuities where strictly architectural concerns might overflow their normative bounds, destabilizing the architectural object.

3. Grown. Architects once had to decide whether to be visionary or conservative. There was little middle ground, and they had to choose between the *tabula rasa* or the heritage, between the past and the future... But now we have the tools to simulate processes, to synthesize a micro-history for every project. If geological, biological, or cultural history has anything to teach us, it is that these processes of temporal formation produce organizations of far greater complexity and sophistication than instantaneous, abstract ideas do. And abstract ideas only seems to appear out of nowhere anyway, while they too arrive from complex vectors associated with the history of ideas. Yet we are no longer trapped in the traditional compulsion either to reproduce historical models or to invent them *ex nihilo*. We can now, simultaneously, enjoy the sophistication of history and the excitement of radical thought. To reach true complexity, we need to breed projects rather than design them.

4. Complex. The history of the artificial might be said to be split between trees and machines, between the picturesque and the rational-machinic. But now that we have computers, the geometries of either pure indeterminacy or pure linearity are a thing of the past, rather than a problem to be carried into the future. The opportunity that lies ahead of us is to overcome the disciplinary barrier that resorts to contradiction as a form of complexity—false dialectics. Instead, we can choose to exploit complexity through consistency and learn to produce in an entirely artificial yet complex process; to design through a mediated, integrated addition of rigorous orders.

5. Work. As simple constructive knowledge has given way to more complex modeling technologies in architecture, architects seem to have nonetheless abandoned technique as a legitimate space for experimentation, remaining mired instead in language, image, and communication. Construction, in its most progressive-generic sense, has lost the capacity to be truly productive. It has become merely "re-productive," with so-called creative work turned into mere labor—computer-aided or otherwise. The real challenge now is to exploit the potential of construction beyond its reproductive, verifiable mode, to produce unexpected effects.

The images illustrating this text relate to the situation for which I wrote it: the British Pavillion of the Venice Biennale in 2002. The pavilion was designed to address different aspects of the Yokohama International Port Terminal which were presented as characteristic features of contemporary architecture.

Presented at "The Good, the Bad, and the Beautiful"
Symposium at UCLA, Los Angeles, Spring 2002

Processes, Materials, *Prototypes...*

Architecture is not a plastic art, but the engineering of material life. It is therefore a more interesting aim within this practice to produce consistency in the process of construction and material organization rather than in the plastic effects. In fact, I am not interested in having preconceived effects, but rather in exploring the materials—and, here, "material" should be understood in the broadest sense possible—that is, as a source of ideas *and* effects.

Material processes are, arguably, far more interesting than ideas. Ideas are typically linked to existing codes, operating critically or in alignment with pre-existing systems of ideas. Therefore, they tend to be mostly derivative (even when they are posed in *opposition* to the prevailing codes). Rather than making a project into the implementation of an idea, or the scaffolding of an image, I aim to engineer processes on different levels. If the various references I make in the construction of my discourse —geological, biological, or cultural—have anything to teach us, it is that temporal agencies (contingent versus universal or abstract forms of knowledge) produce systems of far greater complexity, adaptability, and sophistication than narrowly conceived, institutional or personal visions or compulsions. Perhaps the most important development brought by computation to architecture is the ability to design, synthesize, and proliferate specific histories and scripts for a project. A project becomes the construction of a micro-history, a kind of hyper-specific constructive narrative. The entity of the project is formed in a sequence where additional complexity is constructed to integrate incoming information. Nowadays, we are no longer trapped in the traditional compulsion to reproduce historical models, or to invent them from scratch. We do not have to produce a project as a facsimile, a derivation, or as the invention of a new historical model. We do not need to produce artificial complexity by making collages. We can synthesize the historical processes in a kind of accelerated motion, integrally adding information to the assemblage. Lenin's *laws of motion* have returned with a vengeance.

One of the greatest potentials of diagrams, statistics, notations, and all the tools of abstraction that come together with computation is that they allow us to produce alienation from *within* reality, versus from the outside (the great canard of poststructuralist opposition to almost everything). Alienation is a powerful instrument for producing new architectural possibilities. Alienation provides the capacity for constant displacement from a closed state of conventions or orders, and the possibility to trigger virtualities in a project that would generally be excluded by a historical construction of tools or responses. Practices of alienation in architecture have been extensively explored in the '80s, destabilizing the object by resorting to other disciplines, or destabilizing the subject by embracing automatism, randomness, or chaos. What is interesting is to notate and organize reality in such a way that both the subject and the object of architecture are mediated, so that the output of the process is not predetermined a priori; that is, without having to abandon the disciplinary field, or renouncing authorship. This form of alienation allows us to open the process of design further without denying human agency (human creative activity) for a false form of so-called pure contingency (material agency); that is to say, positioning ourselves midstream of, or astride, multiple factors and considerations, versus at the beginning or head of this chain of production (godlike, of course). Pragmatic considerations are, therefore, not opposed to the exploration of *latent* potentials.

The potential of diagrams and computation as a medium is not the pure capacity to produce virtual, immaterial worlds, but the possibility of synthesizing new materials and working with them with a rigor that was not possible before the appearance of these tools. I am not interested in virtual architecture in/for itself, but in the virtual *within* architecture (what is potential in a project and has not been actualized yet). Materiality is finally the necessary condition of architecture, and the diagram is the instrument that permits us to construct new, composite material agencies. Critical architecture is not generated *only* through a theoretical discourse that later materializes new material forms and figures of speech and thought. This discipline's *grave* specificity is that we work with materials that have geometries, organizations, and physical properties that exceed, if not precede abstract thought and theoretical paradigms—the very history of mimesis suggests such. Diagrams and abstractions allow us to synthesize new materials and develop the project as a process of material transformation, rather than translating a disembodied theoretical discourse back into architecture terms (syntactical, semantic, or constructive). All arguments regarding transcendence *in* immanence notwithstanding, the material agency of architecture is the radical lining for *all* architectures (including *philosophical* architectures and the *architecture* of philosophy).

I have been concerned—at first unconsciously and, later, more intentionally—with the exploration of typological conditions as fields of emergence, versus an archive of forms to draw on. Contrary to the common understanding of typology as an entity loaded with historical significance and verification, I am particularly interested in resorting to typologies as material assemblages that are loaded with generic solutions already charged with a disciplinary content, and that belong to a history of architecture. Prototypes and types bear immense formal powers when engaged rigorously. What often happens when trying to operate completely outside of the realm of the discipline (let's say, for example, with raw, unprocessed data) is that the product is devoid of critical content, as it does not have any reference point. It becomes a product, but it is difficult to determine its relevance. Especially now, when there are a lot of people trying to build architecture straight out of data—and I have not been an exception to this temptation—it is important to construct a parallel argument that will enable us to question the output, in order to open it up, rather than falling into the tautological-ontological sleep of concluding that a project must be good if it comes out of the right form of pure data-processing. Typological assemblages constitute an ideal articulation of the history of the discipline with assemblages of a material, programmatic, social, or political nature, to connect the factual environment, where architecture must perform, with a necessary disciplinary autonomy to grant its openness. In bringing typology to play within digital architectural production, we bring the immense storehouse of architectural history to play in a direct and—arguably—*explosive* manner. It is not simply borrowing firepower, in this case. It is, instead, the elevation of digital architecture (which was mired in its own excesses) to a fully synthetic and ideational (*not-ideological*) stratum within architecture. *Not a return*, it is a leaping ahead (most especially in the sense that such a strategy completely escapes the deterministic bias of mere data-processing, or that which has led into the semi-autistic straits of parametric architectures). With the appropriation of typology (not typologies per se) we are not reentering the "empire of signs" so much as raiding its storehouse of material and formal agency (raids, so to speak, on the unspeakable).

Probably it would be more adequate to call this operation proto-typical rather than typological. Both the type and the prototype operate with similar material agency, but a prototype is not bound to a particular field, and does not claim a priori any condition of pertinence or validity (or any given or singular form). A prototype is suitable for deployment in alternative conditions rather than being exclusive to a project or a site. It is essentially an experimental tool that does not try to develop (from existing material or form) complexes to impose on a particular location or site. On the contrary, they always test an external (hypothetical) organization in a particular situation. Prototypes are technical and material mediators. They mediate information *into* form; they constitute responsive devices of both the internal and external transfer of information. As such, the prototype contains, in itself, the potential to absorb interference, the capacity to adjust to local contexts, and the potential to embody as much as to virtualize and export information into other material composites, sites, conditions, and projects. In a prototypical operation, real local data perform as an index of specific opportunities while external models of organization operate as manifestations of different degrees of analogous "global" processes. (And global, here, restores a certain measure of universality without going over to the abstract.) A prototype does not operate in closed, stillborn, or autistic domains, but understands that organizations are virtually generic *and yet specific* in their actualization.

A project develops from a prototype according to an operative frame, recognized and constituted in principle rather than literally derived from local data. That principle is what, in turn, becomes the material mediation and the core of the organization of data. Specific technical and functional constraints may be imported and applied to constitute prototypical raw material with potential. This is the difference between the prototypical operation and the emergent generation from the bottom up (provided that this is possible at all within an architectural process); data is not the origin of organization, the core of the material, but the vector of differentiation of the prototype. Specific processes and performances are diagrammed according to the needs of material activation and organization of the prototype. Models for internal differentiation, responsiveness, and proliferation constitute the core, relevance, and interest of the prototype.

A prototype has an associated fabric and develops from a diagram that processes specific information into an architectural organization. The associated fabric is the result of the proliferation and differentiation of the prototype across the space of the project, reacting to different conditions. A prototypical approach is most effective when material and formal agencies are forced to operate within many different contexts; or, as the flexible prototype (*devoid of semantic content*) becomes the vehicle (agent) that links heterogeneous projects in a new "transcendental" field of production.

The images covering this text and the following one aim to remind contemporary architectural technologies, which have become increasingly globalised through a series of products that constitute a new material vocabulary which did not exist just a few decades ago: composite wooden panels, drywall construction, standing seam roofing and walling, unitized, double glazed curtain walling, slipform construction, deck plate construction, gluelam, ETFE, particle board, polycarbonate, silkscreened glass, expanded metal... The images refer to those materials and processes that have come to constitute the core of contemporary construction in the last two decades on a global scale.

Selection of AZP term definitions by Sylvia Lavin
for the Crib Sheets Publication

AZP Crib Sheets Glossary

Architecture. Architecture is not a plastic art, but the engineering of material life. In our practice, our main concern is to produce consistency in the process of construction and material organization rather than in its plastic effects. In fact, we are not interested in producing preconceived effects, but rather in exploring materials—and here material should be understood in the broadest possible sense—as a source of ideas and effects.

Autonomy. Autonomy implies the capacity of a practice to develop such a level of consistency on an abstract level as to extend its potential effects beyond its mere efficiencies and into a regime of excess.
  Despite the fact that everybody can identify the Bilbao Guggenheim as part of the high end of architecture (it's a very expensive building), there is probably no more populist architecture today. It is possible to engage people deeply with a very speculative, avant-garde, experimental, self-referential, and autonomous piece of architecture.

Critical. Criticality is an ingredient to be deployed with care in a production; if it becomes too obvious, it spoils the taste of the materials.

Diagram. One of the great potentials of diagrams, statistics, notations, and all the tools of abstraction that come together with informational technology is that they allow us to produce alienation within reality, without having to resort to a discourse external to the discipline. Alienation is a powerful instrument for producing new architectural possibilities. It provides the capacity for a constant displacement from a closed state of conventions or orders, and the possibility of triggering virtualities in a project, generally excluded by a historical construction of tools or responses.

Practices of alienation in architecture were extensively explored in the 1980s, destabilizing the object by resorting to other disciplines, or destabilizing the subject by embracing automatism, randomness, or chaos. I am interested in notating and organizing reality in which both the subject and the object of architecture are mediated, so that the output of the process is not predetermined, a priori in relation to existing models or conventions, does not require abandoning the disciplinary field, nor declining authorship. Pragmatic considerations are therefore not opposed to the exploration of the virtual. The potential of diagrams and information technology as medium is not the capacity to produce virtual immaterial worlds, but rather the possibility of synthesizing new materials and working with them with a rigor not possible before the appearance of these tools. We are not interested in virtual architecture, but in the virtual in architecture. Critical architecture is not generated through a theoretical discourse that later materializes. This discipline's specificity demands that we work with materials that have geometries, organizations, properties, and so on. Materiality is ultimately the necessary condition of architecture, the diagram of the instrument that permits us to construct new composite materials. Diagrams and abstractions allow us to synthesize new materials and develop the project as a process of material transformation, rather than translating a theoretical discourse into architecture.

Extreme Form. Extreme Form is a peak register of formal singularity.

Generic. The generic is the lowest register of singularity amongst a broad sample of cases.

My practice has concerned itself with the exploration of typological conditions as fields of emergence, in contrast to the common understanding of typology as an entity loaded with historical significance and verification. Typologies are material assemblages loaded with generic solutions, already charged with a disciplinary content and belonging to a history of architecture. I am concerned with exploring these conditions as fields of research, trying to make something generic out of the specificity of the project—but through a breakdown of typological operations rather than the proposal of such a paradigm. Typological assemblages constitute an ideal articulation of the history of the discipline, assemblages of a material, of a programmatic, social, or political nature connecting the factual environment where architecture must perform with a necessary disciplinary autonomy to grant its validity.

It is probably more appropriate to call this operation *prototypical* rather than *typological*. Both the type and the prototype operate in similar ways, but a prototype is not bound to a particular field, and does not claim, a priori, any condition of pertinence or validity. A prototype can be deployed in alternative conditions rather than remaining exclusive to a project or to a site. It is essentially an experimental tool that does not develop from existing material complexes to a particular location, but on the contrary, always tests an external organization in relation to a particular situation. Prototypes are technical and material mediators: they "mediate" information into form; they constitute responsive devices for internal and external transferral of information. As such, the prototype contains in itself the potential to absorb interference, the capacity to adjust to local contexts, and the potential to embody as much as it is to virtualize and export information into other material composites, other sites, other conditions, and other projects. In a prototypical operation, real localized data perform as an index of specific opportunities, while external models of organization operate as manifestations of different degrees of analogous global processes. A prototype does not operate in closed domains, but incorporates the notion that organizations are virtually generic and yet specific in their actualization.

A project develops from a prototype according to an operative frame, recognized and constituted as a principle, rather than literally derived from local data. That principle becomes the material mediation and the core of the organization of data. Specific technical and functional constraints may be imported and applied to infuse prototypical raw material with potential. This is the difference between a prototypical operation and emergent generation from the bottom-up, if this latter is possible at all within an architectural process: data is not the origin of organization, the core of the material, but the vector of differentiation of the prototype. Specific processes and performances are diagrammed according to the requirements of the material activation and organization of the prototype. Models for internal differentiation, responsiveness, and proliferation constitute the core, relevance, and interest of the prototype.

A prototype has an "associated fabric" and develops from a diagram that processes specific information into an architectural organization. This "associated fabric" is the result of the proliferation and differentiation of the prototype across the space of the project, reacting to the different conditions. A prototypical approach is most effective when a practice is forced to operate in many different conditions, becoming the vehicle that links different projects.

Geometry. Geometry is the most promising contemporary domain of architectural theory and the most operative region of contemporary architectural practice.

Landscape. The conflict between a rational, artificial, linear geometry and a picturesque reproduction of nature through less determined geometry has structured the history of landscape. It is through overcoming this opposition that we think the possibility of an emerging landscape, and city, and architecture may exist. The emerging landscape will be characterized by developments that are already happening in biotechnology, artificial intelligence... "complex" organizations, generated through the negotiation of multiple orders: the geological, the biological, and climatic, in a morphogenetic process.

Practice. We have tried to put the emphasis of our practice on the architectural construct, on the materiality of the project, and on its organizational qualities. Geometry, construction, organization, materiality, technique, and pragmatics have become an alternative to a temporary suspension of the exclusivity of cultural analysis.

Process. Processes are far more interesting than ideas, which are linked to existing codes, operating critically or in alignment with other, preexisting systems of ideas. Rather than turning a project into the implementation of an idea or the scaffolding for an image, I am interested in constructing differing engineering-based processes. If geological, biological, or social histories have something to teach us, for instance, it is that these processes of temporal formation produce organizations of far greater complexity and sophistication than instantaneous ideas or visions. This is perhaps the most important development brought about by information technology to our practice: we can design, synthesize and proliferate specific histories and scripts for a project. In this way, a project becomes the construction of a microhistory, a kind of specific construction narrative.

The essence of the project is formed in a sequence where additional complexity is constructed to integrate incoming information. We are no longer trapped within the traditional compulsion to reproduce historical models, or to invent new models from scratch. We do not have to produce a project as a reproduction, a derivation, or the invention of a historical model. We do not need to produce complexity by making collages. We can synthesize the historical processes in a kind of accelerated motion, integrally adding information to the assemblage.

Program. Program is the most politically correct side of architecture's double agenda of performances.

Technique. We are interested in exploring the processes of construction and engineering on a variety of levels, rather than creating structures that are the simple implementation of an idea, or merely the scaffolding of an image.

About the images of this text, see page 236.

Published in *AD Monographs*,
London, 2009

Mediating Between Ideas and Material Agency: Icons, Indexes, Diagrams, Drawings, and Graphs

After a few decades in which the architectural debate was focused primarily on signification, representation, and language games, there has been a progressive shift (if not a full rebellion) in the form of a new appreciation for pure methodological and instrumental research. Processes of irreversible globalization require new spatial and material organizations that transcend simplistic national or ideological constructs. So-called critical practices, as a result, are becoming increasingly ineffective within the current culture of global capital, as they often have defined the problem too narrowly. It is not simply national, regional, or global stakes that are at play in architecture, but rather the somewhat obscure formal operations of those systems of *representation* and *speciation*. A formal and material critique, therefore, might contribute possible and positive alternatives. The old ways no longer work. Resistance has shifted within architecture (as the critical stance par excellence) to engagement, and while those engaged in resistance see engagement as complicity, it is not entirely clear that the opponents of architecture in service to capital were not, paradoxically, also complicit anyway (in ways defined by the truly hard-core opposition as secretly complicit *through opposition*).

The massive development of Information Technology and the production of the virtual, while not the entire story, has triggered practices that are more driven by the production of new, alternative realities than to the representation or interpretation of *verifiable* ones. One could argue, of course, that previous modes of resistance aligned on the same dynamics, proposing alternative, virtual worlds through the critique of existing worlds, yet the difference has to do with the exiting of the "boudoir" described by Manfredo Tafuri as productive of nothing useful, or—better yet—nothing politically and ideologically *engaging*.

Computers allow us to construct organizations and images that we have never seen or imagined before and that depend on the computer for their existence. The visualization and operation with numerical data on n-dimensional spaces available through information technology allows us to introduce other parameters in architectural drawings (such as time, light, temperature, weight, etc.) that we were not able to previously visualize. It also allows for us to test the behavior of a system under conditions that are not experimentally verified, and to explore architectural and urban situations beyond our conventional, accumulated knowledge or experience. The *actualization* of the *virtual* can never operate by resemblance, and therefore it requires tools that will allow us to see (and therefore to imagine, to conceptualize) what we have never

seen before. It is precisely this capacity to expand our perception to domains beyond our experiential knowledge, and to control and accurately determine the processes of construction that make the computer an ideal instrument for the production of the virtual. This is also one of the reasons for the recent interest in the diagram and diagrammatic practices.

Since the mid-'90s, and after the era of the poststructuralist revolt and the revolt *against* poststructuralism, diagrams have been a key subject of the contemporary architectural discourse. That said, the exceptional (almost mystical) power attributed to the diagram is multivalent and, as a result, not always consistent. It is, therefore, important to clarify the terms of engagement given to this order of semi-abstract and diagrammatical magic in order to understand how the *use of* diagrams relates to other instruments and mediations between concepts, material organizations, and effects. It is not quite the reloading of associative magic given to other disciplines, but it is an outcome nonetheless of the episteme, insofar as it registers with the discretionary procedures of several other representational orders—for example, philosophy and art—on the verge of exiting postmodernist relativism and reinstating an interest in the real.

Thus, three interrelated questions arise. What is the difference between using diagrams versus icons, symbols, or indices as forms of mediation between concepts and material organizations? What are the different potentials for understanding the diagram, and what are the different representational instruments or apparatuses that are often included within this category, other than drawings or graphs? What do we understand *through* diagrams, drawings, graphs, etc.—the technical arsenal of non-representational architecture?

An interesting undercurrent in the present-day discussion of the diagram can be traced back to semiotics, and probably the earliest disquisitions on the subject date back from Charles Peirce's classification of signs into *icons*, *indexes*, and *symbols*. According to Peirce, an icon is a sign that in itself expresses its status as *dynamic object*. That means that an icon (such as a religious image or a political symbol) is a material expression of the qualities, functions, and properties of the object itself, and the materiality of the icon is not relevant to its performance. The nature of the icon is not arbitrary as there is a binding relationship between its form and its content. An index (such as the reading of a measuring instrument, a physical trace of an action or an associated phenomenon) is a sign that manifests the influence of its *dynamic object*, by an action that leaves a material imprint. Indices also have a binding relationship between form and content, but this connection is not formally explicit, although it is materially linked. A symbol (examples might include a trophy, a monument, or a word) is a sign that both refers to its status as *dynamic object* and is manifested through representation. Regardless of the differences between icon, index, and symbol, all are signs, and signs mediate between form and content in both material and immaterial ways. *Diagrams* belong to a category that mediates between physical constructs and concepts or percepts and their performance depends on how they are deployed. Such also accounts for the inordinate ability of the architectural eye and mind to find almost anything in diagrams one might be looking for, or—conversely—anything one might be trying to avoid.

If the origins of the diagrammatic practices of the 1960s tended to avoid the iconic similarities between the diagram and the building, some of the pop-based architects would resort to icons and signs as a way of drawing relationships between concepts and form. Some of the proposals that emerged in the 1970s within critical practices were primarily aimed at producing mediations between cultural or subjective representations through abstract formal systems deployed as a subversive mechanism, practicing a sort of dialectical-materialist voodoo aimed at destabilizing the status quo. On the contrary, the new, post-poststructuralist pragmatism utilizes the *diagram* as a projective rather than mediating tool that constructs the real, producing new sensations and moods (affects). Following the work of Deleuze and Guattari, who define the diagram in the context of a *techno-scientific semiotics*, the diagram belongs not to the paralogisms of representational systems, like most other signs, but retrieves a *logic of sensation*. As such (and as a therapeutic of the architectural mind), the renaturalized diagram is aimed at bringing forward new *material* worlds through new material organizations. The *diagram* is that which allows the emergence of another possible world. There are several paths of development within the diagrammatic. The diagram has often been linked to the tracing of the virtual, sometimes related to the mere organization of space and matter, sometimes to the production of sensations and affects. There are those who understand the diagram as primarily related to topology and those who include indexicality as part of a diagrammatic practice.

Without taking sides in this debate, and for the sake of clarity, I would like to define a diagram as a material organization that describes relationships and prescribes performances in space. It does not necessarily contain metric or geometric information; those emerge once the diagram starts processing data (or matter). A diagram is always specific to a space. It may be a specific location, a scale, a temporal frame, but it always has a spatial correlation, as opposed to a graph, for example. It relates to processes that may occur not only in three-dimensional space but in several dimensions of reality. There is a tendency to believe that there is a diagrammatic architecture where the architecture inherits the formal characteristics of the diagram, but in principle, a diagram is not necessarily similar in form to the organization it describes or prescribes: a very simple diagram may generate very complex organizations. As opposed to signifying or symbolic operations, one of the greatest potentials of a diagrammatic construction is to produce organizations with explicit versus implicit multiple readings.

The primary quality of a diagram is its reductive nature. Diagrammatic operations should not be confused with arbitrariness or lack of control; on the contrary, the diagram is about precisely defining, at every moment in the process, the exact level of knowledge and determination than we can exert on the project. In a diagrammatic process, the project develops a constant capacity to trigger new possibilities. The project retains its virtualities, which become only partially actualized, keeping the possibility to develop *ad infinitum*. In a diagrammatic project the moment of closure is determined by factors external to the project, and the propositional moments, the aims and strategies, are not restricted to the origin or the end, but to the middle of the process. Between the form of the diagram and the final form of the building, additional information needs to be added.[1]

Only after the diagram has absorbed all this information does it become a drawing, having acquired metrical and geometrical determinations. A drawing is a material organization that prescribes metric and geometric information in three-dimensional space. Its precision is therefore critical to its operativity. Conventional architectural methods are based on an indeterminate relationship between the diagrams and the drawings. In traditional architectural methodologies, these relations are usually regulated by the conventions of the discipline. Drawings are the primary instrument for the production of architecture. But a projective process that remains limited to the relationship between drawings and real space buildings is constrained to the actualization of conventions and commonly resists the integration

---

1   An example of a project developed diagrammatically is the Yokohama project, where the diagram sets the targets precisely, but also generates more ambiguous readings of the outcome. The project begins with the ambition to produce a pier where you never retrace your steps. That is the concept of the project, which is embedded in a diagram that defies the characteristic linear organization of a pier (the no-return diagram). In whatever direction the pier is traveled, the experience will be of a continuous forward movement. The project's departure is not placed on its formal or representational qualities, but on its most basic performance as a spatial organization. The physical concreteness of the project emerges progressively as the diagram becomes engaged with a certain material: in Yokohama, the material is the ground. Its deployment evolves the no-return diagram into a three-dimensional diagram. Ergonomic and functional information are then incorporated into the new diagram—for example, the scale of the load-bearing structures, head clearances, manufacturing constraints—which are then incorporated to determine the scale and geometry of the surface's deformations.

of variation, local specificities or changes of conditions. This is where the diagrammatic process becomes advantageous in a culture determined by the fast pace of change.

A graph is a plot of information that is not actualized in real space. A graph does not have plastic or visual content, as it does not belong to an organization that unfolds in real space. It describes or prescribes information operating in an abstract space. It can act to unlock virtualities that are not perceptible on a sensible level or it can extend the capacity of material organizations to affect or be affected by processes occurring in virtual spaces. The transfer of a graph into real space always requires a specific transfer technique; for example, the implementation of the differential fenestration ratios of a building envelope to produce environmental performances requires the technology to provide differential fenestration. In architecture, to make a graph operative, it is crucial to understand the dimensional relationship between the space of the graph and the concrete space.

The most common mistake of contemporary "experimental" architecture is to turn the space of the diagram or the graph literally into the space of the drawing, and, therefore, of the building. The current tendency toward smoothness is an effect of operating with frictionless diagrams. But real buildings have materials, and these are in charge of the production of the coarseness and true complexity of the building's form and organization. A diagram or graph always requires a determinant form of mediation to become a drawing, to enter into real space.

The images populating this text refer to the progressive return to an iconographic mode of communication made necessary by globalization and enabled through computer and mobile interface. If modernity was grounded on the logographic communication, the contemporary world is moving back toward icons as the primary device of communication.

Paper given at the International Architectural Education Summit, Symposium 3: Beyond Boundaries, Tokyo, 2009

Architectural Education in a Global World

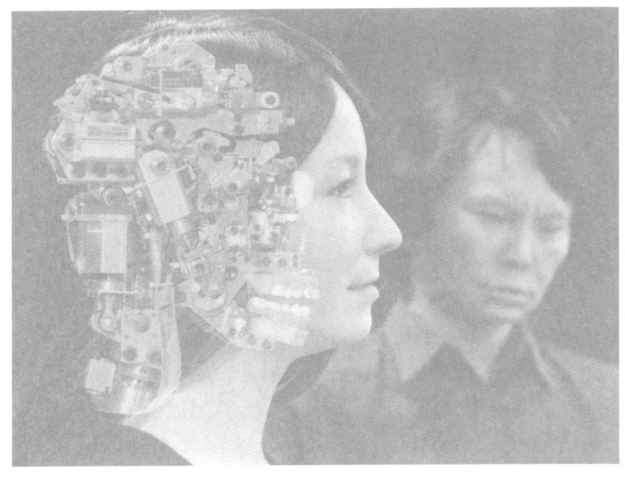

The Future of Architectural Education
I am not sure I deserve the role of giving the keynote speech on the subject of architectural education in this session with other colleagues on the table who probably have thought much deeper than I have on this subject.

I have little certainty about what the future of architectural education may be. All I can do is to put forward a few reflections on the subject, indicate certain tendencies and maybe some potentials that I perceive both as an educator and a practitioner.

The Current Environment
The practice of architecture is increasingly globalized: technologies, regulations, and construction systems are increasingly applied across an expansive and integrated domain. Architects can no longer rely on knowing the local system but need to be able to work in different locations. It is the responsibility of edu-

cational institutions to address the issue of globalizing tendencies by, in turn, becoming global in their own right.

The arrival of current forms of globalization in the 1960s changed everything, making the past radical practices for the most part seem irrelevant. Why equalize geopolitics when economies and technology can do the very same without the attendant ideological battles? Why equalize class, when class has transcended politically and geographically determined communities? One might conclude that the postwar economic boom of the 1960s was the death knell of political ideology as an effective mechanism to transform society.

From Infrastructure to Commodity: the Market

Recent developments in capitalist regimes of culture have been able to provide new levels of civil liberties (not simply reducible to easy credit, easy travel, and easy consumption). Architectural education has moved from an institutional activity that produced the future generations of practitioners in certain geographical areas, to a model where schools are aiming to produce a new type of global practitioner, capable of operating mostly anywhere there is a computer and Internet access.

The question of how education intersects with the market and becomes a marketable consumer product is one that I believe we ought to consider carefully, and that affects directly the way in which education is structured. For example, the type of education that follows from the American market-driven model is markedly different than the one that follows from the European polytechnic model, which is now being redefined to address the prevalence of the market as a global milieu. One model seems mired in the individualistic ethos of the free market (American capitalism), while the other seems mired in the last vestiges of guaranteed work *if you can find it* (the late-European Welfare State).

Global education has become elective, disengaged and individually driven, and lost most of its capacity to produce a transformative effect.

Architectural Education and Professional Qualification

The attachment of professional qualification to the educational process is an important question to resolve. In the Anglo-Saxon model architectural education is detached from professional qualification, while in the continental (European) model it remains attached to and part of the structure of completing one's studies. This attachment is now being questioned both by the competition of the absolute free market model, and by the increasing globalization of practice, which is triggering large-scale projects of recalibration, such as the Bologna Process (the harmonization of educational standards across the EU through the European Higher Education Area). This is now creating the question of what the mechanisms of accreditation should be, with processes trying to normalize what architectural education should be globally—like Bologna—, or some of the standards that the UIA is trying to set in order to reign in the global market of architectural education as a commodity.

The answer to this question is very complex. It is clear that the model of education as a national or local infrastructure, as a guarantor of the good practices, is to a degree incompatible with the predominance of the market as the sole mediator of practice. But it appears to me that when professional qualification is detached from the educational process it produces a certain schizophrenia between practice and academia, as historically evident in the USA, where often the academy is simply and derisively accused of being out of touch with the real world—part, in fact, of its original mandate as a "world apart."

Homogenization: Style and Technique

If the absolute free market model provides flexibility and capacity of rapid response to the disciplinary environment *in practice*, it

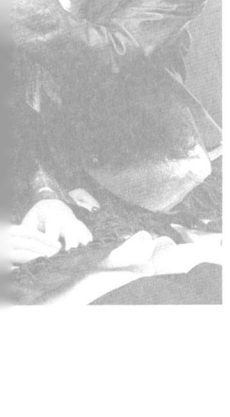

also produces some effects that have to be carefully watched and monitored. In parallel to these attempts there is a drive to regulate the profession on a global level, a tendency across institutions towards specialization and branding, as a result of competition for the market; architectural education as a commodity is often marketed around:
— Certain names and their stylistic traits. *Starchitecture.* Certain institutions own certain names.
— Certain technologies. Curiously this competition for the market has produced also a level of homogenization; for example, landscape urbanism and parametric design have become omnipresent across schools worldwide.

If this homogenization of the contemporary contents of architectural education indexes the new forms of knowledge that have become now relevant to the contemporary practice of architecture, it also relegates knowledge to either a stylistic or technocratic role that does not engage with the cultural, social, and political context that a more traditional context provided to perhaps outdated educational policies.

As a result of this, the production of contemporary architectural education is often a replica of well-known practices or virtuous exploration of certain technologies, all authorized by either celebrity imprimatur or cash, without any capacity to actually engage with the real purpose of education: to expand the disciplinary base and transform it.

The Educational Menu: *Kaiseki* vs. McDonalds
One of the biggest malaises of present-day consumerist education is the fantasy of hyper-individualization. In this model, education is similar to hiring a personal trainer that caters for each student's needs; programs have to be designed to satisfy individual

demands, so relevant research as a collective endeavor becomes impossible. The process is aimed at providing that one-in-one-thousandth chance of launching a new super star.

Contemporary architectural education cannot avoid engaging directly with technology; it is a *fait accompli*. But neither does this automatically describe what "good practice" is (in whatever field of knowledge we choose to operate within and upon). Technology is neutral. Therefore, those of us engaged as educators cannot avoid defining the plan, the targets, the prey, the hunt.

The idea of the *à la carte* school is a product of the consumer education and follows the same strategy of MacDonald's: they offer you an enormous choice, although ultimately everything tastes the same. A *kaiseki* menu is far more interesting: there is only one menu, which you cannot choose: you choose to eat there because you believe the chef knows better, and often everything is sophisticated and new. If the menu has now become inescapable within contemporary education, it should at least be designed for a clientele open to experience new flavors rather than rejoice in the ones they know.

Retrieving Political Agency
What kind of engagement with regimes of power can we expect from architectural education, which will eventually reempower architects and provide us with a transformative political agency? Is it possible to assume that such will *flow* from such engagement?

Contemporary building technology has become today so developed that there are few things we cannot do, as long as our clients are willing to pay for it. Architectural education has followed this moment of enablement as an opportunity to explore freedoms, to such degree that every notion of discipline has vanished, and freedom has become senseless. What is interesting now is precisely to re-encounter the limits, the optimal states, the maximal efficiencies behind an expression: *The limits of freedom are more interesting than the possibilities.* I have always asked people—in the office and in the classroom—to refrain from making formal decisions for which they do not have an excuse, no matter how strongly they feel about it. The excuse is a technique that acknowledges the frictions between efficiencies and expressions, aimed to resolve the *possible* ensuing conflicts. Perhaps one of the most important things to learn in the current milieu is the capacity to create good excuses.

Breeding Knowledge: Collective Research as an Educational Model

To avoid this effect of debased global replication (where sameness is the same everywhere), one possibility is to shift from education as *consumption* to education as *production* of knowledge.

By shifting architectural education from its more traditional role as the production of a local professional class (and its later mutation into the production of technically enabled global manpower) to the role of producing knowledge through the development of concrete, but speculative research programs, we may be able to reengage the practice with a wider context that the global scope seems to have paradoxically erased or placed under house arrest.

An adequate architectural education today is not one that provides a general knowledge of many different fields, but a "vertical" understanding of the problems and potentials entailed in the production of an architectural project.

The design of educational programs around the investigation of concrete problems with a global scope where architects become educated in the process of producing valuable knowledge that others can redeploy elsewhere may become the core of an alternative form of architectural education that addresses some of the inadequacies of contemporary architectural education. There are already a number of examples of these architectural-educational practices: Rem Koolhaas's project on the city at Harvard; Beatriz Colomina's PhD program at Princeton School of Architecture; Atelier Bow-Wow's Made in Tokyo; Columbia University GSAAP's Studio-X. My own program as the head of the Berlage Institute in Rotterdam and the Princeton Envelope Group experiment, which is still in process, belong to this category of educational practice.

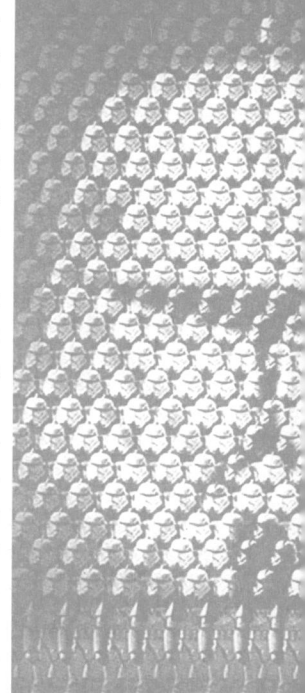

These educational practices imply three basic operations:

1. **Identification of Relevant Research Domains.** To generate expertise that will bridge between theory and practice, between the discipline and the exterior reality/world. This implies a certain specialization of knowledge and a narrow focus. It is more important to explore in all aspects the possibilities of a certain technology, than the provision of a broad outlook. It is crucial to understand the relationship between political, technical, and aesthetic questions; avoid technocracy and mannerism.
2. **Collective, Intersubjective Group Work.** We need to avoid the focus on the individual as an "education consumer" to focus on the possibility of collective research work, more capable to generate a process of "breeding knowledge." The individuals are formed in the production of collective knowledge.
3. **Engagement and Publicness: Feedback and Broadcasting.** One of the most important parts of creating a form of education that will enable future architects to gain transformative capacity is to propose programs that will draw attachments outside the discipline.

Those can be provided by:

- Establishing direct links to potential clients, sponsors, etc, in order to draw in the external forces and potentials. The crucial question is: who are we working for?
- Attaching a broadcasting device to the program, in order to collect feedback and to immediately engage the outcome of the research to a broader debate. No thesis gathering dust in the library or hermetic discipline: research and education need to develop an immediate public interface.

The images illustrating this text refer to androids, clones and surrogates as an ironic metaphor of education. A series of images of these creatures is aimed to serve as an ironic backdrop to the discourse of the text, but also as a reference to a contemporary tendence to transfer human qualities to non-human beings. We need to prepare to educate androids. Is education the insertion of an operative system into the psyche of a population, or the transformation of humans into search engines rather than as accomplished surrogates?

Yale School of Architecture Studio,
Fall 2010

Ecotectonics

During the next three decades, over a billion people in the emerging economies will move from the rural milieu to the city. Natural resources will not be able to feed those future cities unless true technological and lifestyle revolutions take place: cities and the built environment consume around 70% of global energy and generate nearly 50% of global carbon emissions. Environmental concerns will doubtlessly drive the evolution of architecture during the next decades. The bridging between natural and artificial ecologies, the networks between human and non-human agencies will become a critical part of this engagement, politically, formally and materially and this studio will be focusing on the exploration of this subject and its architectural implications and potentials.

If the discipline of architecture has gravitated historically around the subject of tectonics, the growing consciousness that a building is a device that performs primarily as an environmental regulator is shifting the focus of the discipline from tectonics to ecological and thermodynamic processes: buildings establish the regime of energy exchange of the built environment by virtue of their geometry, their materiality etc. and therefore there is an opportunity to establish relationships between these performances and emerging architectural sensibilities and expressions.

We will explore these relationships, aiming to relate environmental and energy performances with material concerns, tectonic, visual or spatial, through the use of a variety of new instruments available. From the incorporation of agricultural technologies to integrate landscape design and building technology, to the use of object-oriented software to model thermodynamic processes into physical structures, we will mobilize a series of new instruments in order to enable the exploration of a new architectural sensibility which does not depart from the core of the discipline to date, but evolves it.

Urban Ecosystems
The urban environment is the location where our investigation will focus, as the domain where the next stage of human habitat will be developed. The urban scale is also where sustainable building technologies can be most efficiently optimized. Addressing the city as an ecosystem populated by a series of new energy-efficient species which have to be adjusted to a new energy-scarce urban environment, will be the general target of this research.

The exploration of the city as an ecosystem sets out the frame for an investigation that will inevitably address typology as a fundamental disciplinary question. We will address building populations as a process of speciation driven by form and material organization, producing physical assemblages capable to mediate between top-down typological procedures and bottom-up parametric design in order to increase the degree of differentiation of the building populations. Rather than types, the research will aim to produce prototypes that generate a diverse building population: diversity is one of the characteristics of a resilient ecosystem. Diversity of speciation allows for the ecosystem to adapt, as it is more likely that some populations will be able to adjust to the new conditions and perpetuate the ecosystem.

Architecture as a discipline has traditionally relied on typology or archetype, classifying buildings by their functions. A building's program or essential function becomes tied to an idealized or original form where a common essence is defined by a set of properties shared by the members of a particular class. However, the sensitivity or capacity to affect or be affected is particular to each individual threshold of sensitivity to the environment. Given a typological family, potential phenotypical variations can arise, producing differentiated behavior of a building population, and potentially new forms of architectural expression.

Can we capture the evolutionary and emergent properties of nature in the artificial, establishing a link between nature and the city? Can we incorporate the sensibility and virtues of natural systems into the artificial realm? The ambition of the studio is to explore the technologies of sustainable building through the introduction of life-like qualities in the artificial: to *animate* matter, sensitize it by designing behavioural patterns that produce physical characteristics and qualities that trigger an emotional response to dynamic forces.

Object-Oriented Architecture

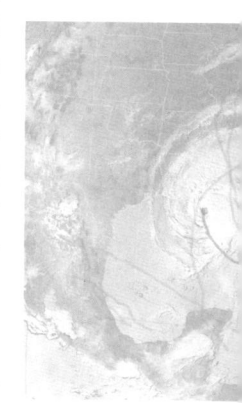

The research will have a specific technical background that we believe to be particularly relevant to explore the new architectural effects of bridging between natural and artificial ecologies and setting up networks between human and non-human agencies: The Object-Oriented paradigm is a holistic approach that links material and social processes through new forms of artificial intelligence. Object Oriented Programming (OOP) produces complex and consistent organizations through simple rules of interacting objects that communicate, self-organize and develop ad-hoc communities. The distinctive feature of Object-Oriented Programs is that they do not distinguish between data structures and coded behavior, between data and function, as usual in programming languages. They are "flat" networks of actors and objects gathered up into assemblies. They act through simple, local rules, processing sensorial and physical data, figuring heterogeneous yet consistent wholes. These systems react locally to sensed aspects of the world, resolving conflicts generated within the distributed system. In Rodney Brooks' terms, *"...It is possible for different parts of the system to "believe" wildly inconsistent things about the world."* The possibility of using *Object Oriented Programming* and *Subsumption* architectures to model contemporary urban behavior, while producing its physical organization, is a newly available technology which may offer new alternatives to produce adequate architectural expressions for contemporary political ecologies.

Envelopes 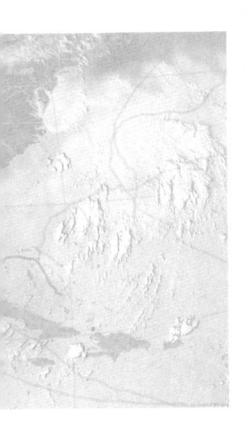 
After a few decades of relentless globalization, we are now entering a stage where the illusion of a border-free world and the utopia of a freewheeling, free-flowing spatiality has ceased to be the primary goal of spatial and material practices: we must address the fact that the space where we live is not without borders.

The building envelope is possibly the oldest and most primitive architectural element. It materializes the separation of the inside and outside, natural and artificial; it demarcates private from public and delimits ownership. When it becomes a façade, the envelope operates as a representational device in addition to its crucial environmental and territorial roles. It forms the border, the frontier, the edge, the enclosure and the interface. Particularly at a time when energy and security concerns have replaced an earlier focus on circulation and flow as the contents of architectural expression, the building envelope emerges as architecture's primary subject. Simultaneously existing as both the architectural surface and its attachments, the envelope is a point of contact, a material link, between architecture and other social, political and economic processes.

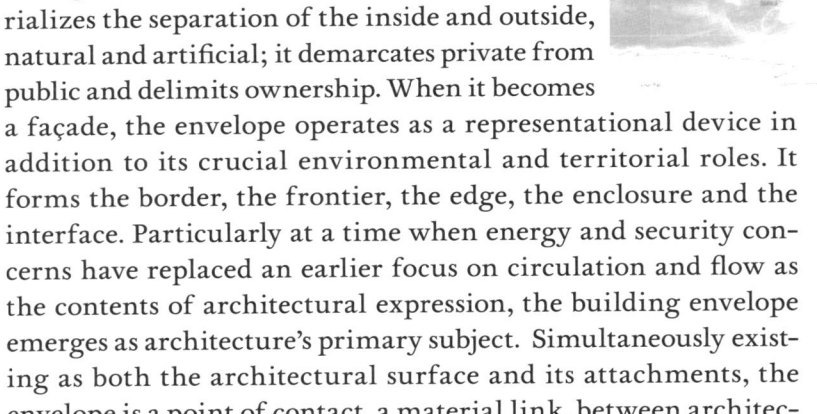

The building envelope is the single most important contributor to the environmental performance of a building, and it will be the element where the research will focus, both in terms of urban massing, and detailing of the prototypes. Driven by environmental determination, the research aims to produce envelope prototypes capable to perform within the urban proposals developed within the studio.

Theoretical, Cultural and Technical Context of the Research

The research is therefore aimed to bring together disciplinar considerations with theoretical and technical concerns to explore the potentials of a new architectural sensibility. The question of typologies and speciation will be a critical reference for the studio. The classical notions of typology from Quatremere and Durand, and their evolution through modernism towards Rowe's formal interpretation and Rossi's historicist approach constitute a theoretical background to the studio, and a link into the more conventional forms of the discipline. The connection of this more disciplinar discourse to recent discussions on Political Ecology, Genetics and Environmentalism—exemplified in the work of Latour and Sloterdijk—as a crucial trans-disciplinary question in contemporary culture, will be one of the theoretical interests of the studio. The research aims to explore also a series of tools that have become recently available. New developments in Artificial Intelligence such as Object-Oriented Programming and distributed computing—as exemplified in the work of Rodney Brooks, Casey Reas and Ben Fry—, and the emergence of an increasingly sophisticated range of sustainable building technologies may open new design possibilities, develop potential models for the artificial realm and produce new architectural sensibilities.

The images illustrating this text are dynamic mappings of weather, traffic, wind and water currents and temperature. Thermodynamic and ecosystemic imagery of this kind is available only in the last two decades and opens an entirely new material sensibility addressed by the experiment of Ecotectonics.

Princeton, New Jersey, Fall 2011 Studio
(Member Culture Now Project)

Localizing Networks: Physical Terminals for Web 2.0 Engines

The project is aimed to capture the architectural potential of the technological and economical paradigm that has opened with the development of communication technologies, and it is part of a collective effort by several architecture schools in the US to address the question of contemporary culture in the built environment.

The phenomenon of Web 2.0 is marked by the rapidly evolving domains of e-commerce, social media, and social networking, which have changed how we create and make use of financial, social, and physical capital. These developments offer new platforms for social engagement and political action whose architectural implications are still a matter of speculation. The changes extend to all aspects of our daily life, reshaping how we form communities and cultures, forge social structures, utilize resources, and engage in politics.

The effects of technology are becoming increasingly visible across different sectors of society. The open platforms of social networking are redrawing social relationships and diversifying social engagement across disparate cultures. Facebook membership alone has surpassed 750 million members in August 2011, nearly double the world's native English-speaking population. With access to an unparalleled amount of personal information, seemingly minor innovations such as photo-tagging and geo-referencing have had enormous implications for marketing, privacy, national security, and disaster relief.

In contemporary politics, SMS and Twitter have emerged as potent tools for citizen journalists under repressive political regimes who wish to voice their dissent. The role played by Facebook and Google in activating the political realm in the Middle East and Far East, as well as domestically in the 2008 Obama campaign, show that these technologies are central to the future of politics.

In transportation, the car-sharing model pioneered by Flexcar and Zipcar has eliminated the financial burden of car ownership for people with an infrequent need, making private transit more accessible and reducing the number of personally-owned vehicles by an estimated 15 for each car in Zipcar's fleet.

In housing, 4,000 New York City residents lease out a spare room to a guest every night through Airbnb, relieving the burden of an expensive rental market and providing visitors with an alternative to hotels.

In the music and the performing arts, Kickstarter has opened the flow of micro-financing to support independent projects which would have otherwise been at the mercy of cash-strapped grant institutions. Others micro-financing platforms like Kiva are providing investment to entrepreneurs in underdeveloped economies.

The mechanisms of 21st century social networking have been the subject of design experiments, such as the DARPA Network Challenge, in which 10 weather balloons were released across the United States at undisclosed locations, only to be 'found' 9 hours later by a team at MIT's Human Dynamics Laboratory. These networks have also proven successful in mobilizing financial aid and information in the wake of the 2010 earthquake in Haiti.

These examples demonstrate a new found capacity to create capital through a marketplace in which individual actors can be brought together for a common goal, independent of corporate governance or representative proxy. And this capital is real: Groupon is on pace to be the fastest growing company to reach one billion dollars in annual revenue; Facebook's annual revenue tops two billion; and Apple briefly surpassed Exxon Mobil as the world's largest corporation. With established models of revenue generation under their belt, tech incubators see membership generation and viral marketing as the essential tools of business growth. If you build the network, money will follow. But it is not only financial capital that is channeled through social networks: constituencies of political opinion and lifestyle trends are also formed in this manner, outside the conventional channels of broadcasting and advertising. Will politics—and eventually aesthetics—follow similar models of crowd-behavior?

Fuller's vision of a future where citizens would *"vote with their wallets"* seems to become a reality in the convergence between society, economy, and politics that plays out through these new channels.

For all of this optimism, the more sobering observation for architects is that the agents that count in this market have thus far limited their public operations to the virtual realm. Their transactions either make better use of an existing physical infrastructure or render it obsolete. At the same time, the physical realm offers potential for modes of social engagement that can complement the virtual.

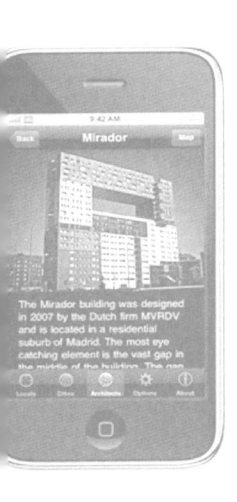

This research will investigate ways in which architecture can calibrate physical engagement as an actor in the process of social networking and social media. One of the most relevant developments of these technologies for the field of architecture and design is the emergence of geo-referencing. After forming exhaustive global connections through the internet, many Web 2.0 companies are now starting to focus primarily on interaction at the local scale. Tools like Foursquare and Google Latitude explore how users with GPS-enabled mobile devices can interact with their physical environment in new ways. This shift in focus toward the localization of networks opens new ground for architecture, a practice that is intrinsically local. It gives us hope that architectural devices may become crucial actors within social networks, reclaiming some of the agency that architecture has lost to the virtual milieu of the world-wide-web.

Social networking and social media companies engage with aspects of society that have undeniable physical qualities and human dimensions. Cultures of performing arts, music, film, digital design, food, fitness, and dating have all undergone fundamental reorganization in the era of social networking, and our hypothesis is that they are ripe for a new physical interface which will enable them to develop a local presence in certain key locations. The studio will be aimed toward generating local audiences and constituencies through the deployment of physical structures designed for each of these themes. Just as Apple stores, university student centers, and World Expo pavilions have established architecture's capacity to communicate commercial, educational, and national identity, this studio presents an opportunity to envision a new form of privately-sponsored cultural institution with its own socially-assembled identity.

We will look to specific companies within the Web 2.0 arena and examine how physical hubs for social interaction can work in concert with the network paradigms already available through the web and mobile devices. We will be drawing from sociology texts on actor-network theory and assemblages for insight into how we can engage the human and non-human—the physical and the digital—actors in the understanding of network behavior. We will aim to establish a new set of quantitative and qualitative metrics for each project through which we can explore how architecture can become a crucial actor within these networks.

Our understanding of a social network as an ecosystem of individual actors speaks to the usefulness of agent-based behavioral models and genetic algorithms.

Thus we will make extensive use of *Object-Oriented Programming* (OOP) and *Parametric Design* tools to explore vectors of proximity, connectivity, visibility, and heterogeneity as they relate to each of the projects. OOP can produce complex organizations through simple rules governing how individual objects interact. Agents that process only local sensorial and physical data can work in concert to resolve conflicts and inefficiencies across a distributed system.

In Rodney Brooks' terms, *"...It is possible for different parts of the system to "believe" wildly inconsistent things about the world."* To evaluate and refine the assemblies that develop from the OOP investigations, we require holistic techniques such as annealing and genetic algorithms. These processes search for classes of high performance models within a complex, multi-dimensional search space. To aid in these investigations, Ryan will lead a series of technical workshops in Processing and Grasshopper, beginning with agent-based behavior and subsequently covering genetic and annealing algorithms and data visualization as they relate to the refinement and analysis of architectural prototypes. He will also be available to provide support throughout the semester for technical issues that arise and, where appropriate, incorporate other topics such as map algebra and graph theory.

Projects

The projects and organizations we have selected to test these prototypes offer a broad—though far from complete—sampling of social networking and social media companies that we believe could benefit from a public venue. It is our intention that by investigating a range of themes and experiences, from the auditory to the olfactory, the studio will produce a diverse and nuanced set of projects.

Kickstarter.com (Concern: Performing arts). Until crowd-funding sites came into existence, there was not an efficient structure in place to match creative projects in the performing arts with a broad community of individual donors. Kickstarter now supports these artists through a threshold pledge system, whereby proposals incentivize would-be contributors through special offers, which are often delivered in a promotional pitch that showcases an excerpt from the larger work. Insofar as these showcases act as content in their own right, they have an inherent isomorphism with street performance, only without the complex social undertones. Therefore, a public venue to showcase Kickstarter projects in the performing arts could provide a vehicle for reexamining the social dynamics of street performance.

IndabaMusic.com (Concern: Music). For all of the music industry's preoccupation with copyright and digital distribution, the potential to utilize the web for the creation of music is frequently overshadowed. Yet artists from Yo-Yo Ma to OK Go have embraced this possibility through their collaboration with Indaba Music, a service that allows users to upload audio content for others to modify, accompany, and remix. Indaba's crowd-sourcing platform has fostered collaborations that transcend geography and genre, bringing together musicians and listeners from diverse backgrounds. Many of these projects have led to live recordings and public performances, which allows us to posit a public venue for crowd-sourced music generation as a natural extension of Indaba's web-based platform.

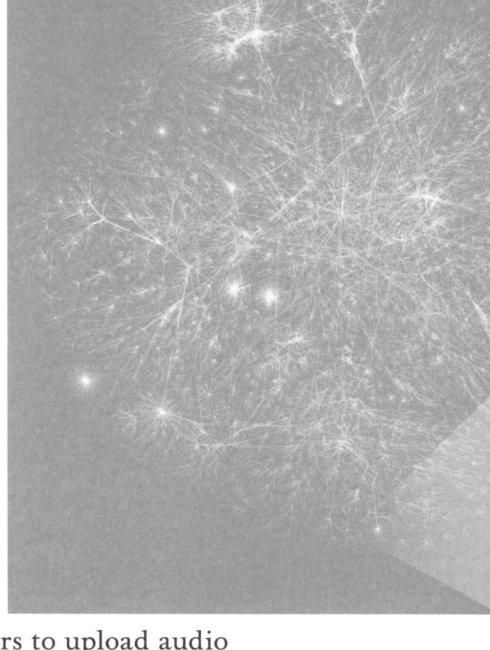

Vimeo.com (Concern: Film). Since its founding in 2004, Vimeo has become the largest online venue for exclusively user-generated video content. What sets it apart from other video sharing services is its strict adherence to original work, a principle that has helped foster a community of creative individuals that foregrounds individual expression and productive discourse. The decision to inaugurate the Vimeo Festival and Awards last Fall suggests that the company sees a place for its content in the public realm, where viewers can share in a collective experience. At the same time, to build a permanent venue for content as diverse as Vimeo's would call for a radically different model than the box office cinema, a model that forgoes feature-length productions in favor of a more plastic and interactive, live-browsing experience.

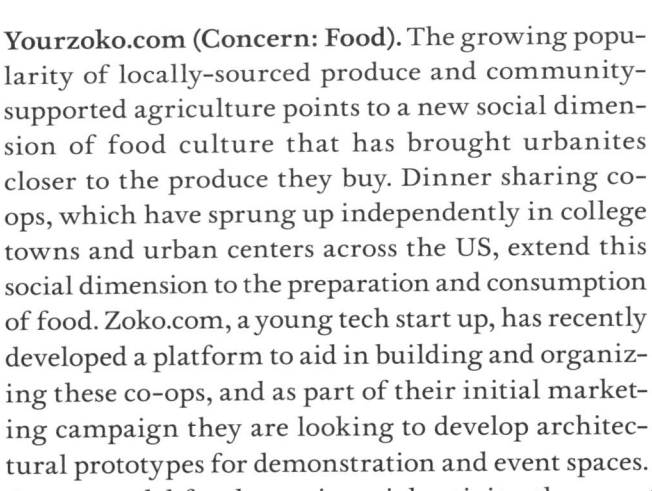

Yourzoko.com (Concern: Food). The growing popularity of locally-sourced produce and community-supported agriculture points to a new social dimension of food culture that has brought urbanites closer to the produce they buy. Dinner sharing co-ops, which have sprung up independently in college towns and urban centers across the US, extend this social dimension to the preparation and consumption of food. Zoko.com, a young tech start up, has recently developed a platform to aid in building and organizing these co-ops, and as part of their initial marketing campaign they are looking to develop architectural prototypes for demonstration and event spaces. A new model for domestic social activity, these prototypes may merge qualities of the home dining experience with some of the social qualities of a restaurant, a café, or—at times—a stage-set.

Match.com (Concern: Dating). One in five relationships starts online, according to Match.com's tag-line, and with an extensive database of personal profiles and evidence-based matching algorithms, it's no surprise. However, the company's ability to curate the dating experience extends only as far as the computer screen, leaving interested parties to carry on independently. Meanwhile, venues that sponsor social events like speed dating offer an alternative paradigm for those who prefer to 'browse' in person, but these events lack the benefits of pre-screening, reducing the likelihood of finding a compatible match. Moreover, they typically offer a highly structured activity in an undifferentiated environment that fails to account for the nuanced intentions, interests, and comfort-level of a broad range of singles. In this respect, Match.com's database of information could be interpreted as an architectural template in which matching algorithms and profile updates are played out in real time as singles transition between different conversations, settings, and activities.

The images in this text refer to the interfaces on mobile communication devices that allow to overlay an image of an enclave with the information available about it, using the web to obtain local information instantaneously by pointing at a certain enclave. This rapidly developing technology allows the localization, in time and space, of the information available on the web. The Web 2.0 experiment described in the text is aimed to explore these potentials to produce new possibilities for the physical embodiment of the world wide web.

Published in *Harvard Design Magazine* n. 35, Cambridge, MA, 2012

Theory of the Excuse: the Erotics of Material Agency

The seamless convergence between desire and effect in the traditional, voluntarist discourse of architecture is hopelessly tautological: I have a vision and I build it. No friction, no compromise: The ideas precede the outcome, and the product is a mere illustration of the idea without incorporating any of the complexities of its implementation.

Probably, one of the first things to learn as an architect is not to immediately succumb to your desires and to be opportunistic with the realities that appear before you. The "theory of the excuse" outlined here is an attempt to relocate volition within the process of viable architectural practice. The theory of the excuse emerges out of a set of practices that I have been developing over the years across the academic and the professional realms.

To my knowledge, no architectural theory in history has acknowledged that the engine of architectural discourse has often been built on excuses rather than visions. The *excuse* is an intermediate figure between desires and constraints that has long deserved a more thorough theorization. The purpose of such theory would be not only to legitimize this practice but to also demonstrate its generating potentials of an architectural program.

I started practicing the excuse (a partly Victorian, partly Jesuitical device) in the academic laboratory when I was trying to instill a certain appetite for rigor in my pupils. Faced with the dilemma of how to demand rigor without suffocating their intuition, I developed a protocol whereby people were able to implement a formal strategy or system as long as they figured an excuse that could legitimize the approach not on its own terms but on those of an exterior set of constraints that were not necessarily architectural. Economy of means, iconographic impact, environmental or structural performance, programmatic organization—things like these became parts of a reference system capable of buttressing the formal concept in a wider analysis of the project. Students were then capable of pursuing formal intuitions as long as they were able to describe them as the realization of an excuse. Projects then had to stand scrutiny not only in terms of their formal, technical, programmatic, and other "internal" values, but also in terms of some "external" performance (social, political, economic, etc.). For example, it would not be sufficient for the WTC bundle tower proposal to have an interesting formal idea: it had to perform both as a structure and to operate on an iconographic level.

When successful, this approach had two positive effects: it would make the project more resilient and multifaceted, and it would open the project up to the "outside" while still allowing it to pursue the accomplishment of an "internal" goal—aesthetic, functional, or otherwise.

From the academic laboratory, the excuse protocol migrated then to the professional realm, where people in the office—including me—were not allowed to abandon themselves to the pursuit of a formal, programmatic, or material experimentation that could not be grounded in broader demands. From the staff to the consultants, the excuse had to be generated; nobody could draw a line without a believable excuse. And eventually this principle was applied even to clients, whose arguments were scrutinized in respect to the concept, economic agreement, or performance criterion. (Actually, clients are often the worst sinners when it comes to submitting to their unbound desires.)

The excuse protocol became rather useful at preventing collaborators from going off on irrelevant tangents and clients from being carried away with either their visions or their value engineering. Everyone was suddenly forced to keep a distance from their specific agendas and argue them on some other "neutral" ground, mediating the process with alternative inputs. The most important function of the excuse was to produce resilience and consistency, but also to open the project to a less tautological formulation which became instrumental in the production of architectural programs. Theorising the excuse—or excusing the excuse—became a worthwhile endeavour.

To theorize the excuse may help to posit a historical frame to the relationship between volition and efficiency. Although one can trace the practice of the excuse further back, it is modernism when it appears in full force within architectural practice, to legitimize the deployment of the enormous power awarded to modernist architects by the emergence of modern construction and urban technologies. Architects were charged by modern democracies—and therefore made responsible—for decisions that were before exclusive to political power. Unbound architectural desire had to be restrained and decisions had to be carefully supported on functional and technical grounds, grounded on an alibi operation beyond aesthetic or linguistic preferences.

After High Modernism collapsed under the accusation that architecture once devoted to social and political revolution had devolved into aestheticized and elitist facade for modern technocracy and corporate multinational power—the excuse had been unmasked—, postmodernism returned to language as the guarantor of a more democratic and delicate vehicle to provide architectural expression. Locality and context reemerged in the face of rampant globalization as justification of experiments that were considered illegitimate under Modernism. The *genius loci* had come to replace the modernist *Zeitgeist*, and both historicism—as a reversal or a retrospective of the *Zeitgeist*—and regionalism became the sources of excuses for a different type of architectural experimentation, charged with a new political consciousness and reliance on new media technologies.

But the postmodern "excuse" of popular engagement soon became stained with populism and media spectacle. Deconstructivism was an attempt to extricate simple models of desire through a negative inversion. The Deconstructivist excuse was based on avoiding an intelligible theory of reality. It was the endless inquisition of signs. Based partially on some of the more trenchant of the Situationist critiques of High Modernist spectacle, and grounded in poststructuralist theory, Deconstructivism sought its excuses systematically in external disciplines like anthropology, linguistics, and art, while its purpose was precisely to resist any association with direct and literal meaning or deliberate and rational purpose. The more obscure the alibi was, the more capable it was of liberating latent, repressed potentials. Deconstructivism merely broke open the prison-house of language and converted the contents of repressed desire to new forms of saying no.

The excuse reappears in relation to a pragmatic, functionalist operation and becomes particularly relevant within this modality. It is often assumed that, once pragmatism enters the work, volition exits, but that is hardly the case. Unlike the more openly visionary work of the modern, a pragmatic position acknowledges friction and, therefore, requires some articulation between desire and reality. There are several contemporary practices—including mine—operating from a pragmatist approach which is connected to a paranoid-critical lineage (probably via Rem Koolhaas in many cases). This lineage has opened various formulations of the relationship between desires and facts as elective means of saying yes to something one might normally say no to.¹

This particular type of work relies often on factual operations that get ascribed to a presumptive transparency where the theory of the excuse becomes instrumental to resituate desire, retaining it within the process of making architecture and triggering it as an after-effect of constraint, in a sort of sadomasochistic arrangement. The excuse uses the techniques of the critical while enabling agency; it articulates a particular form of relationship between desire and constraint, hopefully aimed to break with both the tautological discourse of visionary architecture (the architect as the master/dominatrix), with the infinite suppleness of the pragmatist approach (the architect as submissive slave, subject to the client's desires) and with the celibacy of the project of autonomy and

---

1   If negation was the preferred attitude of the critical, Yes is the preferred word of the pragmatists: "Say yes to everything" is the fake advertising of the Netherlands displayed in *Content*, the latest Koolhaas monograph (Köln: Taschen, 2004). *Yes is More* is the title of Bjarke Ingel's monograph (Köln: Taschen, 2009).

its abstinence-driven techniques (the architect declines the engagement with power under the fear of being used).

In theorizing the excuse we double it, historically and in present-day terms. We permit architecture to run a double agenda by shifting the formal and material operations to another level while remaining thoroughly grounded in the here and now. In many senses, the excuse permits theory to operate at the level of the hypothesis without the attendant recourse to ideological justification. As a result, a possible "double agenda" appears because the excuse for the excuse introduces virtual hypotheses that are always operative within formal operations anyway. Thereby, the grounding of the hypothesis in material agency permanently defuses immaterial gains—disembodied games—typical of figuring the hypothesis out of thin air.

A theory of the excuse might be a perpetual motion machine set in place by the very first maneuver to perpetuate a cover story for what is, after all, a dialectical move from speculative to instrumental reason; a claiming of material agency in a nihilist age, when any invocation of ethical agency must be concealed or held merely provisional. The excuse may be the Trojan horse that enables material agency—which would be otherwise resisted in its naked form by the prevailing discursive practices—, to unleash its potentials. As the long-deferred answer to linguistic analogues, hyper-self conscious theories of autonomy, as well as well-meaning but sometimes vacuous projective practices in architecture, material agency needs the excuse as a legitimation and as a feedback. In preparing an excuse for a theory of immanence, the production of the excuse is doubled. The subject of architecture appears once again imbued of discursive functions—and perhaps ethical precepts—, but is actually utterly void of the apparatus of the humanist agenda and its anthropomorphic projections of the humanist-allegorical paradigm. The subjective analogues fall away, and what is left in place is pure material agency.

The images framing this text relate to duplicity as an operative system: a series of images of "contemporary masks" have been extracted from recent movies: From the stormtroopers in *Star Wars*, the mask of Anthony Hopkins as Hannibal Lecter in *The Silence of the Lambs*, or the mask of Heath Ledger as The Joker in *The Dark Knight* stand here as the markers of duplicity in contemporary subjectivity. The masks of a riot policeman and of Guy Fawkes-Anonymous appear as counterparts of a type of contemporary subjectivity that becomes collective.

Nomad Practices

The texts included in this section were dealing primarily with the reflections on my own practice as an architect, as well as on the contemporary practice of architecture in general, and its impact on a potential reformulation of the discipline. Most of them address specifically the experiments developed in my own practice (FOA at that time) during this period, in an attempt to theorize them and to analyze their disciplinary implications. Some of them were originally published in FOA monographs or publications, others belong to the description of certain projects, or the commenting on other architectural practices.

This essay is based on a presentation made at the Anybody Conference, Buenos Aires, 1996

Forget Heisenberg: A Discussion on the Formless

Straddling the Hyphen

During the last twenty years, an important amount of architectural theory and practice has been devoted to the formless, to the indeterminate. As a viable alternative to the crisis of high modernism, corporate capitalism, and other forms of structural and deterministic thinking have been using randomness, arbitrariness, formlessness, complexity, contradiction, and incoherence as the most adequate —and fashionable— tools either for approximating the fuzzy existential and productive conditions of late-capitalism or for escaping to the deterministic, reductive modernist operation. If memory and history—or the Lacanian imaginary *shading into* the Lacanian symbolic, for the purpose of this essay—are crucial formations of human subjective states, the ability to erase, to forget in order to reconfigure the self is increasingly important these days. For example, it is probably more interesting, and more profitable, to produce Cabernet-Sauvignon in the Napa Valley than to refine the techniques to make a good Bordeaux in Bordeaux.

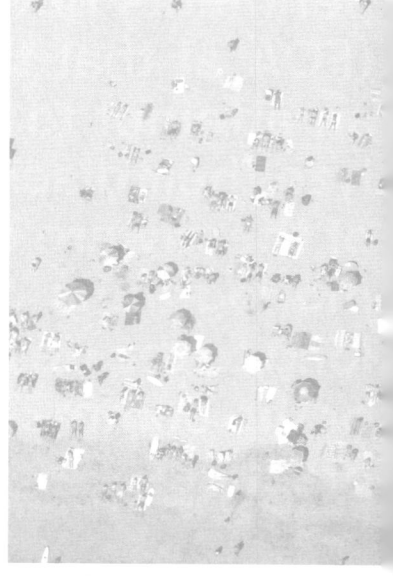

Order, form, determination, coherence, and structure are the remnants of a top-down operative system that erases differences and rigidifies processes, that is exclusive and reductive and thus not suited to the contemporary world.

This trend in architectural thought has been important in all artistic practices since the collapse of high modernism in the 1960s, when important experiments aimed at unveiling random, arbitrary, non-hierarchic, and entropic forms of organization were launched.

Architects and artists have been trying for almost two generations to dissolve what René Thom has called the *pregnance*, or fullness, of the previous order to allow *emergences* to appear. If this quest for indetermination was a necessary reaction to the crisis of modernity, enabling a critique of the previous models of architectural practice, there is no question that the objectives have been achieved. Architectures that resemble the organization of clouds, stains, and rocks more than Platonic solids are everywhere. The search for order within the new systems of organization—building a new pregnance—using more complex orders rather than positioning them as opposites or negatives to previous models may be more interesting. To engage in more complex economic, social, and urban processes does not imply the inability to determine but rather underlines the importance of developing techniques or tools to regain control over these emerging forms of organization—that is, to construct models that incorporate dynamic and complex systems and even unstable structures.

If research in recent years has blurred the definition of architecture and opened it to new possibilities, it has also been devastating, disempowering the practice of architecture by systematically taking a critical, marginal role in respect to the systems that produce the built environment. To recover a potentially crucial role in the current economic, technical, social, and political transformations, architects will have to focus their research on reformulating the discipline. They can either seek refuge in the traditional modes of practice or escape into arbitrariness, indetermination, and contradiction, which, even if critically effective, can never become central to a positive reempowerment of architectural practice. To propose formlessness and indeterminacy as an aesthetic program may be adequate in capturing the productive or moral imperatives of the contemporary world, but it is problematic when applied to the processes of production or construction that are fundamental to the practice of architecture. In respect to the making of the formless body, it seems obvious that the formless is only operative within a cognitive or critical mode, not within a productive mode.

We must first distinguish between the *formless* and the *informal*: the informal does not comply with well-established forms but operates within a well-defined frame of reference. On the contrary, the formless has no parameters; or rather its form is indeterminate. The formless is independent of the well-defined formal orders. It can be constructed either through indetermination or through ruthless, alienated determination. The informal can be the target of an aesthetic program or sought as an effect: the formless can only be produced as a consequence or inconsequence—or, it has a certain willfulness about it that belies its formless, impersonal élan. Once produced, it is unstable yet can be immediately formalized through mental operations similar to projecting images over clouds, waves, or inkblots. The attraction of the formless is its presentation of a material organization prior to its encoding. Its apparent meaninglessness is its very meaning.

To claim formlessness as an objective is difficult to sustain in the practice of a discipline that has important roles beyond the merely critical. It may sound incredibly banal, but very few clients are prepared to pay an architect to "not determine," and therefore the search for indetermination is a kind of professional suicide. This contradiction has a more theoretical formulation: the very nature of the formless is ultimately its unlimited performability. Therefore, the formless becomes dysfunctional and loses its most important potential. It can, however, being achingly beautiful to behold as it drifts across the horizon and vanishes.

My second objection to formlessness emerges when we try to apply it to architecture as a fundamentally projective and productive, rather than signifying or critical, practice. If we look, for example, at Tokyo as a seemingly formless urban structure and try to read the orders at play without knowledge of its history, we may conclude that it is a chaotic, incoherent, and indeterminate mess. But if we look at it from the perspective of the accumulation of successive decisions and circumstances that have produced such an organization, we can understand how these forms have been determined, based on changing economic factors, regulations, property structures, social uses, etc. This accumulation of factors has generated a material structure that is not at first as clearly legible as Baron Haussmann's Paris, Gropius's Siemensstadt, or Duany Plater-Zyberk's Seaside. This does not necessarily mean there is no order or no determination, but that the forms of determination in Tokyo are far more complex and subtle than those of more reductive, emphatic, or avant-garde models. From this perspective, Tokyo is not formless but formful.

Werner Heisenberg's principle of indetermination is often quoted as the expression of modern indeterminism. According to Heisenberg, we can never precisely determine the position of a particle in space because the instruments used to register the phenomenon will alter its nature. Therefore, we can never reach the real essence of the things that we analyze, be it a piece of metal or a political structure. It follows that if we cannot fully understand things, we cannot fully control them. This fundamental inconsistency between form and information, power and knowledge, would dissipate if we could reverse Heisenberg's position, moving from the perspective of the observer to the position of the producer. If we could become less human and more divine, form would become determinable and we would be able to understand what we have made, *even if it disappointed us.*

While formlessness is a viable methodology from the perspective of the observer, critic, or researcher, it is a difficult alternative from the perspective of the producer, for it can only be determined as a negative effect. Indetermination is the result of performing outside the boundaries of already established forms. In this regard, Arata Isozaki and Akira Asada's proposal of a *demiurgomorphic* model for architecture is one of the most valuable suggestions made at this conference. The traditional theomorphic or anthropomorphic models of the architectural body are no longer sustainable. They are too rigid and reductive to operate within a culture increasingly determined by flows and multiplicities that cannot be constrained within the limits of a static, complete, ideal body, whether divine or human. This proposal for a demiurgomorphic model for the contemporary body is a viable alternative to the chaos and indetermination that resulted from the disappearance of the previously solid external models of the architectural body. A demiurgomorphic model enables us to explore forms of determination internal to the process of construction, such as the instruments and techniques that produce the body, rather than forms of determination characterized by the body's reference to a paradigmatic, external model. A *demiurgos* is, after all, a god without a face, a materialistic, opportunistic, performative, technocratic god who is disassociated from images, types, and ideologies and makes rather than signifies. Demiurgos is also responsible and accountable for his products, and those products are essentially formful; that is, formally determined by an affirmative statement or process even if it is not necessarily known in its final embodiment.

In a culture characterized by the proliferation of virtual information, perhaps the most important challenge for architects is to try to reverse this process of material disintegration by transferring information into the production of spatial and material organization. To explore productive and projective rather than representational and signifying techniques could provide a vehicle for the construction of projects, establishing a seamless continuity between analysis and production, concept and technique, information and form. Through production, we may attempt to escape symbolic or typological mediation and the imposition of a priori effects, without renouncing intentionality and determination.

For this to happen, the projectual process must become a construction, generated through analyzing and manipulating forms, patterns, geometries, distributions, and other decoded materials that seek order. The steps in this process introduce specific orders aimed at effects not derived from an already complete paradigm. The demiurgomorphic operation that Isozaki and Asada propose is similar: there is no closed paradigm or significant image, only partial moments of decision where the instruments and specific circumstances determine the final product.

In our office, we have explored this possibility through the development of projective models or models that attempt to produce a reality neither by extending or mimicking an existing reality nor by criticizing it. Through these models, we study the production and material organization of contemporary aspects of space, such as the conflict between global systems and local singularities, the need to articulate the urban and the architectural, the problematization of dynamic processes as a crucial aspect of architectural and urban organizations, the spatialization of activity and information, and the incorporation of information technologies in the design process.

Yokohama

The best example of this research is our entry to the Yokohama International Port Terminal competition, in which we transformed a complex set of instructions into a coherent form. We detected two important issues: first, the mediation between the two parts of the program—the operation of the ferry terminal and the area of civic leisure—and second, the integration of the project with the public spaces of Yokohama's waterfront. The first subject was, to some extent, generic, the second locally bound. We began by registering the pedestrian flow on the Yokohama waterfront, which revealed two types of movement: one conductive, a linear linking of different locations with a more or less constant scale of access; the other inductive, registering a more dense and intense pattern of lines. The first was linked to street circulation, the second coincided with plazas and intensely used public areas, such as Aka-Renga Park, Yamashita Park, and the Stadium Park. Our first idea was to produce a fourth solenoid, or inductive device, on the Osanbashi Pier to generate a consistent level of public activity along the waterfront and to project the urban intensity into Yokohama Bay.

Although we did not know how to structure the spires that constitute the solenoid, circulation was crucial to the project. Our aim was to challenge the purely conductive nature of "tubular" spaces (to use Paul Virilio's term) and create an architecture to host transient rather than static populations. The linear structure of a conventional pier would not produce the desired effect, but turning the pier into an interface rather than a gate enabled a gradual change between two states instead of signifying their border, hence the idea of the "no-return pier." As an alternative to enforcing the pier's linear structure, the circulation diagram links the different functions via interconnected loops that make the linear structure disappear. By reversing the "natural" location of the facilities, that is, by placing the terminal facilities close to the foot of the pier and the civic facilities at the pier's head, we extended Yokohama's public space as far as possible into the bay, forcing citizen traffic to cross that of visitors. This programmatic imbalance creates the charge that makes the system operate. Flows move through the structure, linking Yokohama City with the cruise ships or folding back toward the city without literally turning back. The structure becomes a warp in urban space, breaking the polarity between citizens and visitors.

Having made the diagram but needing the instrument to materialize it, we directed our attention to the urban ground. The redefinition of the ground, or the articulation between ground and building, is crucial. In Yokohama the ground enabled us to embody the no-return diagram. By associating every line with a plane, every bifurcation with a cut in the surface, we transformed the original two-dimensional diagram into a three-dimensional topography that could support the required program.

When faced with the construction of the building and a coherent organization at every level, we decided to use the same system that generated the overall form, this time using the folds in the surface as a structural device. Subsequently, the surface was folded at a different scale to produce a structural web that links the programmatic folds. Using the folds as structural devices redirects the forces from the gravitational vertical into the oblique and allows us to eliminate the traces of gravity in the space. Moreover, the folds allow us to avoid discrete structural devices such as columns, walls, or floors and to blur the traditional separation between the envelope and the load-bearing structure in favor of a materiality in which the differentiation between structural stresses is not determined by coded elements but appears as singularities within a material continuum.

As the topography was constructed without resorting to typological models, we needed to analyze the form that we had generated in order to identify the ideal locations for specific programs. The continuous but differentiated space produced by the successive operations provided opportunities to explore various uses of the facility. Metaphorically speaking, the space of the terminal became an ideal battlefield that could be taken by the locals or occupied by the foreigners. Programs link the flows to the overall scheme, where they become like sediments in the channels created by the folds on the surface, which in turn integrates the segments of the program through a continuous variation of form. Varying degrees of intensity diminish the rigid segmentation that social machines—especially those that maintain borders—usually produce.

In spite of its appearance, the terminal is far from formless. On the contrary, its form is highly determined and intentional, or *formful*—not in respect to the application of a complete paradigm of the architectural body, but through the application of a set of precise techniques. For example, if the programmatic conditions change, the definition of the topography changes as well. It is perhaps presumptuous to claim that the Yokohama project is an example of what Isozaki and Asada identify as *demiurgomorphic* architecture, but I do not think it was by chance that Isozaki chose this project as winner of the competition. Nor was it by chance that after the jury's decision, he was confronted by Kazuo Shinohara, a Japanese architect known for his interest in chaos, randomness, and indeterminacy, who had also entered the competition and was awarded third prize, but who did not understand the choice. Isozaki's proposal of a *demiurgomorphic* body is a perfect explanation. It draws the line between those who, still astonished by the complexity of the contemporary city, have committed themselves to mimicking the surrounding chaos (to make complexity an aesthetic manifesto) and those who believe that behind the seemingly chaotic contemporary city lie orders that we should be able to control if we want to practice as architects and we don't mind negotiating cross currents and complications in the process.

The images illustrating this article relate to the subject of contingency, the main subject of the text. If in the last few decades we have seen a radical development of organizations and the streamlining of processes in the search of increasing efficiencies, we have also witnessed the emergence of unprecedented freedoms. The images describe situations where efficiency ceases to rule and opens to contingency, or perhaps to chaotic efficiency: the breakout of a football match, the beach, the pool, the bath, camping, and the chaotic patterns of Indian traffic.

The Virtual House[1]

Innovative and visionary architectures have been traditionally coupled with the invention of the future. But here we are not concerned with the future but with the virtual, as a source of new architectural possibilities. The idea of the future implies an expressed recognition of the discontinuity of time into fixed frames, as if the process of actualization of a certain reality was independent from a continuous process of change. This is the well-known distinction between diachronic time and synchronic time. The future, the past, the present are part of a static description of time into freeze-frames; alternatively, the virtual is able to capture the dynamic nature of a situation or an organization by extending the real toward the potentials and the memories that it contains. Synchronic time invokes both a very real and a very synthetic approach at once, given that to observe or critique forms of history or knowledge involves *cutting sections* through time and across times, to collect only apparently disconnected or isolated moments.

The virtual house is just such a type of research into a form of inhabitation intended to unfold potentials beyond the given identities of form, function, and place. To literally produce or isolate the virtual is an improbable ambition, unless it is done through a mutable set of relationships

1. The Virtual House was a commission from the Anyone Corporation/FSB Brackel to explore the idea of the virtual in a domestic project.

triggered by an observable process. The virtual will systematically move away (or vanish) when we have almost reached it, or once it has become actualized. Its primary instrumentality is in its very refusal to be instrumentalized. Therefore, we cannot produce the virtual itself, but one of its possible actualizations, or a process or set of principles that will trigger them and allow us to observe its operative, highly mutable coordinates.

This proposal's aim is to unfold the effects that a physical structural system will produce in the given identities and forms of the dwelling, as a trigger of virtualities. The strategy to produce the virtual is not to replace the real with a sophisticated surrogate, such as in so-called *virtual reality*, but rather to dismantle the complex assemblage of social uses, organizations of space, and material qualities that have come to constitute what we generally understand as a home. The virtual is not the better, the future or the past, but those traits given to the present tense capable of unfolding pure potentiality within an inherited series (genealogical lineage) particular to the idea of the house.

In this search for potentials the project is focused first on the determinations that distinguish between the natural and the artificial. The *virtual* is always the beginning of many potential lineages, a sort of *primitive* of multiple possibilities. But is that primitivism reached through reduction and abstraction, or through a return to nature? Is the primitive hut a replicant of nature, as Abbé Marc-Antoine Laugier proposed, or an artificial construct as J. N. L. Durand maintained? Was its form the result of need, as in the Semperian tradition (derived by traditional architectural-cultural determinants), or was it an act of excess and signification as Alois Riegl might claim, remaining within the charmed argument of *Kunstwollen* (artistic volition)?

The proposal addresses the ground first as the most primitive and literal form of nature: the virtual house has to be groundless, not because the ground is irrelevant, but because the house will constitute its own ground. The virtual house is not groundless (abstract), as with Le Corbusier's Ville Savoye, a rootless house with an austere, denatured ground and strict material agency. Rather than becoming a figure of inhabitation, the virtual house should be a room where we can no longer distinguish the figure, the ground, or the interstices. The virtual ground is not an abstract and generic platform, a pedestal, but rather concrete and specific *within its own time*.

The groundless cannot be erected, it does not have the quality of Vitruvian *firmitas*, because it is no longer in dimensional opposition to the ground, as in Le Corbusier's *Poème de l'angle droit* (1947–53). A virtual house's construction is no longer an act of domination over matter and nature, but rather the work of an artificial nature. Its site is the closest thing possible to siteless. *It is conceptual.* In Laugier's engraving of the architecture of the primitive hut, the ground and the house are made out of the same material; it is the disposition of the elements that signifies an opposition between natural and artificial. Here is the *functional equivalent* of the mythic *noble savage*.

The project emerged from a piece of artificial matter with indeterminate structural strength to compression and tension, supplied with water and energy, and characterized phenomenally as a visually differentiated field: This field of visual singularity was made using disruptive pattern material (DPM). DPM is produced by abstracting a given visual field into a differentiated distribution of color on the surface of an object. DPM is specific not only in terms of its relation to a given visual field, but also in terms of its scale, dependent on the distance at which it is perceived. DPM matter will provide the virtual house with a broad palette of abstracted regions, a collection of synthetic landscapes of concrete quality. We could now explore the groundlessness of the house by producing different models of ground, to proliferate the house into a series: for example, the Arizona model, the Kwai model, the Steppe model, or the *Schwarzwald* (Black Forest) model.

This band of synthetic ground has been manipulated to produce the coding of space in a similar form in which a protein band folds to produce a DNA code: the organization of matter will have precedence over the coding. This manipulation is aimed to further destabilize some other categories that have been characteristic of the domestic spatial phenomenology such as the opposition between inside/outside, front/back, up/down, and other cultural constructs of the dwelling. Rather than invoking a Bachelardian *poetics of space*, this house depends on a proliferation of a totally artificial nature—a perhaps *deranged* nature.

In order to radically challenge the conventional categories

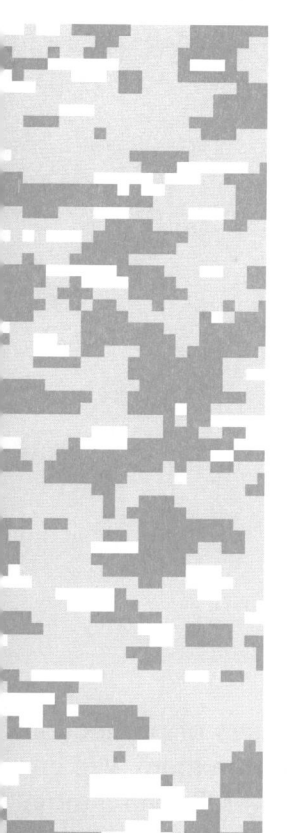

of inhabitation, the manipulation of the band has kept the continuity between ground and building, blurred the segmentation between structure and enclosure. The abstracted but specific landscape band will link outside and inside in one face: each face of the folded DPM surface will shift from a *lining* condition to a *wrapping* condition, disrupting the orientation of the relationships between the enveloping surface and the inside/outside opposition. Interior spaces will be generated by *topological handles* in the surface band. Each room can then combine with another room to form a double-sided, double-used band. Each composite band can be combined with other composite bands to produce a more complex organization of rooms, in which the folding bands will also grow three-dimensionally, as a pile of wafer matter. The rooms are not segmented parts of the structure, but on the contrary, they are singular points in a continuous space. To explore the gradients of different conditions occurring on the folded surface, preceding the coding of inhabitation, the different areas of the house have been classified into three possible qualities of the surface: wrapping/lining, inside/outside, and gravity in/gravity out. The superimposition of the gradients of these three different categorizations will produce the instructions for the use of this topography of inhabitation. The distribution of supplies (forces) from the surface can be distributed not in respect to the production of functional spaces, but as an overall distribution of supplies (forces) dependent on the specificity of the topography. As topological knot, the house also dismantles the antinomies noted above, as if Jacques Lacan's obsession with the Moebius strip were embedded in the house.

The system could proliferate now the body of the house *ad infinitum*, for example, as a deep, inhabited, hollowed-out ground, extending from the room to the city (and back). Or perhaps it deforms itself into variations on the basic room. The virtual house is not an organic, finished body, but a proliferating structure where the rooms are not functionally determined and yet, specific. As unfinished it sustains the possibility of its vanishing.

The images shown in this text originally accompanied the proposal in response to the invitation by Anycorp to participate in the Virtual House competition.

This paper was presented at the Anyhow
Conference, Rotterdam, 1997

New Platforms

Approaching the question of instrumentality in architectural practice implies, to some extent, a reconsideration of the limits of the discipline, in order to question its relationships to external domains, such as the themes proposed in this table discussion: *money, market, policy*. I would like to suggest two oppositions that may help us identify possible forms of understanding the processes of architectural production and their relationship with the products that result from them. These categorizations will hopefully help to position an architectural practice *vis-à-vis* discussions regarding language and determination that seem to be omnipresent at this event.

The first categorization relates to the nature of the processes of production; these can be external or internal to the product that results from them. We can use processes driven by the search of effects, or those driven by the internal constitution of the object. A good example of this opposition is found in the classical friction between, the marketing and the engineering departments of a corporate structure. While the marketing techniques target a product's integration into a system external to its own material production (that is, a market), the engineering techniques aim at controlling the manufacturing processes and the relationships between the components of a product. And very often, the determinations over the product from each side are radically different.

The second possible categorization relates to the nature and effects of the products of a practice. These can be internal or external to the applicable field of production. This dichotomy has a long tradition in the history of aesthetics: *Baukunst* versus *Kunstwollen* in the Semper/Riegl discussion; "composition" and "character" in Rowe's formulation; or "how" and "what" in Mies' terms. Whether instituted in organic terms as constitutive of a system (as with Mies) or in an intellectually articulated debate between opposing worldviews (Riegl and Semper), this dialectical *concordia discors* comes to rest in the building proper (and not as image, in the Benjaminian sense, but in the "house arrest" given to the act of construction). Riegl describes this opposition as the internal coherence of a work of art when the productive requirements of a piece are sufficient to complete the product, and external coherence when a product can only be understood and completed within an assemblage that exceeds its pure production, whether as some form of expressive authorship, or through some functional purpose.¹ With Semper, the cultural consideration trumps all such "internal" considerations.

The distinction made by Rowe between composition and character as two fundamentally distinct aesthetic qualities of an architecture are also illustrative of this opposition: while an architecture determined by compositional requirements focuses upon the construction of the piece and the relationships between its components, almost the equivalent of the autonomy of the artwork, an architecture of character (or "good intentions") is concerned with its capacity to fit within an assemblage of social uses, representations, types, etc. (Hence Rowe's somewhat absurd simile that certain types of architecture resemble bad children having thrown all of the furniture into the bottom of a concrete swimming pool.)² Another good example of these qualities in a product can be found in the opposition between pure and

---

1 Alois Riegl, *Problems of Style: Foundations for a History of Ornament* (Princeton: Princeton University Press, 1992).
2 Part and parcel of *The Architecture of Good Intentions*, but also "symptomatic" of Rowe's diatribe. See Colin Rowe, *The Architecture of Good Intentions: Towards a Possible Retrospect* (London: Academy, 1995).

applied research in the production of knowledge. Pure research—for example, investigations in quantum physics, logic, or advanced mathematics—affects a particular field of preexisting forms of knowledge; that is, the internal form of a scientific discipline. Applied research (such as medical or engineering research) attempts to produce effects beyond a particular disciplinary domain by targeting objectives often external to the body of knowledge.

While there is certainly a link between an internal, disciplinary instrumentality and the delivery of products of internal coherence and the use of techniques of exteriority and the making of works of external coherence, it is also not necessarily the rule. And it is perhaps useful to consider the possible coordinates that a certain practice may take in the field that these oppositions define.

I would like to anticipate four basic modes of practice, which form the combinatorial matrix across these two categories. The first involves operating within the limits of the discipline, both on the level of the processes used and vis-à-vis the effects sought. We could include, here, speculative practices that attempt to produce effects primarily on the structure of the discipline through operations with disciplinary processes including some forms of historicism, formalisms, and deconstructive or metalinguistic experiments. This second (*extra-curricular*) mode operates beyond the limits of the discipline at two levels, aiming at producing effects beyond the borders of the discipline and borrowing techniques from outside the limits of the discipline *to import them*, as in the case of certain commercial practices, such as participatory design processes or direct action. (For example, "post-occupancy feedback" or "reception theory.") The third mode extends beyond disciplinary boundaries with the intention of transforming the disciplinary field, as in some forms of regionalism, symbolic manipulation, or "pop" practices that incorporate images, rituals, idiosyncrasies, etc. toward an end best described as *recontextualization*. The fourth mode requires operating within the disciplinary boundary but draws programs, constraints, and determinations from outside the disciplinary domain. This mode will be populated by what we may define as pragmatic, operational, or functionalist practices. It may be possible to recover the *functional* mode again in this last category by describing it as defined by the construction of *functions*—that is, relations between two different domains

	Commercial Practices	Regionalism
	Direct Action	Pop
OUTSIDE	Participative Design Processes	Symbolism
	Pragmatism	Formalism
INSIDE	Functionalism	Linguistic
		Technological
	OUTSIDE	INSIDE
	TARGETS	

(INSTRUMENTS on left side, spanning vertically)

or parameters as the primary concern of function. "Function," in this regard, transcends its historical determinations and is a perfect example of the synchronic amplitude of the exercise of working against historical determination through the extraction of potentiality versus form or function.

A chart of these possible locations could be:

Neither of the two first options will help us to draw links between the practice of architecture and the processes occurring beyond its disciplinary domain, and, therefore, will not be able to throw much light upon the potential relationships between concepts such as those that frame this session and the processes that we use to produce architecture. Moreover, and without entirely negating their potentials, both have certain limitations in terms of being able to produce "positive" affirmative statements about the project while allowing the disciplinary openness needed to produce innovation. In other words, the only opportunity for the first two modes of practice to produce innovation is by adopting a "negative," critical attitude toward the preexisting disciplinary, political, and economic bodies. Without the construction of some form of contingent negative process, these single-domain practices will remain imprisoned in their own logic, confined to a tautological mode. What is interesting about hybrid modes of practice is that positive determinations are possible on either side of the disciplinary boundary, producing unforeseen effects on the other side, and allowing for necessary openness to produce innovation. While it is also possible that this positive may flip and become negative (especially after a period of normalization and misuse), the negative may also flip and become positive (after a period of sustained negativity leads to negation as an affirmative form of executing projects of *limited* scope). This is a warning to any doctrinal position taken within either camp. Each must remain exploratory.

Yet it is the fourth mode of practice, determined or constrained by external processes (such as money, markets, or policy), but open as a disciplinary structure, that has the potential to become more innovative while forging substantial extensions within the disciplinary body. This claim in favor of an operational, *synthetic-functional* mode of practice can, hopefully, become an alternative and a reply to some of the proposals made in this forum. On the one hand, it opposes the proposition that only *indetermination* is able to grant the necessary openness in the structure of a practice to allow for innovation: a pragmatic or functional approach does not preclude mutations within the disciplinary body, nor does it obviate change in the nature of the products, and yet, it requires determinations and constraints in terms of its affect on the outside. It is at once positive, affirmative, and yet inconclusive and open. (It dwells in the causal chain, between cause and effect, but does not occupy anyone's position within that chain.) On the other hand, it may also be an alternative to the need to establish a dialectical relationship with either history or architectural language in order to make "new figures" significant *within* the domain of architecture. It does not matter whether a certain mutation in a mode of practice is meaningful within the history of architecture (even the current, somewhat messy *transdisciplinary* structure of the discipline), or if the same becomes relevant beyond that domain on the outside. Innovation tends to blur boundaries anyway, and the boundaries are not so much the issue anyway. New figures can be produced through a productive, or *poetic,* practice instead of through a *rhetorical* operation, and this poetical agency invokes an epistemic, transformational agency given to architecture not from the outside but from—paradoxically—a place that does not require an outside or an inside.

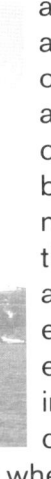

The mutations that the nature of the architectural ground is suffering as a result of changing conditions in the outside are perhaps the most remarkable examples of these functional processes that we are trying to describe here. As increasing mobility of resources and investment, and increased flexibility of temporal and spatial organizations have come to characterize contemporary processes of economic integration, the very nature of the grounds (physical, political, economic or cultural) on which we operate is also becoming increasingly unstable and fluctuating, rendering new figures of the ground operative as a new architectural elementalism. Attempting, then, to frame momentarily the emergence of these figures, illustrated through some architectural projects, requires remaining conscious of the limitations and methodological problems implied in the impermanence of these (transitional) figures of speech. It should be stated at the outset that this approach is unlikely to find an alternative to contribute positively to the development of a new body of architectural knowledge. Yet it signals a shift underway and a possible set of new priorities that might lead there.

When Foreign Office Architects started five years ago, we had a relatively precise agenda vis-à-vis some of the fields or opportunities that we were aiming to address in the practice. Those were defined not within the discipline of architecture, but in emerging processes of production and economic integration that seemed to increasingly determine all contemporary practices, beyond their disciplinary categorization. We foresaw in the constant spatial reconfiguration characteristic of the current economic regimes unprecedented possibilities for a new form of the techniques and processes with which we construct architecture.

The subsequent operations within our practice were aimed at identifying opportunities within certain types of projects of a relatively large-scale, a-typological determination, and public or infrastructural nature. The selection of these projects was dependent on their pertinence to those processes that we had identified as relevant and, obviously, on their availability. Only recently have I started to gain awareness of the precise relationships between our original theoretical agenda and the architectural research required. The process by which we came to formulate what I would like to propose as an alternative model of the architectural ground is by no means a direct path from our original theoretical agenda, but is, on the contrary, heavily mediated by the nature of our commissions and certain originating intuitions that I am now able to explain in a more cohesive manner.

This process started to take shape in a competition entry in 1994 for a building to host a glass factory and a glass museum in a suburban site in Newcastle, with a very acute topography (a ground level that drops 10.5 meters between the borders of the site). The use of a shed-like structure was almost immediately derived from the requirements of an industrial program and the required integration of programs of work and leisure. The manipulation of the ground was driven by the topography of the site and the need to organize a circulatory scheme for the museum and to provide for the access system. Following a strategy of blending programmatic determinations (learned, in part, from OMA) as a technique to produce alternative programmatic structures and seeking the integration of the different inputs in a coherent whole, as an *add-in* process, we started working with a hybridization of the *topographic* structures: the ground and the envelope. In the Glass Centre project, our process was fundamentally a hybridization of previously defined programmatic and topographic categories.

Another strategy in this direction was the coupling of the openings in the enveloping surface with the structure that had to sustain the roof. The roof-lighting openings in the shed were made by cutting and deforming the surface rather than by piercing it. Oriented to capture the light from the north, the eye-shaped openings were filled with trusses that increased their depth proportionally to the bending of the forms. It was our first attempt to operate with an enveloping ground, where structural stresses are handled through singularities of the surface itself, although in this case the singularities were produced more as a hybridization of preexisting "types" (the shed and the Belfast truss) than a differentiation from within a system. In fact, the so-called hybridization occurs from neither adopting nor adapting two pre-existing systems, but by negating both, and it remains a question of phasing as to whether these types lead to the resolution of other measures account for the fusion. The question, then, of origins is mooted.

In the competition for the Yokohama International Port Terminal, many of the concepts initiated in the Glass Centre project acquired sharper formulation. The identification of the ground and the enveloping surfaces became more consistent, partly because we were simply carrying forward existing research on surfaces as structural devices, and partly because of the fact that the program of the project, a transportation facility, was more suited to the exploration of a shifting, unstable construction of the ground.

The structural qualities of the ground in this project came close to the idea of a hollowed-out ground where loads are not distributed by gravitational force through columns, as in the Glass Centre, but rather by displacing stresses through the folded surface of the shell. This shell-like structure became also a potential solution for dispersing the lateral loads that seismic activity very frequently produces in Japan. The particular condition of the Japanese ground, where non-gravitational stresses are often more grave (and threatening) than gravity itself, became clearly instrumental as this development progressed. The relationship in Yokohama between the topography and the areas of structural strength produced by its folds was also different from the Glass Centre. The main zones of structural rigidity appear here parallel to the direction of the folds, rather than in the edges of the cuts. The reason for this was the predominant direction of the circulatory flow, along the longitudinal direction of the project. The removal of the structure away by way of the cuts (the perforations of the surface) was necessary, as they had to also become points of physical access. But beyond the functional requirements, this shift also meant a higher degree of integration between the surface and its static properties, as these were produced as true singularities of the shell rather than as structural elements embedded in the accidents of its geophysical properties. From the point of view of the hybridization of types, the crucial step, here, was to move to a strategy of differentiation within the tectonic system (the folded and pleated surface modulation).

The asymmetrical conditions of the grounding on the pier also enforced differential deviations of the folds with respect to the longitudinal axis of the building subverting the basically symmetrical, programmatic structure. This produced a further deviation from typical orthogonal geometry, complementing the vertical deformations of the surface that constituted the crucial strategy behind the project.

In the next project, the headquarters for the Korean Catholic Church in downtown Seoul, we faced a much denser, more topographic, urbanistic, and cultural domain than in Yokohama. The program required the manipulation of a very fragmented collection of buildings into a coherent complex, and the re-integration of those buildings in the surrounding fabric. Our first decision was to operate by eliminating the classical distinction between the project and its frame, by making the limits of our operation coincident with the property boundary; the project would become the construction of a new ground for the whole complex, rather than introducing another figure inside the already-crowded field. The frame is perhaps one of the most persistent subjects in our investigation, as the limits of the domains where the building has to operate are increasingly difficult to define. In Myeong-Dong, as in Yokohama, the building expands immediately to the physical limits of the ground, so that the object and the frame, the figure and the field, become confused. In both projects there was a basic problem to determine the limits of the domain of operation, and in both cases the frame is a default condition: the legal determination and limit of the apparent ground. The fundamental identity of the building becomes that of defining its own non-apparent ground. But rather than producing a neutral ground, the project here would become a kind of operative system *for* the complex: a focal organization was produced (among others) to enforce the collective and cumulative quality of the space as suggested by the design brief.

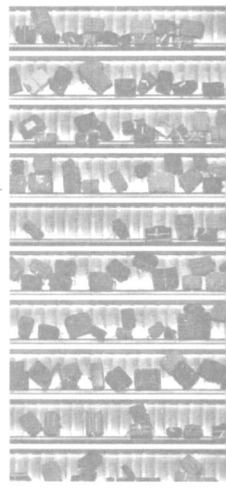

Structurally, this project was conceived as a half-torus, sunken underground and acting as both retaining wall and enclosure of the series of auditoria to be placed under the new ground as a "sunken stadium." The geometry of the torus was produced by a complex curve determined by the adjacent radii corresponding to the different auditoria. Circulation and access points were organized through radial cuts in the torus's surface, in order to avoid the interruption of the structural membrane, which was radially organized itself.

In our entry for the Kansai-Kan Library in Japan, the procedures remain driven by pragmatic questions rather than by a "critical" stance. The problem here was the allocation of a very large volume of archives in a suburban site once occupied by a forest. Our proposal was to structure the project as two parallel surfaces enveloping the public area of the program, all placed on a manipulated ground level. The surface of the ground was formed by the top of the archive's box, mostly sunken underground, as if the new ground was formed by the piling of the archives in several layers. The envelope of these public areas was a membrane that will extend the foliage of the preexisting forest. The structure of the single layer of program was produced as a combination of two fields formed as gradients with proximity to the two access roads. The resulting field was mirrored by a differentiation of the pattern of cuts on the roof membrane in order to produce differentiated lighting conditions onto the ground plane. In the Kansai project, the "framing" was determined as an equipotential extension (the most efficient form to preserve a highly controlled environment) of the orthogonal structure of the book-stacking system that we accepted as a given from conventional uses: a squared envelope was placed on the existing ground at a position determined by the aforementioned access roads. Although the envelope had to assume a regular form, the solution of the joint between the grounds of the buildings and the preexisting slope attempted to blur this functional delimitation; so did the mullion-free curtain glass membrane that formed the building envelope. But perhaps the most interesting consequence of the gradated effect of the ground on the roof system was the opportunity to revisit the roof system we used in the Glass Centre, now as a differentiated pattern. It is perhaps peripheral to the main argument about the ground, but the solution we adopted here regarding the placement of the columns under the deepest area of the cut, allowing for a gravitational drainage system, was also an important development of what started to become a sort of typological development. It is also an example of the construction of a form by the successive addition of new conditions, toward higher levels of complexity, across different projects.

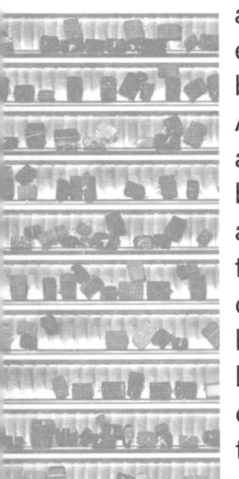

The following project was a design consultancy for a large, multimodal transportation system in Pusan, South Korea. The main objective of this project was to connect the city and the developing waterfront, across the railroad tracks. The scale of the intervention—a 120,000-square-meter, high-speed rail terminal, plus bus station and associated parking lots—was a perfect opportunity for Pusan City to cross over the infrastructure along the harbor and connect to the new developments on the waterfront.

The spatial structure of the tracks became a crucial figure, as the need to keep the station operative during the construction of the new terminal forced us to incorporate these traces into the spatial structure of the project. Seeking to turn the station into a new public space that would connect ground level (0.00 meters) with the floor of the station concourse (+8.50 meters) and further up to a whole new city (800,000 square meters of floor area) built over the level of the tracks (or at +15.00 meters), the new building would dissolve into a new plaza and the road infrastructure serving the complex. The dissolution of the building into the infrastructural elements that project beyond the "frame" of the site became the most remarkable development in respect to the construction of a new ground, blending formally and functionally the building and the ground. The frame is, thereby, extended even beyond the limits of the legal ground by melting topographic and programmatic conditions between the project and its frame. This moves one step further into the beyond, or into the research of relations between figure and ground initiated in the Myeong-Dong project.

The topography we proposed was a shredded surface linking the different levels by weaving undulating bands to provide access, light, and ventilation to the concourse and the platforms. The structure of the bands was produced using a series of arches and catenaries whose geometries determine the undulations of the bands of ground and envelope.

Finally, a speculative competition for a Virtual House (see the previous text and *ANY* n.19/20) allowed us to test the same set of ideas on an entirely different scale. The project, here, was to operate with an abstracted band of ground—a band of "disruptive pattern material"—to produce alternative organizations to the conventional compartmentalization of domestic space. The manipulation of the ground in this case differs from the previous cases. Whereas in previous experiments we maintained the orientation of the surface with respect to gravity, in the Virtual House that relationship keeps reversing, every face of the surface shifting constantly between a "lining" and a "wrapping" condition. A diagonal shift in the plan increased the spatial complexity of this structure, vis-à-vis previous projects, making the stacking of different units to enable the unlimited proliferation of the body of the house possible. The hollow ground that we have been developing through ongoing research acquired a more pragmatic state in this project, allowing for the possibility of proliferating the structure as an alternative development to the "unframed" quality of the ground that we had explored in the previous projects.

The research represented here was made possible by certain conditions found during the brief history of FOA, and by the instruments and techniques developed to produce these projects. It is not a direct exploration or a theorization regarding contemporary architecture and the influence of *new capital markets:* we did not know, for example, the form of the ground we were looking for, and only now can we begin to identify a certain type of ground that is perhaps an embodiment of an early agenda: to command market forces and direct architectural production in line with *apparent* conformity to those markets. There is no question that we have been able to produce these organizations only by using certain techniques, geometries, and computational tools. But what is perhaps more revealing is the fact that certain structures start to arise from these practices, almost of their own volition, pointing toward a redefinition of the ground as an architectural element that expresses the *maximum articulation* of formal and material forces. However transient the validity of this temporal agency, it is nonetheless an example of positively affirming one type of architectural articulation based on material and economic agencies that I believe may produce a new fold in the disciplinary body toward a wholly new formulation of how the "what" and "how" of architecture might function in an expanded, transcendental field.

As an attempt to summarize the qualities of these new paradigmatic grounds, it is interesting to note their fundamentally active, operative nature; these emerging grounds are closer to the contemporary meaning of platforms as operative systems rather than the classical concept of a platform (that is, pediment, base, etc.) aimed at the framing, neutralization, and erasure of the ground to produce an ideal background for architecture to foreground a readily *readable* figure. This is not backtracking but, instead, bracketing figurative agency in lieu of a new material agency that might release a more forgiving (less ideological and/or historical) means to ends. New grounds or platforms derive from a proliferation of the transcendental fields of affiliation that we decide to construct within or beyond the site to exploit certain opportunities and to neutralize certain excesses given to figuration. The notion of *site* as a natural, determining condition is also called into question; instead, new grounds have specific performances:

1) New grounds are not natural grounds (physically or culturally determined), but artificially constructed. "Transcendental" is used in this context as a means of stating their liminal nature.

2) New grounds are neither abstract nor neutral and homogeneous, but concrete and differentiated (formal and material): they are neither figures nor backgrounds, but operative systems immanent to architecture.

3) New grounds have an uncertain (unsung) framework (they frame without recourse to alibis), as the field where they exist is not a fragment but a differentiated domain affiliated to external processes. They are not separable from the operation that produces them.

4) New grounds are neither a datum nor a reference. They are integral.

5) New grounds are neither solid nor structured by gravity: they are hollow and "diagonally" structured. They indulge the "oblique function (Parent and Virilio) without its sociological baggage.

The images in this text refer to the new forms of infrastructure that have been developed since the 1970's, which have had a radical effect on the everyday life: air transportation, systematization of container transport, internet servers, mobile telecommunication towers, satellite communications and GPS... This text illustrates some of the physical infrastructure that enable contemporary life.

Remix 2000

This text is a compilation of punctual observations and propositions made in relation to the professional and academic practice of architecture. It is nurtured by multiple sources: the experiences acquired as a practicing architect at FOA; my time as a critic at the AA, the Berlage Institute, Columbia, and Princeton; and, lastly, a series of reflections on lifestyle and everyday life. Written in the form of a classical manual, they are aimed at addressing discussions on multiple subjects that were present in the academic debates of the '90s. The subjects are addressed contingently, but without any academic references, and they open an alternative form of writing that builds upon personal experience rather than on quotations or alignments to particular trends, although the targets are clearly within the academic debates of the time. They describe a series of reflections and attitudes that have crystallized through these practices.

On the Discipline

During the '80s and '90s, the architectural debate sought a frame of reference within cultural analysis. This reference was not a particularly effective way to ground architectural practices operating within an increasingly complex and unstable cultural background. As a reaction to an architectural discourse focused primarily on social, political, and cultural developments, my generation has tried to drive the discourse toward construction and pragmatics, focusing on materiality, organization, geometry, and building technology, placing a temporary suspension on the exclusivity of cultural analysis within the academic discourse.

Involvement in those external processes is significant only when it is rendered as an excuse to open new architectural potentials. There was a time when social and political possibilities in architecture could only be explored by doing churches, prisons, social housing or schools, while now there is a huge range of projects (residential, transportation, retail, etc.) that have become central to the cultural fabric, and yet have often remained marginal to the enlightened architectural debate. Malls or theme parks do not need an architect to come into being: they happen spontaneously, and it is crucial now to make these developments internal to the logic of the discipline. Writing about minorities, migrations, gender, globalization, and new cultural patterns is unlikely to establish the link between the discipline and the range of new typologies that are now flooding the market. We need to find new correlations between emergent political, economical, and social processes and certain architectural typologies, techniques, geometries, and organizations.

This is not to discredit the purported value of a theoretical perspective for the practice of architecture. Architects who are unable to construct a theoretical perspective for their work quickly run out ideas—that is, lose the ability to see and to think. To think theoretically generates a certain capacity to look at the work not purely from inside but to see it in an economic or social context, for example. What is debatable is what kind of advanced thought can actually contribute anything useful to the practice of architecture. There are certain theoretical approaches that are basically inoperative references for an architectural practice. At most, what we can do is to turn an architectural practice—fundamentally a form of production—into a practice of cultural criticism. And as much as this may be a perfectly legitimate purpose, it is not the role we aim for today, as all forms of ideology seem irrevocably headed for forms of domination. The theoretical paradigm required today is one that problematizes architectural techniques plus engages the world as *it is*, to prepare the world as it *might be*, developing—in the process—an architectural discourse grounded in the productive elaboration of material agency versus material agency constructed out of the rarified airs of critical theory (that is, operative agency without its negative or nihilistic bias, its permanent recourse to negation).

On Material Life

Architecture is not a plastic art, but the engineering of material life. The ultimate creative act is to produce something that has its own life and produces, for itself, performance and expression. One of the contemporary potentials of architecture is to overcome the traditional opposition between natural and artificial, rational and organic, as the artificial is fast becoming "second nature." One of the distinctive traits of our culture is the progressive integration of the natural and the artificial. Contemporary developments in biotechnology, prosthetics, and, most importantly, artificial intelligence, demonstrates that the processes of the artificial have reached a point where critical intelligence, dialectics, and symbolic reasoning have all ceased to play a central role in the process of building the environment, as the artificial has started to produce itself and leave behind absolute human agency. One might argue, from the point of view of the post-human, that architecture is more than ever a purely synthetical operation *sustaining itself*. Within this paradigm, I have become interested in structuring projects as evolving entities that at a certain point become independent of our will, critical judgment, and cultural circumstances; we may have heard a similar refrain from the literary world, regarding how characters acquire a life of their own or how simple descriptive prose negates narrativity, but this is not quite the same thing that is occurring in architecture. While architecture is always slightly behind innovation in the humanities, as it quite often watches and appropriates the same, what is emerging in the newly recursive architectures that have given up the humanist bias of figurative agency is a self portrait of architectural material agency—a self-determinism within architecture that focuses on its disciplinary specificity through material means driven by what once was isolated and called formal agency.

In parallel with the progressive naturalization of the artificial the inability to judge nature as a product is also phasing out. We begin to be in possession of the instruments that allow us to measure or model complex material organizations, natural or artificial. Much as access to artificial, analytical models has empowered us to monitor and improve upon the performance of a mountain or river (in terms of function), the denaturalization of nature and its subsequent conversion to integral artificial terrain has begun to reanimate architecture and urbanism, a two-way street, in a sense, between two systems, one informing the other and both benefiting in the process. While one might argue that the natural never needed our intervention to perform well, and that it is our intervention that has created dysfunctional mountains and rivers, the argument for their mutual imbrication is not to save one or the other but to improve both at once regardless of the origin of the dysfunctions attendant to either.

But this is very different than stating that architecture needs to be supple and organic. I am increasingly suspicious of those architectures whose primary objective is to explore the aesthetics of *life* through complex, smooth form, primarily seeking to produce organic affects. Formal concerns are of significance, but even if there are similarities between the complex forms that result from engineering material life and the pursuit of certain aesthetic effects, this association does not tell the whole story. In fact, I believe that some of the aesthetization of complexity and smoothness operates in an entirely opposite direction to the work I am interested in exploring, by triggering spatial effects that are subsequently implemented by means of construction. The outcome of both processes may sometimes look similar, but it is radically different in essence.

The engineering of material life is a process-driven task that produces consistency between construction, structure, environmental performance, and function, rather than imposing complex plastic effects out of aesthetic legerdemain. Yes, we need to eventually generate an architectural expression, but that may not necessarily become complex or smooth. In fact, I am increasingly interested in the *coarse* and the *reductive*, in all those expressions that emerge out of a more genuine expression of the true life of the building; the search for preconceived effects is far less promising than the exploration of materials in the broadest sense of the term, as a source of ideas, expressions, and affects.

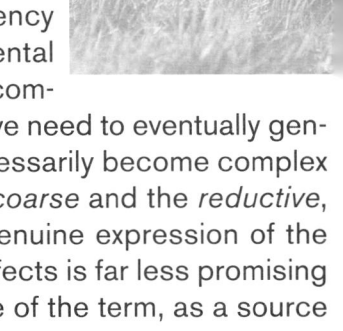

On Landscape

The opposition between the rational and the organic that structures the history of landscape exists across several disciplines, from philosophy to urbanism. Within this history we can witness the conflict between a rational, artificial, linear, and geometric production of landscape and a picturesque reproduction of nature through informal geometry and painterly bias. The possibility of an emergent landscape fully consistent with all forms of information brought to bear in the production of landscape, and, perhaps of an emerging city and architecture, arises from the possibility of overcoming this false dichotomy. A truly emergent landscape under such new premises will be characterized by developments that are already occurring in biotechnology, artificial intelligence, design, and lifestyle, where the natural and the artificial have become virtually indistinguishable. The mutant, the hybrid, and the *morphed*—not the mechanistic or the collaged—are likely to become the models for the organization and structuring of the next century's landscape.

The first attempts to manipulate and artificially organize the land arose either from the need to exploit the land or to appropriate it. Both utilitarian patterns of farming, irrigation, and land ownership, and the more cultural and symbolic patterns appearing in monuments and gardens bear extraordinary similarities across cultures and geographies. They are characterized by the deployment of linear, simple geometries, lines, circles, squares, and triangles, in stark opposition to *chaotic* natural organizations, or rather, as *complex organizations*, generated through negotiation of multiple orders (geological, biological, climatic) in a morphogenetic process. Those simple geometries of the primitive landscapes are the outcome of primitive techniques of land measurement, and are similar across cultures, from China to the Islamic world and Pre-Columbian America, and prevailed basically until the eighteenth century, when English gardeners began using *natural* geometries as a source of spatial effects and narratives. However, *picturesque* gardens generated their geometries through imitation rather than through formally elaborated construction, and, in that sense, they only *look* as if they were geometrically complex when in fact they are somewhat promiscuous in their execution and given to vague means and (often) cheap effects. The English ha-ha is an example of the latter, while the reliance on painterly devices (such as forced perspective and obscured views to distort and/or suggest distance) is an example of the former.

To indulge a totally reductive critique of the two main schools of modern landscape architecture, let us say that Frederick Law Olmsted invested natural geometry with new utilitarian function, but his geometrical techniques remained basically reproductive and picturesque rather than constructed. They were after all mostly borrowed from the English garden. Roberto Burle Marx, in turn, invested complex geometries with new modernist meaning, derived in part from foraging in Continental Europe for the latest artistic fashions and hunting in the Amazon for the brightest plants on the planet. Modern parks returned to *natural* landscaped forms, but the discipline never developed a way of producing complexity out of imitation and never evolved far beyond the picturesque. The difficulty of designing complex form was too much of a disciplinary barrier. Around 1968 the modern world order collapsed and a general interest in artificial complexity arose. In architecture, *chaos* was modelled as *collage*, an unmediated relationship between elements and orders that interfere with each other maintaining their respective identities, while constructing a new collective identity through opposition. Postmodernism and deconstruction explored the capacity of this contradictory juxtaposition as the generator of new orders. Simple, artificial orders such as circles, lines, and grids were inconsistently deployed on a field, remaining unaffected, and unmediated. The collage techniques that characterize the landscape of the late-twentieth century were largely based on the inconsistent deployment of conventional forms or programs in contradiction with each other. But the geometries of pure indeterminacy or pure linearity are more a trace of the past than a possibility for the future. The current opportunities are to overcome the disciplinary barrier that resorts to rote contradiction as a form of complexity (for example, Robert Venturi's concept of *complexity and contradiction*), and rather to exploit complexity through coherence and consistency. (This is the same tall order that introduces the notion of occult symmetry: it is not easy symmetry, as complexity is neither given to reduction or simplification.) In order to do this, we need to learn to produce forms, topographies topological models, that are entirely artificial and yet complex, generating them through a mediated, yet integrated multiplication of rigorous material-synthetical orders. This is the brave new world that calls and strangely spells the end for certain contrived disciplines manufactured out of persistent and pernicious opposition to the unitary nature of architecture.

On Process

Processes are far more interesting than ideas. To build a project as a layering of engineered processes produces more sophisticated devices than reducing the project to the implementation of a single idea or even several ideas fused in an unholy mélange, both the punitive scaffolding of an image. The project's process is a micro-history, a kind of specific narrative developed for the specific purpose of explaining the way in which the different components of a project come together. The entity of the project is formed in a sequence where higher complexity and sophistication emerge to integrate incoming information, if not incoming *streams* of information. Yet this is not to valorize datascapes, a bit of a canard in the short, recent history of processual architectures—a history only gaining stature as it leaves behind some of its earliest experimental modalities and embarks for wholly synthetical operations at the far horizon of simple instrumental orders.

If geological, biological, or cultural history has anything to teach us, it is that long-term processes produce organizations of greater complexity and sophistication than short-term ones. Perhaps the most important development brought by computation to architecture is that we can design, synthesize, and proliferate specific narratives, scenarios, and scripts for a project. Writing a project introduces a sequential development rather than deploying a form or an image. While easy, it also holds promise for the difficult and the recondite, or new means for avoiding old ends. Writing nurtures lateness, waiting for the emergence of the project rather than having the image, the vision, at the onset of the process. Computation has increased exponentially the capacity for processing information within the confines of a given project: we are no longer trapped in the traditional compulsion to reproduce historical models or mimic new ones, or to invent timeless or avant-garde models from scratch. We do not have to produce a project as a reproduction, derivation, or as the invention of an historical model. Any chains we assume are to be productive versus reductive, performative versus ideological. We do not need to produce complexity by making collages drenched in false anxiety or vaporous imaginings. We can synthesize the processes of generation as a kind of accelerated motion of a specific history given to a project (its own history and its own time). We can add information to the construct integrally as required. Or simply because it merits over-saturation and over-determination nonetheless, simply to push the model to another limit beyond predictable limits. In this sense, the horizon is always moving; it is no longer a horizon so much as a fast-receding vanishing point. This sequential, integrative multiplication is more capable of resonating across different levels than congealing into immediate and recognizable—or serviceable—ideological statements, metaphors, allegories, or reproductions and simulacra of past times, past architectural lives, or outmoded forms of instrumental reason.

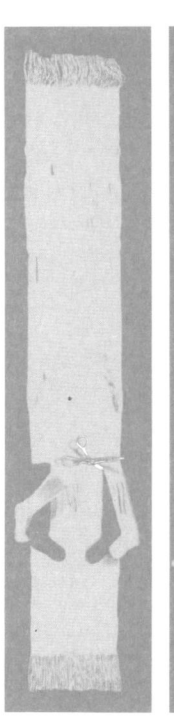

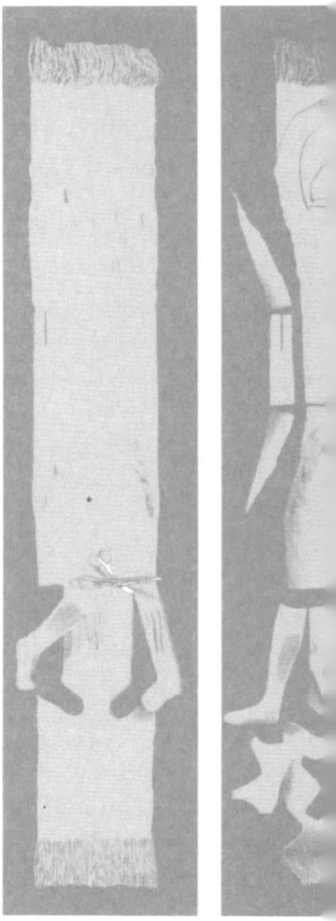

On Building Technology

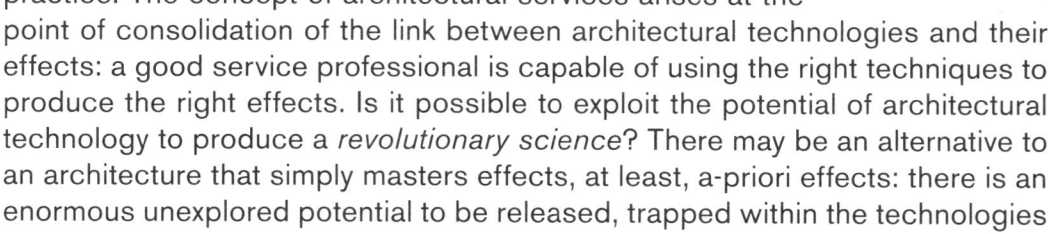

Techniques are usually associated with performance, the provision of services or the production of effects. Architectural technologies keep falling into the realm of what Thomas Kuhn has called *normal science*, in which technique becomes monopolized by consolidated and sclerotic practices, rendering them (in this case *as always*) merely reproductive, rather than productive. Architects seem to have abandoned the realm of building technology as a legitimate space of experimentation, to concentrate on a different set of techniques: language, image and communication. Building technology has, therefore, been relegated to an innocuous service-driven practice. The concept of architectural services arises at the point of consolidation of the link between architectural technologies and their effects: a good service professional is capable of using the right techniques to produce the right effects. Is it possible to exploit the potential of architectural technology to produce a *revolutionary science*? There may be an alternative to an architecture that simply masters effects, at least, a-priori effects: there is an enormous unexplored potential to be released, trapped within the technologies of *architectural services* (that is, project management, cost estimation, quantity surveyance, environmental engineering, etc.), one that has not been integral to the discipline of architecture. Here we also see several false disciplines alluded to earlier as unnecessary and perhaps detrimental to the cause of architecture. If we were able to divorce technologies from their conventional place in the causal chain (as effects), we would become capable of exploiting the potential of these technologies beyond their reproductive, verifiable mode to effectively leverage the discipline from a techno-scientific fulcrum.

On Organizations, Narratives, and Images

Being interested in processes as a field of operation, I have developed a style of presentation that usually explains the construction of the project in a didactic mode. Beginning with flow diagrams and statistics, the project is built over seemingly factual data through the application of certain operations that are rationally traceable. A solid project is, therefore, a project that is supported in a consistent narrative that integrates the different layers of performance through a rigorous process, producing a unique architectural expression. My engagement with both technology and iconography is driven by a conviction that a good project is usually the outcome of a good narrative: a practice cannot be reduced to a single line of research: it needs to build more resilience, be more ambiguous, and incorporate multiple concerns. This is the biggest difference between practice and research. For example, we would not have won Yokohama if the building had not had the form of a wave. The truth is that at the same time that we were building the project through diagrams, we were looking at Hokusai's work. During the competition, the circulation diagrams began proliferating at the same time that there were a series of resonances with those images of waves. But this could only be explained in certain contexts.

The resonance between the waves and the form of the diagram was not relevant as projectual investigation at the time, as we were more interested in the diagram as a research device, so it was edited out of the official version of how the project was developed. But it is undeniable that those images were in the air, in the atmosphere where the project was born. Our minds are full of images no matter how much we try to suspend them, and on some occasions they may become powerful tools to move a project forward or connect it with a wider context. When we won the Yokohama competition, we had to attend to several press conferences. Every journalist wanted to know *what was the idea of the project*, and they were disappointed to hear about diagrams, circulation, and flows, my regular academic spill; in fairness, this narrative was not suitable for public consumption. After I realized the confusion the explanation was causing on the media, I remembered Hokusai's drawings. I changed tack and presented it as the generating concept, to a great cheer from the audience. Everyone understood immediately and there was a big sigh of relief in the room.[1] This is not to discredit the high-borne rhetoric of academic speak; it is just to put it in its place and remind all that there are different means of accessing intelligible fields, inclusive of the intelligence embedded in a wave, or a cloud, through artistic representation or through studying (as Ruskin might have recommended) an actually existing one.

One of the most impressive shows I have ever seen on the design process was the exhibition "Issey Miyake: Making Things" made by the Fondation Cartier in Paris, Museum of Contemporary Art in Tokyo and ACE Gallery in New York. Most relevant in the exhibition was the emphasis on the processes of production as intrinsic to the qualities of the product: how the fabrics are produced, how they are cut, the machines, the manipulation and the experimentation with textiles and plastics. I do not think any other fashion designer has ever explained the design process with such emphasis on production but what was truly remarkable of the show was to see these explanations in the context of a series of products that suggest many other things: you may see witches, gnomes, satellites, robots, jelly fish, butterflies, etc. These resonances are not

1   See text on page 369 on the present volume, "The Hokusai Wave," for further reflection on this event.

pop or kitsch—based on the manipulation of images, stereotypes or popular or conventional imagery. Nor are they communication for communication's sake. Iconographic resonance is produced as an effect of the similitude between material organizations, diagrams, etc. In the best pieces, one can almost imagine Miyake thinking about how to fold a textile in a certain way, and the images that resonate in his mind as the prototypes are coming out of the atelier. The similarities between material organizations would automatically help him to direct the new tests, the scale of the patterns, or the transparencies of the weavings. The "jumping" series, for example, is based on folding materials perpendicular to gravity that function as springs, distorting the effect of the body moving inside. This, in turn, produces a design that exaggerates the body's movement. I do not believe that these iconographic associations pre-dated the design, but adhered to it and made it richer and deeper, more multifaceted. The power of material organizations is that they are much more ambiguous than images or texts, and more potent as trans-cultural communicators. Miyake generates resonances from the logic of production. This is the genius of his work and the weakness of some architects' "experimental" work produced through computational technology. The public legibility of the project may become a serious limitation to the sustainability of the project and the practice as a whole. And these days, paper architecture is no longer sufficient, as it does not generate the friction that a project needs to be relevant. The acquisition strategies need to be engineered into the project. No matter how interested we are in the production process and the exploration of diagrams, data, statistics, etc., or how much we try to avoid the use of metaphors, analogies, narrative, etc. those are, strangely, some of the best mechanisms we have to communicate *outside* the discipline.

Like rivers or mountains, buildings are ultimately pieces of unintelligible matter, the result of an accumulation of processes and therein also may lie their interest, as they open forms of expression that transcend coded languages or visual analogies. (Rafael Argullol used to ask whether a river or a mountain was "right or wrong"...) Do buildings (and, by analogy, rivers or mountains) need to have a meaning, or can they simply be an expression of material processes? The real potential of architecture is to be expressive, to make process explicit. But this approach may present serious limitations in certain contexts when an architectural project needs to be communicated before the building actually exists and has a presence that can speak for itself or simply exist (like rivers or mountains).

While the Yokohama project was perfectly consistent with a larger theoretical investigation that existed in the practice, the interest of the Belgo projects was that they were almost perfectly situated at the antipodes of the official line of research. The commission was the design of two restaurants around a theme with narrow cultural specificity: Belgian food, mussels, monks, sausages, beer barrels, Pantagruelian stomachs, Brueghel, Bosch, velodromes, '70s Belgian kitsch, the Atomium, etc. At least, or *as an excuse*, these were the terms of engagement and endearment our client used to communicate. While we constantly spoke in a metaphorical or referential key, we had to develop a parallel agenda based on the exploration of spatial and structural qualities of the vaulted spaces, the anti-gravitational qualities of the manipulation of the floor, and the continuity of folded surfaces. The constant cross breeding between both spheres ended up being highly productive. The transfer from cultural and thematic iconography to a material expression made the restaurants more legible outside of their original, syncretic cultural context. If our clients were to read this they might feel that they were deceived, but I believe we were exceeding the commission by grounding the design in a physical expression beyond the linguistic and iconographic references (that remained in play nonetheless) and which helped them to develop a transnational appeal.

On Production

Historical references, value systems, and conventions no longer have the same relevance they had in times where space and time were not subject to the constant convulsions caused by global capitalism. In this context, the direct engagement with production appears as a more effective transformative strategy than critical practice. Architects' traditional role as ideologists (demigods) has become redundant as the sheer speed of change overtakes their capacity to represent political and/or ideological purity. Visionary formulations, arguably, pale in the face of the complexity of the real: for, an ideological proposition devoid of any connection to that complex set of relations that produces worlds will remain, at best, a figment of the imagination, or, at worst, a means of conducting an endless critique of actually existing worlds. Paper architecture has lost its effectiveness as a political vehicle: like *utopia,* it is restricted to pure representation without the attachments and frictions capable of truly politicizing matters. To guarantee a minimum level of agency in this context, architects need today to engineer their acquisition strategies, procurement routes, etc., to sustain a necessary level of engagement. And those decisions become crucial in the architectural project, possibly *more critical* than mere ideological formulations. Such a critique of critique, of course, *as metacritique*, introduces pragmatics as the antidote to too much speculation.

Given the growing difficulty of operating with absolute a priori discernment, architecture today is more than ever an experimental activity. But in order to advance the discipline, we cannot completely give up the possibility of judgment. We can perhaps suspend it temporarily in order to facilitate the engagement with reality, or to allow for alternative possibilities to emerge. To judge we need references, value systems, benchmarks, etc. and these are difficult to find in solid form when everything is shifting *all at once.*

The question, then, is how to overcome the critical as the operative, *privileged* paradigm and engage in productive, yet transformative practices. Critical practice was the model for good practice across multiple disciplines: it operated by looking at reality in respect to a past or future system of reference and inference—for example, historical or utopian visions—and pushed what is toward what might be (or what was). The critical model requires that we practice architecture like judges. To overcome this obsolete, dialectical, and willful model, we may need to escape the last, resistant heroic and singular narratives (the metanarratives yet given to architecture) and break down the great schizophrenic paradigms of so-called democratic regimes (for example, rampant globalization between outmoded nation-states, or the maintenance of empire well into the post-colonial era). These conflicting modes of protecting vested interests while clamoring for markets worldwide must be broken down into more concrete performances within architecture to produce new means of critique within the prevailing architecture of political-economic power. Thus, we might let the project emerge from a sequence of small, local decisions that we can realize without resorting to either comprehensive, global systems and/or absolute (preconceived and formal) references. Building a sequence of micro-decisions operating within or on specific and concrete aspects of a project (while bracketing any fully integrated methodology of the same procedures to foreclose a strictly deterministic process) may be an alternative to the big ideological visions. This *object-oriented architecture* would run closer to the development of alternative models of *physically grounded, produced* intelligence (also called behaviorist AI) than to symbolic reasoning and representation. The AI models for this operative system are *distributed computing, subsumption architecture,* and *object-oriented programming* all of which are forms of artificial intelligence that operate by breaking down intelligence into molecular, concrete components that relate independently to external inputs, collaborating with or canceling each other depending on the particular assemblage and specific location.

On Alienation

To explore the project as a product, rather than as a representation of an ideological or a critical stance, it is crucial to organize information from reality in such a way that judgment is temporarily suspended or, at least, delayed. Alienation, abstraction, estrangement, foreignness, nomadism, etc. are all, by default, positions that force us to delay judgment and let the material agency of the evolving architectural object "have its say." The instrumental capacity of diagrams, statistics, notations, and geometry is that they automatically produce a state of alienation with respect to reality that opens, immediately, new potentials in inverse relation to diminishing degrees of pure determination. Alienation provides the opportunity to dismantle conventions, and the possibility to open potentials that have been generally excluded by a historical construction of tools, solutions, and practices. It is not without irony that this form of alienation maps and mimics ideological alienation, but without the attendant imposition of outmoded forms of human agency. It is the outmoded that is the trouble, here, not human agency per se, and it is the bracketing of the same that allows new opportunities (both technical and human) to emerge.

While icons, symbols, and metaphors generally belong to a specific cultural context, and they become ineffective outside of that context, the alienating potential of diagrams, indices, notations, and registers enable us to trigger virtualities in the architectural project without abdicating control and responsibility to a purely machinic world. As a Westerner visiting the Far East, for example, you get an immediate dose of potentially productive alienation, or a decentered perspective that suspends convention and opens possibilities for us to imagine alternative social uses for the body. This makes us aware that social uses are purely contingent and malleable. For example, in Asia people sit on the floor to eat.

Architecture can, therefore, become a vehicle of subversion. When we started developing the programs to occupy the dysfunctional spaces that the geometrical structure of Yokohama had generated, we noticed that they did not have the height or the width to be occupied in the conventional manner. The solution was to invent alternative uses of the body, such as chaise longue–style, built-in benches, or lay-down resting areas.

As opposed to signifying practices, spatial and material practices have this kind of prescriptive and yet ambiguous capacity to embody differences without being exclusive. One of my favorite examples is national driving systems: even in a very universal and prescriptive system of organizing flow, such as the highway code (or maybe precisely because of it), you can immediately identify the spatial preferences of each culture: for example, the "fleet-in being" of the American highway; the "Napoleonic" hierarchy of the network paths in France or Spain; the primacy of the local decisions over the national system in England; the structure of left-yielding, local orientation in Holland; the *Einbahn* system in Germany; and the zonal, rather than linear addressing system in Japan. The theoretical approach we need to develop today is one capable of constructing relational forms for occupying and organizing space within certain prevailing social or political structures, rather than a critical approach that treats architecture as a representation of political agency. Within the globalized world it is vital to produce an updated architectural theory in which the discipline is not merely reduced and criticized as a representation of ideal political concepts, but conceived as an effective tool to produce change. In a world where political or social consensus is no longer produced across homogeneous populations, value systems, cultures and languages, spatial and material organizations have the virtue to act as cross-cultural devices for building consensus, in a more effective way than language, representation, or iconography. In a manner of speaking, this is the architectural equivalent of a return to matter, after decades wandering in the wilderness of rhetoric.

On Knowledge

The architect's profession often requires quite a heavy dose of narcissism. One has to be in a state of constant reaffirmation, positioning oneself as a Freudian subject (ego): I am this, this is my opinion, these are my desires and my vision. The success of an architect is measured by the capacity to make his or her psychological makeup coincide with the world. This is extended to the point where the project only makes sense as the support of this subject that we need to become in order to be "creative." This becomes a caricature in academia. "Creative" students, those who think that their task is to develop and complete their personality through the project, are—like "creative" architects—the least talented. Both as teacher and as architect, I believe it is important to produce a distance to break the psychological engagement with the project, to liberate the project from the tyranny of the subjective. This way the project is forced to take a life of its own. It is like what novelists say about not having full control of the characters. The author can not remain omnipotent for the work to be alive, to engage others. A practice of alienation allows the project speak and makes it more solid, independent on personal narratives, perspectives, ideologies...

The author will always remain behind a production, but as mediated by technical and material agency (the forces within the apparatus of the discipline). The more developed this mediation, the less willful the project. I often ask my students not to be so clever; try to be *dumb* for a while, to see if this produces something. Often, by being dumb you can find something that you did not know, feel, or desire. Being smart is only possible within a closed framework, from the advanced knowledge of a territory or a language. And when this frame does not exist, the only thing that can be done is to be dumb and attempt pattern recognition, like an alien...

On Experience

This industry measures work in man hours and drawing hours, and people by years of experience. Client representatives mistrust anybody under fifty and keep asking for company assets, professional indemnity, and years of experience. This is why the profession is filled with bureaucrats and technicians who cannot imagine anything beyond their calculating ruler, and *experienced* architects who feel they do not need to learn anything anymore; people with a hierarchical chip on their shoulders. Unfortunately, one has to put up with some of this crap because often the system does not recognize even the most obvious things—for example, that the people who are actually doing the jobs in every single office are under forty, and often under thirty. This is happening because younger people can use computers; younger people have access to technical means that have become central to the production processes. They work experimentally, producing knowledge as they are producing the project, rather than using accumulated *experience*. Younger architects are more sensitive to what is going on. Relevant knowledge has ceased to be bound to experience.

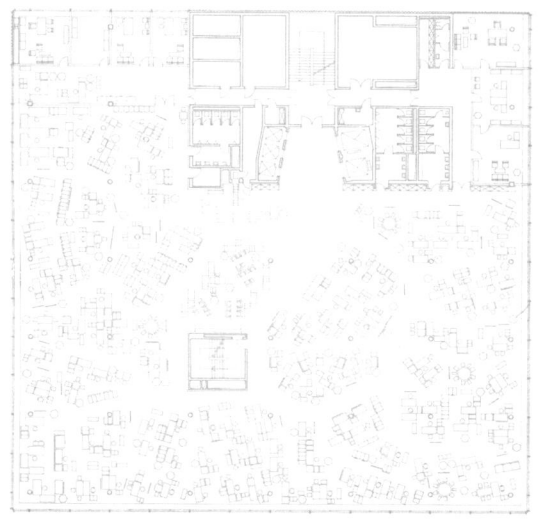

On the Virtual

Within the Western idealist tradition, the practice of architecture has been operating either in a utopian or a conservative mode. The virtual opens an alternative path for practice, where the products are neither ideal nor real. The virtual is what is latent, contained within reality and not yet actualized. It enables a transformational operation without having to confront reality through visionary statements. Pragmatic considerations are not opposed to the virtual, and, in fact, they can be critical to its construction, but only within a particular kind of pragmatism: not as a simple reproduction of the models of practice that have been already verified. The virtual is the realm of possibilities contained within a system.

I am not interested in virtual architecture, but in the virtual *in architecture*. Materiality is finally the necessary condition of architecture. However, the virtual can never be explicit in the material; it is the diagram that allows the capture of the virtual, and the assemblage of new composite materials.

Architects ultimately do not work with discourse but matters, because architecture is not generated through a theoretical discourse that later takes material form. Architecture's specificity is to work with materials, geometries, and organizations. Rather than as a vehicle to translate a theoretical discourse into architecture, diagrams and abstract notation permits us to assemble new materials and develop the project as a process of material transformation. The potential of diagrams and the computer as a medium is not to produce virtual, immaterial worlds, but the possibility of synthesizing new materials and working with them with unprecedented rigor. Producing hybrid material assemblages that go beyond the traditional palette of wood, ceramics, or steel is the final purpose of architectural practice. New matters could be, for example, constituted by concrete, glass, functions and quantities of flow. This is a much more effective architectural purpose than generating a parallel, immaterial world.

On Materials

The type of instructions an architect usually provides have mostly to do with a definition of the material organization of the building, the scale and proportion of the elements, the topological scheme of spaces, and the definition of the inside and outside. In recent years, the idea that architecture determines the composition of activities has become a very important addition to the duties of architects. However, the idea that architecture is interesting simply because it has an innovative program is somehow overvalued. Legions of architects are now trying to justify their projects solely on programmatic composition. Certain forms of architectural programs are very interesting as cultural or social phenomena or artifacts, but that does not guarantee their architectural value. For example, in Tokyo there are thousands of buildings with really weird programs and very little architectural value. Of course, building excellence does not guarantee value either...

Even worse is that the way in which architects usually talk about programmatic: Programmatic composition (even as problematized in the highest academic circles) is always embarrassingly imprecise; it actually explains exactly nothing. There are several disciplines that can talk about this matter far more precisely. To be serious about our capacity to operate with program, we should be able to look at the techniques that other disciplines use to deal with activities, to learn how to quantify, how to program, and to model the effects of a programmatic distribution; not only to develop forms of *engineered* program, but to discern the capacity to produce architectural effects without recourse to fuzzy forms of determinist logic. That is what the prophets of program have not answered yet, as they actually are too enamored of their tools and program is the great excuse for *no logic*.

The strange creature of the hybrid building (the programmatic mix) has emerged as one of the key subjects of contemporary architectural culture and yet it is treated with a laughable degree of imprecision. It appears that the mere joining together of an office with a tennis court or a discotheque with a church is sufficient to guarantee architectural quality. There is an absurd proliferation of colored plans with scattered activity keys or pictograms that attempt to become the new instruments for the making of an architecture of the *program*. But color-coding is an instrument that probably will never produce any architecture. The possibility to transcend the linguistic determination of programs, to define them by geometry and material properties, is crucial to implement a rigorous programmatic architecture. Activities need to be tied to physical, material, and geometrical properties in order to integrate program in the architectural project. Weight, friction, hardness, cohesion, durability, and texture need to become programmatic properties. For example, to design a restaurant, you need to understand the physical properties of this type of program; the proportion and scale of the dining hall is crucial in producing determined atmospheric effects; the distances between fellow diners or the geometry of the tables and the service circulation... To design a meeting room or an auditorium we need to know that certain geometries of the proscenium table are going to produce certain effects in the actions that will be developed within those spaces. If we have knowledge on the material we can manipulate it to produce certain effects, and these effects are effectively determined by cultural specificities, population pyramids, etc. Otherwise, programmatic architecture remains a social commentary.

New materials are produced when these physical and geometric properties of the program enter into reaction with other material parameters: resistance of steel to tension, degree of transparency of glass, wind pressure, or concrete's deflection limits. The material complex in which we can join together these properties is not intuitive because it only has limited models within the traditional discipline of architecture. Typological analysis is one of the most effective instruments for analyzing these complexes. Diagrams are a powerful instrument for producing this type of new material complexity. Within this diagrammatic approximation, material properties are abstracted into parameters in order to provide consistency to a project. Drawings can be formed by a mix of circulation diagrams and flexion strength but a mix between both that can be controlled with precision. For example, FOA's Glass Center, Kansai, and Belgo Zuid were constructed as a hybrid material somewhere between the sentinel illumination of the industrial shed and the diagram of the structural moment of the truss; Yokohama was the intersection between a circulation diagram and a structure made of corrugated sheets; Tenerife was an intersection between the urban structure of the Ramblas and their urban section, and the diagrams of ventilation and circulation of a multifunctional building with a deep floor plate; Pusan is material composed of the circulation and a parallel long span structure, formed of arches and catenaries; Downsview is composed of the purification drainage system with a wind protection system and a set of circuits for different types of physical exercise in the open air...

On the Prototype

As a tool for the exploration of complex material organizations, prototypes are an interesting tool. A prototype is suitable for deployment in alternative conditions rather than exclusive to a program or a location. It is an experimental tool that does not try to develop from existing material complexes on a particular location, but on the contrary always tests an external organization onto a particular situation. Prototypes mediate information into form. As such, the prototype contains in itself the potential to absorb interference, the capacity to adjust to local contexts, and the potential to embody and virtualize reality, exporting information into other material compounds, other sites, other conditions, and other projects. In a prototypical operation, local data perform as an index of specific opportunities while external models of organization operate as manifestations of different degrees of analogous global processes. A prototype does not operate in closed domains, but understands that organizations are virtually generic and yet specific in their actualization.

A project develops from a prototype according to an operative frame, recognized and constituted in principle, rather than literally derived from local data. That principle becomes the material mediation and the core of the organization of data. Specific technical and functional constraints may be imported and applied to provide raw material. Here is the difference between the prototypical operation and the emergent generation from the bottom up (provided that this is possible at all within an architectural process). Data are not at the core of the material organization, but are rather the vector of differentiation of the prototype. Specific processes and performances are diagrammed according to the needs of material activation and organization of the prototype. A prototype has an associated fabric and develops from a diagram that processes specific information into an architectural organization; this fabric is the result of the proliferation and differentiation of the prototype across the space of the project, reacting to the different conditions present in its domain of deployment.

On Fabrics

Fabrics are once again interesting. If in the '80s and '90s the best works of architecture were characterized fundamentally for their formal autonomy—and sometimes for the autonomy between the part and the whole—the investigation on fabrics, their geometry, and materials will become one of the central themes of architectural debate. The reason for this renovated interest in patterns comes out of the necessity to model complexity through consistency rather than contradiction. It also explores the new technical possibilities available to produce synthetic fabrics through artificial intelligence.

In the '80s, urban fabrics were associated with reproduction of historical urban patterns and typologies. Regulating grids or geometric structures were also the trademark of classical postmodernism and played an important role in the '60s structuralism. However, the fabrics that appear in the search of consistent complexity do not have anything to do with the "naturalized" fabrics of the historic city, but with the possibility of constructing areas of consistency without having to resort necessarily to the literal or critical reproduction of the material structures of the preexisting city.

One of the obvious possibilities that the new instruments for synthesizing artificial fabrics presents, insofar as they are applied in a comprehensive environment, is the ability to model fields that were not previously visible. The classical dichotomy between the *tabula rasa* and contextualism can now be resolved thanks to the possibility of modeling and proliferating preexistent conditions that do not share either the same dimension or location with the space where the project takes place. New urban fabrics no longer need to relate to actual historical, typological operativity. Disconnecting themselves from singular forms or actually existing places, they relate instead to the differentiation of prototypes along axes that do not even need real time or real space to generate new worlds. And this is not the reloading of artifice and imaginary principles under the cover of techno-scientific modeling; it is, however, the reintroduction of the space and time of the *non-site*, a critical issue in architectures past and future. Or, perhaps the limits of the context have infinitely expanded to include other dimensions of space-time.

The same happens with grids. Having virtually disappeared from the vocabulary of architecture's debate, the grid has become now one of the most productive fields of architectural experimentation. If the presence of a grid or a regulating structure in a project seemed to throw into question its capacity for integration and flexibility, then the possibility of operating in vectorial spaces enables the retrieval of the internal and external consistency of the project without resorting to a rigid system of reference. The greatest progress made during the construction development of the Yokohama project was in leaping from a high-resolution Cartesian grid to a vectorial grid where the relation between the parts of the project were localized instead of responding to a single, unitary system of reference (the abstract, modernist grid).

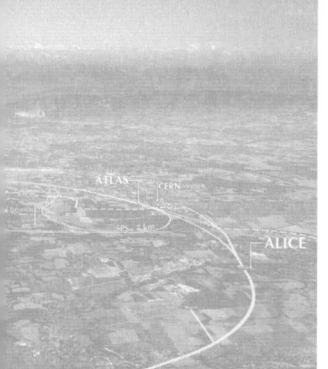

On Context

I get often criticized for being contextual, despite my transnational peregrinations and nomadic credentials. However, there is nothing more important for nomads than context—to be rooted. The difference from this mobile perspective is that context is not a dominion with clear demarcations; rather, it is the singularity of *continuous*, space across divergent spectrums of activity, where tracings of far off dominions may appear and disappear. Context also contains time; it is in perpetual motion. How many times have we returned to a city after several years to find it completely changed? The nomad's context is tied to the idea of opportunity: one can develop certain operations in a certain context, in certain circumstances, and then shift grounds (stay or leave).

The material of context is not necessarily physical. To discern the materiality of the context (wherein we operate, and to note how such enters into the assemblage of physical materials used to construct the project) is crucial to building an *address* for the project. There was a time when the choice of materials did not exist because technical limitations constrained the choice of palette. Modern technology changed that and opened unprecedented freedoms in terms of material choices. Now there has been a return to context as the guarantor of urban consistency: the city of contextual architects was constructed by replicating textures, materials, patterns, motifs, etc. In order to operate consistently, the already consolidated texture had to be literally reproduced. Instead of identifying the most efficient materials available for building at a certain time, and the effective architectonic solutions, contextualism as false urban science developed the self-imposed restriction for the city to be a reproduction of the existing fabric using a material palette that was restricted by antecedents (and hyperbolic design codes to enforce the outcome).

On the opposite side of the spectrum, non-contextual architects were not interested in the city as reference precisely because it implied limited architectural possibilities. I have strived to remain outside this dichotomy. Focusing on fabric, rather than architectural objects, does not limit architectural possibilities. Problematizing materials, their origin and composition, is interesting at a time when globalization (driven by technology) has greatly expanded context to include the context-less. To synthesize new architectural fabric for contemporary contexts means operating simultaneously on many levels: technical, material, and cultural.

On Proliferation

Architects can usually be classified into two modalities of practice: those who practice as visionaries, proposing an entirely new reality; and those who practice as doctors, curing and completing the city. Both modes stem from an idealist tradition: therapeutic architecture is reparative and implies that there is an ideal city, a complete state that we need to be capable of recognizing and reproducing. As an alternative to these two forms of utopian practice, the visionary and the therapeutic, I would like to propose a materialistic, pragmatic form of urban practice based on proliferation. This modality does not work either on the invention or the reparation of the city, but toward its projection from a point of consistent, but mutable *concrete embodiment*. This does not mean being anti-contextual, but rather the opposite: it implies to work with the city as an existing matrix of forces and material embodiments of those forces, projecting it toward possible futures versus repairing or replacing it, replicating or erasing it.

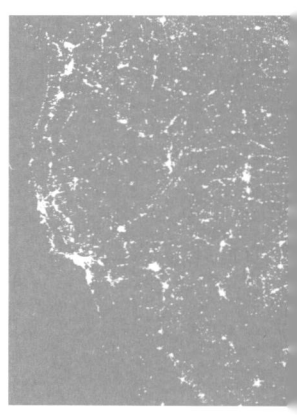

Even when a project seems to lack references and operate in an empty space or when it appears to be over-determined, there are always possibilities to find traces of latent organizations and tendencies that we can trigger to develop, freedoms that we can explore within the most constrained conditions. Space is always full of things and possibilities.

FOA's project for Santa Cruz, in Tenerife, is an example of this approach: the project is not a proposal of a new urban figure, a vision of the city, but it is neither a reproduction of the existing fabric. The process was based in triggering latent organizations: The organization of the Ramblas and the shaded plazas in the historic center, the form of growth of the piers along the length of the coast, the road structure along the length of the port and the ring road around the city: all of these were the ingredients with which we attempted to construct an organization capable of proliferating the existing structure into a system that could make the city grow over the port precinct, rather than inventing a new city.

On Determination

Arbitrariness and indetermination have become popular arguments in the discourse of the architectural avant-garde since the collapse of the techno-corporate and scientific models of high modernism; that is, from the immediate postwar period through the end of the '60s. However, indetermination is an unlikely model for a discipline that is aimed at the ordering of the environment. If the process develops arbitrarily, then what do architects do?

The notion that architecture can be produced by indetermination, to remain contingent for the sake of openness is a peculiar one and runs the risk of undermining the role of architecture as a profession. It is, in fact, a good reason for why architects are often not taken seriously, and possibly a cause for the natural domain of our practice being invaded by more determined and vigilant practitioners, such as engineers, quantity surveyors, cost consultants, managers, and administrators. Despite this, architects' traditional capacity to process complex data is potentially more adequate to deal with the construction of the contemporary city than the predominant system of fragmented responsibility through specialization.

There is a whole generation of architects that, in the name of experimentation and progress, have played the role of the cog-in-the-wheel, a very self-destructive process. Indeterminism is normally associated with more democratic and flexible ways of proceeding, albeit this political connotation seems somehow inadequate: it is difficult to claim responsibility for a political agenda when we have renounced positive determination for crypto-hermetic and *oracular* practices.

Even the most sophisticated versions of this approximation, such as those that work with hypotheses of self-generating organizations, tend to hide the degree of determination that they indulge. Even if we cannot predict a priori the form that a system of *cellular automata* will produce, it does not mean that there is not a moment of determination involved: once we have a material domain, some behavioral rules and some agents with certain objectives, the form is virtually determined. Mere selection of the automata is a form of determination.

In reviewing the technical and disciplinary procedures as a domain for architectural experimentation, we should distinguish between indeterminism and openness. Open work is not necessarily without determination, but rather work capable to incorporate changes and external inputs through its process of development, without necessarily declining the responsibility of making decisions. Openness, chance, flexibility, integrative strategies are operative advantages in a world characterized by fast-changing demands (the so-called facts on the ground): the most effective work is the one that is developed with great precision of intentions without necessarily determining a priori what the result may be. In fact, what diagrammatic practices allow us to do is to construct a project without eliminating the possibility to incorporate changes in the environment through the project, or, conversely, without declining the possibility to control it, by determining partially and sequentially the adequate domains of control. Diagrammatic practices enable architects to apply determinations while allowing local structures or contingencies to inform the final result.

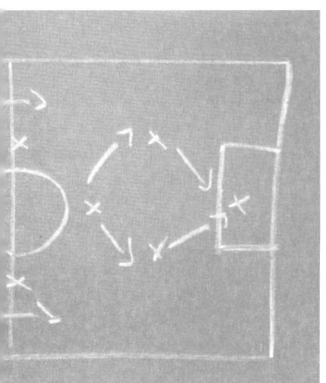

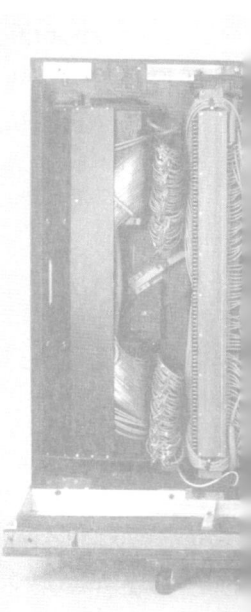

The correspondence between Pierre Boulez and John Cage is a good illustration of this. Both musicians were working on the opening of new possibilities for musical composition, and both were interested in alienation as a productive state to be able to explore the sound spaces left aside by the musical forms of the past. But they chose entirely opposite ways of searching. Cage adopted indeterminacy and abdicated control in order to produce openness, and the unexpected. His technical apparatus for reorganizing the composition became a throw of the dice, randomly opening the I Ching or simply allowing increasing freedom to the interpreter. Like in an improvisation, the contingencies of the moment of performance are embraced as part of the creation by relaxing the constraints on the performance or the interpretation. Boulez is interested in the opposite, which is absolute determination as a way of triggering the virtual, so he composed through algorithms and developed complex formulae by which notes repeated at intervals on certain levels produce displacements of the rhythm, the harmony or the tonality of the piece. Even in his experiments on open composition, the incorporation of contingencies is carefully structured through certain devices. Cage worked with the matter of the music by putting objects amongst the chords of the piano or using electronic devices, while Boulez operated almost exclusively with conventional instruments most of the time, and with striated musical scales.

Neither Boulez nor Cage had full knowledge of the piece's sound beforehand. It was only in the performance that the piece would take its final form, and it would be a form that would change across the different interpretations. They are both good examples of a diagrammatic operation. Neither of them used a causal technique aimed at a precise effect. For Cage, the diagram of the pieces is a basic structure and materiality that will take shape once it is performed, incorporating noises and contingencies of the performance, while Boulez knew exactly the constructive logic of the piece, and yet it had been proliferated to such extent that it prevented the sound to be imagined in advance. He took musical order to such level of complexity that it became experientially contingent. While Cage was a kind of mystic who prayed an all-embracing credo, Boulez is a craftsman who constructs structures of such complexity that are able to open new acoustic effects without renouncing to precision and determination. His extraordinary proliferation or rigorously constructed material aimed towards the subversion of the traditional musical experience is a wonderful model for diagrammatic practices in architecture.

On Facts and Ideologies

I am often criticized for being too interested in precision, data, and measurement, or for having this kind of modernist, positivist, scientific idea that we can determine or produce things without taking an explicit ideological stance. And while this appears to be politically incorrect, naïve, and/or narrow-minded, let's look at the alternatives: the critical, the representational, the subjective, and the politically engaged. They are no less controlling, and yet they are probably less capable of transformative action as they are fundamentally based on working with stereotypes, conventions, and idiosyncrasies. It is difficult to sustain the resort to representation or language as a replacement for an impossible objectivity in measurement, particularly if we want to explore new grounds.

Moreover, nothing is more intentional than data as any expert in statistics can confirm. Quantitative analysis is far from naive, value-free, and objective. Organizing data is a process loaded with subjective or collective choices and values: in order to optimize, a certain value system is required. In an analysis-driven process, there is always a moment when a certain organizational, formal, or material diagram has to be deployed onto the data for it to produce a project. Data cannot *construct* architecture. There are a lot of organizational and geometric decisions to be made to turn information into something that can operate as a building.

In this process, reduction is often necessary: the selection of relevant data for the construction of a project is as crucial as the selection of the material palette in a conventional building design. Without this selection process, the project becomes an infinite process. But reduction in the material palette does not imply simplicity. To produce complexity we need to construct new models of measuring or notating, models capable of dealing with ever more dynamic processes and complex organizations, even if we know that our models will eventually become obsolete or crash under the strain. The most interesting potential of the use of abstraction and parametricization is their alienating—and therefore, liberating—potential, rather than the modernist and neo-modernist recourse to causal, formalistic technique.

On Instruments: Diagrams, Drawings, and Graphs

After a few decades in which the architectural debate has been focused on signification, representation, and language, there has been in the last few years a shift towards methodology and instrumentality, and it is necessary now to clarify the terms of discussion. What do we understand by diagrams, drawings, and graphs, or, the technical arsenal of non-representational architecture? After some decades in the wilderness, diagrams are again a key subject of the contemporary architectural discourse. I would like to propose that we define a diagram as a material organization that describes relationships and prescribes performances in space. It does not necessarily contain metric or geometric information; those emerge once the diagram starts processing matters. A diagram is always specific to a space. It may be a specific location, a scale, a temporal frame, but it always has a spatial correlation, as opposed to a graph, for example. It relates to processes that may occur not only in three-dimensional space, but also in several dimensions at once. There is a tendency to believe that there is a "diagrammatic architecture," where the architecture inherits the formal characteristics of the diagram, but in principle, a diagram is not necessarily similar in form to the organization it describes or prescribes: a very simple diagram may generate very complex organizations. In fact, as opposed to signifying or symbolic operations one of the greatest potentials of a diagrammatic construction is to produce organizations with multiple readings.

The primary quality of a diagram is its reductive nature. Diagrammatic operations should not be confused with arbitrariness or lack of control; on the contrary, the diagram is about defining precisely, at every moment in the process, the level of knowledge and determination that we can exert on the project. In a diagrammatic process, the project develops a constant capacity to trigger new possibilities. The project retains its virtualities, and these become only partially actualized, retaining the possibility to develop *ad infinitum*. In a diagrammatic project the moment of closure is determined by factors external to the project, and the propositional moments, the aims and strategies are not restricted to the origin or the end, but in the middle of the process. The diagram is primarily an apparatus to develop the project through its performance. Between the form of the diagram and the final form of the building there needs to be additional information added. An interesting example of a project developed diagrammatically is the Yokohama project, where the diagram sets the targets precisely, but also generates more ambiguous readings of the outcome. The project begins with the ambition to produce a pier where you never retrace your steps. That is the concept of the project, which is embedded in a diagram that defies the characteristic linear organization of a pier (the no-return diagram). In whatever direction the pier is traveled, the experience will be of a continuous forward movement. The project's departure is not placed on its formal or representational qualities, but on its most basic performance as a spatial organization. The physical concreteness of the project emerges progressively as the diagram becomes engaged with a certain material: in Yokohama, the material is the ground. Its deployment evolves the no-return diagram into a three-dimensional diagram. Ergonomic and functional information were then incorporated into the new diagram (for example, the scale of the load-bearing structures, head clearances, manufacturing constraints) to determine the scale and geometry of the surface's deformations. Only after the diagram has absorbed all of this information, does it become a drawing, acquiring metrical and geometrical determinations. A drawing is a material organization that prescribes metric and geometric information in three-dimensional space. Its precision is, therefore, critical for its operativity. Conventional architectural methods are based on an indeterminate relationship between the diagrams and the drawings. In the traditional architectural methodologies, these relations are usually regulated by the conventions of the discipline. Drawings are the primary instrument to produce architecture. But a projectual process that remains limited to the relationship between drawings and real-space buildings or environments is constrained by the actualization of pre-conceived conventions and commonly resists the integration of variation, local specificities, or changes of conditions given to processes of actual construction.

A graph is a plot of information that is not actualized in real space. A graph does not have plastic or visual content, as it does not belong to an organization that unfolds in real space. It describes or prescribes information operating in an abstract space. It can act to unlock virtualities that are not perceptible on a sensible level or extend the capacity of material organizations to affect or be affected by processes occurring in virtual spaces. The transfer of a graph into real space always requires of a specific transfer technique; for example, the implementation of differential fenestration ratios of a building envelope to produce environmental performances requires the technology to provide differential fenestration. In architecture, to make a graph operative, it is crucial to understand the dimensional relationship between the space of the graph and the concrete space.

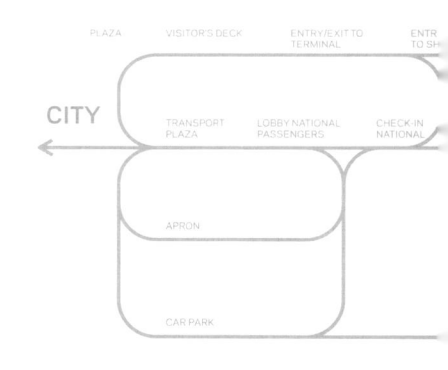

The most common mistake in so-called contemporary experimental architecture is to literally turn the space of the diagram or the graph into the space of the drawing, and, therefore, of the building. The current tendency toward smoothness is an effect of operating with frictionless diagrams. But real buildings have materials, and these produce coarseness and true complexity to the building's form and organization. A diagram or a graph always requires a determinant form of mediation to become a drawing, to enter into real space.

On Modes of Production

Relevant architecture has always been capable of articulating the social, productive, and cultural context of an era into a material organization. During the last thirty years there have been dramatic changes in the productive and social structures that a contemporary architect needs to assimilate. The process of late-capitalist globalization and the development of new communication and transport technologies are crucial domains that invite new solutions.

However, these arguments are irrelevant if they do not lead to the development of new architectural possibilities. The shopping malls and theme parks that proliferate around cities do not need good architecture to exist. They are interesting urban or architectural phenomenon, but this does not grant architectural excellence unless it can be used to generate new architectural potentials. In order to explore these opportunities it is crucial to describe precisely this phenomenal transformation in terms of material organizations, rather than as social or cultural "turns" that have been so fashionable in the last decade. This means to translate this new urban phenomenology to geometry, tectonics, materiality, organization, distribution, and building technology. In order to advance the discoveries made by the previous generation as a response to the social, political, cultural, and technological changes that have occurred since the end of the '60s we need a new technical discourse specific to the discipline. If the generation of architects that preceded us is a product of the '60s, our generation grew up in the shadow of the '80s. In the developed world there was no longer any cold war; class, gender, or ethnic wars were no longer that relevant. Neo-liberal democracy and free-wheeling capitalism were the norm (if not one and the same thing). We all used computers, flew off somewhere at the drop of a hat, and watched CNN in the retooled *pax Americana*. If we compare the architect's biographies of the preceding generation with ours, theirs look contingent and ours very deliberate: we are a cold-blooded generation with a pedigree. We have studied or taught at the best universities, written for good magazines, and worked in the correct offices.

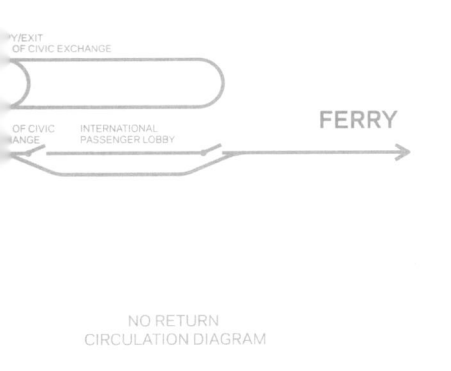

We have already more than thirty years of post-capitalist history and we cannot go on being fascinated by the *new, the collapse of traditional orders*, the strangeness of this *brave new world*. Perhaps one of the most paradigmatic lines of investigation within this new context is nomadic practice, something that arises from our biographies. We have had the possibility to verify differences, and to learn to understand the specific opportunities that each place or project offers. This is a vital experience that develops a hypersensitivity to opportunities, forming a sensibility towards variation and change.

For example, the procurement systems for architecture in the Anglo-Saxon cultures tend to be driven by financial and legal processes: either you are Frank Gehry or you are a kind of lawyer or accountant. Probably as a result of an anachronism, Spain is still a paradise for architects, just as Japan, Switzerland, and the Netherlands are cultures that still place extraordinary importance on the quality of built environment. These are countries where it is still possible to make architecture outside the star-system because there is a strong cultural and social interest and a structure of production (perhaps obsolete) that allows architects to make architecture. Japan, for example, has probably the best construction industry in the world within a culture that in many aspects is almost Medieval. The *civilized* world is where you practice with a lawyer at your side, to avoid possible lawsuits while looking out to sue others. In this civilized world the professional value has been replaced by insurance policies that have become the driver of any selection process. For the majority of private American or English clients the most important thing is that you have good insurance or that the value of your company is set at a determined level. They are not concerned about whether you know how to make good architecture or even if you are technically competent. What interests them is that if, at a certain point, something goes wrong, they can take you to court and make off with your insurance money. Given that we know that progress is not linear, we can only hope that what is happening at the moment in the so-called advanced economies is nothing more than a bad dream, and that architecture will once again have an important role in the agenda of future civilizations—such as has occurred in Bilbao with the Guggenheim or in London with the Tate Modern. Perhaps this will happen once we know how to create a public consciousness that good architecture generates surplus value.

The images displayed along this text relate to the multiple issues addressed throughout: from the hybridisation of the natural and the artificial, to the resonances of production and imagery across different practices, to circulation systems in different cultures, to micro-structures... These images aim to provide visual references for this phenomenology.

Published in *Verb Processing*, Actar, Barcelona, 2001.

Roller-Coaster Construction

"This is where amateurs have an advantage over pros. A pro knows what he can deliver, and rarely goes beyond it. An amateur has no concept of his limitations and generally goes beyond them."[1]
—TREY GUNN

Architecture is not a plastic art, but the engineering of material life. Despite these asymmetrical classifications, architecture is a plastic problem only if you decide that *plasticity* is your material. But that is just a particular case. FOA's work, in this respect, is distinguished from other surface-complex architecture by the respectful distance it takes from plasticity as singular affect. The repeated comparisons of FOA's work to *certain instantiations* of formally similar work by Eero Saarinen, Jørn Utzon, or Frank Gehry, despite the plastic similarities and the mostly well-meaning appreciation of their work, are based, rather unfortunately, on *formal output* without an appreciation for the origin of that output. Formal concerns are of significance, but this associative critique (guilt by association)

---

1 Trey Gunn, *Road Diaries: Project Two, Discipline Global Mobile*, CD-ROM 1998

does not tell the whole story. For example, Gehry works in exactly the opposite direction: he produces a spatial effect that is subsequently implemented by means of construction. He is primarily concerned with consistency in spatial effects. The result may be sometimes similar, but the process of reaching it is radically different. What is more specific to our work is fundamentally the process, as our main priority is to produce material consistency. In fact, we are not interested in preconceived effects but rather, in exploring materials—and here we should understand material in the broadest sense, as a source of unexpected ideas and effects. A formal bias within criticism is, therefore, reductive—and such a bias is based on a misconception of plasticity as a type of scenography.

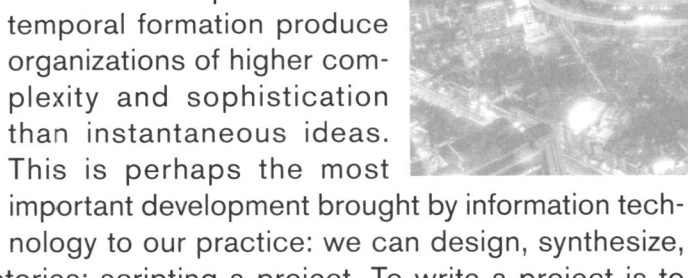

Processes are far more interesting than ideas. Ideas are linked to existing codes, operating critically or in alignment with preexisting systems of ideas. Rather than making a project the implementation of an idea, or the scaffolding of an image, what we are interested in is constructing and engineering processes on different levels. A process is the generation of a micro-history of a project, a specific narrative where the entity of the project forms in a sequence. If geological, biological, or human history has something to teach us, it is that these processes of temporal formation produce organizations of higher complexity and sophistication than instantaneous ideas. This is perhaps the most important development brought by information technology to our practice: we can design, synthesize, and proliferate specific histories: scripting a project. To write a project is to introduce a sequential development rather than deploying a form, an image. It is more interesting to produce the sequence, write the code and wait for the emergence of the project. We are no longer trapped in the traditional compulsion to reproduce historical models, or to invent them from scratch. We do not have to produce a project as a reproduction, derivation, or the invention of a historical model. We do not need to produce complexity by making collages: we can synthesize the processes of historical generation in fast-forward motion, adding information sequentially to the project. This sequential, integrated addition produces more ambiguous effects that are more capable or resonating on different levels than straightforward ideological statements, metaphors, allegories, or reproductions.

Through our interests in the processes of construction and engineering of material life, we get constantly involved with all sorts of technologies, and these are always associated with performance: producing effects, delivering services, etc. In architecture, technology has lost its generative potential, becoming enslaved to the production of architectural services; but architecture as a service industry is a deadly business and rarely delivers interesting architecture. Soon, only star-architecture will be worth being involved with; the rest will be the banal delivery of architectural services. And, while this end game has long been predicted, today it is in the process of *actually taking command*. A revolt is in order. To counter the concept of so-called architectural services as the answer to building, what is required is the temporary decoupling between architectural technology and effect: a good professional is capable of using the right techniques to produce the right effects. But what would happen if we divorced technique from service and effect? Is it not possible to exploit the affective potential of architectural technique by temporarily severing it from the pernicious and reductive site of the service bureau? Strangely, one must turn the machine upside-down and backwards before the true privilege of the effect might register once again within architecture (which, needless to say, is not reducible to building).

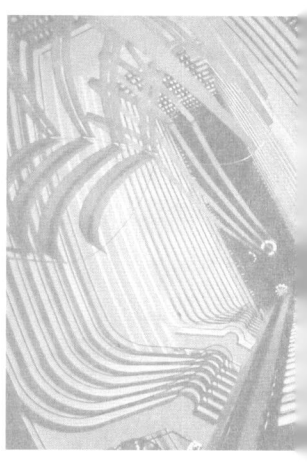

This is where I think there may be an alternative to an architecture that masters effects but neglects technical or material agency in the process. (And, here, it is important to note that effects are not affects, and that the latter is a surplus generated by privileging non-specific, ambient agency, while the former is a relational precept within the causal chain that is acknowledged and privileged through its material agency. Affect is often a short circuit of material agency, or *aesthetic* recourse to surplus effects.)

There is enormous potential to be released in the delivery of "architectural services" that has yet to be exploited. Project management, cost modeling, value engineering, and the modeling capacity of artificial intelligence notwithstanding (or, project management, cost modeling, etc. temporarily set aside), what is necessary is to free architecture from the merely prosaic versions of the same that have swept like kudzu through the profession as a means of paying allegiance to late-capitalism and its quest for the total work of banality (versus art) is to *redefine* all of the above. This has been, in many ways, the entire point of FOA's research, while honesty requires admitting that much of this is only now evidenced in retrospect, as we were dealing with these problems while in the thick of the battle on two fronts: first, the last vestiges of the poststructuralist jihad; and second, the not-unrelated devolution of architecture to *real estate*.

None of this, as a result, has been yet integrated in the discipline of architecture, and this is leading the profession toward complete paralysis. As a result of this disciplinary paralysis, there are: the starchitects and architectural service bureaus (often gigantic offices with tentacles all over the world). What is common to them is that both are based on branding. The real challenge is to exploit the potential of these technologies and the concomitant branding strategies beyond their utilitarian bastardization; that is, to integrate them into a discipline that has not actually evolved for quite some time, perhaps constructing an entirely new discipline.

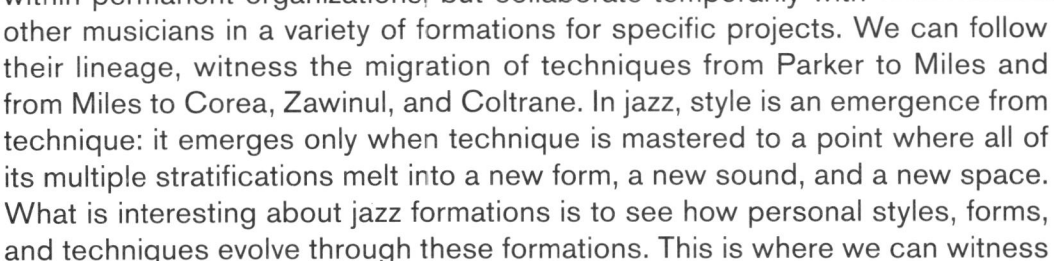

Speaking of stars, I have never been a *pop* enthusiast. Pop music is basically technically incompetent, packaged by image, driven by lifestyle. Pop stars rarely survive as musicians when the band dies, as their technical background is too weak to survive without its relationship to a certain lifestyle or a culture. *Jazz* musicians usually have more solid technical knowledge. They do not operate within permanent organizations, but collaborate temporarily with other musicians in a variety of formations for specific projects. We can follow their lineage, witness the migration of techniques from Parker to Miles and from Miles to Corea, Zawinul, and Coltrane. In jazz, style is an emergence from technique: it emerges only when technique is mastered to a point where all of its multiple stratifications melt into a new form, a new sound, and a new space. What is interesting about jazz formations is to see how personal styles, forms, and techniques evolve through these formations. This is where we can witness the evolution of a discipline, almost as if we were witnessing the evolution of an animal species. Despite the obvious dangers of sclerosis, disciplinary lineage provides an invaluable ground upon which to experiment beyond the constant reference to the market or to the outside, laying the ground for a broader field of experimentation and greater internal consistency.

During the last fifteen years, the most interesting architectural experimentation has gravitated around the possibility of broadening an excessively hardened discipline to include a variety of concerns of an external nature. This is a necessary update of architecture's operative capacities in response to ever-changing demands, which has been often implemented through the resort to abstraction as a mechanism, taking distance from the manipulation of architectural language proper (or architecture on the ground). Two types of abstraction are usually deployed today, albeit toward different ends. Theoretical discourse, while having fallen out of favor, and a combination of parametric design and data collection, while fashionable and suspect at once, have constituted the two fundamental mechanisms aimed at either the inclusion or occlusion of economic, social, political, or psychological factors into the discipline. Whether they are means to show or to hide such considerations is dependent on how they are deployed. They are abstractions only in the sense that both are highly detached from the real and both have the potential to remain de-naturalized forms of architectural rhetoric without any resultant "facts on the ground" to support or justify them. However productive this dual "abstracting" process has been in terms of broadening architectural knowledge, it has failed on both accounts to define a system of assessment internal to the discipline, or to explain in what way the inclusion of those concerns has enhanced the quality of the product. Architecture is supposed to erase the gender divide, increase the sales of a mall, and decrease the level of CO_2 in the atmosphere. Sure… But even if new fields of operation are identified, this approach does not guarantee the architectural qualities of the product and does not even question them. Like pop music, the value exists fundamentally outside the discipline, outside the internal consistency of the project. Social equality, net profits, and environmental sustainability can certainly be best achieved by means other than architecture, if that is what we are after. Yet, and this is the key point, if architecture *might* be revolutionary, it will have to find its own radical means within itself to effect the transformation most sane individuals (including some architects) cannot *not* prefer.

On the other side of the spectrum, a truly experimental architectural practice is threatened by even more dangerous processes than simple dilettantism: that is, greedy consultants; managers who measure the work in man hours and hours per drawing, and people by years of experience; mediocre client representatives that mistrust anybody under fifty; useless engineers who cannot imagine anything beyond their calculating ruler; "experienced" architects who feel they have nothing left to learn; and people with a hierarchical chip on their brain... Unfortunately, one has to put up with some of this crap because sometimes the system does not recognize even the most obvious things, including the fact that the people who are actually doing the jobs in every single office are under forty, mostly even under thirty. They are the ones who can use the computers, and access to technical means has made them central to the production process, producing knowledge rather than delivering "experience."

With Yokohama, our managers said that we would need between 30 and 40 architects working on the job. We are managing with 14. If we had followed their advice, not only would we have gone bankrupt, we would have sacrificed the project's sophistication, as the energy that now is concentrated in a few good people would have been lost in meetings, timesheets, minutes, and other things invented by managers to justify their incapacity to produce, and their hierarchical privileges. It was perhaps our academic experience that reassured us of the value of keeping a team structure that also produces knowledge, rather than just drawings. One of the things you learn from teaching is that there are virtually no limits to the capacity of people to produce—knowledge *and* stuff—as long as they remain motivated. It is only experience that teaches us where our limits are, and once we have learned that, we are finished, because our work can be calculated and measured; it becomes stratified and ceases to be a weapon. It was also our academic background that allowed us to put together a dream-team of architects whose individual skills and commitment went beyond conventional measure, and whose presence could have specific impact on the work; like a good band.

Despite the constant requirement of our client for a clear hierarchy of command, we structured the work around packages as a production structure, giving independence to the designers to research, develop, and produce the drawings for each package: partitions, glazing, ceiling, traffic, structure, mechanical services, etc. We tried to avoid any centralization of command, as the team was sufficiently small and close enough to allow us to rely on everybody to keep track of activity on all fronts. This platoon model suggests a form of militancy in practice necessary to avoid professional stratification and calcification. It is the same model used to produce revolutions. Everybody goes to meetings, does copies, meets contractors, makes coffee, talks to consultants, fixes computers, and does accounts. Of course, it has come at a price: no 9-to-5, no holidays, no weekends, etc. This experiment is about pushing things to the limit, within a specific time frame and toward a specific agenda, occupying everybody's life with the project for as long as it lasts and is interesting. The process is aimed at reaching maximum intensity, suspending all limitations of work and projecting it as far as possible.

The structural development of the project, done in consultation with SDG (Structural Design Group), has become the main source of ideas for its implementation, and a trail of discovery that reaches far beyond the images that became the more recognizable side of the project. The structure that we proposed in the competition was made out of a folded piece of steel, a consistent isomorphism with the concept of the project as a folded organization. This proposal was also advantageous in terms of its resistance to earthquake stresses and akin to the techniques of the naval industry to which the building was affiliated. The "cardboard" structure emerged out of what was originally a reference to the local tradition of origami. These references to local construction systems, both literal and culturally mediated, were an attempt to contextualize the proposal without having to resort to the mimicry of local building. In other words, the context was introduced as a process of material organization, rather than as an image. This sensitivity to the *local contexts* played, in turn, a decisive role in the generation of the building's early geometry, though the extraordinary importance of the *latent asymmetries* of the grounding conditions *on site* played the *formative* and one might say *definitive* role in the design-development phase that followed.

At the beginning of design development, the structure was clearly the most critical point of the project, as the competition scheme proposal was as interesting as it was naïve and needed substantial technical development to become realizable without betraying the original purpose. The main problem was to solve a three-dimensional complex geometry with a geometry that was basically axial—that of folding. The outcome of the process was (early on) quite interesting, as it originated important geometrical and formal emergences directly out of the technical constraints, rather than as a kind of external formal or geometrical concept imposed on the project from the outside.

During the development of the basic design phase, we came up with a solution where the folds of the web were woven together every half fold, so that we could achieve curvature at a larger scale. This was the adoption of a structural-geometric strategy used, for example, by Pier Luigi Nervi, Renzo Piano, and others to make large-span shells with a kind of structural unit or cell that is repeated along curves. But what was most interesting was the way the cells of the structure became differentiated at every point of the surface, as in an organic system. One of the immediate advantages of this system was that we removed the lower plate of the structure to simplify the construction, turning the folded metal plates into a crucial expressive trait of the project: the origami had finally become visible.

At this point there was an interesting debate about whether the structural system had to become an isotropic shell with local singularities, as the computer perspectives seemed to indicate, or whether it should retain the bi-directional qualities that the plan of the building contained, as a system composed of two series of large-scale folds bridged by a series of transversal folds. After testing a hybrid between the original cardboard type and a space frame with local densification, we realized that the concentration of axial stresses along the longitudinal large-scale folds suggested that the structural type had to be altered to become a concrete-filled structure. This was the reason we decided that, despite the image of the building, the bidirectional structure was ultimately a more adequate structural solution. The coincidence between the ramp system and the main longitudinal girders became the primary determinant of the structural geometry, as the conflict between the symmetrical condition of the programmatic structure and the asymmetrical condition of the grounding system forced us to bend the ramps. The edges of the building were located at 15 meters from the pier's edges to comply with the symmetrical location of the boarding decks on both sides, while the foundations could only reach up to 21.5 meters from the Shinko side and 29 meters on the Yamashita side. This conflict between structural asymmetry and programmatic symmetry was already present in the competition entry but had not been fully exploited, as it had been absorbed entirely in the lower level ramps, without affecting the geometry of the upper level. It was only when we had started to think through the correlation between the two levels of girders that the asymmetry then extended through the geometry of the whole project, rather than being confined to the lower level. One of the critiques we received after the competition scheme was made public was that the topology of the building was basically symmetrical and Beaux-Arts. However, it was not that we did not consider this problem during the competition stage but, rather, that we thought it was more interesting to preserve the conflict as a generative trigger rather than imposing a formal concept (asymmetry) to the resolution of the problem. The sensitivity to the initial conditions of the brief and the reference to the local shipbuilding industry had become productive in the process of formal determination.

The other subject that evolved through the development of the project was the determination of the grid—that is, the geometrical *fabric* of the project. At the competition stage of our proposal, the initial form was generated by analyzing the spatial locations of the different spaces of the terminal (the boarding decks, visitors' decks, rooftop plaza, departure and arrival hall, and traffic plaza) and linking them locally through a deformed surface. That surface was constructed through a sequence of parallel transverse sections, describing the local conditions every 15 meters, and morphing them along the axis of the building. The interesting question arising from this process was its ambiguity between an organizational technique based on parallel bands and the single-surface technique that absorbs differences into singularities of a congruent whole. We were basically interested in the single surface effect, but our methods were still reliant on techniques that we had learned at OMA, where the sequences of parallel bands developed from La Villette through the City Hall in The Hague and the Très Grande Bibliothèque produced organizations that allowed for a maximum sectional flexibility: a kind of rotated *plan libre* aimed at reaching maximum programmatic freedom across levels.

In so doing, though, our programmatic aims (the coherence of the circulation diagram across programs) were radically different from the programmatic incongruence and juxtapositions that originated OMA's infamous band technique. The predominant longitudinal direction of the building and the basically symmetrical programmatic structure supported the use of this organization, producing a conflict with our interest in programmatic continuity that would drive the evolution of the project through detail design. The conflict between a striated organization and a smooth congruence that we had also seen between the grounding conditions and the programmatic symmetry was also present in this inadequacy between ambition (artificially constructed ground) and technique (programmatic organization). A key point to stress is that despite its "in-formal" appearance, our ambition for this project (and most other ones) was one of radical formal determination versus deformation. The informal appearance is, therefore, the outcome of processes of complex formal determination rather than a sought-for formal effect.

In this process of constantly increasing in the determinant aspects of the geometry of the project, our first step was to increase the resolution of the transverse sections from 15 meters to 5 meters by inserting two new sections within each band. The technique we used to determine the new intermediate sections was achieved by producing what we called "control lines" or curves that were determined by transforming the location points of each element in the transversal sections—that is, producing spline curves. This was the first technique where we started to establish an argument of consistency between the different sections, produced out of the determinations of successive local conditions. By cutting the "control lines" through intermediate planes, we were able to locate the position of the different elements longitudinally. At the same time, we dropped the splined geometry of the surface into a second geometrical field composed of complex curves, the latter made out of a palette of seven different radii, producing the surface out of the intersection of cylindrical or conical surfaces of regular radii, in order to simplify the manufacturing process. This process produced 96 transversal sections to determine the form of the building, but these were clearly insufficient for a detailed description of the project. So, due also to a change in the basic size of the transversal folds, we increased the resolution to a grid of 3.6 meters, still using the control curves as our technique of coherence. Soon, the 124 transversal sections we had obtained doubled, as the basic scale of the transversal folds was fixed to 1.8 meters, becoming the new resolution of the grid. The process of geometrical development became basically a problem of increasing the resolution of the grid, and every step in this process required an exponential increase in the amount of information we had to produce. When we started the detailed design of the girder's geometry, we realized that even this amount of information was not sufficient to precisely control the geometry of the project. We also noticed that by rolling parallel sections along curved control lines we were producing irregularities in the geometry of the ramps, unless we were differentiating between the transversal sections of the girders. Even worse: because of the existing geometrical definition, every face of the girder would have to be triangulated, and different from the others, and every transversal fold had become a different geometry. Even if now we had control of the determination of the stiffeners that constructed the girders, we had no control over the triangulation of their faces.

One of the most important evolutions in the project occurred at this point, when we started to consider the construction of the girders through the rotation of the same stiffener templates at regular intervals along the control lines that now had to be dropped into complex curves. In order to increase the regularity of the manufacturing process we started simultaneously considering the possibility of producing local symmetry in the transversal folds by making them meet the girders at a perpendicular angle. The only way to achieve this, given the deformed geometry of the girders, was to shift from the parallel transversal grid of the competition entry to a topological grid originated in the control lines that determined the girders' geometry. In our new topological grid, the parallel bands did not grant independence to the different parts but, on the contrary, established functions that connected them to each other, considerably diminishing the amount of information required for the determination of the form. We had, therefore, moved from a raster space, where each point is determined by local information, to a vectorial space, where each point is determined by a differentiated global order. Again, there was no ideological or critical statement in making this step; it was the pragmatic resolution of technical conflicts in the process of development. These kinds of discoveries are the ones that can turn processes of a purely technical nature back toward an architectural discourse based on material agency, allowing the discipline to advance by way of the productive and generative exigencies within practice versus the imposition and superimposition of critical or ideological operations.

The next conflict emerged between the possibility of achieving repetition in the girder's geometry or symmetry in the transversal folds. Because the folds would have to link with the girders at the stiffeners locations, if we wanted to achieve local symmetry, we would have to sacrifice regularity in the girders' sections, as the pitch of the stiffeners would be determined by the intersection of the folds with the girder's edge. If, conversely, we started with a regular pitch of the stiffeners in the girders, we would have to sacrifice the local symmetry of the folds. In order to set up a non-parallel grid to solve the problem, we first gave priority to the local symmetry of the folds, to determine the position of the stiffeners along the girders. The position of the new gridlines was not geometrically determined, and had to be calculated numerically through a program that established iteration loops to calculate the intersection of the transversal folds' local axis with the curved edges of the girders. As a program, the iteration loops had to be calculated sequentially, so, the results would depend on the area of the plan where we started calculating the iteration loops. However, due to the fact that, after calculation, over 65 percent of the steel weight was concentrated in the girders, we decided to take a grid determined by rolling templates along the control lines at regular intervals, so that the girder's construction would become as regular as possible. In this option, the fabric of the folds had to become anti-metrical in the central folds—still identical in terms of formal determination—and symmetrical on the lateral folds, leaving only the two intermediate folds of every arch to be irregular. A third scale of folding was required at this stage in the process: in order to reduce the total weight of steel, we had to place small stiffeners inside the small-scale transversal folds that were resulting in greater increases in the manufacturing costs. In order to avoid this increase, we decided to replace the 6-millimeter-thick plates that constituted the first proposal for the detail of the folds with a 3.2-millimeter corrugated plate. The corrugations would provide the plates with enough strength to avoid the stiffeners.

However the process was not yet finished, although most of the crucial decisions had already been made. In one of the meetings with the contractors to explain the geometry of the project and the process of setting out on site, they asked us for the coordinates of the points of the building, as if the form was decided in advance, and they could just implement that geometry on site. To their surprise, we had to explain to them that the geometry was strictly related to the manufacturing and construction systems, and could be modified if necessary. They said that they had thought that site control was going to be the most crucial aspect in the construction process, but now they realized that the most important process was to be the manufacturing. One of them pointed out that they would have to use the same techniques used to build roller coasters, where the setting out utilizes local references between identical templates rolled along an irregular three-dimensional geometry. "Exactly!" we said. "Roller-coaster construction!"

The images contained in this text take as a reference the idea of a roller-coaster construction and extends it from the physical qualities of a certain construction system, to the urban and lifestyle qualities emerging in contemporary cities, and more specifically in the Asian cities, the most populated ones. Walter Benjamin wrote that roller-coasters and ferries wheels are nothing but training fields for the modern proletariat. If so, contemporary cities are becoming slowly training camps for the modern workers to become accustomed to movement rootlessness, contingency and the whole phenomenology so crucial to the late-capitalist workforce. From the infamous atria of CDG airport and the Marriott in Atlanta, the Bonaventure in Los Angeles, and the Hyatt in Shanghai, to Manga comics, Blade Runner and the 5th Element imaginations, through the interstices of the Walled City in Hong Kong and the escalators of the Atomium, the Tokyo motorways and the mid-level escalator in Hong Kong, there seem to be a consistent tendency towards a city capable to educate the contemporary proletariat, a tendency that these pictures try to capture.

Published in *Phylogenesis*.
Actar, Barcelona, 2003

Phylogenesis: FOA's Species

FOA's phylogenesis research is a reflection on the work the firm completed during its first decade of practice, 1993–2003. The purpose of revisiting this period is to address general questions about the identity, consistency, and operativity of an architectural practice today. It is, more generally, a reflection on the contemporary conditions of production, and a work in progress that *fortunately* involves others—editors, curators, critics, and friends—through a series of exhibitions and publications developed simultaneously. As an organization grown out of the speculative and academic milieu, FOA spent its first ten years in the development of a technical arsenal for the implementation of a certain approach to the practice of architecture. This approach, and its instruments, has been explored through a series of competitions, speculative commissions, and, as of 2002, some very real projects, some of them completed, as of the time of this revisitation, while others are still under construction. Through these exercises, an identity of the practice has been developed and is now becoming tangible. The proverbial value of hindsight being what it is, in this case it is, nonetheless, 20/20+. The *plus* is in the fact that we can see where we have been and also see where we are going. This "where we are going" is, in turn, not so much a vision of plenitude and happily-ever-after as it is a vision aimed at a precise set of issues brought into focus through this initial R&D phase. In becoming more tangible (or, let's say, *real*), this strategic examination of architecture's possible rearticulation through phylogenesis is starting to pose certain nagging questions that cannot be ignored without the resultant neurosis given to avoidance setting in. What do architects need an identity for? Is it more efficient to have an identity, a recognizable brand? How should it be defined? What is its degree of stability and reactivity? Who gets to buy and sell it?

The question of identity has lately become crucial due to the increasing rate of globalization of architectural practice. The identity of a building, or an architectural practice, used to be determined either by the domain of its operativity—for example, a nice "contextual" modality or a trenchant and/or refined particularized "style," the former usually produced by the bland, nondescript architect, and the latter by the heroic or cheeky architect operating at the edge of the so-called artistic mode, oscillating between material agency and will (to) power, but without abandoning the field to the clinicians waiting in the wings, the big A&E firms and others... The globalization of the variable domains of architectural practice has brought forward again the debate between *Baukunst* and *Kunstwollen*, between technique or material and interpretation and style. This irresolvable morass beckons again, today, in the form of architecture's relationship to strenuous market forces all but obliterating the notion that one or the other of these positions can be defended, and, thus, wiping out something that has never been of much use anyway.

The *intrinsic* identity of architectural practice is what matters. As the domain of architecture proper expands and shrinks (a differential that all should pay close attention to), both in terms of competencies and territories, contemporary practice needs to develop new forms of internal consistency, beyond the effective replication of verifiable local protocols or the deployment of an *externally* consistent "visual" field. Style is neutral in the long run anyway, and the visual field is what is constant. It is this field that is under assault. It is also this field that augments and recapitalizes architecture in all instances; and it is this insight that allows architects to (if they are clever enough) out-manoeuvre capital.

I belong to what we could call the second generation of architects operating within a globalized domain of practice. The previous generation developed practices of stylistic consistency, deployed as a vehicle to overcome differences in cultural protocols and iconographies, raw materials and site specificities, while sustaining a certain degree of branding regularity. But as the evolution of markets has sped up dramatically, the consumption rate for virtually everything has increased, and the level of information and competition between and within localities (definitive situations and specific sites) has started to loosen, rendering stylistic consistency mostly ineffective except as a nostalgic enterprise. Some of the most advanced branding campaigns are now testing concepts of dynamic branding or local variation.[1] Others have simply declared the end of style and claimed that location and matter are the critical factors in the synthesis of identity.

Using FOA's practice and production as a case study, I am aiming, here, for the development of alternative forms of consistency within the practice of architecture. The proposed reflections are an attempt to overcome revanchist recourse to issues of style and spurious theories of authorship (or its negation) without falling into servile and plain inconsistency, and without merely complaining—this inconsistency being a quality that some architects are putting forward as pragmatic and realistic given the ever-changing horizon of practice. That said, neither does one want to stake out a claim to depleted mines, becoming, in the process, captive of the rapacious material and productive agency of architecture to no end other than the possible amassing of a dubious wealth: material knowledge or material practice for its own sake.

Yet I am part of a generation that grew interested in material knowledge as the core of practice, one that has often failed to produce comprehensive architectural statements. As a result, the classification of projects to which I will refer (deferring final judgment in the process) is an attempt to establish a certain benchmark for contemporary practice, while identifying certain methodologies internal to the practice of architecture that represent a range of territories explored to date by FOA.

In order to make this reflection, the practice had to run for a few years, as a population of projects is needed before developing a classification. This is not

1   See the branding campaigns for British Airways, AOL, JetBlue, etc.

an a priori classification, but a classification that—like most classifications in the natural sciences—emerges from a population. By constructing the practice's identity from a populational analysis of the projects, I am trying to avoid both idealistic and critical statements, self-serving or otherwise. Building the consistency of a practice out of its own material diversity, that is, understanding its production as a non-arbitrary group of entities that share certain features and, therefore, belong to a species, such is the basic mode of operation thus far, as well as the means of assessing FOA's past comprehensively from the present. From this perspective, the practice may be seen as a phylogenetic process in which seeds proliferate in time across different environments, generating differentiated, yet consistent organisms. The idea here is to try to describe a practice as a lineage of ideas, evolving over time and through different environments.

A practice is always determined by a series of repetitions and differentiations. Excessive repetition leads to sclerosis and inflexibility, and fails to exploit opportunities in new environments and simultaneously fails to expand the practice's genetic potentials. Excessive differentiation dilutes the internal consistency of the work, enslaving it to external conditions and making it purely contingent, local, or specific. The operativity of a practice depends on a balance between repetition and differentiation. Operativity is not only determined by the capacity to adapt—to synthesize changing conditions—but also by its transformative capacity to alter the environments purposefully within which it is rooted. That capacity is primarily developed through repetition, through the development of a specific culture of the practice. Techniques, protocols, and handshakes are improved through testing, as certain operations or traits prove to be successful under certain conditions and become part of a practice's arsenal. The perspective of this reflection upon the past decade of work is built by identifying repetitions in the work, and trying to produce an evolving classification of traits. It is in those repetitions where I try to identify the consistency of the practice, to construct a kind of fingerprint, or DNA, of FOA's practice.

A practice's body of work is neither a series of contingent experiments, defined by their particular conditions, nor the definition of a style, but rather as a consistent reservoir of architectural species to be proliferated, mutated, and evolved in the years to come: a genetic pool. By looking in this manner at the work, I am trying to distance myself from the naive idea, recently claimed commonly by architects of various stripes, that a practice has no repetition and is driven exclusively by external forces to which it is infinitely pliant. This form of determinism is truly dangerous.

A product can never be entirely constructed by the market; it needs to contain a high degree of internal consistency that does not emerge from volatile market conditions. A typological approach is, therefore, increasingly ineffective as an articulation between an environment, a program, or an effect and a particular material assemblage. But the claim that a style is able to provide internal consistency to the work under any circumstances is equally important: very often the traits of a style become irreconcilable with the material consistencies of the environment. My perspective, here, is aimed at dismantling the identity between the internal consistency of the projects and absolute authorship. I am trying to construct through the identification of a phylogenetic lineage in FOA's work, a kind of alienated and evolving authorship that is able to accumulate knowledge from the various experiences of the practice—and the term *alienation*, in this case, indicates an elective function that equals a distance from the "law" of architecture. Through the development and denotation of a phylogenetic tree, I am aiming at establishing forms of congruence between the internal consistency of various works and consistency across the spectrum of external processes (those that take the project beyond its own borders). The need to construct an alternative approach to the classical opposition between the external and internal consistency of a production is probably grounded in the specificity of a nomadic practice: in such a practice it is crucial to construct arguments that can transfer knowledge across environments without losing the practice's identity, while being simultaneously free to redefine the practice's identity in response to the specific environment. This consistency is, therefore, grounded on the definition of consistent morphological diagrams rather than making aesthetic, ethical, or political claims, which displace the practice's consistency to issues that are essentially outside of architecture. Its progress does not depend, therefore, purely on the adequacy of future commissions or conditions, but rather establishes certain grounds to assess the evolution of the practice on its own terms.

Types are fundamentally constant in time and space, their operativity is usually local, while species are sets of consistent morphologies that vary across time and space, and, therefore, present a more operative tool in a constantly shifting environment. The necessary evolution of the discipline as it confronts the increased rates of environmental change that contemporary culture demands propel the concept of species as a potential mediator between a top-down typological design process and a bottom-up parametric design approach. By defining an architectural practice, a location, a scale, or a program as a lineage of consistent, evolving, and non-contingent organisms, we are able to establish an effective feedback loop between bottom-up and top-down construction processes.

The "species" developed through FOA's first ten years of practice had to be resilient enough to grow in multiple ecosystems. They constitute the "culture" of the office from which the practice should grow further, both in terms of the development of these species and of other lineages that might emerge from this genetic pool under advancing or advanced conditions we may never foresee and would best not foresee anyway.

In this light, projects are to be seen not as something designed (or finished) but as a breed of a particular species (evolving toward god-knows-where). Design is a cultural activity, a task of translation and interpretation (even of psychological expression, like in Riegl's *Kunstwollen*, the will to art), but this theorization of species is actually closer to a Semperian reencounter with matter (or the "perennial philosophy" of form and its semi-secret origins). The same sort of arcane knowledge is used to produce wine, horses, or bulls, and purposefully manipulated outside of *normative* genetic pools and/or environments. Often given to "Masonic" handshakes and diversionary manoeuvres to protect proprietary secrets, such arts are necessary to the progression of civilization *as we know it*. This is not simply a case of the generation of new forms and new types from a genetic base allowed to run free; it also requires a certain high-handed consistency in the form of a system of enforced restrictions and repeated "taxonomic" calculations to keep the experiment within bounds. Such interventions, as such, are what distinguish top-down systems from the often romanticized mere chaos of nature. Just as with horses and wine, there is a process through which successful traits are selected via experimentation and selection. Typologies are the traditional or default instrument through which groupings of traits and organizational features became part of disciplinary bodies of knowledge (for example, architecture or any of several allied disciplines—foremost logic and mathematics).

The series of projects to which this text ultimately refers is, therefore, a document that describes the "cultures" of FOA at a relatively early stage of development, not yet intensely mediated by the external conditions surrounding the projects, but neither mutating madly (as we were more or less in control of our admittedly primitive models). It is a well-known process that as an architectural practice evolves it tends to suffer increasing pressure from external forces—opportunities for proliferation may also destroy internal consistency. In this sense these reflections are targeted at defining a reference system for the practice's future consistency.

There are probably several descriptive formulae or means of analyzing the culture of a practice. FOA's work could have been described as a series of protocols or techniques for systematic application, a kind of methodology. But this document aims to describe the genetic potential of FOA circa 2002, through an analysis of the products themselves. The classification proposed thereby has the spirit of a scientific classification. Its target is to identify the genesis of the projects as the evolution of a series of phyla or abstract diagrams, actualized (and simultaneously virtualized) in their application to the specific conditions where the projects take place in time and space.

As with any form of classification, this one also exerts a certain type of violence on the elements it sorts, raising some inevitable questions. Some projects belong to various lineages in a higher or lesser degree. Some projects belong to a lineage but inaugurate another, or suggest future evolutions, and have been placed accordingly to best explicate the nature of the species that constitute FOA's current practice. But it is precisely this violence—the tension between the projects and the species—that begins to reveal the embryological potentials of the practice, the gaps that may be filled by future projects, and the niches or opportunities for developing the current genetic pool.

Like in any taxonomical attempt, there needs to be a level of repetition in the traces of the sample in order to make it possible, but that does not mean that such a taxonomic system must necessarily lead to systematic repetition: on the contrary, it hopefully becomes, like language, a tool for the proliferation of reality. For example, FOA's classificatory regime includes seven transversal sections of the phylogenetic tree, where the project species are formed:

Function (Ground–Envelopes). The first discriminator relates to the predominant function of the surface. Projects are classified, here, into those that relate to the formation of enveloping surfaces, or surfaces whose primary function is the enclosure of space, and those whose primary function is the construction of a connective ground.

Faciality (Single Face–Multiple Face). A surface will have at least one face, depending on how many of its surfaces are inhabited. For example, a monolith or a ground is experienced only through one of its faces, while usually a slab or a facade has an outside and an inside, or a floor and a ceiling. Depending of the number of layers in which the surface slices space, the order of faciality increases or decreases.

Balance (Constant: Shifting/Parallel-Perpendicular). This discriminator classifies surfaces in reference to gravity force, and it becomes critical in establishing the relationship between the surface and the structure and the drainage system. This classification determines, in a first instance, whether the surface remains constant in its alignment to gravitational forces, or whether it alternates its orientation within the project. If a surface (plane) remains consistently within a perpendicular relationship to vertically disposed gravitational forces (that is, horizontal), it will most often take the form of a ground or a roof. If it is constantly parallel to the gravitational force, it will mainly become a wall or a facade. If the surface shifts between being parallel and perpendicular to gravitational forces, the building will be a blob or a shed (the roof and the walls deployed more or less as continuous, unitary surfaces). Depending on this alignment the qualities of the surface will substantially vary, both in its geometrical definition and its material qualities. Such introduces orthogonal stress (or *anxiety*).

Discontinuity (Planar-rippled-pinched-perforated-bifurcated). This attribute of the species describes the typology of surface singularity that determines discontinuities on the surface, and it is classified in a gradation depending on the intensity of the surface singularities. If the surface is continuous, does not have interruptions, except in its delimitation, and does not have any surface singularity, it is planar. If it has some local deformations but no interruptions, it becomes rippled. If the singularities are more accentuated to the point that the tangent varies more than 90 degrees, it is pinched. If the surface is locally interrupted, the surface is perforated. If the surface is locally interrupted but is continuous on a different level, layer, or space, establishing (simultaneously) continuity *and* discontinuity, then the surface is bifurcated. Pierced organizations correspond usually to the resolution of specific connections between well-demarcated spatial segmentations, while bifurcations tend to be more common in projects that require loose spatial segmentations.

Orientation (Oriented: Striated/polar–Non-oriented). This discriminator divides surfaces according to the spatial ordering of their singularities. Singularities on the surface can be independently organized following a consistent law, or they can be entirely contingent in response to preexistent traces. Among those singular surfaces or fields that are called oriented, are those that can be oriented following a striated distribution—that is, following a parallel order—or those that respond to centers or poles.

The first category tends to correspond to organizations more dependent upon preexisting traces or local singularities, responding to preexisting focalizations of parameters in certain zones of space, while the second type corresponds more to organizations with a weak relationship to preexisting fields, and more self-supporting scale or quality. The striated variety is usually related to fields with a prevailing flow direction, while polar structures relate to either strong focal preexistences or central or polycentric organizations of the project.

Geometry (Continuous–Discontinuous). The geometrical discriminator refers to the geometrical continuity of the surface. It divides the projects between those that have a continuous variation of the tangent, and, therefore, produce a smooth surface, and those that have points of contact with indeterminate tangents intersecting with the smooth surface at certain points, producing breaks in the geometrical continuity or purity of the surface. Those projects either produce edges or ridges, rather than seamless discontinuities.

Diversification (Patterned–Contingent). Every branch of the phylogenetic tree is split between those projects where a patterned system of discontinuities, accidents, or shifts in orientation occur on a regular basis across the surface, or whether they appear contingent to local specificity. Contingent diversification responds usually to organizations constructed from the bottom-up or in reaction to local specificities, while patterned textures correspond to organizations deployed from the top-down, or those where the scale of the organizations is such that the capacity of self-determination is stronger than local singularities.

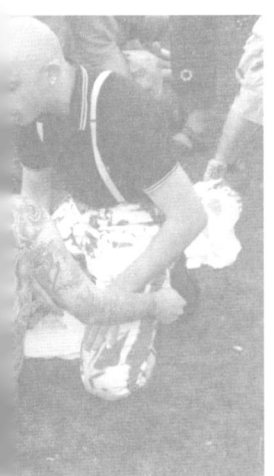

The images illustrating this article try to refer to the idea of speciation, which is central to the text, and relates it to the processes of social formation that characterise contemporary urban cultures. If the contemporary city has become the primary source of a subjectivity that is increasingly freed from roots, cultural traditions, social structures, but also mass cultures, it has also created a fragmented field of subcultures, tribes or sects, where urban subjects can find an elective support structure: from mods and rockers to chavs, through skinheads, goths, lolitas, queers, hipsters, gamers, geeks, otakus... they represent types which has come to occupy the void left by traditional and mass culture, in a similar way to what is happening to architectural species.

From the entry to the "A new World Trade Centre"
design competition, 2001

United We Stand
(The Bundle Tower™)

The Bundle Tower™ was born as an answer to the reconstruction of Ground Zero and is revisited here as a free-floating, latent utopia to be built in place of the late World Trade Center, or perhaps anywhere else. High-rise buildings are the ultimate embodiment of the intensive, expansive, and dynamic traits of modern capitalism, and the Bundle Tower™ is aimed to establish an architectural measure for new peaks of intensification: to inaugurate a new species of high-rise structure that will sustain the next-scale intensification of urban development in the twenty-first century.

Capitalism does not usually concern itself with remembrance and nostalgia, but rather operates with a systematic forgiveness, often bordering on schizophrenia. This very central aspect of capitalism is what those groups clamouring for a 9/11 memorial fail to understand when demanding a vindication of the system. Capitalism is hardly concerned with permanence and roots, as such contradicts its core tactics of incessant expansion and permanent reconfiguration.

Consequently, the Bundle Tower™ was born without any ambition of being a memorial, but with the aim of giving a provisional architectural expression to the ever-changing, ever-expanding capitalist space. The Bundle Tower™ is hardly about the perpetuation of a moment or an image; it makes possible a new degree of urban intensification and opens up new domains for vertical expansion.

"United We Stand" was the motto chosen by the confederation of people who rallied to respond to the 9/11 attack. Although dating from a patriotic ballad of 1768, the time of the American Revolution, and reused in 1942 to sell American War Bonds, the former slogan gained a new lease on life after 9/11. Placed, here, in a multinational context, the slogan takes on new meaning by addressing the cohesive, yet expansive nature of global capitalism, and its cultural, political, and economic values; that is, its simultaneous strength and vulnerability. We have adopted this motto as the utopian title of the Bundle Tower™, which in its structural and spatial behavior resonates with the global and interconnected nature of global capitalism. The Bundle Tower™ grows higher only through the collaboration of different members, through structural, spatial, circulatory, and technical networks. Its self-similar structure cuts across scales, intertwining micro and macro as in the best examples of complex cultural, political, or economic organizations. Grounded on a shallow pool, the Bundle Tower™ is reflected to become a kilometer-high marker of future urban space.

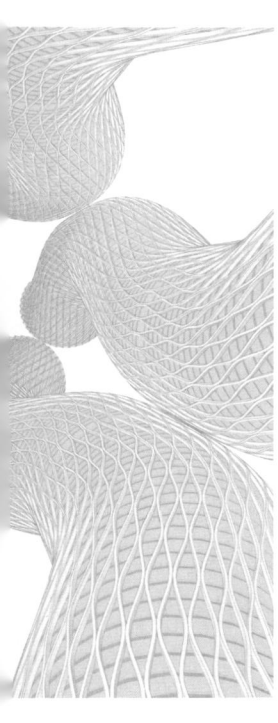

As a latent utopia, the Bundle Tower™ is presented here in its most generic form, devoid of local specificities and possible differentiations between towers or sectors of towers and potential negotiations with ground structures. It is a diagram ready to be deployed and loaded with the capacity for diversification, but also with the capacity to generate consistency across heterogeneous conditions. The binding relationship between the size of the floor plates and the undulation of the towers and their height implies that the prototype will react precisely to a given set of grounding or developmental conditions. The Bundle Tower™ is a diagram that contains the consistency of possible matters; it is built with geometries and dimensions of existing high-rise technologies that were evolved out of typological material. The Bundle Tower™ is a new high-rise species in the most diagrammatic form, grown in a generic ecosystem, awaiting the specificity of a situation to actualize its potential. It has been provisionally scaled to match the size of the original WTC complex (1.3 million square meters), but could potentially reach higher, to become the tallest building in the world.

The Bundle Tower™: A New High-Rise Prototype

The world's tallest building requires a new high-rise typology. If we look at the evolution of the skyscraper type, we can see a process in which the increase in height of the structure results in a tendency of the organization to concentrate an increasingly larger array of structural sections in the periphery of the plan. As the lateral forces become stronger than the gravitational ones in high-rise structures, it becomes necessary to maximize the moment of inertia of the structure. The models to address this question have evolved from post-and-beam typologies, which distribute structure evenly across the plan, into different types of tubular organizations, concentrating structure in the periphery of the building mass.

But as the structure grows taller, the strength of the material is insufficient to provide stability to lateral forces, so the depth of the plan needs to grow proportionally. (A slenderness of 1/12 is understood to be the limit in this building type). This leads to building types that become extremely deep, and are therefore heavily dependent on artificial lighting and mechanically controlled ventilation.

In order to generate a new type of high-rise, our proposal is to operate with the building mass, rather than with just the distribution of the structure. To carve-out mass out of a structure. Instead of splitting the complex into two independent towers, as in the former WTC or in the Petronas Towers, to avoid excessively deep workspaces, our proposal is to maintain the physical continuity of the whole mass, and to use it as a structural advantage. We propose to form the complex as a bundle of interconnected towers that provide a flexible floor size and that buttress each other structurally, being able to increase the moment of inertia of the structure without necessarily increasing the floor depth and the total area.

Bundle Scale and Number

The average floor size of rental workspace in New York City is 1,000 square meters. We have taken that as our quantum, or bundle scale, in the new WTC-NY project. A 25% increase for vertical circulation and mechanical services has been added to that surface. As our target is to reach approximately 500 meters in height, we are aiming at approximately 110 floors, with a conventional floor-to-floor height of 4.5 meters. If we take the size of the former complex as a measure of total floor size, we have: 884,000 square meters/110 floors = 8,036 square meters/floor, which is approximately equal to six towers of 1,340 square meters per floor, which accounts approximately for 1,050 square meters of net floor area and 290 square meters of core space per floor, distributed in floor depths ranging between 20 meters and 30 meters, depending on the local relation between the elevator core and the envelope.

Isomorphic Tubular Structure

In order to maximize the ratio between floor area and perimeter, and to improve the structural performance of the building, we have opted for a tubular structure with a circular profile with an 18-meter diameter, where the structure is concentrated as a structural lattice on the facade of each tower. The tubes, organized in a circle, bend vertically to buttress each other at approximately every third of the total height of the building, cutting the bending length of the towers to approximately 165 meters. The size of the average floor plate that we identified in the bundle scale gives us a diameter of 41 meters, if we use circular towers. This is a scale that, considering the presence of a vertical circulation and distribution core, will allow us to avoid the presence of vertical structure outside the façade and the core.

In order to maximize the resistance of the structural lattice of the tubes, the geometry of the columns will also bend, balancing the transmission of weight and the resistance to buckling and lateral stresses. The lattice of the tower structure and the geometry of the Bundle Tower™ are self-similar structures.

Elevator System and Transfer Lobbies: A Network of Vertical Circulations

Each tower, with an approximate area of 147,400 square meters, will have a battery of 12 high-speed lifts that will provide access primarily to the floors in the tower but will also form part of a network of sky lobbies that each tower shares with the two neighboring ones every 36 floors. A fire escape system is also organized through these vertical cores, allowing transfers between six different fire escapes for every tower through the sky lobbies (two stairs per tower). Risers for HVAC, fire-suppression systems, electricity, and telecommunications are also contained in the system of vertical cores, allowing every tower to access supplies from the two adjacent ones.

Variable Depth and Variable Area Floor Space

As the vertical structure is always concentrated on the periphery of the tubes, the slabs inside the towers are column-free circles 41 meters in diameter, made with a lattice of increasing depth as the span of the floor increases. As the tower envelope bends to touch the adjacent towers, the vertical circulation core remains vertical, providing periodic variation in the depth of workspaces between the envelope and the circulation core. This offers a higher variety of workspace types.

The images used to frame this text are sampled from the original 2001 entry to the "A new World Trade Centre" design competition, and a few other reference images, such as the attack on the Twin Towers, the "united we stand" street signs, the "dead or alive" posters of Osama Bin Laden, and the picture of the US national security team witnessing the assassination of Osama Bin Laden.

Revised, previously unpublished internal memo to the design team after a first visit to the London site of the 2012 Olympic Games, 2004

Grunge Olympics

The operative question of the moment is: what can London offer to the Olympic Games in the twenty-first century? This question is compounded by its inverse: what can the summer Olympic Games offer London in return? The symbiosis between the permanent event structures of the Olympic Park, the topography offered by a host city, and the series of large-scale ephemeral events is a classic urban problem. Can such a large event be used to kick-start a whole series of more stable urban processes such as what happened in Tokyo or Barcelona? The other pressing question regarding this project is whether a city can provide a spectacular and specific character to a rather generic process.

London is now a city in the process of redefining its identity as a global capital in the twenty-first century. It is the largest metropolitan agglomeration in Europe, but has very close transatlantic links. It has also, probably, the closest relationship to the Middle East and the Far East of all Western metropolises. It has, by far, the most multinational population in the world. It is under enormous pressure to grow in order to host an ever-growing population. It is the most ideal ground to host a contemporary Olympic Games. To symbolize not the might of a tiger economy nor the pride and urban sophistication of ethnic and cultural consistency, but the gathering of cultures, religions, and ethnic groups, at a time when global cultures and global policies have become an absolute necessity for the new world order to remain sustainable.

This is a difficult task to complete, as we cannot rely only on technical prowess or financial might. Neither can we expect success in the form of the cuteness of a carefully designed urban life. London is a pretty thoughtless assemblage of things, and perhaps this is the reason why, despite all these potentials, London has not yet been able to synthesize these clashing sensibilities; to build a recognizable or coherent urban project.

London is facing a challenge that no other city has faced before with such intensity: the *explicitation* of a truly global metropolis, and the Olympic Games is a true opportunity to unfold these potentials. One can see this challenge most clearly while driving around on the M-25 or in Dagenham, strolling in Brick Lane and Lambeth, or, actually, around Stratford and the Lea Valley itself. We can no longer rely on antecedents: picturesque Victoriana; '60s Notting-Hill bohemian *frisson*; or '80s, high-tech hubris... There is something new about to appear on the horizon, and the London Olympics will be the chance to synthesize this ulterior form of urbanity, claim it for London, and offer it, in turn, to everybody else as the future of global cities.

If there is something at all worth testing in the 2012 London Olympics, it is the possibility of actualizing the virtual city (the one hiding inside of the mess London often resembles), using the event to reinvent the city, and maximizing its potentiality as virtual. Are we going to rely again on the typical, sanitized, and aseptic Olympic campus? Haven't we learned yet that globalization is no longer about homogenization but about the awareness and unlimited enhancement of local flavors within a global order?

Can London compete in sophisticated urbanity with Paris's cosmetic beauty? Can it compete with the already sanitized Madridian plateau? And with the bullish New York boldness and spectacle? And should it?

What better location to reinvent London than the Lea Valley? Reconstruct London from the land that was always at the back of the house, the side hidden behind the prettier face of London proper. The Lea River Valley bears the scars of the metropolis's bold ambition; like the body of an athlete in full strain, it bulges and sinks, is beyond the archetypal body, a brutally stressed one. A tangle of canals, locks, roads, tracks, sewers ensues; in a word, we have a completely artificial topography made entirely out of infill (land created by deposition) and re-covered with a thick layer of natural overgrowth. This is a landscape where water, air, earth, and fire have become hyper-real. The radical mixture between the natural and the artificial as a critical trend of the contemporary world becomes obvious in the Lea Valley. The mixture of verdant greenery and leaden water with the artificial landscape are already a metaphor for flow and growth as crucial processes of contemporary urban phenomenology. In short, here is a landscape of ravishing, even terrifying beauty in search of the right moment to free its postindustrial potential.

Maybe London 2012 should be an Olympic reality check for contemporary urban culture. No more theme park experience, no more sanitized, cosmetic, homogenized image of the average Olympic Village, but the enhancement of London's frank, quirky, bold lack of posture. Couldn't this become the seed for the image of London 2012? Rather than attempting again the production of the archetypal body of the city, through singular projects, the project could become a picture of the body under stress, far away from the cosmetic, rebranding procedures conventionally associated with the picturesque version of the Olympic Games. Rather than sanitizing and making-up, we must engage in the true regeneration of the land; we could attempt to reveal the quirkiness, the beauty of the brutal, and the incongruous. The most astonishing beauty is never the one we expect, but the one that takes us by surprise; the one that reveals that reality could be *otherwise than it is*.

The task of revealing the magnificent formative power of the Lea Valley landscape will be certainly more appropriate a model for the city of the twenty-first century—with its commitment to sustainability, multiculturalism, and new infrastructure—than the beautified Olympic Villages we have become accustomed to: let's do a Grunge Olympics!

The images illustrating this text are the result of the author's photographic record of the London 2012 Olympic site, before the bid started.

Published in *Log* n.11 New York, 2004

30 St. Mary's Axe: Form Is Not Facile

Form Isn't Finance

The most recent blockbuster to hit the architectural scene is 30 St. Mary's Axe, better known as the Gherkin, and recently awarded the prestigious Stirling Prize. Its popularity comes as no surprise: the Gherkin is not only an impressive architectural feat, but also a success in framing a critical debate at a critical time. The building lies precisely at the crossroads of the current architectural debate: between communication and production. This position is probably the reason for its enormous success, which extends from the general public to the innermost circles of the architectural discipline. It is a building that has been equally effective at connecting with the average citizen and seducing advertising moguls as it has at engaging the highbrow conceptual discourse regarding blobs and bubbles.[1] The most notable aspect of the project, however, is that a building designed to have 60 % of its surface rented out also speculatively managed to do so through an entirely idiosyncratic form. Raised from the ruins of the old Baltic Exchange in the very core of the city of London, a building that was bombed and destroyed by the IRA in 1992 in a kind of mini–Ground Zero scenario, the building is owned by Swiss Re, an insurance company—coincidentally the main insurer for the Twin Towers—

---

1 *Bubbles* is the subtitle of *Spheres I*, the first of Peter Sloterdijk's trilogy on *spherology*, where the contemporary world is described as a foamy space. See text on page 477 herein, "Politics of the Envelope," for further deliberations on this theme.

that was looking for accommodations in London and for a real estate investment in the city. Despite having succeeded in making Swiss Re into a household name, the building remains, as of this writing, half empty and is allegedly losing £35,000 per day in rent.

Form Isn't Facile

In order to justify the Gherkin's extravagant form to his client as well as to the city, architect Lord Norman Foster had to construct an entire phalanx of excuses.[2] Accordingly, the building's circular plan helps minimize its presence as an object in the urban landscape; tapering at the bottom enables a higher transparency at ground level, facilitating enjoyment of one of the oldest areas in the city of London, while tapering at the top diminishes its impact on the skyline and eye-level perspectives. Those were crucial arguments in the process of getting permission to build to such an unusual height in that part of the city. Moreover, the gently curving surface of the building is more aerodynamic, avoiding the negative wind effects of a typical high-rise building. This is accomplished by recessing the profile of the building at the bottom and the top, thereby deflecting most of the wind toward the top and decreasing the pressure of the air toward the street level. The building supposedly consumes 50% less energy than comparable buildings by providing six helicoidal, wedge-shaped atria that increase the penetration of daylight into the floor plates while producing a natural draft to ventilate the floors. Who would dare counter such impeccable technical argumentation with petty commercial concerns? This is a building that should soon succeed in cultivating its own very special kind of sophisticated tenants.

Form Isn't Flaccid

But wait—there's more. The building is clearly an evolved product of the Foster and Partners' professional tradition and machinery, but in this case, unlike in most other examples of the high-tech genre, its intelligence is not limited to the technical. On the contrary, in 30 St. Mary's Axe technical performance seems to have become the perfect excuse to legitimize an evocative form operating at an extraordinary scale, both physically and culturally. Is London's erotic Gherkin the most direct embodiment and final proof of the phallic psychological association of the high-rise building? This is the question everyone is asking Elena Ochoa, a.k.a. Lady Foster, who just happens

---

2 See text on page 268 herein, "The Theory of the Excuse," on the use of this moral trope in current architectural production.

to be a sex therapist and celebrity broadcaster in Spain, and who likely started dating Lord Foster around the beginning of the Gherkin's design phase. Her TV program, *Hablemos de Sexo* (Let's Talk About Sex), has made her into a sort of Spanish Doctor Ruth and a *Hello!* regular. So far she has evaded the oft-posed question with a naughty grin, but Kevin McCloud, the Channel 4 live broadcast anchorman of the Stirling Prize award ceremony ventured that the sensual curves of the Gherkin make it actually the first *female* skyscraper, more akin to a siren's sensual shape than to the classic phallic metaphor. This argument certainly rings true if one compares the suppleness of the Gherkin to the stiffness of the almost exactly contemporary Torre Agbar—a.k.a. *el supositorio* (the suppository)—designed and recently built in Barcelona by Jean Nouvel, in what appears to be a worldwide epidemic of phallic high-rises. Of course, Nouvel's turn to the firm may have just been a concession to the rule of constant facade-to-core depth that forms one of the core principles of commercial high-rise design. In its double challenge, both to the most obvious formal analogy and to the principle of extrusion that has traditionally structured the tower typology, the tumescent Gherkin becomes far more subversive than the ram-rod straight Torre Agbar. This highly charged ambiguity is precisely where we can see how technology, typology, and the other tools of production can productively resonate with symbolism, analogy, representation, and other mechanisms of communication. Rather than opposing one another in yet another exhausting, oppositional dead end, in the Gherkin the two strategies (production and symbology) feed off of one another without exhausting the process of *projection* that underlies each one.

We will probably never know where or how Lord Foster actually started work on this project, but I would bet a considerable chunk of change that all of the obvious (and perhaps some less obvious) analogies and resonances crossed his mind at some point in the process. Whether he did actually connect them consciously to the more technical processes of the project or not is irrelevant. In the post-Guggenheim era, what is promising about the Gherkin is that by engaging with one of the most populist architectural tendencies—that is, symbolism—it not only did not lose any of its *architectural* (read *high-tech*) integrity, but also managed to use symbolism to enhance its architectural values and woo the public. And by challenging an intrinsically typological problem—for example, the facade-to-core depth in a high-rise office building—the unflappable Lord Foster has opened the range of symbolic associations of that very type. The Gherkin's provocatively ambiguous form offers an extraordinary addition to London's skyline; and, just as significantly, offers a provocative addition to our discipline's horizon: one should target production and communication intentionally and simultaneously rather than denying a priori the strategic validity of either or assuming that they are mutually exclusive.[3]

The images illustrating this text relate the 30 St. Mary's Axe Foster high-rise in London, better known as The Gherkin, with a latent imagery that extends to other high-rise buildings. The high-rise building has been traditionally linked with a phallic imagery that has suddenly been very obviously embodied—by coincidence or by deliberate choice—in the 30 St. Mary's Axe building and the Torre Agbar in Barcelona building, both built almost simultaneously. Images of the project, of its contemporary Torre Agbar in Barcelona, and of some female sex toys, serve as a marker of a sexual practice—the use of sex toys—which has developed enormously since the 1960's through the intersection of greater sexual freedom and electronic technology.

3   This text is inspired by Colin Rowe's "Character and Composition; or Some Vicissitudes of Architectural Vocabulary in the Nineteenth Century," where he revisited some categories of the architectural discourse in the nineteenth century in order to set up references for architectural form beyond technological prowess or political engagement. Thirty years on, the inevitable engagement with technology and politics have rendered both *character* and *composition* hopelessly unfashionable and have replaced them by more potent, brutal and pragmatic surrogates: *communication* and *production*. Where character addressed the adequateness of architecture to represent a particular social function, communication addresses an opportunistic positioning where branding or representation of far more ephemeral and contingent clusters of meaning take precedent. Where composition addressed the disciplined and educated compliance with the arcane principles of architecture, production addresses the effective and precise deployment of technology to deliver innovative buildings. The simultaneous and connected revision and updating of these two lineages of practice offers, I would argue, one of the most promising and intriguing areas of investigation in architecture in the *post-Guggenheim* era. Written in 1953–54, and first published in *Oppositions 2* (1976), "Character and Composition; or Some Vicissitudes of Architectural Vocabulary in the Nineteenth Century" was republished in *Mathematic of the Ideal Villa, and Other Essays* (Cambridge: MIT Press, 1976). I would like to thank Sarah Whiting for her decisive editorial input in the construction of this text.

Published in *Quaderns d'Arquitectura i Urbanisme* n. 245, Barcelona and *Volume* n. 3, New York, 2005

The Hokusai Wave

Architects these days fall into one of two categories when it comes to acquiring projects: on the one hand, you have those who are connected to a certain circle of clients and who use this network to obtain projects; on the other hand, there are those who operate through media to target the public at large. Of course, neither category exists in a pure state, but, generally, the first group operates through cocktail parties, dinners, golf, sailing, and so on, and is most likely to offer well-tested models and services catering to a certain type of demand. This first acquisition protocol tends to produce a more subservient and conservative architectural practice, because the architect does not have much room to manoeuvre around the client. The hierarchy of power could not be clearer. The client has a definitive mandate and the architect is constrained to a strategy of personal seduction and a well-tested portfolio. The second group's strategies, in contrast, are *molar,* rather than being ingrained within a given structure: they are not linked to a social network but to a mass audience. Their connection lines are less structural and more mediated. They are more likely to use competitions, conferences, academic networks, exhibitions, and publications as acquisition tools. Prototypes or ideas are broadcast and eventually crystallize in commissions, where the client usually operates as the administrator of a more collective will. This mode of project acquisition usually enables the architect to be more experimental because it retains the project's initiative, even if it is a vague one, and the architect can use his public clout to twist the clients' arms—albeit, to a certain degree—in pursuit of a more daring architectural agenda. Statistically, most innovative projects—and, certainly, some of the worst catastrophes—are procured via this protocol. When following this model, it is vital for the architect to maintain a public discourse, to float constantly new ideas and strategies, to release publications, and to appear seductive not by sporting cocktail attire but by spilling broadsheet ink.

As I am—by both chance and choice—not part of the cocktail set, one of my crucial duties is to keep broadcasting a new interpretation of reality with consistent frequency. In doing so, I guarantee a certain initiative in my relation with whoever is invested with the authority to commission and administer projects, and I am empowered to pursue certain goals beyond the mere provision of architectural services. By constructing arguments that exceed a specific project and conveying them to a broader public, I produce a more ambiguous regime of power in my client relationships. The crucial matter here, rarely discussed within the architectural debate is the relationship between the acquisition protocols and their architectural output, or, in more general terms, between power and control. This is the relationship addressed by Peter Eisenman in his deliberate disinterest in power in order to maintain architectural control or by Rem Koolhaas in his fascination with pure power at play, freed from any architectural control. These two extreme positions frame the discussion and the attempt to construct a binding relationship between them through a very specifically architectural subject: *representation*.

Representation has been a contested subject for a whole generation of architects (*my generation*); that is, those of us who have focused on experimenting with material organizations and factual data as an escape from the discursive predominance of representation, meaning, identity, and language that characterized earlier generations. I belong to what has been called the post-critical generation... In evading the representational bias, most of this research has resorted to a sort of a renaturalization of architecture, focused in the processes of material organization, and intentionally avoiding any discussion of representation, figural properties, etc. Ecologies, natural or artificial, have become a common reference for many of us, as processes of material agency, transformation and exchange not mediated by representational orders per se. But from this nearly idealist ecological perspective, the regimes of power at play in the practice of architecture are not a matter of concern, as their processes are not regulated by such considerations. Yet, if we are to become fully engaged with the discussion of power regimes and their potential transformation, representation is a crucial subject to re-address: for example, in a democracy, individuals are represented as "equal," while this may not be necessarily true from every perspective. How architecture engages in regimes of representation, and how the architect represents himself within these relationships, is a domain we need to engage if we are to tamper with the regimes of power within which we need to practice.

The tale of the Hokusai Wave is the history of how the engagement with clients and public media—in other words, the very sources of power at play in all commissions—substantially altered FOA's projectual methodology, moving us toward an incorporation of iconography and meaning. Having come to our own fairly precarious professional niche out of a more or less speculative and academic practice, we spent a long time *in advance of building* theorizing about building technologies and crafts, a most pressing endeavor for a young practice. As our work evolved toward a more professional output, my role has become less involved with crafting and more engaged in acquiring and explaining projects, theorizing and communicating the practice to a variety of agents, in order to make the practice economically sustainable. As the most interesting speculation generally happens out of necessity, my subject of research has moved consistently with the new requirements of my role.

This process has not been a radical change but a slow and progressive shift wherein the old speculations became intertwined with newer ones, both on a conceptual and an operative level. It started, actually, ten years ago in one of those episodes that radically change one's perception of reality. Faced with a full press conference in Yokohama City Hall, circa February 1995, we had to explain what it was we were trying to do in our newly awarded Yokohama Ferry Terminal Competition project. Faithful to our doctrine, fine-tuned through years of academic practice, I proceeded to explain the circulation diagrams, the geometric transformations, and the construction technologies that were involved in the project, hoping that the audience would have enough patience to wait for the emergence of the project. Halfway through the presentation, I started to notice the blank expression on the faces of those assembled in the room—that is, a clear indicator that the message was not getting across (this was to become a very common experience during this evolution toward a marketing performance). After a few minutes of cold sweat, an image that was carefully edited from the project's discourse—but still floating somewhere in the back of our minds—suddenly came to my rescue. It was the *Hokusai Wave*, a drawing from a local painter that we had been toying with while we indulged in geometric manipulations and construction hypotheses during the design phase of the competition entry. In a sudden (and risky) burst of inspiration, I terminated the factual, process-driven narrative to conclude that what really inspired us was the image of Hokusai's Wave. The room exploded in an exclamation of sincere relief—a collective "Aaaahhh...!"—and we left the room, still sweating and grateful for that moment of lucidity, with the clear realization that something wasn't quite working in our carefully crafted discourse.

As a strategy, the Hokusai Wave has, since that moment, been slowly gaining momentum in my theorization of the office, in a manner that has never been rendered entirely explicit in our public statements, but that over time has nevertheless come to hit the practice with the force of a tsunami.

The Hokusai Wave resurfaced barely a year after the Yokohama press conference incident: the ferry terminal project had gone fallow and we were engaged in a brutally commercial commission: the worldwide expansion of the Belgo restaurant chain. We did have second thoughts as to whether we should accept this commission: A themed restaurant, the Belgo chain was a project dangerously opposed to our core disciplinary beliefs. Belgo restaurants depended on Belgian branding and facile iconography: Brueghel, beer barrels, mussels, vaults, and so on. But with the Yokohama project on hold, we had no option. Our strategy of survival was to turn these images into excuses for architectural experimentation: out of them we were able to produce shell structures, wooden vaults, and sausage-like ramps. After years of waging the war against the populist claims of architecture as a tool of communication, we were realizing that without the *excuse* of the iconography there was little to justify our experiments with bent surfaces and shell structures in small-scale work. Paradoxically, the most banal, Disney-esque iconography became the justification (both conceptual and financial) for formal experimentation.

The same problem reappeared in an entirely different context with a proposal that we submitted to a competition in Tehran for the reconstruction of the Azadi Cinema, a former local symbol of international urban culture and, subsequently, target of brutal repression during the revolution. It was to become a multiplex... Unlike the Belgo projects, here the iconography was not imposed but was, instead, deliberately deployed to ensure universal communication with a now-sheltered culture: we used the image of an unspooling film reel to explain the project more effectively. Simultaneously, the reel became the organizational system for the cinema's theaters, piled on top of each other and connected via a battery of escalators with a consistent geometry. For the first time, we had deliberately coupled an image and an organizational system into a consistent entity as a projective strategy.

The Azadi project revealed whole new potentials for the Hokusai Wave approach, and despite the fact that this coupling of iconography and organization remained largely peripheral to our office's public discourse, it had become by then a *standard FOA procedure* for competition design, non-professional media strategies, and client interface. This was 1997, and parametric design and datascape research were in full swing (even within our own office), so we determined that this iconographic research remained unfit for cultural consumption and we kept it in the closet.

Different variations of the Hokusai Wave were subsequently undertaken in order to generate several of the new projects in the office. Paradoxically, this strategy, originally devised to respond to commercial demands, became the foundation of a series of commissions for local authorities, most of them in Spain. Short-circuiting our conventional arsenal of diagrams and constructive solutions with locally resonant iconographies became a very effective technique to territorialize our constructed foreignness and connect with local agents. Local iconographies became a perfect excuse to naturalize materials and geometries that would have been otherwise vulnerable to budget cuts or political uncertainty. Moreover, iconography helped us accelerate the identification of traits from our usually hypertrophied site and program analysis in order to provide a formal argument for the projects. Iconographies did not precede the material investigation but rather emerged as viable figures from our immersion in each project's analysis. We would collect general material about local customs and iconographies and keep that information on the table while we did site analysis and programmatic diagrams. I knew that a project was structured when a formal correlation started resonating between them. The Villajoyosa Police Station's pentagonal plan was automatically derived from the site's geometry and turned into Villajoyosa's Pentagon, a reference for the municipal police headquarters with great popular appeal, and the lattices that fortified its windows were built as if they resulted from a film-noir, machine-gun shoot-out. The Torrevieja Theater was modeled on the local sandstone quarries and boasts a white and faceted acoustic finish modeled, in turn, like a salt crystal (sandstone quarries and salt lakes were the basis of the local economy before tourism brought its radical transformations of the local landscape.) So we were resurrecting a lost arcadia... The La Rioja Centre of Technology Transfer in Logroño became a building that dissolved into a vineyard: a transparent volume covered with wires and grape leaves. The Canarian Government Multiples III proposal in Santa Cruz, Tenerife grew into a palm-tree trunk by applying triangular *brise-soleils*, shifting gradually to maximize their sun-shading effect, to a high-rise tower with a triangulated exoskeleton.

In post-Guggenheim Spain, this experimentation with local public commissions was directed toward finding a viable exit from the conventional recipe of deploying a more or less cool shape, usually one bearing a signature, to draw attention to the local and to boost public confidence that modernization was taking place. We could avoid becoming either service providers or gurus, constructing obscure arguments and wacky shapes to maintain a hollow mystery with no meaning. We were fitting just right and the feedback produced by the introduction of forms external to the intrinsic construction of the project was actually helping to expand our *formal repertoire*.

But the most bizarre developments of this coupling between material organization and iconography happened in the media-intensive Anglo-Saxon context, where the density of reporting per square foot of construction is tenfold that of the Spanish standard, often interfering even during the project's development. In this particular milieu, our turn to iconography became especially productive.

Max Protetch's invitation for reconstruction ideas for the WTC site in Manhattan became the beginning of an interesting case study to explore the relationship between organization and iconography. As a theoretical exercise, our take on the WTC project was originally grounded in a deep distaste for public sentimentality and a concern that the project ran the risk of becoming a shrine devoted solely to remembrance. Our exploration set out to rid the project of any symbolic and representational content (a conventional FOA target) and to explore a prototype for the next generation of high-rise buildings by designing the world's tallest building on the site. The resulting project was a circular cluster of bending, sinusoidal towers leaning onto each other to increase their structural stability and produce redundancy in the vertical circulation system through a distributed system of sky lobbies. The project was generated purely by technical considerations, such as structural behavior, fire-escape routes, vertical circulation systems, average Manhattan office lease size, etc. We opened our submission with a polemical sentence, carefully edited out by Protetch in the exhibition catalogue (*A New World Trade Center*), but captured by Deyan Sudjic, *The Observer*'s architecture critic, in his report of January 27, 2002:

> *Let's not even consider remembering. What for?* claim the architects in their provocatively heartless introduction, a sentiment that is likely to be misunderstood in the context of a New York still decked with flags and paper shrines.[1]

Being certain that we had found an important idea in the Bundle Tower™, we revisited the project when asked by Zaha Hadid and Patrik Schumacher to participate in their Latent Utopias exhibition in Graz, in late 2002. By then, the reconstruction process had started under the motto *United we Stand*. In a paradoxical twist, the structure of the project had become a perfect match for the campaign slogan, as our slender towers were able to stand only because of their mutual support. Suddenly, images of aggregated high-rise construction—the *castellers*, a Catalan tradition of building human towers, being one of our favorites—became part of the project, resounding, of course, with the intentional bombast of the Bundle Tower™. We decided to use the reconstruction motto to name our entry for the Latent Utopias exhibition. The theme of the interlinked towers was to be incorporated later into our collective entry to the competition as part of the United Architects team, under yet another label, "the city of the social capital," and was to appear also in some of the other entries. A project that started as an attempt to avoid representation and identity ended up becoming the most effective recipient and generator of meaning.

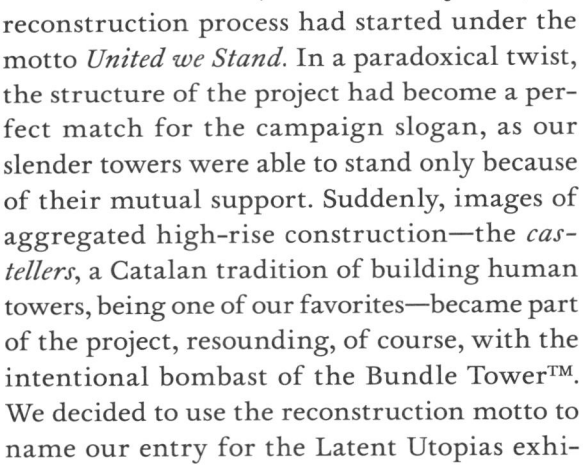

The exact reversal of this process of appropriation of a typological organization occurred in another media-heavy project. Our winning competition entry for the BBC Music Centre was

1 Deyan Sudjic, *The Observer* (London, January 27, 2002).

actually published in the *Evening Standard*, *El Croquis*, and *Icon Magazine*, in some cases by mistake and in others by deliberate negligence, during the middle of a torturous competition process that involved several workshops with the user groups. In this project, a tape loop—that is, a deliberate reincarnation of the Azadi film reel—was used to represent the musical content of the building, even though, unlike its precedent, the tape loop had no functional or constructive resonance with the brief's technical analysis. Instead, it was deliberately deployed as a pure metaphorical dressing aimed to qualify a very compact and efficient, but otherwise unintelligible studio box assembly. Because of the formal qualities of this particular iconographic reference (a band can only wrap four sides of a parallelepiped) the loop automatically introduced the possibility of visually opening the studios to the public along one of their sides, a functionally questionable decision that despite initial resistance was enthusiastically embraced by the users as the main advantage of the scheme. The resulting transparency between the public space and the studios became not only an environmental advantage for life in the studios, but also an ideal demonstration of transparency at a time of deep crisis in its public perception of the Corporation (BBC), as the competition coincided exactly with the demise of the chairman and the director general over improper reporting over the Kelly affair. This transparency, in turn, required an innovative approach to ensure that the walls could become simultaneously visually transparent and non-reflective as well as totally soundproof and acoustically diffusive. The architectural innovation of this project ultimately lies in the construction of the triple glass wall, with particular internal and external geometries, as well as the design of a loop surface made of holographic film and color-shifting LED, which would be able to broadcast digital graphic images on the studio's blank faces. Ultimately, what was initiated as a branding strategy became productive in the technical domain.

The Hokusai Wave

In the most recent and most entertaining example of interplay between iconography and material organization, we became part of the consortium that won (against all odds) the commission to produce the master plan for the London 2012 Olympic Bid and the Lea Valley master plan. We won the project by combining down-to-earth, experienced sports architecture expertise and land management and planning with a careful dose of "emergent design flair." We promised to grow the project from the local grassroots in an integrated urban plan that was aimed at regenerating the whole of the Lea Valley, with no big architectural gestures. The team—which included Allies & Morrison, EDAW, HOK Sports, and many other engineering and management consultants—worked diligently taking into account every road, every business, every canal, and every bird. No big visions, no big ideas. We had to incorporate commands from the engineers, the conservationists, the real-estate experts, the sports architects, the biologists, *and* the local residents. After six months of hard work we delivered a master plan that not only answered to all those requests, but also looked good and was consistent with the fluvial geometries of the Lea Valley: the project used the water, the landforms and the green to make a large urban park. Afraid that a more architectural output would make the plan threatening to the public, we presented this thoroughly constructed master plan via the usual set of vague and popular imagery, aimed to convey to the general public the festive atmosphere and the regenerative values of the prospective London 2012 Olympic Games rather than potentials of not-yet-designed architectural proposals. Consequently, Sudjic wrote in *The Observer*:

> But despite the glitz with which the Prime Minister launched London's bid, it turns out that all those toe-curlingly kitsch computer renderings of Olympic flames, rivers of happy people and Stratford by night do not show London's Olympic stadium at all: it hasn't been designed yet.[2]

2   Deyan Sudjic, *The Observer*, (London, January 25, 2004).

The alarms sounded the minute this critique hit the newsstands; everybody began asking for *Architecture*. Of all the members of the consortium we were identified as the ones who could deliver in a short period of time a sufficiently exciting architectural image of the games, and were subsequently commissioned with a workstream called "Look and Feel of the Games." Looking at the meandering, bifurcating, lenticular geometry of our Olympic Park, we knew by now that the real question here was to deliver an image able to spark broadsheet headlines if we were to quell the rumors of our boring and bureaucratic approach to urbanism, and our incapacity to deliver exciting architecture (which, for the record, had not yet been commissioned). After some subsequent spectacular failures in the London 2012 boardroom, the Hokusai Wave came back to the rescue: the venues became *muscles,* lenticular organs, within the anatomy of a park structured by a bifurcating striation (like muscular tissue) of meandering waterways, traffic arteries, and rolling dunes. Not only did the muscle analogy produce an immediately consumable image, it further suggested a range of consistent structural and land-stabilizing strategies that would produce the muscular forms to populate the park. Everybody immediately understood the geometry of the project and we even made some headlines: "London puts muscle into its bid," reported the broadsheets. Best of all, this approach enabled a strategy by which the venues would not be floating on a sanitized, separated platform but would become, formally and structurally, part of the striated and meandering landscape of the Lea Valley.

But the Hokusai Wave is not exclusively ours: projects like the Chinese basket-like, bird's nest-like H&dM design for the 2008 Olympic Stadium, Foster's Gherkin, or the branding exercise of UNStudio's trefoil/wheel Mercedes Benz Museum in Stuttgart, to name just some of the most accomplished, are also cross-breeding very obvious iconographies with processes of material organization, be it of a typological, organizational, or constructive nature. At this point in the game I have not completed a full theory of this methodology, but I could venture a few conclusions. After several decades of neo-modern boxes, abstract blobs, and incessant indexicality (let's say deranged datascapes), I believe that one of the most promising paths for disciplinary research is the expansion of architecture's material palette *into* semiotics. But, here, I want to underscore that the semiotics that I am invoking are not that of *linguistic theory*, but rather *architectural immediacy*: architecture's engagement with a "reading" audience, both within the discipline and among the public at large. In order to accomplish this intersection of semiotics and materiality, it is necessary for architecture to incorporate languages, identities, and protocols of communication within the complex meshwork of geological and biological matters (or metaphors) that constitute the discipline's core.

In order to produce this disciplinary expansion we need to revisit representation with the same fluid perspective that we have dealt with material organizations, without falling back into the trap of the analogy to the written word, such as happened with all previous incarnations of "semiotic" models in architecture. The semiotics that inspired architects in the past belonged fundamentally to the field of structural linguistics; that is, from Saussure to Barthes to the wild and arbitrary wiles of poststructuralism. My hypothesis is that the consistency between the material and the significant will have a brighter future when mediated through *form*—or, that which mediates *matter* and *substance*—rather than through signs, indices, or other modalities of coded transfer. Rather than embracing the contingent, ambiguous nature of *shape* as an alternative to the hermeticism of indexicality, I propose the development of a discipline of *form with a double agenda*, operating simultaneously as an organizational device and as a communicative device. This direction could be explored to sustain the future growth of the discipline, to expand architecture's audience to include a public component, which the form argument has traditionally avoided by locating itself exclusively on a disciplinary plane. By opening form into the reprocessing of identity and iconography, we can perhaps sustain a reempowerment of the architect as a relevant expert with a public dimension, rather than a *hermetic* (even if *seductive*) practitioner.

My tendency to resort to iconography as an alternative to a

coded or indexical language is a kind of primitive choice, a protocol of communication that comes bound with form and can, therefore, be directly coupled to material organization. Rather than deploying rhetorical modes of existing systems of signs, as in classical architecture, or signs in a calligraphic mode, as in postmodernism, the potential of extracting forms out of well-established formal identities to destabilize material assemblages and vice versa, seems to be a viable escape from the arbitrary deployment of shapes with neither binding relationships nor deliberate effects on the typological, organizational, or constructive nature of a building, to which a large part of "signature architecture" has been reduced.

Paradoxically, while aiming to provide a sufficient level of engagement with the general public and delivering effective *excuses* for disciplinary experimentation, the *double agenda*'s full depth remains reserved for the expert, who is able to understand that the object of practice is not exhausted in either area of performance (either as iconography or material organization) but in a constant and iterative feedback between both realms—that is, a process of mutual destabilization.

Despite superficial similarities, Venturi's populist manipulation of identities is the complete opposite of this approach, as the two sides of the equation remain aseptically detached at the façade line in both the duck and the decorated shed. Consequently, neither the reader nor the critic can discern anything about the series of the thresholds, ratios, techniques, and systems that constitute at least some part of architecture's expertise. In the Hokusai Wave mode, the deployment of a particular image becomes responsible for typological or constructive reconfigurations that have to be discussed in terms other than mere visual semantics in order to understand their full depth. A similar erosion of identity through semantic and constructive operations can be seen in the case of the Villajoyosa Police Station, which both represents (through formal similarity) the US Pentagon and simultaneously echoes a ballistic impact through the perforations of the window system. Noirish and nihilistic, neither reading dominates—instead, the two representational echoes play off of one another, forming a resonant chamber of possible readings. Along the same lines, the deployment of a tape loop as a brand image for the BBC, and its effect upon the studio technology and organization, or the use of the image of a palm tree trunk as an excuse for a (nearly extinct) *brise-soleil* facade typology for a high-rise building in a semi-tropical climate are just some of the effects of the coupling that transcend either a purely cultural or a purely material perspective. A critical perspective along these lines demands that we break down the divisions and hierarchies that have consistently been maintained along architecture's envelope line.

Despite superficial similarities, the double agenda proposition also differs from Philip Johnson's professional cynicism (or Jencks' double coding). It is targeted at avoiding the perpetuation of the architect as a seductress, permanently dependent on a client's desire, by connecting the discipline to a broader pool of power, both by grounding the practice within a more extended cultural background and by claiming a body of technical expertise rather than a place in the whimsical realm of pop-cultural production. It is precisely the deliberateness in the simultaneous pursuit of a double agenda that provides an alibi for reciprocal subversion on each domain, a win-win alternative to the painful career of the hermetic and uncompromising, *misfit* architect, condemned to endure twenty years of public incomprehension, like some of our most distinguished colleagues from earlier generations. Perhaps the Hokusai Wave will save us from the trap of having to be devoted either to power or to control and lift us past that phase altogether. Let us delve into the eddies and vortexes of matter while simultaneously producing constantly evolving yet recognizable identities.

The images illustrating this text are a compilation of FOA projects together with iconographic references, and their related images.

Published in *Harvard Design Magazine*, spring/summer 2007 and *The Endless City*, Phaidon, London, 2008

The High-Rise Phylum

After a two-decade lapse that coincides almost exactly with the lifespan of the Twin Towers in Manhattan, high-rise building is back in vogue. The World Trade Center towers, finished in 1972, one year before the Sears Tower in Chicago, were completed just as the 1973 oil crisis was about to unfold, pausing the race for taller buildings by instilling doubts about the solidity of an oil-based economy. Their destruction, which took place in an economy driven by information, seems to have convinced everyone again of the charisma that tall buildings command. A few global Web sites are now devoted to following the growing array of high-rise buildings worldwide and to discussing and valorizing their technical prowess. According to Emporis,[1] one of these Web sites, 40% of the high-rise buildings (buildings of 12 or more stories) currently in existence have been built since 2000, and around 8% of the world's stock of tall buildings is under construction right now. The most high-rise-intensive city in the world, Benidorm, Spain, already has one high-rise building for

---

1   Source: http://www.emporis.com/statistics/most-skyscrapers (accessed Feb. 13, 2012)

every 180 inhabitants; there is even a high-rise cemetery, the Memorial Necropole Ecumenica III, in Santos, Brazil.

It is not just the renewed importance of urban charisma, the glamour of the "high-life," the breathtaking views, the feeling of power from living with cutting-edge technology and humming gadgets, or even the vertigo caused by buildings swaying in the wind. There is also the inevitable trend toward the densification of existing urban centers as the planet's human population flocks irreversibly toward urban cores. The superiority of the "culture of congestion" and the green credentials of the elevator core as an alternative to the gas-guzzling, six-lane highway are becoming universally accepted facts.

Beyond their renewed aesthetic hipness, tall buildings offer a high-density model for distributing population on the planet that helps preserve the greenbelt from the ever-expanding suburb and has a smaller land and ecological footprint.

Once the preserve of the very rich and powerful inhabitants of the world's financial centers, skyscrapers in some cities are becoming a sort of vernacular typology engaging the middle class; they are no longer simply the outcome of land shortage or urban speculation, as in the classic examples of Manhattan, Hong Kong, and Singapore. Examples of this democratization of the skyscraper can be found everywhere, from London to Kuala Lumpur, Moscow to Panama City, and Dubai to Madrid. This building type has stopped being an expensive extravagance or symbol of power and is, now, a serious investment strategy and development vehicle. The success of high-rise, mixed-use complexes (for example, Roppongi Hills in Tokyo, The Arch in Kowloon, Tower Place in Seoul, and Kanyon in Istanbul) is being recognized by international developers as an example of quality urban development with a serious profit margin to be replicated as often as circumstances allow. Globalization has brought highrises a customer base on an unprecedented scale.

One of the reasons for the democratization of building height has been a substantial development of related building technologies: higher-strength materials and faster construction technologies, both in steel and concrete; high-efficiency curtain-wall systems with superior insulation and solar filtering values; intelligent vertical transportation systems with higher lifting capacities; and more efficient energy plants. The efficiency of high-rises is now substantially greater than it was in 1973, and is making the construction and maintenance of high-rise buildings affordable for a widening spectrum of customers. In current urbanization, skyscrapers have ceased to be specially crafted products for the rich and powerful and are becoming a mass product. There is, in particular, a massive growth of high-rise residential buildings. As opposed to the postwar high-rise residential construction, which was the result of enlightened politics and urbanism, mostly for low-income populations, new high-rise residential building is driven by market demand. The commercialization of the type has also brought a higher level of industrialization in the making of tall buildings.

The building industry's answer to the inherent complexity of the high-rise typology and the scale of its economies has been to break down the project into different problems to be resolved by different experts. The typical high-rise today is designed first by well-established market ratios administered by real-estate specialists: population ratios, facade-to-core depths, floor plate sizes, planning grids, floor-to-floor heights, net-to-gross ratios, and facade ratios form the first level of constraint. Safety regulations and elevator capacities, interpreted by vertical transportation and fire consultants, add constraints. Environmental regulations, channeled into the project through mechanical and electrical engineers, constrain the skin design to achieve certain daylight and insulation values and solar gain ratios. Finally, the local construction industry's speed and skills and the price of commodities filtered through the structural consultants or contractors determine what kind of structure—and therefore massing—the project may acquire.

The ruthless force of these economies has usually "designed" most of the building by the time architects get involved, relegating their role to the design of the skin (usually with the involvement of facade consultants), lobby, and toilets. To illustrate the force of these constraints, it is sufficient to calculate the per-year cost of one elevator in a 50-story office building in a generic global city: every rentable square meter of floor plate will have a market value of, say, $750 per year. A standard elevator shaft will have a per-floor surface of 9 square meters. If we make the calculation 9 square meters x 30 floors x $750, we get costs of $337,500 per year. Given the fact that the total floor plate will usually be restricted by planning constraints, the elimination of one elevator by an architect or fire consultant will produce revenues for the developer of more than $1 million over three years.

The only possibility of preventing these forces from controlling design comes when the project requires the delivery of an image to brand a corporation, city, or developer—not to mention the individual consumer in search of a fashionable redoubt to call home. In the best-case scenario, the architect is empowered by formalizing an envelope that will be attractive to potential customers, create brand value for the occupier, or seduce local planning committees and politicians to allow higher floor/area ratios. The taller the structure, the more relevant this factor becomes. The skyscraper is still the paradigmatic urban object, and in very competitive or politically sensitive situations, its brand value becomes so critical that it can actually change a few standard building equations and produce an entirely different sort of economy. The recent history of the type is not short of examples in which the involvement of a particular architect has been able to subvert customary economies.

We are now witnessing an unprecedented number of high-profile design competitions in which attention-seeking clients are commissioning well-known architects to produce spectacular buildings that defy all conventions, including budgetary ones. But "the current mania for flamboyant skyscrapers has been a mixed blessing for architecture. While it has yielded a stunning outburst of creativity, it has also created an atmosphere in which mere novelty is often prized over true innovation. It is as if the architects were dog owners parading their poodles in front of a frivolous audience."[2] This is *New York Times* architecture critic Nicolai Ouroussoff writing about the latest examples of this global quest for the flamboyant skyscraper: the competitions for the Gazprom City in St. Petersburg for Russian energy giant Gazprom and the Phare Tower in La Défense, Paris.

The question here is how to tell innovation from novelty, particularly within the double standard that rules contemporary high-rise projects. These projects are subject either to ruthless efficiencies that constrain possibilities to the repetition of verified models, or they fall into the economy of the brand image, in which everything is possible and the desired novelty can direct choices without drawing any significant links to the typological phylum. Those projects that, because of their profile, would allow the benchmark to slide further are often misused to produce weird and spectacular high-rises full of contingent gestures that fail to open the market to meaningful experimentation. This is one of the reasons why these projects—as opposed to, say, museums—have remained in the hands of large com-

---

2   Nicolai Ouroussoff, "Towers to Transform Skylines of Paris and St. Petersburg," *New York Times* (December 4, 2006), http://www.nytimes.com/2006/12/04/world/europe/04iht-towers.3767443.html (accessed April 5, 2011).

mercial firms and beyond the reach of more imaginative architects, who have systematically either failed to understand or chosen to ignore the underlying economies at play in this typology.

To work effectively in this evolving market, we need to develop a typological knowledge that could reactivate the synergies across the divides into which the industry has split the high-rise project. The creation of a new dynamic between efficiency and expression will allow us to grow beyond the vacuous expressionism that has captured some of the high-rise commissions of late, while—at once—voiding them of any true innovation. Such a new dynamic cannot ignore the context of the already given technologies or econometrics that drive high-rise development worldwide. Yet the real opportunities for innovation are to be found in the engagement and problematization of those *seemingly* neutral parameters that regulate the typology.

This text is an attempt to update the high-rise *phylum*. It is aimed more at the identification of new tendencies and opportunities than at the construction of a general theory, since it is drawn primarily from direct personal experiences rather than systematic research. I have intentionally set aside the visionary, iconic approach of novelty in trying to produce this update.

Tall Buildings: Rule or Exception?

The current, extraordinary increase of high-rise construction is an opportunity for considering its possibilities as an urban typology. High-rise fever is putting unprecedented pressure on urban cores to accommodate new skyscrapers, often forcing city leaders to rethink their planning policies. The key question is whether high-rise buildings still remain extravagant and unique—that is, objects whose proliferation creates a city of exceptions, a city shaped by the sum of individual initiatives—or whether the number of high-rises has grown so large that it has become an integral part of the urban fabric and, therefore, requires a more sophisticated policy than just limiting heights. What should be the nature of a high-rise policy? A location of landmarks in strategic points to construct new views? A design guideline on the environmental performance of tall buildings? The delimitation of zones with unlimited height? A policy of Floor Area Ratio (FAR) allocation related to public transport capacity and daylight thresholds? Many policies are already under development in different cities, and when analyzing them it is noticeable that the attitude toward high-rise buildings has deep cultural roots.

For example, in the USA, the downtown has been traditionally linked to high-density and high-rise buildings primarily dedicated to workspace. The distribution of high-rises follows a mono-functional pattern radiating from a center, usually devoted to financial activities. In Europe, where the closest precedents of skyscrapers are church towers and other representations of power, high-rises have been generally perceived as anti-urban and exiled to special precincts away from the center. La Défense in Paris and Canary Wharf in London are good examples of this trend. Asian cities have located their high-rises less idiosyncratically, as punctual intensifications of the urban fabric. High-rises have become a more continuous distribution usually related to transport infrastructure capacity and location. The Asian models have enthusiastically adopted the residential high-rise as an inner-city, land-use issue in contrast to the mono-functional models in the USA (with the notable exception of New York City) and in European central business districts.

Tokyo provides probably the best example of the coupling of transportation infrastructure and high-rises. The main stations on the Yamanote line have concentrated clusters of urban density and skyscrapers; such clusters replicate, graph-like, the patterns of accessibility in the inner-city core. There is no central business district or exclusive high-rise ghetto but instead a distribution of high-density clusters of optimal accessibility. Seoul, Kuala Lumpur, and Shanghai (although, paradoxically, Pudong replicates the European model of a high-rise ghetto) present a similar approach to urban policy for high-rises—that is, not characterized as forming a precinct but rather as exemplifying standard rules. The skyscraper clusters are the result of the intersection of FARs, transport capacities, and the casting of shadows. There is no a priori, formal consistency or delimitation. Skyscrapers appear where there is a coincidence of four factors: optimal transportation infrastructure; a high FAR; sufficient land to justify the concentration of a large built floor area; and sufficient distance to neighboring buildings to ensure sufficient natural lighting. The local tendency to build tall projects by the riverfront or along main infrastructural lines allows for both accessibility and shadow buffers. The recent redevelopments of remaining tracts of land in central Tokyo (Shinagawa or Shiodome) and the development of riverfront locations in Seoul, such as AIG's complex in Yeouido, Jangshil, and Mokdong's Richensia and Hyperion complexes confirm the vitality of this model.

In contrast, London, which has been undergoing a massive transformation of the city center (the financial core) over the last decade, is addressing the enormous current pressure to densify by delimiting a high-rise cluster formed around Tower 42 (currently London's tallest building). The planning envelope follows a sort of Gaussian curve, taller at the center and fading toward the edges. Additionally, an area of exclusion is formed by seven view corridors for St. Paul's, London Bridge, and Big Ben. Most interesting, in London there is no FAR assignment by a city plan, as there is in most other European cities: Floor plate allowance is at the discretion of the local planning authorities, and developers are required to build up their case, submitting environmental, transportation, and daylight impact reports. Aesthetics feature prominently in the assessment of proposals, and a more "iconic" proposal will have an advantage in the building permitting process. All this confirms London as the world's most picturesque city in terms of high-rise policy. Barcelona has a similar "City Beautiful" approach in which high-rises (which usually end up being headquarters for public utilities like water, gas, and telephone) are essentially ornaments aimed at producing vistas or orientation points in an otherwise relatively low skyline. A flamboyant design, like Jean Nouvel's Torre Agbar or EMBT's Gas Natural Tower, is, therefore, critical to the success of any tall project.

The approach to the questions of location, height, and design could not be more different in European capitals and in Asian metropolises. In Europe, high-rises are still treated as monuments, extravagances that used to be paid for by the king or the church and now are paid for and exploited by private corporations but approved by public agencies, placed as landmarks in strategic locations, and required to have iconic designs. In the current European debate on skyscrapers, a struggle is on between the pressure on urban centers to accommodate a normalization of higher densities and larger buildings, with their monumental character, a struggle that may generate interesting opportunities to invest tall buildings with iconic content but also to develop adequate prototypes for local urban milieus.

In Asia and, for the most part, America, by contrast, the skyscraper is a more mundane endeavor treated with a certain stylistic indifference. If, in the European case, skyscrapers are still "avant-garde" and are determined by vistas and relationships to the existing skyline, in Asia and America they are more integral to the urban fabric and are determined mostly by technical and financial matters (generic urban planning rules, infrastructural capacity, FAR allocation, disaster prevention planning, daylight rights, environmental impacts, and so on). In most cases, the iconic quality of the proposal will be secondary to these more quantitative assessments.

There are monumental exceptions to these rules: the Petronas Towers in Kuala Lumpur, the Burj Khalifa in Dubai, Taipei 101 in Taipei, and the Jin-Mao Tower in Shanghai take the monumental, extravagant approach predominant in Europe, while Canary Wharf creates a more generic high-rise fabric. There is no easy conclusion or universal prescription, and what is adequate for an economy and culture like Barcelona's may be totally wrong for London's, which faces a much higher pressure to densify. It seems unlikely that the "iconic" approach to skyscrapers will be able to develop the typology, generate knowledge with which to frame the future engagement of high-rise buildings with urban fabrics, and avoid the emphasis on novelty for its own sake. But it is also true that if there is no further ambition in these projects other than to satisfy commercial interests, it is unlikely that the enormous energy that propels them will be able to develop new urban models. Without a more deliberate connection between the efficiencies of high-rise buildings and their expression, developing an urban policy for them will be difficult.

Expression and Efficiency: The Icon and the Type
The growing popularity of the skyscraper and its progressive industrialization has developed the high-rise phylum substantially in the last decade. There is an increasingly complex body of efficiencies, differentiated in terms of location, use, and scales, that regulates the relationship between the structural, programmatic, and environmental factors driving both the building's configuration and in its engagement with the urban landscape. This more evolved high-rise phylum is poised to alter the real typological and expressive capacity of the form, if only…

The traditional high-rise building from the second half of the twentieth century was primarily determined by the extrusion of a floor plate and a structural grid. Squares, circles, slabs, *H*s, *L*s, and *Y*s were the basic plan choices. Gone were architects' attempts to derive high-rise form from the constraints of shadows and the need for daylighting (for example, Eliel Saarinen, Raymond Hood, or Hugh Ferriss). William Van Alen's efforts to invest the skyscraper with a representational charge, as well as Le Ricolais's and Buckminster Fuller's attempts to shape the building in response to diagonal forces, fell with both the questionable outcome of the socially progressive residential model and the increasing ubiquity of the corporate office model. Reaction and banality eviscerated almost all progressive tendencies. Fazlur Khan's experiments with diagrids and tapering spires were isolated, as were most other extravagant experiments in an industry in which the efficiency of the grid was a real advantage. In the '60s and '70s, skyscrapers had been conceptually liberated from the city, and their form was meant to respond only to internal efficiencies of construction technology and program. Only at the end of the '80s did the representational drive reappear in a series of image-driven high-rises that proffered the type, again, as a center-city agent for redevelopment and "architectural signage."

Increasing pressure from the market is now forcing planners and designers to provide towers with more compelling and crafted images than those of the mere repetitive extrusions—the banal series. Very often, this added layer of expression is produced by the mere treatment of the envelope with unusual materials or patterns, by playing with balconies in residential towers, or by slight deformations of the facade in office buildings. An elaborated or a decorated skin is probably the most economical device that can provide an aura in high-rise design. In some sections of Shanghai and Guangzhou, fields of towers are designed as mere extrusions of an optimized footprint, but are then given a variety of tempiettos, pagodas, and so on, aimed at individuating them. They are effective as far as the market is concerned, but, unlike Hugh Ferriss' setbacks for daylight and Louis Sullivan's ornamented ceramic panels for fire protection, they are detached from any real efficiency in the tall-building typology. They demonstrate a paradigmatic outcome of the negative side of the industrialization of the high-rise, in which expression has become an alternative detached from functional and constructive concerns. The expressive layer is not alien to the history of the type, but the tension between expression and efficiency has never been greater. Early twentieth-century tall buildings in America were often given sophisticated, intricate silhouettes that appropriately expressed the ambitious enterprise of building high-rises and differentiated their presence on the skyline. The skylines of cities like Prague, Moscow, and Cairo reveal a level of crafting of tall structures that exemplifies the mystique of tall buildings and the consciousness of profile, even if tall buildings then were exclusively driven by the goal of monumentality and singularity. The spire as punctuation mark, whether ecclesiastical or commercial, is often the limit for cities adverse to the densification of fabric on the vertical axis.[3]

The current trend toward profiled high-rises is often at odds with the economic and functional forces ruling the office and residential high-rise economies. This is a potentially fertile conflict between the increasingly demanding requests of developers and planners to produce dramatic tall buildings and increasingly precise market demands—that is, particular dimensions of facade-to-core, specific facade and fenestration ratios, market-driven population ratios, compliance with certain models of structural efficiency and procurement systems, and so on. As the high-rise becomes an industrial product, the typology becomes increasingly optimized and constrained.

In most European cities, and increasingly in cities in America and Asia,

---

3 Prague's example is, in itself, telltale: the city has numerous churches and the Castle (with St. Vitus's three spires reigning over all others), yet modern high- or mid-rise buildings only occur "on the horizon" (for example, the communist-era, 20-story *panelák* or *sidliste* at the outskirts, or in the occasional concession to a Rockefeller Center-type business enclave within the city, scaled and positioned with care so as not to disrupt the overall fabric, and always controversial anyway).

it is unlikely that developers will present authorities with an extruded form without any formal complexity because of the fear that planners and potential tenants will dismiss such projects as banal. In many cities, particularly in the Eurozone, extravagant projects help developers get through building permit applications, increase the FAR of the site, and eventually attract higher income for the building. Within this process, market parameters are subverted and owners give up some efficiencies to be able to maximize their revenues. The case of Foster's 30 St. Mary Axe (the Gherkin) in the city of London is quite interesting in this respect: because of its unique geometry, it is the first tall building to obtain planning permission in the city proper for decades. Swiss Re, the owner and commissioner, has acquired enormous exposure, which, on the other hand, has failed to attract subtenants to fill the substantial portion it does not need. However, Swiss Re is negotiating to sell the building (at a sum that will allegedly deliver a profit of around £250 million), probably to a larger organization interested in occupying the whole space and obtaining a prominent position in the city.

In London there is a flood of profiled skyscrapers that, because of their idiosyncratic forms, have been immediately given nicknames: the Gherkin (Foster's 30 St. Mary Axe); the Shard (Renzo Piano's tower); Helter-Skelter (Kohn Pedersen Fox's Bishopsgate Tower); and Walkie-Talkie (a Rafael Viñoly design) among them. In New York, where simple extrusions were the norm, the Twin Towers' unapologetic simplicity is being replaced by the more complex profiles of buildings like the Freedom Tower and Foster's Hearst Tower.

Some projects are trying to manipulate to dramatic effect some of the constraints that high-rise buildings impose on geometry to escape from conventional extrusions and produce bold images. Some of the best examples among these idiosyncratic towers (many designed by

Norman Foster) use structural or functional efficiencies to generate their extravagant profiles. Foster has argued for the round and tapering profile of his 30 St. Mary Axe in London on the grounds that it liberates views around it and decreases wind at street level and its scale in the skyline. His Hearst Tower uses the diagrid that provides extra stability against lateral forces as an argument to produce a profiled volume. His Russia Tower, with a Y-shaped up-tapering plan, is justified on the grounds of structural efficiency and programmatic flexibility.

An alternative path of experimentation is represented by those towers that address local iconographies not as expressions, but as efficiencies, as crucial elements of contemporary skyscrapers. César Pelli's Petronas Towers, SOM's Burj Khalifa in Dubai and Jin Mao Tower in Pudong, and C. Y. Lee's Taipei 101 have attempted to distill images that resonate with local cultural figurations, using the rotated squares of Asian Muslim towers (in the case of Petronas), the desert flower (in the case of Burj Khalifa), and the tiered repeating pagodas of older Chinese architecture (in the Jin Mao Tower). Taipei 101 is filled with symbolism. Its eight distinctive sections create the impression of a bamboo stalk but actually represent gold ingots used in ancient China as royal currency. Each of its eight sections has eight floors (the pronunciation of the number eight sounds like "earn fortune" in Chinese), while four circles on each side of the building near the base represent coins. There is no question that iconography is integral to high-rise buildings. Those who did not take it into consideration have been sometimes forced to do so: Kohn Pedersen Fox's Shanghai Hills World Financial Center, which used to feature a round hole at its tower top, suffered a last-minute redesign to substitute a square opening, since the circle recalled the Japanese flag and, since it was owned by the Japanese Mori Corporation, its image had to be changed to avoid offending the locals.

In the best examples, the designers have sought a resonance between local iconographies and certain building efficiencies. The Petronas Towers offer an increased facade ratio by striating the skin of the building, while the Burj Khalifa's desert flower provides a geometrical basis for using three tapering buttresses as structural ribs, much as does Foster's Russia Tower. Both buildings are built using reinforced concrete, relatively new in buildings of this height, and both step back towards the top to lower the center of gravity in response to the added weight of the concrete. This architecture explores the efficiencies of its technology to produce an idiosyncratic profile that expresses its construction method.

The sheer scale of some of these buildings is, in itself, one of the new parameters in the high-rise world, since it is almost impossible to resolve it with a minimal geometry if one is to avoid being relatively inefficient. The need to go beyond the simple extrusion to create very large, tall structures was realized first by SOM's Sears Tower (1974) in Chicago; it was explored further by I. M. Pei's Bank of China (1990), built in Hong Kong, another early example of structural expressionism. OMA's Togok and CCTV projects, designed, according to its patent description, as "an alternative to the traditional diagram of the super-high-rise" and to "avoid the isolation of the traditional high-rise," are excursions into the unprecedented scale of some contemporary high-rise projects. My firm's own Bundle Tower™, a project done for the Max Protetch exhibition *A New World Trade Center* (and started as an attempt to develop a structural concept for a new generation of super-high-rise buildings, but, in a curious turn of events, ending up resonating with the *United We Stand* motto)—was another attempt to turn the fragmentation of volumes that becomes almost unavoidable in projects above 300,000 square meters into a structural advantage that enables an alternative vertical transportation system, allowing the different towers to share the cores of the neighboring ones by linking them with a system of sky lobbies.

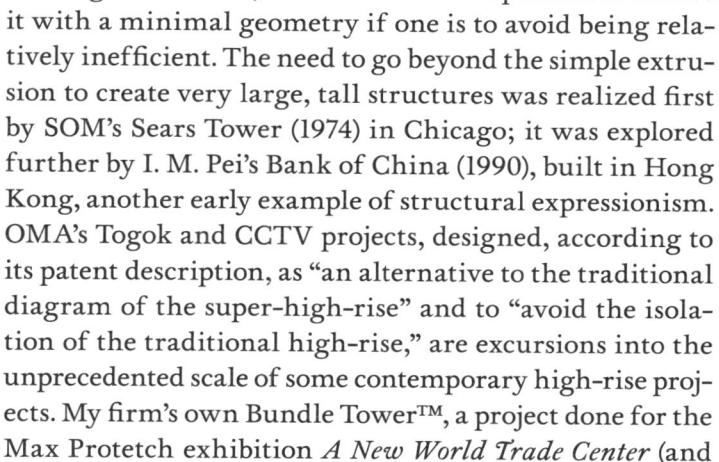

It is precisely in the correlation of emerging tower efficiencies and local specificities of the high-rise population with the tower's capacity to generate alternative expressions that we can find true innovation, rather than one-off iconic extravagances. In this investigation, the resonance between technical problems and local iconographies, as in the Petronas Towers or Burj Khalifa, is just an interesting additional vernacular trait of differentiation in the increasingly urban character of the type, as opposed to a global replication of the same models.

Local and Global: The Vernacular High-Rise
The high-rise type lies at the crossroads of the global processes of densification shaping contemporary urban development and the protocols and iconographies that define local cultural specificities. As a type that requires a substantial level of investment, the high-rise is often linked to global economic processes, foreign investment, and migrant populations, presenting an ideal battleground between global trends and local uses. Particularly since the global success of the high-rise residential building (a relatively recent phenomenon), high-rises have become increasingly differentiated, producing vernacular varieties that do not always conform precisely to global trends. As prime real estate, centrally located and not entirely suitable for certain lifestyles, inner-city, residential high-rises are often filled with expatriates and cosmopolitan locals who tend to be temporary inhabitants. But even with a certain "international" standard expected from this type of development, very specific design expectations come from the local communities owning a controlling market share. Although many of the developers of these projects are corporations or investors with multinational portfolios seeking to profit from rising property values (in a word, *speculators*), they need to consider carefully the specificities of the local market. Recent examples like the Tower Palace development in Seoul (built by

Samsung on the site where OMA's Togok Towers were to go), The Arch in Kowloon (built by Sun Hung Kai Properties), and Tokyo's Roppongi Hills (built by the Mori Corporation) have become phenomenal real-estate successes that everybody is trying to replicate and a proof of the vitality of the inner-city, residential high-rise typology, particularly in Southeast Asia.

There is a great deal of similarity among these projects, but there are also several differences that account for the specificities of each market. For example, the Korean example features considerably larger units than the other two, plus conservatories, while the other two rely on more conventional fenestration patterns; the Japanese example is still based on the dimensions of a tatami grid, while the Chinese model features the traditional facade articulation typical of Hong Kong that provides external walls for almost all rooms. The high-rise as a vernacular species may resonate with local iconographies and symbols, but its primary field of diversification occurs on a more subtle level, by complying with a number of parameters that embody local specificities of lifestyle, trade protocols, cultural preferences, and climatic conditions.

An analysis of the floor plates of the global stock of high-rise building demonstrates that this type is no longer just a Western export but is increasingly developing local varieties of such strength that in some cases they are spreading back toward the original epicenters of the type. For example, some of the condominiums now in Seattle, Miami, or the London Docklands incorporate Asian traits, such as increased facade ratios and exterior toilets, as developers learn from Asian markets or target Asian investors. Contemporary high-rise residential floor plates across the globe have become radiographies of cultural hybridization and the synthesis of local variations. The scale of the units, level of provision, and position of the toilets in the plan (next to or away from the facade, en-suite or collective), the provision of service areas within the apartments, and the level of differentiation between the private and the public areas of the dwelling are often indicative of domestic protocols in Western, Middle-Eastern, and Asian populations. Instead of focusing on the iconic nature of high-rise buildings, a comparative, quantitative, or topological analysis of the different parameters of residential organizations could become an extraordinary instrument for producing a deeper understanding of these processes of simultaneous vernacularization and hybridization of high-rise life. What follows is an attempt to map this battlefield between transnational trends and vernacular variations, setting up a global frame of reference that will enable us to identify variations, tendencies, and innovations, abandoning the utopian-visionary models based on novelty to embrace, like craftsmen, the elaboration of the high-rise phylum.

In some cases, localizing tendencies are intensifying. Norman Foster's Troika residential development in Kuala Lumpur, which features interior toilet and kitchen blocks, reportedly fails to meet local living standards requiring toilets and kitchens to be exterior and naturally ventilated. Despite its good looks, it is not compliant with local feng-shui specifications either. However, it is likely that it will find suitors, given its location and international quality.

But there are other processes that have a global reach. The dramatic shift of the typology toward the residential is increasing the use of building technologies that provide better acoustic insulation and less wind deflection. Given the fact that residential use does not require the amplitude of spaces needed for offices, reinforced-concrete wall construction is rapidly gaining market share among high-rise builders and even starting to reverse the trend toward large spans in office buildings. The rapid increase in global steel prices is decisively contributing to this technological shift. New concrete additives allow unprecedented speed of construction for a technology that a few years back would have not been considered, because of program constraints, for buildings above 25 floors. Current developments in high-strength concrete technology also allow increasing capacity to reach heights previously restricted to those resulting from steel technology. In fact, the Burj Khalifa, soon to be the tallest inhabited building in the world, and in many ways a sentinel of things to come, is using reinforced concrete for its over 150-story structure. In South Korea, where the local industry has developed a technology for residential high-rises based on mass construction, slip-formed reinforced concrete's optimal use runs now to 24 floors (it was 16 only six years ago).

As height becomes a desirable commodity, there is a growing disparity in the rental values on different building levels. In a commercial high-rise, lower levels are desirable because of their proximity to the street (for retail or high-density uses like trading floors). Upper levels are desirable because of the views and diminishing acoustic intrusion. In residential high-rise buildings, as the value per square meter increases with the floor level, it is common to have fewer, larger apartments, where buyers with higher purchasing capacity will aim. Following this logic, there seems to be an unexploited potential to design sectional differentiation in high-rise buildings rather than follow the direct extrusion of floor plates.

Another global tendency is toward a less artificially controlled environment, due to the increase in global energy prices. Also in South Korea, where there is a real industry of tall residential buildings; the facade ratio has been constantly increasing during the last 20 years, coming closer and closer to Hong Kong levels, even with a much higher average of surface per unit. Under-floor heating, winter gardens, and cross-ventilation are part of a local standard that in the current energy market is likely to be exported soon. What is more important, the optimization that the building industry has reached in the use of slip-formed reinforced concrete for high-rise residential construction will change the landscape of high-rise technology once dominated by steel construction.

All these developments depart from the original Western high-rise tradition based on an artificially maintained environment and expensive and technologically complex systems. Glass and steel construction, a technology transferred from shipbuilding and railroad construction and once exclusive to high-rise construction, is rapidly losing market share to the more earthbound concrete technology. The wider impact of these construction technologies, both in appearance and in typology, remains to be seen.

As a relatively complex technical enterprise, the design of a high-rise building is subject probably more than any other building type to precise calculation. These calculations are made to estimate the level of service needed to provide for its different systems—for example, the population that the elevator core is supposed to serve at peak time and the length of elevator waiting times, the population that the air-conditioning system is supposed to serve, or the dimensioning of toilets and fire escapes. Space is scarce and needs to be carefully accounted for, and this level of accountability is what enforces quantification of its multiple performances. It is precisely this level of quantification that constitutes the framework to criticize the contemporary stock of high-rise typologies not as a series of novel occurrences but as a particularly intriguing species in constant evolution that diversifies in respect to climate, geography, and cultural protocols. What follows, here, is a series of indices that may allow us to map out the geographical or cultural diversification of high-rise typologies in order to generate a frame of reference that will enable us to criticize and develop the current typologies, ground innovation, and avoid mere novelty. Many of these parameters have been extracted from technical indices traditionally used by developers, quantity surveyors, and engineering consultants to analyze the performance of a design, but which have so far been absent from any public debate on high-rise buildings. To problematize some of them may be the means to generate true innovation.

Population Standards

Certain population standards are compulsory by building laws, such as the population for which a fire escape system is designed, but most of the time the estimate of populations will vary across the different systems in a high-rise building to provide different standards. For example, it may be that the overall population for the vertical transportation system is based on 12 square meters per person, but for the air-renewal rate that figure is enhanced to 10 square meters per person and the toilets downgraded to 14 square meters per person. It may also be that population density varies across the section of the building, reaching to 7 square meters per person in the lower floors to accommodate trading floors and other population-intensive uses, while increasing to 14 square meters per person at higher levels. These decisions may sometimes trigger arguments to set the specifications that will be affected by local work cultures and social uses. For example, when one is calculating the elevator or air-renewal capacity of a high-rise facility in some European countries, it is acceptable to decrease the population by 12% to account for daily vacancies that reflect local working culture and the type of work done in these buildings. But will these conditions apply elsewhere, for instance in South Korea?

The specification of an office building's toilet block population has similar social implications. The number of toilet units will be given by a locally established ratio in respect to a population that will typically oscillate around a standard guideline. However, when that overall number must be split into male and female populations, the situation becomes more politically charged. If we follow workplace statistics, it is unlikely that the female population in a high-rise building today will reach 40% of the total, no matter where we are. But, should we design our buildings to meet the current statistics or should we aim for a more politically correct 50:50 ratio? If we do 50:50, it is likely that the male block would be undersupplied for the present workplace market. The solution is often to dimension for 60:50 or 60:60 to match all requirements, but at a price: 2 extra toilet cubicles will consume approximately 4 square meters of area. Following the estimate we did before, in a 50-story tower in a generic global city this will mean a loss of $150,000 per year in rent—the price of political correctness.

Facade Ratio
The facade ratio is one of the most powerful tools for analyzing the evolution of high-rise typologies and their geographical diversification. Since the facade of a high-rise building is one of the most expensive elements, cost consultants use a ratio comparing the surface of facade to the floor area. This parameter has been used for decades by developers and quantity surveyors, to analyze the financial implications of a design, and by mechanical engineers to estimate energy requirements. If the ratio is high, it means greater expenses; if it is low, daylight and ventilation may need to be artificially supplied. It is therefore a parameter that connects financial implications with environmental qualities, often involving cultural specificities and technical specifications.

Surface-to-Volume and Window Ratios
Parameters such as the surface-to-volume and the window ratios, traditionally used to calculate energy requirements and to specify the composition of the facade, become indicative of the increasing differentiation of high-rise residential types in their global reach. If we compare these ratios for residential high-rises across different geographies, we will see the differentiation generated by cultural, climatic, and construction factors. For example: in a prototypical high-rise development in Dubai the average facade ratio would be around 0.45 square meters per indoor

square meter; in London 0.50 square meters per square meter; in Miami 0.55 square meters per square meter; in Seoul 0.60 square meters per square meter; in Kuala Lumpur 0.75 square meters per square meter; and in Hong Kong 0.85 square meters per square meter. The manipulation of these parameters gives us the possibility of playing with a spectrum of culturally specific possibilities.

The implications of this diversification in a typology generally considered global are interesting: In America and the Middle East, a high level of mechanically controlled environment in a residential unit is acceptable, while the further we move toward Southeast Asia, the more common is the requirement for all rooms to have direct contact with outside air. In the Western models, residential units rely heavily on full air-conditioning, while in Southeast-Asian prototypes, natural ventilation and under-floor heating are standard, even when air-conditioning equipment is installed.

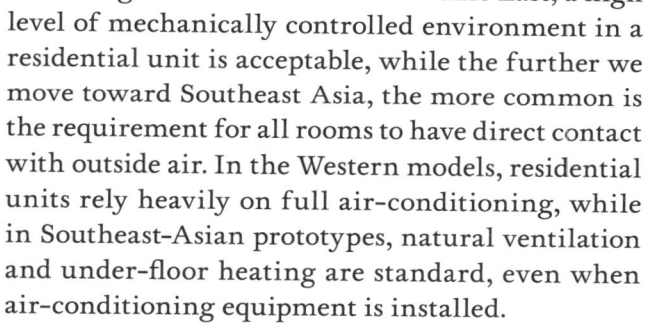

The argument for this radical increase in the facade ratio in Southeast Asia is often based on the humidity of the climate, but it is more likely the result of certain living patterns that Asian cultures are not prepared to give up even in a high-rise. Local cooking has developed certain types of kitchens with dry and wet areas; complex systems of service access and entrances into service areas exist within apartments of a certain standard; and a culture of bathing while being able to see daylight and views is possibly fueling some expensive traits of the Asian residential high-rise such as the systematic location of toilets on the facade of the building, as opposed to the Western models, where the toilets and kitchens tend to be internal and artificially ventilated and lit. Kuala Lumpur and Hong Kong are certainly very humid, and when the air-conditioning is turned off, there may be problems, but there is no reason to think that

Seoul or Beijing need very different residential structures from those in Manhattan, Chicago, or San Francisco.

Floor-Plate Scale

Floor-plate scale is a critical parameter in the design of a high-rise and possibly the one that may affect its profile most drastically. In residential buildings, the floor plate is primarily related to the facade ratio and the scale of the units. The combination of unit scale and a certain residential typology usually determines the floor plate to a substantial degree. In commercial buildings, the size of the floor plate is set by the scale of leases in a certain office market rather than by climatic and environmental factors as in the residential high-rises, since it is understood that high-rise office space is fully air-conditioned and artificially lit. For example, most of the commercial floor plates in cities in emerging economies, such as those of Guangzhou, Shanghai, or Kuala Lumpur, tend to require very large floor plates even in inner-city locations, since a substantial part of those markets is driven by back-office operations. In more established financial centers, such as London, New York, Singapore, or Tokyo, where the offices have a more representative purpose, the pressure toward very large floor plates is smaller, although, given the size of the tenant populations, it is unlikely that floor plates below 1,500 square meters will be considered commercially adequate.

Facade-to-Core Dimension

Another parameter that remains closely related to the floor plate is the facade-to-core dimension, which, contrary to what is happening in residential buildings, is tending to increase in most markets, despite the green calls for increased natural lighting and ventilation. With the exception of countries like Germany or the Netherlands, where the local daylight and ventilation regulations forces offices to remain shallow, most of the commercial high-rise floor plates will be aiming at bays at least 10.5 meters deep, but it is common these days for this type of building to aim for 12 to 15 meters deep because of the flexibility of that size in accommodating different organizations with a more or less cellular or dense space. In commercial buildings, the consideration of the planning grids is also important for the design of the building fenestration and for interior organization. For example, a lawyer's office in the UK and most Commonwealth states will require cellular offices to be 3 meters wide, while an American lawyer will consume a minimum of 3.6 meters of facade. In locations like London or New York, where firms on both sides of the Atlantic share the available space, the decision to choose the facade quantity is an important one and will affect the planning grids of the building and the rhythm of fenestration, which is, inevitably, linked to the subdivision possibilities of the floor plate.

All these parameters, often ignored when discussing the merits and demerits of high-rise projects, constitute the material grain of the contemporary high-rise phylum and provide a potential frame to discuss the way projects are, in fact, evolved specimens of this growing population of buildings. The parameters instigate technical discussions and yet they are loaded with political arguments and cultural questions. They offer dimensions of a possible map to help us begin understanding the truly new possibilities of the high-rise building.

The compilation of images framing this text are related to high-rise lifestyle collected from different media. From Bono enjoying a bath in a NY high rise, to a wide variety of popular imagery about what life in a high-rise is supposed to be.

Published in *AD. The Patterns of Architecture*,
London, November 2009

Patterns, Fabrics, Prototypes, Tessellations

Both patterns and fabrics have recently enjoyed a powerful return. Since the passing of certain mid-stream variations on high modernist architecture (such as the works of Team X, the Dutch Structuralists, or the Japanese Metabolists), and attempted correctives to the excessive focus on the object practiced by classical modernists, patterns have been largely absent from architectural discourse with few exceptions. While the mild *anti-modernism* of so-called dissident modernists has on occasion focused on the serial and/or modular construction of the architectural project (to enable flexibility and represent a supposed democratic, bottom-up approach), subsequent insurrections have deposed the same and constituted the repeated return of the opposite (the singular object).

The climate of progressive politics in which the '60s debate was framed meant that the investigation of patterns and fabrics became a promising opportunity, on both an urban and constructive scale, in the face of the exploration of formal autonomy that characterized modernism in both its avant-garde phase and its banal mid-century apotheosis as the International Style. But the flexibility and openness of such proposals was limited to the addition and subtraction, or the *interchangeability*, of identical parts. Thus, the possibility of addressing diverse needs within the structure was also limited. The structuralist experiment was also severely restricted in its ability to produce an image of a whole. Some variations to the structuralist approach were developed to introduce variation in the pattern: for example, the reintroduction of the concept of "wholeness," or monumentality, was often seen in the works of Louis Kahn or the Metabolists. And, from the engineering side of the architectural equation, both Robert le Ricolais and Pier Luigi Nervi explored the possibility of topologically deforming patterns in order to accommodate the differential behaviors of structures.

However, these experiments to differentiate fabrics or to provide them with legibility could not slow the general demise of modernism and the emergence of postmodernism as a response to the exponential proliferation of difference produced by competition and *production* within the various camps of the postwar economic, geopolitical, and social landscape. Postmodernism abandoned the project of non-paradigmatic consistency embedded in late-modernist experimentation and delved into the exploration of autonomy on the levels of language, material consistency, and part-to-whole relationships—arguably, all symptoms of a malaise that set in after the last revolt of the '60s. The creative potential of postmodernism petered out for this reason. Strangely then, the only remains of any consistency whatsoever were to be found within the more conservative and historicist varieties of postmodernism committed to the preservation of traditional urban fabric, inclusive of patterns of fenestration and ornamentation. In a slightly more bizarre manifestation of this turn, we saw briefly (thankfully) the extrusion of "Palladian windows" horizontally and vertically in new corporate versions of strenuous but pathetic architectural rhetoric. If modernism explored the autonomy of the object dissociated from its field, postmodernism explored further the autonomy between the parts and the whole as an index of a seemingly fragmented and hybridized culture, giving expression to the collapse of the modern project and its ambitions of consistency (however expressed) and collective redemption (however defined). With the arrival of postmodernism, techniques such as collage and montage were prioritized as compositional devices against the characteristic patterned modularity of the structuralist revision of modernism, or the topological deformations with which informalism tried to inject new energy into the modern project.

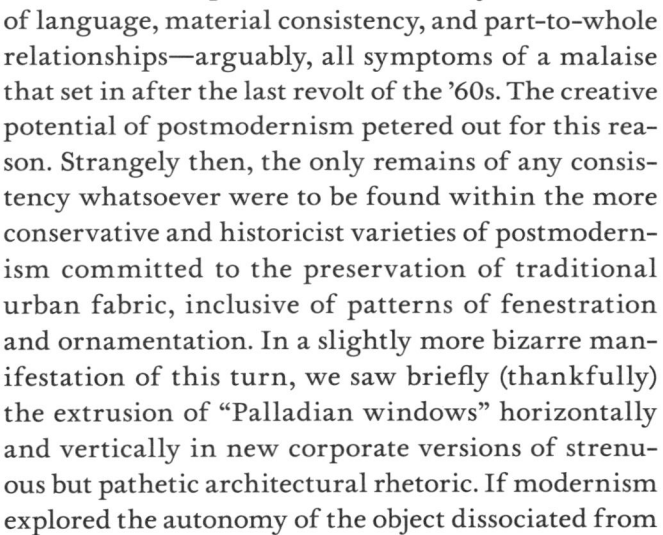

It was not until the mid-'90s that the discourse on the generic resurfaced, propelled primarily by the theoretical work of Rem Koolhaas as well as his work on generic space and the architectural effects of globalization. This opened the field to a range of explorations by a generation of younger architects aimed at overcoming the opposition between the generic and complexity as structuring and compositional devices, to investigate new technologies and sensibilities. Theorized under the labels of "Intensive Coherence," "Folding Architecture," and other instantly fashionable locutions, these experiments returned to the subjects of pattern as the material organizations most suitable to embody new forms of genericness. While not the appropriation of the "pattern language" of Christopher Alexander, and definitively not the "pattern book" of nineteenth-century cut-and-paste architectures, the new propensity to engage complexity devolved nonetheless to the *appliqué* (and probably without knowledge of Robert Venturi's cheeky approach to help or hinder). Yet all evolution is informed by devolution and forms and figures are thrown out en route to subsequent moments of revelation. In the self-consciously post-postmodern iterations of this idiom, seriousness was half the problem, while the lack of it was the other half. If we have seen the same weak resolve in post-contemporary art, it obvious, then, *as we shall see*, that a serious form of seriousness is what is called for.

Pattern Domains: Urban Fabrics and Envelopes

If the current interest in patterns is likely to be an effect of the cultural necessity to embody complexity through consistency rather than through contradiction (Venturi's legacy), this tendency has been reinforced by the availability of new technologies that *enable* architectural practices—for example, Foreign Office Architects (FOA), Greg Lynn FORM, Reiser + Umemoto, OMA, Herzog & de Meuron, and UNStudio—to develop increasingly sophisticated patterns on different scales of operation. If this sounds self-serving (and to include FOA in this list of seriously serious architects appears, at least, grandiose), it is only due to the fact that certain shallow forms of practice remain as the default means to so-called fashionable ends, and it is toward these ends (not the firms or practitioners involved) that a critique of formal agency is aimed only insofar as they remain "fashionable." Criticism in this regard is never *ad hominem*, while it appears so only to those guilty of true self-aggrandizement. These enhanced capacities of material practices to deal with patterns have been primarily applied *transversally* (in two directions): from the production of urban fabrics such as Peter Eisenman's masterplan for Rebstock Park (2001) or MVRDV's "datascapes," to the design of envelopes such as in the work of Herzog & de Meuron and FOA. One set is "horizontal" and the other "vertical," but not in the literal sense. Both are essentially "paradigmatic" (though the paradigmatic implies verticality). While the latter are concerned with paradigmatic matters that are expressible across the spectrum of built form, the former are paradigmatic insofar as they trouble the whole question of what is paradigmatic in architecture and how does such operate. Here we see two sets of concerns intersecting: the first carries with it informational strategies that produce pattern and the second harbors delusions of grandeur in the form of erasing informational orders toward formal and material agency that arrives out of information but then negates it. Neither is better (or truly paradigmatic in the ideological sense). They are merely different manifestations of the same process of reaching for architecture that has *a reason to exist*.

One of the possibilities that artificial intelligence (AI) has made available is the ability to model fields that were not previously visible and for this reason had not yet entered into the instrumental realm of material practices. Linking directly quantitative analysis with a graphic output, and the consistency and exactness that the calculating engines introduce in this process, has enabled new practices to address some of the crucial problems posed by globalization: namely, the dichotomy between tabula rasa and contextualism, and the articulation between local and global. This has become particularly evident in the design of urban fabrics. If the historicist idiom of postmodernism resorted to the reproduction of urban patterns drawn from the historic city and its typologies, or if the deconstructivist idiom dissolved pattern in an inconsistent, anxiety-inducing collection of pseudo-objects, the new experiments on urban fabrics are testing the possibility of constructing urban consistency without having to resort *necessarily* to the literal—or critical—reproduction of material or ideological structures given to pre-existing models.

These new technologies have expanded the limits of urban context to include other dimensions of space and time. The same applies to the articulation between parts and the whole within architectural artifacts. The dichotomy between bottom-up and top-down formal genesis has been put into crisis by

AI, which allows modeling, with great precision, the traits of a material mediation, rather than relying on an idealist worldview where the whole is built as the accretion of parts and where the part is a mere subdivision of the whole.

Having virtually disappeared from the technical arsenal of *truly interesting* architecture for two decades, the geometrical structure of the project—*tracé regulateur*—has regained relevance and become a commonplace of architectural experimentation. If the presence of a regulating mesh in the structuralist approach seemed to throw into question the system's capacity for integration and flexibility, the new possibilities of operating directly in a vectorial space enable us to retain internal and external consistencies without resorting to a rigid grid or reference system.

Esquema

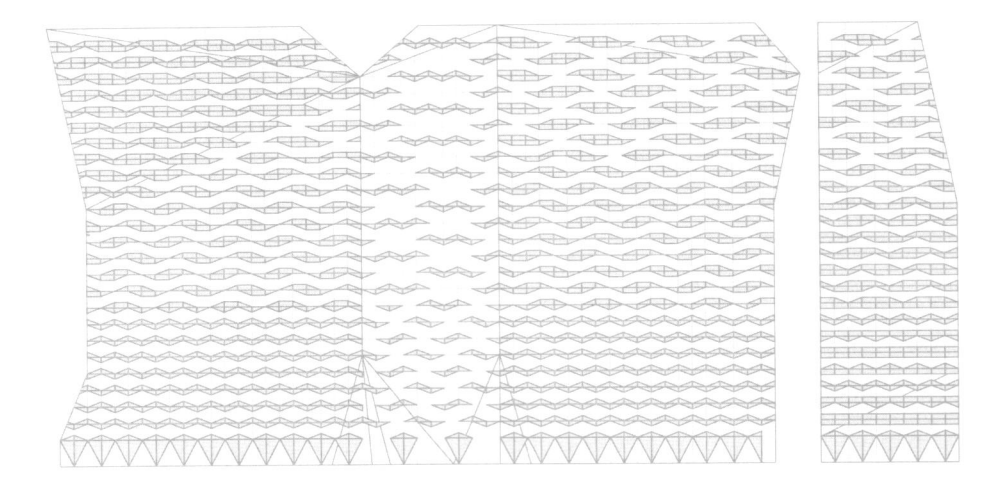

Pattern Politics: Difference/Repetition and Single/Multiple

One of the fields of contemporary architectural research where the investigation on patterns has been most intense is the subject of the building envelope. Compared with other domains of contemporary building technology, the building envelope is probably the most unitized, and, therefore, the geometry of the tessellation is crucial to determine its various performances: environmental, iconographic, or expressive. The building envelope is also the architectural element that is more directly linked to the representational functions of the building. As the traditional articulations of the building envelope, such as cornices, corners, and fenestration patterns, become technically redundant, the envelope's own physicality, its fabrication and materiality, its geometry and tessellation have taken over the representational roles that were previously trusted to architectural language and iconographies. The current proliferation of alternative political practices, such as trends, movements and other "affect-driven"[1] political forms, runs parallel to the development of envelopes that resist primitive models of "faciality," no longer structured on the oppositions between front and back, private and public, or roof and wall, rendering the hierarchies of interface between building elements more complex.

The politics of rhetoric, symbolic reasoning, and representation are giving way to a new breed of *object-oriented* politics,[2] invested in modes of production and exchange and primarily implemented through the production of affects, an unencoded, pre-linguistic form of identity capable of transcending the propositional logic of more traditional political rhetoric. The envelope, as the primary site of architectural expression, has become engaged in the production of surfacial effects, both as an environmental and a security device, and as the vehicle that will produce the building's facialization, make it human, and turn it into a political entity.[4] There is a new politics of faciality at play that affects the envelope as the locus of political expression.

The renewed relevance of the subject of patterns as a critically expressive device in contemporary architecture stems from these changes in the nature of contemporary politics. Beyond the

---

1 Following Deleuze, "affects" are "pre-personal intensities" that are transmitted by empathy between material organizations rather than through codes, signs, or conventional forms of representation. Gilles Deleuze, "Percepts, Concepts, Affects," in Gilles Deleuze, Félix Guattari, *What is Philosophy?* trans. Hugh Tomlinson and Graham Burchell (New York: Columbia University Press, 1996). As Nigel Thrift has pointedly noted, contemporary politics are progressively less reliant on representation and proposition and more dependent on the production of affects. See Nigel Thrift, *Non-Representational Theory: Space, Politics, Affect* (London: Routledge, 2007). Whether this is a good thing remains to be seen.

2 The term is borrowed from Rodney Brooks, a pioneer of behaviorist AI, who has promoted the idea of a "physically grounded artificial intelligence" from the field of robotics as an alternative to centrally structured coded wholes based on symbolic reasoning. Brooks argued that interacting with the physical world is far more difficult than symbolically reasoning about it. Rodney A. Brooks, "Elephants Don't Play Chess," and "Intelligence Without Representation," in *Cambrian Intelligence: The Early History of the New AI* (Cambridge: MIT Press, 1999). See also his "The Relationship Between Matter and Life," *Nature* 409 (2001).

solution to environmental concerns, there are questions of representation that the patterns of the envelope need to address *now*. One such challenge is the production of identities for an increasingly inconsistent and mobile community, while insulating and immunizing its population against the abrasive global atmosphere. Another is the representation of the emerging heterarchical orders that increasingly construct their power by both producing and using diversity, while simultaneously trying to produce consistency.

Frank Gehry's Guggenheim Museum in Bilbao (1997), Future Systems' Selfridges department store in Birmingham (2003), OMA's Seattle Public Library (2004) and Casa da Musica in Porto (2005), or Herzog & de Meuron's Prada Tokyo (2003) are notable examples of a tendency toward a multidirectional, differential faciality that resists linguistic coding, orientation, and other traditional forms of representation to engage in the production of new expressions and political affects.

The demise of the primitive figures of building faciality has found resonance in the availability of technical possibilities (such as glass serigraph technology and CAM manufacturing) which have enabled architects to play not only with smooth geometries, tessellation patterns, and material textures, but also with a wide repertory of layers that can also perform technical functions (such as solar shading and visual occlusion). The introduction of certain cladding and roofing technologies, such as curtain wall systems, silicon joints, and plastic waterproofing membranes, has eliminated the need for cornices, corners, pediments, and window reveals. The difference between the roof and the wall has disappeared, as have many other traditional articulations of the building envelope.

These conventional figures of the building envelope are being replaced by more nuanced interfacial embodiments in which different layers of performance are played out against each other to produce a wide range of complex effects. The decoupling of the patterns of visual, thermal, and atmospheric permeability has opened unprecedented possibilities for a molecular facialization of the envelope by

---

4   The idea of extending a human, political dimension to things or sub-human entities is very much the project that Bruno Latour explores in his proposition of a *Dingpolitik*. This is the term coined by Latour to address the politics resulting from the crisis of objectivity triggered by the collapse of modernity and the search for a new model of objectivity in which politics become intrinsic to the object, its sciences, and nature at large. See *Making Things Public: Atmospheres of Democracy*, ed. Bruno Latour and Peter Weibel (Cambridge: MIT Press; Karlsruhe: ZKM/Center for Art and Media in Karlsruhe, 2005). Published to accompany an exhibition at the Zentrum für Kunst und Medientechnologie Karlsruhe, March 20 through October 3, 2005.

dissolving or intensifying the joints at will through the phasing and de-phasing of these layers.

There seems also to be a tendency toward polygonal tessellations in contemporary envelopes—including PTW's Beijing Water Cube (2007), Future Systems' Selfridges department store, and FOA's Ravensbourne College of Design and Communication in Greenwich, London (2010)—that opposes the Cartesian grid division of the late modern screens. This tendency is first made possible by the release of the envelope from structural and environmental control functions.

Polygonal geometries have additional performances: for example, a hexagonal tiling has less joint length than a rectangular tile of the same area. If the contemporary envelope has more stringent requirements in terms of insulation and security performance, and this tendency is driven by a contemporary desire for sealed, immunizing atmospheres,[5] it is certainly enhanced by a faciality that is no longer structured in planar, vertical, and discrete faces, as some of these newer envelopes explore differential geometries of the surface (for example, bubble envelopes that totally depart with Cartesian tessellation). The *political* agency of such new *material* agency is yet to be defined, and it is possible that the translation of Latour's theory of *Dingpolitik* to architecture will lead to more problems than it solves in the near term, while provoking a dynamic clash of *architectural* cultures in the long run.

Gehry's fish-like skins are an index of these tendencies: the staggering of the joints, originally driven by the constructive purpose of waterproofing the membrane by overlapping the tiles, becomes a characteristic pattern that breaks the continuity of the joints and enhances the three-dimensional, dynamic affect of the skin. The proliferation of diagrids and non-orthogonal tessellation patterns—OMA's Seattle Public Library (2004) and CCTV building (2002), Herzog & de Meuron's Prada Tokyo (2003) and Beijing National Stadium (Bird's Nest, 2008), Foster's Swiss Re (2004) and Hearst (2006) towers in London and New York, respectively—display a general tendency toward the incorporation of the structure in the skin, producing anti-gravitational, uprooted, unstable, and differentiated affects.

5   "Immunization," "insulation" and "ventilation" are some of the terms used by Peter Sloterdijk to describe the artificial diversification of the atmosphere within the capsular society. The human island, the capsule, and the greenhouse are the prototypical devices for a new generation of buildings committed to this diversification of the atmosphere. Peter Sloterdijk, *ESFERAS III. Espumas. Esferología plural* (Madrid: Siruela, 2006).

The differential faciality that we find in some of the examples cited here explores the expression of a sort of politics that moves away from the ideal, modular democratic organization based on indifference, independence, and interchangeability: if modularity was typically a quality of a democratic system that prioritizes the part over the whole, some of the emerging envelope geometries seem to be exploring modular differentiation as a political effect and developing alternative forms of tessellation capable of addressing emerging political forms.[6]

Arguably, the modernist (abstract) modular grid, indifferent to the relative weight of individuals or politically active subgroups, embodied the ideals of democratic equality and liberal individualism and a preference for non-hierarchical organizations in which individuals are equal and will submit to the will of majority. However, emerging social structures characteristic of globalized societies (and given over to globalized, immaterial capital) and their heterogeneous populations tend to produce trans-scalar entities, from sub-individual to transnational. In these emerging social assemblages, individuals, groups, and other agents are primarily defined by relations of exteriority.[7] The allometric modularities and variable repetitions that emerge as almost generic traits of contemporary envelopes are probably more adequate to express a collective purpose within "weighted" models of democracy (either those committed to the exercise of civil liberties or those that are driven by a hierarchical bureaucratic and authoritarian regime overlaid onto apparent democratic protocols).

The convergence of affects of power and its material agency, especially in the aftermath of 9/11, given both to democratic or social-democratic nation-states with a multicultural tradition and

---

6   See Richard Sennett's "Democratic Spaces," *Hunch* 9 (Rotterdam 2005); Latour, *Reassembling the Social: An Introduction to Actor-Network-Theory* (Oxford: Oxford University Press, 2007); and Sloterdijk's *ESFERAS III. Espumas. Esferología plural*, op. cit. All three of these texts engage new socio-political forms that coincide insofar as they describe emerging social structures as material organizations where the articulation between individual and society, part and whole, is drawn by influences and attachments across positions, agencies, and scales that transcend both the individuality of the part and the integrity of the whole, or in other words as they always have been except that now they are drawn more fluidly as if to represent a world order traversed by increasingly immaterial versus material forces.

7   Manuel De Landa has applied Deleuze's theory of assemblages to describe these emerging forms of social and political organization. Assemblages are non-essentialist, historically contingent, actual entities (not instances of ideal forms) and non-totalizing (not seamless totalities, but collections of heterogeneous components). See Manuel De Landa, *A New Philosophy of Society: Assemblage Theory and Social Complexity* (London: Continuum, 2006).

advanced capitalist economy and autocratic states (often *city-states*) striving to attract and *integrate with* global capital while remaining essentially closed societies, in all of its various forms, signals the sometimes distressing means dominant political systems will utilize to save their respective ideological souls. This convergence is remarkable, as Jacques Chirac's measures to enforce secularity and ban conspicuous religious symbols in schools and Trevor Phillips' program of "Britishness" are not all that far removed from political-material machinations in places such as Dubai, Singapore, or Beijing. The question is whether the differentiated facialities and tessellations of the envelope emerging, for example in the Beijing Olympic projects, are genuine devices to allow the envelope to relate to a larger variety of concerns—environmental, social, economic, and so on—or a strategy to step up the immunization levels while representing an ideally differentiated public. In other words, do they inflect in response to multiple and *neutral* material agencies, incorporating specificities that have *no ideological import*, or do they comport with new, spectacular embodiments of global capitalism and authoritarian bureaucracies?

Furthermore, do they represent new, emergent authoritarian orders within the *new world order*, those given to lawless and stateless global capital (and beholden to no one), or do they offer a new political reality that is responsive to the professed neutrality and benevolence of capital?

As the politics of affect bypass the rational filter of political dialectic to appeal directly to physical sensation, the construction of an effective frame of reference within the discipline for discussing expression becomes critical. It is critical, therefore, to also construct a critical agency within material agency, to foresee and short circuit any return to ideological expressionism. One can no longer sustain the ideological assumption that a more regular or a more differentiated pattern, one more permeable or more closed, is better at expressing a certain society and the production of transformative effects. That was, in effect, *too* easy (and *too* naïve). The political accuracy of *any* envelope needs to be judged in respect to very concrete assemblages that shed *overt* or *applied* political agency. The political agency that might be retained is pure material agency as *immanent* political agency (not as politics/ideology). The most acknowledged envelopes among the iconic Beijing Olympics projects are probably those in which the architects have succeeded in creating a plausible alibi for the differentiated pattern wrapped around the massive unarticulated volume of the buildings, where a resonance between literal performance and affect has been achieved. This is where a new discipline of the envelope becomes politically operative as an act of resistance that does not get caught in the negative project of the critical tradition or in the use of architecture as a mere representation of politics.

FOA's Pattern Politics
Probably as a result of its engagement with commercially driven projects, FOA has been investigating the problem of the envelope for a number of years. As a result, it now has a body of project-based research on the problem of the envelope's tessellation. Considering the projects that have been engaged in this investigation, it is interesting to trace the tendencies present in the envelope's patterns, performing as environmental and expressive devices. The hypothesis of this analysis is that the four tendencies are toward the monolithic, differentiated, frameless, and rootless, and that these are representative and consistent with the primary *political* affects of the work.

First, there is a general propensity in the work toward envelopes that express a monolithic quality that foregrounds the perception of the object as a whole rather than as a composition of parts. In several cases, the massing of the envelope is predetermined by the nature of the program or the project's site previous to FOA's involvement: for example, the Spanish Pavilion for Aichi 2005 in Japan, Ravensbourne College of Design and Communication, the Trinity EC3 office complex in London (2006), or the Highcross retail and cinema complex in Leicester (2008) are all exemplifications of this tendency. The atomization of the face, the seamlessness, and the bias toward a body without organs that expresses changes of intensity rather than figures of organization are some of the qualities this group of projects share. As a result, the buildings produce affects of effacement, liquefaction, and de-striation.

A second trait that we can identify across all the projects is a deliberate attempt to produce differentiated patterns. In the Spanish Pavilion for Aichi, the pattern is differentiated automatically by the particular geometrical quality of the six deformed hexagons, with no other purpose than to represent a differentiated color field that, despite its contingent appearance, is governed by the geometrical laws of the parts. The Ravensbourne College of Design and

Communication is the only project where we can see a pierced fenestration: the geometry of the pattern enables perforations of different sizes in respect to the specific needs of the interiors. The differentiated fenestration pattern is then projected into the structure of the tessellation pattern. Here, the differentiation is produced locally in respect to programmatic factors.

In the Affordable Housing in Carabanchel, Madrid (2007), the difference engine is located in the contingent action of the inhabitants to set their own preferences in respect to daylight, shading, and views, changing over time as those conditions change, as a direct register of the collective's desires; as in a swarm, the part and the whole are seamlessly related in performance and expression. And in the Leicester Highcross retail and cinema complex the differentiation is embedded in the serigraphic pattern that covers the John Lewis department store's glass facade and the optimization of the stainless tiling of the cinema block, but most importantly it is produced by the movement of the spectator around the building causing a flickering moiré effect, together with the changing reflections on the mirrored surfaces.

In the Iconic Towers in Dubai (2004) and the Trinity EC3 office complex (2006), the differentiation of the pattern is local, generated by the differential solar exposure of the specific surfaces interacting with the facade tessellation. In the Institute of Legal Medicine in Madrid (2006), the circle-packing geometry is differentiated to adjust to the basic geometry formed by two spheres and a torus. Whether the differentiation is driven by the *pure* functional performances of the envelope in relation to varying parameters such as solar exposure, views, and so forth, or as a global order, in relation to the joints and joining patterns, details, or to the *localized* functional performances, the work displays a tendency toward differentiated patterns.

The envelope patterns in these projects present a tendency to merge the frame and the infill, the whole and the parts, which is particularly distinctive in comparison with other contemporary experiments in tessellation: the Barcelona Coastal Park and Auditoria (2002), the Spanish Pavilion, and the Ravensbourne College of Design and Communication present, repeatedly, an edge condition *within* the envelope that directly emerges through conformity to the geometry of the tiles rather through deference to cornice or corner, or any other framing technique. The exploitation of an *integral* correspondence between parts and whole, derived from within as it were versus applied, is one constant that occurs again and again through the late work, projecting the buildings as open, frameless, incomplete entities. It is not long before such buildings will actually have to go wandering in search of clients.

Finally, the analysis of the envelope's patterns displays a bias toward polygonal tessellations and packing structures, a trope that we can see in most of these projects. From all the cases listed, it is the Leicester Highcross retail and cinema complex, the Affordable Housing in Carabanchel, and Trinity EC3 office complex that retain the more conventional orthogonal grid as an organizing structure for the envelope's construction. However, the orthogonal grid is usually disguised by introducing an overlapped pattern or a 3-D manipulation of the surface. The conceptual argument behind this approach could be addressed by different hypotheses, but one of its most direct effects is the suspension of gravity as the primary organizing force behind the envelope tessellation. The envelope becomes, by virtue of this configuration, a hovering, rootless object that presents itself as a skin rather than as a topographic construction. The case of the Barcelona Coastal Park and Auditoria is interesting, as it is not an envelope proper, but a topography where the gliding of tiles in respect to each other produces an "effect" of instability that communicates a similar "affect" of rootlessness.

An analytic of this order, tossing out previous forms of so-called architectural truth-telling for a language of pure material agency, underlines the emergence of a series of affects in the patterns of envelopes that are to a degree independent of both the programs and the technologies used in their design. These characteristics may be seen as the "atmosphere' of the work. However, to take things a step further, these atmospheric qualities are an initial index for a resultant political stance; that is, work immediately antecedent to translation into a political vocabulary. In fact, and without belaboring the obvious, the *monolithic*, the *different*, the *frameless*, and the *rootless* are all concepts with serious political baggage.

The images illustrating this text relate to various projects from FOA which explore different possibilities of tessellations and patterns. From The Barcelona Park and Auditoria to the Ravensbourne Design and Communication there is a consistent research about knowledge. This image thread deals with the relationships between patterns and architecture.

Opportunity.
Alejandro Zaera Polo interviewed by Jeffrey Inaba

—**AZP:** I think it's naive not to acknowledge the status of celebrity. The new celebrity status certain architects have reached has been positive for the practice at large, because it's given architecture a more public profile. Of course, in the past there were architects who became famous, but they didn't have the public exposure that some architects have today. I think this new status has been positive in making decision-makers aware that there are degrees of quality in architecture; certain architects can produce buildings of a quality that, for example, a corporate machine cannot. The model of the celebrity has promoted the architect as independent thinker with a certain ideology and methodology, a worldview, but also a personality and a particular lifestyle. This model starts to emerge at the end of the 1970s. Until that time, good architects engaged in collective problem-solving activities, and mastered the latest construction technology. The corporate model was about keeping up with evolving knowledge. The Gropius model of technical expertise, and collective design gave moral and political legitimacy to architecture as a service profession, and dominated the first half of the 20th century. After the big modernist prophets Mies Van der Rohe and Le Corbusier, the corporate model convinced everybody that architects should forget all-encompassing visions, work in teams, and master skills and technologies: a kind of humble, modest service to society which presumed that the destiny of modernity had already been revealed and all architects had to do was to follow it dutifully. This was to become a very effective sales pitch.

That model largely collapsed at the end of the 1970s, when globalization undercut its advantages. A number of architects formed an international network, went to conferences and created an international debate using new communication vehicles. The model of CIAM as an international convention on architecture proliferated everywhere through schools and institutions and set up an opportunity for a quasi-permanent, ubiquitous forum where specificity rather than alignment was sought. They redefined the 'latest' as a debate on culture and personality rather than as technological progress. They portrayed themselves as individuals engaged in a multi-cultural, globalised network. They became international brands (I am thinking about Isozaki, the New York Five, Johnson, Rossi, Moneo, Stirling, Kleihues...). This model flourished, produced a second generation and is now perhaps showing signs of exhaustion. The challenge now is to formulate an alternative model. Yet in order to make something new, we need to reflect also on the celebrity model; to simply dismiss it without understanding what it does will not take us very far toward making a good case for quality architecture.

Marketing vs. Production

—JI: When defining ambition for today's architect one must not overlook the dynamics of celebrity that emerged in the late 20th century. If the corporate model was an attempt to cope with technology and collectively acquire knowledge in order to process technological advances, then in the late 20th century we witnessed a similar collective model. Yet the two models of teamwork seem quite different. The 1990s model of collaboration, formed to cope with greater information and new technologies, evolved simultaneously with the rise of celebrity architecture. Do you see this recent era as one characterized by the broadening of the architect's capabilities particularly in ways of processing information and designing? Do you think the shift to collaboration and the rise of celebrity are interdependent?

—AZP: We need to revise the role of the architect. Many of these so called celebrity architects from the first and second generation of globalized architecture have, in fact, become corporate organizations. Norman Foster is now bigger than SOM, and Herzog and de Meuron is of a scale not very different from conventional corporate practices. Looking at some of these practices and our own experience, it appears that when firms reach a certain scale a number of possibilities open up. Such firms are more capable of delivering projects, of doing research, than a small atelier doing little projects. Scale triggers some inevitable protocols and structures in an organization.

Some of these celebrity architects have also understood the advantages of corporate organization, and have started to develop organizations with the capacity of the traditional corporate machine plus the capacity to communicate more effectively and engage in cultural and political debate. In the Gropius model, the architect was not supposed to talk, [laughs] because if he or she was doing things correctly, using the right technologies, and producing what was good for mankind, the work would speak for itself. They didn't have to convince politicians or legitimize their work as long as it operated within the modernist dogma; the work was self-evident and nobody could possibly doubt it. Nowadays, these characters have achieved a high level of publicity and have not only managed to master the corporate technologies of organization and the capacity to deliver; they have also exponentially developed their capacity to operate politically, strategically, to communicate the projects, to negotiate with a variety of agents and know how to move them to enable the work to flourish. In order to do that, a number of little engines had to be developed within those offices, e.g., PR machines or people hired especially to coach presentations. I think this is a new addition to the recipe for a possible update to the architect's role. In some cases, like with OMA/AMO, that machine has developed a certain independence. The degree to which these two engines feed each other or merge into a seamless organization is an interesting question to address when theorizing new models of architectural practice. Can the PR machine effectively inform the production, or should it be kept fenced off in a parallel domain? How do these two engines feed each other?

If you listen to students or people who are starting to practice or teach, you hear a generalized rejection of the model of the celebrity architect. This is obviously in part because celebrity offices are major predators of jobs for the small fish. And there are two lines that the critique to celebrity architecture is trying to develop as possible fields of expansion. One is more technical, exploring software, sustainability and other technologies that can potentially shift the field, as a way out of the culture of celebrity. The other model starting to emerge is political activism. Suddenly there is a renewed desire to engage in some political activities that celebrity culture had completely ignored. And yet, celebrity architects have opened some paths for engagement with politics: they are a fixture at openings and mayoral celebrations and central occasions in the business of promoting cities... As architects have become increasingly involved with media, their ideological concern has been eroded (as has happened to politicians themselves). So, younger practitioners have identified this lack as a niche that has been overlooked by the celebrity architects and are logically trying to explore it.

But both alternative fields, the purely technical and the purely political, are possibly sterile and a dangerous trap: they are doing software projects or political manifestos rather than architectural projects. Both are problematic because they shift the ground of architectural practice into a dimension that is not architectural, just as celebrity architects that have shifted the ground of their practice to achieve that status, possibly getting into some trouble.

But to entirely dismiss the positive side of celebrity is to ignore an important potential of practice today. Obviously celebrity alone does not result in good architecture, but good architecture does not even have a chance without a degree of involvement of these new sides of the profession. I am optimistic and I believe that the public engagement that is open to the celebrity can be an interesting field to explore as an architectural opportunity.

Ultimately, whatever you do as an architect, you need to be able to transfer those influences into an architectural realm. Thinking about that transfer and how it reformulates the discipline is an interesting possibility.

Celebrity and accountability

—**JI**: You're saying that you can't discount celebrity immediately without realizing the benefits that have been gained from it, and that it requires expertise to be able to perform well under the scrutiny of the celebrity spotlight. I would add that the architect is unique as a celebrity in that he or she isn't perceived as being purely driven by greed or a thirst for fame itself. What we enjoy at the current moment is a degree of integrity in that we are able to construct a complex yet creative public entity, such as a large-scale building: our ability to make edifices stand and endure is perceived as admirable and authentic. It's quite interesting that this status of ours is in large part due to our technical knowledge. I think we are also beginning to realize that it has to do with our ability to communicate in a credible, sensible way. We don't seem to be stretching the truth, we don't publicly say formulaic things, and we don't appear to be entirely self-promotional.

—**AZP**: One should also look at the benefits celebrity has produced for architecture beyond the integrity of the product. Take three positive examples that are not just about the signature of the architect but are concrete projects that have become important and transformed the perception of architecture for decision-makers. The Guggenheim model is the epitome of celebrity. It has created some negative effects but it has had undoubtedly a very positive effect for architects, which is that now clients worldwide believe that architecture is an added value. This was not the case before except for a very marginal percentage of the commissions. Whether this has opened new fields for the practice is questionable, but the effect on the appreciation of the discipline is indisputable. Whether you like them or not, Richard Meier's Perry Street condominium buildings in New York have demonstrated to potential clients and investors that there is an added value to hiring a certain kind of architect to do a residential building. The Selfridges department store by Future Systems in Birmingham has convinced the entire UK retail sector that it is important to do good architecture, and more of the same no longer goes. Thus suddenly, a number of projects have become inspirational, not just for architects, but for decision-makers and the public at large. The celebrity model has also established that architects are different from one another. The corporate model was based on a sort of uniform technical expertise. There was not much of a difference between SOM and, say, HOK. Now there is an expectation to do something different, even if it sometimes leads to a caricature performance. It is even affecting some of these corporate firms. And this quest for difference makes it more interesting to practice architecture now than before.

—**JI**: The corporate model presented an elevated degree of technical expertise in the construction quality of the building. Today we have maintained this competency while also establishing what might be called a cultural model; we offer not only technical expertise, but also cultural value. Bilbao has an appreciated value as a mainstream cultural object. What seems distinct about this current phenomenon is that it is not so much associated with a movement as it is with individuality: the recognition of the unique approach of individual architects. In the corporate model, the ambition to attain high cultural status was attempted by including contemporary art in and around the building, whereas today it happens by packaging the expressive talent of the architect, by positioning the architect front and center in the broadcasting of the building. In that sense, architects have attained greater power by advancing technical expertise in the development of formal languages, and 'cultural' expertise in the intelligent development of public personas connected to these forms. Whether one likes the project or not, the most apparent example of this is, as you say, the Guggenheim.

—**AZP**: Yes, I think this must be

acknowledged. In spite of their flaws, these projects have convinced more people to be architecturally ambitious. Not just architects, but cities, corporations, voters and taxpayers. It is no longer politically viable for clients of a certain profile to just want a new building. Now you need a special building, which is complicated because at the same time the techniques of accountability and project management, as well as the liabilities, have expanded to such a degree that clients—or their advisers—tend to know very precisely what they want and to strictly enforce their project objectives, objectives which have been dictated by looking at previous models. And this creates substantial friction with experimentation as a methodology of architectural design. Everybody is asked to produce something special out of the same constraints. Celebrity architects have been remarkably resistant to accept accountability, but I believe there is a fantastic opportunity in the opposition between the simultaneous demands for accountability and uniqueness that the celebrity architects have consistently ignored. To explore the space between these two new realities seem to me a much more interesting problem than, say re-ideologizing architectural practice or exploring morphing software.

But the culture of celebrity also generates a certain inertia. There are always the same names being invited for these competitions, because they are the architects that have already acquired that celebrity status, and clients don't know better. Perhaps a fundamental role for somebody to play is to make a bank of good architects that don't yet qualify as celebrities but can deliver a very high profile project under these kinds of conditions. It might open the base a little more. Unfortunately, this new class of agents that I called 'mediators' in a Berlage Institute lecture series defaults too often to celebrity architecture because they also need to nurture their profile as dealers by constructing their own stable of celebrity architects that they can 'get' for clients or planners.

Education after Celebrity
—**AZP:** The other subject that is intimately connected to this discussion is how to teach. First of all, celebrity architecture gravitated from the beginning around academia, as it was one of the most powerful channels of communication and debate, necessary for the model to operate. And in return, the model of academia in the past twenty years was to bring these celebrity architects into the studio, where they would supposedly release knowledge or teach their students how to be stars, and

engage the institutions with the network. I think that doesn't necessarily produce an interesting academy or a compelling didactic environment anymore. And, in fact, in my application to the Berlage Institute Deanship, one of my proposals was not to hire any studio instructors over 35, as it was the most efficient—and economic —way to ensure that teaching was integrally connected to the production —rather than consumption—of knowledge. It was deemed too radical and not accepted, but I still believe it was a good idea. In the current climate, the schools should develop the alternative to celebrity architecture and should produce the most advanced knowledge, rather than importing it in small bits from the same important architects.

Particularly in Anglo-Saxon culture there is a very deep schism between practice (which deals primarily with professional liabilities) and academia (which deals primarily with architectural ideologies). This, which in some instances produces some interesting effects, has become an obstacle to generating a type of knowledge that could explore the gaps between the celebrity culture and the culture of project management. A new model of collaboration between experimental practices and academia needs to be invented. This is one of the things I tried to develop during my tenure at the Berlage: a sort of institution where the primary objective is not to produce people—as in traditional education—but to produce knowledge.

—**JI:** The AA is a good example of a school regarded for producing accomplished, famous architects. Not that the intention was to produce celebrities, but what was it about its environment that yielded people who have built highly accomplished practices today?

—**AZP:** It challenged the corporate model and became the paradigm of the emerging celebrity architect engaged in an international debate of diverse, often contradictory voices. In the 1970s, Alvin Boyarsky designed the system—I suspect because he did not have any money to pay for proper knowledge—not on the grounds that there was a kind of necessary knowledge or discipline that had to be transferred to students—the previous model of technical expertise—but on the grounds that young—and cheap—tutors will develop new models of practice together with the students. The AA was probably one of the first educational models that realized that the corporate model was in retreat, that there was a global process going on, that the problems were fragmenting and would require a higher level of specialization and that branding and communications were going to be important. The AA is an important model and example of people learning to brand and sell themselves by constructing an argument and defending it against attacks from multiple directions. The AA produced so many important tutors because it was a school without the polite academics you often see in American academia, where you have to be politically correct all the time. I have been in AA roundtables where people have literally gotten into physical fights over a project and everybody systematically and cruelly tries to undermine everybody else's position. The meanness of this situation teaches you to be constantly aware of what you are doing and develop skills to defend your work against a crossfire of multidirectional criticism.

Culture vs Project Management
—JI: No one has had a career as accomplished as yours. In your 'Scientific Autobiography' essay you describe the benefits of having witnessed the cultural changes in Madrid in the early 1980s; you were at the GSD, when Michael Hays was formulating an important branch of architectural theory; then you worked at OMA at a crucial period in the evolution of the office prior to its current worldwide celebrity; you were involved with *El Croquis* which as you have said was the most amazing opportunity to conduct industrial espionage by visiting different architects' offices in order to document how they operate; you won the Yokohama terminal competition and started your own office; were appointed to lead the Berlage; and now are involved with the planning of the London Olympics. One myth is that the architect toils for many years before receiving opportunities to realize his or her ambitions, whereas you've been able to achieve so much in just a few years. To update the Scientific Autobiography essay, would you care to reflect upon this current point in your career?
—AZP: Thanks. It does not feel so accomplished from inside. The 'Scientific Autobiography' was a reflection on the specificities of my career, which is obviously constructed to a degree but has been shaped by several personal contingencies, and some luck. A career is a succession of opportunities one exploits or fails to exploit. I am very interested in opportunism. I like to think that what we do as architects is exploit the opportunities of a specific situation, rather than having some sort of a priori program we implement. I often use the metaphor of winemaking to illustrate the business of the architect. Rem's famous quote about 'surfing' is one of the best descriptions of a contemporary way of constructing a career and a project. You must catch the right wave at the right moment.
—JI: Have you ever caught a bad wave or have you ever wiped out on a big wave? That's also part of one's career: wiping out and learning how to surf the next wave with new information.

—**AZP:** I have caught some bad waves but I won't describe them because they involve some well-known names in the business and there is no point in recounting them. Fortunately I withdrew almost immediately. I guess bad waves are the ones that don't take you anywhere. They fizzle so you don't need to register them. I think you need to develop a certain way of scouting the horizon for good waves, and at any given moment you could see the next opportunity. What I learned from being involved in all these different things is that you don't really know what the next step will be or where you will end up. But you have a certain intuition of where the next waves may come from, and you also know when the wave you are in is losing energy, and you need to start scouting for another.

Likewise, as a practice, I have always been wary of daring projects, those where there are lots of things done just in the name of architecture or ideology or exploration. I like projects where you see opportunities being exploited to such degree that it looks as if the project could not be otherwise because it makes so much sense. This may be why I am so interested in accountability.

—**JI:** Numerous 1970s era AA architects have established greater legitimacy for the idea of career ambition with political opportunism and by virtue of their adeptness in the market and within mainstream culture. Opportunism is now an operative vehicle for individuals in the profession. In general, ambition has been considered one-dimensional, a negative trait; the term carries associations of insincerity. If someone is ambitious, the assumption is that they're trying to get ahead at all costs or profit undeservedly at the expense of content or commitment to a disciplinary agenda. As you said earlier, in the end it comes down to doing good work. If one idea of doing good work involves ceaselessly finding new opportunities and using the knowledge of those experiences to create new insights, be it in the form of good texts, buildings, or other products, then isn't ambition an essential quality of the profession?

—**AZP:** The ambitions of the people who came out of the AA in the 1970s were different from the ambitions of our generation who came out of school in the early 1990s. Of course, 1970s-era AA architects have also evolved, seized opportunities presented to them, but their ambitions were much more directly connected to a certain vision or end, a sort of utopia. I do not recall ever having had such utopian or ideological drive and that is perhaps why I was more opportunistic, realistic, and pragmatic. The 'Scientific Autobiography' was an attempt to describe how one develops a certain pseudo-ideological position through the need to be efficient in a sequence of different situations. Deep down, it is a reflection on the relationship between ideology and opportunism, theory and practice. Opportunity is very connected to survival, to a changing environment, to working in the market, academic or professional. When you are operating within a market, which is a loose and ever changing field of agents, you need to develop an ability to take chances. It is not the same as when you operate within a bureaucracy, where agents remain locked by fixed relationships. Ideologies and visions are in principle better suited to operate within bureaucracies and not very efficient in market situations, but there are many interesting variations to this relationship. However, you may turn your ideology into a marketable asset, which is something that the celebrity culture has managed to do effectively. In fact, some of these celebrity architects are invoking utopia as much as the new kids on the block trying to carve out a niche for themselves. And they have very pragmatic reasons to do so: without a public belief in utopia it is difficult to maintain their celebrity status. There are many variations to this dichotomy between market and bureaucracy, opportunism and ideology that you can explore and theorize. How do you operate within a market enslaved by a bureaucracy, like Dubai or China?

There are a number of ingredients that go into the formation of a practice. An office is a culture, exactly like a school. You develop certain protocols, interests and targets that produce consistency among your collaborators. There are people out there who believe that can be synthesized, but the strongest cultures, like the best wines are a contingent combination of factors, distilled by time and trial and error. You can apply techniques to make an organization more efficient, you can artificially enhance it; that is the project manager's business. You can learn a lot by watching other cultures too—that is the *raison d'être* of industrial espionage—but it ultimately comes down to a sort of magic coincidence. In our case it relates very much to our experience at OMA, from where we inherited the combination of cultural ambitions and a degree of professionalism. There is also the same expectation from our collaborators of hard work and ambition, long hours and weekends. Some people believe that is a sort of patriarchal or Oedipal reaction, but I believe that architecture, like any other practice, evolves historically and develops through lineages. I do not really care how you categorize this in psycho-social terms; having a pedigree is a more efficient way of learning and developing practice protocols. Can you grow strong and fast in some other way? Perhaps. That again is the project managers' business. For better or worse, actually often for worse, a practice also develops certain inefficiencies in order to be more efficient in other ways. When the office was smaller and more intimate and the collaborators were younger, this culture of commitment—doing anything to get it done no matter how long we had to stay—was really remarkable, and one has amazing memories of some collaborators in that heroic period. When you enter that process the office becomes much less efficient, because earlier, with three guys you could do anything, and now you need fifteen guys to do what you did before with three. Obviously we need to grow and in this process of replicating yourself, you need to resort to hierarchies, to develop a class of people who refuse to stay late or work over the weekend. This is mind bogglingly inefficient as you can imagine. You enter necessarily into the process of striation, of bureaucratization that kills a lot of potentials. You can apply the most sophisticated organization theories and management techniques, but in this business, if you haven't got a culture, you haven't got a chance. A culture is a much more sophisticated mechanism than a management protocol to set up a certain working morale, a certain way of controlling the projects when you cannot control them directly, because you can not always be there. And our academic lineage, our experience in creating cultures is now becoming effective in this sense. I'm looking for new waves now in this ocean.

On the Hokusai Wave
—**JI:** Knowing when a good wave is going flat seems to be a key issue in your career. It's interesting to observe that you have decided to focus on one thing, and then after a while you pull back to pursue other opportunities. For you, it seems as if it hasn't resulted in an overinvestment in one realm at the expense of another. For some, having relevance within an intellectual discourse is their primary investment at the expense of their practice. And vice versa. Instead, you've been able to flourish intellectually by operating in multiple realms. For example, you contribute to the discipline's intellectual discourse through your professional insights. Hokusai, the wave, is one of the most important of these. You've reintroduced and embraced a word that's been denigrated for so long: iconography. You have given new life to iconography by understanding the opportunity it affords to the positive reception of a project. Yet you've also recognized that it has limited design value. It lends itself to having great influence in the public realm, but that's not to say that your project is exclusively determined by iconography. Do you want to talk about that, because it seems there is a little bit of backpeddling from your interest in iconography, especially in your discussion of the 2012 Olympic project? You defended

it by saying that producing an iconographic form of human musculature was simply necessary, as if it were of little interest as a creative opportunity.

—**AZP:** Thanks again for the compliments. By the way, we stepped out of the London Olympic wave because it was losing energy. Maybe we screwed up there. I am curious to see where it ends because I still wonder whether we should have stayed. If it ends up being an architectural flop, we will have demonstrated that we also know when to step out.

The perceived retreat from iconography subject probably has something to do with some sort of moral background. [Laughs] Intuitively, the whole iconography things was a realization of the fact that—despite having constructed a discourse about practice based on operativity, scientificity, technology, the computer operations and so on—in other situations, an entirely different set of strategies could be implemented almost spontaneously. That's why the moment of the Hokusai wave in that press conference was so crucial, because you have your theoretically constructed, watertight discourse, seeking that kind of academic relevance and suddenly you realize that nobody gives a damn. So, you need to react and make that kind of a leap into the void by daring to entirely discard your theoretical apparatus in a matter of seconds. I like those moments when you must suspend all your beliefs in order to be effective in a very specific situation. I have realized that this was a strategy we used often under the theoretical radar, and the text is an attempt to theorize that phenomenon.

In that sense I am very Kuhnian, or very Rortyan, in the belief that any serious theorization is actually generated by efficiencies, by economies, rather than as a sort of *weltanschauung*. It always happens a posteriori, after the fact. This is probably a trait of opportunism—not trying to envision a comprehensive reality. Theory is mostly a way to explain to myself why certain things happened. For example, I didn't know before moving to the States to study at Harvard that I would end up in Holland, Japan and London. By the time when you reach theorization, the game is over. You need to be scouting for the next wave.

The images here refer to the quotes in the text about celebrity architecture: from H&dM, Norman Foster, Toyo Ito, SANAA, Peter Eisenman, Rafael Moneo, Frank Gehry, Rem Koolhaas, Arata Isozaki, Jean Nouvel and Zaha Hadid.

Material Politics

The texts included within this section are addressed to discuss the question of the political engagement of architecture in particular and material practices in general. The intention behind these texts is to re-empower the discipline of architecture by capitalizing on the current devaluation of political discourse and the raise of new political forms associated to physical structures and material organizations. These texts originate fundamentally during my tenure as Dean of the Berlage Institute, which was focused in finding a public and transformative role for the practice of architecture. The texts cover different attempts for architecture to engage effectively with different regimes of power.

Toward an Ecology for a High Metabolic Rate

The subject of ecology has become today one of the most widely shared concerns, cutting across classes, cultures, and ideologies without exception. There is no political party or group for whom the ecological question is not one of the campaign priorities. The ecological has already become an important area of consensus. But even if it is difficult not to share this concern about the environment, we cannot avoid being wary about the way in which ecological arguments are also used demagogically to justify the most conservative approaches toward the built environment, in a manner similar to how the preservation of the historical city was also an argument of general consensus that became ultimately a paralyzing force in many European cities once it became instrumentalized by politicians and sold massively as a popular taste. As a subject related to the production of the environment, these are very powerful arguments whose instrumentalization is likely to also produce very negative consequences, especially when approached as a matter of preservation rather than as an issue for continuous development. Both the preservation of the historical city and the preservation of ecological resources have a very dangerous similarity: both refer to a past system—the city or "nature"—that is often presented as finished and perfect, and suited only for conservation. These types of approaches are readily understandable to the public, as they are presented as certain and static pictures; and they tend to produce sclerosis rather than progress. As architects, we cannot remain marginal to these discussions, as the approach to the problem may lead into the most conservative forms of the built environment, or to the most progressive ones.

A very strong myth to be dismantled in respect to the emerging ecological ideologies is the conception of *nature* as opposed to *artifice*. We should start to develop an approach where we understand that both are interdependent: nature is intrinsically dependent on artifice from the very moment in which we are able to state the opposition; nature cannot exist without the presence of man. In the same way that the human body is not independent of the processes of its cultural construction, ecological systems are also culturally mediated products varying across history and geography—time and space—through continuous human modification. Nature is only conceivable within the context of humanity, not as an idyllic origin to be preserved, but as a milieu to be improved, enhanced, and constructed in parallel to our own construction, as a part of the assemblage of matters and processes that constitutes the built environment: nature as neither determining nor passive, but enabling. Any attempt to politically or scientifically argue for a particular, static conception of nature will ultimately become the argument for an utterly conservative approach to the production of the environment. While most arguments *for* nature propose not a static but a dynamic natural world, it is nonetheless important to note that all are essentially conservative arguments (including radical environmentalist arguments) when they are predicated on a divide that simply does not exist or hasn't existed since humans began to alter and attempt to control nature.

Ecology is part of an emerging global and holistic consciousness that understands that the processes that determine and regulate our environment are closely tangled up with human agency. Instead of denying this or resorting to a nativist phenomenology of pure givenness, one given in turn to embracing an incommensurate *somethingness* beyond all human activity, we should capitulate to reason and develop instruments of a more finely calibrated sensitivity and for a more far-reaching form of human perception capable of seeing past the incommensurate to the legibility of integrated systems. It is not enough to protect our forests, if our wood is obtained through deforestation of other countries; is not enough to protect ourselves from nuclear waste by dumping it in somebody else's backyard. Ecology has demonstrated that ecological processes are only instantaneously local, but finally will have a global effect: global warming or the deterioration of the ozone layer are problems as serious and consequential to local communities as the oscillations of the international stock market or the fierce competition between world cities. An increasing consciousness of buildings or cities not as independent but as interdependent entities with a much larger system of social, political, and cultural relations is probably one of the most distinctive characteristics of contemporary urban and architectural theory. In this sense, ecology may become an adequate model to approach the construction of the environment, which has traditionally been treated as a very local industry. The concept of an environment as a system of interacting entities within a certain regime, whose equilibrium is dependent on the presence of each one of its elements, is an interesting idea for an urban system. However, the notion of equilibrium is one of the myths of the most banal versions of ecological ideology. The condition of equilibrium is never a permanent condition in ecosystems, but rather a shifting condition that goes through periods of relative stability. Changes in natural ecosystems occur constantly, but at a much slower rate than in artificial ecosystems. The idea of the ecosystem as a finished and perfect system in eternal equilibrium is as dubious as any of the urban or political utopias visited and revisited over the entire trajectory of modernity.

Something we could also learn from ecosystems is precisely that entities have only a certain duration. Buildings could perhaps not be "permanences," but moments of stability within the process of construction of the built environment. In this sense, the Western city has a lot to learn from the Eastern city, traditionally a more ephemeral entity. One of the arguments to increase the osmosis between nature and the artificial is to understand architecture as an element of the ecosystem, rather than as a "sign" written on a tamed nature. Architecture is not forever; it has a limited duration, and can eventually dissolve. The idea of the built environment as a metabolic process of continuous transformation of matter and energy—an idea that also has a very strong Asian tradition—is a very exciting "ecological" alternative to the type of "preservative" strategies with which the question of the built environment has been addressed in Europe. In this sense, the incorporation of alternative energies into buildings is certainly an interesting approach, as it moves away from the idea of the building as a limited, local entity, and turns the building into a device that interacts with flows that move beyond its limits: sun, wind, water become suddenly the flows that the building relates to. Instead of operating as virtual internal-combustion engines or purely localized systems, ecological buildings will have to find their "engines" in the flows that cross their domains.

In this sense, the emerging industries of recycling are developing further the possibility of a healthy metabolism of the built environment, by producing the anabolic sector of the cycle. Glass, concrete, aluminum, steel, plastic, etc. are now recyclable materials producing economic and attractive alternatives to "original" or "virgin" materials. There are no longer strong reasons to maintain that new construction and artificial materials are anti-ecological, or that there are economic arguments behind the preservation of the built environment as it is. It is not difficult to imagine a moment in which cities could be understood as organisms in perpetual change, where matter is constantly reorganized to suit changing needs. This idea of an ecologically constructed environment, rather than the dubious enforcement of preservation strategies to conserve resources, both for the city and for its natural support, counters a de facto system of stagnation and accretion which is unsustainable in its own right when weighed against the march of time. An ecological architecture that does not approach either the city or nature as localized, fixed entities, but as interactive processes held in tension in a dynamic state is a new dynamic ecology for a *high metabolic rate*. This high metabolic rate is the acceleration of the interactive matrix of architecture and nature, of human activity and natural systems. As it has often been in the past, this interactive matrix has the potential again to be productive of enormous outputs without exhausting the system. It is all a matter of recalibrating the urban systems that draw most heavily on the planet as a whole, and recalibrating the human systems that overwhelm those half-natural, half-artificial agglomerations we call cities.

In a very direct illustration of the content, the images framing this text aim to illustrate contemporary urban structures with a high metabolic rate, such as Hong Kong and Benidorm.

Published as the introduction to the
Disciplines issue of *Hunch* n. 9, Rotterdam,
2005

Disciplines

The collapse of the modernist paradigm at the end of the 1960s triggered a crisis for those disciplines like architecture, which had been trying, during the first half of the twentieth century, to accommodate the requirements of an emerging modern world order. The confidence in the new technologies that drove experimentation across many disciplines came to a halt. Mass production of typologies, zoning laws and generic urbanization became subject to widespread criticism as they failed to produce successful urban environments: the corporate and technocratic models of building design seemed to be unable to engage with issues of difference or identity, emerging as a crucialpart of the new phenomenology of modernization. In the case of architecture and urbanism, this crisis of modern disciplines brought about two different approaches that have lasted until recently: one that claimed the immediate dissolution of the discipline into a broader field ranging from sociological analysis to cultural theory. They sought refuge in older forms of the discipline, to escape from the chaos produced by rapid changes in modes of production and economic, social, and political integration. One solution exited the discipline altogether and dissolved in the outside world; the other remained enclosed within well-established forms of the discipline and forgot about the old modernist ambition of tracking reality.

With the emergence of information technology, the literal transfer of data into organization, and the cross-breeding of disciplinary fields has become easier than ever, producing the illusion that it is actually possible to operate across disciplines effectively. In the field of practice, this increasing ease of shifting across disciplines has created a new class of operators able to assess the process of designing and making buildings in the same way as providing supplies to a supermarket, delivering a road project, or handling a marketing campaign. But these increased technical capacities have generally failed to deliver innovative architecture. Such technologies have been used ad hoc, in a purely instrumental capacity rather than been problematized or driven towards any form of structured knowledge.

Advanced architectural research has shifted its focus in recent years towards philosophy, sociology, psychology, cinema, literature, and cultural studies, aiming to establish validation criteria. The most interesting architectural experimentation has gravitated towards broadening an excessively hardened discipline to include a variety of external concerns necessary to actualize its operative capacities to ever-changing demands. Sustainability, politics, economy, and other fields external to the conventional disciplines of material practice have often become fields of reference for architecture and urban design. However productive these processes have been in terms of broadening architectural knowledge, they have not succeeded in defining a system of assessment internal to the discipline, to recreate a new ground for architecture itself, or to explain in what way the inclusion of those concerns has advanced the architectural qualities of the products. Often, this has resulted in some of the most advanced research in architecture ending up in bad movies, bad sociology, or bad literature.

Within the current socio-economic structures of global capitalism, a unilateral politics of resistance seems no longer able to challenge contemporary forms of consolidated power. The challenge to instituted power can only be selective, and the division of political labor has to be addressed by multiple disciplines operating independently and simultaneously and not necessarily in a multidisciplinary relation. A contemporary politicization of architecture needs to relocate politics within specific disciplinary domains, not as a representation of an ideal concept of the political, but as a political effect specific to the discipline. For the discipline to acquire transformative agency it is necessary to engage in a political critique of its technologies.

I have the optimistic belief—in a rather Kuhnian fashion—that it is at moments like the current one when disciplines can make their most important advances. Progress can only be measured and experienced with respect to some reference system, and therefore it is difficult to move forward in a void of references. Even if triggered by external factors, the intensity that characterizes excellence in any field usually occurs within the framed, focused domains of a discipline, however transient and ephemeral its consistency may be. I am still of the belief that the modernist project of tracking reality through the discipline is not only possible but also effective, as disciplines are still the repositories of valuable experience and knowledge.

Surely there are transfers and mutations and hybrid conditions. But perhaps the most powerful relationship across disciplines is reality itself, and the potential links across disciplines can be better explained as phenomena of resonance rather than of translation or coupling. Ultimately, better practices usually emerge out of the slightly brutal action of disciplining reality, reducing problems to vaguely closed domains where we can study an action and its consequences, where we can repeat a movement until it becomes first an automatic reflex and then transcends itself. Rather than attempting an all-encompassing, strategic, holistic perspective aimed at structuring reality at once, we are here interested in offering an alternative perception of multiple domains of expertise, which draw links to the outside while preserving the consistency of disciplinary knowledge. As in distributed computing, it is the co-evolution and optimization of relationships between multiple routines, mediated through the mainframe, which is able to produce real innovation, rather than the heaviness of a centrally organized system that tries to articulate everything at once.

Disciplines need to remain adjacent to exploit their resonances, rather than their articulation. We need to register their tendencies, their convergence and bifurcation, as if we were witnessing a geological process rather than a process of translation across them.

The images along this text depict a few moments where the mere discipline of making buildings seems to have gone mad, a sort of disciplined madness or perhaps a maddening discipline.

Published as the introduction to the Rethinking Representation issue of *Hunch* n. 11, Rotterdam, 2007

Rethinking Representation

The symptoms of unrest started to appear around the end of 2002: among the Berlage Institute's population this took the form of discernible boredom with the usual subjects of debate, and a quest for more meaningful, ideological, and substantial endeavors in architecture. Soon after, it became clear that the malaise was not exclusive and that it was spreading everywhere, in some form of architectural fundamentalism, either disciplinary or political, and sometimes a combination of both. It was first noticeable among the younger generations, suddenly claiming ideals, resistance, vision, or meaning as an alternative to the reduction of everything to an exchangeable commodity or a parameter. Then, an array of old expressionists joined the chorus, possibly as a defence against the ruthless opportunism and technical proficiency of the next generation. Utopianism, generally abandoned after the '60s, was getting a second lease on life, brought back by a variety of agents of disparate origin. In the post-9/11 age, *realpolitik* was no longer cool.

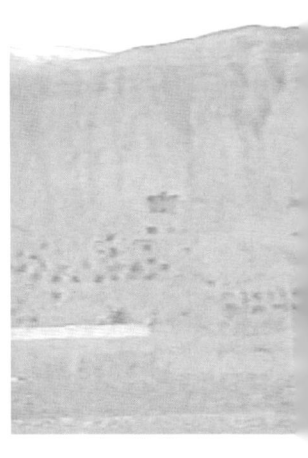

Once again, representation became a legitimate architectural enterprise that would eventually free us from the insidious, all-pervading, and inexorable dictates of the global market. Ever-shorter cycles of lurching between forms of accommodation and forms of resistance seemed to portend the blending of the two.

For nearly two decades, the architectural debate had been moving away from the subject of representation (for example: politics, meaning, identity and language) toward those of organization, production, and technique as primary means for the production of architectural form. The flow of informational tools into design practices and the potentials of unprecedented developments in construction and material technologies shifted architectural research into quantitative analysis and empirical abstraction—to some, a new determinism. Diagrams, parametric design, datascapes, and computer-aided manufacturing were the new areas where a "non-standard architecture" was to be found, deliberately avoiding any concerns about representation. The coupling of the neo-liberal consensus and the ongoing techno-corporate globalization processes with the newly available information technologies produced a kind of naturalization of architecture and urbanism, which promised a blissful end of history and conflict. Ecologies—processes of material organization, transformation, and exchange unmediated by representation—became the models of operation, and exact sciences the models of description, communication, and knowledge. In this view, irresolvable issues of representation could be entirely bypassed by the literal or the material.

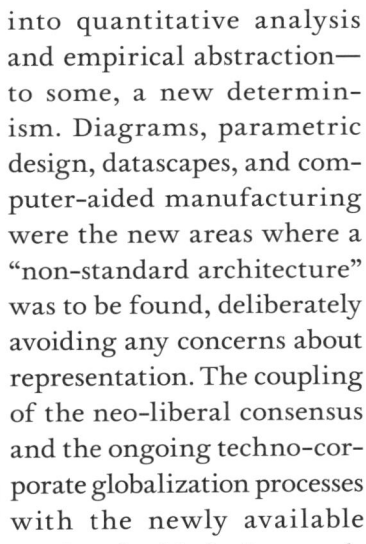

But the events of 9/11 and the subsequent war on terror have put into question the capacity of global models to deliver the seamless integration of cultures and the avoidance of conflict through the establishment of an automatic ecology of universal consensus in which conflicting ideals had been replaced by numbers, and values by dollars. The resulting political debate shifted toward the discussion on the public display of religious beliefs, the questioning of the theory of evolution, revanchist forms of empire, the collapse of the multicultural society, and such other subjects that focused primarily on matters of belief, ideology, and cultural tradition, all held in demented tension in the whipsaw of newly calibrated "culture wars." The carefree approach to globalization was no longer sufficient in the post-9/11 world, and the systems of representation were coming back as a nasty monkey wrench tossed into the well-oiled machinery of globalization. Those having abandoned representation in the seemingly conflict-free new world of the new millennium (often formulated as post-historical or post-cultural by both detractors and adherents) found themselves caught out by the sudden turn of politics—and even markets—towards representation.

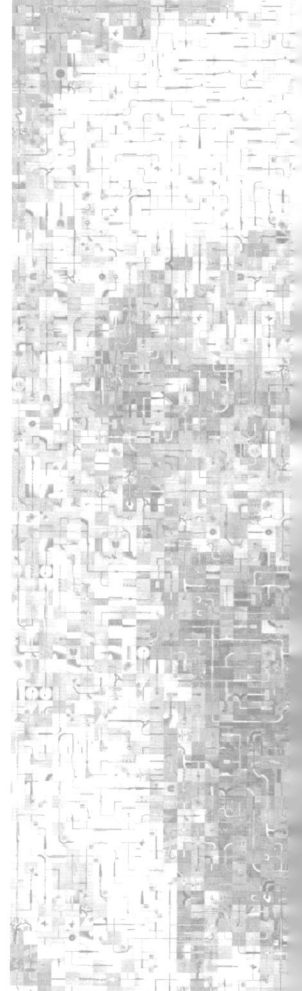

In this new age of global capitalism, a revision of ideology and politics toward a society of endless spectacle and endless consumption had become *de rigueur*. With the reaction, a reaction *against the reaction* followed: on both sides of the cultural divide *facts* now had to be replaced by *concerns* to account for the failure of the techno-corporate machinery to properly describe and organize the world. On the one hand, bible-wielding creationists used this new relativist moment to denounce the theory of evolution, as if meaninglessness permitted the formulation of purely fabricated histories, especially reworked denials of the progressive insights of rationalist thought—both history and science. Once there are "no facts", anybody can put forward anything as a legitimate *concern*. On the opposite side of the spectrum, those who had willingly sipped or swigged the Kool-Aid of neo-liberal capitalism switched sides or returned to the fence and began to question the merits of turning everything (including architecture) into something to be bought and sold. The shift, leftward and rightward, occurred in almost all fields concerned with the quality of life or the future of civilization. The invitation to return to the banqueting table, in turn, led to competing tables, and the descent into new ideological battles ensued.

There has been a curious disciplinary background to these revolts. This is very much a social sciences/liberal arts revolution, claiming human sciences, politics, and the arts as an alternative to exact sciences and technology as the necessary basis to construct any form of knowledge: if globalization theorists in architecture cannibalized the vocabulary of the military, the organization theorists and the CIA, the new advocates of representation are overtly revisiting the language of cultural theory and political revolution, making manifestos of "militant" and "activist" architecture and devising strategies of "resistance," "dissent," "conflict," and "destabilization." This new strain of representational hubris is no longer the polite, academic, playful, and largely contingent games of '80s late-postmodernism and the sexiness of free-floating signifiers. This new revolt could be characterized across disciplines as a new concern for deeply embedded meaning, "substance" versus "surface," discrete historical consciousness versus vaporous post-historical relativism, political alignment and engagement versus "third wave" transmogrification of economics as politics, disciplinary purity as opposed to promiscuous crosspollination via cultural or visual studies, and, sometimes, religious and/or moral valuation in the face of creeping economic determinism, this latter manifestation of strife playing out on both the Left and the Right insofar as new utopian, anti-capitalist agendas might be called moral agendas.

Wedged between the Bible-wielding creationists, the Talibans of architecture, and the new utopians building up their crusades based on history, religion, and/or political ideology, some of us went into a sort of soul-searching process in order to address representation and power as the new concerns looming large on the horizon of practice. In this new phase of global capitalism, as we inevitably reengage with the critique of power and new-found, potential forms of transformation, representation becomes a crucial subject to address, however difficult it is to find worthwhile content—or means—for leveraging its *ahistorical* agency. Not being able to actually find much *meaningful* content (utopian or otherwise), we were mostly left with techniques borrowed from branding specialists and political spin doctors: logo-building, focus groups, market segments, etc.; that is, the most ready-to-hand and effective technologies we could find in our agnostic arsenal, while keeping things moving, were a sort of cynical rereading of representation. Or, rather, an approach to representation as a series of techniques to effectively construct meaning without the need for much concern as to what was being re-branded. Behind this smokescreen of blasé consumerism, of course, is the entire late-capitalist machinery circling that last frontier of human subjectivity (free will). Here, then, is the true nature of the revolt underway Left and Right. Both sense "The End" approaching, and both want to seriously muck up the works if that is the only way out. In Europe these revisions of temporal failure have taken a more populist character, engaging with local idiosyncrasies and playing out in reborn regional politics while seeking "revolution" through a new tectonics. In America, where culture has a stronger tradition of the synthetic, recent architectural investigations have generated a particular strain of preempted representation based purely on branding technology.

It is evident that we need to return to the table to discuss the subject of representation as part of a new stage of global capitalism and the different approaches it has generated within the architectural field since 9/11 in order to identify those approaches that are not likely to send us a century back, or even worse, to the Middle Ages.

And after that, I do hope that we can put the subject to rest, so that we can go back to that beautiful pre-9/11 utopia in which everybody from everywhere glides effortlessly across the world, and where architects no longer need to represent anything whatsoever. But I am afraid that is just the dream of an unreconstructed globalization fundamentalist.

The images illustrating this text depict different moments where an iconography has been attacked, such as the Bamilan Buddhas or 9/11, the passions behind Benazir Bhutto and Osama Bin Laden's imagery, to conclude with the total ambiguity of the Pet Rock.

Published as the introduction to the Mediators issue of *Hunch* n. 10, Rotterdam, 2006

Mediators

Architects are famously unable to communicate or even to explain themselves. We are, of course, not talking here of architecture as a mere service profession. Beyond providing refuge from nature and basic structure for human life and activity, architecture can also stage and structure social protocols, articulate both collective and individual worlds, public and private spheres, and represent or formulate institutional and political power. The stereotype of the architect as described in past and present-day media, but also subliminally promoted in schools, is a bizarre amalgam of myopia, authoritarianism, and arrogance, driven by a burning desire to impose his/her visions and obsessions come hell or high water. To become a relevant, if not successful architect, then, one has to nurture incipient megalomania, look down on reality with utter disdain for anything that might preexist or stand in the way of "the vision," and walk around in a state of permanent dissatisfaction with the status quo. Architects are thought to be by nature ill-equipped to listen to the public, when, in fact, they are constitutionally unable to hear any voices other than those inside their own heads. This proceeds from school, as most architects are not born from the head of Zeus but have, instead, to be indoctrinated to become demigods. Tone deaf? Perhaps... But the real crime is that architectural high-handedness is one of the chief reasons for the endless marginalization of the profession by those not impressed by the god-like act, and those not impressed comprise the lion's share of possible clients or possible adherents to the profession.

The reality for most of the profession has been much less than ideal, and the amount of architecture that is allowed to be "critical" or "heroic" is actually very small. Most of the time, the role of the architect is to implement the instructions of people with sufficient power to transform physical space to better suit their preconceived purpose. Developers, politicians, and regulatory bodies hold the real power to define the built environment, and practicing architects are mere accomplices in their ventures. As the power to modify the built environment has become increasingly affordable and available to an ever-larger number of social agents, architects have become enablers rather than visionaries, subject to others' visions and decisions. In the developed and democratic world, construction, once an expensive and sophisticated technology, is now available to an ever-growing population of agents, and this has radically altered the traditional relationship between the commissioning agent and the architect. On the one hand, the architect has been removed from responsibilities that have been transferred to regulations or supervisory bodies. These regulatory and supervising bodies ensure that the deployment of construction technologies does not detract from the public good. And this does not stop at ensuring structural integrity, accessibility, and environmental performance, but extends to the preservation of cultural heritage, and even the assessment of the aesthetic value of an architectural product. In many instances, the aesthetic police are the former planning bodies stripped of any real impact on cities after the catastrophe of mid-century urban renewal. In the devolution of central planning authority, the capacity to implement architectural policies, both by the institutional powers or the architects themselves, has been transferred to market agents that operate effectively within the existing legal framework but usually devoid of any identifiable architectural agenda. This mode of production has effectively neutralized the capacity to implement progressive architectural agendas, both from the architects and the commissioners. The productive relationship between Michelangelo and Lorenzo de' Medici, Jawaharlal Nehru and Le Corbusier, or Oscar Niemeyer and Juscelino Kubitschek is now reduced to very small portions of the market as the construction of the environment is decided generally by faceless corporations and implemented by faceless consultants in a neutral, risk-averse, and heavily regulated legal framework.

However, as democratic governance, technological advances, and market forces are increasingly eliminating the possibility of a truly original, if not progressive architectural program, both from the architects and from their commissioners, the opportunities to direct the built environment are reemerging in a growing intermediate domain to which we are dedicating this publication—that is, the resulting new population of productive agents or mediators, a phenomenon that begs elucidation and analysis.

This new breed of agents is a result of the democratization of the decision-making processes in the built environment. As construction technology becomes affordable for increasing sectors of the population, governmental bodies are forced to regulate exponentially the construction activities. But those bodies have also become interested in utilizing building for political goals. Within the all-pervading capitalist-democratic system, brokering the deals between political powers and the construction industry has reached substantial levels of complexity that require specialists as an interface with the ever-growing number of stakeholders in the process. As the construction industry becomes more complex and sophisticated, both technically and politically, the articulation of the commissioners, the public, and the architect has become such a complex domain that a new breed of operators has emerged in the industry as a specific and effective practice; a new domain where far-reaching effects might be achieved given the right mix of checks and balances.

It is increasingly common for commissions today to include a composite of clients, often mixed public-private organizations, with no clear architectural program but full of architectural expectations. The increasing demand for change in contemporary cities has reduced substantially the strategic capacity of those enabled with commissioning powers, be it elected politicians or company CEOs, and rendered architectural utopias totally dysfunctional as vehicles of effective transformation.

What is relevant about mediators is that, in the best cases, they cannot afford to be entirely subservient to the status quo, usually represented by the client, nor to the utopian drive, usually represented by the architect; they need to move in-between both. Mediators need to develop a certain program and count on a stable of architects, often *involuntary co-creators* of the mediator's vision, merely in charge of implementation. At the same time, the mediators program needs to be understandable to those empowered to make decisions, and is therefore contaminated, bastardized, streetwise, and definitely anti-utopian.

Mediators are, as a result, the missing link between an ever-growing, architecture-consuming public, the commissioning clientele and the architects' generally hermetic collective. Mediators are often architects themselves, but they have developed specialized listening skills; their antennae enable them to interpret what individuals, organizations, or entire populations need or think they need, and to translate those needs into guidelines for architects. They often perform as matchmakers between a particular client or problem and a particular architect, suitable to servicing the client's desire.

Mediators also help the public understand what services architects offer, how crucial architecture or *architectural desire* is and how it might become an added value. They operate as opinion-makers through a variety of means and media, and often with a greater influence on the built environment than either politicians or architects. But, although they are generally well informed in the art of mediating desire, their opinion is hardly neutral. It is obvious that they have a vested interest in the outcome of their matchmaking (sometimes to a voyeuristic extent): their assigned role in the economy of distributing architectural pleasure or pain, broadly or narrowly defined, requires them to be truly *passionate* about architecture and to act often as a collector of architects, whom they then coach and promote. They usually have their stable, which they deploy when necessary, strategically, and push forward in competitive circumstances. These often require a premium in return, as they are often the sexiest of the lot. Yet, all things considered, it is usually better to have a mediator in charge of delivering architectural services than a bunch of bureaucrats going by the book with absolute neutrality but no architectural program.

One of the interesting sides of the "mediator phenomenon" is that it does have global reach. And as other global processes, it has evolved local varieties, dependent on the various cultural traditions. The European climate has proven the most favorable for the evolution of this species, probably because of the appetite of the public sector for architectural pleasures, a consolidated urban tradition given to high-end dalliances, and possibly a historically enlightened public that finds it all truly exciting to behold. European mediators come with a pedigree of one kind or another and are often grown from the ranks of critics, journalists, and academics. One proof of the remaining importance of ideology and publicness in the European city is that one of the most fertile milieus for mediators has been architectural magazines and cultural institutes. One could distinguish Jean-Louis Cohen during his period as director of IFA, Josep Lluís Mateo as director of *Quaderns*, Vittorio Magnano Lampugnani at the helm of *Domus*, Hans van Dijk at *Archis*, and Ricky Burdett and the Architectural Foundation as characters who were able to develop a particular take on architecture and in certain cases assemble a consistent group of architects they coached and promoted through their magazines and in their roles as jurors and advisors to public administrations and other commissioning bodies. Others emerged from the broadsheets, such as Luis Fernández-Galiano and Deyan Sudjic, at *El País* and *The Observer* respectively, where they have been instrumental in creating broader public awareness and to promote certain approaches to architecture. A slightly different breed of mediators, more directly engaged with governmental power, in Europe has emerged from the public service. The cases of Josep Antoni Acebillo in Barcelona, Hans Stimmann in Berlin, and Maarten Schmitt in Groningen are example of non-elected technocrats who have succeeded to implement incredibly ambitious programs of urban regeneration, previously reserved only to elected politicians or developers—and, most importantly, loaded with the strongest kind of architectural ideology rather than with neutral technocratic strategies.

In the USA, the climate has been generally less fertile yet there are a few figures that have managed to steer meager public funds into new architecture while also eventually currying favor with major patrons. In America, the new breed of mediators is generally less powerful than in Europe, as the public dimension of architecture is still less developed than in Europe, having actually regressed over the past forty years. There is no public sector entity capable of steering productive capacity away from private or public-private development, which has also lost most of the visionary power of the likes of Portman and Hines. One of the first specimens of the North American species in this regard, insofar as private money has been channeled toward public measures, is Phyllis

Lambert, where, for biographical reasons, the client and the ideologue reside *in the same person*. As is well known, Lambert started her career quite literally as the client in the construction of the Seagram building, in New York, and evolved into the quintessential philanthropist as founder of the Canadian Centre for Architecture, in Montreal. American mediators are less ideological than their European counterparts and usually ground their operation either in a cultural or academic institution or in the press, as professional debate does not seem to have any credibility amongst local commissioning powers. Mediation in the US has more often taken the form of directly lobbying power rather than a public campaign aimed at influencing power. The most powerful mediators in the USA are by far those connected to the media, and the only mass media in America with an interest in architecture seems to be the *New York Times*. Both Paul Goldberger and Herbert Muschamp have been important forces in lobbying for certain architects and certain commissions, but much less effective than their European counterparts at producing trends or ideological positions, probably because of a lack of ideological consistency in their critique.

Operating on a different level of influence, Terence Riley (during his curatorship of architecture and design at the Museum of Modern Art in New York), Mark Robbins (the first curator of architecture at the Wexner Center for the Arts in Columbus, OH), Aaron Betsky (curator of architecture, design, and digital projects at San Francisco Museum of Modern Art and now, interestingly, director of the Netherlands Architecture Institute), and Joe Rosa (formerly at Heinz Architectural Center at the Carnegie Museum of Art in Pittsburgh, and now at San Francisco Museum of Modern Art), are the closest American versions of local mediators—albeit with *mild* ideological baggage and the support of powerful institutions with the expressed agenda of setting the standard for the public consumption of architecture and design. In spite of this powerful accretion of influence peddling through exhibitions and publications, they all are nonetheless rather disengaged from the real powers that shape American cities.

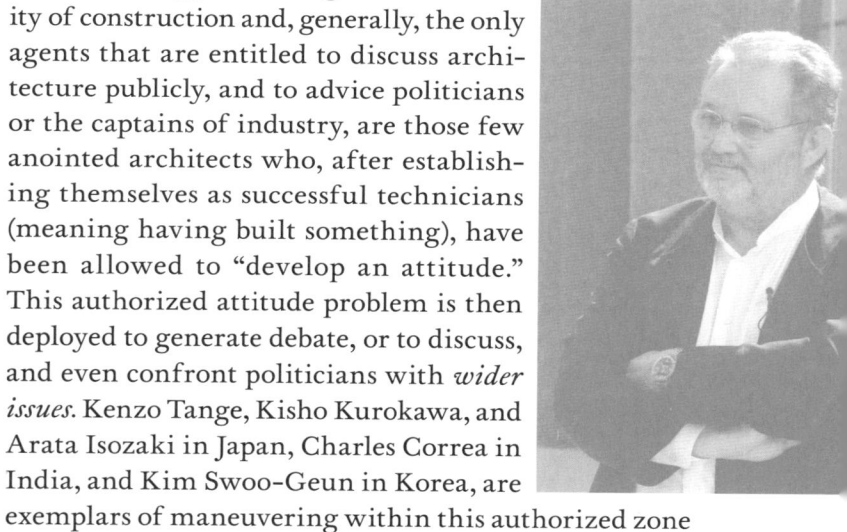

Asia is the area where the disengagement between public architectural culture and the decision makers of the built environment is most acute, and where architectural theory and debate is all but absent. This is due to a strong local tradition that connects the architect directly with the builder rather than considering the architect an intellectual/artist, to some extent disengaged from the construction business, and, therefore deprived of a "critical" distance. In Asia, mediation happens through the materiality of construction and, generally, the only agents that are entitled to discuss architecture publicly, and to advice politicians or the captains of industry, are those few anointed architects who, after establishing themselves as successful technicians (meaning having built something), have been allowed to "develop an attitude." This authorized attitude problem is then deployed to generate debate, or to discuss, and even confront politicians with *wider issues*. Kenzo Tange, Kisho Kurokawa, and Arata Isozaki in Japan, Charles Correa in India, and Kim Swoo-Geun in Korea, are exemplars of maneuvering within this authorized zone for architectural criticism in Asia. I must admit that except for Japan and Korea, my knowledge of the ground is limited and I may be missing important data. But I am certain that the most advanced place in terms of mediation is Japan. During the years of the "bubble economy," a local specimen called the producer, who was usually grown out of the publishing sector and managed to control the excess of resources liberated by the system into sophisticated construction programs for the more progressive clients. Shozo Baba, the former director of Shinkenchiku, and Fram Kitagawa from the Art Front Gallery in Tokyo, are probably the best examples of this breed in Japan. One of the skills of the Japanese mediators was to be able to communicate with the "outside world," as a large percentage of the "experimental" commissions of the time were given to foreign architects and mediators were usually the only ones in the industry able to communicate with them. After the bubble economy burst, the "producers" lost ground, as public projects virtually disappeared and private investors seemed to have no interest and/or no resources to devote to experimentation. The next generation of Asian mediators will probably appear in Korea or China where there seems to be sufficient excess resources to sustain this form of operation and an increasing awareness of the value of architecture.

Despite the growing importance and scale of the construction sector in the world economy, architecture's mediators have not yet been recognized as specific agents in the building industry. Nobody has offered them a platform from which to explain to either the public or the profession their opinions, programs, ambitions, and tribulations, *as a collective*. In fact, since mediators are the ones who call the shots, either openly or secretly, nobody has been able to question them publicly for fear of alienating them. To identify and theorize the practice of architectural mediation seems to be an important task to address if we want to understand how decisions are made in the contemporary built environment.

The images illustrating this text are photographs of some of the most well known agents operating in between the practice of architecture and urbanism and media, politics, academia and the culture industry: Josep Anton Acebillo, Ricky Burdett, Paul Goldberger, Luis Fernandez Galiano, Phyllis Lambert, Herbert Muschamp, Hans Stimmann and Deyan Sudjic.

This letter was sent to the participants in the
Local Smart lecture series at the Berlage Institute
Rotterdam, October 2005

Local Smart

Dear X,

During the Spring Term of 2006 we are planning to host a lecture series at the Berlage Institute, and we believe that you will be an excellent contributor to the debate we are aiming to trigger with it. The series will seek to theorize and debate local practice in relation to the larger, global tendencies. We believe that your practice is illustrative of this type of agency, and your involvement in the international debate will enable you to present the local practices in which you are currently engaged in the global forum that we will try to form with these events.

    The ever-expanding process of globalization has been pushing its limits further and further away from its traditional epicenters, constantly shifting the focus of investment to new regions. The emerging markets in China and India, Eastern Europe, and some regions of the Middle East and Central America are now the new engines of a process that is simultaneously creating frictions with potential global effects, as 9/11 has shown. Some of the most important issues in contemporary politics, cultural processes, and urban and architectural practices emerge from those frictions between global protocols and local structures.

One of the most immediate effects of globalization is the radical transformation of these once peripheral domains' physical structure, to make them viable for their integration within the global systems. New highways, airports, stations, corporate hotels, and convention centres are part of the necessary infrastructure for a territory to be embraced by the global order. Once these basic infrastructures are completed, urban regulations, parks, museums, etc. have to be deployed to demonstrate further compliance with democratic and international standards.

Architects of different sorts get involved in this process in multiple ways. The typical process is structured in three phases, where different types of architects become engaged with various forms of overlap between them. First to be called in are the corporate bulldozers, to clean up the place and erase the physical remnants of previous urban cultures that may represent obstructions to the global processes to be set free. Phase two arrives, then, once some basic infrastructure is in place. What do you do as a local politician to demonstrate that your city is ripe for multi-national re-capitalization? You call in some international, celebrity architects to demonstrate your concern with quality and sophistication. Moreover, if a *starchitect* can work somewhere, anybody can, and the place is ripe for foreign investment. The third phase is generally driven by a group of relatively young architects, sometimes local, and usually educated abroad while the future of the homeland was being sorted out. This group is usually exquisitely educated and operates within an extensive international network of equally well-educated colleagues. They are fully engaged with the latest contemporary debates and intellectual fashions, armed with the latest and sleekest technologies, and feel at home in the metropolis—sometimes more at home than in their city of origin. Mohammed Atta belonged to this kind of international cadre before deciding to crash a hijacked jetliner into the World Trade Center in New York instead of returning to Cairo to practice urban planning. Salam Pax, the *Baghdad Blogger*, does too.

As part of this research on the forces and stresses that shape the contemporary city, and as a way of creating an alternative perspective to the one usually being broadcast by the leading international institutions and architects, we have selected a series of cities, in different stages of globalization, to explore these issues. We have identified agents like yourself—mostly architects—directly engaged in these processes of physical transformation but simultaneously engaged in the international debate via academic practice, exhibitions, journalism, or simply professional networking. People like yourself are a paradigmatic impersonation of these tensions between global and local processes, and we are asking you to contribute in this capacity, as a speaker for one of these developing cities. This will be a lecture series for a series of cities to speak up about how they are being physically transformed by globalization and the frictions this has produced with existing structures. We are asking you not to explain your work by itself but as an index of what is happening in the environment where you practice, to describe the ongoing urban processes, the specificity of local tactics, your engagement with transnational organizations, both private and governmental, and with local politics, as well as your overlap with starchitects and corporate behemoths. A personal, almost biographical tone will be adequate to explain the specificities of current developments in your city, its urban potential, the tactics necessary to operate in it, and a record of some experiments or happenings. Hopefully this perspective will help us construct a more accurate picture of the wild variations of the contemporary global city.

Best Regards,
Alejandro Zaera-Polo
Dean of the Berlage Institute

The two pictures included in this text correspond to two architects who represent the conflicts of the global world in its maximum intensity. Mohammed Atta, an Egyptian urban designer educated in Germany who hated skyscrapers and became the mastermind of 9/11; and Salam Abdulmunem, an architect from Irak educated in Jordan, alias *Salam Pax* or the Baghdad blogger, who reported from everyday life in Baghdad during the Western invasion of Irak, evading the security services for several months. The conflicts of a generation (Generation X) torn between globalization and the political realities in developing economies are at the centre of this subject.

Published in *Power: Producing the Contemporary City*, Berlage Institute, Rotterdam, 2007

Architecture and Power

Architecture has always had a peculiar relationship with power. Among all the arts, architecture is the most power-intensive artistic discipline and, arguably, the one that is able to dictate behaviour and routine most forcefully. Architecture can hardly be exercised without complicity with power, and yet its best examples orchestrate new realities, therefore defying the status quo. In this characteristic conundrum, architects are charged with harnessing the powers of building technology, but also to challenge them, to stage social rituals, organize the processes of production, represent the community or local institutions, and yet to set the stage for their transformation.

The relations between building and politics are well documented, although not always very transparent. Due to its size and complexity, the construction sector is probably the most susceptible to pork-barrel politics and kickbacks. Construction programs are one of the most effective devices to kick-start a stalled economy, mitigate joblessness, and attract votes from the local community. But within these common forms of transaction between politicians and the construction industry, architects are sometimes required—beyond engaging in some of these transactions—to produce visions and policies, materialize ideological agendas, and provide a public face, if not a whipping boy, for the subsequent *physical* outcome of these byzantine processes.

The translation between ideological posturing and material or spatial representation is equally fuzzy, and the relationship between architecture and politics has gone through several stages in its mutually imbricated history. It has evolved from straight-forward submission by the elite to the selective patronage of aristocrats and potentates to a more ambiguous and seductive game of cat and mouse within the very business-like *bourgeoisie*, to an activist and strenuously ideological role within revolutionary periods given to modernity (especially in the early-twentieth century), to public service or public works within a liberal democracy, to the transubstantiation to pure capital flows and the conversion of building to image in the late-modern era, and so on... Along this route, the very nature of the discipline has evolved from the mastering of craft and technology to the full servicing of ideological and post-ideological games through an engagement with ideology and the media.

The current balance of this mix is permanently shifting, and it is entering a new era as a result of some critical changes in the contemporary political and economic context. In the age of globalization, the power of shaping the city has been progressively devolved toward private initiatives nominally under the supervision of bureaucratic and regulatory regimes whose main goal is to minimize risks and ensure open and fair competition. In comparison with past times, recent and otherwise, politics has become increasingly faceless in its architectural determinations. One no longer knows what a building represents, nor to *whom it belongs*.

In the developed world, where the power to transform the built environment is at an historical peak, neither architects nor politicians are capable any longer of driving the vision for a new city. Even in cases where media architecture is called upon to perform, it is generally as a device to distance the public from local politics. (The Guggenheim in Bilbao is a perfect example of architecture playing politics by moving away from it.) And the same tends to apply to the politics of contemporary corporate governance: Gone is the time when corporations sought representation through architecture. In a globalized economy, corporations prefer to maintain liquidity and lease generic space rather than invest in fixed—and idiosyncratic—assets that may become a liability in the future. As a result of this, agents with the flimsiest of political good will and no elected status (such as corporate media and developers operating on behalf of transnational speculative capital) are becoming the new arbiters of taste, deciding the texture and image of the built environment, most especially cities.

In this new set of parameters, it is worthwhile to reconsider the relationship between architecture and politics, or architecture and power: what are the new driving forces that shape our cities? And what is their agenda? How should architecture relate to them? Should architects maintain an independent ideological position or should they remain disengaged from all ideological posturing in order to better engage with contemporary processes and the infinite give and take of the same? It is now critical, as it has been critical at similar junctures, to understand and discuss from a variety of positions, the *phenomenology of power* in contemporary architecture and the ways in which it comes to physical expression in its global sense, as progressive or regressive system of "governance."

The pictures displayed along this text are photographs of two of the most power-driven buildings in the recent world: the Petronas Towers, and the Ryugyong Hotel in Pyongyang.

Published to accompany the Berlage Institute's
installation at the 2006 Architecture Biennale in Venice

Re-empowering Architecture

It is axiomatic that the city is the predominant and foremost instance of human habitation. While this has been so for centuries, if not millennia, today more than half of the world's population is urban, and that percentage keeps growing. This connotes two problems: the urbanization of the globe, and the globalization of the urban. This numerical shift is only news in the sense that the numbers are now overwhelmingly in support of the experience. Whereas the city has always been the magnet for upwardly mobile populations (however poor to begin with), what is different now—beyond the mere statistical point of no return—is the additional problem that cities can hardly absorb the numbers descending upon them and remain cities. The megalopolis beckons. The city, an always constrained notion of human inhabitation, has suddenly become the most potent milieu for the construction of a post-humanistic discourse crossing multiple disciplines, from art and sociology to architecture and politics. If the concepts of nation, class, gender, or ethnicity (as the fundamental components of human identities) once were the central issues bridging disciplines that addressed the human condition, the city and its vicissitudes has become the prime battlefield for the construction of post-humanist, post-contemporary culture.

No wonder, then, that material practices *across the board*, ranging from product design to territorial planning (military or otherwise), have been trying desperately to reengage with the city as an overwhelming apparatus to which one needs to relate in order to do anything significant in post-contemporary culture—that is, to market anything whatsoever and to control and discipline the apparatus. But this reengagement with, or disciplining of, the new metropolis proceeds devoid of traditional fields of representation (the structuring of order) and co-optation (the exploitation of the captive population). The exponential growth and often chaotic new frontier of the global city has made all traditional forms of analysis and production obsolete and triggered a profound reformulation of the disciplines involved. In order to grasp the complexity, mutability, and interconnectedness of the new urban milieu, the disciplines given to the material production of the city have gone through profound transformations. Traditional technologies based on the discrete nature of matter and geometry in the construction industry, the discrete and precise legibility of typologies and civic order, and the linear development of historical time (the conscious production of collective memory and its analogues) have given rise to technologies that describe and manipulate the urban milieu as constituted by permanently mutating fields, identities, and temporalities. Traditional urban theories and ideologies have been dismantled by the evidence of phenomena that quite simply exceeds or overflows them. The traditional roles of design professionals as visionaries, orchestrators of presence, or creators of urban structure, inclusive of "open space," have been thoroughly dismantled by the contemporary processes of urbanization, where power is "democratically dispersed" throughout the city as an endless market and administered by bureaucratic regimes of quasi-public agency, leaving little room for radical reformulation or for the paradoxical insurrection of "stopping the machine" in its tracks by simply *slowing down*. The former is branded utopian while the latter obstructionist. Both are moot responses or lost causes today as cities become continuous, wall-to-wall playgrounds for speculative capital. Victims of disempowerment and perverse fascination, architects and urbanists have often become idle and disoriented, unable to engage with contemporary urban processes except as a type of shadow government shouting from the back benches, weirdly paralyzed witnesses at the scene of the crime, permanently engaged in research to find out who is to blame, and withdrawn from any transformative role other than to document and accuse (to point the finger elsewhere, when obviously we are as responsible as anyone for the state of things).

How does one, then, engineer a knowledge-producing institution or discipline that acknowledges that, for better or worse, in a society where knowledge is power, inoperative knowledge has no power? And what is operative knowledge? During the last four years the Berlage Institute has tried (as a sort of development of its own genetic code) to develop a remedy to this contemporary malaise paralyzing the profession from within. The absolutely unique and obvious solution is: engage with the outside! Do a project rather than a research! Have a client! Have a commission! Or as Slavoj Žižek might say: *Enjoy your symptoms!*

Working through commissions is not just a pragmatic requirement, but a theoretical endeavor, since we can no longer aim to understand the world without accepting to transform it. Heidegger's criticism of the modern world was that it originates in a commission (*Bestell*) and is done on behalf of someone else, and, therefore, it cannot give existence (*Bestand*), truth, or origin to a reality.[1] But the project does not necessarily need an origin: to be truly modern, subcontract the origin!

But, of course, having a commission does not help 99% of the stuff that goes up and falls down shortly afterward. The question then becomes: Is there *room* to alter the course of events? Where is that *space* to be found? And, is there a possibility for the reempowerment of the profession *in*

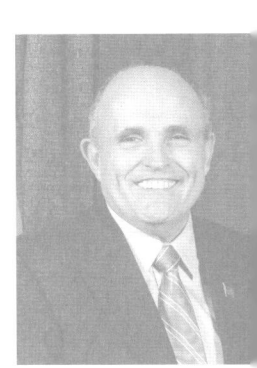

---

1   For Heidegger's use of these terms, see his essay "The Question Concerning Technology," in *Basic Writings,* ed. David Krell (New York: Harper Collins Publishers, 1993). The essay derives from a lecture given in 1955.

finding it? The general hypothesis we have been working on is that operative knowledge is more likely to emerge out of the concreteness of the project than through the distanced nuances of research and theory. Indeed, the city has become the common place and the exemplary domain for the investigation of these subjects but through direct engagement in the act of projecting, transforming, and waging battle with the city proper (and those who think they own it), we will find the knowledge for that reempowerment.

Two alternatives have emerged from this question and been explored at the Berlage Institute. One hypothesis is that it is more likely to find maneuvering space in the realm of micropolitics and through complicity, rather than in the conception of all-encompassing visions or confrontational strategies. One must say yes and no at the same time (and sometimes in the same breath). In this approach the architect performs opportunistically, "like a surfer"—to follow a well known metaphor—that is to say, concentrating one's effort in riding forces that are external to the discipline in an attempt to obtain the necessary energy to produce new models. This approach tends to have a holistic outlook, where disciplinary genres and scales of operation become blurred, open-ended, and interrelated. The design of a system of waste disposal, public transportation canopies, or urban lighting is considered as a potentially crucial strategy to produce urbanity, defying the traditional categories of product design, architecture, urban design, and branding. A populational approach, where prototypical consistencies are sought across urban facts is often deployed as a technique that renders them continuous, rather than discrete. Housing typologies and urban healthcare become typologies to be tested on an urban scale. The economic processes of urban transformation become in themselves an object of profound analysis. Not just urban complexes, but whole cities are explored as components of worldwide processes, rather than as discrete units of identity, culture, or lifestyle.

The alternative approach is skeptical of the open-endedness of this form of engagement and longs for a more ideological and disciplinary stance to give direction and closure to the research, insisting that it is impossible to transform reality without establishing and enforcing certain ideal models external to urban systems that will, in turn, shift the game in wholly new, progressive directions. This approach is more dialectical and, therefore, less mediated, working with a set of carefully constructed identities, models of behavior, and architectural compositions, often of historical import, either as cultural precedents or disciplinary models. As such, in order to be effective one needs to treat reality as a set of discrete domains, both in terms of disciplinary boundaries and in terms of physical locations and relationships within the wider urban field. The project and its disciplinary performance is structured in well defined genres such as urban design, landscape, architecture, and product design, which are then understood as precise fields of investigation with a specific history (hence the recourse to precedent); locations or sites are also constructed through an historical datum that needs to be accessed, understood, and projected forward. In this sense, architecture and urbanism is not just a problem of opportunity, growth, or technology; it is a problem of representation, and, therefore, a theoretical problem. The subject of *capital cities*—cities that, beyond their mere performance as urban system, need to become vehicles to represent a culture, a nation, or a set of values—has become an ideal field of research for this approach that understands that a city is more than its factual performance as an urban system.

This exhibition attempts to present these two extreme paths of projective investigation into the contemporary city.

The pictures displayed along this text are photographs of the most important mayors during the last three decades. Charged with the urban transformations of major cities around the world, mayors probably constitute the most important powers in the making of cities and contemporary architecture: Pasqual Maragall, Ken Livingstone, Rudy Giuliani, Yuri Luzhkov, Chris Patten, Michael Bloomberg, Chen Liangyu, Shintaro Ishihara, Bertrand Delanoe, and Bo Xilai represent the faces of the urban contemporary power.

A previous version of this essay appeared in *El País*, Madrid, September 10, 2004

The Urban Age

If the twentieth-century city will be remembered for anything, it will be for the shift that took place in the last decades in the processes of economic and cultural globalization (plus the attendant intensification of flows, transfers, and exchanges that swept across the planet's surface), changing both its texture and the image. The twenty-first century will be the era when urban enclaves claimed strategic advantage and command over those trajectories and extensions that give rise to cities in the first place. The process seems to trend toward the so-called megalopolitan model, yet what is occurring within is the restructuralization of the fabric toward intensified orders that focus specific traits and eject others.

For the first time in human history, more than half of the world's population is living in urban environments—both in squalor and splendor. Rather than producing dispersion, the remarkable intensification of migratory processes, commerce and exchange, has consolidated the crucial role of urban centers within the political, economical, social, and cultural organizations of the contemporary world. In those areas with a more consolidated urban capital, the pressure on urban infrastructures is of such a magnitude that is altering radically both its spatial and material structures and its socio-cultural composition. As cities plan for expansion, they also plan for the permanent state of emergency to come (always a threat only partially mitigated by an increase in surveillance and policing).

This ongoing process of recentralization is by no means exclusive to the well-established, well-capitalized economies of the West. Developing areas in Asia, Africa, and South America have recently registered the most extreme surges in urbanization. And it is likely that this process will intensify further: China, where the current ratio of rural to urban population is approximately 80:20, is aiming to reverse that ratio in three decades. India and Brazil are currently experiencing similar indexes of rapid urbanization.

The emerging global network of cities is producing a new geo-political order that, if properly managed, will soon become more effective than the system of national states in terms of providing better quality of life to the world population. The processes of urban development have now become one of the crucial engines of developed and developing economies, and urban politics are at the crossroads on how to balance growth and investment of public and private sectors in a sustainable process of endless redevelopment. The organization and physical consistency of the city—its form, scale, density, and distribution—has now become a crucial political question. The concrete design of the built environment and the determination of urban densities, plus the impact of this intensification in social and cultural terms, all point to the continuing tightening of economic and architectural integration and a possible integral quality of life within hyper-localized micro-cities within cities. In New York, London, and Paris, as typical of the crisis in the former First World, newly intensified districts where formerly sprawl or post-industrial ruin ruled suggest that the megalopolis of the future is a finely knit affair, albeit a *continuous and endless* finely knit affair.

The urban sociologist David Harvey has characterized the forms of economic integration given to neo-liberal, late capitalism as a series of mechanisms that enable the absorption and displacement of the ever-expanding surpluses, resources, and assets of the capitalist system within the finite spaces of a postcolonial order, where literal expansion is no longer viable. These contemporary forms of capitalism, which Harvey terms *regimes of flexible accumulation,* operate through *mechanisms of spatial and temporal displacement* capable of producing displacements and deformations of space to generate flexibility in the attachment of assets, resources, and surpluses. For example, transport and communication infrastructure is representative of the mechanisms of spatial displacement, while credits, shares, and interest rates (modern financial instruments) enable the temporal displacement of economic processes and administration of urban capital.

Cities are precisely the location of these highly specialized mechanisms. Rather than becoming the chosen apparatuses for the accumulation and crystallization of communal wealth via economic, political, and social structures, as in the traditional regimes of capitalist accumulation, they are increasingly the means of permanently managing and distorting the distribution of wealth. Rather than the enclaves where time and space become regulated and organized, where spatial domains are assigned to classes, guilds, or ethnic and cultural groups, the contemporary city is the enclave where temporal and spatial orders collapse in an elastic and malleable space, permanently reformulated.

This new hyper-functionality of *productive* urban centers (and this excludes those denuded and stripped of value), in themselves and in respect to the territorial domains to which they are attached (an increasingly difficult determination), implies a radical revision of urban typologies and planning hypotheses. If in the past urban typologies were primarily associated with specific uses—residential, retail, commercial, leisure, industrial, etc.—any new urban typologies must be capable of negotiating the on-rolling short-circuiting of predictable urban activities and the resultant highly mutable regimes of power that characterize contemporary urban life. To build typologies as a function of densities and relationships with transportation infrastructure is one of the intuitive outcomes of some of the functions that contemporary urban structures will need to make available. The introduction of time as a potentially crucial extension to the management of life in the city is one of the most interesting challenges in the field of contemporary urbanism, if not a potential battleground given the "subjective" nature of certain types of time. On a mundane level, the liberalization of working hours (for example, part-time work or telecommuting) is blurring the temporal boundaries between work and leisure. Production and consumption are, of course, also part of the mechanisms of temporal displacement that need to be incorporated in the urban structure and that contain enormous potentials to generate new urban typologies.

If urban-planning methodologies were tied in the past to a now outdated structure of urban land ownership, what has replaced it is a system wherein ownership structures are increasingly complex and temporary. Despite vagaries of command and control (if not outright ownership), the progressive densification of infrastructure needs to be properly reengineered and, more importantly, *paid for*. The possibility of seeing and thinking the city as a three-dimensional, interconnected organization, rather than as an abstract planar model determined by land ownership is an unavoidable task urbanism will need to tackle sooner rather than later, if the whole edifying machinery is not to seize up and melt down. After a century of extension, we have now entered the age of "contraction" through intensification.

The contemporary processes of hyper-urbanization will not only affect abstract planning techniques and force the generation of new urban typologies; they will also drive decisive political and cultural reconfigurations. Cities are the cauldrons where cultures are formed, and cultures crucially determine the structures of human organization. While the modern city was structured around the dialectic between the individual and the collective, private and public, artificial and natural, the contemporary city is the stage for a politics of an entirely different nature. Concepts such as community (a stable population within a certain spatial domain) and individuality (the somewhat consistent and stable identity of the subject) have become entirely destabilized within the new urban dynamics. The contemporary subject is no longer strictly embedded within a class, ethnic background, or religious belief. Yet neither is said subject the freewheeling, independent, and sovereign agent grounded in liberal-democratic rules of acceptable behavior and civic decorum. The contemporary subject is an entity mediated through complex and mutating interactions, and much more difficult to represent in anthropological-architectural terms. In the collapse of liberal space-time produced by the fast-mutating contemporary metropolis, attachments of a more specific order—those established by the urban infrastructure, for example—have started to replace those categories in which urban subjectivity was formerly inscribed (parks, schools, or civic institutions), and which constituted the very basis of the politics of liberal-democratic regimes. Financial structures, utilities and services, transport, access to knowledge and information, cultural and leisure opportunities, and, last but not least, the entire enfolding spatial and physical structure of cities, have become the increasingly dominant *force* in the construction of the contemporary urban subject. The street scenes during the blackout in Manhattan on August 15, 2003 were a wonderful example of a new urban population of mixed class, age, and ethnic background suddenly bound by the sudden collapse of an integral component of the urban infrastructure (the electrical grid). Had the blackout lasted for much longer than it did, an entirely different dynamic would have certainly ensued, like in Julio Cortazar's *The South Highway*, a fiction of a traffic jam evolving into a city... Yet chalk up a moment's cessation of urban infrastructures normalcy as a means of taking the pulse of the body politic.

Within a civilization in which populations are increasingly mobile and have increasingly weak attachments to the hinterland, the arguments for political, cultural, and linguistic consistency are shifting toward the physical or material milieu, as if the dematerialization of informational and semiotic orders was demanding a hyper-materialization of political and cultural orders. Within this situation, space becomes the most important factor of cultural consistency, capable of transcending language, ritual, and ideology. If the political forms of parliamentary or representational democracy were structured by the dialectical operations between cellular systems, the correlation between physical spaces and immaterial identities mediated through civic and commercial hierarchies that no longer conform to predictable or identifiable patterns has become the prevailing mechanism of contemporary, neo-liberal democracies. Governance has shifted away from paternal orders toward an associative-material rather than deliberative-linguistic functionality. As Richard Sennett explains, deliberative democracy is based on a verbal tradition and in a theatrical spatial order of representation, based on submission to a representative majority and dialectics and language.[1] But in the absence of identifiable linguistic, ethnic, and cultural contexts within emerging urban populations, contemporary democracy is increasingly based on mere physical coexistence in space, on non-representational politics and affects: in associative

---

1   Richard Sennett, "Democratic Spaces", in *Hunch* n. 9 (Rotterdam: Berlage Institute, 2005), 40.

democracy, where social dynamics become literally explicit rather than represented, the provision of inclusive spaces, not necessarily structured to stage a verbal debate but to enhance physical proximity may in some instances replace the political discourse and the protocols of representation, and initiate new forms of consensus. Kemal-El-Fnaa Square in Marrakesh, informal and permanently changing, may become a better model for a contemporary urban democratic space than the monumentality of Washington's Mall.

In this sense, the now infamous Bilbao-Guggenheim effect is far less relevant as a precedent for future urban regeneration—it was, after all, a very specific "representative" building type, built in very particular cultural and political context. Such maneuvers are, instead, an index of how political power is increasingly aware of the fact that urban space may be both the backdrop for political-cultural consensus and the very milieu in which the social fabric is constructed. This has a certain diabolical side that feeds the feverish imaginations of conspiracy theorists and Hollywood producers, but also issues forth from a premise that is not wholly given to simple manipulation by unseen, noirish factors operating in the shadows or from the pristine glass towers of the capitals of capital. This new urban milieu is no longer built on stability and equilibrium, but on change and instability. The question is not how to make more iconic, culturally preposterous buildings, capable of transmitting political enthusiasm to the masses and envy to one's neighbors or enemies, but how to explore some of the affective capacities inherent to building airports, train stations, retail malls, or new residential districts or office towers, all which have suddenly become pervaded by an ersatz new sexiness on behalf of—but of course—*the public*.

The images in this text are urban landscapes of extreme cases of fast urban development: Beijing, Chongquin and Shenzhen.

The Politics of the Envelope

Political Materialism
Before delving into a political argument, I should probably admit to a suspicion of political ideology that goes beyond its application to architecture and most likely has a biographical origin. My experience of Spain's transition from dictatorship to democracy left me with a rather cynical view of political ideologies as effective tools for understanding or transforming reality. I was born during Franco's dictatorship, and I remember having to learn to vote at school—one of the new protocols of the new democracy. As a left-leaning adolescent, I longed for the Western powers to intervene against Franco's dictatorship, a desire that came back to haunt me 30 years later when pondering Western intervention in Iraq—a far worse dictatorship and in a far more globalized world. In Spain I watched Javier Solana, then minister of culture under the Socialist government, campaign for Spain's entry into NATO, and then saw the termination of compulsory military service by Aznar's right-wing government—which the Socialist Party opposed—confirming my worst fears about political ideologies.

On the other hand, I also witnessed the subversive effects of foreign tourism on sexual behavior during Franco's strictly Catholic regime as well as the positive impact of low interest rates, home ownership, and massive infrastructure construction on social mobility. Finally, the demise of the Aznar government in 2004, brought down by text messaging, convinced me of the deeply transformative political potentials of seemingly innocuous technological and economic processes.

If there is a lesson in the current American presidential campaign it is precisely that an all-encompassing mass politics focused on class, gender, race, creed, and identity, and built upon partisan ideologies, is less effective than a more nimble molecular politics capable of engaging independent swing voters, who are soon to become the largest segment of the electorate. Likewise, contemporary political agencies can be found in the most pragmatic, concrete operations. Despite having become a crucial political battleground, architecture and urbanism appear to be unable to find a role within this new political maelstrom. Architects' traditional role as visionaries (and ideologists) has become redundant as the sheer speed of change overtakes their capacity to represent politics ideologically. Visionary formulations pale in the face of reality's complexity: an ideological position devoid of a close link to actualization and corporeality will remain disempowered. Paper architecture, for example, has lost its effectiveness as a political vehicle; like *utopia*, it is restricted to pure representation without the attachments and frictions capable of politicizing matters. In order to guarantee a minimum level of agency, architects need today to engineer their acquisition strategies, procurement routes, etc., to sustain a necessary level of engagement. And those decisions become an integral part of the architectural project.

Within this context it is vital to produce an updated politics of architecture in which the discipline is not merely reduced to a representation of ideal political concepts, but conceived as an effective tool to produce change. Rather than returning to ideology and utopia, a contemporary politicization of architecture needs to relocate politics within specific disciplinary domains, not as a representation of an ideal concept of the political, but as a political effect specific to the discipline.

A unilateral politics of resistance is no longer able to challenge contemporary forms of consolidated power. The challenge to instituted power can only be selective, and the division of political labor has to be addressed by multiple disciplines operating independently and simultaneously and not necessarily in a multidisciplinary relation. For the discipline to acquire transformative agency it is necessary to engage in a political critique of its technologies.

The uncertainty about the current political processes is provoking a creeping nostalgia for the days when there were coherent political projects that could be described through ideology and represented by utopian visions. Instead, we are excited by the prospect of moving beyond a single narrative of how the world is, or feels, or where it is headed. The attempts to politicize architecture have emerged from the hypothesis that architecture is a "social construct," a cultural fabrication, and an embodiment of political concepts. But architecture is as much a physical construct as it is a social or political one, and to understand architecture as a mere representation of the political is as problematic as it is to declare architecture entirely ruled by the inexorable laws of physics, economics, buildability, climatology, and ergonomics.

To escape from the great revolutionary narratives and their ideological understandings of history, an effective link between architectural technologies and the political needs to be established. It may be good to stop speaking of *power* in general, or of *the state, capital, globalization, empire* in general, and, instead, address specific *ecologies of power* comprising a heterogeneous mixture of bureaucracies—markets, shopping malls, residential towers, lifestyles, cladding systems, facade ratios, carbon emissions, etc.—and the specific exercises of power within and between these organizations. I have chosen the building envelope as the field that may help us to draw these political attachments to the material world, restoring political agency to architecture through material agency.

The Envelope as a Political Agent

The building envelope is possibly the oldest and most primitive architectural element.[1] It materializes the separation of inside and outside, natural and artificial; it demarcates private from public and land ownership; when it becomes a facade, the envelope also operates as a representational device, in addition to its crucial environmental and territorial roles. The building envelope is the border, the frontier, the edge, the enclosure, and the

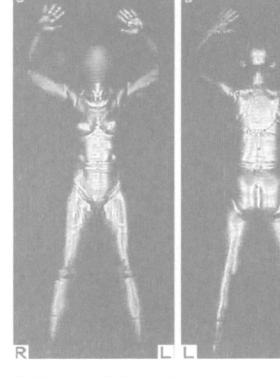

---

[1] "The beginning of building coincides with the beginning of textiles… The [w]all is the structural element that formally represents and makes visible the enclosed space as such, absolutely, as it were, without reference to secondary concepts. We might recognize the pen, bound together from sticks and branches, and the interwoven fence as the earliest vertical spatial enclosure that man invented… Weaving the fence led to weaving movable walls… Using wickerwork for setting apart one's property and for floor mats and protection against heat and cold far preceded making even the roughest masonry. Wickerwork was the original motif of the wall. It retained this primary significance, actually or ideally, when the light hurdles and mattings were transformed into brick or stone walls. The essence of the wall was wickerwork." Gottfried Semper, "The Textile Art," in *Style in the Technical and Tectonic Arts; or, Practical Aesthetics*, trans. Harry Francis Mallgrave and Michael Robinson (Los Angeles: Getty Research Institute, 2004).

joint: it is loaded with political content. It is an optimal domain to explore the politicization of architecture and, possibly, the development of a *Dingpolitik*.²

The political performances of architecture have been historically attached to the plan or the section. The plan of the building organizes the power structure and protocols, while the section organizes the social strata and the building's relationships with the ground. The envelope, on the other hand, has been relegated to a mere "representational" or "symbolic" function. The reasons for such a restricted political agency may lie in the understanding of the envelope as a *surface*, rather than as a complex assemblage of the materiality of the surface technology and its geometrical determinations.

The envelope exceeds the surface by incorporating a much broader set of attachments. It includes the crust of space affected by the physical construction of the surface, by the scale and dimension of the space contained, by its permeability to daylight and ventilation, and by its insulation values and solar-shading capacities. It also involves the space that surrounds the object, its orientation with respect to sun, wind, views, etc. The envelope has the capacity to *re-present* the ancient political role that articulates the relationships between humans and nonhumans in a common world. The envelope is the surface and its *attachments*.

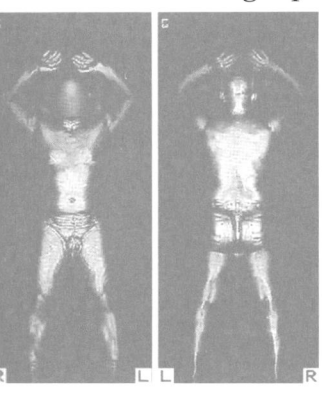

There is no such a thing as a *unitary theory of the building envelope* in the history of architecture. Previous theories of the envelope have basically addressed either representation or construction technologies. Gottfried Semper's analysis of cladding materials and J. N. L. Durand's proposals for an adequate expression of typologies belong to this genre. The Loosian crime of ornament and the modernist abstracted "whitewash" of the facade are also episodes of the politics of the envelope. Colin Rowe's aesthetic critique in "Character and Composition," and Rowe and Slutzky's "Literal and Phenomenal Transparency," both collected in *Mathematics of the Ideal Villa*, insist on similarly compositional issues. Robert Venturi's return to the decorative and the representational is also a precedent to this discussion, and, of course, there is a large body of knowledge addressed to the environmental and structural performance

---

2   Bruno Latour coined the term *Dingpolitik* to address the politics resulting from the crisis of objectivity triggered by the collapse of modernity and the search for a new model of objectivity in which politics is one aspect of the object, its sciences, and nature at large. See Latour and Weibel, eds., *Making Things Public* (Cambridge, MA: The MIT Press, 2005).

of envelopes: for example, R. Buckminster Fuller, Robert le Ricolais, Reyner Banham et al. Furthermore, the traditional divide between facade and roof construction technologies have prevented the discipline from looking at the envelope in a more holistic way, as a single object of analysis. Both theoretically and technically, the building envelope has been seen as two separate elements: the roof and the facade. But this division has been rendered irrelevant by the development of envelope technologies, which make increasingly similar roofing and façade.

Like the skin of a living creature, the envelope is the primary actor in the complex process of maintaining *homeostasis* in the building. But in the case of human inhabitation, the skin does not function only on a purely biological level; it protects the building's interior, but also communicates with the external public realm, opening up psychological, political, social, and cultural surpluses. The surface of the building has a double function, engaging with dialectical oppositions: the private and the public, inside and outside, etc. It is a boundary that not only registers the pressure of the interior, but also resists it, transforming its energy into something else, and vice versa.

Within these dynamics, *faciality* is sustained because certain arrangements of power need to have a face. Facialization organizes systems of binary opposition operating on different levels and functions as their dynamic point of contact: power structures configure private and public, inside and outside through the envelope. As a homeostatic membrane it is a crucial component of the organization of power regimes in the building.[3]

At a time when energy and security concerns have replaced an earlier focus on circulation and flow as the contents of architectural expression, the building envelope becomes a key political subject. Like artificial intelligence and genetic engineering, the building envelope is now a technological conun-

3   While this critique is primarily concerned with material agency in the form of a building's facade, there is always the additional import (troublesome and given to arguments regarding surface versus content) that suggests performativity, as discussed here, is ineluctably also contaminated in advance by image. The well-known attempt to structure the language of architecture in modernism is not the point in analyzing material agency. Material agency, in this sense, transcends functional and tectonic issues of style and registers "elemental" aspects given to architecture (inclusive of what material and stylistic aspects "say" or do not "say").

drum situated at the vortex of an ongoing political storm.⁴ Peter Sloterdijk eloquently anticipated the growing political relevance of envelopes in his so-called *Spheres trilogy*,⁵ with the powerful imagery of a foamy space filled with bubbles and balloons of different scales and qualities. This *capsular* society and its phenomena, such as *global provincialism*, the *politics of climatization*, and *social uteri*, describe a new paradigm that requires reconsideration not only of the technologies and economics of the building envelope, but also its political, social, and psychological implications.

There are multiple instances where the qualities of the envelope may trigger political effects: the envelopes of a retail complex or a lobby enclosure are powerful mechanisms of social engineering. Like a radiator adopting an intricate form to increase the surface of heat exchange with the air, a more intricate building footprint increases the vertical contact surface between private and public. A more permeable definition of the envelope will produce a more fluid relationship between private and public: the facade ratio⁶ of a residential block determines the environment's degree of artificiality; a gradual delimitation between the natural and the artificial in the facade of an office building could help to improve energy efficiency and minimize its carbon footprint; and a more ambiguous appearance may allow for the reprogramming of the building's identity. It is at this level that the discussion of the qualities and structure of material organizations gives architecture political agency. Issues such as difference and repetition, consistency and variation, flexibility, transparency, permeability, local and global resonances, and the very definition of "ground" have wide-ranging implications for what a building might "say" or "not say." This ability to "say" or "not say" is not the reloading of theories of

---

4   This firestorm is the not entirely unjustified response to the excesses of global capitalism and its manipulation of markets through advanced financial instruments, all of which has proven exceptionally costly in social, political, and economic terms. The outcome of the world financial meltdown of late 2007 is likely to be a massive reconstitution of "firewalls" to protect indigenous markets from the distorting effects of transnational capital.

5   See Peter Sloterdijk, *Esferas I, Burbujas, Microsferología* (2003); *Esferas II, Globos, Macrosferología* (2004); and *Esferas III, Espumas, Esferología plural* (2006), trans. Isidoro Reguera (Madrid: Ediciones Siruela). In German, *Sphären, Blase, Mikrosphärologie*; *Sphären, Globen, Makrosphärologie*; and *Sphären, Schäume, Plurale Sphärologie* (Frankfurt am Main: Suhrkamp Verlag, 1998–2004).

6   Facade ratio is the quotient between the external surface of a building and its overall floor plate, and indicates the amount of external surface per square meter of built area. It is often used by developers and engineers to specify the technical and cost performances of a building.

architecture parlante (so-called speaking architecture) but, instead, the reformulation of the perennial relationship between architectural form (formal-material agency) and intellection (rational thought per se).

Mobilizing a political critique of the envelope to address its multiple attachments may enable us to frame architecture not merely as a representation of the interests of a client, of a certain political ideology, or an image of utopia, but as an all-too-real, concrete, and effective political agency able to assemble and mediate the interests of the multiple stakeholders that converge on the architectural project today. A discipline of the building envelope capable of remaining attached to reality and yet resistant to consolidation will enable architecture to produce effects that may actually destabilize power regimes rather than function as their mere representation, whether of the status quo or its resisting parties. In order to regulate its relationships with power, with the status quo, and with emergent social structures, architecture needs to develop political strategies to maintain a relation with power while simultaneously challenging and opening its structures. Rather than aiming at revolution as a political ambition, an updated discipline of the envelope will need to focus on *explicitation*,[7] a model where political practices are attached to artificial environments in which we co-exist, and where disciplines become the primary source of political agency.

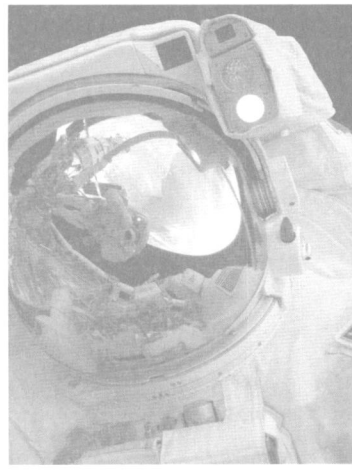

Molecular Faciality

A crucial factor in the renewed importance of the envelope derives from the evolution of the conditions of architectural production.

While many aspects of the architectural project are now in the control of alternative agents (project managers, specialist contractors, etc.), the increasing facelessness of the commissioners gives architects license to

---

7 Sloterdijk uses the term *explikation* (explicitation) as an alternative process to revolution and emancipation. The history of explicitation is made increasingly intelligible in the spheres and objects to which we are attached. The categories of the French Revolution and Left and Right, both with their particular techniques of classification and of positioning, no longer correspond to the order of things, which is no longer hierarchical but heterarchical. Whether we talk about carbon footprints, deregulation, genetically modified foods, congestion pricing, or public transport, these issues give rise to a variety of political configurations that exceed the Left-Right distinction. The Left-Right divide still exists, but has been diluted by a multitude of alternative attitudes. See Sloterdijk, *Esferas III, Espumas, Esferología plural*, op. cit.

invent the building's interface. The building envelope has become the last precinct of architectural power. What is the nature of public representation in the age of so-called public-private partnerships when both corporations and public administrations are procuring their buildings from developers who are sourcing their capital from private equity, hedge funds, and REITs (Real Estate Investment Trusts)? The contemporary city is built for corporations run by administrative boards for multinational shareholders' interests; it is built by building corporations serving multinational interests as well, who procure the buildings and often run them, taking care of maintenance, security, refuse collection, energy supply, and even the provision of infrastructure. How does one construct the face of the faceless? Even if the rise of sovereign funds and the reempowerment of central banking succeed in removing *liquid-ness* from the production of buildings and cities, the building envelope will still be required to fulfill a more complex set of performances, as the primary regulator between public and private, inside and outside, natural and artificial... Between determinations characterizing one's position "inside the fold" and "outside the fold" (an expression of one's relationship to power and privilege)—that is, increasingly complex relationships that will never return to clearly defined parameters (regardless of whether they ever enjoyed such clarity in the first place). The growing number of buildings adopting supple envelopes with differentiated patterns does not appear as a mere coincidence, but as an index of a convergence of factors leading to a particular design choice. While only a few decades ago the crucial question for architects was the choice between pitched roofs and flat roofs, today architects are considering the choice between the *box* and the *blob*. The introduction of certain cladding and roofing technologies, such as curtain wall systems, silicon joints, and plastic waterproofing membranes, has eliminated the need for cornices, corners, pediments, and window reveals. As far as envelope technology goes, the difference between the roof and the wall has disappeared, eliminating the cornice line as a necessary articulation; fenestration is no longer a critical building problem, and the corner, a singularity derived from construction geometries and property alignments, is also weakening as the limits between private and public fade and the structure of land ownership is challenged by contemporary urban development instruments. Given these and other advancements in envelope systems, the choice between the box and the blob is a specious one, which alone is unable to structure a robust theoretical frame for a discussion of the convergence of political forms and architectural technology.

Beyond the emerging technological possibilities, there is also a whole new politics of faciality at play that affects the envelope as the locus of political expression. The current proliferation of alternative political practices, such as trends, movements, and other *affect-driven* political forms,⁸ runs parallel to the development of envelopes that resist primitive models of faciality, that are no longer structured on the oppositions between front and back, private and public, or roof and wall. Once cornices, corners, and windows are no longer technically necessary and the private and public are entangled in an increasingly complex relationship, the hierarchies of interface become more complex: the envelope has become a field where identity, security, and environmental performances intersect. From Seattle to London to Beijing, the faciality of the envelope has proliferated to such a degree that the pattern of construction joints appears to be the new scale of articulation of the face.⁹

The classical approach to the envelope as a vehicle of expression and identity was to inscribe a conventional architectural language on the surface—hence, *architecture parlante*. The facade represented the building *allegorically,* as a signifier that located the building within a socio-political hierarchy. Eighteenth-century French academic theory held that the facade should reflect the building's program and purpose. The architecture of the Enlightenment still referred back to classical architectural languages, but

---

8   Regarding affects, see Nigel Thrift, *Non-Representational Theory: Space, Politics, Affect* (London: Routledge, 2007). The production of the affect, while once considered *au courant*, has fallen into disfavor recently after its excessive appropriation by artists and architects ignorant of its intended "exceptional" use.

9   There is an extraordinary parallel between this formulation of the face and the facade and the critique leveled by John Ruskin at Michelangelo's "inhumanity" as expressed in his distortion of the human body, but, most critically, the contortions or grimaces of the human face. Ruskin drew a line in this regard, preferring Venetian *dignitas*, as represented by Veronese and Tintoretto. Michelangelo, of course, went too far... The analogy here is, perhaps, to the blob and to the distortions given to signature cultural buildings that utilize warped and/or distressed surfaces to express an avant-garde or *fashionable* sensibility—the new "Mannerism," as it were.

simultaneously grounded itself on modularity and a rigid metrics of space as organizing principles representing the egalitarian values of the Saint-Simonian ideal democracy. The modern movement dismissed the classical tradition and viewed the facade as the logical result of the program—not as its representation. During the modern period the external surface of the building, cleansed of any reference to stylistic convention, was supposed to act both as an integral part of the whole building but also, and nonetheless, as a *symbol of modernity*.[10] By the time of High Modernism, however, the facialization of the building—the process of making it human by giving it expression and, therefore, political content—had entered a crisis, as the envelope aimed to achieve the maximum degree of transparency and headed toward the abyss of banality and ubiquity. Yet, the lack of an overt allegory (or discursive content) in the facade did not necessarily imply the facade's disappearance as a quasi-autonomous element capable of representing a building's internal organization. The modern search for spatial fluidity had an ethical purpose in the early days: that is, the dissolution of spatial boundaries that were, in turn, symbols of social stratification (of outmoded class systems), to be avoided in a nonhierarchical and progressive democratic society. These strictures vanished with the International Style and the adaptation of modern architecture to a new, signature corporate image. Outdone by its own success, modern architecture swerved into new categories of accommodation and service to the very systems of stratification and control that it originally rebelled against, though much of its early forms were expressions of an industrial and technical society that, indeed, was soon headed in the opposite direction to the egalitarian expectations of the more utopian progenitors of the insurrection.

As the modernist world order began to fade at the end of the '60s, the more intrusive mechanisms of facialization were rehabilitated. The *postmodern* approach reinstated the relevance of the envelope as a representational mechanism, taking advantage of new building technologies to create effects alienated from both content and context, in correspondence with the prevailing capitalist ideology of individualization and spectacle.

Contemporary politics is now giving way to a new wave of powerful material organizations, belongings, and attachments, which are redefining political

---

10 See Alan Colquhoun, "The Facade in Its Modern Variants," in *Werk, Bauen + Wohnen* #12 (Zurich, December 2005). One finds in this expectation that the purely functional or expressive facade of modernism speaks by way of its very reduction to material agency. By expressing the ideological preference for techno-social progressivity, the facade—indeed—"speaks."

space and herald both the emergence of different political qualities (such as *affects*) and domains (such as *everyday life*). The resulting power structures operate as physical aggregates, *assemblages*[11] where behavior is created through the localized complex association of molecular components. Both governmental agencies and corporate organizations are moving toward multiple layers of governance with intensified connections between them. Today, the emerging heterarchical order increasingly constructs its power by both producing and using diversity. The postmodern politics of rhetoric, symbolic reasoning, and representation is giving way to a new breed of *object-oriented politics*,[12] invested in modes of production and exchange and primarily implemented through the production of affects.

As the traditional articulations of the building envelope have also become technically redundant, the envelope's own physicality, its fabrication and materiality, have taken on representational roles. The envelope design has consequently focused on the construction of the surface itself, both as an environmental and a security device, and as the vehicle that will produce the building's facialization, make it human, turn it into a political agency. Globalization has on the one hand neutralized the effectiveness of architectural language, propelling the iconic and symbolic as communicative devices, while environmental and security concerns have simultaneously raised the threshold of the envelope's capacity for *immunization*. The envelope needs to satisfy the demand to provide identifiable images for an increasingly inconsistent and mobile community while insulating itself against an increasingly abrasive global atmosphere.

11 Manuel de Landa has theorized emerging social structures using Deleuze's *theory of assemblages*, to posit trans-scalar social entities, from sub-individual to transnational, that characterize globalized societies and their heterogeneous populations. See Manuel de Landa, *A New Philosophy of Society: Assemblage Theory and Social Complexity* (London: Continuum, 2006).

12 The term is borrowed from Rodney Brooks, a pioneer of behaviorist AI. "There is an alternative route to Artificial Intelligence that diverges from the directions pursued under that banner for the last thirty some years. The traditional approach has emphasized the abstract manipulation of symbols, whose grounding, in physical reality has rarely been achieved. We explore a research methodology which emphasizes ongoing physical interaction with the environment as the primary source of constraint on the design of intelligent systems. We show how this methodology has recently had significant successes on a par with the most successful classical efforts. We outline plausible future work along these lines which can lead to vastly more ambitious systems." From Rodney Brooks, "Elephants Don't Play Chess." See also his "Intelligence without Representation." Both essays in *Cambrian Intelligence: The Early History of the New AI*, (Cambridge, MA: The MIT Press, 1999). See also his "The Relationship Between Matter and Life."

The demise of the primitive figures of building faciality has found resonance in the availability of certain technical possibilities (for example, printing technology and CAM manufacturing) that have enabled architects to play not only with smooth geometries, tessellation patterns, and material textures, but also with a wide repertoire of layers with a primarily ornamental purpose, which can also perform technical functions such as solar shading and visual obstruction. The decoupling of the patterns of visual, thermal, and atmospheric permeability has opened unprecedented possibilities for *molecular facialization* of the envelope by dissolving or intensifying the joints at will through the phasing and de-phasing of these layers. The conventional figures of building faciality have been replaced by a more nuanced interfacial embodiment in which different layers of performance are played out against each other to produce a wide range of complex effects.

The current tendency toward airtight envelopes is played out in the joint pattern and modulation rather than the fenestration structure. The abundance of polygonal tessellations—for example, PTM's Beijing Watercube—may be driven by a contemporary desire for sealed atmospheres. The construction of bubble envelopes is made possible by polygonal geometries, which may also reduce joint length: polygonal tessellations have a smaller joint length per surface unit than rectangular grids. Frank Gehry's fishlike skins are another index of this tendency aimed at erasing the hierarchical faciality and modular joint grid that characterize standard curtain-wall systems. The proliferation of diagrids and nonorthogonal tessellation patterns—OMA's Seattle Public Library and CCTV building, Herzog & de Meuron's Prada Tokyo and Beijing Stadium, Norman Foster's Swiss Re and Hearst towers—display a general tendency toward anti-gravitational, uprooted, unstable, and differentiated affects, even if many of these patterns have, in fact, a structural function.

If the political history of the twentieth century could be interpreted as the exploration of public freedoms with respect to the normative basis of democracy, the development of the building envelope could be partially described in parallel terms. *Differential faciality* explores the expression of a sort of politics that moves away from the ideal, modular democratic organization based on indifference, independence, and interchangeability. If modularity was typically a quality of a democratic system that prioritizes the part over the whole, some of the emerging envelope geometries seem to be exploring *modular differentiation* as a political effect.

New forms of facialization are being deployed, without apology, to address growing requirements to produce effective public interfaces for a global audience—the whole debate on the *iconic*—and growing security and environmental concerns that legitimize the envelope's opaqueness. Iconicity, while having enjoyed a brief return (especially with cultural buildings that need to express *something* or efface their own attempts to attract attention), has—nonetheless—failed to form a strategic alliance with the emerging sense that something more austere and rewarding is in the wings. Perhaps the very idea of spectacle has become distasteful, finally, as it fully represents the questionable notion that more is always better, or that the unique automatically implies the new. The contemporary envelope, the primary depository of contemporary architectural expression, is now invested in the production of affects, an unencoded, pre-linguistic form of identity that transcends the propositional logic of more traditional political rhetoric—and as it emerges from Gilles Deleuze's idea that material forms have independent or immanent qualities that need not register "anthropomorphic" qualities, the presence of affect is both a promising development and a troublesome sideshow, the latter insofar as it is simply another version of spectacle, unmediated and beyond any form of critique. The material organization of the membrane has become not only a result of a technical articulation of building parts but an image of the engagement between the individual and the collective, and, therefore, a mechanism of political expression for what has been called "the coming community."[13] Importantly, this possible community expressible in material agency restores the most salient features of a type of immanence given to representational orders freed of unnecessary means to ends; foremost, instrumental orders that are openly or secretly *repressive* orders.

The modular grid, indifferent to the relative influence of individuals or politically active subgroups (and considered radical insofar as "subjectivity" was the enemy) embodied the abstract ideals of democratic equality and lib-

---

13 See Giorgio Agamben, *The Coming Community*, trans. Michael Hardt (Minneapolis: University of Minnesota Press, 1993).

eral individualism all the while embracing a worldview that was becoming increasingly machinic. It expressed a preference for nonhierarchical organizations in which individuals were, in theory, equal yet submitted *by law* to the will of a patently abstract majority (since defined downward as the elect). However, today, emerging social structures characteristic of globalized societies and their heterogeneous populations tend to produce trans-scalar entities, from sub-individual to transnational. In these emerging social assemblages, individuals, groups, and other possible *actants* are primarily defined by relations of exteriority,[14] and need to engage with different assemblages without losing their identity.[15] In these emerging social structures, the relationship between an assemblage and its components is complex and nonlinear. The *allometric* modularities and *variable repetitions* that emerge as traits of expression in many of the new envelopes cited above are probably more adequate to express collective purpose within a modular system and to represent "weighted" models of democracy—for example, either those committed to the exercise of civil liberties or those that are driven by a hierarchical bureaucratic regime overlaid onto apparent democratic protocols.

The question is whether the *differentiated facialities* and tessellations of the envelope emerging in the Chinese Olympic projects are genuine devices to allow the envelope to relate to a larger variety of concerns—environmental, social, economic, etc.—or a strategy to step up the *immunization* levels, while representing an ideally differentiated public.[16] Do they inflect in response to multiple agencies and incorporate specificities

14 An actant is a material entity or human person or group that takes on form, definition, facticity, and, ultimately, agency. It is required to enter into an alliance with a spokesperson (as Marx put it, actants "could not represent themselves; they had to be represented"). First used by Bruno Latour, the term is one of the central concepts of Actor-Network Theory (ANT). See Bruno Latour, *Science in Action: How to Follow Scientists and Engineers through Society* (Cambridge: Harvard University Press, 1987).

15 Richard Sennett's definition of associative democracy, Latour's Actor-Network Theory, and Sloterdijk's foams coincide to describe emerging social structures as organizations where the articulation between individual and society, *part and whole*, is drawn by influences and attachments across positions, agencies, and scales that transcend both the individuality of the part and the integrity of the whole. Manuel de Landa has applied Deleuze's theory of assemblages to describe these emerging forms of social and political organization. Assemblages are nonessentialist, historically contingent, actual entities (not instances of ideal forms), and nontotalizing (not seamless totalities but collections of heterogeneous components). See Manuel de Landa, *A New Philosophy of Society*, op. cit.

16 The question of engagement or complicity is always lurking when considering architecture's engagement with power structures. "It's very cheap and easy for architects and artists and film-

rather than resorting to the mere production of political affects, spectacular embodiments of global capitalism, or authoritarian bureaucracies?

As the politics of affect bypasses the rational filter of political dialectics to appeal directly to physical sensation, the construction of an effective frame of reference within the discipline for discussing the production of expression is critical. One can no longer sustain the ideological assumption that a more regular or a more differentiated pattern, one more permeable or more closed, is better at expressing a certain society and the production of transformative effects. The political accuracy of a certain envelope needs to be judged in respect to very concrete assemblages. The most acknowledged envelopes among those iconic Beijing Olympics projects are probably those in which the architects have succeeded in creating a plausible alibi for the differentiated pattern wrapped around the massive unarticulated volume of the buildings, where a resonance between literal performance and affect has been achieved. This is where a new discipline of the envelope becomes politically operative, as it is the discipline that can become an act of resistance without getting caught in the negative project of the critical tradition or in the use of architecture as a mere representation of politics.

The Political Agency of Dimension
Whether architecture and urbanism can or should be critical, projective, progressive, or utopian, and whether speculative architecture can remain an effective practice are still much debated issues that need to be addressed with respect to a proposal of a *general theory of the building envelope*. Architecture and urbanism mobilize such a vast scale of resources that unless the practice is kept at a purely speculative level it is difficult to sustain without it becoming, to some degree, an accomplice of power. At the same time, a progressive discipline constantly challenges the status quo, and, therefore, needs to develop political strategies to maintain a relation with power while simultaneously investigating and opening its structures.

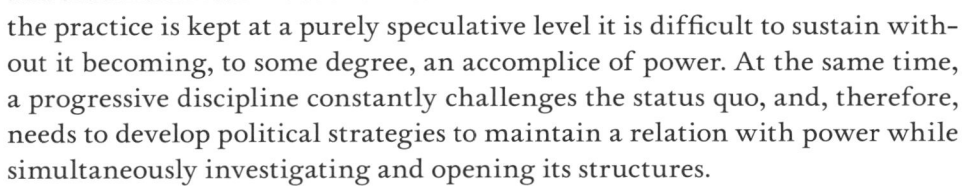

Architecture's challenge to established power has been traditionally enacted through the proposal of alternatives developed in relation to a certain ide-

---

makers to pull out or to make this kind of criticism," Jacques Herzog says. "Everybody knows what happens in China. All work conditions in China are not what you'd desire. But you wear a pullover made in China. It's easy to criticize, being far away. I'm tempted almost to say the opposite... How great it was to work in China and how much I believe that doing the stadium [and] the process of opening will change radically, transform the society. Engagement is the best way of moving in the right direction.'" Excerpts from a conversation between Herzog & de Meuron and Tom Dyckhoff, *The Guardian* (London, March 14, 2008).

ological position that provided directionality in an ideal progression (the revolutionary march through institutions). In these narratives, reactionary positions were attached to the past and progressive attitudes to future forms of emancipation—most often just beyond reach. However, the modern idea of progress has entered into crisis, as attachments are now linked to both the past and the future simultaneously. The topography of time and the site of political passions have been irreversibly overturned, as the great historical narratives have failed to address the phenomena of contemporary societies. Contemporary politics is less determined by temporal processes and progress than by space and co-existence (multiple time frames within one unitary space). To retrieve political agency, architecture needs to develop transversal political practices able to evolve constantly, accumulating new political concerns as new events unfold and, through such accretion, to build a whole new arsenal that is both more than the sum of its parts and yet remains open to further inputs.

Instead of a revolutionary architecture, an *architecture of explicitation* would imply more complex political directionalities as it transforms the space and the material organization of the built environment, even if those transformations cannot be inscribed in a holistic political program. For architecture to express the domestication of density and high-rise life through specific massing strategies in tall buildings, to convey that certain tendencies in the articulation of the building envelope capture the new political affects, to communicate that certain manipulations of the ground and the roof indicate the politicization of nature, or to explain the breakdown of the correlation between interior and exterior and private and public are legitimate political performances.

My interest in envelopes as political devices is that they constitute the element that confines an atmosphere and regulates the flow of energy and matter in and out of that system. If traditional politics was based on equilibrium and closed systems, the contemporary mechanisms of social and economic integration suggest that systems need to operate in an open mode. And, like in thermodynamics, equilibrium is only valid for closed systems where the overall amount of energy is kept constant. Once energy flows in and out of a system, the number and type of possible historical outcomes greatly increases.

Instead of a unique and simple equilibrium, there are now multiple ones of varying complexity regulating their attached power regimes. By analyzing the building envelope, architects may be able to reempower the practice of architecture as a truly transformative force in the reorganization of power ecologies. As an alternative to historical directionality, I would like to propose an analysis of the political dimensionality of space. The dimensional analysis of building envelopes is an attempt to reground architecture's political performance in space and material organizations.

The structure of this theory of the building envelope is based on the hypothesis that the political potentials of a material organization are primarily determined by the dimensionality of their limits, as this determines the flows in and out of the system. Following this hypothesis, every dimensional type can trigger specific technological, social, and political effects. Admittedly, the dimensions of the envelope are not usually left for the architect to decide and are generally associated with the type of project, site constraints, and client's requirements. And that is precisely their virtue, as they are aimed at identifying political opportunities within the constraints—the attachments—that come with each project. Within those constraints, a wealth of possibilities can be activated to transcend the mere technical problems of shelter and put into effect the wider political performance of the buildings. The structure of this analysis has been organized into four categories of envelope: *flat-horizontal*, *spherical*, *flat-vertical*, and *vertical*, resulting from the specific ratios of the envelope's primary dimensions.

$X \approx Y > Z$. The category of *flat-horizontal envelopes* includes those in which the horizontal dimensions are considerably larger than the vertical. Buildings like airports, train stations, factories, trade fairs, convention centers, markets, and retail and leisure complexes generally belong to this category. The political performance of flat-horizontal envelopes lies in the delimitation of edges, frontiers, and boundaries and the sheltering of large-scale atmospheres operating primarily on the articulation between natural and artificial. Since a comprehensive perception can only be obtained from an aerial perspective, flat-horizontal envelopes are experienced in a fragmented manner and are, therefore, less concerned with representation and figural performance than with the organization of material flows: traffic, ventilation, daylight, security, etc. The flat-horizontal envelope usually presents relatively low affective and environmental performances.

$X \approx Y \approx Z$. The *spherical envelope*'s dimensions are approximately equivalent in all directions; cubic, spheroidal, and polygonal geometries are also particular cases in this category. In principle, the spherical envelope has the lowest ratio between its surface and the volume it contains. The specificity of this type is the relative independence that the skin acquires in relation to its programmatic determinations, as functions are not strongly determined by adjacency to the outside and, therefore, by the form of the envelope. This often implies a wider variety of programs inside and a heterogeneous environmental content. Spherical envelopes generally enclose a wide range of spatial types with specific functions, rather than a single spatial condition. Unlike other envelope types in which the border between public and private occurs on the surface of the container, the spherical type often contains gradients of publicness. Spherical envelopes often correspond to public buildings, buildings that gather a multiplicity of spaces, such as city halls, courthouses, libraries, museums, and arenas. In the spherical envelope the gap between expressive and environmental performances is at a maximum, with low-environmental and high-expressive performances.

$X \approx Z > Y$. The category of *flat-vertical envelope*, better known as a *slab*, includes those envelopes whose predominant dimensions are parallel to gravity and distributed along a line. Flat-vertical envelopes are generated by the horizontal displacement of a section of space, which, in order to support a specific function, optimizes density, daylight, ventilation, structural constraints, and the building's relationship with public space and infrastructure. Land uses and orientation are crucial drivers for this envelope type. Most mid-rise residential and many office buildings are probably in this category, as they respond to the need to host a large volume of homogeneous program. The flat-vertical envelope is primarily determined by the facade-to-facade or facade-to-core depth, hence its laminar organization. Modern urban fabrics are predominantly matrices of flat-vertical envelopes combined in various configurations suited to a particular climate, use, and culture. The flat-vertical envelope usually has a high level of environmental performance and a relatively low level of expressive performance.

$Z > X \approx Y$. The last category of envelopes in this proposal, the *vertical envelope*, has a predominantly vertical dimension and, unlike the flat-vertical type, a multidirectional orientation in plan. The specificity of this envelope category is an intense relationship between physical determination and performances. Because of its scale and technical complexity, functional and environmental performances such as daylight penetration and natural ventilation need to be maximized, while the formal qualities of the envelope play a crucial role in the building's structural stability. The vertical envelope's geometric determination crucially impacts both the spaces that it encloses and its surroundings. In addition, the visibility of the vertical envelope makes it particularly conducive to iconographic performance. If in the spherical envelope the gap between representative and environmental performances reaches a maximum, in the vertical envelope both sets of performances are at their highest level. The collusion between extreme technical performance and high visual impact produces the maximum tension between efficiency and expression, a condition that runs deep in the history of this building type.

Significantly, it is the fusion of technical and political factors that triggers new opportunities for theorizing the politics of the envelope. If this has been the case at certain key points in the past as well, it is the *new* technical and political capacities or conditions that allow, if not demand a top-to-bottom reevaluation. These four categories are, therefore, a preliminary taxonomy aimed at bringing together environmental and political performances toward a new analytic of the building envelope. They are, of course, particular or proto-typical instances of a more extensive and highly gradated speciation of envelopes that ranges across or between them. Some buildings hold an ambiguous position in this taxonomy, yet it seems unlikely that a new analytic of the envelope can be initiated without resorting to some form of classification, however precarious, reductive, and ephemeral it may be. It is, after all, reduction and a permissible level of abstraction that allows an analytic to be produced, and it is perhaps the key to understanding how past moments when the envelope of the building stood face-to-face with highly charged political-economic shifts led to either enhanced material expression or hyperbolic figurative expression—the two ends of the spectrum of possibilities this present study will renegotiate.

X ≈ Y > Z. Flat-Horizontal Envelopes. Loose Fit.

The first of the four proposed categories of building envelopes comprises those in which the horizontal dimensions are considerably larger than the vertical. Buildings or complexes such as airports, train stations, industrial buildings, trade fairs, convention centers, and markets, as well as retail and leisure facilities, generally belong to this category. Flat-horizontal envelopes perform primarily by sheltering the domains they enclose and delimiting their boundaries. They tend to operate on a basic articulation between inside and outside, and are, therefore, paradigmatic cases of an articulation between natural and artificial in its most basic terms. Since their comprehensive perception can only be obtained from an aerial perspective, flat-horizontal envelopes are generally perceived in a fragmented manner and are therefore less concerned with figural performance than with the organization of material flows: traffic, ventilation, daylight, security, etc.

The flat-horizontal envelope's political charge stems from its customary function to host large crowds, enclose vast open spaces, and to control movement through a rigorously articulated environment. Because of its capacity to handle large flows of transient populations and goods, this envelope type features prominently as one of the mechanisms of spatial displacement—that is, as a prime example of the types of space-time that global capitalism has created as one of its basic infrastructures or means of transfer. While infrastructural buildings usually connect with large territorial domains *by extension* (that is, by rail, road, or air corridors), flat-horizontal envelopes that enclose infrastructure tend to have a conflictive relationship with the local grain.

Flat-horizontal envelopes are often driven by flow-control and security mechanisms; station and airport envelope footprints are usually related to security protocols, while in retail parks, stadia, and convention centers the importance of access points and interface with the exterior public space constitute the crucial determinants of the building's outline or extension into that "outside." The other predominant physical determination is of a structural nature: their floor-consuming functions are usually coupled with long spans, and their prevailing roofing performance is crucially determined by functional grids of parking bays, retail unit grids, storage and access grids, etc., that determine how the transfer of vertical loads punctures the functional spaces.

From a structural criteria, flat-horizontal envelopes can be generally classified as those that bring gravitational loads down to the ground in a pattern that pierces the space at regular intervals, such as shopping malls, storage buildings, or factories, and those such as auditoria, hangars, and sport venues. The spatial typology, the structural system, and the depth of the envelope are interrelated parameters. Patterned, flat-horizontal envelopes are built on a structural base unit that covers the ground by repetition, allowing for lighter structures. As the span grows larger, to avoid intermediate supports, the roof depth increases. The modulation of daylight and ventilation through that deeper crust is another crucial potential of the flat-horizontal envelope.

The flat-horizontal envelope induces a strong differentiation in terms of performance between its predominantly vertical (facade) and horizontal (roof) surfaces. The primary performance of the vertical surfaces is first defensive and then ornamental; it is determined largely by the relationship of the object to the outside. Alternatively, if we consider the roof—the predominant horizontal component of the flat-horizontal envelope—the most critical determinations are internal and primarily of an environmental, *atmospheric* nature.[17]

The critical potential of the roof design in this envelope typology is to provide daylight and solar shading, and to enhance natural ventilation; these concerns will gain greater importance in the near future as energy becomes a costly commodity and environmental politics intensifies. Retail malls, a particular case of this typology, are generally designed as sealed envelopes where interior and exterior are strictly detached in environmental terms. On the other hand, trade-fair halls, stations, and airport terminals are increasingly designed as permeable skins, capable of filtering daylight, enhancing natural ventila-

---

17 The notion of an artificial atmosphere is particularly vivid in this type of envelope, which returns us again to the work of Sloterdijk on the artificial diversification of the atmosphere within the capsular society. The human island, the capsule, and the greenhouse are the prototypical devices for a new generation of buildings committed to this diversification of the atmosphere in which this envelope typology features prominently. See Sloterdijk, *Esferas III, Espumas, Esferología plural*, op. cit.

tion, and opening views between inside and outside. The envelope's political performance relies primarily on its permeability to both social and environmental flows, which produces a gradation that mediates between models of social filtering and control with low permeability of vertical enclosures, such as suburban retail malls or factories, and those with high permeability, such as markets or stations. Environmental permeability is another crucial factor of speciation in this typology, ranging from sealed, artificially controlled environments and sterilized atmospheres, to filtering systems with a more gradual integration between inside and outside. The degree to which the envelope intensifies or defuses the limits between private and public, natural and artificial constitutes its most critical political performance and sets up the speciation of this envelope typology. These factors are particularly important, as this is the envelope type that has a deeper engagement with the public realm and with the exterior environment, but due to its scale, the degree of environmental control in this typology is not as stringent as in other types.

The global economy has triggered some processes that will affect the evolution of the flat-horizontal envelope, and it is likely that they will continue to evolve in light of the changes taking place now. As public infrastructures have become increasingly procured by the private sector and the public sector has become increasingly concerned with retail developments as part of the public realm, the degree of engagement between flat-horizontal envelopes and the surrounding urban fabric will intensify. As flat-horizontal envelopes continue to get larger and larger to ostensibly provide for a burgeoning urban population and the consequent growth of consumers, goods, and transient population, an interesting dynamic emerges powered by the contradiction between permeability and energy efficiency. Such frictions index a clash of political, economic, and material agency that is only likely to intensify with the coming interventionist politics emerging from the current financial crisis, and the growing environmental concerns regarding the sustainability of such energy-intensive buildings. Either way, it appears as if the most progressive flat-horizontal envelopes tend toward higher permeability, as a means of utilizing the interface between the building and its surroundings as social and environmental filters.

Yet, as energy concerns (and demand) grow, and counter to reactionary measures aimed at minimizing short-term losses (leakage of both social potency or simple BTUs), the incorporation of passive technologies for providing daylight and natural ventilation is fast becoming mainstream: sealed envelopes are no longer the default solution for flat-horizontal types, as a more gradual engagement with the surrounding atmosphere is proving to be more sustainable. The abstraction of sealing down a building and either heating or cooling it (without taking into account seasonal fluctuations and climatic conditions), while patently absurd, will only disappear when comprehensive solutions are taken seriously versus delayed or undermined due to entrenched political and economic myopia. While compactness is one of the most energy-efficient qualities of an envelope, the ruggedness of the edge surface and the roof may be able to enhance the relationship between the internal and external environments both as a climatic device and as a physical and visual boundary acting as a device for social *integration*. The material and geometrical configuration of the edge is crucial to the articulation between inside and outside: footprint insets or corrugations producing the spongement of the vertical enclosure and the use of permeable materials may enhance the osmosis between the enclosed program and its surroundings.

The problem of inserting a large shed into an urban fabric is well known: the lack of active frontages turns flat-horizontal envelopes into large-scale obstacles to urban flows, sterilizing the surroundings with a forbidding edge. Stadia, stations, retail malls, trade halls, and factories are all primarily driven by the necessity to roof over a large area and, therefore, tend to present a very low level of engagement with adjacent functions. These containers tend to avoid an interface with the outside, which is perceived as a source of *pollution* for the activities that take place inside them. An increasingly common solution to this problem is to wrap the envelope with complementary programs capable of producing active frontages. Complementary programs wrapped around the main destination program have enjoyed in recent years the largest percentage of growth in typologies such as contemporary stadia, inner-city transportation hubs, and retail complexes. This model was well-tested in the US in the '80s and '90s when large urban train stations came up for redevelopment and most of them turned into *train stations cum shopping malls*. Public space is also retail space in an age when getting anything off the metropolitan, regional, or federal budgets is becoming difficult. As such, a project for new material agency that is also new political agency could be to reconsider some aspects of the neo-liberal model.

One of the specificities of this envelope type is a high level of solar exposure per square meter of covered floor plate, which makes the roof features crucial to the environmental performance of the building. The flat-horizontal envelope's roof produces an extended horizontal limit that provides shelter from temperature, rain, and excessive solar exposure. If due to its waterproofing functions the horizontal limit of building envelopes was traditionally rigorously delimited, as the envelope becomes more extensive a certain degree of openness may be necessary to allow for ventilation and daylight, unless an entirely artificial environment is implemented and political artifice demands strict delimitation for *political reasons*. Total closure is an increasingly expensive option—socially and economically—, and higher permeability of the membrane may be advantageous to allow for daylight and ventilation and reduce energy dependency, while restoring some measure of civic responsibility in the process. Additionally, the outlay of green on the roofs might further ameliorate fluctuations in climatic regimes insofar as it is axiomatic that "nature abhors a vacuum" will rush to fill artificially created voids with differential conditions that are, not strangely, self-regulating.

Thus, one of the most interesting current concerns of the flat-horizontal envelope is its relationship with nature. As all of the bamboo gardens and water features in airports and convention centers testify, the more conventional examples of this envelope type usually engulf nature in an "idealized" form, in which nature is merely replicated rather than constructed (existing on life support): an unequivocal example of what Bruno Latour describes as *mononaturalism*.[18] This phenomenon is, ironically, a type of index of the *depoliticization* of the natural; the belief that nature is opposed to the artificial, and singular, as opposed to constructed and multiple. In these instances, nature takes the form of the hyper-natural, and performs its varied functions admirably, while to the unreconstructed romantic it might seem like nature

18 *Political ecology* is the term Bruno Latour proposes to describe an anti-fundamentalist politics of nature in an attempt to overcome traditional distinctions between nature and society, subject and object, as well as human and non-human. Bruno Latour, *Politics of Nature: How*

is held captive in such orders, and pines for the open heath. Yet, what we see is the very notion that nature does have both a material and social or psychological effect, and its presence, in whatever form, in this building typology does, after all, ameliorate both the atmospheric and the psychological extremes given to artificial, internalizing worlds.

This "idealized" version of nature—never real anyway and hardly any less false than the fully instrumentalized, synthetic one—excludes political considerations at its most fundamental level. It does, in fact, do this intentionally—as the divorce between the natural world and the human world is its entire justification. Thus, the manipulation of the interior environment and the reformulation of the ground are the primary domains to be addressed in solving this conundrum. Where more progressive envelope typologies challenge the admittedly stunted apolitical version of the natural, the truly radical move would be to simply accept the advantages of the inordinate potentiality and endless energy implicit in the self-regulating natural world and get on with it. All one needs to do, in reality, is *detheologize* it, to get a better purchase on our relationship to nature and our possible good fortune in finding a proper engagement with its immense reserves of *material intelligibility*. In this regard, the technologies of the flat-horizontal envelope's roof can be effectively used to produce the rearrangement of daylight, ventilation, and solar intake for the provision of more energy-efficient environments than those produced through the radical detachment of interior and exterior. Could the interior gardens be used to reduce carbon dioxide inside the building in order to minimize the air-renewal cycle and, therefore, the heating loads in winter? Can vegetation act as a humidifier helping to cool the air in the summer? Is nature an ideal notion to be represented inside these large envelopes as little oases of artificiality or is it an integral part of the building systems? Is flatness a necessary condition

to Bring the Sciences into Democracy, trans. Catherine Porter (Cambridge: Harvard University Press, 2004). A well-meaning attempt to dissolve antinomies, Latour's proposal reminds all that naivety springs eternal and it is not so simple to reduce nature to constructed environments without also introducing massive means to support such endeavors. The simple installation of a tree in an enclosed and sealed courtyard or atrium will require significant resources to keep alive and repeated replacement, as the palms at the World Trade Center, New York, while a tree planted in actually existing ground, outside (or in a courtyard open to the sky), will perform its ritual of life and death according to more sustainable and cost-efficient laws.

of an artificial ground? The answer to these and other questions will imply entirely different levels of political engagement with a *multiple* nature, one that seems incredibly close to the older idea of an *endless* nature, one not given to romantic projection and one formally taken up by Georges Bataille in his theories of excess, insofar as those theories dovetail with a vision of plentitude hijacked (according to Bataille) by *artificially induced strife*.[19]

The success of a certain infrastructural approach to architecture in recent years suggests a similar process of *multi-naturalization* of the human environment. The treatment of large-scale roofs as a new *natural ground* seems to have become a default solution for buildings today as green credentials and organic features have become a politically correct trope for both politicians and urban activists. In this modality, the flat-horizontal envelope may simply operate as a new datum, an artificial ground that challenges the natural as an ornament and tampers with a politically loaded architectural element: *the ground itself.* In fact, explosive controversy might erupt if the real issues were actually tackled: the exploitation of land given to urban systems; the importation of resources in lieu of the conservation of preexisting ones; the usurpation of public space for private means; the dislocation and fragmentation of entire populations due to the excesses of an economic regime that knows no limits and when confronted with any finds a new crisis to exploit.

The use of large, flat-horizontal envelopes as ground can be found across a variety of contemporary programs and locations. The COEX Center, in Seoul, the Suntec City Mall, in Singapore, and the West Kowloon Mall, in Hong Kong, are retail facilities that act as connective tissue to a large urban complex, forming a new ground onto which other parts of the program are placed. However, the sort of naturalism that is constructed on these artificial grounds is often an idealized one rather than an exploration of potential interferences between nature and the artificiality of its physical support. Indeed, these very models

---

19 See Georges Bataille, *The Accursed Share: An Essay on General Economy*, trans. Robert Hurley, 2 vols. (New York: Zone Books, 1988–1991).

simply recirculate the old myths: that nature is either "pliable and submissive" or "out there somewhere" and not really anything to be concerned about. This schism is not new; it was played out in a less toxic manner in the modernist reduction of landscape to green plateaus for building, a de-naturalization and an easy abstraction that, in turn, was folded into subsequent models of rote artificiality and the geometrical games of modernist landscape architecture.

Digging the program underground or generating multiple grounds through bifurcation avoids the disruption of the urban fabric that flat-horizontal envelopes often produce by blocking arteries and destroying active frontages. If in the modernist ideal the democratization of the ground was produced through its neutralization to a flat plane and its reproduction *ad infinitum* (the Maison Dom-ino or the elevated walkways built in the '60s as a solution for separating pedestrian and vehicular traffic), the new strategies of stratifying urban ground are usually attached to active frontages on several levels and incorporate a high density of program, particularly retail. The advantage of this type of intensified ground is that it produces a series of gradations between the natural and the artificial capable of adjusting to the varying intensities of the urban field of which they are part.[20]

Generally, the requirement to make the roof more permeable to light and air implies a lower capacity to work as a ground, as a physical infrastructure. The question for flat envelope roofs is, then, whether the natural—or rather what form of the "natural"—lies below or above the envelope. Does the design attempt to produce an *atmosphere* by reducing artificial lighting, moderating temperature variation, and inducing natural ventilation, or is the purpose to act as a ground by increasing thermal mass and insulation, retaining storm-water, and absorbing carbon dioxide with vegetation? It is the intersection between structural solutions, drainage paths, daylight and natural ventilation patterns, and public flows that constitutes the fundamental political agency of the envelope: Once the flat-horizontal envelope has ceased to act as an insulating apparatus between the natural and

---

20 Some examples of this strategy of public space bifurcation on two or more levels can be found often in projects by the Jerde Partnership, for example in the Beurstraverse in Rotterdam, Namba Park in Osaka, and Kanyon in Istanbul.

the artificial, it will start to develop entirely different mechanisms to qualify either as an atmosphere-inducer or as a ground-infrastructure, and become a fine-tuned political instrument in the process.

Building technologies can substantially improve these structural performances by increasing the insulation capacity and thermal mass of the envelope, but energy consumption is primarily a geometrical problem, a function of compactness and configuration: the smaller a building envelope ratio becomes, the easier it is to maintain its internal temperature.[21]

As carbon footprints and energy prices become key subjects of global geopolitics, energy consumption and carbon dioxide emissions will become crucial components in the political performance of a building. Yet the politics of flat-horizontal envelopes is not restricted to the problems associated with world-wide climate change. Sloterdijk's *politics of climatization*[22] addresses the process in which growing sectors of urban space are given to private agents to develop and maintain: gardeners, event managers, and private security agents are part of the design of these contemporary urban *atmospheres*. Koolhaas' *junk-space*[23] is another description of the same phenomenon of sanitization of ever-larger areas of the city, providing a safe environment, assuming we are prepared to surrender police duties to private security services. Norman Foster's Crystal Island,[24] in Moscow, is a perfect example. If built it would contain 2.5 million square meters under a single envelope, instantly becoming the world's largest building, approximately five times the size of the Pentagon.

---

21 Optimizing internal atmospheres is something that R. Buckminster Fuller identified some time ago. His proposal for a giant dome over Manhattan was groundbreaking in the development of "atmosphere design." See R. Buckminster Fuller, *Operating Manual for Spaceship Earth* (New York: E.P. Dutton, 1971), first published in 1969.

22 Sloterdijk, *Esferas III, Espumas, Esferología plural*, op. cit.

23 See "Junk-space," in Rem Koolhaas, Simon Brown, and Jon Link, *Content* (Cologne: Taschen, 2004), 152-161.

24 For a description of Crystal Island, see http://www.fosterandpartners.com. For a critique of Foster and Partners, including the signature (now ubiquitous) diagrid, see Hal Foster, "Go, Modernity," in *London Review of Books*, vol. 28, no. 12 (London, June 22, 2006).

The project is proposed as an example of "sustainability, able to improve the environmental performance of the out-sized building, by swallowing *ever larger areas of the city* under a single envelope designed to enhance natural ventilation and daylight.

Whatever contempt we may feel for the junk-space megastructures and other social uteri, they have an undeniable popular appeal. Their energy performance is quickly improving and may eventually surpass that of the conventional city fabric, where the requirements for natural ventilation and daylight force the adoption of a smaller envelope texture with a much higher envelope ratio. Technically, the limits of scale of an envelope derive from the need to provide daylight and fresh air. There is already an arsenal of solutions to this problem without having to resort to energy intensive artificial lighting and air-conditioning: mechanically oriented mirrors bring daylight deep into the space, water jets and wind turbines produce adiabatic cooling, and atria can be strategically distributed to produce natural ventilation through stack effects. The capacity to enclose and manage vast volumes of air and produce energy-efficient artificial atmospheres capable of minimizing the consumption of natural resources crucially depends on the capacity of the envelope to regulate flows of solar radiation, air, water, people, vehicles, etc.

The question is: What is the scale of privatization of the public space that a democratic society can tolerate? Provided that they are even true, will the environmental achievements of Foster's Crystal Island be sufficient to guarantee an adequate political performance despite its supposed ecological benefits? The political dangers of the flat-horizontal envelope lie in the scale of space they regulate: the fundamental difference between, say, Yona Friedman's Ville Spatiale and the Mall of America is that the first is not an envelope but a frame, while the second is a container with a thoroughly sealed and dressed envelope which establishes a clear boundary between public and private, inside and outside. The smaller grain of traditional city fabric was perhaps better adapted to intensifying a social mix and safeguarding the coexistence of a diverse population despite the more subtle protocols of social control or engineering operating simultaneously. A way to ensure that the skin of the flat-horizontal envelope does not create a radical split between those who are included—for example, shoppers with substantial disposable incomes—and those who are excluded, could be to devise equally sophisticated mechanisms of physical and visual permeability across the skin. The larger the envelope becomes, the more sophisticated the interface has to be in order to guarantee an appropriate socio-economic population mix. The setting of those levels of permeability—physical and visual—oscillate between security and accessibility, exclusivity and popularity, thermal performances and air-renewal ratios, all of which have accordingly become deeply political instruments that may result in very specific social and architectural phenomena.[25]

The politics of climate offers the possibility for environmental technologies to disrupt the logic of the socially sealed envelope. Just as air-conditioning made large and deep floor plates inhabitable for the benefit of the consumer's masses, the *eco-imperative* becomes another argument to dissolve the impenetrability of modern membranes. Sealed envelopes are being superseded by more permeable envelopes as a model of environmental efficiency and social integration (for example, in the Masdar project by Foster and Partners in Abu Dhabi).

An interesting case study to analyze in this respect, particularly significant for the relationship between large-scale, flat-horizontal envelopes and urban fabrics, is the retail developments carried out in second-tier cities in the UK in the last ten to twelve years. This process started with the so-called Sequential Test, a planning policy issued by John Gummer, then the Conservative Secretary of State for the Environment. The policy gave priority to mixed-use development and inner-city sites over suburban and exurban locations in response to failing city centers and the failed strategy of

---

25 In 2005 Bluewater Shopping Centre (in Greenhithe, Kent)—birthplace of the *chavs*, a teen movement in the UK characterized by hooded clothing and gold jewelry and exhibiting a cult of consumerism, drug abuse, anti-social behavior, and life on benefits—forbade entrance to individuals sporting hoodies or baseball caps. The policy allegedly increased the number of visitors to the center some 20%. Opened in 1999, Bluewater Shopping Centre is the largest mall in the UK; it has also been identified as a major target of radical Islamic groups.

privatizing urban regeneration processes. Urban centers in Britain had reached levels of substantial degradation in the mid-'90s, and the Sequential Test was designed to entice the private sector to invest in inner-city sites by making the price of inner-city property so low that moving retail to the suburbs, as in the American model, no longer made sense. The suburban model, which had been promoted in the UK by early Thatcherite policies, reached its extreme in the completion of the Bluewater Shopping Centre and was then abandoned as a general practice. Inner-city locations made sense, given existing infrastructure and a captive population. This policy resulted in large sectors of the centers of Birmingham, Bristol, Liverpool, Leeds, Leicester, Manchester, Sheffield, and Southampton being bought up and redeveloped by private developers—a process closely monitored by the authorities, well aware and concerned that the city was being privatized block by block, service sector by service sector, and yet, unable to offer an alternative to the regeneration of decaying urban centers. This process unfolded throughout the early tenure of New Labour, which promoted these developments as strategically vital to the survival of city centers, triggering a shift in the orientation of UK retail development and planning in the late-'90s toward a focus on urban regeneration. A beefed-up public planning infrastructure was put in place by the Labour Government to continue what Gummer had started during the preceding conservative governments; the Commission for Architecture and the Built Environment (CABE) and the Urban Task Force (a think-tank set up by Richard Rogers to advise the government on urban policy) were established in order to promote denser urban cores and the hoped-for "urban renaissance." City councils pioneered the link between retail and urban regeneration as a central component of a strategy focused on the development and promotion of urban cores. In turn, the notion of such "place building"—which had been at the heart of New Labour's urban policy agenda—became inextricably entwined with revisions of retail-planning policy (private, speculative, and governmental).

The resulting struggle between old urban structures and the *junkspace* invaders is certainly being played out in the domain of the envelope and performed as a negotiation between developers who want to swallow as much space as possible within their complexes and urban planners who want to keep as much openness as possible throughout these complexes, extending the city fabric through them to produce active frontages and intensify permeability.²⁶ As a result of this tension, the final form of these complexes often became a hybrid between the existing urban fabric and the generic diagram of a suburban shopping mall.

The possible outcomes of this gradation range from the small grain of the traditional urban envelopes, such as those proposed by the *New Urbanists* and Prince Charles, to the voracious envelope typified by *Crystal Island*. In the first model, the envelope's geometry coincides precisely with the demarcation of public and private spheres and the limits between inside and outside. There are clearly delimited responsibilities for public and private agents in terms of policing, maintaining, cleaning, and controlling the environment, with a clear division between public and private domains at the envelope line. The second model requires a more complex political structure in which a single operator—in the case of the British inner-city retail complexes, a private one—is charged with ensuring the maintenance of a piece of the city, including both private and public areas and their hybrids. This is the public-private model that has swept around the globe since the late '80s, beginning with the revitalization of derelict post-industrial sites, foremost waterfronts. One could argue that privatization of the public realm by commercial development at a global scale (festival waterfronts, marketplaces, etc.) is a politically corrupt urban strategy in which large sectors of public space are given to profit-seeking operators. Yet, as energy becomes a scarce resource we may reach a threshold where minimizing the building envelope strongly favors the process of hybridization between the public and private spheres. On the other hand, the *New Urbanist* developments of Seaside, Florida, or the new town of Poundbury in Dorset, UK (both retro-models based on imaginings of a more innocent era), despite the strict consistency of the envelope that separates public and private and outside and inside, are hardly examples of virtuous, public-spirited domains. Each comes with an intense set of prescriptions that control both how things look and feel, and how things

---

26 This is perhaps the battleground between the traditional and the increasingly hermetic forms of "open" and "closed" cities. The latter is toward the production of enclaves—private utopias—for the privileged. The enclaves, of course, require the appropriation of public space and monies (in the form of subsidies and tax abatements).

operate. In the case of Disney's Celebration in Florida, the rules change as often as a threat appears that might unravel the "fabric" of the prevailing "image," that image the very crux of the marketability of the town as high-end real estate. Whether commercialization of the public realm is the inevitable outcome[27] and whether the management of large swathes of urban ground should be left in private hands are different matters; there is no reason why those spaces may not eventually revert to public ownership and management, especially if they begin to fall apart (that is, by *default* and/or *reappropriation*).

The troubling question is whether this trend is truly fostering the regeneration of benighted urban centers, as New Labour claims, or whether it is the incremental takeover of inner cities by profit-seeking organizations, who bring along the twin protocols of air-conditioning and private security forces to secure the illusion of "sustainability," in all senses of the word. In essence, the process of appropriation denotes cultural politics played via the very nature of the building envelope, with the assistance of public policy and, often, public monies. As with Sloterdijk's example of *the politics of climatization*, the description of the politics of each condition can be expanded through a dialectical conception—the urban core versus the transplanted suburban envelope. The envelope becomes—conceptually– a way to politicize and synthesize all typologies (old and new) and to re-represent in any given example the intersection of technology, social values, environmental and/or security performances, and "actually existing" human constituencies; in other words, the envelope is, and returns as, a vehicle for the discipline of architecture to use and exploit in order to define political, social, and cultural terms—and to do so with or against the grain (and with or against the prevailing socio-economic model). As political models change, so change

---

27 In 1994 the Supreme Court of New Jersey passed judgment on a sentence against J. M. B. Realty Corporation, the owner of several suburban shopping malls in New Jersey in favor of the New Jersey Coalition Against War in the Middle East who demanded the right to demonstrate and hand out pamphlets against the first Iraq War in several malls owned by the plaintiff, arguing that the malls are effectively public space, despite private ownership. This decision demonstrates the legal status of retail compounds as public. See *New Jersey Coalition Against War in the Middle East v. J. M. B. Realty Corporation*. Supreme Court of New Jersey, 1994.138 N.J. 326, 650 A.2d 757.

the games of the envelope, but they are always pushed forward by technological innovation plus socio-economic goodwill or the opposite, anomie.

Whether architecture can effect social integration, the redistribution of wealth, and the maintenance of social mobility for all (as its universalizing, utopian principles might demand), or whether it merely facilitates the production of socio-economic hegemony is difficult to determine once and for all, as the contingent order of cities is highly malleable and constitutes a constantly shifting tableau for these very factors to be tested. Without reducing the political potentials of the building envelope to a question of energy efficiency and resource usage (purely material concerns), it is still clear that architecture can have decisive and timely environmental agency and that this might be its *baseline* effect—its first cause. Today, buildings approximately produce 50 percent of carbon emissions and consume over 60 percent of total energy resources. Needless to say, carbon emissions are already a crucial geopolitical issue to be managed via so-called "cap-and-trade" mechanisms, a process that addresses primarily industrial sources of pollution, but one that will no doubt one day include domestic sources, an expansion of scope necessary to stop a few gluttonous super economies from causing global damage to the world ecosystem.[28]

Engaging with ecological concerns is contemporary architecture's most direct path to political effect, and this performative agenda depends—increasingly—on the envelope's design and integrity. *A political ecology* might enable architecture to regain an active political role, via basic but fundamentally radical forms of instrumentalization, and overcome the artificial and perhaps *politically motivated* division between nature and politics.[29] The design of

---

28 A typical global carbon footprint map shows the relationship between wealth, carbon emissions, and the consumption of energy resources: by exceeding their carbon footprints, wealthier states are effectively "invading" the poorer ones. When a building substantially reduces its energy consumption, it might be said to be contributing to the defusing of "global tensions"—although this exists mostly as a possibility rather than a fact. In using renewable energy sources a building reduces energy dependence and mitigates global warming. In order to do this it needs to engage local climatology and resources. One of the first resources in this regard is the actually existing landscape and its productive and self-regulating agencies.

29 "Politically motivated" often also means intentional, because this schism perhaps allows for appropriation and exploitation—the very engine of economic and political forms of domination.

flat-horizontal envelopes can play a decisive role here by ensuring a gradated transition rather than a boundary of exclusion, both environmentally and socially. Yet it remains a highly contingent affair. For to advocate a new openness by way of an investigation of high material agency in architecture, within the confines of a fast-closing system that values control of space for political reasons versus control of space for ethical and/or environmental and social reasons, is to effectively open a battleground where there are no discernible fronts other than the not-so-innocent envelope of buildings.

X ≈ Y ≈ Z. Spherical Envelopes. Relaxed Fit.

The dimensions of the *spherical envelope* are approximately equivalent to each other; cubic, spheroidal, and polygonal geometries are particular cases of this typology. In principle, the spherical envelope features the lowest ratio between surface and volume. The specificity of this envelope type is the relative independence that the skin acquires in relation to its programmatic determinations and environmental performance, as function is not usually determined by proximity to the outside and, therefore, by the form and quality of the envelope. This often implies a wider variety of programs inside, each with different environmental requirements. Spherical envelopes generally enclose a broad range of spatial types with specific functions, rather than being determined by the provision of a uniform environmental condition, such as in residential or commercial projects. For the envelope to become spherical, there needs to be either a number of programs that do not require contact with the natural environment or a series of voids, perhaps containing public spaces. Unlike other envelope types, in which the border between public and private tends to locate on the surface of the container, the spherical type often contains gradients of *publicness* within. Spherical envelopes often correspond to public buildings that gather a multiplicity of spaces: city halls, courthouses, libraries, museums, indoor sports facilities, etc.

Because of the low strength of the attachment between surface and contained space, the design of the spherical envelope has a tendency to focus on the surface itself as autonomous membrane. Given this typology's public character, expression and identity are crucial forces in its formation. While in other envelope typologies the massing is primarily driven by the functional determinations of the programmatic grain—for example, the depth of a cellular office or a bedroom—the spherical envelope usually contains a range of diverse functions. The spherical envelope has been affected more than other envelope types—except perhaps the flat-horizontal type—by the evolution of environmental control technologies because of its low surface-to-volume ratio. The availability of air-conditioning systems and the development of curtain-wall technology have made fenestration optional as an envelope system, releasing traditional structural constraints and enabling tilts, curves, and bends in the envelope's surface and volumetric articulation. The transition between the roof and the wall—a complex problem in traditional building—has been made easy by the incorporation of plastics into the construction industry, eliminating the cornice line as a necessary articulation; the corner, a singularity derived from construction geometries and property alignments, is also weakening as the limits between private and public fade and the structure of land ownership becomes challenged by contemporary urban development instruments.[30] The relative indifference between function and geometrical definition in the spherical envelope is particularly conducive to new expressive freedom: for example, pleated surfaces and irregular tessellations explore the low surface tension of this typology insofar as the shell dissociates itself from the internal structure and the programmatic vagaries of the type.

Furthermore, a highly technical delamination of physical, visual, thermal, and atmospheric regimes, expressed across the envelope membrane, is a fast-developing outcome of current environmental and security concerns, a development made possible by new fabrication technologies (for example, serigraphy, laser cutting, numerically controlled fabrication, etc.). Yet, beyond the emergent possibilities latent in both technical and socio-economic change, there is also a whole new politics of faciality at play affecting the envelope as the locus of non-discursive political agency—a form of pure material formality that registers the irrepressible nature of architecture to embody ideas. The emergence of new political modalities runs parallel to the development of envelopes that resist primitive *models of facialization*. The degree to which of the building's *face* is a *face* or as a *mask*, —an artful dissembling versus material truth-telling— is just one of the possible questions. As swing voters become the largest portion of the electorate and political tactics shift away from party-line ideologies and political rhetoric toward the possibility

---

30 The scale of urban land ownership increased enormously in the late twentieth century, as concentrations of private wealth and governmental instruments altered the traditional structures of land ownership.

of articulating new models of governance in accord with the changing world order, architecture returns to its own first cause (progressive representational agency) through new *sub-political* mechanisms consistent with micro trends, movements, and other *affect-driven* political-social re-formations.[31] We are witnessing the proliferation of modes of faciality that can no longer be structured on the oppositions between screens and holes, figure and ground, front and back, private and public, or roof and wall. The building envelope, as material-political vehicle, needs to adopt more complex representational systems, while not abandoning the responsibility to "speak" for things public. Once cornices, corners, and windows cease to be technically necessary and exterior/interior and private/public concerns become entangled in an increasingly complex relationship, the hierarchies of their interface become more subtle: the envelope has become the physical intersection of identity, security, and environmental performance. Envelopes have evolved toward a sort of micro-articulation: the pattern of construction joints has replaced the cornice line, the corners, and the fenestration patterns as the relevant scale of architectural expression. These tendencies are most visible in the spherical envelope because of its association with public building types and because of its low envelope ratio: spherical envelopes present the lowest level of environmental constraints and the highest levels of representational demands: identity and expression are a crucial part of the performances of this envelope type.

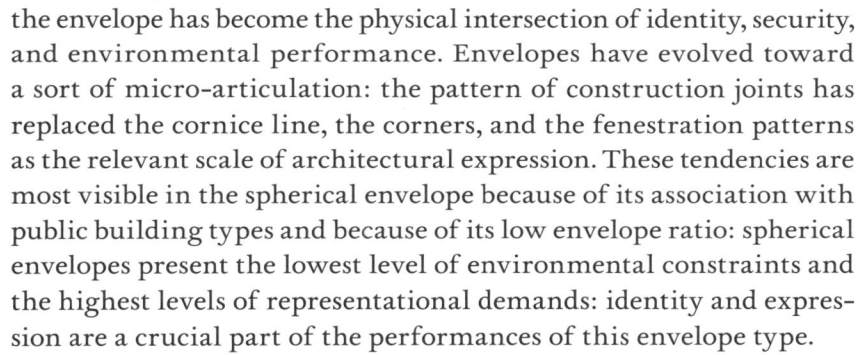

If the political history of the twentieth century could be interpreted as the exploration of public freedoms with respect to the normative basis of democracy, the development of the building envelope could be partially described in parallel terms. If the architecture of the Enlightenment still referred back to classical architectural languages, it grounded itself on modularity and a rigid metrics of space as organizing principles enabling effective construction but perhaps representing the egalitarian values of Saint-Simonian ideal democracy. During the modern period the facade ceased to be an allegory altogether and instead became a symbol: the external surface of the building, cleansed of any reference to stylistic convention, was now supposed to act both as an inseparable part of the whole building and as a symbol of modernity. The building's *face* was aimed to achieve the maximum degree of transparency, literal or phenomenal. However,

---

31 As Nigel Thrift has pointed out, contemporary politics is progressively less reliant on representation and proposition and more dependent on the production of affects. See Nigel Thrift, *Non-Representational Theory: Space, Politics, Affect*, op. cit.

the lack of an overt allegory in the facade did not necessarily imply the facade's disappearance as a quasi-autonomous element capable of representing a building's internal organization. The modern movement was invested in erasing the facade, merging it into an organic whole in which the external surface of a building would become a mere by-product of either its programmatic organization or its constructive articulation.[32] And yet, faciality could not entirely disappear: the *brise-soleil*, an element primarily designed to reduce solar heat gain, seemed to be also devised to compensate for the loss of structural expression in the modern curtain wall, providing an opportunity for the facade to retrieve some of the plastic interest and representational potential it had lost with the removal of the classical orders. Even if an identity grounded in faciality was in crisis, the modularity of facade construction, reinforced by the idea of industrial production, remained solidly in place as a symbol of a modern, industrial, democratic, and egalitarian society.[33]

As the modernist world order collapsed at the end

[32] As Alan Colquhoun has described, these investigations follow two primary lineages: an evolutionary, technical, and aesthetic approach shared by the Esprit Nouveau and Neue Sachlichkeit movements of the mid-1920s and a more ideologically charged approach represented by Expressionism, Futurism, De Stijl, and Constructivism, in which the building is considered transparent and fluid rather than divided into rigid compartments or bound by solid walls. This fluidity has an ethical component, as spatial boundaries are seen as symbols of social oppression to be avoided in a non-hierarchical democratic society. "The history of the facade between 1910 and the 1960s exhibits two partly parallel and partly sequential tendencies. The first tendency is the impulse to destroy the facade as such. The building should not be considered as consisting of plan and elevation but as an organic whole in which the external surface of a building is a by-product of its internal organization. The building is thought of as transparent and fluid, and should not be divided into rigid compartments or bounded by solid walls. This fluidity also has an ethical component. It symbolizes a non-hierarchical democratic society. Spatial boundaries are symptoms of social oppression. This tendency has an 'idealist' and a 'materialist' side deriving on the one hand from Rousseau and German idealism and, on the other from Marxism. In terms of architectural history, this ideology belongs to the first pre-war phase of modernism. It is represented by Expressionism and Futurism, but continues with De Stijl, Constructivism and the avant-garde magazine *ABC. Beiträge zum Bauen* after WWI, still with contradictory idealist and materialist connotations. The second tendency is less philosophically radical. It sees the facade in evolutionary, technical, and aesthetic (rather than ethical) terms. This view was shared by the Esprit Nouveau and Neue Sachlichkeit movements of the mid 1920s. The facade is not abolished but continued 'by other means.'" Alan Colquhoun, "The Facade in Its Modern Variants," in *Werk, Bauen+Wohnen*, (Zurich, December 2005).

[33] For example, Louis Kahn expanded the idea of modern transparency into a potent faciality by exposing the spatial structures and programmatic units in the building, while Mies van der Rohe targeted another form of transparency by revealing the load-bearing structure and the fabrication of the envelope as the primary expressions of the envelope.

of the '60s, coinciding with the emergence of global culture, faciality was rehabilitated: the postmodern period reinstated the relevance of the envelope as a representational mechanism, to create plastic effects alienated from their contexts, in correspondence with the prevailing post-'60s, late-capitalist ideology of individualism and pop spectacle. This architecture differed as much from the traditional city as from the utopianism of the '20s, as well as from its mid-century critics in the '50s. Even if, ironically, architects such as Robert Venturi attempted to redeploy language and allegory, as legitimate components of envelope design in the age of rootless and spectacular capitalism.

As traditional or even mainstream modernist architectural languages become politically ineffective in the wake of globalization, or the traditional articulations and inflected tropes of the building envelope become technically and socially redundant or simply obsolete, the envelope's own physicality, its fabrication and materiality will attract new representational roles (effects) and values (affects). Globalization has, on the one hand, neutralized the effectiveness of architectural language, propelling the iconic and symbolic to the forefront of contemporary practices while increasing the demands for the envelope's technical capacity for *insulation* and *immunization*, environmentally and security-wise, against an increasingly abrasive global atmosphere.[34]

Facades were, still are, and always will be designed to communicate something, although this communication has taken a turn, since around 1900, toward the unencoded and unencrypted mode, unlike in premodern practices, and modernity in this sense extends all the way back (*through the French Revolution*) to the Renaissance and the first stirrings of building as "science" versus building as ideology. The design of spherical envelopes has recently shown a general tendency to focus on the construction of the surface itself, both as an environmental and defensive device and as the locus of symbolic representations. This tendency of spherical envelopes toward a multi-directional, *differential faciality,* resists traditional protocols where representational mechanisms can be precisely oriented and structured. Nouvel's unbuilt, yet influential Tokyo Opera, Gehry's Guggenheim Museum in Bilbao, Future System's Selfridges Department Store in Birmingham (UK), OMA's Seattle Public Library and Casa da Musica, or Herzog & de Meuron Prada Tokyo are notable examples of those tendencies. Freed from the tech-

---

34 The general and specific forces of entropy: environmental degradation, social disintegration, class warfare, renascent nationalism, terrorism, etc.

nical constraints that previously required cornices, pediments, corners and fenestration, the articulation of the spherical envelope has become increasingly contingent and indeterminate. OMA's Seattle Public Library or Gehry's Los Angeles Disney Hall are also notable examples of this challenge to the conventional faciality of public buildings in which the envelope folds irregularly, undermining any frontality or privileged position. These effects are also achieved by dissolving the envelope's articulations—or, smoothening the envelope. As in Foster's Swiss-Re building in London, where the cladding system is extended to the top of the building, there's no need for a crown or cornice line in this brave new world; the closest element approaching a "crowning gesture" in Swiss Re is a floating rail for the cleaning cradle that hangs near the top of the building. Any form of pediment is missing and the form narrows toward the bottom, producing an effect of instability.

The current appetite for the envelope to become an insulating, immunizing device, combined with the devaluation of discursive language as a means of architectural expression is shifting the envelope away from normative language and signification (grammar, or syntactical and semantic values) toward visual languages. A *differential faciality* in which the materiality and tessellation of the surface become critical design mechanisms mediating between simultaneous demands for iconicity and immunization seems to be the general tendency within experimental practices. The geometry of tiles, for example, their degree and variation as well as the pattern and nature of joints, assumes—today—the task of so-called architectural expression. As the articulation of the volume becomes infinitely pliant, the construction of the envelope is charged with architectural, social, and political expression as a totality. The demise of the traditional figures of building faciality—in Deleuzian terms, the *white wall/black hole system*[35]—has found subsequent reification in the availability of certain technical possibilities (such as printing technology and CAM manufacturing) that have enabled architects to play not only with tessellation

---

35 See Deleuze and Guattari, "Year Zero: Faciality," in *A Thousand Plateaus*, trans. Brian Massumi (Minneapolis: University of Minnesota Press, 1987).

geometries and material textures but also with a wide repertoire of layers that may sometimes play an ornamental role, as well as perform technical functions such as solar shading and visual obstruction.

The fenestration pattern in a building envelope has psychological and symbolic connotations and has been historically attached to political representation. Fenestration patterns—whether symmetrical or asymmetrical, regular or irregular—have long been associated with political concepts such as order and freedom, equality, diversity, and transparency. The *fenêtre en longueur* was an index of the lack of compartmentalization and new internal freedom associated with the *plan libre*, but it was also loaded with psychological content.[36] Herman Hertzberger used to joke that in his student years, left-wing architects were those who used horizontal windows, while right-wing architects had a clear preference for vertical windows. While amusing, this anecdote also sets up the more complex question of how time is framed using fenestration (and why one form might be considered left-wing and the other right-wing). A possible reading is that the framing of the horizon and the occlusion of the ground and the sky produced by the *fenêtre en longueur* is polemically opposed to the framing of the continuity between ground and sky that vertical fenestration supposedly produces—the latter, arguably, a traditional means of structuring subjectivity in deference to forms of authority, as the vertical view is an eidetic embodiment of "as above, so below." At least in structuralist terms this would make sense. Yet, the vertical opening binds the interior space to a temporal, external cycle with a vertical slice of solar radiation that sweeps the room sequentially like a clock. Here the primal purpose of the oculus in the Pantheon becomes self-evident. By slicing daylight in a parallel direction to the sun's trajectory, the horizontal window, one might say, suspends natural time in favor of all-pervasive universal time. Therefore, which is more aligned with the real? And, does this not demolish the rhetoric of fenestration and introduce an option to carve the building more closely "at the joints"? However stilted, these

36 Part of Le Corbusier's arsenal, the *fenêtre en longueur* (or horizontal band of windows) became part of the progressive modernist idiom until it became part of the problem (that is, a caricature of its original intent through ubiquity).

alternative experiences of the world, viewed through equally artificial apparatuses, underscore entirely different approaches to being in the world, with inevitable political effects of the most literal form. In the spherical envelope, the relative independence between the interior and the exterior mitigates the effect of traditional fenestration patterns while neutralizing the avant-garde pretensions of the *fenêtre en longueur*, demoted anyway in subsequent critiques regarding the scopic regimes given to modernist architecture. The value of this rhetorical chiasmus is that it opens the field for a much broader investigation of actual material agency devoid of anthropomorphic projections and suicidal maneuvers to command time and space to conform to ideological biases. (Perhaps it is for this reason, as well, that Paul Virilio invoked the *oblique function* as a means of resubjectivization.)

Beyond this tussle over means of marking the envelope with meaningful or *meaningless* expressions of human or inhuman agency, the technology that regulates the homeostasis of the envelope has become substantially more complex. The de-coupling of the patterns of visual, thermal, and atmospheric permeability has opened unprecedented possibilities for *multiple facialization* of the envelope by dissolving or intensifying the joints in the envelope's surface at will through the phasing and de-phasing of these layers. The conventional figures of building faciality have been replaced by a more nuanced interfacial embodiment in which different layers of performance are played out against each other to produce a far greater complexity of effects. For example, in Herzog & de Meuron's Eberswalde Library or Ricola Factory, there is a deliberate attempt to induce kinetic effects by combining the modular composition of the wall with an additional figurative texture. Gehry's shifted titanium claddings seek, on the contrary, the neutralization of the modularity to enhance monolithic effects, a physical expression of exclusivity and insulation, while the surface geometry defies the traditional forms of faciality. It is interesting to consider what these architectural expressions of envelope geometry and tessellation meant in the complex frame of Basque politics in the '90s, and the role the Bilbao Guggenheim played in that political scenario.

Generally, the tendency toward air-tightness is played out, today, in the joint pattern and modulation of global surface rather than the fenestration. The emergence of polygonal tessellations as a contemporary tendency in envelope design—for example, PTM's Beijing Watercube—may be related to the bubble geometries of *differential faciality*, but it is also an index of a contemporary desire for insulation. The politics of globalization has also brought a fear of the other which has not been seen since the postwar era, a phenomenon prompted by attacks on transport infrastructure by the "enemy inside" as well as attacks from the "outside" in the form of blowback from new and old imperial adventures. For example, Sarin gas attacks in Tokyo, Madrid 11/4, and London 7/7, global epidemics such as AIDS and SARS, reactionary water-tight immigration policies, resurgent protectionist economic politics, etc., all suggest a rather generalized, paranoid frame of mind leading *backward* toward air-tight envelopes. The consequent tendency toward bubble envelopes is made possible by polygonal geometries that may also reduce joint length (polygonal tessellations have a smaller joint-length per surface-unit than rectangular grids, for example). Gehry's fishlike skins are another index of this tendency aimed at the erasure of hierarchical facade organizations and the modular grid that characterizes standard unitized curtain-wall cladding systems. In doing so they may also be exploring the expression of a weighted, gradated organization between part and whole, away from a modular organization based on indifference, independence, and interchange-ability. If modularity was typically a quality of a democratic system that prioritized the part over the whole, some of these emerging envelope geometries seem to be exploring modular differentiation as a political effect toward as-yet-unknown ends.[37] The modular grid, indifferent to the relative weight of individuals or politically active subgroups, very much embodied the ideals of

---

37 John G. Blair observes that when the word module first emerged in the sixteenth and seventeenth centuries, it meant something very close to model. It implied a small-scale representation or example. By the eighteenth and nineteenth centuries the word had come to imply a standard measure of fixed ratios and proportions. "A modular system is one that gives more importance to parts than to wholes. Parts are conceived as equivalent and hence, in one or more senses, interchangeable and/or cumulative and/or recombinable." John G. Blair, *Modular America: Cross-Cultural Perspectives on the Emergence of an American Way* (New York: Greenwood Press, 1988).

democratic equality and liberal individualism. It demonstrated a preference for non-hierarchical organizations and other ideal notions of democracy in which individuals are equal subjects to the will of majority. *Weighted* models of democracy—either those committed to the exercise of civil liberties or those that are driven by a hierarchical bureaucratic regime overlaid onto basically democratic protocols—tend to relate better to *allometric* modularities or *variable repetitions* as traits of expression, to reintroduce a collective purpose to a modular system without resorting to primitive forms of hierarchy.

As transparency has proven a politically naive tactic within global capitalism, where the design of an adequate public interface requires detachment between expression and building efficiencies, while growing security and environmental concerns legitimize the consistency of the envelope, faciality is being deployed without apologies. Yet this renewed self-consciousness is now embedded in the physicality of the skin, pervading the materiality of the construction itself. Given the devaluation of language as a means of expression and representation within global capitalism, the contemporary envelope—arguably the primary repository of contemporary architectural expression—is now invested in the production of affects, an unencoded, pre-linguistic form of identity that transcends the propositional logic of political rhetorics. These rely on the material organization of the membrane, where the articulation between *the parts and the whole* is not only a technical solution but also posits a resonance with the articulation between the individual and the collective.

Regarding the part-to-whole construction of the envelope, it is also worth considering whether the infill pattern of the envelope is consistent with its frame, or whether they are divergent organizations. This consistency is difficult to produce once we move away from the geometries based on flat, vertical surfaces that have constituted the core of traditional faciality, both classical and modern. The explosion of the spherical envelope's faciality tends to produce an airtight, seamless material texture in which the consistency between the surface tessellation and the geometry of the envelope and its singularities—folds, edges—has interesting political resonances. For example, OMA's Seattle Public Library is remarkably oblivious to the articulation between the tiling pattern and the edges of the faces resulting from the overall geometry: there is a seamless, graphic continuity of the pattern despite the accidents of the surface, unlike in Herzog & de Meuron's Prada Tokyo, where the envelope pattern infects even the section of the building, in a reversal of the modernist ambition of transparency. This is a transparent membrane of a kind that colors even the structural nature of what it encloses. If there is a chance to remain transparent in the age of spectacular capitalism and immunization, Prada Tokyo, built for an exclusive super-brand that requires certain strategies of exclusion and atmospheric insulation, is paradigmatic of it. This building proposes a contemporary form of transparency, in which the interior is shamelessly exhibited and yet filtered through the diagrid pattern, lenticular glazing, and LCD screens. There is a distorted transparency that achieves both accessibility and exclusivity and produces a unique atmospheric quality.

If with modernism we saw the emergence of the homogeneous, gridded envelope, and with post-modernism the rise of incongruent juxtapositions of rhetorical figuration as representational models for conflicting and mutating political views, the slide we are witnessing today toward seamless, yet differentiated envelopes appears to be more than a mere coincidence. Perhaps an embodiment of a certain political unconscious driving contemporary architectural affects, it is also a very pointed end run on all of the foregoing. The envelope's tessellation patterns seem to have fallen under the spell of differentiation, mobilizing a variety of technical alibis: whether a differentiated view or a differential solar exposure. Weighted modularity resonates with the swarm-like organizations characteristic of both associative and weighted democracies, depending on whether they are formed bottom-up or top-down. As opposed to deliberative democracy, associative democracy is primarily mediated through matter rather than language, and we can see some of those envelopes as an index for this tendency. Moreover, it is possible to say that the age of affect is, in part, an outcome of a move away from cause and effect. What transpires culturally, at the moment (and in terms of globalizing trends), is a slipperiness without parallel, or a pure eliding of times and places toward a *global* affect.

Herzog & de Meuron's Signal Box in Basel and Ricola Storage Building, two examples of spherical envelopes, are notable experiments in producing a differentiated envelope capable of dissolving the figures of faciality into a multiple, differentiated skin. The facade of their Dominus Winery goes even further in redefining the nominal part-to-whole relationships in the construction of an envelope by resorting quite literally to the contingency of a material pattern to produce differentiation.

It is fascinating, for example, to see *how* China has lately chosen cutting-edge architectural representation (by mostly cutting-edge Western architects) to emphasize and celebrate its new global economic might. The 2008 Beijing Summer Olympic Games were a huge experiment in the formation of a new national identity, and the deliberateness and precision used in its architectural and mediatic formulation was breathtaking—notwithstanding Western carping that much of it was simply too much, totalitarian, staged and even faked. The Olympic stadium, the Olympic pools, and the unfinished CCTV tower all display a similar massing strategy—a more or less non-articulated shape built at a colossal scale. There is no illusion of transparency or openness, only the ambition to construct a well-defined, unitary envelope. In that respect, not much has changed since Mao. But a closer analysis of the buildings' skins draws out the differences: the three buildings have been systematically structured with a differentiating pattern, probably aimed at portraying a culture founded on diversity, albeit, a diversity always expressed within the "collective" of Communist Chinese society. In other words, these buildings present an image diametrically opposed to the modular spirit of Western individualism, and display a "brutal delicacy" not unduly at odds with the gigantic scale of the projects. These buildings speak volumes about the regime;[38] they send the message that China can conceive, organize, and complete massive projects for a huge population (plus round up the required massive audiences to fill these projects) all the while appearing sensitive

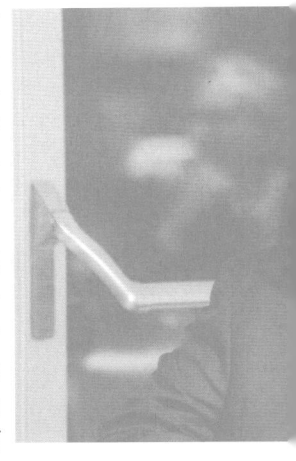

---

[38] "We wanted to do something not hierarchical, to make not a big gesture as you'd expect in a political system like that," de Meuron says, "but [something that for] 100,000 people [is still] on a human scale, without being oppressive. It's about disorder and order, apparent disorder. It seems random, chaotic, but there's a very clear structural rationale." "The Chinese love to hang out in public spaces," Herzog adds. "The main idea was to offer them a playground." The Chinese government, they say, has carried out their wishes to the letter. They make a distinction between creating a building that fosters a country's ideology—say, Albert Speer's work for Hitler—and one that seeks to transform it." Excerpts from a conversation between Herzog & de Meuron and Tom Dyckhoff, *The Guardian* (London, March 14, 2008).

enough to integrate, organize, and celebrate multiple specificities (ethnicities, traditions, etc.) and variegated agencies (for example, state-controlled, international-corporate, private, and semi-private entrepreneurial entities) through the aegis of productive distribution of industry. All production is driven through central command nonetheless, but it is so finely tuned that the operation appears acrobatic and nimble rather than colossal and monolithic. In any case, the Maoist blue suit has been dropped as inappropriate to China's new political identity and the homogeneous mass of the faceless proletariat has been replaced by smiling Uighurs and dancing Wu Wei masters—those differentiated skins of the Olympic projects carefully constructed by the authorities to underwrite this multifaceted "new China."[39]

The overriding question, in the foregoing instance of China and elsewhere, is whether the differentiated facialities and tessellations of the contemporary spherical envelope correspond simply to a strategy to reinforce the impermeability of the building envelope as an insulating membrane while representing an ideally differentiated public, or whether they are genuine devices to proliferate the faciality of the envelope and allow it to relate to a much larger variety of concerns—environmental, social, economic, etc. Another question of concern is whether they inflect (carry instances of nascent socio-economic liberation) in response to embedded multiple agencies and incorporated divergent specificities or do they simply resort to the production of political illusions and empty affects—in other words, spectacular embodiments of the *phantom public* of global capitalism.[40]

There is a growing sensitivity to how the production and marketing of difference has become a core strategy of a post-Fordist culture industry. Capital has fallen in love with difference, advertising thrives on selling us things that will enhance our uniqueness and individuality... Semiotic poly-

---

39 Whether or not this image was manufactured primarily for "sale" in the West or not remains to be seen.

40 The term phantom public was coined by Walter Lippmann in his critical assessment of the public within modern democracies as an artificially constructed entity. This work triggered a more optimistic reply from John Dewey about the relations between information and the formation of democratic communities in what has become a famous polemic. Walter Lippmann, *The Phantom Public* (London: Transaction Publishers, 2002). Lippman's critique was first published in 1925.

semy has become, in so many ways, both functional for and a function of capitalism itself. This leads Antonio Negri and Michael Hardt to caution us against the immunity from critical reflection and judgment that concepts such as difference and polysemy have traditionally enjoyed in cultural studies.[41]

Because of the proliferation of agencies in contemporary politics, it is no longer morally sustainable to hold to the *ideological* assumption that a more regular or a more differentiated pattern, one more permeable or more closed, is better at representing a progressive society and the production of transformative, liberating effects. The political accuracy of a certain envelope needs to be judged with respect to very concrete assemblages. The most interesting envelopes among the iconic Beijing projects are probably those in which the architects succeeded in creating a plausible structural alibi for the differentiated pattern wrapped around the massive, unarticulated volume of the buildings, where a resonance between literal performance and affect was achieved. The aesthetics of performance and technology is still one place where this is permitted. Here, a new discipline of the envelope becomes politically operative, as it is the discipline that can act as a *pièce de résistance* without getting caught in the negative project of the critical tradition—that is, modern negative dialectical criticism—or in the use of architecture as an overt means of political representation. *The political* is not reducible to *politics*.[42]

X ≈ Z > Y. Flat-Vertical Envelopes. Tight fit.

The category of *flat-vertical envelope* includes those envelopes whose predominant dimensions are distributed along a line parallel to gravity. Flat-vertical envelopes, or slabs, are generated by a horizontal and vertical displacement of space that, in order to support a specific function, optimizes density, daylight, ventilation, structural constraints, and the building's relationship with public space and infrastructure. Land use and orientation are also important determinants for this type of envelope. We can probably

---

41 "The affirmation of hybridities and the free play of differences across boundaries is liberatory only in a context where power poses hierarchy exclusively through essential identities, binary divisions, and stable oppositions. The structures and logics of power in the contemporary world are entirely immune to the 'liberatory' weapons of the postmodernist politics of difference" Toni Negri & Michael Hardt, *Empire* (Cambridge: Harvard University Press, 2001), 142.

42 This seems to be the message of those addressing the political at this time: for example, Giorgio Agamben, Jacques Rancière, et al.

include in this category most mid-rise residential and many office buildings, as they respond to the need to host a large volume of homogeneous program with precise environmental determinations. The flat-vertical envelope is primarily determined by the facade-to-facade or facade-to-core depth, hence its laminar organization.

The modern urban fabric is dominated by matrices of flat-vertical envelopes combined in various configurations suited to particular climates, uses, and cultures. For example, the facade-to-facade depth for office buildings will vary from 12 to 36 meters or more. In Germany and the Netherlands, glass-to-glass depth (the depth or breadth of buildings) is limited to less than 15 meters in order to enhance daylight and natural ventilation, as artificial lighting and mechanical ventilation have proved to be the most onerous aspects of environmental control. In the energy-intensive culture of the USA, the facade-to-core dimension of an office building usually requires more than 15 meters because of a tradition of artificially controlled working environments and a demand for higher flexibility and compactness. In residential buildings the facade-to-facade depth will vary between 9 and 24 meters, depending on the access system (double- or single-loaded corridors)—which is also culturally determined—and residential typologies (double or single aspects).

The flat-vertical envelope characterizes the modern city where optimized functional performances have prevailed over the cumulative, varied structure of natural topography, property boundaries, territorial limits, and community thresholds—as a result, the ensemble floats in the resulting *tabula rasa*. Functionally driven, flat-vertical envelopes emerge from traditional urban fabric at the point where internal forces—daylight, ventilation, and structure—override the maximal constraints of property boundaries and where divisions between public and private are elided.

Historically, from Durand to Khrushchev, the flat-vertical envelope has often been associated with political programs and the desire for a new, open society freed from natural and historical constraints and governed by healthy, egalitarian, and rational laws. It also relates to a variety of social and cultural performances involving land-ownership structures and political representation. Haussmann's famous mid-nineteenth-century interventions in Paris deployed flat-vertical envelopes as a wrapper for surgical incisions in the old urban fabric. Gropius's and Hilberseimer's modern-orthodox, flat-vertical residential typologies exploited the freedom provided by modern property structures—both capitalist developments and state-driven residential programs—to abandon street alignments and property boundaries and engage with climatic conditions and functional determinations to produce the scale and the spacing between the units.

The relations between street patterns and property boundaries, which define different types of public and private space, and the conflict between the ideal orientation of the facades and their alignment with street patterns are classic problems of urbanism. Whether the massing of urban fabric contributes to the legibility of the community structure or optimizes their environmental performance (or both), the geometrical determination of the envelope plays a crucial political role.

As an urban type, the flat-vertical envelope determines both the structure and representation of the social fabric. It delimits interior and exterior but also determines the limits between open public and private spaces. The flat-vertical building envelope is often deployed as a border that both forms a threshold between public and private space and constructs the building's faciality. The Barcelona block—like many other nineteenth-century urban typologies in Europe—was achieved by bending a traditional flat-vertical envelope to align with and wrap an urban block that remained nonetheless consistent with the distributive nature of the modernist grid. Turning the corner of a flat-vertical envelope is a legitimate disciplinary challenge: the consequent loss of daylight and ventilation in the corner spaces and the surrender of the ideal orientation of the units to the role of creating a border between private and public is a well-documented technical problem. The facades of the envelope are treated differently: the external (street) face focuses on the expression of the buildings, their signification, and the provision of active frontages, while the internal (rear) face is primarily driven by functional constraints of solar shading and ventilation. *Siedlungen, Höfe*, and *Mietskasernen* also exemplify the problematic relationship between the flat-vertical envelope's functions as an environmental membrane and as a surface upon which urban representation is inscribed.

In the antipodes of Barcelona, Le Corbusier's City for Three Million Inhabitants—the paradigm of the "tower in the park"—was aimed at defusing any hierarchy of open space, erasing the presence of the site's property boundaries: all land is public space—a park—and there are neither frontages nor backyards. The dramatic failure of Pruitt-Igoe, Toulouse Le-Mirail, Biljmermeer—as well as many other examples of this envelope typology applied to urban land without traditional property structures—derived from several causes, including the miscalculation of the performance of active frontages on grade and the inability to estimate the impact of maintaining such large amounts of public space on the municipal economy (ideologically, structurally, and financially). Most important, however, their failure can be traced back to the absence of a form of faciality that would make these complexes understandable (legible): there is neither front nor back, but rather a deliberate attempt to avoid addressing the signification of the buildings and their role within the construction of a new, expansive, and legible public realm.

As an envelope type that accounts for the majority of today's collective urban dwellings, the flat-vertical envelope determines not only how the population of the contemporary metropolis is housed, but also how it perceives itself in relation to the city and to the public realm. Is the contemporary city a locus of social integration, or a mere device for the peaceful cohabitation of culturally diverse populations? Is social integration necessarily achieved by submission to a series of common protocols and laws, or is it possible to form an urban culture made of exceptions through a public endorsement of difference? How does an increasingly differentiated urban population respond to locally defined iconographies, environmental specificities, and lifestyle patterns? These are some of the crucial opportunities for political performance that we can find today in the flat-vertical envelope.

The most active surfaces in the flat-vertical envelope are the vertical surfaces where technical requirements to insulate, ventilate, and light or shade coincide with representational concerns. During the first half of the twentieth century the collective residence adopted a monumental language in order to represent the emergence of new urban communities, such as in the Red Vienna Höfe, the Berliner *Siedlungen* or the Stalinist Seven Graces in Moscow. By contrast, modernists sought to recover transparency between the function and the face: Le Corbusier's Unité d'Habitation and Mies's Lake Shore Drive apartments represent two alternatives to the idea of the modernist envelope's transparency. While the Unité d'Habitation explores cellularization as a modular system of individual units, Lake Shore Drive submits to the repetitive rationality of industrial production, resulting in an envelope that prioritizes the unity of the container and its constructive rationality above the identity of the units, even as modularity remains very much the architectural expression. Le Corbusier expresses the modular nature of modern culture, emphasizing the independence of the inhabitants, while Mies expresses a new collectivism based in production through constructive rationality. Neither needs to resort to applied languages, but to an explicitation—Sloterdijk's term, again—of the modularity of the new industrialized production of collective residence. However, the difference between a modularity based on an accretion of units versus a modularity based on the production of a neutral screen is a crucial one that addresses, again, the question of the relationship between part and whole.

After the postmodern revival of the envelope as a surface of inscription and representation, we witnessed in the '90s an attempt to use the skin of the residential building to represent diversity and multiculturalism through a literal embodiment of social collage. In this paradigm, individuals are different and can no longer be represented by a homogeneous, repetitive tessellation of the facade, either by expressing cellular units or in the modular nature of the envelope's manufacture. Dutch architecture became the epicenter of this experimentation, capitalizing on a local tradition of cultural tolerance and multiculturalism, as well a penchant for large housing construction programs. The Dutch case is exemplary, not only because it was where the industry was more active, but also because of a Calvinist tradition of engagement between residential typologies and urban space that continues up through "Big Brother," a quintessentially Dutch invention. Dutch traditional housing has consistently blurred the boundaries between the private and the public: large windows on the ground level are supposed to be left open for the public to keep an eye on the private activities of citizens, while the traditional Dutch front window comes with a projecting (fish-eye) mirror for comprehensive surveillance of the public space.

In this sense, some of the work developed in the Netherlands in the '90s represents an interesting position both with respect to the Dutch tradition of transparency and as the embodiment of the new paradigm of a global culture of individualization and mass customization. MVRDV's Silodam and West 8's Borneo-Sporenburg, both in Amsterdam, are some of the most paradigmatic examples of this phenomenon. In these projects units are differentiated in order to provide a diversified product for a differentiated population, and the differences are intensified by color-coding, so that the ensemble becomes a patchwork of forms and colors, a graphic image of a multicultural, global community. Calvinist literal transparency has been replaced by an artificially enhanced transparency that intensifies difference as a cultural statement. The idea of a fragmented, ideally diverse population brought together under the collective umbrella of a modern, multicultural society is at the origin of these envelope strategies. The arrangement of colors and spaces in this work may affect people's feelings and actions and encourage "easy-going" individualism rather than modernist cellularization (atomization and alienation). Then again, it may only encourage residents to act as a conformist, homogeneous herd united by an illusion of individualism. In diametric opposition to the patchwork approach is Némasus, an experimental housing prototype designed in 1987 by Jean Nouvel for Nîmes. Here a totally homogeneous system of double-aspect, loft-like spaces is proposed under the idea that a better home is a bigger home. Both the Gifu Housing by SANAA and the VM housing project in Orestad by PLOT are intermediate alternatives that explore different possibilities between repetition and differentiation.

Yet isn't it consistency, rather than difference, that contemporary global communities need to build across coexisting cultures? The future of multiculturalism and diversification in the post-9/11 age is open for consideration, and there are reasons to believe that the politics of the globalized world will be moving toward the enforcement of sameness rather than difference as the fractious nature of multicultural societies becomes more and more apparent.[43] If the politics of identity remains constantly in flux, it is problematic to

---

43 The French law on secularity and conspicuous religious symbols in schools (also known as laïcité) came into effect on September 2, 2004, at the beginning of the new school year. At approximately the same time, Trevor Phillips, then chairman of the Commission for Racial Equality in the UK, stated in a controversial interview in *The Times* on April 3, 2004, (see next page)

come up with a recipe for the design of such types of envelope. An alternative may be to draw the energy for such figurations from the developments of concrete environmental solutions, but we know by experience that this is probably not a sufficient cause for differentiation of faciality in itself. It seems that an additional "something" is required, and while that something might be a specious argument for diversity in the face of overwhelming monotony and sameness, it at least begins to engage what is always bracketed in purely functional or technical solutions—that is, everything else.

An interesting debate in this respect took place at the Berlage Institute circa 1990 between Alvaro Siza and Hermann Hertzberger regarding the project Siza had just completed in the Schilderswijk Ward in The Hague. This was a decade before 9/11 and the murder of filmmaker Theo van Gogh by a Muslim fundamentalist. Both Siza and Hertzberger were totally innocent of political conservatism: Siza was a veteran of the *Revoluçao dos Claveles* and Hertzberger was known as the paladin of the Dutch postwar welfare state and Montessori education. The discussion, therefore, took place between two self-proclaimed progressives who nonetheless occupied clearly opposite positions with respect to the political implications of the design.

Siza's Schilderswijk housing is a great example of envelope complexity. On the one hand, its skin is built with brick and stone, following the tradition of the Amsterdam School, as opposed to the abstract figuration of Dutch modernism, the language of choice for the political left. The argument was that the lower classes should have access to high-quality local materials with which they can draw an affiliation and that imply an intensification of local architectural traits as identity engines. Second, the building features an extremely sophisticated system of access stairs that proliferates the Dutch tradition of walk-up residences: a complex folding of the envelope

(continued from previous page) Britain 'must scrap multiculturalism' www.timesonline.co.uk/tol/news/uk/article1055221.ece that multiculturalism was outdated as it encouraged "separateness" between communities. As an antidote, and in typical reactionary manner, he called for a greater emphasis on integration stating, "We need to assert that there is a core of Britishness."

into a stair system provides access to all of the residences in the block without intermediate lobbies, extending urban space right to each door. Third, and most crucial, the traditional transparency of the Dutch residential envelope is unfolded into an interior layer that allows for internal divisions of public and private realms in order to accommodate immigrants with an entirely different privacy protocol.

Siza allegedly explained that most residents were likely to come from a North-African background. The movable screen enabled the primarily Muslim residents to split off a private area within the unit so women could retreat from male visitors, preserving traditional etiquette. After Siza's presentation, like a good modernist, Hertzberger said that public housing in the Netherlands should not support social habits that run counter to Dutch morality and its belief in gender equality.

The construction of an additional layer of concealment inside domestic space was certainly very alien to the local spirit of Dutch cohabitation. Was the exfoliation of the private/public threshold to the interior of the unit a politically advanced decision, appropriate for a tolerant, multicultural society to embrace? Or was it a sign of unacceptable political behavior (a politically correct maneuver) that defied the most basic definitions of abstract universality and democratic decor? Resolving the contradictions between domestic protocols of multiple cultures that cross contemporary metropolises is a nearly impossible task *politically*. This proves that architectural devices have greater potential for shifting political impasses than ideological or discursive practices, if and only if the architectural becomes embodied as difference within unanimity (actual plurality within a universalizing political agenda). Siza's option, for example, was "private" (intended to remain within the interior of private domestic space). It is consistent with the freedom that comes with domestic space. For it to become "public" has more to do with it being within a public housing project than anything purely structural or physical. It is, therefore, an ideological matter, after all, or until public housing does not reinforce the dictates of the state. The reason it is difficult to find a corresponding political equivalent for Siza's typology is because it is basically *politically incorrect*.

Z > X ≈ Y. The Vertical Envelope. Slim Fit.

The fourth envelope category in this classification has a predominantly vertical dimension and a multidirectional orientation in plan. The specificity of the *vertical envelope* category is the conflation between extreme technical performance and high-visual impact, a condition that produces the maximum friction between efficiency and expression, in turn productive of an affective regime that runs deep in the history of this building type. If in the spherical envelope there is almost no conflict between representative and environmental performance, in the vertical envelope the friction between environmental and structural performances is at a peak. Because of their scale and technical complexity, vertical envelopes have very high performance standards: formal determinations play a crucial role in the building's structural stability and its embedded environmental performativity. The vertical envelope's geometric determination may also have important impact on its surroundings (for example, the casting of shadows, the deflection or channeling of wind, and increased demands on services). At the same time the visibility of the vertical envelope makes it particularly conducive to an iconographic performance, frequently at odds with its structural and environmental performances. The production of signature towers is also the means to marketing such high-end real estate, while the nature of the "signature" is either: a stylistic affectation; an austere and glossy image of modernity; or a desirable *mélange* of affects brought to bear through location, cost (exclusivity), and pure materiality (formal, minimal, or expressive agencies as tectonic gestures).

If tall buildings have traditionally constituted a statement of urban power and prestige, their sudden proliferation is now paradoxically connected to a process of urban democratization.[44] There is an irrepressible trend toward the densification of existing urban centers as the planet's human population flocks to urban cores, where more than half of the world's population now lives. The pressure on urban land and infrastructure this process is triggering will require more intensive land use to allow these migrants to settle in cities, and high-density construction is probably the inevitable solution, however unlikely it may sound at the vortex of the financial crisis.

---

44 Political stakes are high for this building envelope type as it is one of the most active sectors; according to Emporis, (http://www.emporis.com/) 40 percent of the world's high-rise buildings —buildings above 12 stories—have been built since 2000 and around eight percent of the world's stock of tall buildings is under construction right now.

Examples of this process can be found everywhere, from London to Kuala Lumpur, Moscow to Panama, Dubai to Madrid: Once the preserve of the most rich and powerful inhabitants of the world financial centers, tall buildings are no longer a costly extravagance but a crucial development vehicle engaging the middle class. Even if this process does not reach yet the underclass that these migrating movements have created, this process implies a sort of democratization of the the high-rise, exceeding its natural milieu of the workspace and pervading all aspects of urban life: the most high-rise-intensive city in the world—Benidorm, Spain —already has one high-rise building for every 180 inhabitants. There is even a high-rise cemetery, the *Memorial Necropole Ecumenica III*, in Santos, Brazil. The opposite phenomenon is also true: high-rise buildings continue to be seen as symbols of urban power, exclusivity, and uniqueness now accessible to the middle classes, and this dichotomy sets up the stage for the high-rise's political performance, either as a device for the democratization of urban life or for the consolidation of an urban elite.

The vertical envelope lies at the intersection of the global processes of densification shaping contemporary urbanity and the increasing cultural and environmental concerns, often driven by local pressures. As the level of investment these structures require is often linked to global economic progress, foreign investment, and migrant populations, the typology has become the prime battleground between big global business and local urban activism. As a result, the vertical envelope has started to move away from the generic extrusions that optimized technical and economical performance during the second half of the 20th century to develop a wide range of local variations both in terms of its geometrical definition and its architectural expression, usually driven by populist and iconographic concerns—concessions to the *local* while the model remains *global*.

The conventional high-rise envelope has generally been driven by economic pressures, resulting in the extrusion of a floor plate and a structural grid derived from internal efficiencies of construction technology, cost and program. However, the current densification of the urban core is reviving the new monumental drive for high-rise construction. This is most visible in a series of image-driven high-rises that seek to play an urban role through iconicity. Tall buildings are paradigmatic of the representation of power in the city, be it that of a corporation, a city, or the might of a political regime. In London, for example, there is a new generation of iconic skyscrapers with nicknames which inscribe them in the popular banter: The Gherkin (Foster's 30 St. Mary Axe); The Shard (Renzo Piano's tower in London Bridge); Helter-Skelter (Kohn Pedersen Fox's Bishopsgate Tower); and Walkie-Talkie (Rafael Viñoly's design for a tower on Fenchurch Street) among them. In New York, where simple extrusions were the norm, the Twin Towers' unapologetic simplicity is being replaced by the more complex profiles of buildings like the Freedom Tower and Hearst Tower. Two recent competitions, for the Tour Phare, in Paris, and for the Gazprom Tower, in Moscow, are paradigmatic of the representational role that vertical envelopes have acquired within the contemporary processes of urban development.

Although the precise construction of the vertical envelope's skin does not bear the importance that it has in other envelope species, an elaborated, graphic skin has nonetheless become an "economical" device to respond to market demand for *uniqueness*. In other cases, the manipulation of the envelope's crown, where the technical determinations are weaker, is the technique to distinguish buildings otherwise designed as mere simple extrusions of an optimized footprint.[45] The deployment of an iconic image on the envelope is probably the most radical version of this search for iconicity within the contemporary vertical envelope: the tiered pagodas of older Chinese architecture in the Jin Mao Tower and the image of gold ingots used in Taipei 101 are the most prominent examples of this totemic approach.

A more nuanced alternative to the one-off iconic representation of power and privilege is the correlation of technical efficiencies and symbolic performance. The deployment of images that resonate with local iconographies or figurations as geometrical determinants can set in motion a productive engagement with environmental or structural efficiencies of the envelope: the rotated square footprints of Asian Islamic towers in the case of Petronas offer an increased facade ratio by striating the skin of the building. In the case of

---

45 While it has often been stated that a skyscraper is "bread and butter" for an architecture firm because it involves a distinctive lobby, a repetitive series of floors quite often identical in plan if not detail, plus a signature "top," of late the interiors of mid-rise residential towers have deployed very complicated and very mixed floor plans to appeal to the desire of the upper-classes for an "exceptional" *pied-à-terre*. While the floor plate may still be repetitive, the presence of celebrity architects in the high-end residential condominium market has led to an *à la carte* menu of designer-ready "floor plans."

Burj Khalifa, a desert flower provides a geometrical basis for the three tapering buttresses to lower the center of gravity. Kohn Pedersen Fox's Shanghai World Financial Center, which in an earlier scheme featured a round hole at its crown, suffered a last-minute redesign to incorporate a square opening, since the circle was deemed too reminiscent of the Japanese flag. Although owned by the Japanese Mori Corporation, its image had to be altered to avoid offending the locals with a monumental manifestation of Japanese power on Chinese land. These symbolic gestures and geometrical patterns connote a specificity that is at once *cultural* and *technical* insofar as they distance themselves from the austere, mono-cultural modernism of the mid-twentieth century—that is, the so-called corporate modernism of the International Style.

Representation is an important part of the vertical envelope, yet these epithelial, graphic, and iconic treatments—unlike Hugh Ferris's setbacks for daylight, Louis Sullivan's ornamented ceramic panels for fire protection, or Fazlur Khan's structural diagrids—are the epitome of a schism between technical efficiencies and political representation that disables the discipline's political agency. The expressive layer that some of these buildings adopt is not alien to the history of the vertical envelope, but the tension between efficiency and expression in the design of tall buildings has never been greater than it is now. If we follow Sloterdijk's logic of explicitation as the political program in the modern project, the iconographic treatment of the vertical envelope would perform as a cover-up for the technical or social processes taking place in the construction of these buildings.

The most common approach of avant-garde architects to the design of high-rises is to challenge the conventional, to produce the unique, and, on occasion, to attempt the revolutionary. However, would it not be more effective to mobilize the political in the vertical envelope as an expression of efficiencies? Is not the most crucial task of a politically engaged vertical envelope to make visible, to give new expression to, the most generic efficiencies of the high-rise city? A number of parameters, increasingly obscured by the drive toward iconicity, affect the processes of high-rise construction, while the search for the contemporary high-rise phylum[46] is primarily a project of explicitation. In an age when virtually anything is technically possible, to

---

46 See my "High-Rise Phylum 2007,", page 383 on this volume.

make these parameters physically evident, to convert them into physical tropes and give them expression, would perhaps be the most critical political program for the vertical envelope. The efficiencies of the vertical envelope range across a set of parameters that embody local specificities, including climatic conditions, lifestyle, trade protocols, and market demands. As the envelope increases in visibility and iconographic potential, so does the potential for views, solar exposure, and environmental and structural demands.[47] As a result of this intensification, the vertical envelope may become increasingly complex and *anisotropic*. It reacts very specifically to the surrounding urban context with specific inflections that provide views, solar exposure, natural ventilation, and profile. The envelope in this case not only affects the interior space but also has a massive impact on its urban surroundings. Oddly, the intensification of environmental efficiencies and economic demands can become a plausible alibi for a more inflected envelope with a more intense relationship to its surroundings, moving beyond the iconic and the graphic (arguably, stylistic concerns with a limited shelf life and low-resolution ideological pretexts) toward a possible political-material synthesis. Therefore, probably one of the most significant processes now taking place within this envelope category is a global tendency for tall buildings in residential markets; singular or linked buildings no longer set aside (as housing enclaves) but intimately integrated into the urban fabric. This tendency may in fact represent one of the more promising (and legitimating) forces operating within the development a more articulated and diverse vertical envelope, as it implies a drive toward a reengagement with nature and the city—in other words, a shift away from the high-rise's original milieu, the artificial environment of the workplace, and the emergence instead of the optimization of tall buildings with the patterns of day-to-day residential use.

47 Local specificities, in turn, might be converted to program-driven facade-to-core dimensions; environmentally driven facade and fenestration ratios; market-driven population ratios; compliance with certain models of structural efficiency; and procurement systems. For example, in a prototypical residential high-rise development in Dubai, the average facade ratio would be around 0.45 square meters per indoor square meter, in London 0.50 square meters per square meter, in Miami 0.55 square meters per square meter, in Seoul 0.60 square meters per square meter, in Kuala Lumpur 0.75 square meters per square meter, and in Hong Kong 0.85 square meters per square meter. If the ratio is high, it means greater capital expense; if it is low, daylighting and ventilation may need to be artificially supplied, which leads to higher maintenance needs and costs.

Contemporary high-rise residential envelopes across the globe are X-rays of cultural hybridization as they develop local variations. There are deep cultural and political implications for the geometrical determinations of the vertical envelope. For example, in Southeast Asia the residential high-rise has been largely naturalized, while in the West high-rise life is still associated with extreme artificiality and a particular sort of urban life. A high level of environmental mechanical control is acceptable in high-rise residential units in the West and Middle East, while the closer we move toward Southeast Asia the more common it is for all rooms to be required to have direct contact with the outside and to be naturally lit and ventilated. In Western models residential units rely heavily on full air-conditioning while in Southeast Asian prototypes natural ventilation and sub-floor heating are standard, even when air-conditioning equipment is also installed. The argument for this increase in the facade ratio in Southeast Asia is often based on the humidity of the climate, but it is more likely the result of certain living patterns that Asian cultures are not prepared to give up even in a high-rise residence.[48] Kuala Lumpur and Hong Kong are certainly very humid and when the air-conditioning is turned off there may be problems, but there is no reason to think that temperate zone cities like Seoul or Beijing need very different residential structures than Paris, Manchester, New York, or Chicago. Yet in South Korea a high-rise apartment without adequate orientation to the elements may see its price halved compared to those with optimum orientation within the same building. The combination of these factors has interesting effects on the resulting geometry of the envelope of the building, effects that tend to produce local species—in effect, the modernist envelope inflected by contingencies specific to locale and indigenous cultural practices: even the tessellation of the skin is affected by cultural differences: a lawyer's office in the UK and in most Commonwealth states requires three meters of facade, while an American lawyer's office uses approximately 3.6 meters. In locations such as London or New York where firms from both sides of the Atlantic share

48 Local cooking has developed kitchens with dry and wet areas; complex systems of service access and entrances into service areas exist within apartments of a certain standard denoting a certain class structure; a culture of bathing while being able to enjoy views and daylight is fuelling some expensive traits of the Asian residential high-rise such as the systematic location of bathing areas on the facade of the building.

the available space, the selection of the envelope modulation is important and will affect the rhythm of fenestration and the interior planning grids.

If the articulation of the facade is one of the most direct effects of "naturalizing" the vertical envelope, there are also several possibilities in which current tendencies in high-rise construction may become explicit in the sectional configuration of the vertical envelope. An interesting example can be seen in the correlation between the use of concrete as structural material for high-rise residential buildings and the preference for pyramidal envelopes. As the residential sector accounts for most of the tall building stock under construction, concrete is surpassing steel as the preferred material for high-rise construction. The ductility and lightness of steel, which gave it an edge over concrete in the early days of the type, is inadequate for residential construction, as steel has a level of deflection and sound transmission that is not ideal for domestic environments. Instead, concrete structure provides a solidity that reduces deflection and noise transmission, and provides a higher thermal inertia. Consequently, the construction industry has geared up to produce concrete construction technologies able to deliver high-rise buildings efficiently. Slip-form construction systems have now accelerated the rate of construction to one floor every three days, which makes concrete basically equal to steel construction up to 50 stories. Beyond this threshold, concrete structure becomes problematic for very tall buildings. In response, the building mass has become a crucial structural device of concrete construction in tall buildings: there is a generation of mixed-use super-high-rises being built with a spire-like envelope optimizing the structural use of the building mass. Tapering the envelope toward the top produces a higher structural section and moment of inertia in the lower sections of the building, making form coincident with the stress diagram of a tower. The Burj Khalifa in Dubai is probably the best example of the return to an almost gothic type of structure; Renzo Piano's Shard in London, Jean Nouvel's MoMA Extension Tower in Manhattan, Herzog & De Meuron's Paris Pyramid and Norman Foster's Russia Tower in Moscow also respond to this tendency of partial residential towers in which the shaping of the envelope carries crucial structural efficiencies, made *explicit* by the use of a pyramidal envelope. In a sense, it is axiomatic that architects struggle to find ways to turn such structural and technological variants into a language, as it would seem that *architecture parlante* past and present refuses to die. The new language of form, based on material values, might after all be just another version of this game.

The pyramidal shape, traditionally an icon of stability and hierarchy, has now become an expression of high-rise domesticity, a new "high-rise earthiness," as if the high-rise phylum was becoming increasingly grounded. Both the Ryugyong Hotel in Pyongyang and the Petronas Towers in Kuala Lumpur are extreme examples of the political role that vertical envelopes may play in representing a political regime; both feature pyramidal sections. William Pereira's Transamerica Pyramid in San Francisco now hosts the headquarters of the Church of Scientology and OMA's CCTV building in Beijing is chiselled out of a pyramidal envelope. OMA's CCTV competition model even featured Egyptian-like low reliefs, as if it were the remainder of some gutted pharaonic monument.

Commercial determinations are also capable of producing substantial socio-economic distortions of the extruded vertical envelope, but in exactly the opposite direction to the structural constraints. As height becomes a desirable commodity, there is a growing disparity in the rental values on different building levels. In a commercial high-rise, the lower levels are desirable because of their proximity to the street (for retail or high-density uses like trading floors). Upper levels are desirable because of their views and isolation from street noise. An inverse logic reigns. In residential high-rise buildings, as the value per square meter increases with each floor, it is common to have fewer, larger apartments for buyers with higher purchasing power. Therefore, the larger the floor plate is at the higher levels, the more valuable the building becomes. There are also several examples of contemporary high-rise projects in which this commercial logic has been mobilized to produce an *aesthetic of instability*. Structural and commercial logic seems to be operating in diametrically opposed directions in the vertical envelope, opening unexploited potentials that will produce effects of stability or instability depending on the vertical envelope's massing. The effects of the buildings may then become an explicitation of certain efficiencies, be it structural, technological, programmatic, or commercial; the problematization of these efficiencies becomes an interesting political field, albeit rife with latent socio-economic factors that may translate into further social stratification.

The sheer scale of some of these building complexes presents another new parameter to address in the design of vertical envelopes. The simultaneous desire for critical mass and synergy that drives the dramatic increase in scale of these typologies is leading several projects toward a configuration of interconnected towers capable of providing adequate daylight while exploiting synergies across ever growing concentrations of urban activity. OMA's Togok, Louisville Museum Plaza, and CCTV projects have been designed as "an alternative to the traditional diagram of the super-high-rise" and to "avoid the isolation of the traditional high-rise." They are excursions into the unprecedented scale of some contemporary high-rise projects. FOA's own Bundle Tower, a project done for the Max Protetch show *A New World Trade Center*, was an attempt to develop a structural concept for a new generation of super-high-rise buildings aimed at turning the almost unavoidable fragmentation of volumes in projects larger than 300,000 square meters into a structural advantage. The sudden proliferation of these branching versions of the vertical envelope indicates the convergence between certain efficiencies in the design of very large vertical complexes and the emergence that most contemporary icon, the network.

All of these parameters, often ignored when discussing the merits of high-rise projects, constitute the material grain of the contemporary high-rise phylum. Vertical envelopes constitute a field of convergence between the physical, the technological, the perceptual, and the symbolic, and constitute an important field of political performance. One of the most important possibilities is obviously the development of more environmentally conscious envelopes; for example, by increasing the facade ratios—at the price of higher capital costs—we can largely avoid mechanical ventilation and artificial lighting, producing energy savings and carbon emission reductions that may have, in turn, important and desirable political effects. Beyond their renewed aesthetic value as havens for the radically chic moneyed classes, tall buildings offer a high-density model that may help, for example, preserve the greenbelt from the ever-expanding suburb, and present a smaller ecological footprint than alternative urban models. The strange, ecological superiority of the *culture of congestion* and the now green credentials of the elevator core as an alternative to the gas-guzzling, six-lane highway are becoming universally accepted facts, which gives the vertical envelope a *raison d'être* beyond a mere representational drive.

In this sense, the current demand for spectacular high-rises[49] is precisely opposite from what we have described as a phylum of the vertical envelope, or, in other words, what Sloterdijk proposes as a *process of explicitation*. The current search for novelty follows the twentieth-century tradition of revolution or emancipation in search of truly significant factors needed to radically transform the real. But, what we believe is politically relevant regarding vertical envelope design is the way it can contribute to making certain urban phenomena explicit. Starting with the global process of urbanization and moving toward the densification of the urban residential fabric, environmental concerns and the technologies developed to enable these processes combine to form a truly engaged vertical architecture capable of making these current processes explicit and turning them into precepts or tropes.

The spectacular high-rise, the one that is contingent to the phylum, the one that pretends to be novel, exceptional, and revolutionary, but is not, is exactly the one that contributes most to the maintenance of contemporary socio-economic power structures and the endless mutations those power structures undergo to escape true progressive transformation. Oddly, stateless capital has produced the apparition of the contingent spectacular high-rise. It is precisely the differential and strategic departure from the conventional, the permanent flight from the status quo, rather than now-traditional radical opposition, that can actually reveal and subvert the dominant urban powers.

The images displayed along this text relate to the subjects herein described and aim to capture the political, social and cultural relevance of the building envelope. From Franco's coffin, the bubble child and Apollo 11 astronauts—autobiographical winks—through the security scans at contemporary airports at which we have become accustomed post 9/11, anti-AIDS condoms, pregnant chavs in Bluewater shopping mall, SARS epidemics, flash crashes, short-selling and the interconnectivity of the global market and other phenomenology of the contemporary life in "co-isolation". Modern faciality casuistic is represented by Monica Lewinsky's TV statement. Ayaan Hirsi Ali and Trevor Phillips appear in representation of the new politics of multiculturalism in globalised societies. Bubble-like contemporary buildings, shopping malls, vernacular skyscrapers and towers sprinkle the text as examples of contemporary building envelopes.

49 "The current mania for flamboyant skyscrapers has been a mixed blessing for architecture. While it has yielded a stunning outburst of creativity, it has also created an atmosphere in which novelty is often prized over innovation. At times it's as if the architects were dog owners proudly parading their poodles in front of a frivolous audience." Nicolai Ouroussoff, "Towers Will Change the Look of Two World Cities," *New York Times* (New York, May 12, 2006). http://www.nytimes.com/2006/12/04/arts/design/04towe.html.

No Frills and Bare Life: Cheapness and Democracy

Now that we inhabit the hangover of neo-liberal capitalism and globalization, and everybody is looking to the political leaders for redemption, it may be an ideal opportunity to consider what the real transformative capacities for architecture are and could be in the twenty-first century. Looking with some perplexity at the incredible burst of urban development that capped several decades of uninterrupted expansion of global capitalism, and at the scale with which those bland and sanitized projects took shape all over the world (more so in the so-called developing world), one wonders if the qualities of what was produced fit within what we generally understand as a city, as a locus of collective and democratic life. Are these developments just a device to efficiently organize rapidly growing urban populations and submit them to certain protocols that enable their integration into new productive orders in the least conflictive manner? Or do they represent the rise of an entirely new form of urban assemblage, with its own political dynamic? Despite their ruthless efficiency, do these urban topographies contain a possibility for the emergence of political life, with its own mechanisms of opinion, dialogue, dissent, resistance, and even subversion? Or has this new brave world done away with the customary forms of citizenship altogether?

As much as the phenomenon of rampant urbanization may inspire doubts about the possibility for a truly democratic life in these new communities, there is nonetheless something liberating about them: the possibility for anybody's access to urban life; the escape from the haphazard and often despotic regimes of rural life and the clutches of small communities, tribes, even nations; the freedom to move across these metropolitan communities; and the access to an ever-expanding range of services and commodities.[1] Urban inhabitants are substantially wealthier than rural ones, hence the massive migration toward cities that is currently taking place. On the surface there seem to be potential openings toward new freedoms by engaging with the protocols of urban life. For, if anything, hyper-urbanization is making available to an ever-increasing population access to what is arguably the most desirable commodity on the planet: urban life and the choices it avails. The question that remains to be answered is whether these new global, urban agglomerations will embody a new *sustainable* egalitarian world order, and how. Or, are they a stalking horse for new totalitarian regimes of control and exploitation, the stuff of sci-fi film and nightmares, but also a very real possibility if one takes into account the socio-economic and mechanistic nature of the overall assault?

There is, perhaps, the possibility for these material accretions to become polit-

ically charged: both the global phenomenon of the rise of the swing electorate, focused on concrete decisions rather than on ideological consistency, and the emergence of new political constituencies through informational technologies are crucial changes in the contemporary structuring of civil society.

Beyond urban development and architecture, there are other contemporary products that have already become vehicles of political constituencies without having to resort to political ideology or political discourse: low-cost airlines have effectively *de-classed* the airplane cabin and *de-rooted* large populations, exposing them to other cultures. Low-cost fashion and furniture have been

---

1   The relationship between merchandise and political culture has been widely analyzed in other economic contexts, in particular the American postwar period. See William Leach, *Land of Desire: Merchants, Power, and the Rise of a New American Culture* (New York: Vintage, 1994).

made widely available to the emerging urban populations, providing an easy physical self-confidence that did not exist before among the urban lower-middle classes. Yes, perhaps the new global order, essentially a gigantic market for the movement of capital, goods, and labor, has been fashioned at huge ecological and social costs, but revolutions have always had problems...

While it may be dangerous to assume that the accessibility of goods and services can be equated with the accessibility of rights that characterizes a democratic community, because the market economy is the predominant milieu of urban growth, it is important to understand where the political agencies of the market reside within this rather broad and amorphous milieu. Rather than reinforcing the firewall between economic and political theory (which never quite existed anyway), it is crucial to understand how these new products of a global consumer society might constitute de facto political constituencies; how, without being mediated by the more conventional forms of mainstream political discourse, they might regain some political agency for architectural practice through precise physical actions.

The political discourses that set the benchmarks for modern democratic societies—irrespective of how successful any of these were at actually implementing social justice or constituting real political advances in the communities in which they operated—were primarily based on political realism and reached maturity in the second half of the twentieth century. Most of these ideologies explored the notion of *equalization* as a political objective: Mao Ze Dong enforced the equalization of class, Che Guevara, the equalization of geopolitics, Betty Friedan, the equalization of sexual pleasure, Malcolm X the equalization of race, and Daniel Cohn-Bendit, the equalization of age. However, the pursuit of liberty, equality, and fraternity, while an admirable universal idea, did not quite played out according to plan.

Moreover, the intensification of global practices in the '60s made those ideological formulations seem irrelevant. Why equalize geopolitics when economies and technology can do the very same without the attendant ideological battles? Why equalize class, when class has transcended politically and geographically determined communities? One might conclude that the '60s postwar economic boom was the death knell of political ideology as an effective mechanism to transform society.

In 1975, as the world was leaving the first oil crisis behind, Bill Gates founded Microsoft Corporation and Amancio Ortega founded Zara, the largest clothing manufacturer in the world. A year later, Steve Jobs co-founded Apple Computer. When Alan Greenspan became Chairman of the Federal Reserve in 1987, he implemented a policy of cheap money that triggered unprecedented investment and growth worldwide. Other paradigmatic corporations from this new breed of agents, such as EasyJet and a reborn Monsanto, emerged in 1995 and 2000, profiting from the consolidation of global regulations and the opening of markets. Despite the apparent lack of political positioning across their practices, what links such players as Greenspan, Haji-Ioannou (EasyJet), Ortega (Zara), Kamprad (IKEA), and Gates (Microsoft) is a political program without a political office. Their political agenda is implemented through the role of the global entrepreneur—providing products or services at relatively low prices by optimizing the supply routes within an increasingly globalised market. Through these tactics, the milieu of the politics of globalization has become primarily mediated by the abundant supply of capital to facilitate and service ever-growing markets and the ideologies of political equalization have been replaced by a strategy of *cheapness*. Leaving aside the potential impact on global warming, social ossification, and other unpleasant side effects of neo-liberal economies, the capacity for social transformation in many regions of the world has been nothing short of remarkable. If we owe the ideological framing of neo-liberal capitalism to some of those earlier visionaries, even those who might be said to have been ardent anti-capitalists, it appears as if our everyday life is now fundamentally determined by the actions taken by this second generation of late-twentieth-century, non-ideological visionaries.

Given the impact on the growth of cities fostered by the monetary policies of Greenspan and other central bankers (ample capital chasing "pliant" urban populations), changes both in the workplace and in private life—made possible by the new affordability of communication, information, foreign travel, and fashion—seem especially symptomatic of a larger shift in the *demos*, which marks the implicit ideology of technological innovation: *resubjectivization* coupled with an increase in productivity. It is this issue of resubjectivization that needs to be watched closely in the future, as it is generally bracketed at the moment given that all governments have more or less reverted to crisis-management mode.

Yet, what is new about these prospects is the relationship between production and political ideology. If, traditionally, vision was a value added to a product, these new agencies base their performance primarily on the reduction of costs. The political effects of this strategy are particularly interesting when considering the goods and services most related to the body—clothing and air travel. If Chanel or Issey Miyake are supposed to be adding a wholesome aura or lifestyle to the body and were duly priced upward, some of the low-cost operators have resorted to a radical minimization of production costs, which, in turn, produces their quality, which is not necessarily low any longer. In this mode of operation, the relationship between style, price, and value is inverted and the political agency of production is reframed, emptying out the product of any explicit ideological ambition, jettisoning the spectral surplus value of the commodity. This is delivered either by tracking the market by the week (as if the designer had been replaced by popular taste, much like the politicians seem to have been replaced by pollsters and focus groups experts), such as practiced by Zara and Topshop, or by cutting down everything unnecessary (the so-called *frills*) and synthesizing a new style, free from conventional expectations. (for example, the no-nonsense character of EasyJet or Muji.) As with the new local-government policies of David Cameron's Tory party in the UK,[2] the political model of cheapness replicates the business strategies of the low-cost airlines, and success is measured by its ability to deliver reduced public services at minimal cost to taxpayers, while charging additional fees for certain services.

2   Robert Booth, "Tory Controlled Borough of Barnet Adopts Budget Airline Model," in *The Guardian* (London, August 27, 2009). http://www.guardian.co.uk/politics/2009/aug/27/tory-borough-barnet-budget-airline

Within a market economy we could probably substitute *low cost* for Giorgio Agamben's double-edged term *bare life* (from the Greek, *zoe*), without totally disfiguring it in the process. Bare life is the ultra-quotidian, sacrificial life of the dispossessed, a form of abject citizenship that inhabits a non-qualified political nether region. "The political system no longer orders forms of life and juridical rules in a determinate space, but instead contains at its very center a dislocating localization that exceeds it and into which every form of life and every rule can be virtually taken."[3] In other words, exceptions are the rule in the contemporary city, and the "state of exception" (when all rules of citizenship are suspended) is its foremost materialization.[4] Agamben's term connotes a perverse economy of absolutism working in both markets and politics, and, in defense of adopting his conceptual apparatus, it is this very recourse to draconian measures, especially after practicing a form of demented *noblesse oblige*, that threatens from the wings of the new economic world order. By adopting Agamben's warnings, we can also preposition warnings regarding a possible outcome to the current situation while examining it nonetheless for signs of, or opportunities for, *actual* political liberalization.

And, if life in neo-liberal capitalist terms can be reduced to consumption and markets (with their constantly shifting horizons), economic fortunes are made in the reduction of plentiful life (*bios*) to bare life (*zoe*) by focusing on the biopolitical horizon of life at the expense of all else and, in turn, conceptually reducing citizens to mere biological units. All citizens in such a model are now de facto outcasts, insofar as all citizens operate within a narrowing field of deterministic economic and political functions. But, as in Agamben's critique, bare life acquires a new dignity when taken out of this

---

3   Giorgio Agamben, *Homo Sacer: Sovereign Power and Bare Life*, trans. Daniel Heller-Roazen (Stanford: Stanford University Press, 1998), 44.

4   In his book *The State of Exception*, Agamben questions Carl Schmitt's crypto-totalitarian legitimization of the suspension of individual rights by the State, an excess of power implicit in sovereignty. See Giorgio Agamben, *State of Exception*, trans. Kevin Attell (Chicago: University of Chicago Press, 2005).

schematic and placed in a semi-sacred *free state*: a non-use (neutral) political value as irreducible as the fact of (bare) life. A politics based on the concept of bare life—an ancient juridical term—is not necessarily the automatic enslavement by socio-economic means, or the totalitarian assault on subjectivity it *might* become. And perhaps, most importantly, it unfolds several possibilities all at once and illuminates multiple approaches to urban design and architecture as possible means without ends, or *projects without addresses*. Is it really beneficial for architects to continue to produce grand visions, or is it perhaps a matter of exploring concrete, technical aspects of a project as the origin of urban or architectural expression (and subsequent wholesale recalibration of the "game")? Mobilizing a political expression founded on the prosaic or the banal and addressing its multiple attachments may enable us to frame architecture not merely as a representation of an overarching ideological program (let's say, hyper-material agency) or an image of a new utopia (let's say, the corporatization of individuals), but as concrete and effective political agency able to assemble and mediate the interests of the multiple stakeholders that converge on the contemporary project, while also holding in reserve the ability to refuse servicing outright repressive orders (figurative and otherwise). It is perhaps the most basic, bare, technical, and pragmatic questions that enable us to explore the discipline as a source of effects that may actually destabilize power regimes rather than function as their vehicle of implementation or as their mere representation, whether of the status quo or its resisting parties. The opening of power structures is better served by focusing on the means to ends, while voiding the project from within of all-too-obvious ideological and utopian content. Rather than aiming at revolution, a political practice for architecture is perhaps best shifted to explicitation by means of reduction to a bare state, a mode where political practices are grounded in the admittedly artificial environments in which we co-exist, and where concrete aspects become the primary source of political agency—in other words, bare state as enlightened materialism.

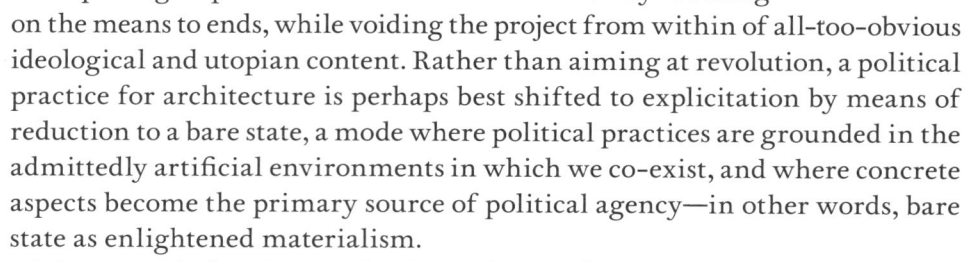

A few years before Zara and Microsoft were founded, the implicit resetting of relations between style, economy and value was explored within the art scene. In 1967, Germano Celant—today the director of the Prada Foundation—coined the term *Arte Povera* to describe a group of young Italian artists experimenting with nontraditional and politically charged art as the Italian economic miracle of the immediate postwar years collapsed into economic and political chaos. Under the rubric of Arte Povera—which literally means "poor art"—there was an exploration of a wide range of artistic materials and practices demolishing the aesthetic of the quasi-precious traditional ones (primarily painting and sculpture), which placed in question the "value" of art per se—plus the art market and the burgeoning politics of the so-called *art world* (a term only then coming into common use). Arte Povera sought an art made without restraints—a laboratory situation in which any theoretical basis was rejected in favor of complete openness toward materials and processes. The movement promoted the notion of a revolutionary art—free of convention, power structures, and the marketplace by virtue of austerity. Arte Povera was a relevant precedent to some of the strategies of *cheapness* that began to emerge just a few years later as effective business models, as well as an alternative to ideological formulations in the pursuit of a democracy inevitably mediated by production and artificiality.

It is precisely the notion of frills—epithelial, ornamental, and contingent excrescences of clothing design (conventionally used to elicit sensual response or induce arousal)—that low-cost airlines and similar down-market entrepreneurs use to describe all services that are not part of the *core* product, that suggests an intriguing metaphor for architectural praxis—that is, a new means for negotiating the relationship between economy, value, and style. In this sense, bare life might equal no frills, or an elective avoidance of all things unnecessary. While such a model contains the seeds of its own destruction (as it might eliminate its own market), it also signals a possible escape route from overweening, abject consumerism.

In a low-budget airplane cabin, where the physical body is denied any gratification exceeding its mere biological survival (and first class and coach seem to merge into no-class), a new sense of *demos* emerges, a state that seems—in essence—precarious and easily overturned or recolonized by excess or privilege. However, these relationships between subject and state are not as literal as they may seem. They are immensely versatile, and each claim for stasis is typically followed by its collapse. Agamben writes that it is not at all clear that the state of *bare life* necessarily corresponds to a politically neutered status or to an enforced aesthetic of poverty and estrangement. There is another ground between abandonment and freedom: the two forms of bare life. It is a rarefied aesthetic apolitical engagement—a paradox. Must bare life necessarily mean the absence of rights—frills, in the low-cost jargon—literally and physically speaking? Might it not also mean the presence of a form of *demos* that guarantees the right of nonparticipation in the production, distribution, and manipulation of capital—the right to say "No thanks"? Might there not be architectural analogues for the same that are not politically castrated upon arrival?

It may be precisely in the articulation between value, economy, and style in architecture that we may find the opportunities to retrieve political agency within a market-driven economy. In the triangulation of style, price, and frills, which is by no means a simple matter or stable formula, it is worth trying to define these relationships by tracing a small history of this equation since modernism, when, arguably, and for the first time, economic splendor entered into the theory of architecture and urbanism as *pure affect*.

Finding frills to be superfluous, regressive, and ineffective, modernism militated against their presence. Adolf Loos' brilliant diatribe *Ornament and Crime* (1908), connoting ornamentation in architecture as a form of criminal activity, plus the Brechtian admonition to modern cosmopolites to "leave no traces," are both clear polemical exercises in the modernist approach to frills. However, these were implemented on the grounds of economy, not style. The ideological label was *functionalism*. Style in modernism (as an anti-style) was the automatic result of eradicating the superfluous and the contingent. The famous anecdotes about Lucio Costa removing the corner in his Brasilia housing to avoid privileging any one occupant, and Mies van der Rohe's obliging response to a request for a more "expensive-looking" Seagram Building, for which he subsequently specified a bronze facade, point to the paradoxes and contradictions implicit in the democratic ambitions of modernism. While a more repetitive, industrialized pattern was the trademark of the democratic aesthetics of high modernism, it was an expensive type of democracy that came with a fairly high price, and one that was not necessarily morally affordable after all, given the problem with modernism was that *no* style became *the* style.

Brutalism is an interesting episode within this short history of frills as an index of the correspondence between value and style. After the modernist evacuation of style as a legitimate purpose, roughness and poverty became the primary generator for architectural expression: the reinforcement bars sticking out of the concrete, or the imprints of the wooden scaffolding on the raw concrete in Chandigarh became the source of an expression of architectural materiality. The absence of detail in favor of this literal expression of material became the primary stylistic trait of brutalism.

Postmodernism would exploit the contradictions between value and cost by using scenographic techniques in order to produce expensive effects at a moderate price, detaching style from value, like a commodity in the stock market. Post-modernism redeemed frills on the grounds that, even if their use value is negligible, their exchange value offers a surplus with respect to their production cost. In a late-capitalist economy, style is a free-floating commodity without any attachment to structural values, and, therefore, frills are an economically legitimate practice.

Moving along the arrow of recent architectural history we should probably pause to consider Frank Gehry as, perhaps, the most illustrious example of an architect obsessed with the practice of *architectural* cheapness. Strongly connected to the Arte Povera scene (Celant wrote the introduction to one of his early monographs), Gehry's early works, such as his own house in Santa Monica, the Los Angeles Temporary Contemporary, Santa Monica Place, the Cabrillo Marine Aquarium, and the Easy Edges Furniture, exemplify the concise *practice of cheapness*. The projects are remarkable attempts to explore economy in combination with an aesthetic of excess—or frills, in low-cost airline lingo. Even Gehry's post-Guggenheim titanium extravaganzas are based on the possibility of detaching the visible envelope from the weatherproofed membrane by building it as a rainscreen; and it is precisely his willingness to accept the inconsistency between the frills and the weatherproofed skin that allows him to produce such entities at a reasonable cost: to a degree, a strategy of cheapness. That acceptance requires a certain hyperbolic "political" stance (the proverbial *je ne sais quoi* of the architectural avant-garde). Cheapness and frills are made compatible in certain avant-garde practices, as *haute-bohemian* brands combine seemingly incompatible traits to produce an aesthetic of casual luxury.[6]

Other recent explorations of cheapness can be found in Rem Koolhaas's infamous statement, "No money, no detail," in which the project's economy becomes the source of its aesthetic approach, making a virtue out of a necessity. This concept of an aesthetic of cheapness was explored in OMA's Lille master plan, with a proposal to specify low-grade concrete for all buildings in the master plan. This was made with the plausible excuse that the character of Lille was intended to be markedly different from Paris—that is, more rough and tumble. This strategy of intensifying the material grain by downgrading the material quality evidently recalls brutalism. This *qualitative* cheapness was supposed to automatically emerge from the lower material specification, rather than by design. In this case, the no-frills strategy of bare life produces a sort of deep *rusticato,* which goes deeper than the skin into the structure of the buildings. This is a sort of neo-Rousseauian approach where, if desirable, the social contract and the so-called rights of citizens that come with it are voluntarily suspended (for example, the consumer's rights to quality) as a critique of the status quo and the premiation of *natural* traits (*primal* rights) antecedent to signing the so-called contract.

Lacaton & Vassal is the latest exemplar of the practice of architectural cheapness. The project for the Palais de Tokyo (probably the cheapest museum refurbishment ever done per square meter) or the Management Sciences University in Bordeaux, the University of Arts and Human Sciences in Grenoble, and the residences in Coutras and Floriac, mobilize an entirely different aesthetic of cheapness based on recycling, environmental performances, and low-cost industrial production by using precast concrete, plywood, polycarbonate, and

---

6   A good example of the haute-bohemian style in architecture is Ian Schrager's Gramercy Park Hotel in New York City, with key "public" interiors and furnishings by Julian Schnabel.

glasshouse technology in a somewhat ruthless manner. Of all contemporary architects exploring the idea of value as a projectual argument, Lacaton & Vassal come closest to the idea of actual bare life, where building is understood as an assemblage of systems arrayed in an ad hoc manner, suspending the representation of a qualified life in architecture. The buildings are barely conditioned, austere, and semi-exterior environments, again using a neo-Rousseauian aesthetic of community with the natural reminiscent of several aspects of Arte Povera (and to the installations of Lucy Orta or the clothing lines of the Japanese brand Final Home). Unlike Gehry's cheapness, where double skins, *pochéd* spaces, and complex geometries produce a sophisticated envelope with frills at relatively affordable prices, Lacaton & Vassal's veritable no-frills strategy appears to be working more with ephemerality, transparency, and continuity between inside and outside, lacerating expense across the entire project and driving the budget into the enviable terrain of the *literally, truly cheap*.

As the celebrity model of the '90s and '00s—which in architecture translated into the star system—draws to a close, the elastic relationship between style and economy becomes an intriguing issue, particularly in light of what is happening in the emerging low-cost markets. There are spatial and temporal implications associated with these models of cheapness that may be worth considering in their translation into architectural practice. There is a geopolitical model associated with the production chain of these companies. While the high-end boutiques are traditionally built according to a recipe of high design, exclusivity, lots of marketing, and a decentralized production, retailers such as Topshop and Zara have defied many of these premises by co-locating design and production. In a typical fashion house, design and marketing are often located in a world capital—Paris, London, New York, or Tokyo—while production is located in emerging economies, where the designs are executed. The goods are then shipped back to metropolitan centers to be sold at artificially inflated prices.

Alternatively, some of the new low-cost emporia operate on the model of *vertical integration*—a term famously central to American Apparel's public relations strategy, which states that the company keeps jobs in downtown Los Angeles by pursuing novel production techniques where the company's design and production are deeply integrated and co-located.[7] Most of Zara's production is done in La Coruña, Spain, where design and marketing headquarters are also located, while the Topshop lines are purchased from small design-production units.

Unlike previous common mercantilism, this type of centralized operation, even at the expense of higher production costs, is capable of providing retail advantage: a relationship between design and production. Operating in this manner, these companies enable a much more intense feedback between the different phases of the project's procurement. This logistical methodology for ultimately measuring a product's immediate effectiveness or salability (in industry parlance, its "turn") is a type of index for a marketing model that focuses on means rather than ends—the product seems almost expendable in a chain of relationships that maximize liquidation (and liquidity). It is one of the potentials of cheapness—cheapness as a powerful antidote to excess—that makes it the nemesis of both utopian and visionary alternatives.

Finally, it is in this feedback across the procurement route where the temporal implications of this model lie: the distance and time lag between design and production of garments has been reduced to such a degree that such companies can now churn out new designs as rapidly as they can conceive of them. Zara and Topshop's competitive advantage is that design and production are so intimately connected, they can change their collection every two weeks, short-

---

7 Considered a boon to the Los Angeles economy, American Apparel recently was required to fire a significant portion of its labor force, as it was inordinately stacked with so-called undocumented workers. While not in any way diminishing their reputation, or perhaps instead perversely enhancing it, the reliance on, in this case, well-paid but copious urban labor is part of the new model called vertical integration.

circuiting the tempo of fashion and the seasonal collections: they are, in fact, turning the market into an evolutionary continuum. Again, this may be an indication that a project without a definitive target, one primarily focused on its means, may be a vital tendency within cheapness.

Precisely by suspending ideological judgment and relying on production, the cheap frills model of Zara and Topshop provide the largest diversity of products to the broadest audience at any given time. As an ecosystem, these models have an advantage driven by a reverse econometric, a result of trends in globalization—speed, mobile labor, heightened- and micro-production facilities, plus a creeping anomie aimed at faceless multinational clothiers. Such post-neo-liberal business models and brands mutate rapidly, as they are not constrained by a history of the brand, or by the need to create an ideology, a signature style, or a comprehensive *Weltanschauung* to justify their existence. When Karl Lagerfeld took over Chanel, or Tom Ford took over Gucci, the first task was to reinvent the history of the brand, interpreting it for a new audience. What were the classic designs of the brand? And how can that brand be expanded and connected to the contemporary market? New low-cost brands have shed the weight of the past, producing an inborn, half-mythological history. They have no identifiable style beyond the generic ubiquity they breed and covet. They can go anywhere (at anytime) they identify an opportunity. Style consistency and brand stability is evidently not an asset in the low-cost markets, but a liability. Can they remain an asset in the future of architectural practices, as they have been through the starchitect period?

Across these low-cost practices, and beyond these general tendencies of relocalization, integration between design and production, and overcoming of the fashion cycles and stylistic inconsistency, we can identify two basic models of operation. One option is the enforcement of no frills as the origin of a new style with a better value. In this case, cheapness becomes the origin of a new style: this is the model we can see emerging from EasyJet's no-frills airline, and from Muji's no-brand goods (a brand paradoxically reversing Naomi Klein's *No Logo* strategy to build up a brand). In these models, a new aesthetic leap of the cheap emerges from a careful consideration of how to eliminate excess, the exceptional, the precious, the over-priced, and the exclusive. A certain acceptance of the "generic" is implied in this model, which includes brands with similar political ambitions, such as IKEA and American Apparel, where a certain purification of style is enforced, albeit perhaps without the rigor of the bargain-bin models of EasyJet and Muji.

We can see a second alternative in other markets where the use of cheap frills is the economic driver of choice for the product. In this case, cheapness is the result of sophisticated procurement techniques that allow the product to access style while remaining reasonably priced. Such is the strategy of brands like Zara, Topshop, Primark—or even the haute-bohemian airline Virgin Atlantic—where combining cheapness with a certain level of hedonistic extravagance produces a very marketable approach. In such instances, the concept of brand crosses back over the threshold of elitism to bend the product closer to affordability, but without losing its semi-prestigious cachet. Such approaches are made possible through very shrewd tactics capable of both lowering the retail cost of the product while maintaining some of its qualities or services (often the most idiosyncratic). While recent examples of flagship stores such as Saks Fifth Avenue in New York selling seemingly everything at 70% off lead one to believe that price is relative, the subsequent role of availability has trumped brand consciousness. The very idea of brand is defended from within wholly new borders having less to do with image than with ubiquity and its analogue, *accessibility*, which in this case suggests a de facto democratizing spirit in the neo-liberal markets. In a market-driven culture, *affordability* is the byword for democracy, although it is not clear that equality of means necessarily implies the equality of rights that characterizes democratic life.

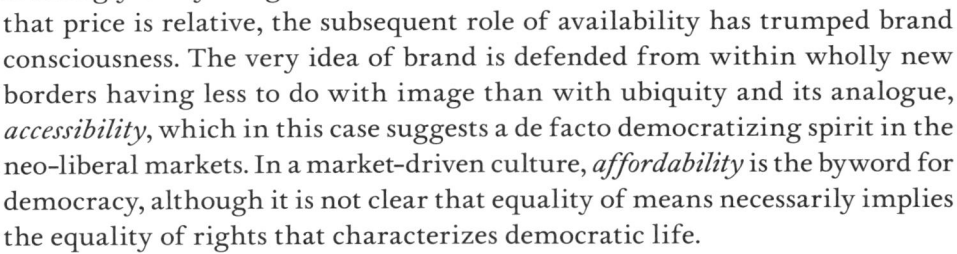

Different forms and modalities of citizenship also produce different forms and modalities of urbanity: there is the hyper-city of law and order (like New York's or London's urban police-state) and there is the no-frills modernist city, typically sprawling, where economy and optimization are part of the manifestation of law and order (of the qualified life) and the source of a no-frills aesthetic. Such cities as the latter are on the rise. Then, there is the postmodern city where law and order have been replaced by a city of exceptions (states of permanent emergency) and frills, with diminished constitutional rights in return for endless diversions. Strangely, the latter are quite often city-states.

The question, here, is whether these models could be potentially used to challenge the status quo and operate as a powerful transfer device, much like Agamben suggests bare life can be turned into a powerful political weapon. Architecture by the likes of Lacaton & Vassal is loaded with an implicit critique of the star system and architectural consumption. Short of a new brutalism, one can only imagine that cheapness in architecture (*sans* ideology) might come back as an architecture that is quite simply architecture, and not a brand. Political agency means—often—to do only what is necessary, and absolute material agency implies the crossing out of anything truly frivolous. In the case of Lacaton & Vassal, if the buildings are partly planted in the earth and open to the environment, despite their cheapness, there is also the economy of natural forces at work—recall that Thoreau opens *Walden* with a disquisition on "economy." Recall, too, that not far from Thoreau's Walden Pond, in Cambridge, Massachusetts, is Le Corbusier's Carpenter Center at Harvard. One thinks immediately, then, of Le Corbusier's dream for the Carpenter Center: that nature would provide the finishing touches, a dream made slightly absurd by Pierre Huyghe in his work *This is Not a Time for Dreaming*.[8]

The notion that politics and economics can be neatly divided into *polis* and *oikos*—either in the sense that the markets should be entirely freed of political intervention or that political action can be effected without careful consideration of economic inputs—is ludicrous. In parallel to the increasing level of governmental intervention in the markets that we are starting to witness, we will also see the growing effect of economies on political discourse. (David Cameron's Easy Council is paradigmatic.)

It is in the exploration of the types of citizenship that are increasingly mediated by economics that we may be able to discern solutions for the cities of the near future, and where an elective cheapness and its aesthetic implications

---

8   *This is Not a Time for Dreaming* (2004) was commissioned by Harvard University to mark the fortieth anniversary of the Carpenter Center. In Huyghe's version, a bird flies by and drops a single seed and the Carpenter Center is engulfed in vines and all but disappears. This underscores Le Corbusier's idea that nature should provide buildings with entourage.

may prove a fruitful field of investigation. Democracy, in its global neo-liberal form, is expensive, often inefficient, and consumes an absurd amount of non-renewable resources. We live in an age in which the limitless appetites of the capitalist system have come face to face with the limits of the planet's natural resources, which will increasingly make economy—rather than excess—the engine of all processes: for example, economies of urban land, as global populations flock to the cities; economies of energy and carbon emissions, as three billion people will enter the global middle classes in the next four decades and claim their legitimate rights to air-conditioning, private vehicles, and air transportation; and economies of money (as redundant as it sounds), as credit becomes reattached to real assets and speculative capital reaches, quite literally, for the stars (or anything else not tied to the ground).

As we move forward, the crucial question is how to preserve true democracy, whatever that might be, and its corollary actual capital—real estate—within the emerging landscapes of cheapness that proliferate everywhere, because cheapness may deliver democracy *on the ground* (bare life as egalitarian global ethos) or do away with it once and for all. A materialist approach to political agency might seem an ancient artifice, a founding act of the *polis*. But bare life, as free, political-economic agency, implies that the luxury of the many resides in a model that bridges not wealth and poverty, but multiple economies given to benefiting some when they might benefit all. Cheapness may become this potential bridge—not as a cheapening agent, but as a form of recalibrating the engines of production and consumption, of which architecture is a principal component.

The images along this text address some precedents and contemporary examples of cheapness as a current social and political trend. The references start with the cheapness revolutionaries, Alan Greenspan, Ingvar Kamprad, Stelios Haji-Ioannou, Amancio Ortega, Jimmy Wales and Jeff Bezos, then refer to the Arte Povera as an ancestor to the low-cost contemporary culture. The other images refer sometimes to low cost products such as UNIQLO and the Tata Nano, and the mass attraction of low-cost consumer goods, the sweatshops and the automatization of production that lie behind the low-cost production, and the transfer of low cost strategies to politics with Cameron's Easy Council.

Colophon

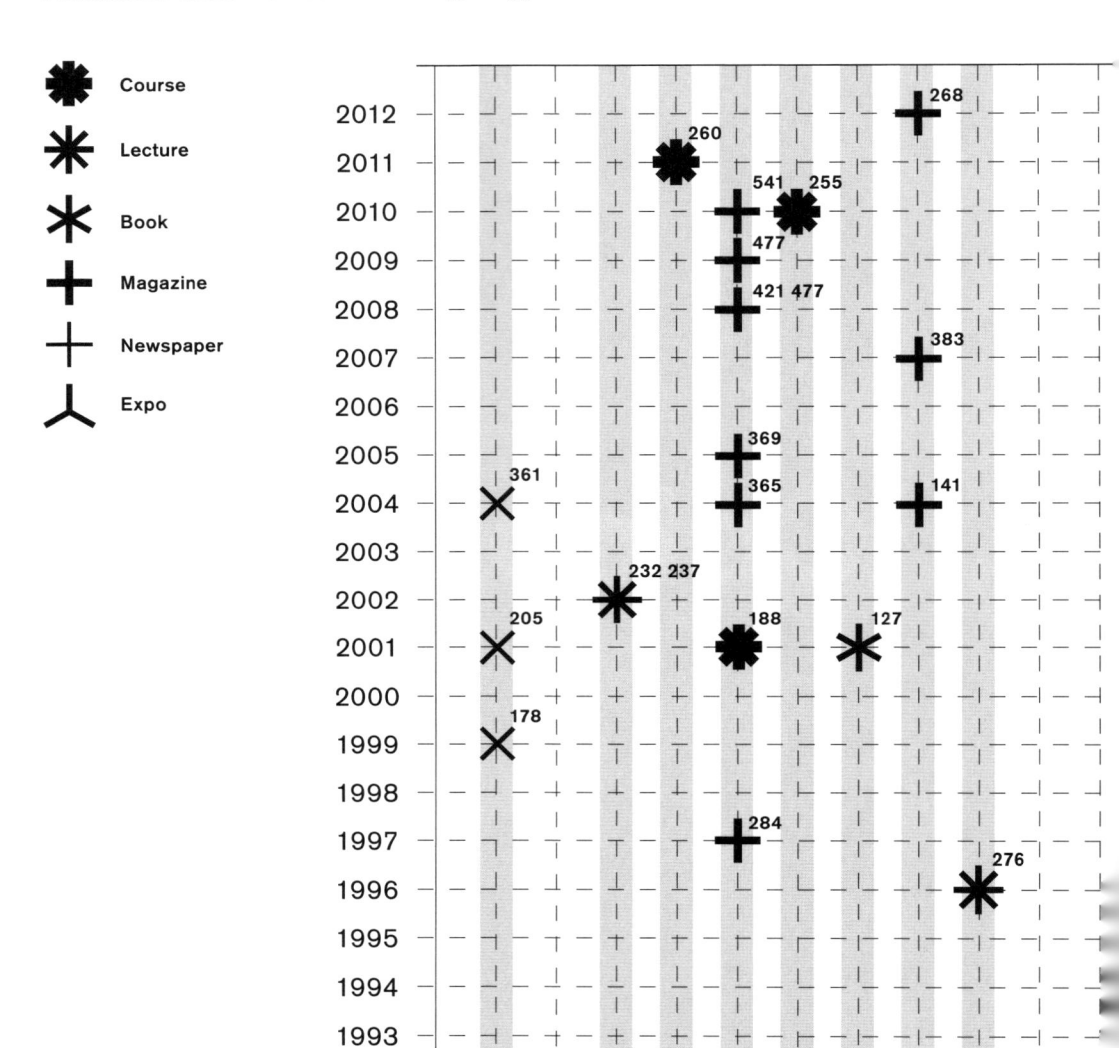

Publication dates / Cities / Device typology

- ✱ Course
- ✲ Lecture
- ✳ Book
- ✚ Magazine
- ┼ Newspaper
- ⅄ Expo

Year	Unpublished	Los Angeles	New Jersey	New York	New Haven	Montreal	Cambridge	Buenos Aires
2012							268	
2011			260					
2010				541	255			
2009				477				
2008				421 477				
2007							383	
2006								
2005				369				
2004	361			365			141	
2003								
2002		205	232 237					
2001	205			188		127		
2000								
1999	178							
1998								
1997				284				
1996								276
1995								
1994								
1993								
1992								
1991								
1990								

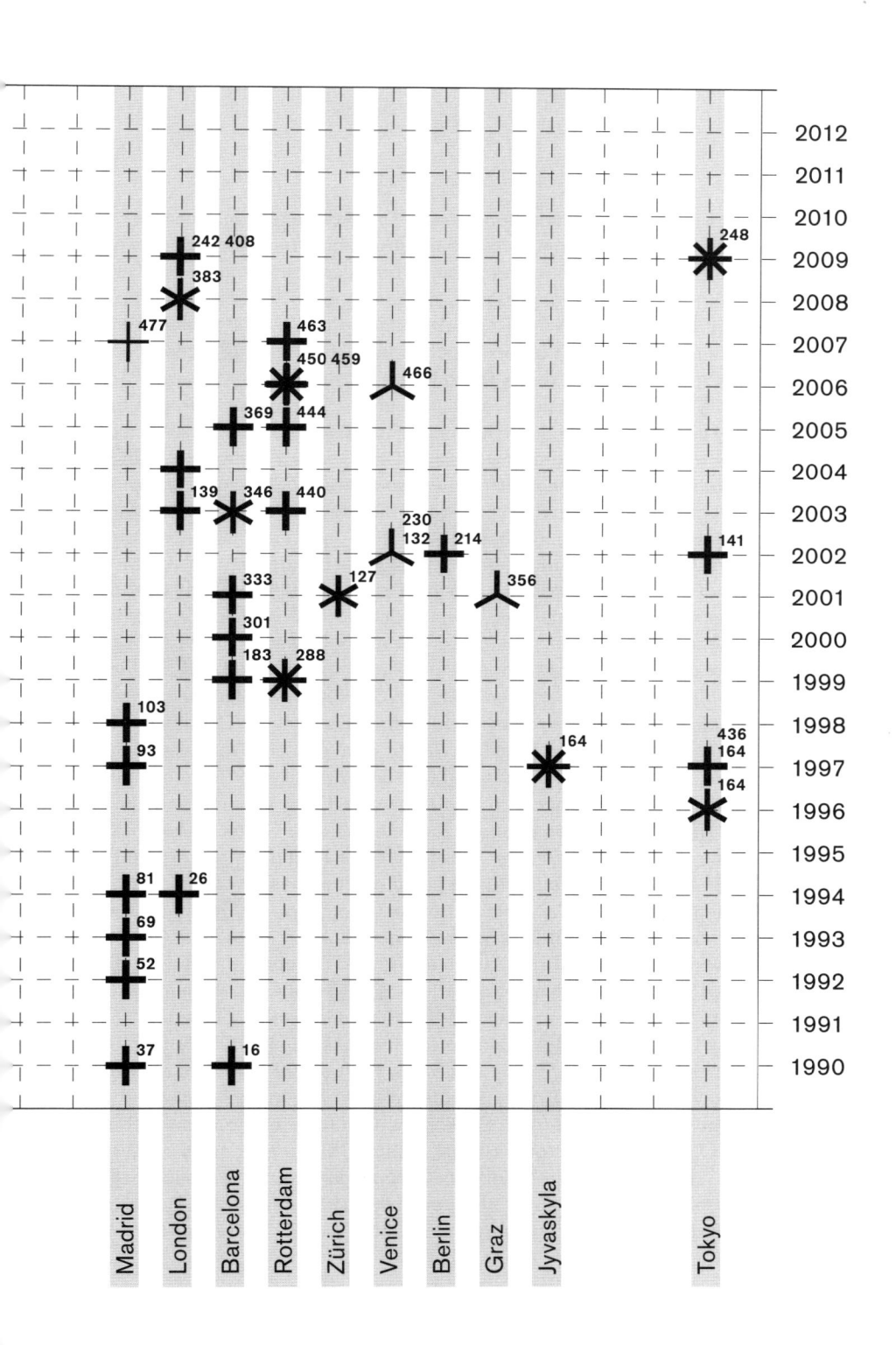

Publication Dates / Cities / Device tipology

561

Autobiographic Calendar

1963 JF Kennedy Assasination/First James Bond Movie, Dr. No, released in America/Paul IV succeeds Pope John XXIII/Malaysia is formed as a country/Arecibo Observatory begins operation   **1964** Nehru dies/First Shinkansen train operating between Tokyo and Osaka/Summer Olympics in Tokyo/Nikita Khrushchev is deposed as leader of the Soviet Union and replaced by Leonid Brezhnev/First Nuclear test of the People's Republic of China/Martin Luther King is awarded the Nobel Peace Prize/Soviet Union launches *Voskhod 1*   **1965** Lee Kuan Yew announces Singapore's independence/Watts Riots begin in Los Angeles/Gateway Arch is completed in St Louis   **1966** Mao's Cultural Revolution starts/ Palomares hydrogen bombs incident   **1967** Six-Day War/ Expo 67 opens in Montreal/Fidel Castro announces that all intellectual property belongs to all people /Monterrey Festival/Che Guevara executed   **1968** May '68 Revolution/Martin Luther King Assasinated/*Prague Spring*/*Mexico '68* Summer Olympics/first manned Apollo 7 flight   **1969** Apollo 11 lands in the Moon/Woodstock Festival/Led Zeppelin I released/Richard Nixon sworn in/Boeing 747 Jumbo Jet starts flying commercially/ECM records founded in Munich by Manfred Eicher   **1970** Jimi Hendrix dead/Yukio Mishima commits suicide in public/The Khmer Republic is proclaimed in Cambodia   **1971** Collapse of Bretton Woods Agreement/Nasdaq debuts/Twin Towers built/2,500 Year Celebration of Persia   **1972** The Godfather released/Pruitt-Igoe destroyed/Nixon meets Mao in China/Munich '72 Summer Olympics massacre/Apollo 17 last moonwalk/Deep Throat released   **1973** First Oil Crisis/Yom Kippur War/*Dark Side of the Moon* released/Sydney Opera House completed/Bosphorus Bridge completed   **1974** Nixon resigns, Watergate Scandal/Charles de Gaulle Airport opens in Paris   **1975** Francisco Franco's Death/ End Vietnam War/Zara starts/Bill Gates starts Microsoft/launch Volkswagen Golf   **1976** US Copyright Act /First commercially produced Cray Supercomputer/ First Concorde flight/Mao dies/Deng Xiao Ping becomes de facto leader of China   **1977** Apple Computers incorporated/Jimmy Carter president/Spain first democratic elections   **1978** Spanish first democratic constitution in place/John Paul II becomes Pope   **1979** Iranian Revolution/Margaret Thatcher becomes British Prime Minister   **1980** Tito's Death/Gwangju massacre/Cable News Network launched   **1981** Ronald Reagan access to the White House/Space Shuttle program launched/AIDS identified/Linux kernel written   **1982** PSOE wins elections in Spain/Spain enters NATO/Lebanon civil war   **1983** Microsoft Word launched/GNU operating system started   **1984** Los Angeles Summer Olympics/Bhopal Disaster/Crack Cocaine introduced   **1985** Mihail Gorbachev General Secretary of the Communist Party USSR/   **1986** Spain enters European Union/Challenger Space Shuttle disintegrates/Chernobyl Incident/Fluoxetine, primary ingredient of Prozac approved in Belgium   **1987** Black Monday in UK. Britain is forced out of International banking system/Mike Pickering plays House in Hacienda/Alan Greenspan Chairman of the Federal Reserve   **1988** Seoul Summer Olympics/Perestroika Starts/ Space Shuttle *Discovery* retrieve the Space Shuttle program   **1989** Fall of the Berlin Wall/Tiananmen Square Massacre   **1991** Persian Gulf War/Election of Boris Yeltsin and Collapse of the USSR/Ministry of Sound opens   **1992** Besiege of Sarajevo/Barcelona Olympics/Seville Expo'92 Universal Exhibition/

LA riots **1993** Bill Clinton President of the USA/Jiang Zemin President of China/European Union is formed **1995** Kobe Earthquake/Collapse of Barings Bank/Sarin Gas Attack on Tokyo subways/Windows 95 released/Easyjet established **1996** JM Aznar wins Elections in Spain/Ladi Di killed in a car crash/*Big Blue* defeats Gary Kasparov/Boris Yeltsin and Bill Clinton sworn in for a second term **1997** Blair's Labour Party forms government/Asian Financial Crisis/Kyoto protocol signed **1998** Monica Lewinsky Scandal on the Drudge Report/U.S. embassies in Dar es Salaam and Nairobi bombed /Google founded **1999** Vladimir Putin becomes Russian president **2000** Failure of the Camp David Israel-Palestine agreements/AOL bought by Time Warner/USS Cole bombed in Aden/Peak of the Dotcom Bubble/World population reaches 6Bn/Al-Aqsa Intifada starts **2001** September 11 Attacks/Wikipedia is founded/Junichiro Koizumi becomes Japanese Prime Minister/Ipod released by Apple/Windows XP released **2002** Euro replaces national currencies in the EU/Pim Fortuyn assasinated/FIFA World Cup co-hosted by Japan and Korea **2003** Coalition of the Willing formed in Azores/Iraq invasion/SARS epidemic erupts in Asia/Hu Jintao becomes President of China **2004** JL Rodriguez Zapatero wins Elections in Spain/Madrid March11 Bombings/Southeast Asia Tsunami/French Ban on Religious Symbols at Schools/Trevor Phillips enunciates Britishness/Theo van Gogh Killed in Amsterdam **2005** YouTube goes online/Kyoto protocol enacted without USA and Australia/French and Dutch electorates reject European Constitution/Bali Bombings/Hurricane Katrina devastates New Orleans/Cardinal Ratzinger replaces Karol Wojtila and becomes Benedict XVI **2006** Ban Ki-moon is elected as the new Secretary-General of the United Nations/ Dow Jones Industrial Average closes above 12,000 for the first time/ U.S. Defense Secretary Donald Rumsfeld resigns/ Second Lebanon War **2007** Benazir Bhutto is assassinated/ South Korean President Roh Moo-hyun and North Korean leader Kim Jong-il meet in Pyongyang **2008** Beijing Olympics/ Nationalisation of Northern Rock, Bear Stearns, Fannie Mae and Freddy Mac. / Collapse of Lehman Brothers, Bail out of AIG, absorption of HBOS and Merrill Lynchy by Lloyds and Bank of America/Fidel Castro announces his resignation as President of Cuba/The Large Hadron Collider starts operation **2009** Barack Obama is inaugurated as the 44th, and first African American President of the United States/ Israel completes its withdrawal from the Gaza Strip/The Icelandic government and banking system collapse/ Mahmoud Ahmadinejad reelected president in Iran amongst generalized civil unrest/Michael Jackson dead/Dubai requests a debt deferment/Copenhagen Summit for climate change **2010** The Burj Khalifa in Dubai is officially opened/ The Deepwater Horizon oil platform explodes in the Gulf of Mexico, producing one of the largest oil spills in history/The Eurozone and the International Monetary Fund agree to a 110 billion bailout package for Greece/ Wikileaks leaks to the public over 90,000 internal reports about the United States-led involvement in the War in Afghanistan and more than 250,000 American confidential diplomatic cables/ The European Union agree to an 85 billion rescue deal for Ireland **2011** The Tunisian government falls after violent protests, signing the beginning of the Arab Spring/ Hosni Mubarak resigns after widespread public insurgency/A 9.1-magnitude earthquake and subsequent tsunami hit the east of Japan, killing nearly 20,000 people and severely damaging the Fukushima Nuclear Power Plant, causing the worst nuclear disaster after Chernobyl/ Osama bin Laden is killed during an American military operation in Pakistan/ Syrian revolts trigger brutal military repression/Libyan rebels overthrow and kill Muammar Gaddafi/Occupy Wall Street protests begin in New York/ ETA declares an end to violence/The European Union announces an agreement to tackle the Euro crisis totaling to 1 trillion/ Global population reaches seven billion…

Glossary

This is a list of terms and statements identified as significant or recurrent throughout these texts. The more repetitive a word is, the bigger its font size, providing a visual map of the common threads spread across the book.

A

à la carte
  education 217
  menu 534
  school 218, 252

The idea of the à la carte school is a product of the consumer education and follows the same strategy of MacDonald's: they offer you an enormous choice, although ultimately everything tastes the same. 252

abstract 17, 53, 54, 79, 80, 82, 83, 88, 97, 98, 99, 111, 114, 170, 178, 183, 188, 200, 231, 232, 234, 236, 237, 243, 245, 247, 285-287, 298, 300, 318, 320, 323, 330, 352, 379, 416, 474, 480, 487, 489, 490, 530, 531
  abstraction 18, 20, 22, 55, 79, 113, 114, 166, 178, 179, 181, 182, 187-189, 233, 234, 238, 285, 314, 328, 337, 445, 495, 499, 503

The most interesting potential of the use of abstraction and parametricization is their alienating potential, rather than the modernist and neo-modernist recourse to the causal. 328

accidental 86, 95, 97, 99, 114, 200
accomplices 451
accountability 212, 216, 402, 424, 426, 429
accumulation 28, 30, 31, 34, 52-54, 57, 63, 65, 66, 129, 130, 171, 175, 211, 278, 279, 311, 472, 473
activist 157, 447, 464, 502
actualization 142, 150, 152, 175-177, 239, 236, 243, 246, 284, 285, 321, 330, 478
  actualized 234, 246, 247, 285, 318, 329, 330, 352
affect 7, 27, 28, 48, 49, 52, 68, 72, 82, 84, 85, 91, 92, 98, 107, 119, 128-130, 137,

165, 172, 176, 180, 220, 226, 245, 247, 249, 257, 290, 292, 304, 330, 333, 335, 341, 403, 406, 407, 413-418, 420, 425, 480, 485, 487-489, 491, 492, 494, 498, 512, 515, 520, 521, 523, 524, 529, 532, 535-538, 550
  affect-driven 413, 485, 513
  affective 129, 169, 171, 335, 476, 494, 532

Already such ineffable qualities such as time, light, and temperature are beginning to be modelled and played with as affective, material measures. 169

affects of effacement, liquefaction, and de-striation 418

The politics of rhetoric, symbolic reasoning, and representation are giving way to a new breed of object-oriented politics, invested in modes of production and exchange and primarily implemented through the production of affects, an unencoded, pre-linguistic form of identity capable of transcending the propositional logic of more traditional political rhetoric. 413

affiliation 51, 67, 95-97, 100, 102, 123, 182, 300, 530
affiliative 172
affirmative 144, 280, 291, 292
age 4, 5, 20, 22, 24, 48, 90, 94, 142-144, 152, 153, 163, 165, 174, 175, 178, 272, 484, 500, 515, 521, 529, 535
agency 3, 7, 36, 81, 96, 129, 152, 285, 292, 299, 300, 303, 313, 315, 316, 335, 348, 410, 415, 417, 437, 442, 448, 459, 467, 478, 479, 480, 482, 483, 487, 491, 492, 500, 503, 510-513, 518, 535, 544, 546, 548, 550, 557, 558
  agent 4-6, 27, 121, 152, 211, 213, 236, 262, 264, 326, 371, 374, 393, 416, 423, 426, 430,

444, 451, 452, 457, 458, 461, 465, 474, 479, 483, 504, 508, 545, 558
  material agency 4, 7, 12, 164, 168, 171, 172, 189, 191, 233, 234, 235, 242, 268, 272, 285, 300, 302, 303, 314, 317, 335, 344, 347, 371, 411, 415, 416, 417, 420, 479, 481, 483, 486, 489, 498, 500, 511, 518, 548, 557

aggregate 40, 131, 135, 376, 487
alchemy 130, 131
alienated 4, 130, 154, 173, 278, 350, 486, 515
  alienating 96, 151, 315, 328, 458
  alienation 154, 179, 181, 233, 238, 314, 315, 317, 326, 350, 529

Alienation provides the capacity for a constant displacement from a closed state of conventions or orders, and the possibility of triggering virtualities in a project, generally excluded by a historical construction of tools or responses. 238

Alienation provides the opportunity to dismantle conventions, and the possibility to open potentials that have been generally excluded by a historical construction of tools, solutions, and practices. 315

all-encompassing visions 421, 469
ambiguity 4, 55, 67, 79, 89, 90, 113, 115, 341, 367, 449
American 6, 16-21, 25, 31, 32, 37, 43, 47, 50, 51, 94, 108, 111, 131, 142, 144, 145-147, 150, 151, 159, 205, 215, 225, 249, 316, 332, 357, 407, 428, 455, 456, 457, 478, 507, 519, 537, 543, 553
apparatus 17, 42, 114, 177, 180, 244, 272, 317, 326, 329, 432, 467, 473, 503, 518, 547
arbitrary 98, 99, 101, 102, 109, 114, 181, 182, 244, 277, 349, 380, 381

564

> The same sort of **arcane** knowledge is used to produce wine, horses, or bulls, and purposefully manipulated outside of normative genetic pools and/or environments. **351**

architectural
culture 18, 94, 110, 149, 151, 152, 193, 319, 415, 457
debate 37, 242, 301, 302, 322, 328, 365, 370, 445
discipline 71, 111, 228, 365
education 205, 206, 216, 248-253
fundamentalism 156, 444
knowledge 93, 94, 97, 101, 188, 189, 211, 217, 293, 337, 441
performance 190, 197, 209, 227
practice 87, 94, 96, 103, 107, 108, 110, 111, 115, 117, 119, 135, 145, 165, 169, 170, 175, 178, 207, 209, 211, 219, 224, 240, 268, 270, 277, 288
production 51, 93, 112, 146, 206, 235, 288, 299, 366, 483
project 19, 118, 209, 253, 293, 312, 313, 315, 320, 408, 424, 478, 483
representation 54, 167, 522
service 308, 309, 335, 336, 370, 454
architecture and power 463, 465

> **Architecture** is not a plastic art, but the engineering of material life. **232**

architecture of political-economic power 314
architecture-consuming public 453
artificial 16-19, 21, 22, 30, 38-40, 42-44, 46, 47, 58, 59, 61, 62, 85, 96, 97, 100, 102, 128, 136, 137, 146, 147, 149, 175, 231, 233, 240, 255, 257-259, 285, 286, 300, 303-307, 322, 332, 342, 358, 363, 364, 371, 401, 402, 404-406, 415, 430, 438, 439, 474, 479, 482-484, 493, 496-498, 500-505, 510, 518, 523, 525, 529, 536, 540, 548, 553
artificial complexity 233, 306

artificial intelligence 137, 240, 257, 259, 303, 305, 314, 322, 336, 411, 413, 481, 487

> **Artificial intelligence** has made available the ability to model fields that were not previously visible and for this reason had not yet entered into the instrumental realm of material practices. **411**

artificial nature 19, 39, 46, 286
artists 5, 17, 49, 84, 90, 91, 127, 128, 158, 187, 265, 277, 485, 490, 548
assemblage 69, 81, 83, 91, 128, 129, 142, 147, 152, 185, 189, 197, 205, 225, 233-235, 239, 241, 256, 263, 285, 289, 314, 318, 323, 350, 362, 381, 416, 417, 437, 480, 487, 490, 491, 524, 542, 553
asset 317, 430, 465, 472, 555, 558
associated fabric 236, 240, 321
atmosphere 116, 189, 310, 337, 378, 387, 414, 415, 420, 487, 488, 492, 493, 497-499, 503-505, 515, 541

> Paper architecture has lost its effectiveness as a political vehicle; like utopia, it is restricted to pure representation without the **attachments** and frictions capable of politicizing matters. **478**

attractors 31, 33, 65, 66, 138
author 37, 95, 102, 113, 118, 119-121, 182, 199, 216, 316, 317, 364
authors' subjectivity 181
authorship 6, 119, 120, 181, 199, 217, 233, 238, 289, 348, 350, 289, 350
authoritarian 416,
bureaucracies 417, 491
authoritarianism 450

> The generational reading of the work collected here aims to set up consistency with a whole population, enabling a form of **authorship** that transcends the individual agent and turns it into a collective, mediated one. **6**

automata 326
autonomy 20, 67, 94, 102, 118, 235, 237, 239, 271, 272, 289, 322, 408, 409
autonomy of architecture 95, 121, 224

> **Autonomy** implies the capacity of a practice to develop such a level of consistency on an abstract level as to extend its potential effects beyond its mere efficiencies and into a regime of excess. **237**

autopoietic 164

B
Bare Life 542, 547-550, 552, 553, 557, 558
bastardized 453

> The most productive function that an architectural critique may have is to act as a deterritorializing machine, ...to operate like a television camera on a **battlefield**, altering the course of events by simply being present. **69**

Baukunst
Baukunst and Kunstwollen 347
Baukunst versus Kunstwollen 118, 289
behaviorist AI 314, 413, 487
Belfast truss 294

> I like those moments when you must suspend all your **beliefs** in order to be effective in a very specific situation. **432**

bible-wielding creationists 446, 448
bifurcate 354
bifurcation 230, 282, 354, 443, 503
biography 7, 50, 183, 331, 332
biographical 68, 227, 456, 462, 477
biotechnology, prosthetics 303
bottom up 97, 122, 124, 200, 201, 236, 240, 321, 355, 408
bottom-up and top-down 351, 411, 521
bottom-up parametric design 256, 351

brand 148, 154, 209, 347, 382, 386, 387, 422, 427, 449, 467, 521, 552, 553, 555-557
  branding 148, 201, 220, 251, 336, 348, 364,368, 373, 377, 379, 427, 448, 449, 469
brave new world 146, 155, 307, 332, 516
breed 77, 118, 158, 161, 202, 217, 231, 253, 254, 312, 351, 379, 413, 441, 452, 453, 455, 458, 487, 545, 555

We are no longer trapped in the traditional compulsion either to reproduce historical models or to invent them ex nihilo. We breed projects rather than design them. 231

broadcasting 254, 262, 370, 425

It is vital for the architect to maintain a public discourse by spilling broadsheet ink. 370

bubbles 6, 92, 365, 415, 457, 458, 482, 488, 519, 541
bureaucracy 153, 430
  bureaucratic 85, 105, 186, 379, 416, 464, 467, 490, 520

C

Calvinistic 151
capital 21, 23, 28-30, 32, 52, 59, 63, 111, 136, 150, 154-157, 242, 260-262, 299, 347, 61, 376, 391, 416, 417, 464, 465, 468, 470, 472, 473, 476, 479, 482, 484, 523, 536, 540, 541, 544, 545, 550, 553, 558
capitalism 20, 29, 42, 52, 53, 59, 63, 108, 156, 176, 221, 222, 228, 249, 276, 312, 331, 356, 357, 417, 441, 446-449, 472, 482, 491, 496, 515, 520, 521, 523, 524, 542, 545

Capitalism does not usually concern itself with remembrance and nostalgia, but rather operates with a systematic forgiveness, often bordering on schizophrenia. 356

  advanced capitalism 26, 28, 30
  late-capitalism 5, 29, 35, 50, 53, 55, 67, 82, 83, 94, 112, 115, 171, 227, 276, 336, 472

capitalist 20, 26, 28, 29-31, 43, 50, 51, 94, 106, 111, 249, 332, 357, 417, 448, 452, 472, 473, 486, 526, 545, 547, 558
  late-capitalist 28-31, 33, 34, 36, 39, 53, 58, 59, 62, 63, 91, 171, 331, 345, 449, 515, 551
cause and effect 112, 292, 521
celebrity 145, 251, 367, 421-428, 430, 432, 460, 534, 553

The celebrity model has also established that architects are different from one another. The corporate model was based on a sort of uniform technical expertise. 425

change 27, 34, 35, 41, 59, 60, 63, 64, 76, 77, 78, 84, 90, 91, 102, 136, 140, 142, 144, 154, 165, 167, 168, 171, 175, 190, 195, 196, 217, 218, 222, 223, 225, 247, 260, 282-284, 292, 313, 316, 326, 327, 330-332, 343, 351, 367, 371, 387, 402, 413, 418, 428, 438-440, 453, 464, 476, 478, 491, 498, 504, 509, 512, 522, 543, 545, 554
chaos 27, 50, 51, 65, 79, 80, 233, 238, 280, 283, 306, 352, 440, 549
character 3, 7, 12, 19, 22, 48, 49, 55, 80, 118, 140, 216, 289, 303, 361, 368, 391, 398, 423, 454, 480, 511, 546, 552
cheap 32, 39, 130, 306, 427, 490, 552, 553, 555, 556
  cheapness 542, 545, 546, 549, 551-558
CIA 447

If urbanization has historically developed as a process of accumulation and location of surpluses within the late-capitalist regime, the urban milieu is now determined by its capacity to incorporate a circulation of surpluses. 28

city 18, 21-24, 27, 29-31, 34-36, 52, 53, 55, 56, 89, 108, 110, 149, 158, 211, 224, 240, 253, 255-257, 282, 283, 287, 298, 305, 322-324, 325, 345, 355, 361, 362-366, 376, 383, 386, 388-391, 393-395, 398, 399, 404, 406, 411, 417, 436, 438, 439, 454, 460-462, 464, 465-467, 469-475, 484, 494, 499, 504-508, 511, 515, 525, 527, 533, 535, 536, 542, 547, 556, 557
civic order 467
class 208, 249, 253, 257, 331, 384, 426, 431, 441, 466, 474, 475, 478, 486, 515, 533, 537, 544, 549
client 42, 43, 312, 317, 338, 339, 366, 369, 370, 373, 453, 456, 468, 483
closure 34, 176, 246, 329, 470, 500
cloud 64, 70, 310
  cloud or waves 168
  clouds, stains, and rocks 277
  clouds, waves, or inkblots 278
coarse 304
  coarseness 247, 330
coherence 30, 31, 67, 68, 97, 118, 178, 180, 182, 208, 276, 289, 290, 307, 342, 343, 410
  coherent 31, 37, 45, 50, 55, 57, 88, 97, 99, 171, 172, 281, 282, 294, 296, 362, 478
cold-blooded generation 331
collective 5, 6, 25, 40, 129, 147, 155, 211, 252, 253, 254, 260, 266, 272, 296, 306, 328, 370, 372, 376, 400, 409, 416, 421, 422, 450, 453, 458, 467, 474, 489, 490, 520, 522, 527-529, 542
commission 17, 128, 129, 159, 160, 211, 227, 284, 312, 370, 372, 378, 468, 507, 529
commodity 42, 249, 250, 251, 401, 444, 497, 539, 543, 546, 551
communication 28, 30, 33, 36, 48, 53, 55, 89, 105, 135, 138, 152, 156, 211, 231, 247, 260, 267, 308, 311, 331, 365, 367, 368, 373, 380, 381, 415, 418, 419, 420, 422, 426, 445, 473, 515, 545
  between communication and production 365
community 19, 44, 48, 158, 211, 265, 266, 414, 463, 474, 487, 489, 525, 526, 529, 544, 553
complex 24, 33-36, 63, 65, 77, 90, 98, 99, 108, 112, 118, 123, 129-134, 136, 137, 141, 142, 153, 169, 170, 175, 187, 189, 197, 216, 220, 228, 231, 235, 239, 240, 245, 250, 257, 264, 265, 277, 279, 281, 285, 287, 296, 298, 302-307, 313, 320, 321, 325, 327-329, 333, 340, 342, 343, 357-359, 380, 384, 390, 392, 395, 402, 405, 413, 414,

424, 453, 474, 480-482, 484, 485, 487, 488, 490, 492, 507, 508, 512, 513, 517, 518, 527, 530, 534, 536, 537, 553

complexity 19, 34, 101, 109, 131, 135-137, 146, 169, 180, 182, 221, 231-233, 241, 247, 268, 276, 283, 297, 299, 304, 306-308, 313, 320, 322, 327, 328, 330, 334, 385, 395, 410, 452, 463, 467, 478, 493, 495, 518, 530, 532

> The opportunity that lies ahead of us is to overcome the disciplinary barrier that resorts to contradiction as a form of complexity. 231

> The current opportunities are to overcome the disciplinary barrier that resorts to rote contradiction as a form of complexity and rather to exploit complexity through coherence and consistency. 306-7

complicity 164, 222, 242, 463, 469, 490
 complicity, quantitative analysis, factual data, consumerism 222
composite 117, 131, 136, 189, 235, 236, 287, 453
 composite material 129, 234, 238, 239, 318
composition 29, 34-36, 38, 44, 47-49, 51, 54, 61, 73, 118, 124, 130, 168, 178-182, 198, 226, 289, 319, 324, 326, 327, 368, 404, 418, 470, 472, 480, 518
 composition of activities 319
compute 24
 computation 232, 233, 307
 computational 6, 165, 167, 168, 171, 173, 299, 311
 computer-aided manufacturing 445
concreteness 128, 246, 329, 469
conflict 98, 204, 218, 219, 240, 281, 305, 340-342, 344, 394, 445-447, 526, 532, 445
conservative 27, 34, 95, 113, 150, 153, 158, 171, 190, 191, 231, 318, 369, 409, 436, 437, 506, 507
consistent 3, 5, 34, 39, 51, 54, 61, 75, 77, 89, 93, 101, 111, 112, 123, 129-131, 148, 192, 198,

200, 202, 210, 211, 213, 243, 257, 258, 281, 295, 305, 309, 312, 322, 324, 339, 345, 347, 349-351, 354, 370, 373, 378, 379, 418, 420, 455, 474, 513, 520, 526, 531

consistency 4, 6, 20, 27, 36, 86, 127, 130, 131, 134, 140, 152, 153, 180-182, 190, 192-198, 201, 202, 204, 208, 212, 213, 226, 228, 229, 231, 232, 237, 270, 304, 307, 320, 322, 323, 334, 337, 342, 346, 347-352, 357, 362, 380, 390, 409-411, 414, 430, 442, 443, 456, 472, 475, 482, 508, 520, 529, 543, 555

> Beyond urban development and architecture, there are other contemporary products that have already become vehicles of political constituencies without having to resort to political ideology or political discourse: low-cost airlines have effectively declassed the airplane cabin and de-rooted large populations, 543-4

construction of subjectivity 221
consume 255, 404, 407, 510
 consumerism 20, 222, 449, 506, 549
 consumption 38-40, 42, 43, 53, 136, 137, 249, 253, 266, 310, 348, 373, 427, 446, 456, 474, 504, 505, 510, 547, 557, 558
contaminate 148, 453, 481

contemporary 4, 5, 7, 18, 19, 23, 26, 27, 29, 31, 34-36, 41, 43, 44, 49-51, 53, 54, 56, 61, 65, 68, 75, 84, 86, 87, 90-94, 103, 105-108, 110-113, 117, 119, 121-123, 126, 132, 133, 151, 155, 157, 166, 168, 177, 179, 184, 187, 193, 197, 213, 216, 217, 222, 225, 226, 231, 236, 240, 243, 247, 251-254, 258-261, 271, 272, 276, 277, 280, 281, 283, 293, 299, 300, 303, 310, 319, 324, 325, 328, 330, 331, 345-348, 351, 355, 362-365, 367, 368, 387, 396-399, 402, 407, 410, 412, 413, 415, 416, 419, 425, 428, 438, 439, 441, 442, 453, 458, 460-462, 464, 465, 467, 468, 470, 472-476, 478, 484, 486, 488, 489, 492, 499, 502, 504, 510,

512, 513, 515, 519-521, 523, 524, 527, 529, 531, 533-535, 537, 539
 contemporary subject 43, 272, 474

context 7, 78, 88, 96, 120, 148, 167, 191, 194, 223, 224, 227, 235, 236, 239, 245, 251, 253, 259, 270, 300, 302, 310, 312, 313, 315, 323, 324, 331, 332, 339, 357, 373, 375, 376, 388, 411, 437, 464, 475, 476, 478, 486, 515, 524, 536, 543
 Context also contains time 323, 324, 347
 contextual 97, 323
 contextualism 322, 324, 411
contingent 3, 56, 64, 86, 98, 108, 109, 114, 121, 152, 182, 232, 291, 315, 325, 327, 331, 351, 354, 368, 380, 387, 416, 418, 419, 430, 447, 490, 510, 511, 516, 541, 549, 550
 contingency 50, 115, 181, 233, 283, 345, 522
 contingent diversification 355
 contingent, local, or specific 349
continuity 33, 40, 62, 79, 190, 195, 197, 204, 230, 280, 287, 312, 342, 354, 355, 358, 415, 517, 520, 553
contradiction 97, 101, 130, 172, 204, 222, 231, 276, 277, 278, 306, 307, 322, 410, 498, 531, 550, 551
control 20, 27, 32, 36, 50, 55, 56, 60, 62, 66, 72, 73, 95, 96, 102, 107-110, 116, 117, 121, 137, 138, 155, 157, 169, 174, 180, 182, 189, 243, 246, 277, 279, 283, 315, 316, 326, 329, 342-345, 352, 370, 382, 415, 431, 437, 457, 467, 474, 483, 486, 496, 498, 506, 508, 511, 512, 525, 537, 543

> Between power and potential lies control. 107

controversy 104, 502
convergence 4, 111, 141, 216, 262, 268, 416, 417, 443, 484, 540
corporate 18, 20, 22, 25, 59, 94, 105, 110, 111, 113, 145, 153, 156, 157, 159, 160, 222, 270, 276, 288, 325, 393, 409, 421-423, 425, 427, 440, 445, 446, 462, 465, 474, 486, 487, 523, 535,
 corporate bulldozers 460

567

crafts 371
craftsman 182, 327
critical
critical mass 29, 32, 61, 103, 540
critical mode (see also productive mode) 278
critical practice 93, 94, 145, 278, 313

> Once writing abandons the role of the critical–that is, establishing benchmarks, comparisons, judgments, and value systems– it becomes a projective tool in itself. 144

> Critical architecture is not generated through a theoretical discourse that later materializes. 238

cross breeding 118, 312, 379, 441
cross-cultural 316, 519

> Iconographic research remained unfit for cultural consumption and we kept it in the closet. 373

culture 6, 16-20, 24, 25, 33, 38, 40-42, 52, 81, 82, 90, 104, 110-112, 120, 148, 151, 153, 154, 156, 157, 167, 186, 213, 218, 221, 222, 225, 226, 242, 247, 249, 266, 280, 303, 316, 332, 336, 349, 351, 352, 355, 364, 373, 384, 392, 403, 405, 409, 422, 423, 426-431, 436, 446, 449, 458, 460, 469, 470, 474, 477, 495, 515, 522, 523, 525, 527, 528, 529, 531, 537, 540, 543, 536

> In this business, if you haven't got a culture, you haven't got a chance. 431

architectural culture (see architectural) contemporary culture 49, 68, 92, 166, 216, 259, 260, 351, 467, 558
material culture 26, 36, 81, 90, 91
metropolitan culture 53, 65
popular culture 38
cultural protocols 348, 402
cultural specificities 320, 398, 404
cultural terms 472, 509
cyborg 33
cynical 4, 155, 448, 477

D
Darwin 16
data 28, 44, 62, 98-100, 132, 135, 137, 138, 146, 168-170, 177, 222, 223, 234-236, 239, 240, 243, 245, 257, 258, 264, 309, 311, 321, 325, 327, 328, 370, 441, 457
data collection 337
data-processing 133, 188, 235
datascape 307, 373, 379, 411, 445
daylight and ventilation 404, 406, 480, 497, 500, 526
defamiliarization 114
deformation 36, 58, 68, 63, 71, 82, 86, 88, 90, 123, 124, 172, 246, 296, 330, 342, 354, 393, 409, 472
deliberative-linguistic 475
demiurgomorphic 280, 283
democracy 6, 142, 221, 225, 228, 331, 371, 414, 416, 464, 475, 476, 477, 488, 490, 501, 513, 520, 521, 542, 549, 551, 556, 558
democratic 38, 155, 224, 270, 314, 325, 408, 416, 451, 452, 460, 474-476, 486, 488, 489, 490, 505, 514, 519, 520, 523, 531, 542-544, 550, 556

> Kemal-El-Fnaa Square in Marrakesh, informal and permanently changing, may become a better model for a contemporary urban democratic space than the monumentality of Washington's Mall. 476

democratic governance 452
democratization 384, 385, 452, 503, 532, 533
densification 33, 61, 340, 384, 394, 398, 474, 532, 533, 541
describe a practice as a lineage of ideas 349

> Design is a cultural activity, a task of translation and interpretation. 351

desire 5, 16, 21, 22, 27, 38, 43, 46, 58, 60, 84, 85, 107, 135, 143, 182, 219, 220, 268, 269-271, 282, 316, 317, 382, 387, 415, 419, 423, 450, 453, 454, 477, 488, 491, 519, 525, 534, 540, 543

desire and effect 268
desires and constraints 268
destabilization 381, 447
destratification 62, 129
determination 22, 26, 31, 41, 48, 56, 59, 60, 65, 71, 72, 74, 87, 90, 96, 102, 112, 114, 115-117, 212, 126, 129, 149, 174, 181, 182, 246, 259, 276, 278-280, 288, 291, 293, 296, 308, 315, 319, 325-327, 329, 341, 342-344, 355, 464, 472, 473, 495, 497, 526, 532
determination of the grid 102, 341
determination/indetermination 112
determinism 164, 167, 303, 350, 445, 448
deterministic 113, 235, 276, 547
deterministic process 95, 314
deterritorialize 63, 130, 152
deterritorialisation 184, 187
deterritorializing 60, 61, 69, 82

develop 3, 18, 28, 30, 33, 38, 39, 50, 53, 54, 67, 80, 85, 86, 88, 97, 98, 105, 108, 116, 120, 129, 131-133, 148-153, 158, 165, 168, 172, 175, 178, 185-187, 191, 194, 198, 200-203, 205, 209, 212-218, 222, 225, 234-240, 246, 252, 254, 256, 257, 259, 263, 264, 266-269, 277, 299, 300, 306, 307, 309, 310, 312, 316-321, 324, 325, 329, 332, 339, 347-349, 368, 388, 391, 392, 397, 402, 405, 408, 410, 423, 427-431, 437, 453, 455, 457, 461, 468, 483, 491, 492, 504, 528, 533, 537, 540, 541
developer 17, 22, 149, 158, 159, 221, 223, 228, 384, 386, 394, 395, 399, 403, 404, 451, 455, 465, 482, 484, 507

development 20, 25, 27-29, 33, 42, 45, 47, 51, 55, 56, 58, 61, 63, 65, 66, 68, 78, 82, 91, 98, 101, 102, 112, 155, 156, 159, 166, 170, 175, 176, 178, 179, 181, 191, 195, 204, 208, 211, 218-220, 224, 225, 229, 232, 241, 242, 245, 249, 253, 259, 260, 262, 281, 283, 293, 295, 297, 298, 302, 303, 305, 307, 314, 323, 326, 331, 334,

340-344, 350-352, 356, 375, 380, 384, 385, 388-390, 398, 401, 402, 404, 413, 425, 436, 445, 455, 462, 467, 468, 472, 476, 480, 481, 484, 485, 488, 489, 498, 504, 506-508, 513, 526, 530, 533, 534, 536, 540, 542, 543

diagram 21, 87, 88, 101, 115, 120, 121, 123, 181, 182, 192, 197, 198, 202, 233, 234, 236, 238, 240, 242, 243-247, 282, 309-311, 314, 315, 318, 320, 321, 327-330, 342, 350, 352, 357, 372, 374, 397, 445, 508, 538, 540

diagrammatic 87, 88, 123, 152, 190, 196, 245-247, 320, 327, 329, 357

diagrammatic architecture 245, 329

diagrammatic practices 243, 244, 245, 326, 327

In a diagrammatic process the project retains its virtualities, which become only partially actualized, keeping the possibility to develop *ad infinitum*. 246

In a diagrammatic project the moment of closure is determined by factors external to the project, and the propositional moments, the aims and strategies, are not restricted to the origin or the end, but to the middle of the process. 246

diagrams and abstractions 234, 238

diagrams, indices, notations, and registers 315

diagrams, statistics, notations 233, 238

diagrams, statistics, notations, and geometry 314

direction 56, 59, 64, 94, 102, 104, 111, 125, 140, 176, 179, 201, 204, 212, 214, 215, 217, 227, 246, 294, 295, 304, 329, 334, 342, 355, 380, 411, 428, 470, 486, 487, 491, 494, 517, 539, 470, 486, 491, 517

discipline 37, 53, 66, 71, 82, 95-97, 107-109, 111, 112, 118, 119, 121, 122, 141-143, 146, 151, 154, 159, 164, 165, 167, 173, 174, 178, 179, 182, 184, 185, 188-191, 193, 198, 205-209, 217, 219, 223, 225, 226, 228, 233-235,

238, 239, 243, 246, 252, 254-257, 259, 271, 277, 278, 288, 290, 292, 293, 301, 302, 305-307, 309, 311, 313, 316, 317, 319, 320, 325, 330, 331, 333, 336, 337, 344, 351, 352, 365, 368, 380, 382, 417, 418, 424, 425, 427, 431, 440-443, 463, 464, 468, 469, 478, 481, 483, 491, 509, 524, 548

Rather than returning to ideology and utopia, a contemporary politicization of architecture needs to relocate politics within specific disciplinary domains, not as a representation of an ideal concept of the political, but as a political effect specific to the discipline. 478

disciplinary 23, 37, 83, 84, 95, 96, 114, 118, 119, 121, 122, 143, 151, 182-184, 186, 197, 200, 201, 205-207, 213, 216, 217, 231, 233-235, 238, 239, 250, 251, 256, 259, 290-293, 299, 303, 306, 326, 336, 337, 352, 373, 379-381, 429, 441-444, 448, 469, 478, 526

disciplinary stance 470

discontinuity 39, 62, 73, 284, 354

disempowerment 468

displacements 98, 99, 327, 472

disruptive pattern material (DPM) 286, 298

dissent 261, 447, 543

distributed computing 259, 443

diversification 29, 58, 355, 357, 399, 402, 404, 405, 415, 497, 529

DNA of the practice 202

double agenda 211, 213, 241, 272, 380-382

down-market 549

driving systems 315

Dutch generation 149

E

eccentric 139, 149, 150, 153, 158

eccentricity 139, 154, 206, 217

ecology 39, 40, 42, 259, 436-439, 446, 500, 510

ecological 255, 371, 384, 436-439, 505, 510, 540, 544

economy 17, 29, 31, 50, 133, 136, 142, 154, 157, 158, 160, 192, 227, 262, 269, 362, 374,

383, 387, 392, 417, 441, 454, 457, 458, 463, 465, 498, 502, 527, 544, 547-554, 556-558

economic and cultural globalization 471

economic, social, and political integration 440

ecosystem 256, 259, 264, 351, 357, 438, 510, 555

The primary objective is not to produce people–as in traditional education–but to produce knowledge. 427

efficiency 16, 17, 68, 91, 105, 111, 138, 153, 270, 283, 385, 388, 392-394, 396, 482, 495, 498, 506, 510, 532, 535, 536, 542

embryological potentials 353

emergence 7, 28, 34, 53, 66, 70, 79, 80, 83, 98, 103, 122, 123, 199, 210, 234, 239, 245, 259, 262, 270, 277, 283, 293, 307, 334, 336, 340, 372, 409, 420, 441, 487, 512, 515, 519, 521, 527, 536, 540, 542, 543

emergent 73, 129, 154, 160, 208, 225, 236, 240, 257, 302, 305, 321, 378, 417, 483, 512

energy 27, 37, 136, 152, 153, 174, 185, 255, 256, 258, 286, 338, 366, 385, 387, 392, 401, 404, 409, 429, 432, 438, 469, 481, 482, 484, 492, 497-501, 504, 505, 508, 510, 525, 530, 540, 558

engagement and publicness 254

engineering material life 304

engineering of material life 133, 232, 237, 303, 304, 333, 335

enjoy your symptoms! 468

envelope 71, 78, 89, 90, 91, 131, 190, 197, 198, 203, 204, 247, 253, 258, 259, 282, 294, 297, 298, 330, 353, 359, 360, 382, 386, 390, 393, 410-420, 477, 479-541, 551, 553

enveloping surfaces 102, 295, 353

environment 24, 27, 58, 78, 85, 91, 115, 131, 133, 135, 145, 149, 148, 152, 159, 171, 172, 190, 191, 205-207, 216, 222, 227, 235, 239, 248, 250, 255-257, 260,

263, 267, 277, 297, 303, 304,
309, 322, 325, 326, 330,
332, 350, 351, 401, 402, 405,
427, 430, 277, 297, 303, 322,
325, 326, 350, 351, 401, 402,
405, 427, 430, 436-439, 451,
452, 454, 457, 458, 462, 464,
465, 472, 487, 492, 496, 498,
500-502, 504, 506-508, 511,
536, 557

environmental 48, 111, 143, 172, 187, 189, 203, 247, 255, 256, 258, 259, 269, 304, 309, 330, 338, 351, 377, 386, 389-392, 404, 406, 412-415, 417, 418, 451, 479, 480, 485, 487, 489, 490, 494, 495, 497, 498, 500, 505, 506, 509-513, 515, 520, 523, 525-527, 530, 532-534, 536, 537, 541, 552

equalization 544, 545
equilibrium 34, 35, 192, 438, 476, 492, 493
erasure of the ground 300

To truly understand matter's erotica, you need to taste it in its most disciplined arrangements or in its utmost state of chaotic dissolution. 128

estrangement 42, 84, 154, 186, 187, 314, 550
European climate 454
event structures 361
evolving classification of traits 349
exchangeable commodity 444
excuse 146, 225, 252, 253, 268, 269-272, 302, 312, 319, 366, 373, 374, 381, 382, 552

The excuse is an intermediate figure between desires and constraints. 268

excuses rather than visions 268
existence 28, 46, 243, 265, 383, 468, 492, 555
expansion 28, 55, 65, 106, 120, 230, 356, 357, 372, 380, 423, 472, 510, 542

Democracy, in its global neoliberal form, is expensive, often inefficient, and consumes an absurd amount of non-renewable resources. 558

experience 21, 24, 25, 45, 46, 48, 53, 55, 58, 67, 68, 70, 87, 131, 138, 153, 167, 169, 186, 228, 243, 246, 252, 266, 301, 317, 327, 329, 332, 338, 364, 372, 422, 430, 431, 442, 466, 477, 530
explicitation 362, 483, 492, 528, 535, 539, 541, 548

Rather than aiming at revolution, a political practice for architecture is perhaps best shifted to explicitation by means of reduction to a bare state. 548

explore 63, 68, 92, 97, 110, 113, 118, 167, 169, 207, 243, 254, 256, 257, 259, 262-264, 267, 280, 283, 284, 286, 287, 304, 314, 324, 326, 328, 331, 375, 415, 420, 424, 426, 427, 430, 461, 476, 480, 487, 512, 529, 548, 551
explore freedoms 252
exploring materials 237, 334
exploring the materials 232

expression 26, 40, 43, 80, 84, 87, 90, 105, 118-121, 129, 155, 181, 194, 244, 252, 257, 58, 266, 270, 279, 303, 304, 309, 311, 312, 351, 357, 372, 88, 392-394, 409, 413, 416, 417, 419, 465, 480, 481, 484-486, 488-491, 495, 496, 511, 513, 514, 516, 518-520, 526, 528, 532, 533, 535, 536, 539, 548, 551
expression and efficiency 392, 394

Musical genres often evolve through the devaluation of form and technique in order to increase the integrative capacity of expression. 84

exteriority 34, 44, 82, 83, 118, 290, 416, 490
external 4, 34, 45, 89, 90, 97, 98, 109, 117, 118, 122, 127, 130, 133, 142, 146, 170, 173, 174, 188, 196, 199, 200, 210-213, 225, 235, 236, 238, 239, 246, 254, 269, 271, 280, 288-290, 292, 300, 302, 314, 321, 323, 326, 329, 337, 340, 349, 350, 352, 375, 377, 399, 412, 441, 442, 469, 470, 481,
482, 486, 499, 513, 514, 517, 526
external and internal consistency 350
external coherence 118, 289, 290
external conditions 349, 352
external inputs 314, 326
external processes 122, 142, 225, 292, 300, 302, 350
externally consistent 347
extreme form 238

Extreme form is a peak register of formal singularity. 238

F

fabrics 31, 57, 80, 310, 322, 392, 408-411, 494, 506
face 69, 71-75, 80, 83, 89, 146, 188, 211, 270, 280, 287, 299, 313, 343, 353, 363, 408, 418, 448, 464, 478, 481, 484, 485, 495, 512, 513, 526, 528, 530, 558
faceless consultants 452
faceless corporations 452
faciality 64, 71-74, 90, 353, 413-416, 481, 483, 485, 488, 512-516, 518-520, 522, 523, 526, 527, 530, 541
facialization 91, 413, 414, 481, 486-489, 512, 518
facts 3, 271, 326, 327, 337, 384, 446, 447, 469, 540
factual data 222, 309, 370
factual performance 470
fascination 84, 181, 370, 468
feedback loop 351
flexible 53, 111, 170, 175, 236, 325, 358, 472
flexible accumulation 28, 31, 34, 52-54, 57, 63, 175, 472
flexibility 29, 33, 49, 53, 61, 86, 87, 113, 116, 145, 153, 250, 293, 323, 326, 342, 396, 407, 408, 412, 473, 482, 525
flow 29, 32, 54, 64, 90, 99, 102, 130, 171, 252, 258, 261, 281, 295, 309, 315, 318, 355, 364, 439, 445, 464, 471, 481, 492-494, 496, 498, 499, 503, 505
flows and change 63, 140
for rigor 269
forces 7, 21, 22, 30, 43, 62, 66, 94, 95, 108, 130, 132, 153, 156, 159, 174, 199, 218, 227, 254, 257, 282, 287, 299, 317, 324, 347, 350, 352, 353, 358, 386, 393, 394, 396, 406, 416, 452, 456, 461, 465, 469, 509,

511, 515, 525, 536, 557
foreign 148, 149, 458, 477, 545
  foreign investment 398, 460, 533
  foreignness 43, 314, 374
form
  form of complexity 231, 306
  form with a double agenda 380
  formal autonomy 322, 408
  formal determination 90, 116, 341, 342, 344
  formless 276, 278, 279, 283

> The formless is independent of the well defined formal orders. It can be constructed either through indetermination or through ruthless, alienated determination. 278

  formless and the informal 278
  formlessness 276, 277, 278, 279
  forms of economic integration 28, 472
  forms, patterns, geometries, distributions 280
frameless 230, 418, 420
free 27, 49, 75, 81, 107, 112, 113, 297, 328, 336, 350, 351, 356, 364, 445, 446, 447, 449, 460, 524, 546, 548, 549, 558
  free-floating commodity 551
  free-wheeling capitalism 331
  freedom 6, 41, 60, 62, 70, 76, 113, 142, 144, 177, 182, 197, 228, 252, 283, 323, 324, 326, 342, 368, 395, 488, 512, 513, 517, 526, 531, 543, 550
frills 542, 546, 549-553, 555-557
function 7, 18, 35, 41, 44, 50, 65, 69, 71, 72, 78, 88, 98, 114, 116, 122, 127, 134, 137, 176, 177, 193, 227, 257, 270, 284, 291, 299, 300, 304, 306, 311, 350, 353, 368, 473, 480, 481, 483, 488, 494, 496, 504, 510, 512, 518, 524, 527, 548
functional 33, 48, 60, 68, 74, 87, 96, 98, 100-102, 111, 230, 236, 239, 246, 269, 270, 286, 287, 289, 290, 292, 293, 295, 297, 321, 329, 377, 389, 394, 396, 419, 481, 486, 495, 497, 511, 524-526, 530

> We can go back to that beautiful pre-9/11 utopia in which everybody from everywhere glides effortlessly across the world, and where architects no longer need to represent anything whatsoever. But I am afraid that is just the dream of an unreconstructed globalization fundamentalist. 449

G

> The generic is the lowest register of singularity amongst a broad sample of cases. 238

genetic 49, 57, 201, 202, 204, 264, 349, 350, 351, 352, 353, 468, 481

> Generational analysis seemed to be a good alternative to the prevailing model of the star-system and its theory of exception and uniqueness. 5

genius loci 4, 270
geometry 23, 28, 35, 36, 40, 46, 59, 60, 63, 70, 74, 82, 86, 87, 88, 102, 120, 134, 136, 187, 192-198, 202, 201-204, 217, 224, 226, 240, 246, 255, 295, 296, 302, 305, 306, 314, 319, 320, 322, 330, 331, 339-345, 355, 360, 372, 374, 379, 395, 397, 412, 413, 419, 467, 508, 516, 518, 520, 537
  geometric manipulations 372
  geometrical continuity 355
  geometrical diagrams 198
  geometrical fabric 341
  geometries of pure indeterminacy or pure linearity 306
  geometries, organizations 234, 238
  geometry, tectonics, materiality, organization, distribution 331
geopolitics 4, 142, 213, 249, 504, 544
  geopolitical 20, 122, 409, 472, 510, 553
global 6, 7, 18, 25, 28-30, 36, 62, 66, 68, 82, 83, 88, 90, 94, 99, 101-103, 122, 123, 128, 131-137, 154, 156, 160, 184, 229, 236, 239, 242, 248-251, 253, 255, 262, 321, 333, 344, 357, 362, 363, 383, 386, 387, 398, 399, 400, 401, 404, 405, 411, 414, 419, 427, 437, 438, 445, 446, 454, 459-462, 465, 467, 482, 487, 489, 498, 504, 508, 510, 515, 519, 521, 522, 529, 533, 536, 541, 543-545, 558
  global capital 154, 242, 361, 417
  global capitalism 312, 357, 417, 441, 446, 448, 449, 482, 491, 496, 520, 523, 542, 543
  global network 472
  global protocols 460
  global positioning systems 7
  global systems 281, 314, 460
  globalization 29, 30, 88, 109, 122, 147, 186, 225, 229, 242, 247, 249, 250, 258, 270, 302, 314, 324, 331, 347, 363, 385, 410, 411, 421, 445-447, 449, 459-462, 464, 471, 479, 487, 515, 519, 542, 545, 555

> Globalization has neutralized the effectiveness of architectural language, propelling the iconic and symbolic to the forefront of contemporary practices while increasing the demands for the envelope's technical capacity for insulation and immunization, environmentally and security-wise, against an increasingly abrasive global atmosphere. 515

  globalization as trigger of difference 29
  globalization of architectural practice 347
  globalization of the urban 466
  globalized 133, 248, 348, 416, 422, 465, 487, 490
  globalized world 123, 316, 477, 529
God-like 451

> The superiority of the "culture of congestion" and the green credentials of the elevator core as an alternative to the gasguzzling, six-lane highway are becoming universally accepted facts. 384

571

ground 4, 21, 22, 24, 43, 59, 74, 101, 119, 123, 142, 174, 175, 208, 210, 231, 246, 263, 270, 282, 285-287, 293-300, 302, 326, 329, 337, 342, 353, 357, 361, 366, 402, 424, 441, 456, 457, 458, 480, 482, 492, 497, 501-504, 509, 513, 517, 528, 550, 558
  Ground Zero 156, 157, 159, 356, 365
  groundless 285, 286
groupings of traits 352
grow 4, 18, 22, 24, 41, 57, 137, 145, 150, 153, 190, 206, 208, 212, 287, 325, 351, 357, 358, 361, 378, 388, 430, 431, 497, 499
  grown 21, 143, 153, 201, 203, 222, 231, 346, 357, 389, 454, 457
  growth 21, 28-33, 136, 153, 158, 169, 191, 262, 325, 364, 380, 385, 467, 470, 472, 498, 499, 544, 545

Let's do a Grunge Olympics! 364

H

hard core 188, 190, 191, 242
heavily regulated legal framework 452
Heisenberg's Principle of Indetermination 58, 279
heroic 19, 20, 23, 36, 214, 313, 347, 431, 451
high-rise 109, 356, 357, 358, 366, 368, 375, 376, 382-385, 387-407, 492, 532, 533, 535-541
  high-rise phylum 383, 388, 392, 400, 407, 535, 539, 540
  High-Rise Prototype 358
  high-rise species 357

If geological, biological, or social history have something to teach us is that these processes of temporal formation produce organizations of far greater complexity and sophistication than instantaneous ideas or visions. 241

Hokusai Wave 369, 371-374, 379, 381, 382, 431, 432
hollowed-out ground 287, 295
horses and wine 352

Human agency is not everything. 129

human habitation 466
hybrid 33, 35, 82, 149, 189, 191, 219, 226, 291, 305, 318, 320, 340, 442, 508
  hybrid building (the programmatic mix) 319
  hybridization 88, 210, 294, 295, 399
  hybridization of high-rise life 400, 508, 537

One of the biggest malaises of present-day consumerist education is the fantasy of hyper-individualization. 251

I

icon 203, 244, 392, 539, 540
  iconic 244, 388, 390, 391, 392, 398, 400, 418, 419, 476, 487, 489, 491, 515, 524, 533-536
  iconographic 247, 269, 311, 373, 412, 432, 495, 532, 533, 535, 536
  iconographic references 312, 377, 382
  iconographic resonance 311
iconography 42, 80, 309, 312, 316, 348, 371, 373-375, 378-380, 381, 396-399, 413, 431, 432, 449, 527, 534
idea 5, 7, 42, 44, 49, 55, 57, 66, 67, 96, 103, 105, 113, 124, 125, 131, 146, 168, 170, 174, 175, 180, 191, 195, 197, 198, 200, 218, 225, 228, 229, 232, 241, 252, 268, 269, 281, 282, 284, 285, 295, 307, 310, 318, 319, 323, 327, 334, 345, 349, 350, 355, 376, 413, 414, 427, 429, 438, 439, 489, 492, 502, 514, 522, 528, 529, 544, 553, 556, 557

Idea in Greek equals image. To have an idea, one must see an idea. 170

  idea and image 170
  ideal models 470
identity 4, 5, 71, 73, 75, 76, 108, 112, 121, 122, 176, 177, 184, 86, 187, 230, 263, 284, 285, 296, 306, 346-350, 361, 370, 376, 380-382, 413, 414, 440, 445, 466, 467, 469, 470, 474, 475, 478, 482, 485, 489, 490, 511, 513, 514, 520, 522-524, 528-530
identify the consistency 349
ideology 4, 7, 39, 41, 56-58, 67, 68, 84, 94, 126, 128, 142, 159, 160, 172, 174, 196, 207, 249, 280, 302, 317, 327, 417, 421, 427, 429, 430, 436-438, 446, 448, 454, 455, 464, 467, 475, 477, 478, 483, 486, 512, 514, 515, 522, 543-546, 555, 557

One might conclude that the postwar economic boom of the 1960s was the death knell of political ideology as an effective mechanism to transform society. 249

My experience of Spain's transition from dictatorship to democracy left me with a rather cynical view of political ideologies as effective tools for understanding or transforming reality. 477

  ideology and opportunism 430
ideological 4, 6, 26, 27, 50, 51, 67, 68, 85, 95, 111, 114, 116, 126, 149, 158, 160, 172, 206, 208, 235, 242, 249, 272, 300, 308, 313-315, 327, 335, 344, 411, 417, 423, 429, 444, 447, 456, 464, 465, 470, 478, 479, 486, 491, 518, 524, 531, 536, 544-546, 548-550, 555
  ideological and post-ideological 27, 159, 464
  ideological consistency 456, 543
  ideological role 464
idiosyncratic 365, 395, 397, 465, 556
image 16, 44, 48, 79, 102, 111, 126, 140, 168, 170, 172, 177, 191, 228, 231, 232, 241, 244, 267, 280, 289, 307, 308, 334, 336, 339, 340, 357, 364, 372, 373, 379, 381, 382, 386, 387, 393, 396, 408, 420, 464, 465, 471, 481, 483, 486, 489, 501, 522, 523, 529, 532-535, 548, 556
immunization 415, 417, 487, 490, 515, 516, 521
  immunizing 414, 516
  immunizing atmospheres 415

incoherence 30, 276
increasing the resolution of the grid 343
indeterminate 4, 114, 117, 130, 246, 276, 278, 286, 330, 355, 516
    indeterminacy 133, 231, 277, 283, 306, 326

> To propose formlessness and indeterminacy as an aesthetic program may be adequate in capturing the productive or moral imperatives of the contemporary world, but it is problematic when applied to the processes of production or construction that are fundamental to the practice of architecture. 277-8

    indetermination 17, 22, 56, 57, 58, 60, 65-67, 78, 108, 112, 113-116, 126, 277-280, 292, 325

> Indetermination is an unlikely model for a discipline that is aimed at the ordering of the environment. 325

    indeterminism 279, 325, 326

> Indeterminism is normally associated with more democratic and flexible ways of proceeding, albeit this political connotation seems somehow inadequate. 325

indexicality 245, 379, 380
individual and the collective 474, 489, 520
information 39, 44, 46, 47, 63-65, 67, 87, 90, 107, 122, 123, 126, 133-136, 138, 165, 166, 170, 183, 191, 204, 216, 233, 235, 236, 239, 240, 245-247, 261, 267, 279-281, 305, 307, 308, 314, 321, 328-330, 335, 343, 344, 348, 374, 383, 411, 422, 428, 475, 523, 545
    information Age 165
    information technology 145, 165, 169, 175, 177, 238, 241-243, 281, 334, 441, 445
    informational 29, 82, 411, 445, 475
    informational technology 167, 168, 178, 238, 543
infrastructural 293, 298, 390, 391, 496, 502
innovation from novelty 387

insulating 414, 487, 503, 516, 523
integration/differentiation 122
intense 74, 77, 80, 129, 140, 143, 164, 210, 281, 412, 495, 508, 536, 554
    intensification 33, 85, 92, 105, 108, 110, 121, 122, 356, 357, 471, 472, 474, 530, 536, 544
    intensification of flows, transfers, and exchanges 471
    intensified 53, 111, 472, 487, 503, 529
    intensified orders 471
    intensities rather than extensions 82
    intensive 88, 122, 123, 135, 154, 230, 356, 375, 383, 403, 463, 498, 505, 525, 532, 533
    intensive coherence 30, 31, 410
    intensive tessellation 152
intentionality and determination 280
interface 89, 117, 133, 166, 247, 254, 258, 263, 282, 373, 413, 452, 484, 485, 496, 498, 499, 506, 513, 520
    interfacial 414, 488, 518
interiority of architecture 96
internal 3, 46, 50, 55, 61, 97, 102, 117, 118, 121, 122, 188, 191, 198, 212, 213, 225, 236, 240, 269, 280, 288-290, 302, 337, 348, 361, 377, 393, 405, 439, 441, 486, 497, 499, 504, 512, 514, 517, 525, 526, 531, 533
    internal and external transfer of information 235, 239
    internal coherence 118, 290
    internal coherence of a work of art 289
    internal consistency 181, 182, 323, 337, 347, 349, 350, 352, 412
interplay between iconography and material organization 378
intersection of semiotics and materiality 380
intrinsic identity 347
IT revolution 164, 167, 168

> What do you do as a local politician to demonstrate that your city is ripe for multi-national re-capitalization? You call in some international, celebrity architects to demonstrate your concern with quality and sophistication. Moreover, if a starchitect can work somewhere, anybody can, and the place is ripe for foreign investment. 460

J
Jazz musicians 336

> We can perhaps suspend the possibility of judgment temporarily in order to facilitate the engagement with reality, or to allow for alternative possibilities to emerge. 313

K
Kaiseki vs. McDonalds 251
kickbacks 463

> Due to its size and complexity, the construction sector is probably the most susceptible to pork-barrel politics and kickbacks. 463

knowledge 16, 17, 28, 49, 55, 58, 63, 68, 87, 91, 93-97, 101, 104, 135, 137, 141, 142, 151, 153, 155, 164, 165, 169-172, 188, 189, 202, 205, 209, 211-213, 216, 217, 231, 232, 243, 246, 251-254, 268, 278, 279, 284, 290, 293, 316, 317, 320, 327, 329, 336, 337, 338, 348, 350, 351, 352, 388, 392, 410, 420, 421, 422, 424, 426, 427, 429, 441-443, 445, 447, 457, 468, 469, 475, 480

> Relevant knowledge has ceased to be bound to experience. 317

knowledge is power 468
Kunstwollen 118, 285, 289, 347, 351

L
laboratory 78, 208, 209, 211, 215, 261, 269, 549
landscape 16, 21, 56, 69, 70, 73, 75, 80, 99, 103, 104, 106, 125, 131, 141, 167, 185, 186, 187,

573

217, 230, 240, 251, 256, 287, 305, 306, 363, 364, 366, 374, 379, 392, 402, 409, 470, 503, 510

language 19, 54, 60, 68, 70, 96, 112, 113, 116, 121, 125, 143, 146, 148, 164, 170, 172, 182, 188, 201, 202, 207, 208, 222, 223, 225, 231, 242, 270, 271, 288, 292, 308, 317, 328, 337, 353, 370, 381, 409, 410, 413, 420, 445, 447, 475, 481, 485, 487, 515, 516, 520, 521, 527, 530, 538, 539
  language, representation, or iconography 316
late-capitalist 28-31, 33, 34, 36, 39, 53, 58, 59, 62, 63, 91, 171, 331, 345, 449, 515, 551
lateness 307

Writing nurtures lateness, waiting for the emergence of the project. 307-8

latent potentials 96, 199, 233
liberal arts school 149
lifestyle 262, 255, 301, 305, 336, 345, 398, 399, 407, 421, 469, 479, 527, 536, 546
like a surfer 62, 469

The limits of freedom are more interesting than the possibilities. 252

lineage 3, 16, 43, 81, 84, 89, 94, 120, 121, 154, 176, 191, 201, 271, 285, 336, 337, 349-352, 368, 430, 431, 514

Despite the obvious dangers of sclerosis, disciplinary lineage provides an invaluable ground upon which to experiment beyond the constant reference to the market or to the outside, laying the ground for a broader field of experimentation and greater internal consistency. 337

liquid 64, 130
  liquid economy 31
  liquidation 554
  liquidity 465, 554
  liquidness 484
local
  local iconographies 374, 396, 397, 399, 534
  local singularities 281, 340, 354, 355,
  Local Smart 459

local specificity 132, 154, 355
local structures 53, 326, 460
local variations 399, 533, 537
logic of production 181, 311
looking outside 221
low-cost 547, 558

The notion that politics and economics can be neatly divided into polis and oikos— either in the sense that the markets should be entirely freed of political intervention or that political action can be effected without careful consideration of economic inputs—is ludicrous. 557

M
machine 7, 16, 17, 21, 26, 55, 69, 71, 82, 83, 86, 88, 90, 93, 95, 102, 122, 133, 135, 154, 156, 173, 174, 177, 184, 187, 194, 231, 272, 283, 310, 335, 366, 374, 421, 423, 467
  machinery 446, 449, 474
machinic 33, 59, 63, 75, 95, 101, 119, 121, 133, 231, 315, 490
management 138, 148, 157, 220, 378, 428, 431, 509, 473, 546, 552
manipulation of the ground 123, 294, 298
map 36, 54, 55, 57, 103, 104, 105, 106, 119, 125, 126, 130, 171, 259, 264, 315, 400, 402, 407, 510
market 6, 7, 18, 27, 29, 40, 53, 94, 105, 106, 107, 114, 117, 125, 127, 131, 132, 135, 143, 145, 167, 174, 213, 194, 249, 250, 251, 261, 262, 288, 292, 299, 302, 314, 337, 348, 350, 385-388, 393-395, 398-402, 404, 406, 429, 430, 438, 441, 445, 446, 448, 452, 459, 467, 479, 482, 493, 496, 498, 508, 534, 536, 541, 544, 545-547, 549-551, 553, 555-557
  market agents 452
  market forces 94, 299, 347, 452
  market ratios 385,
  marketing 5, 117, 145, 167, 261, 262, 266, 288, 372, 422, 441, 523, 532, 553, 554
  marketing and the engineering 117, 288
matchmakers 453
material
  material accretions 543
  material agency 4, 7, 12, 164, 168, 171, 172, 189, 191,

233-235, 242, 268, 272, 285, 300, 302, 303, 314, 317, 335, 344, 347, 371, 411, 415-417, 420, 479, 481, 483, 486, 489, 498, 500, 511, 518, 548, 557
material assemblages 152, 189, 234, 239, 318, 350, 381
material complex 320
material composites 235, 239
material compounds 321
Material Grain of Geometry 192
Material History 127
material life 133, 232, 237, 303, 304, 333, 335
material mediators 191, 201, 235, 239
material of context 323
material organization 26, 29, 34, 36, 53, 54, 65, 70, 71, 75, 77-79, 84, 90, 91, 127, 129, 133, 134, 152, 153, 170, 171, 174, 175, 189, 190, 193, 197, 200, 203, 204, 232, 237, 242-247, 256, 278, 280, 281, 303, 311, 316, 318, 321, 328, 330, 331, 339, 370, 371, 375, 378, 379-381, 410, 413, 416, 435, 445, 482, 486, 489, 492, 493, 520
material palette 39, 135, 324, 328, 380
material practice 53, 54, 57, 63, 163, 258, 315, 348, 410, 411, 435, 441, 467
material processes 232, 312
Material processes are, arguably, far more interesting than ideas 232
material transformation 174, 234, 238, 318
materialist practice 131
materiality 39, 48, 65, 73, 85, 89, 118, 177, 224, 234, 238, 240, 244, 255, 282, 302, 318, 323, 327, 331, 380, 413, 457, 480, 487, 515, 516, 520, 532, 551

Materiality is finally the necessary condition of architecture, and the diagram is the instrument that permits us to construct new, composite material agencies. 234

matter 26-28, 39, 55, 60, 62, 64, 70-75, 77, 80, 85, 88, 90, 91, 123, 125, 127-131, 135, 146, 147, 151, 164, 166, 168, 173, 174,

178-180, 181, 182, 186, 198, 204, 209, 217, 222, 226, 228, 245, 252, 257, 260, 286, 287, 292, 310, 311, 316, 318, 319, 327, 328, 348, 351, 357, 370, 371, 380, 382, 391, 404, 411, 413, 432, 436, 437, 438, 439, 446, 467, 478, 487, 492, 509, 521, 531, 548, 550
matter and energy 27, 438
matter and substance 380
maximum intensity 339, 462
meaning 4, 39, 42, 46-49, 64, 67, 70, 75, 77, 107, 139, 150, 171, 186, 193, 218, 230, 271, 272, 278, 292, 299, 306, 312, 333, 357, 368, 370, 371, 375, 376, 444, 445, 448, 449, 457, 500
meaningful 387, 444, 448, 518
meaninglessness 278, 447, 518
means without ends 548
measurement 35, 54, 56, 59, 60, 87, 90, 305, 327, 328
mechanism 17, 28, 30, 38, 42, 44, 50, 55, 61, 62, 74, 78, 89, 109, 115, 119, 120, 121, 125, 175, 177, 181, 188, 191, 245, 249, 250, 261, 311, 337, 367, 431, 472, 473, 474, 475, 482, 486, 489, 492, 496, 504, 506, 510, 513-516, 542, 544
mechanisms of spatial and temporal displacement 28, 472
media 6, 18, 20, 24, 49, 63, 89, 94, 109, 114, 133, 164, 179, 180, 216, 260, 262, 263, 264, 270, 310, 369, 371, 373, 375, 376, 407, 414, 423, 450, 454, 456, 458, 464, 465

As architects have become increasingly involved with media, their ideological concern has been eroded (as has happened to politicians themselves). 423

In the media-intensive Anglo-Saxon context the density of reporting per square foot of construction is tenfold that of the Spanish standard. 375

mediatic 20, 522
mediation 34, 84, 101, 121, 170, 199, 220, 236, 239, 243, 244, 245, 247, 280, 281,

317, 321, 330, 412, 456, 457
mediating 70, 79, 85, 204, 242, 245, 270, 454, 516
mediators 191, 201, 235, 239, 250, 351, 426, 450, 452-456, 458

Mediators are, as a result, the missing link between an ever-growing, architecture-consuming public, the commissioning clientele and the architects' generally hermetic collective. 453

medium 68, 91, 95, 107, 121, 130, 145, 233, 238, 318
megalopolis 466, 472
megalopolitan model 471
metalanguage 96
metalinguistic 118, 290,
metaphorical 283, 312, 377
methodology 86, 192, 201, 279, 314, 328, 352, 371, 379, 421, 426, 487, 554,
micro-history 231, 233, 307, 334
microhistory 241
militant 109, 447
military 151, 447, 467, 477
mind 23, 52, 72, 81, 140, 150, 164, 173, 174, 186, 199, 215, 218, 244, 245, 283, 310, 311, 367, 372, 431, 519,
mind and matter 174

We are in need of a theory of misbehaviour capable of defining an elective amorality as a higher moral stance. 5

It is precisely the deliberateness in the simultaneous pursuit of a double agenda that provides an alibi for reciprocal subversion on each domain, a win-win alternative to the painful career of the hermetic and uncompromising, misfit architect, condemned to endure twenty years of public incomprehension. 382

model/s 3, 4, 5, 18, 19, 26, 27, 29-31, 34, 35, 41, 50, 51, 53, 57, 59, 63, 65, 66, 68, 74, 76, 85, 87, 93, 94, 97, 98, 104-106, 108, 109, 113-115, 118, 120, 122, 123, 133, 137, 149, 155, 164, 167, 168, 172, 173, 175-178, 191, 202, 205, 206, 208, 211, 231, 233, 236, 238, 239-241,

249-251, 253, 256, 258, 259, 261, 262, 264, 266, 270, 277, 279-282, 286, 294, 303, 305, 307, 308, 313, 314, 318-322, 325, 327, 328, 334, 339, 352, 358, 364, 369, 370, 380, 384, 387, 389, 390, 392-394, 398-400, 405, 411, 413, 414, 416, 421-423, 425-427, 438, 440, 445, 446, 469, 470, 471, 474, 476, 480, 483, 485, 490, 497, 499, 500, 502, 503, 506, 507-509, 512, 513, 519, 521, 533, 535, 537, 539, 540, 546, 547, 549, 553-558
model complexity through consistency rather than contradiction 322
modeling 167, 168, 177, 184, 204, 231, 322, 323, 335, 336, 412
models for the organization 305

The project does not necessarily need an origin: to be truly modern, subcontract the origin: have a commission! 468

modes of production 30, 168, 331, 413, 440, 487
modular 131, 408, 416, 488, 490, 518-520, 522, 528,
modular differentiation 416, 488, 519
molecular facialization 414, 488
moment of closure 246, 329
monolithic 418, 420, 518, 523
morphed 305
morphogenetic 65, 67, 240, 305
Mr. Rumsfeld's New Europe 155
multi-dimensional 169, 264
multicultural 154, 229, 416, 446, 529, 530, 531
multicultural graft 154
multiculturalism 364, 528, 529, 541
multiplicity 56, 65, 97, 100, 122, 123, 176, 178, 220, 229, 494, 511
multiple ecosystems 351
multiple orders 123, 240, 305
mutation 17, 19, 21, 24, 33, 54-56, 61, 67, 141, 142, 253, 292, 293, 442, 541
mutant 305
mutating fields 467

N

It is more interesting to produce Cabernet-Sauvignon in the Napa Valley than to refine the techniques to make a good Bordeaux in Bordeaux. 276

narrative 54, 55, 76, 114, 233, 241, 305, 307, 309-311, 313, 317, 334, 372, 479, 491, 492

nature 7, 12, 17, 19, 22, 24, 27, 32, 34-36, 38-40, 43, 46, 47, 50, 56, 59, 63, 66, 70, 72, 74, 77, 79, 80, 86, 88, 91, 96, 100, 109, 114, 117, 118, 123, 129, 138, 170, 173-175, 182, 188, 189, 194-196, 223, 225, 235, 239, 240, 244, 246, 257, 278, 279, 281, 284-286, 288, 289, 292-294, 299, 300, 303-305, 307, 329, 337, 344, 352, 357, 375, 379, 380, 381, 389, 400, 413, 414, 418, 436-439, 449, 450, 464, 467, 473, 474, 480, 484, 492, 496, 497, 500-502, 504, 509, 510, 512, 516, 521, 526, 528, 530, 532, 536, 543, 556, 557

natural 17, 18, 22, 38, 40, 43, 46, 53, 58, 60, 62, 64-66, 71, 96, 97, 99, 100, 108, 111, 127, 136, 156, 172, 174, 255, 257, 258, 265, 282, 285, 286, 300, 303-306, 325, 332, 349, 363, 366, 371, 390, 391, 405, 406, 437-439, 474, 479, 482, 484, 493, 495-499, 501-505, 511, 517, 525, 533, 536, 537, 552, 553, 557

nature as opposed to artifice 437

The most interesting speculation generally happens out of necessity. 371

negative 109, 117, 176, 221, 270, 277, 279, 291, 292, 303, 366, 394, 418, 425, 429, 436, 491, 524

neo-liberal 156, 331, 445, 472, 475, 500, 542, 545, 547, 555, 556, 558
  neo-liberal consensus 445
  neo-liberal democracies 475
  neo-liberal democracy 331

network/s 30-33, 63, 69, 90, 91, 137, 138, 149, 157, 204, 215, 220, 255, 257, 260, 261, 262, 263, 264, 316, 357, 360, 369, 416, 422, 427, 461, 472, 489, 490, 540

networking 148, 260-264, 461

neutral 172, 190, 252, 270, 296, 300, 347, 388, 417, 296, 452, 454, 455, 528, 548

neutralize/d 64, 137, 300, 452, 487, 515

new 4, 6, 7, 15, 17-20, 22-24, 26-30, 32-36, 38-39, 41, 46, 47, 53, 54, 56-60, 63-65, 69, 72, 75, 80, 81, 92, 94, 97-99, 101, 105, 106, 108, 110-113, 116, 117, 122-124, 126, 129, 138, 142, 145-149, 155-159, 164-168, 170-172, 174-177, 179-181, 185, 189, 191, 194, 195, 198, 199, 201, 204, 205, 207, 208, 213-215, 217-219, 221-223, 225-227, 230, 233, 234, 236, 238, 241-243, 245, 246, 249, 251, 252, 256-263, 266, 267, 270, 271, 277, 284, 288, 292, 293, 296-300, 302, 305-308, 311, 314, 315, 318-320, 322, 324-329, 331, 332, 336, 337, 342-344, 347, 349, 351, 356, 358-360, 362-364, 370, 371, 373, 374, 376, 385, 388, 389, 392, 397, 400, 407, 409-418, 421-431, 437, 439-441, 445-449, 452, 453, 455, 459, 460, 463-465, 467, 470, 472-474, 476-478, 480, 482, 485-487, 489-492, 495, 497, 499, 500, 502, 503, 507-509, 511-513, 515-517, 519, 522-525, 527, 528, 533, 534, 538-549, 553-557

new capital markets 299
new figures 292, 293,
new grounds 263, 296-298, 300, 328, 441, 502,
new materials 164, 189, 191, 194, 204, 233, 234, 236, 238, 245, 259, 300, 318, 320, 499
new models 155, 167, 205, 241, 266, 328, 414, 423, 427, 469, 480, 513, 553
new naturalism 41
new political constituencies 543
new utopians 448, 548

niche 94, 106, 125, 126, 167, 217, 353, 371, 424, 430
no hope, no fear 228
noble savage 286
nomadic 5, 63, 323, 332, 350
  nomadic practice 332, 350
non-representational 172, 244, 328, 413, 484, 512
non-standard architecture 445
not-ideological 235

O

now 4, 20-22, 24, 28, 35, 36, 38, 43, 44, 48, 49, 85, 96, 100, 103-105, 110, 131, 138, 144, 155-157, 160, 166, 168, 171, 173, 175, 177, 192, 199, 200, 202, 204, 215, 217, 218, 220, 223, 225, 226, 229-231, 234, 249, 250-252, 258, 260, 262, 265, 272, 286, 287, 294, 297, 299, 302, 319, 322, 323, 328, 336, 338, 343, 345, 346, 348, 361, 373, 379, 383-385, 387, 391, 393, 399, 401, 414, 416, 418, 422, 425, 426, 428, 429, 431, 439, 446, 451, 452, 456, 459, 465, 466, 472, 474, 476, 482, 483, 486, 489, 492, 498, 504, 513, 520, 532, 533, 535, 536, 538, 539, 540-542, 545, 547, 554

object-oriented 256, 257, 259, 264, 314, 413, 487
  object-oriented architecture 257
  object-oriented politics 413, 487

An object oriented architecture would run closer to the development of alternative models of physically grounded, produced intelligence than to symbolic reasoning and representation. 314

on instruments: diagrams, drawings, and graphs 318,
openness 181, 235, 291, 292, 325, 326, 408, 500, 508, 511, 522, 549

operate/s 3, 33, 37, 48, 55, 59, 63, 69, 70, 71, 72, 83, 87-90, 94, 95, 106, 113, 121, 122, 127, 141, 142, 151, 153, 167-169, 174, 178, 179, 181, 190, 192-194, 197, 202-206, 216, 220, 223, 224, 226, 228, 229, 234-236, 239, 240, 243, 252, 258, 269, 272, 278, 280, 282, 290, 293, 294, 296, 298, 304, 314, 319, 321, 323, 324, 328, 336, 356, 358, 369, 370, 411, 423, 426, 428, 430, 441, 452, 454, 461, 462, 472, 479, 487, 492, 496, 502, 509, 547, 554, 557

operation/s 7, 16, 30, 31, 32, 39, 56, 59, 73, 74, 76, 80-82, 86-88, 90, 98, 99, 122-124, 132, 144, 155, 157, 172, 173, 175, 189, 191, 193, 194, 196, 198, 199, 201-203, 209, 210, 216, 223, 229, 235,

236, 239, 240, 242, 243, 245, 246, 253, 262, 270-272, 276, 278, 280, 281, 283, 290, 292, 293, 296, 300, 303, 307, 309, 318, 321, 323, 327, 329, 337, 344, 349, 381, 406, 410, 432, 445, 456, 458, 469, 475, 478, 523, 546, 554, 555

operative knowledge 468, 469

operative systems 299, 300

operativity 20, 55, 63, 91, 133, 207, 208, 246, 322, 330, 346, 347, 349, 351, 432

opinion-makers 454,

opportunity 9, 112, 129, 143-145, 148, 183, 206, 207, 231, 252, 255, 263, 291, 297, 298, 315, 323, 362, 388, 408, 421, 422, 424, 426, 428, 429, 430, 431, 432, 470, 514, 542, 555

==The nomad's context is tied to the idea of opportunity.== 323

==I like projects where you see opportunities being exploited to such degree that it looks as if the project could not be otherwise.== 429

opportunism 23, 154, 155, 428-430, 432, 444

opportunistic 86, 215, 268, 280, 368, 429

opportunistically 469

order/s 3, 23, 26, 27, 29, 30, 34, 40, 41, 44, 46, 50, 58, 59, 62, 66, 68, 70, 72, 73, 76, 79, 80, 83, 84, 86, 88, 91, 95, 96, 98, 99, 102, 103, 106, 108, 109, 111, 112, 114, 117, 119, 120, 123, 125, 131, 133, 137, 143, 156, 165, 170, 174, 177, 179, 181, 190-193, 198, 199, 203, 209, 210, 216, 219, 221, 223, 231, 233, 234, 238, 240, 243, 250, 254, 256, 276-280, 282, 283, 286, 288, 292, 296, 297, 305-307, 313, 316, 320, 324, 326-328, 331, 332, 335, 343-345, 348, 353, 354, 358, 359, 361-363, 366, 368, 370, 371, 374, 380, 381, 402, 409, 411, 414, 416, 417, 419, 420, 422, 423, 428, 430, 432, 440, 448, 449, 460, 465, 467, 470-475, 478, 483, 486, 487, 489, 494, 501, 506, 507, 509, 510, 513, 514, 517, 522, 524, 525, 527, 529, 531, 542-544, 547, 548, 551, 557

Order, form, determination,

coherence, and structure 276

organiza- tion 18, 26, 28, 29, 31, 34, 36, 50, 53-55, 63-65, 68, 70-73, 75, 77-79, 84, 86, 90, 91, 94, 98, 101, 115, 116, 122, 123, 127, 129, 131, 133, 134, 135, 152, 153, 166, 168, 170, 171, 174, 175, 177, 178, 180, 186, 189, 190, 193, 196, 197, 199-201, 203, 204, 214, 224, 225, 228, 231, 232, 234-247, 256-258, 263, 264, 269, 277, 278, 280, 281, 282-287, 293, 296, 298, 299, 302, 303, 305, 307, 309, 311, 316, 318, 321, 324-326, 328-331, 334, 336, 339, 342, 346, 354, 355, 357, 358, 370, 371, 373, 375-382, 395, 400, 407, 410, 413, 416, 418, 422, 423, 430, 431, 435, 441, 445, 447, 453, 462, 471, 472, 474, 479, 481, 482, 486-490, 492-494, 496, 509, 514, 519-521, 525

organization theorists 447

organization, production, and technique 445

organizational 53, 78, 122, 125, 202, 224, 240, 328, 341, 352, 373, 379, 380, 381

organizational, formal, or material diagram 328

organizations are virtually generic 236, 239, 321

organizations, narratives, and images 309,

orientation 46, 56, 64, 87, 98, 99, 184, 227, 287, 299, 316, 353-355, 391, 414, 480, 494, 495, 507, 524, 526, 531, 537

origin 17, 28, 35, 52, 53, 60, 74, 92, 95, 98, 102, 109, 118, 121, 168, 173, 174, 176, 180, 186, 195, 200, 211, 236, 240, 244, 246, 295, 304, 324, 329, 333, 351, 437, 444, 461, 468, 477, 529, 548, 555, 556

origin or the end 246, 329

original 20, 44, 49, 91, 99, 102, 124, 195, 219, 250, 257, 266, 282, 294, 312, 340, 358, 360, 399, 402, 439, 452, 479, 516, 536

ornament 72, 130, 289, 391, 480, 502, 550

outside 3, 7, 34, 44, 51, 60, 68, 101, 105, 112, 119, 131, 146, 146, 155, 164, 184, 188, 203, 206, 207, 211-213, 217, 218, 220, 221, 229, 233, 234, 254, 258, 262,

269, 279, 286, 287, 290, 292, 293, 311, 312, 315, 318, 324, 332, 337, 340, 350, 351, 353, 359, 405, 441, 443, 458, 468, 479, 481, 484, 494, 496-500, 506, 508, 509, 511, 519, 537, 553

outside the discipline 146, 254, 311, 337

outside the internal consistency of the project 337

over-determination 22, 308

P

parallel sets of serial 98

parameter 25, 53, 96-98, 106, 107, 116, 117, 129, 134, 137, 138, 169, 191, 243, 278, 291, 320, 354, 388, 395, 397, 399, 400, 402, 404, 405, 406, 407, 419, 444, 465, 484, 497, 536, 539, 540

==Parameters instigate technical discussions and yet they are loaded with political arguments and cultural questions.== 407

parametric 137, 168, 235, 251, 256, 264, 337, 351, 373, 445

parametric design 251, 256, 264, 337, 351, 373

parametricization 328

particular assemblage and specific location 314

parts and the whole 18, 47, 117, 409, 411, 520

pattern 53, 80, 126, 129, 134, 136, 153, 168, 169, 181, 204, 225, 257, 280, 281, 283, 286, 297, 298, 302, 305, 311, 317, 322, 324, 389, 393, 399, 405, 408, 409, 410-415, 417-420, 475, 484, 485, 488, 491, 497, 503, 513, 516-518, 520-522, 524, 526, 527, 535-537, 550

==The current interest in patterns is likely to be an effect of the cultural necessity to embody complexity through consistency rather than through contradiction.== 410

pattern politics 412, 418

patterned system 355

patterns, fabrics, prototypes,

577

tessellations 408
pedigree 159, 331, 430, 454

We are a cold-blooded generation with a pedigree. 331

performance
6, 7, 12, 18, 49, 54, 75, 88, 91, 97, 118, 138, 142, 152, 181, 190, 192, 193, 194, 197, 203, 209, 212, 216, 223, 227, 236, 240, 241, 244-247, 256, 258, 264, 265, 269, 300, 303, 304, 308, 309, 314, 321, 327-330, 335, 359, 366, 372, 381, 389, 402, 403, 412, 414, 415, 418, 419, 425, 451, 470, 480-482, 484, 485, 488, 491-498, 500, 504-506, 509, 511, 513, 518, 524-527, 532-534, 540, 546, 552

performance and expression 303, 419
performative agency 96
permanent state of emergency 472
phenotypical 191, 257
phylogenetic 349, 350, 353, 355
  phylogenetic lineage 350
  phylogenetic tree 350, 353, 355
phylum 26, 90, 91, 383, 387, 388, 392, 400, 407, 535, 536, 539, 540, 541
physical coexistence 475
  physically grounded 314, 413
Pierre Boulez and John Cage 326
plane of consistency 180
platforms 260, 261, 265, 266, 286, 288, 298-300, 379, 458

New grounds or platforms derive from a proliferation of the transcendental fields of affiliation that we decide to construct to exploit certain opportunities and to neutralize certain excesses given to figuration. 300

policy 147, 159, 288, 292, 389-392, 505-507, 509, 545

politics
7, 32, 38, 75, 133, 148, 227, 260-262, 365, 368, 385, 408, 412-414, 416-418, 423, 433, 441, 442, 445, 446, 447, 448, 449, 458, 460, 462-466, 472, 474, 476-478, 480, 482, 484-488, 491, 492, 495, 497, 498, 500, 504, 506, 509,

511, 512, 518, 519, 523, 524, 529, 530, 541, 545, 547-549, 557, 558
politics of faciality 413, 485, 512

political
4, 5, 7, 9, 20, 21, 30, 32, 33, 41, 66, 68, 85, 109, 110, 111, 113, 114, 142, 144, 145, 155-157, 168, 172, 183, 188, 193, 203, 213, 222, 224, 225, 227, 228, 235, 239, 244, 249, 251, 252, 254, 258-262, 269, 270, 277, 279, 291, 293, 302, 313, 314, 316, 325, 331, 337, 350, 357, 368, 374, 404, 407, 413-418, 420, 421, 423, 424, 429, 435-438, 440, 442, 444, 446, 447, 448, 450, 452, 462, 464, 465, 471-483, 485-493, 495-506, 508-513, 516-527, 530-533, 535, 536, 539-550, 552, 556-558

micropolitics 469
political activism 423
political affects 414, 418, 491, 492
political agencies 478, 544
political agency 172, 252, 316, 415, 417, 479, 480, 482, 483, 487, 491, 492, 500, 503, 512, 535, 544, 546, 548, 550, 557, 558
political agenda 325, 531, 545
political awareness 227

The monolithic, the different, the frameless, and the rootless are all concepts with serious political baggage. 420

The challenge to instituted power can only be selective, and the division of political labor has to be addressed by multiple disciplines operating independently and simultaneously and not necessarily in a multidisciplinary relation. 479

political life 542
political power 111, 270, 450, 452, 476
political question 472
political spin doctors 448
politically charged 227, 403, 543, 548
politically correct 38, 109, 110, 145, 241, 404, 428, 502, 531
politically incorrect 145, 327, 531
politicizing matters 313, 478

pork-barrel politics 463
polytechnic 149, 150, 205, 208, 211, 249
  polytechnic and the liberal-arts 205
  polytechnic model 149, 205, 249

population
5, 6, 18, 21, 147, 154, 155, 158, 193, 213, 254, 256, 257, 261, 281, 316, 320, 348, 349, 361, 384, 385, 394, 398, 400, 402-404, 406, 407, 414, 416, 444, 451, 452, 453, 466, 467, 471, 472, 474, 475, 487, 490, 496, 498, 502, 506, 507, 522, 527, 529, 532, 533, 535, 542-545, 558

  populational 6, 349, 469
  populational analysis 349
positions 31, 51, 56, 57, 103, 110, 122, 132, 141, 155, 173, 174, 81, 184, 185, 208, 218, 314, 347, 370, 416, 456, 465, 490, 491, 530
positive 109, 117, 135, 136, 165, 168, 172, 175, 176, 242, 269, 277, 291, 292, 325, 421, 424, 425, 431, 477
Post-¥€$ 141, 154, 160
post-human 18, 303
post-humanistic 466, 467
post-industrial 32, 472, 508

potential
18, 27, 35, 37-39, 47, 61, 71, 78, 86, 93, 95, 96, 98, 102, 107, 108-110, 124, 132-134, 138, 142, 144, 145, 148-151, 154-156, 158, 159, 166, 169, 170, 175-177, 180, 183, 191, 198-202, 225, 230, 231, 233, 235-240, 244, 245, 248, 253-255, 257, 259, 260, 262, 265, 267, 268, 271, 272, 275, 277, 278, 284, 285, 291, 292, 295, 302, 303, 308, 309, 312, 314, 315, 318, 321, 328, 329, 331, 335-337, 349, 351-353, 357, 358, 362, 364, 371, 373, 378, 381, 386, 395, 401, 407, 409, 424, 425, 431, 439, 442, 445, 448, 460, 462, 473, 474, 478, 493, 497, 502, 510, 514, 531, 536, 539, 543, 545, 554, 558

If we were able to divorce technologies from their conventional place in the causal chain, we would become capable of exploiting the potential of these technologies beyond their reproductive, verifiable mode to effectively leverage the discipline from a techno-scientific fulcrum. 309

potentiality 201, 285, 291, 363, 501
povera 40, 548, 549, 551, 553, 558
power 5, 16, 17, 21, 22, 38, 57, 63-65, 75, 84, 90, 95, 102, 107-111, 114, 115, 144, 145, 151, 153, 158, 164, 234, 243, 252, 270, 272, 279, 311, 314, 347, 364, 369-371, 382, 384, 389, 414, 416, 425, 435, 442, 448, 450-453, 455-457, 463-465, 467, 468, 470, 473, 476-481, 483, 484, 486, 487, 490-493, 523, 532-535, 539, 541, 543, 546-549
power and control 95, 108, 109, 110, 370
power is nothing without control 102, 107
power regimes 371, 481, 483, 492, 548
power takes a physical form 22
powerful 7, 22, 48, 92, 105, 107, 110, 111, 120, 142, 149, 151, 166, 189, 233, 238, 310, 320, 384, 385, 404, 408, 426, 436, 442, 455-457, 482, 486, 532, 554, 557
pure power 370

==Among all the arts, architecture is the most power-intensive discipline and, arguably, the one that is able to dictate behaviour and routine most forcefully.== 460

practice 3, 6, 7, 9, 12, 15, 19, 26, 27, 37, 38, 45, 50, 53, 54, 57, 63, 65, 68, 77, 80, 82, 83, 87, 93, 94-96, 101-103, 105, 107-115, 117-119, 122, 124-126, 131, 133, 135, 141-145, 147-149, 151, 152, 154, 163, 165, 166, 169, 170, 173-175, 178, 179, 181, 183, 185, 189, 191, 193, 194, 198, 201-207, 209-213, 216, 217, 219-221, 223-225, 227, 232, 233, 237-245, 248-254, 258, 263, 268, 270-273, 275-278, 283, 288-293, 299, 301, 302, 308, 309, 311-313, 315, 317, 318, 324-327, 332, 334, 338, 339, 344, 346-353, 368, 369, 371, 372, 381, 382, 410, 411, 413, 421-427, 429-432, 435, 441, 442, 445, 448, 453, 458, 459-462, 467, 483, 485, 491, 492, 507, 515, 516, 531, 537, 544, 545, 548, 549, 551, 552, 553, 555

==Practice is never a pure form of local knowledge.== 142
pragmatic 4-6, 20, 23, 24, 28, 84, 87, 89, 91, 111, 116, 119, 120, 142, 149, 150, 151, 153, 158, 159, 207, 224, 233, 238, 240, 271, 290, 292, 296, 299, 302, 313, 318, 324, 344, 348, 368, 429, 430, 468, 478, 548
pragmatism 16, 27, 111, 222, 245, 271, 291, 318
pragmatist 23, 84, 271
precision 60, 71, 212, 226, 246, 319, 320, 326, 327, 330, 412, 522
pregnance 28, 70, 73, 79, 80, 277
presence 22, 62, 72, 92, 95, 108, 120, 123, 263, 312, 323, 338, 359, 366, 394, 412, 437, 438, 467, 489, 501, 526, 534, 550
price 29, 136, 137, 139, 140, 147, 150, 155, 158, 339, 386, 400, 401, 404, 504, 506, 537, 540, 545, 546, 550, 551, 553, 554, 556
private and public 53, 413, 474, 481, 482, 484, 485, 492, 498, 508, 512, 513, 526
problematize 179, 224, 302, 319, 403, 441
problematizing materials 324
process 16-19, 26-30, 34, 35, 37, 42-44, 50, 51, 53-55, 63-67, 72, 76, 79, 82, 86, 90, 91, 94, 95, 97-102, 111, 113-117, 121, 122, 124, 126, 128-130, 132, 133, 137, 142, 144, 152-154, 156, 157, 164-167, 169-171, 173-176, 179, 181, 182, 184, 186, 188-190, 196, 198-204, 206, 207, 210, 211, 213, 216, 220, 221, 223, 225, 228-234, 236-243, 245-247, 250, 252-258, 262, 264, 268, 270, 271, 276-278, 280, 281, 283, 284, 285, 288, 290-294, 300, 302-305, 307-312, 314, 317, 318, 321, 325, 326, 328-332, 334, 335, 337-345, 348-352, 355, 358, 361, 364, 366, 367, 371, 372, 376, 377, 379, 381, 391, 395, 398, 400, 411, 422, 427, 431, 437, 438, 439, 441, 443 445, 448, 452, 454, 459-465, 467-469, 471-474, 478, 481, 483, 486, 490, 492, 498, 500, 502, 504, 506, 507, 508-510, 532-536, 541, 547, 549, 558
process-driven 121, 304
process/effect 117
processes are far more interesting than ideas 240, 307, 334

==Processes are far more interesting than ideas. Ideas are linked to existing codes, operating critically or in alignment with pre-existing systems of ideas.== 334

processes of production 67, 278, 288, 293, 310, 463
processes, materials, prototypes 232
processing 98, 100, 122, 133, 188, 235, 245, 258, 264, 307, 328, 333, 422
produce 12, 17, 23, 27, 30, 35, 37, 46, 56, 61, 70, 75-77, 79, 80-82, 86, 90, 91, 98, 99, 101, 104, 106, 107, 108, 111, 114, 117, 119, 121, 124, 127-131, 142, 151, 152, 154, 158, 160, 166, 168, 169, 176, 178-180, 196-199, 201, 203, 205, 206, 208, 210, 213, 216, 217, 218, 221, 225-227, 231-233, 237, 238, 241, 245-247, 249-251, 256-259, 264-267, 270, 276, 277, 280-287, 290, 291, 294, 295, 297-300, 303, 304, 307, 308, 311, 313, 314, 316-320, 322, 326-330, 334, 335, 338, 339, 343, 348, 349, 351, 355, 369, 370, 373, 375, 378-380, 386-388, 394-397, 408, 411, 413, 414, 416, 418, 420, 421, 426, 427, 430, 436, 437, 440, 443, 464, 469, 478, 482, 483, 487-490, 495, 497, 500, 501, 503, 505, 508, 510, 517, 518, 520, 521, 522, 526, 532, 535, 537-539, 546, 548, 551-553, 556, 557
produce knowledge 338, 427
produce physical affects 128
product 6, 18, 20, 24, 48, 53, 54, 77, 93, 111, 117, 118, 136, 137, 188, 189, 199, 200, 209, 217, 218, 234, 236, 249, 252, 268, 280, 281, 288-290, 292, 303, 310, 314, 318, 331, 337, 350, 352, 366, 385, 394, 424, 429, 437, 441, 451, 467, 469, 470, 514, 529, 543-546, 549, 554-556, 558
production 12, 17, 18, 22, 26-30, 36, 39, 40, 42-45, 47, 48, 50-53, 55, 57, 58, 61, 63, 65, 67, 68, 76, 81, 84, 85, 91-95, 98, 101, 104, 105, 108, 109, 110, 112, 117, 118, 120, 121, 129, 130, 135-137, 144-148, 151, 152, 163-165, 167, 168,

579

170-172, 177, 181, 186, 199, 200, 206-208, 217, 220, 224, 227, 228, 233, 235-237, 242, 243, 245-247, 251, 253, 254, 266, 270, 272, 278, 280, 281, 287-290, 293, 299, 302, 305, 308, 310-313, 317, 318, 331, 332, 335, 338, 339, 346, 348-350, 364-368, 382, 409, 411, 413, 414, 417, 422, 423, 427, 436, 437, 440, 445, 452, 463, 467, 473, 483, 484, 487, 489, 491, 503, 507, 510, 512, 514, 520, 522, 523, 524, 528, 532, 546, 549-551, 553-555, 558

production and symbology 367
production of affects 84, 85, 91, 92, 413, 487, 489, 512, 520
production versus that of critique 144
productive alienation 315
productive mode 51, 278
productive processes 51, 223
productive versus reductive, performative versus ideological 308
profession 6, 144, 165, 185, 197, 225, 228, 251, 316, 317, 325, 336, 421, 424, 429, 450, 451, 458, 468
professional 3, 7, 24, 50, 107, 133, 142, 143, 144, 152, 153, 166, 184, 185, 213, 217, 250, 253, 268, 269, 278, 301, 308, 317, 332, 335, 339, 366, 371, 373, 382, 427, 430, 431, 456, 461, 467
profile 4, 100, 135, 138, 150, 198, 215, 219, 266, 267, 359, 366, 387, 394, 395, 396, 397, 406, 421, 426, 534, 536
program 24, 32, 54, 67, 87, 88, 96-99, 101, 105, 108, 114, 116, 123-125, 133, 146, 148, 156, 163, 166, 169, 196, 197, 201, 203, 204, 207, 211, 214, 215, 219-221, 225, 226, 241, 251, 253, 254, 257, 268, 270, 277, 278, 281-283, 290, 294-297, 306, 315, 319-321, 342, 344, 350, 351, 367, 374, 393, 401, 417, 418, 420, 428, 452-455, 457, 458, 463, 486, 492, 494, 499, 502, 503, 511, 525, 526, 528, 533, 535, 536, 545, 548

==Despite the apparent lack of political positioning across their practices, what links such players as Greenspan,== ==Haji-Ioannou (EasyJet), Ortega (Zara), Kamprad (IKEA), and Gates (Microsoft) is a political program without a political office.== 545

programmatic composition 226, 319
progressive naturalization of the artificial 303
project 3, 9, 18, 19, 27, 28, 34, 38, 43, 47, 48, 50, 54-61, 64, 65, 67, 68, 71, 72, 74, 78-80, 82, 83, 86-91, 95-99, 101-103, 105, 107, 108, 110, 112, 113, 115-121, 123-126, 129-132, 134, 139, 146, 148, 151-155, 157, 159, 160, 171, 179, 182, 191, 195-197, 201-204, 206, 209-212, 216, 217, 219, 221-224, 226, 227, 231-236, 238-241, 246, 250, 253, 260, 261, 263-265, 269-271, 275, 280, 281, 283, 284, 285, 286, 291-299, 302, 303, 307-326, 328, 329, 332-343, 345, 346, 348-355, 359, 361, 362, 364, 365, 367-379, 382, 385-388, 390-392, 395, 397-399, 407-409, 412, 414, 417-420, 422-431, 441, 442, 456, 458, 468-470, 478, 483, 490, 491, 493, 499, 503, 504, 506, 511, 522, 523, 524, 529-531, 535, 536, 539, 540, 542, 548, 551-555
projecting 110, 228, 278, 324, 339, 420, 469, 528
projective 59, 70, 101, 124, 144, 172, 179, 245, 246, 272, 278, 280, 281, 373, 470, 491
projective practices 272
projects without addresses 548
projective and productive 278
proliferate 24, 129, 212, 233, 241, 286, 287, 307, 331, 334, 349, 523, 530, 558
proliferating 151, 176, 179, 182, 212, 287, 299, 309, 322, 325
proliferation 33, 51, 57, 68, 75, 99, 121, 125, 146, 174, 191, 207, 226, 236, 240, 280, 286, 299, 300, 319, 321, 324, 327, 352, 353, 388, 409, 413, 415, 485, 488, 513, 524, 532, 540
prophets of program 226, 319

==I was born during Franco's dictatorship, and I remember having to learn to vote at school–== ==one of the new protocols of the new democracy.== 477

prototype 83, 84, 86, 88, 132, 191, 208, 219, 222, 232-236, 239, 240, 256, 259, 264, 266, 311, 321, 322, 357, 358, 370, 375, 391, 405, 408, 529, 537

==Prototypes are technical and material mediators, able to transfer information into form and constituting responsive devices of internal transference of information.== 191

proto-typical 235,
prototypes mediate information into form 321
prototypical 191, 235, 236, 239, 240, 321, 404, 415, 469, 495, 497, 535
public 7, 9, 34, 36, 53, 71, 85, 145, 148, 150, 155, 157, 158, 160, 177, 204, 212, 213, 254, 258, 262, 264-266, 281, 282, 293, 297, 298, 310, 311, 332, 341, 365, 368-373, 375, 377, 378, 380-382, 389, 391, 400, 403, 413-415, 417, 421, 424, 425, 430, 431, 435, 437, 446, 450-458, 464, 465, 467, 469, 472, 474, 476, 479-485, 488, 489, 491, 492, 494, 496, 498, 499, 502, 503, 505, 507-509, 511-513, 515, 516, 520, 522-528, 531, 546, 551, 554

==By opening form into the reprocessing of identity and iconography, we can perhaps sustain a reempowerment of the architect as a relevant expert with a public dimension.== 380

public engagement 424
public media 371
public service 455, 464, 546

Q
quantitative analysis 222, 328, 411, 445

==Quantitative analysis is far from naive, value-free, and objective.== 328

R
race 383, 478, 544
radiographies of cultural

hybridization 399
random 21, 65, 69, 101, 113, 114, 181, 277, 522
randomness 17, 233, 238, 276, 283
rational and organic 303
rational and the organic 305
re-encounter the limits 252
re-territorialisation 185
real 4, 7, 9, 20, 21, 38, 54, 56, 62, 65, 81, 85, 87, 133, 136, 137, 139, 142, 145, 146, 155, 157, 158, 165, 166, 167, 172, 176, 177, 180, 189, 194, 206, 207, 210, 211, 219, 220, 226, 231, 235, 239, 244-247, 250, 251, 262, 267, 279, 284, 285, 312, 313, 318, 322, 330, 336, 337, 346, 347, 363, 366, 378, 379, 385, 388, 392-394, 398, 399, 401, 443, 451, 457, 483, 484, 501, 502, 509, 517, 532, 541-544, 558
reality 3, 20, 21, 27, 28, 42, 43, 45-47, 51, 54-56, 58, 61, 63, 64, 70, 79, 82-85, 89, 131, 141, 142, 150, 151, 175-177, 210, 211, 215, 216, 220, 221, 223, 233, 238, 245, 262, 271, 281, 284, 285, 313, 314, 318, 321, 324, 353, 364, 370, 371, 417, 426, 432, 441, 442, 450, 451, 462, 463, 470, 477, 478, 483, 487, 501
realpolitik 444
reasonable prices 147
reconfigure 276
reduction to a bare state 548
reempower 252, 492
reempowerment 277, 380, 468, 469, 484
reempowerment of architecture practice 277
regime 28, 29, 34, 35, 53, 54, 57, 94, 102, 108, 109, 113, 115, 142, 151, 154-159, 164, 175, 237, 249, 252, 255, 261, 293, 314, 353, 370, 371, 416, 435, 438, 464, 467, 472-474, 477, 481, 483, 490, 492, 500, 502, 512, 518, 520, 522, 532, 533, 539, 543, 548
regime of excess 237
regimes of flexible accumulation 28, 34, 54, 57, 472
regimes of power 164,

252, 371, 435, 473
regulatory regimes 464
renaturalization 371
repetition 30, 75-77, 79, 86, 111, 117, 123-125, 129, 134, 136, 142, 202, 204, 344, 349, 350, 353, 387, 412, 416, 482, 490, 497, 520, 529
repetitions and differentiations 349
replicating yourself 431
representation 4, 7, 27, 45, 46, 49, 54, 57, 72, 76, 79, 84, 167, 175, 177, 194, 242-245, 289, 310, 313, 314, 316, 328, 367, 368, 370, 371, 376, 380, 389, 413, 414, 442, 444-449, 464, 465, 467, 470, 475, 476, 478-480, 483, 484, 486, 487, 491, 493, 512, 515, 517, 519, 520, 522, 524-526, 528, 533-535, 541, 548, 553

If we are to become fully engaged with the discussion of power regimes and their potential transformation, representation is a crucial subject to re-address. 371

representation of an ideological or a critical stance 314
representation of ideal political concepts 316, 478
research 9, 17, 28, 30, 61, 65, 71, 89, 93, 94, 97, 116-118, 128, 129, 130, 146, 163, 166, 179, 180, 189, 198, 201, 205-221, 239, 242, 252-254, 256, 257, 259, 262, 277, 279, 281, 284, 290, 294, 295, 298, 299, 309, 310, 312, 336, 339, 346, 371, 373, 379, 388, 412, 418, 420, 422, 441, 445, 461, 468, 469, 470, 479, 487

A practice's body of work is neither a series of contingent experiments, defined by their particular conditions, nor the definition of a style, but rather a consistent reservoir of architectural species to be proliferated, mutated, and evolved in the years to come: a genetic pool. 349-50

resistance 19, 23, 50, 51, 64, 68, 86, 88, 93, 94, 95, 96, 101, 109, 110, 126, 165, 166,

167, 185, 186, 222, 242, 243, 320, 339, 359, 360, 377, 418, 441, 444, 445, 447, 478, 491, 524, 543
resistant 20, 22, 23, 313, 426, 483
resource 18, 28, 29, 30, 53, 148, 190, 203, 211, 219, 255, 260, 293, 436, 439, 457, 458, 472, 473, 491, 500, 502, 505, 508, 510, 558
resubjectivization 518, 545, 546
return to matter 316
revolutions 40, 95, 142, 160, 164, 167, 168, 189, 191, 255, 270, 339, 357, 373, 447, 449, 483, 515, 541, 544, 548
rhythm 60, 75, 76, 77, 129, 130, 131, 179, 180, 208, 225, 327, 407, 537
rhythmic 80, 90, 129, 130, 180
rigor 43, 49, 96, 104, 120, 151, 179, 198, 199, 206, 233, 238, 269, 318, 556
rigorous orders 231
rigorous process 114, 121, 309
rigorously 50, 82, 234, 327, 496, 500
risks 464
risk-averse 452
rocks 277
roller-coaster construction 333, 345
rootless 285, 418, 420, 515
rootlessness 6, 20, 21, 345, 420
Rorschach 69, 70, 75, 79, 130

S

scale 29, 35, 39, 42, 59, 60, 66, 73, 78, 87, 90, 105, 111, 115, 122, 124, 132, 134-136, 156, 173, 174, 180, 190, 191, 193, 196, 203, 213, 221, 226, 236, 245, 246, 250, 256, 262, 281, 282, 286, 293, 298, 311, 318, 320, 327, 329, 330, 340, 343, 345, 351, 354-357, 359, 361, 366, 373, 385, 392, 396, 397, 399, 406, 408, 410, 416, 422, 424, 458, 469, 472, 480, 482, 485, 490, 491, 493, 495, 498, 499, 502, 505, 506, 508, 512, 513, 519, 522, 526, 532, 539, 540, 542
schizophrenia 19, 22, 26, 44, 54, 55, 56, 59, 60, 61, 63, 71, 81, 176, 206, 250, 356
schizophrenia between culture and civilization 19

581

schizophrenic 54, 210, 314
scripting a project 334
seamlessness 418
second 19, 20, 32, 38, 39, 40, 82, 112, 118, 138, 147, 172, 185, 192, 195, 211, 212, 213, 222, 278, 281, 289, 290, 303, 336, 342, 348, 354, 369, 372, 392, 411, 418, 422, 444, 505, 506, 508, 514, 530, 533, 544, 545, 556
  second colonization of America 32
  second generation of architects operating within a globalized domain 348
  second nature 19, 38, 40, 303
seductive 91, 370, 380, 464
selective patronage 464
self 3, 23-25, 54, 75, 78, 90, 95, 151, 160, 198, 224, 257, 272, 276, 303, 324-326, 349, 354, 355, 357, 360, 410, 414, 423, 424, 500, 501, 510, 517, 520, 530, 544
  self-generating organizations 326
  self-similar structure 90
  Self-Similarity 75, 78
The semiotics that I am invoking are not that of linguistic theory, but rather architectural immediacy. 380

Semper/Riegl 289
  Semperian reencounter with matter 351
sensibility towards variation and change 332
service 30, 33, 49, 53, 128, 214, 215, 224, 226, 242, 265, 266, 308, 309, 320, 335, 336, 339, 359, 369, 370, 375, 400, 402, 405, 421, 450, 453-455, 462, 464, 475, 477, 486, 504, 507, 532, 537, 543-547, 549, 556
  service profession 421, 450
  service providers 375
sexual pleasure 544
signifying 72, 75, 245, 278, 280, 282, 315, 329
  signification, representation, and language 242, 328
  signifying or critical 278
  signifying practices 315

single 12, 46, 57, 58, 62, 91, 103, 104, 105, 107, 122, 125, 129, 151, 152, 179, 190, 195, 219, 225, 228, 258, 267, 291, 297, 307, 309, 317, 323, 338, 341, 353, 412, 479, 481, 494, 504, 508, 525, 556
  single/multiple 412
  singularity 193, 238, 286, 323, 354, 394, 484, 512
  singularity of continuous 323
smooth 56, 59, 62, 63, 64, 75, 79, 99, 149, 180, 304, 342, 355, 414, 488
  smooth space 56, 59, 62, 63, 64, 99
  smoothness 63, 101, 180, 181, 247, 304, 330
social 5, 6, 7, 20, 23, 26, 29, 30, 37, 38, 41, 53, 60, 61, 67, 68, 80, 85, 101, 108, 111, 118, 123, 124, 133, 142, 150, 157-159, 170, 188, 189, 193, 203, 208, 223-228, 235, 239, 241, 251, 257, 258, 260-267, 269, 270, 277, 279, 283, 285, 289, 302, 315, 316, 319, 320, 331, 332, 337, 355, 368, 369, 376, 403, 409, 416, 417, 430, 438, 440, 447, 450, 451, 463, 471-473, 476, 478-483, 485-487, 490-493, 497-499, 501, 505, 506, 509, 510, 511, 513-516, 523, 525-528, 531, 535, 539, 541, 544, 545, 552, 558

spatial 27, 28, 29, 30, 31, 33, 36, 45, 46, 48, 53, 54, 56-58, 60-64, 68, 71, 75, 78, 87, 89, 91, 94, 97, 98, 100-102, 114, 122, 148, 166, 170, 171, 175, 193, 197, 242, 245, 246, 256, 258, 280, 286, 293, 298, 299, 304, 305, 312, 315, 316, 329, 334, 341, 354, 357, 464, 472-475, 479, 486, 494, 496, 497, 511, 514, 553
  spatial and material organization 29, 36, 171, 242, 280, 316
  spatial and material practices 258, 315
  spatial segmentations 354
speciation 201, 202, 242, 256, 259, 355, 495, 498
  species 105, 200, 201, 256, 337, 346, 349, 351, 352, 353, 354, 355, 356, 357, 399, 402, 454, 455, 534, 537
  specific in their actualization 236, 239, 321
It is precisely this level of quantification that constitutes

the framework to criticize the contemporary stock of high-rise typologies not as a series of novel occurrences but as a particularly intriguing species in constant evolution that diversifies in respect to climate, geography, and cultural protocols. 402

stains 70, 79, 129, 277
stakeholders 452, 483, 548
star 5, 75, 105, 110, 119, 145, 147, 155, 220, 252, 272, 332, 335, 336, 426, 553, 557, 558
  star architect 110, 220
  star architecture 335
  star system 5, 105, 119, 155, 332, 553, 557
  starchitect 336, 460, 462, 555
  starchitecture 251
The birth of what is known as the star system is characterized by the intensification of differences. 105

statistic 66, 115, 170, 174, 216, 217, 226, 233, 238, 309, 311, 314, 328, 403, 404
  statistics or data 170
It is precisely the differential and strategic departure from the conventional, the permanent flight from the status quo, rather than now-traditional radical opposition, that can actually reveal and subvert the dominant urban powers. 541

stock market 7, 107, 145, 438, 551
strategy 17, 18, 28, 33, 38, 39, 46, 54, 56, 60, 62, 64, 66, 70, 73, 78, 92, 124, 143, 157, 184, 185, 194, 213, 220, 235, 252, 269, 285, 294-296, 313, 340, 369, 372-374, 377, 379, 384, 417, 432, 469, 491, 503, 506-508, 522, 523, 545, 546, 552-554, 556
  strategic intensification 110
stratification 34, 105, 336, 339, 486, 539
streetwise 453
structure 6, 12, 18, 23, 30-37, 39, 44, 45, 48-50, 53-58, 61, 62, 64, 65, 67, 70, 71, 73, 75-78, 80, 87, 90, 95,

96, 98, 99, 100, 102, 105, 111, 112, 114, 118, 120, 122, 123, 124, 126, 127, 133, 142, 143, 153, 169, 170, 171, 174, 180-185, 190, 193, 196, 202, 204, 208, 211, 214, 217, 219, 222, 241, 246, 250, 256, 257, 260, 263, 265, 269, 276-279, 281, 282, 287, 288, 290, 292, 294, 295, 297-299, 304, 305, 315, 316, 320, 322, 323, 325-327, 329, 331, 332, 338-340, 342, 353, 355-361, 369, 373, 376, 386, 394, 397, 401, 406, 408, 409, 411, 412, 415, 416, 419, 420, 422, 435, 439, 441, 450, 460, 461, 467, 472-475, 480-487, 488, 490, 491, 493, 497, 507, 508, 512, 514, 523, 525-527, 533, 537, 538, 541, 548, 549, 552

structuralist 18, 106, 113, 114, 408, 409, 412, 517

style 22, 72, 86, 102, 145, 187, 194, 201, 202, 207, 208, 250, 289, 309, 315, 336, 347-350, 408, 479, 481, 486, 535, 546, 548-551, 553, 555, 556

subcontract the origin 468

It is important to break the psychological engagement with the project, to liberate the project from the tyranny of the subjective, so the project is forced to take a life of its own. 316

successful traits 352

surface 39, 61, 71-75, 79, 80, 89, 100, 102, 124, 131, 136, 169, 172, 195-198, 246, 258, 282, 283, 286, 287, 294-299, 312, 330, 333, 340-343, 353-355, 359, 365, 372, 373, 377, 386, 401, 404, 415, 419, 420, 448, 471, 480-482, 485-488, 494, 497, 499, 511-516, 518-520, 526-528, 543

surface singularity 354

surplus 28-30, 34, 52, 53, 63, 332, 335, 472, 473, 481, 546, 551

surplus value 53, 332, 546

sustainable 155, 158, 256, 257, 259, 280, 362, 371, 472, 499, 500, 524, 543

sustainability 189, 203, 311, 338, 364, 423, 441, 498, 504, 509

swarm 140, 146, 213, 216-218, 419, 521

swing electorate 543

symbolic 43, 96, 192, 193, 245, 276, 280, 290, 303, 305, 314, 329, 368, 375, 413, 480, 487, 515, 517, 534, 535, 540

symbolic and representational 375

symbolism 291, 367, 368, 396

synthetic 7, 30, 175, 235, 284, 286, 292, 303, 307, 322, 449, 501

synthesize 125, 153, 189, 191, 201, 231-234, 238, 241, 307, 308, 324, 334, 349, 362, 509

synthesizing artificial fabrics 322

synthesizing new materials 233, 238, 318

synthetic 7, 30, 175, 235, 284, 286, 292, 322, 449, 501

systems of signs 68, 381

T

tabula rasa and contextualism 322, 411

talibans of architecture 448

The incremental takeover of inner cities by profit-seeking organizations bring along the twin protocols of air-conditioning and private security forces to secure the illusion of "sustainability". 509

The seamless convergence between desire and effect in the traditional, voluntarist discourse of architecture is hopelessly tautological. 268

taxonomic 351, 353

taxonomic system 353

taxonomical 353

technique 30, 38, 45, 49, 55, 60, 61, 63, 65, 75, 82, 84, 85, 89, 92, 94, 96, 98, 101, 105, 106, 108, 112, 113, 115-120, 122, 144, 151-153, 171, 172, 179, 181, 182, 184, 187, 192, 194, 196-199, 201, 202, 205-209, 211-213, 218, 219, 223-227, 231, 240, 241, 247, 250, 252, 264, 271, 272, 276, 277, 280, 283, 288, 290, 293, 294, 299, 302, 305, 306, 308, 319, 327, 328, 330, 335, 336, 339, 341-343, 345, 347, 349, 352, 374, 381, 409, 419, 426, 430, 431, 445, 448, 449, 469, 474, 483, 534, 551, 554, 556

Like pilots, football players, and musicians, to be a virtuoso, to produce the magic, you need to know the technique so well that you do not need to think about it anymore. 213

technique or material and interpretation and style 347

techniques, protocols, and handshakes 349,

techno 20, 59, 84, 151, 167, 245, 323, 325, 445, 446, 485

techno-corporate globalization 349,

technocratic models 440

technology 7, 15, 17, 19, 24, 26, 29, 40, 44, 47, 48, 55, 59, 60, 78, 90, 92, 101, 131, 137, 145, 146, 147, 150, 160, 165, 167-169, 172, 173, 175, 177, 178, 185, 189, 201, 217, 219, 231, 236, 238, 241, 242, 243, 247-249, 251, 252, 254, 256-262, 267, 270, 281, 302, 308, 309, 311, 323, 324, 330, 331, 334-336, 357, 367, 368, 371, 372, 374, 382, 384, 385, 388, 393, 397, 400-402, 410-412, 414, 420-423, 432, 440-442, 445, 447, 449, 451, 452, 461, 463, 464, 467, 468, 470, 478-482, 484-487, 499, 501, 504, 506, 509, 512, 516, 518, 524, 533, 538, 541, 543, 544, 553

technological advances 422, 452,

temporal 4, 7, 28, 30, 35, 53, 54, 58, 67, 75, 76, 91, 115, 137, 154, 175, 231, 232, 241, 245, 293, 299, 329, 334, 449, 472-474, 492, 517, 553, 554

temporal and spatial displacement 53, 175

temporalities 66, 90, 467

temporary decoupling between architectural technology and effect 335

tendencies 5, 6, 49, 65, 105, 109, 121, 124, 142, 187, 191, 229, 248, 249, 324, 367, 388, 393, 400, 415, 418, 443, 459, 492, 513, 514, 515, 538, 555

territorialize 374

tessellation 152, 408, 412-420, 488, 490, 512, 516, 518-521, 523, 528, 537

the Bundle Tower™ 356-358, 360, 376

the real 7, 9, 38, 54, 65, 81, 85, 87, 137, 155, 158, 250, 251, 165, 166, 167, 172, 176, 177, 180, 206, 219, 231, 244, 245, 279, 284, 285, 312, 313, 336, 337, 378, 379, 388,

Glossary 583

theory 3-6, 18, 29, 35, 38, 41, 50, 65, 68, 87, 93, 118, 122, 141, 142, 144-149, 151-154, 165, 176, 189, 194, 200, 205-210, 228, 240, 254, 263, 264, 268, 271, 272, 276, 290, 303, 316, 366, 379, 380, 388, 413-416, 428, 430, 432, 438, 440, 446, 447, 457, 469, 480, 484, 486, 487, 489-491, 493, 512, 544, 550

==Theory is a practice aimed to enable agency rather than to find truth.== 3

theorize 3, 143, 145, 154, 193, 270, 275, 430, 432, 458, 459
theory and practice 6, 141, 147, 149, 152, 205, 206, 210, 254, 276, 430
theoretical 3, 4, 9, 12, 23, 38, 60, 81, 137, 141-145, 147, 152, 154, 155, 168, 178, 179, 188, 193, 194, 198, 205, 208, 214, 224, 234, 238, 259, 278, 294, 302, 312, 316, 318, 337, 375, 410, 432, 468, 470, 485, 549

==Any serious theorization is actually generated by efficiencies, by economies, rather than as a sort of weltanschauung. It always happens a posteriori, after the fact.== 432

==The focus of the discipline is shifting from tectonics to ecological and thermodynamic processes.== 255

time 3, 4, 6, 7, 9, 12, 15, 17, 28, 29, 36, 46-48, 53, 54, 58-60, 62, 63, 76, 81-84, 86, 89, 90, 94, 99, 103, 105, 111, 114-116, 127, 132, 135, 137, 139, 140, 143, 146, 147, 151-153, 157, 159, 165, 167, 169, 172, 173, 175, 179, 180, 184, 191, 193-196, 204, 214, 219, 220, 223, 226-230, 243, 258, 262, 266, 267, 275, 282, 284, 286, 301, 302, 308, 309, 310, 312, 322-324, 327, 336, 339, 342, 346, 349, 351, 352, 357, 362, 365, 371-373, 377, 379, 386, 402, 403, 411, 419, 421, 426, 428, 430, 432, 437, 439, 451, 453, 458, 464, 465, 467, 469, 471, 473, 474, 481, 486, 491, 492, 496, 503, 504, 517, 518, 524, 529, 532, 540, 550, 554-557
time-space compression 53, 54
top-down 97, 124, 201, 256,
392, 451, 457, 502, 517, 541, 542
top down or the bottom up 200
top-down systems 352
top-down typological design 351
topographic 44, 54, 68, 85, 99, 100, 124, 167, 294, 296, 298, 420
topographical 52, 60
topological 33, 35, 59, 73, 87-90, 152, 167, 168, 195, 287, 307, 318, 343, 400, 409
topological grid 152, 195, 343

==Architects can usually be classified into two modalities of practice: those who practice as visionaries, proposing an entirely new reality; and those who practice as doctors, curing and completing the city. Both modes stem from an idealist tradition.== 324

transcend the linguistic determination of programs 319
transfer information into form 191
transform 17, 150, 165, 170, 206, 210, 249, 251, 387, 451, 463, 468, 470, 490, 492, 522, 541, 544
transform reality transformation 26, 27, 35, 66, 90, 97-99, 123, 128, 137, 142, 151, 174, 180, 203, 207, 210, 216, 221, 222, 234, 238, 254, 277, 318, 331, 338, 371, 372, 374, 390, 438, 445, 448, 453, 460, 461, 463, 467, 469, 470, 492, 541, 545
transformative 206, 207, 216, 249, 252, 254, 313, 328, 349, 417, 435, 442, 468, 478, 491, 493, 524, 542
transformative agency 442, 478
transformative impact 216
transparency versus resistance 19
transubstantiation to pure capital flows 464
triumphant late capitalism 94
tsunami 372
tubular spaces 281
type 4, 5, 6, 16, 21, 31, 32, 34, 35, 56, 61-63, 66, 67, 72, 82, 88, 98, 108, 113, 118, 119, 120, 123, 124, 138, 143, 164, 166, 167, 171, 186-188, 190, 191, 193-197, 200, 201, 208, 213, 216, 220, 226, 234, 235, 239, 249, 256, 270-272, 280, 281, 284, 289, 293, 294, 295, 299, 318, 320, 321, 334, 337, 340, 351, 352, 354, 355, 358, 360, 368, 369, 384, 385, 387, 392-394, 398, 399, 402-405, 407, 427, 437, 438, 459, 460, 468, 473, 476, 489, 492-500, 503, 511, 512, 513, 524, 526, 527, 530, 532, 538, 551, 554, 558

typological 33, 96, 123, 124, 167, 168, 189, 190, 191, 194, 201, 217, 234, 235, 239, 256, 257, 280, 282, 293, 297, 320, 322, 350, 351, 357, 368, 376, 379, 381, 387, 388, 392
typologies, techniques, geometries, and organizations 302
typology 171, 190, 191, 194, 200, 202, 234, 235, 239, 256, 257, 259, 354, 358, 367, 382, 384, 385, 388, 392, 394, 399, 400, 402, 405, 406, 497, 498, 501, 511, 512, 527, 531, 533

==U==
unilateral politics of resistance 441, 478
united we stand 356, 357, 360, 376, 397
upwardly mobile populations 466
urban
urban age 471
urban density 194, 389, 472
urban development 155, 356, 384, 398, 472, 476, 484, 512, 534, 542, 543
urban enclaves 33, 471
urban infrastructure 472, 474, 475
urban life 362, 473, 533, 537, 543

==Hyper-urbanization is making available to an ever-increasing population access to what is arguably the most desirable commodity on the planet: urban life and the choices it avails.== 543

urban phylum 26
urban planning 34, 47, 53, 57, 215, 391, 461, 474
urban politics 472
urban space 27, 29, 282, 357, 476, 504, 528, 531

Colophon

urban structure 32-35, 56, 169, 278, 320, 467, 474
urban system 35, 438, 470
urban topographies 29, 30, 34, 542
urbanization 27, 28, 52, 385, 440, 466, 467, 472, 541, 543
urbanization of the globe 466
utopia 16, 45, 51, 55, 119, 228, 258, 313, 356, 357, 429, 430, 449, 478, 483, 548
utopian 3, 4, 7, 67, 154, 155, 156, 228, 229, 313, 318, 324, 357, 400, 429, 448, 453, 467, 478, 486, 491, 510, 548, 554

V
value 19, 20, 39, 40, 48, 53, 54, 109, 132, 133, 135-138, 144, 159, 169, 172, 223, 224, 226, 230, 270, 302, 312, 313, 316, 319, 328, 332, 335, 337, 338, 346, 386, 387, 401, 425, 431, 451, 454, 458, 473, 518, 539, 540, 546, 548-551, 553, 555
vector 31, 59, 80, 132, 142, 236, 240, 321
vectorial space 56, 59, 89, 181, 344, 412
vernacular 187, 384, 398-400, 541
vernacularization 400
virtual 109, 110, 142, 143, 164, 172, 173, 175, 176, 177, 181, 182, 233, 238, 242, 243, 245, 247, 262, 263, 272, 280, 284-287, 298, 299, 318, 327, 330, 363, 280, 439

Rather than constructing a sophisticated surrogate of the real, the virtual would imply opening unprecedented forms of reality, proliferating the real in unexpected directions. 176

The strategy to produce the virtual is not to replace the real with a sophisticated surrogate, such as in so-called virtual reality, but rather to dismantle the complex assemblage of social uses, organizations of space, and material qualities that have come to constitute what we generally understand as a home. 285

virtual reality 285
virtuality 107-110, 153, 176, 177
virtualization 142, 143, 148, 151, 153
virtualize 143, 150, 151, 191,
235, 239, 352
virtualize reality 321

To become a relevant, if not successful architect, then, one has to nurture incipient megalomania, look down on reality with utter disdain for anything that might preexist or stand in the way of "the vision," and walk around in a state of permanent dissatisfaction with the status quo. 450

I am not at all interested in visionary projects, nor in individual authors. 216

volition 268, 270, 271, 285, 299

W
wave 7, 20, 86, 97, 170, 309, 310, 428, 429, 431, 432, 448, 486
(see also Hokusai Wave)
what and how 118
v winemaking 428
world outside 2, 207, 220
write the code 334

To write a project is to introduce a sequential development rather than deploying a form, an image. 334

people tended to associate my name automatically with writing, and practice never forgives that mistake. 144

Z
Zeitgeist 4, 94-98, 101, 228, 229, 270

585

Photographic credits

INTRO Nick Leeson, 1995, p. 2 (left) – **Kurt Cobain**, 1992 p. 2 (center) – **Julian Assange**, Espen Moe, Wikimedia Commons 2010, p. 2 (right) – **Naomi Klein**, Ed Kashi, 2010, p. 3 – **Sofia Coppola**, hallovalerie, flickr, 2009, p. 4 – **David Einhorn**, Ethan Miller, 2006, p. 4 – **Angelina Jolie**, Gage Skidmore, Wikimedia Commons, 2010, p. 5 (left) – **Whitney Houston**, Vince Bucci, 2000, p. 5 (right) – **Spike Jonze**, Terry Richardson, 2010, p. 6 (left) – **Johnny Depp**, 2002, p. 6 (right) – **Björk**, Jean Baptiste Mondino, 1993, p. 7 (left) – **Vincent Gallo**, Anton Corbijn, 2011, p. 7 (right) – **Ayrton Senna**, Mario Luini, ASE, 1992, p. 8 (left) – **Dov Charney**, Stephen Shugerman, 2005, p. 8 (center) – **Gen-X**, Douglas Coupland, 1995, p. 8 (right) – **Global Positioning Systems** Police arrest a man during the Watts Riots, NY World-Telegram, Wikimedia Commons, 1965, p. 16 – **Dinoland**, Lilian Seymour - NY Fair, National Park Service US Department of the Interior, 1965, p. 17 – **Gateway Arch under construction**, Bob Arteaga, 1965, p. 18 – **Watts Riot**, Doris Brandon, 1965, p. 19 – **Martin Luther King Jr**, Walter Albertin, World Telegram & Sun, 1964, p. 20 – **Watts Riot**, Doris Brandon, 1965, p. 21 – **Richard Nixon giving "V" sign after resignation**, Bettmann Collection, 1974, p. 22 – **War is Over** (if you want it), 1969, p. 24 – **Marine waiting for flight**, Corbis Images / Bettmann Collection, 1968, p. 25 – **Deepwater Horizon offshore drilling unit on fire**, US Coast Guard, Wikimedia Commons, 2010, p. 26 – **Bhopal**, Luca Frediani, Wikimedia Commons, 2008, p. 27 – **Burial of an unknown child**, 1984, p. 28 – **Controlled burn of oil**, John Kepsimelis U.S. Coast Guard, Wikimedia Commons, 2010, p. 29 – **Muxia Oil Slick**, Lmbuga, Wikimedia Commons, 2005, p. 31 – **Rena oil spill cleanup**, New Zealand Defence Force, Wikimedia Commons, 2011, p. 32 – **Chernobyl Disaster Aftermath**, Soviet Authorities, Wikimedia Commons, 1986, p. 33 – **Bergan oil field fire**, NOAA, Wikimedia Commons, 1991, p. 34 – **Line5130**, Collection of Doug Helton, NOAA/NOS/ORR, Wikimedia Commons, 2010, p. 35 – **Budapest**, 1956, p. 37 – **Paris May 68**, Jean-Claude Seine, 1968, p. 38 – **Prague Spring**, Corbis Images / Bettmann Collection, 1968, p. 39 – **Juggling on the Berlin Wall**, Yann Forget, Wikimedia Commons, 1989, p. 40 – **Berlin Wall Brandenburg Gate**, Sue Ream, Wikimedia Commons, 1989, p. 41 – **Democracia real YA! Madrid**, Olmo Calvo, Wikimedia Commons, 2011, p. 42 – **London anti-war protest banners**, AK7, Wikimedia Commons, 2002, p. 44 – **Tahrir Square**, Ahmed Abd El-Fatah, Wikimedia Commons, 2011, p. 45 – **Lybian rebels** (Tripoli), EPA, 2011, p. 47 (left) – **Egypt Arab Spring**, Moe, Wikimedia Commons, 2011, p. 47 (right) – **Tahrir Square II**, Jonathan Rashad, Wikimedia Commons, 2011, p. 48 – **Protesters fests toward Pearl roundabout**, Bahrain in pictures, Wikimedia Commons, 2011, p. 49 – **Occupy Wall Street Day 14**, chan4chan, 2011, p. 50 – **Steve Jobs and Steve Wozniak**, circa 1976, p. 52 – **Microsoft Staff**, courtesy Microsoft, 1978, p. 54 – **Galácticos**, 2003, p. 56 – **Andy Warhol and Edie Sedgwick**, 1965, p. 58 – **Keith Jarret Trio**, 1997, p. 60 – **Google Larry Page and Sergey Brin**, Ehud kenan, Wikimedia Commons, 2003, p. 62 – **Miles Davis band performance**, 1973, p. 64 – **Mark Zuckerberg and facebook team members**, 2011, p. 66 – **Woven wool fabric**, pinkscissors, 2009, p. 69 – **Issey Miyake fabrics**, 2001, p. 70 – **Barbour quilted fabric**, 2002, p. 71 – **Chanel bag**, Mindsay Mohan, flickr, 2007, p. 72 – **Studded pattern Alaia bag**, Monique Chan, MoonRox, 2004, p.73 – **Tartan Pattern**, Burberry, 2001, p. 74 – **Leopard Print Pattern**, YSL, 1978, p. 75 – **Desert Camo**, US Military, 1992, p. 76 – **Gingham Pattern**, Alexander McQueen, 2001, p. 77 – **Acrylic discs dress**, Paco Rabanne, 1967, p. 79 (left) – **Silver plates dress**, Paco Rabanne, 2005, p. 79

(right) – **Boa digérant un éléphant**, Antoine de Sant-Exupéry, 1943, p. 82 – **BB**, John McNab, flickr, 1967, p. 84 (left) – **Aéroport Roissy Charles de Gaulle**, Paul Andreu, flickr, 1975, p. 84 (right) – **TGV**, 1998, p. 86 – **Debut: YSL**, Pierre Boulat, 1962, p. 87 – **Citröen DS Pallas**, 1966, p. 89 (left) – **Balenciaga Museum**, Irekia-Vasc Government, 2011, 89 (right) – **Air France Concorde**, Alexander Jonsson, Wikimedia Commons, 2000, p. 90 – **Pierre Poulin furniture**, geishaboy500, flickr, p. 91 – "**Power is Nothing without control**" Pirelli Ad, Y&R, 1995, p. 93 – **Crack dosage**, DEA, Wikimedia Commons, 2005, p. 94 – **Viagra pills**, 2000, p. 95 – **Prozac pills**, Tom Varco, Wikimedia Commons, 2006, p. 96 – **Extasis pills**, 2004, p. 97 – **COCP Birth Control pils**, 1998, p. 98 – **Melatonin 3Mg**, 2000, p. 100 – **Millenium Stadium Concert**, Andrew King, Wikimedia Commons, 2010, p. 103 – **Celebration after Obama speech in Denver**, zenobi_joy, Wikimedia Commons, 2008, p. 105 – **Love Parade 2002 Berlin**, Arne Müseler, Wikimedia Commons, 2002, p. 107 – **Huskers**, Touchdown Celebration, beatboxbadhabit, flickr, 2008, p. 108 – **Glastonbury aerial view**, BBC Glastonbury webcam, 2002, p. 109 – **Woodstock Festival**, Paul Campbell, Wikimedia Commons, 1969, p. 111 – **Woodstock stage**, Derek Redmond, Wikimedia Commons, 1969, p. 112 – **Woodstock crowd**, Derek Redmond, Wikimedia Commons, 1969, p. 113 – **Crowd, Ogbomosho**, CFAN, 2003, p. 114 – **Live Earth: London**, Krypto, flickr, 2007, p. 116 – **Swami opening**, Mark Goff, Wikimedia Commons, 1969, p. 117 – **Guggenheim Crowd**, Vineus, flickr, 2007, p. 119 – **Concert crowd Osheaga**, Anirudh Koul, flickr, 2009, p. 121 – **Kaaba, Mecca**, Basil D Soufi, Wikimedia Commons, 2008, p. 122 – **Crowd at Washington Monument**, acnatta, flickr, 2009, p. 124 – **Neuron in tissue culture**, Gerry Shaw, Wikimedia Commons, 2000, p. 127 – **Compression-resistant foam**, BASF, flickr, 2010, p. 128 – **Artificial spiders webs**, BASF, flickr, 2011, p. 129 – **Neopor Insulation**, BASF, flickr, 2010, p. 130 – **RGB Global Pavillion Installation**, FOA / Enrique Moreno Merino, 2002, p. 132 – **Dow Jones market cycle**, Doc Trader, 2008, p. 134 – **Australian stock exchange**, Damian White, flickr, 2011, p. 136 – **Cedric Price portrait**, 1970, p. 139 – **Buzz Aldrin Moonwalk**, Neil Armstrong / NASA, Wikimedia Commons, 1969, p. 140 – **Franco is dead**, La Vanguardia cover, 1975, p. 141 – **Olympic Jump Barcelona 92**, 1992, p. 142 – "**Is greed still good**", Fortune Magazine, 2005, p. 143 – **Alan Greenspan**, EPA, 2004, p. 145 – **Super Dutch** (book cover), Christian Richters, Princeton Architectural Press, 2000, p. 146 – **Diana's funeral**, Maxwell Hamilton, Wikimedia Commons, 1997, p. 147 – **Blair and Brown** during the 1997 general election campaign, Johnny Eggit, 1997, p. 149 – **Tokyo subway sarin incident**, 1995, p. 150 (left and right) – **9/11 WTC aerial view**, NOAA, 2001, p. 151 – **Azores summit**, Staff Sgt. Michelle Michaud, Wikimedia Commons, 2003, p. 153 – **One Euro** coin after 10 years, Michiel Hendryckx, Wikimedia Commons, 2011, p. 154 – **11-M,** Fernando Garrote, 2004, p. 155 – **11-M**, Álvaro Reyes Mateo, 2004, p. 156 – **Theo Van Gogh murder**, 2004, p. 157 – **Pim Fortuyn murder**, 2002, p. 159 – **Koizumi in Graceland**, Eric Draper, Wikimedia Commons, 2006, p. 160 – **Breeding Sciences Manufacturing #6A and 6B,** Edward Burtynsky, 2004, p. 164 – **FANUC R2000iB AtWork**, Mixabest, Wikimedia Commons, 2010, p. 165 – **JW Space Telescope Primary Mirror**, David Higginbotham, NASA/MSFC, 2011, p. 166 – **Wiimote in Hands**, Evan Amos, Wikimedia Commons, 2010, p. 168 – **Google Street View 9 eyes camera**, Google, 2008, p. 169 – **Banksy's One nation under cctv**, Carol Lainy, Wikimedia Commons, 2008, p. 170 – **cctv security system with multiple camera views in china**, Yuyangc, Shutter Stock pictures, 2010, p. 171 – **House of cards** video still, Radiohead, XL Recordings, 2008, p. 172 – **Lily Pad Arduino**, David Mellis, Wikimedia Commons, 2010, p. 173 – **Reactable**, Xavier Sivecas, Courtesy Reactable, 2009, p. 174 – **Sailor operates IED**, US Army, Wikimedia Commons, p. 176 – **MQ-1 Predator**, U.S. Air Force / Col Leslie Pratt, Wikimedia Commons, 2008, p. 177 – **Pierre Boulez at the Donaueschinger Musiktage**, Sonja, Wikimedia Commons, 2008, p. 178 – **Stockhausen WDR**, Kathinka Pasveer, Wikimedia Commons, 1994, p. 179 – **John Cage préparant un piano**, courtesy John

Cage Trust, circa 1950, p. 180 – **Iannis Xenakis**, courtesy Les Amis de Xenakis, 1975, p. 181 – **Quaderns # 196** (Dunes), COAC, 1992, p. 183 – **Tir amb Arc**, Ramon Prat, 1995, p. 184 (left) – **Spiral Jetty**, Joe Vare, flickr, 2009, p. 184 (center) – **Richard long "A circle of slate"** (detail), Alex & le temps qui passe, flickr, 2007, p. 185 – Roden Crater, USGS, Wikimedia Commons, 2007, p. 186 – **Olafur Eliasson The Weather Project**, Thomas Pintaric, Wikimedia Commons, 2004, p. 187 – **Damien Hirst For the Love of God**, Handout, Getty Images, 2007, p. 188 – **Deep Throat**, Bryanston Pictures, Wikimedia Commons, 1972, p. 190 – **Earthrise**, Bill Anders / Apollo 8 / NASA, Wikimedia Commons, 1968, p. 192 – **Oceans temperature**, NASA Images, Wikimedia Commons, 2008, p. 194 – **Arctic Pole**, NASA Images, Wikimedia Commons, 2008, p. 195 – **Climate simulation**, UCAR, National Science Foundation, 2008, p. 196 – **Hole in the Ozone Layer Over Antarctica**, NASA Images, Wikimedia Commons, 1998, p. 197 – **Earth Debris**, NASA Images, Wikimedia Commons, 2005, p. 198 – **Wind direction study**, NASA Images, Wikimedia Commons, 2009, p. 199 – **Earth**, NASA Images, Wikimedia Commons, 2010, p. 200 – **Arctic ocean SST and ice edge**, Giorgiogp2, Wikimedia Commons, 2010, p. 201 – **SeaWIFS sea life**, NASA/Goddard Space Flight Center, flickr, 2011, p. 202 – **Miami Beach**, Mojumbo22, flickr, 2009, p. 205 – **Between Tijuana and San Diego**, Julien Pearce, flickr, 2010, p. 207 – **Station**, James Byrum, flickr, 2008, p. 209 – **Checkpoint 300 in Bethelhem**, papalars, flickr, 2011, p. 210 – **Denver airport security**, alist, flickr, 2009, p. 211 – **San Diego-Tijuana border**, musicneverstoppped1, flickr, 2008, p. 212 – **Sushi no Moriawase**, lenagold, 2006, p. 214 – **Wonton**, lenagold, 2004, p. 216 – **Shish Kebab**, Alesist, flickr, 2009, p. 217 – **Donner Kebab**, Alex Kehr, flickr, 2007, p. 218 – spring rolls and rice, lenagold, 2004, p. 219 – **Sushi Sashimi**, lenagold, 2005, p. 220 – **Tacos**, JeffreyW, flickr, 2006, p. 222 – **Shrimp shaomais**, Stewart Butterfield, flickr, 2007, p. 224 – **Zorba's falafel platter**, Mr. T in DC, flickr, 2010, p. 225 – **Dim-Sum**, iohim, flickr, 2008, p. 227 – **Hommos**, Charles Haynes, flickr, 2009, p. 229 – **FOA's British Pavillion** (Venice Biennale 2002), Valerie Bennett, 2002, p. 230 & p. 231 – **Standing seam metal roof**, me-wlkp, 2006, p. 232 – **OSB**, 2004, p. 233 – **Mudding Sheetrock** (drywall), Forest Service-Northern Region, flickr, 2010, p. 234 – **Tyvek house wrap** (thermal insulation), Scott Ehardt, Wikimedia Commons, 2006, p. 235 – **Expanded metal**, Andy Matthews, flickr, 2010, p. 236 – **Gluelam Beam**, millerm217, flickr, 2007, p. 237 – **ETFE**, USACE publicaffairs, flickr, 2010, p. 238 – **Polycarbonate façade**, Thomas Kaare Lindblad, 2003, p. 239 – **Glass Curtain Wall**, Victortsu2, flickr, 2011, p. 241 – **33 contemporary icons** display, 2006-2010, p. 242-247 – **Dr. Ishiguro and geminoid**, IR Lab Osaka University, 2011, p. 248 – **Geminoid F**, Yoshikazu Tsuno, AFP, 2011, p. 249 – **Hitachi ipexpo robot**, osde8info, flickr, 2011, p. 250 – **Star Wars Episode II**: Attack of the Clones poster, Lucas Film, 2002, p. 253 – **Tornado simulation**, Pittsburg Supercomputing Center, PSC, 2004, p. 255 – **Global wind speed and wave height**, Science Express, AAAS, 2008, p. 256 – **Katrina's tracks**, NASA/GSFC, Wikimedia Commons, 2005, p. 257 – **Japan Tsunami**, NASA/NOAA, 2010, p. 258 – **Google lattitude logo**, Google, 2009, p. 260 – **iPhone Architecture guide app**, Makayama Media, 2009, p. 261 – **Global internet nodes**, UCSD, 2007, p. 262 – **Internet blackhole censorship spots**, OpenNet, 2007, p. 263 – **Internet IP address Map**, The Opte Project, 2006, p. 265 – **Augmented reality app**, Layar Partner Network, 2011, p. 266 – **Stormtrooper**, Andres Rueda, flickr, 2009, p. 268 (left) – **The Joker**, Legendary Pictures, 2008, p. 268 (center) – **Annibal Lecter**, Orion Pictures, 1991, p. 269 – **London Riot Police**, hozinja, flickr, 2011, p. 270 – **Anonymous Mask**, Carolina Georgatou, flickr, 2011, p. 271 – **Nomad Practices Crowd at Long Beach**, kingair42, flickr, 2009, p. 276 – **Crowd at Dushera Festival**, seeveeaar, flickr, 2008, p. 277 – **Crowd at Waldkraiburg swimming pool**, Aerial Photography, flickr, 2002, p. 278 – **Crowd invades Sheffield pitch**, Ben Sutherland, flickr, 2010, p. 279 – **Jongler convention Münich**, Aerial Photography, flikcr, 2011, p. 280 – **Dhaka Traffic**, Pyb, flickr, 2005,

p. 282 – **Virtual House**, FOA, 1997, p. 284 (upper) – **VH Proliferation**, FOA, 1997, p. 284 (lower) – **Canadian Disruptive Pattern Arid Region**, Phazall, Wikimedia Commons, 2012, p. 285 – **Arecibo Observatory**, NAIC / NSF, 1997, p. 288 – **Pylons sunset**, Loadmaster, Wikimedia Commons, 2009, p. 289 – **Bosphorus Bridge**, Piutus, flickr, 2006, p. 291 – **M6/A38 Cloverleaf Junction**, Highways Agency, flickr, 2008, p. 292 – **MSC Tomoko Panama**, Mike Baird, Wikimedia Commons, 2009, p. 293 – **Landing at Philip SW. Goldson Int. Airport (Belize)**, Enrique G. Morales, 2006, p. 295 – **Luggage claim**, Michael Awad, Nicholas Metivier Gallery, 2006, p. 296 – **Mobile phone antennae on rooftop**, Karen Blakeman, flickr, 2011, p. 297 – **Internet servers**, Paul Hammond, flickr, 2008, p. 299 – **North Korea Workers Party parade**, Erci Lafforgue, flickr, 2008, p. 301 – **Neil Harbisson Cyborg**, Carlosramirex, Wikimedia Commons, 2011, p. 302 – **Nikon retina sensor**, Rolf Coppens, Grrr, 2011, p. 303 – **Hello Dolly**, Chris Green, Wikimedia Commons, 2008, p. 304 – **Transgenic Crop Design**, BASF, flickr, 2007, p. 305 – **Transgenic Apple**, dujarandille, flickr, 2007, p. 306 – **A Poc Design**, Issey Miyake, Miyake Design Studio, 2000, p. 308 – **Jumping**, Issey Miyake, Ace Gallery NYC, 1999, p. 309 – **Minaret Dress**, Issey Miyake, Miyake Design Studio, 1995, p. 310 – **Grid with Columbia's Debris**, NASA, Wikimedia Commons, 2003, p. 311 – **Nha Trang Factory**, Andreas Gursky, 2003, p. 312 – **Magic Roundabout**, Google Maps, 2007, p. 313 – **Tokyo Subway Map**, Tokyo Metro, 2005, p. 314 – **Shibuya Crossing**, Shibuya246, flickr, 2009, p. 315 – **Office Plan**, 1994, p. 317 – **Semiconductor Viewed Through Electron Microscope**, Charles O'Rear, Corbis Images, 1993, p. 318 – **NUNO: patched paper**, libbyrosof, flickr, 2007, p. 319 – **Motorola DynaTAC**, Dan Forbes, 1973, p. 320 – **Rocinha Neighbourhood**, matteo0702, flickr, 2010, p. 321 – **CERN aerial view**, Maximilien Brice, CERN, 2008, p. 322 – **USA at Night**, NOAA/NGDC DMSP, 2007, p. 324 – **Soccer tactic board**, 2005, p. 325 – **Ampico reproducing piano**, 1996, p. 326 – **Robot writing Bible**, Gastev (Mirko Tobias Schaefer), flickr, 2008, p. 328 – **Yokohama's Circulation Diagram**, FOA, 2001, p. 330 – **CNN Breaking News**, CNN, 2006, p. 331 – **SFA Joker Jinx**, Chris Hagerman, Wikimedia Commons, 2005, p. 333 – **Bangkok streets at night**, Stuck in Customs, flickr, 2006, p. 334 – **Atrium**, alexbrn, flickr, 2005, p. 335 – **Kowloon Walled City Alley**, Deadkid dk, Wikimedia Commons, 2006, p. 336 – **Fifth Element**, Gaumont Film Company, 1997, p. 337 – **Jin Mao Tower Atrium**, Kakapo31, flickr, 2006, p. 339 – **Mid levels escalator**, Will Clayton, flickr, 2009, p. 340 – **Atomium escalator**, saturn, flickr, 2010, p. 341 – **US Army water park**, familymwr, flickr, 2008, p. 342 – **Terminal 1 CDG Airport**, bostankorkulugu, flickr, 2011, p. 343 – **Hakozaki Junction**, Kabacchi, flickr, 2010, p. 344 – **Timbo King at Times Square**, kevin dooley, flickr, 2011, p. 346 – **Quadrophenia Mods**, Franc Roddam, The Who Films, 1979, p. 347 – **Chelsea Bridge Rockers**, Triton Rocker, Wikimedia Commons, 1978, p. 348 – **Parade at Little Tokyo (L.A.)**, Ray_from_LA, flickr, 2010, p. 349 – **Goth People**, Rama, Wikimedia Commons, 2005, p. 350 – **Marukin at Sanja Matsuri**, TOKYO ezine, flickr, 2011, p. 351 – **Shibuya Girls**, ThisParticularGreg, flickr, 2007, p. 352 – **Punk youth**, LordKhan, flickr, 2006, p. 353 – **Skins**, the_moog, flickr, 2007, p. 354 – **Castellers**, calafellvallo, flickr, 2011, p. 356 (left) – **the Bundle Tower**, FOA, 2001, p. 356 (center) – **the Bundle Tower**, FOA, 2001, p. 357 – **The Situation Room**, Pete Souza, Wikimedia Commons, 2011, p. 358 – **United We Stand 34C Stamps**, 2001, p. 359 – **Osama Bin Laden "Wanted" Poster**, 2008, p. 360 – **London Olympics Site**, AZP, 2008, p. 361-364 – **30 St Mary Axe**, aurélien, flickr, 2010, p. 365 – **Dildos**, 2007, p. 366 – **Agbar Tower Bcn**, Alexander Z, Wikimedia Commons, 2007, p. 367 – **Under the great wave off Kanagawa**, Katsushika Hokusai, Wikimedia Commons, 1832, p. 369 – **FOA Yokohama Port Terminal**, Satoru Mishima, 2002, p. 371 – **Pentagon Aerial View**, USGS, Wikimedia Commons, 2002, p. 372 – **FOA Police headquarters Villa Joiosa**, Cristobal Palma, 2004, p. 373 – **35 mm Film**, 1996, p. 374 – **BBC Chorus & Orchestra HQ**, FOA, 2004, p. 375 – **Construction**, Walt Stoneburner, flickr, 2011,

p. 376 – **London Olympic Stadium**, FOA, 2010, p. 377 – **Granite Quarry**, US Archives American West photographs, Wikimedia Commons, 1872, p. 379 – **Municipal Theatre and Auditorium**, Torrevieja, FOA, 2006, p. 380 – **Beijing Bird's Nest**, Beast from the Bush, Wikimedia Commons, 2007, p. 381 – **Transparent City**, Michael Wolf, 2007, p. 383 – **Elite residence**, Vispiron properties, Tameer, 2007, p. 384 – **Heartland Nightlife**, Besar Bears, flickr, 2005, p. 386 – **Bono bathtub**, Anton Corbijn, 1995, p. 388 – "**Charlotte**", Giampaolo Sgura, 2011, p. 390 – **Marina Bay Sands Hotel air swimming pool**, by, Panoramio, 2010, p. 392 – **Businessman looking at cityscape**, Gregor Schuster, Corbis, 2008, p. 394 – **Couple on balcony**, Yang Liu, Corbis, 2008, p. 396 – **Wall Street II** (film still), Oliver Stone, 20th century Fox, 2010, p. 398 – **3rd floor patio terrace**, InterContinental Hong Kong, flickr, 2007, p. 400 – **Transparent City**, Michael Wolf, 2007, p. 402 – **Sao Paulo memorial cemiterio**, 2004, p. 404 – **Lobby Lounge at Night**, InterContinental Hong Kong, flickr, 2007, p. 406 – **TWSkateboarding March Issue**, TWS Magazine, 2006, p. 408 – **Spanish Pavillion** Aichi Japan, AZP/FOA, 2005, p. 409 – **Ravensbourne College** (façade detail), AZP/FOA, 2010, p. 410 – **Trinity EC3**, AZP/FOA, 2005, p. 412 – **Carabanchel Social Housing** (façade detail), AZP/FOA, 2007, p. 413 – **Elizabeth House**, AZP/FOA, 2005, p. 414 – **Institute of legal medicine**, AZP/FOA, 2006, p. 416 – **John Lewis Dep. store**, AZP/FOA, 2008, p. 417 – **Elizabeth House**, AZP/FOA, 2005, p. 419 – **H&dM**, Georg Gatsas, 2006, p. 422 – **Lord Norman Foster**, Carolyn Djanogly, 2005, p. 423 – **Toyo Ito**, 2008, p. 424 – **SANAA**, Takashi Okamoto, 2008, p. 425 – **Peter Eisenman**, Chris Wiley, 2007, p. 426 – **Rafel Moneo**, 1994, p. 427 – **Frank Gehry**, 2008, p. 428 – **Rem Koolhaas**, Marc Seliger, L'Uomo VOGUE, 2008, p. 429 – **Arata Izosaki**, 2004, p. 430 – **Jean Nouvel**, Gaston Bergeret, 1996, p. 431 – **Zaha Hadid**, Steve Double, 2003, p. 432 – **Material Politics** Hong kong Skyline, Brian Giesen, flickr, 2009, p. 436 – **Benidorm**, po.psi.que, flickr, 2008, p. 438 – **Pritzker Pavilion Structure**, jmcmichael, flickr, 2004, p. 440 – **Waves**, papalars, flickr, 2008, p. 441 – **Chelsea windows**, leonelponce, flickr, 2010, p. 442 – **Destruction of Giant Buddhas** (Bamiyan Valley in Afghanistan) film still, Christian Frei, 2005, p. 444 – **9/11 attacks**, Spencer Platt, 2001, p. 445 – **Bin Laden mosaic**, Genista, flickr, 2006, p. 446 – **Benazir Bhutto sanctuary**, Faisal Mahmood, 2007, p. 447 – **Pet Rock**, Al Freni, 1979, p. 449 – **Richard Burdett**, Venice Biennale, 2008, p. 450 – **Paul Goldberger**, PBS, 2011, p. 451 – **Herbert Muschamp**, NY Times, 2006, p. 452 – **Luis Fernández-Galiano**, Rebeca García, 2003, p. 453 – **Deyan Sudjic**, 2010, p. 455 – **Phyllis Lambert**, Michel Boulet, CCA Montreal, 2008, p. 456 (left) – **Hans Stimmann**, Andreas Praefcke, Wikimedia Commons, 2006, p. 456 (center) – **Josep Antoni Acebillo**, 1999, p. 457 – **Mohammed Atta**, DMV, Wikimedia Commons, 2001, p. 459 – **Salam Pax**, Jeff Vinnick, Getty Images, 2004, p. 460 – **Petronas Panorama**, Someformofhuman, Wikimedia Commons, 2008, p. 463 – **Ryugyong Hotel** (Pyongyang), exposocialism, flickr, 2011, p. 464 – Mayor **Michael Bloomberg**, Rubenstein, flickr, 2007, p. 466 – Mayor **Chris Patten**, James Yuanxin Li, Wikimedia Commons, 2008, p. 466 (center) – Mayor **Bertrand Delanoë**, Marie-Lan Nguyen, Wikimedia Commons, 2008, p. 468 – Mayor **Rudy Giuliani**, Crzrussian, Wikimedia Commons, 2006, p. 468 (center) – Mayor **Yuri Luzhkov**, A.Savin, Wikimedia Commons, 2010, p. 469 – Mayor **Ken Livingstone**, World Economic Forum, Wikimedia Commons, 2008, p. 470 (left) – Mayor **Bo Xilai**, EFE, 2007, p. 470 (right) – **Beijing CBD**, Cobble, Wikimedia Commons, 2008, p. 471 – **Chongqing**, Brad Templeton , 2010, p. 473 – **Shenzen Aerial View**, 2010, p. 475 – **Javier Solana**, pi, Wikimedia Commons, 2007, p. 477 – **Obama at American University**, Will White, Wikimedia Commons, 2008, p. 478 – **Scanner mm wave tech**, Transportation Security Administration, Wikimedia Commons, 2009, p. 479 – **Security screening area at Denver International Airport**, Danpaluska, Wikimedia Commons, 2009, p. 480 – **Museum für Kunst und Gewerbe Hamburg**, MKG / Dennis Conrad, Wikimedia Commons, 2010, p. 481 – **Flippat Festival** (Malmö), Markus Wüste, courtesy Plastique Fantastique, 2008,

p. 482 – **Space Astronaut John Grunsfeld**, NASA GSFC, flickr, 2010, p. 483 – **Moderna Museet** (Malmö), Carsten Reith, courtesy Plastique Fantastique, 2009, p. 484 – **Observatory/ Air-Port-City**, courtesy Tomas Saraceno, 2008, p. 485 – **Allianz Arena**, Christian Denis Mueller, Wikimedia Commons, 2006, p. 486 – **Watercube** (Beijing), Angus, Wikimedia Commons, 2007, p. 487 – **Watercube-Birdsnest**, 2007, p. 488 – **Prada Boutique Aoyama**, Wiiii, Wikimedia Commons, 2008, p. 489 – **Dymaxion gallery**, 2011, p. 491 – **Biosphere 2** (coastal fog desert), lumierefl, flickr, 2009, p. 492 – **BMF Climatron**, Jet Lowe, Wikimedia Commons, 1983, p. 493 – **Clard Svenson inside geodesic dome at Drop City**, History / Genealogy Dept., Denver Public Library, 1967, p. 494 – **NASA Vehicle Assembly Building**, Bernt Rostad, flickr, 2009, p. 495 – **SeaGaia** (Miyazaki Ocean Dome), Megapixie, Wikimedia Commons, 2007, p. 496 – **Atocha Station Greenhouse interior**, CesVLC, Wikimedia Commons, 2007, p. 498 – **Eden Project geodesic domes**, Jürgen Matern, Wikimedia Commons, 2006, p. 499 – **The Eden Project** (Cornwall, UK), Jim Linwodd, flickr, 2002, p. 501 – **Crystal Island**, Foster & Partners, 2007, p. 502 – **Blue Water shopping centre**, www.webbaviation.co.uk, 2005, p. 504 – **Chavettes**, 2003, p. 505 – **Selfridges Store** (exterior), Future Systems, 2003, p. 506 – **Selfridges Store** (interior), Future Systems, 2003, p. 507 – **David Vetter** (Bubble Boy), Baylor College of Medicine (archives), 1980, p. 508 – **Final Home**, 1994, p. 509 – "**The Complex**" Drop City, 1967, p. 510 – **SARS epidemic**, *Newsweek*, 2003, p. 512 – **Condoms**, liber, flickr, 2008, p. 514 – **Monica Lewinsky**, video still, 1996, p. 516 (left) – **freedom in mah'soul**, Half Bowl Human, flickr, 2011, p. 516 (center) – **SARS**, Wikimedia Commons, 2003, p. 517 – **Black Monday**, Daily News, 1987, p. 518 – **Lehman Bros-Collapse**, *The Times UK*, 2008, p. 519 – **AIDS ad**, 2008, p. 520 – "**Infidel**" (book cover) by Ayaan Hirsi Ali, Free Press, 2007, p. 521 – **Trevor Phillips**, boellstiftung, flickr, 2010, p. 522 – **Sao Vito skyscraper**, LiaC, Wikimedia Commons, 2006, p. 523 – **Hotel Iveria** (Georgia), tomaradze, flickr, 2003, p. 524 – **Hong Kong**, vince42, flickr, 2011, p. 525 – **Trellick Tower** (North Kensington), J@ck!, flickr, 2011, p. 526 – **Tower of David** (Caracas), Meridith Kohut, NYTimes, 2011, p. 527 – **Macao** (China), vince42, flickr, 2011, p. 528 – **Hong Kong urban density**, Michael Wolf, 2004, p. 529 – **Hong Kong**, vince42, flickr, 2011, p. 530 – **Dubai view over clouds**, Captain, Wikimedia Commons, 2008, p. 532 – **Shanghai skyscrapers**, pmorgan, flickr, 2005, p. 534 – **Dubai Skyline**, nelson ebelt, flickr, 2011, p. 536 – **The Bund Shanghai**, Pyzhou, Wikimedia Commons, 2010, p. 538 – **Hong Kong**, BarbaraWilli, flickr, 2011, p. 540 – **Che Guevara** Heroico (detail), Alberto Korda, Wikimedia Commons, 1960, p. 542 – **Fidel Castro**, unknown, Wikimedia Commons, 1984, p. 542 – **Mao Tse Tung**, Zhang Zhenshi, Wikimedia Commons, 1967, p. 542 – **Ingvar Kamprad**, Histwr, Wikimedia Commons, 2007, p. 542 – **Stelios Haji-Ioannou**, easyGroup, Wikimedia Commons, 2009, p. 542 – **Amancio Ortega**, Wikimedia Commons, 2008, p. 542 – **Betty Friedan**, Fred Palumbo, Wikimedia Commons, 1960, p. 543 – **Malcolm X**, Ed Ford, Wikimedia Commons, 1964, p. 543 – **Daniel Cohn-Bendit**, SH, 1968, p. 543 – **Alan Greenspan**, Stephen Jaffe, Wikimedia Commons, 2007, p. 543 – **Jimmy Wells**, Joi, Wikimedia Commons, 2008, p. 543 – **Jeff Bezos**, James Duncan Davidson, flickr, 2005, p. 543 – **Pistoletto's "Venus of Rags"**, Javier Almodóvar, flickr, 2010, p. 544 – **Jimmy Choo Mania at H&M**, Dominic's pics, flickr, 2009, p. 545 – **IKEA house prototype**, 2008, p. 546 – **Nano** - The Wonder Car, sandeeprathod, flickr, 2008, p. 547 – **kidrobot** x **swatch**, g&b's, flickr, 2011, p. 548 – **IKEA Warehouse**, ElvinWong, flickr, 2008, p. 549 – **Frank Gehry**, Roger Ressmeyer, 1987, p. 550 – **People queue**, Liu Wen Cheng, flickr, 2008, p. 551 – **Zara** Sidney store queue, raluca.ioana, flickr, 2011, p. 552 – **comme des garçons x H&M**, cuttlefish, flickr, 2008, p. 553 – **Nike factory**, China, 2011, p. 554 – **Zara employee attaches price tickets to skirts**, Katell Abiven, 2011, p. 555 – **Easy Council**, 2008, p. 556 – **|**

Published by Actar
Barcelona–New York
www.actar.com
With the collaboration
of Princeton University
School of Architecture

Author
Alejandro Zaera-Polo

Text editor
Gavin Keeney

Proofreading
Alta Price

Image research
Andrés Flajszer
Manuel Távora
Rosa Lleó

Graphic design and production
ActarPro

All rights reserved
© of the edition, Actar, Barcelona 2012
© of the text, Alejandro Zaera-Polo
© of the images, their authors

ISBN 978-84-92861-22-4
DL B-15545-2012

Printed and bound
in the European Union

Distribution

ActarD
Barcelona–New York
www.actar-d.com

Roca i Batlle 2-4
E-08023 Barcelona
Tel. +34 93 417 49 93
Fax +34 93 418 67 07
salesbarcelona@actar.com

151 Grand Street, 5th floor
New York, NY 10013, USA
Tel. +1 212 966 2207
Fax +1 212 966 2214
salesnewyork@actar.com

Every effort has been made to contact copyright holders of images published herein. The publisher would appreciate being informed of any omissions in order to make due acknowledgement in future editions of this book.

PRINCETON UNIVERSITY SCHOOL OF ARCHITECTURE